SECOND EDITION

Programming Android

*Zigurd Mednieks, Laird Dornin, G. Blake Meike,
and Masumi Nakamura*

Beijing · Cambridge · Farnham · Köln · Sebastopol · Tokyo

Programming Android, Second Edition

by Zigurd Mednieks, Laird Dornin, G. Blake Meike, and Masumi Nakamura

Published by O'Reilly Media, Inc., 1005 Gravenstein Highway North, Sebastopol, CA 95472.

O'Reilly books may be purchased for educational, business, or sales promotional use. Online editions are also available for most titles (*http://my.safaribooksonline.com*). For more information, contact our corporate/institutional sales department: 800-998-9938 or *corporate@oreilly.com*.

Editors: Andy Oram and Rachel Roumeliotis
Production Editor: Melanie Yarbrough
Copyeditor: Audrey Doyle
Proofreader: Teresa Horton

Indexer: Ellen Troutman-Zaig
Cover Designer: Karen Montgomery
Interior Designer: David Futato
Illustrator: Robert Romano

September 2012:   Second Edition.

Revision History for the Second Edition:
2012-09-26   First release
See *http://oreilly.com/catalog/errata.csp?isbn=9781449316648* for release details.

ISBN: 978-1-449-31664-8

[LSI]

1348680648

Table of Contents

Part II.   About the Android Framework

Part III.   A Skeleton Application for Android

Part IV.   Advanced Topics

Preface

The purpose of this book is to enable you to create well-engineered Android applications that go beyond the scope of small example applications.

This book is for people coming to Android programming from a variety of backgrounds. If you have been programming iPhone or Mac OS applications in Objective-C, you will find coverage of Android tools and Java language features relevant to Android programming that will help you bring your knowledge of mobile application development to Android. If you are an experienced Java coder, you will find coverage of Android application architecture that will enable you to use your Java expertise in this newly vibrant world of client Java application development. In short, this is a book for people with some relevant experience in object-oriented languages, mobile applications, REST applications, and similar disciplines who want to go further than an introductory book or online tutorials will take them.

How This Book Is Organized

We want to get you off to a fast start. The chapters in the first part of this book will step you through using the SDK tools so that you can access example code in this book and in the SDK, even as you expand your knowledge of SDK tools, Java, and database design. The tools and basics covered in the first part might be familiar enough to you that you would want to skip to Part II where we build foundational knowledge for developing larger Android applications.

The central part of this book is an example of an application that uses web services to deliver information to the user—something many applications have at their core. We present an application architecture, and a novel approach to using Android's framework classes that enables you to do this particularly efficiently. You will be able to use this application as a framework for creating your own applications, and as a tool for learning about Android programming.

In the final part of this book, we explore Android APIs in specific application areas: multimedia, location, sensors, and communication, among others, in order to equip you to program applications in your specific area of interest.

By the time you reach the end of this book, we want you to have gained knowledge beyond reference material and a walk-through of examples. We want you to have a point of view on how to make great Android applications.

Conventions Used in This Book

The following typographical conventions are used in this book:

Italic
> Indicates new terms, URLs, email addresses, filenames, and file extensions

`Constant width`
> Used for program listings, as well as within paragraphs to refer to program elements such as variable or function names, databases, data types, environment variables, statements, and keywords

`Constant width bold`
> Shows commands or other text that should be typed literally by the user

`Constant width italic`
> Shows text that should be replaced with user-supplied values or by values determined by context

 This icon signifies a tip, suggestion, or general note.

 This icon indicates a warning or caution.

Using Code Examples

This book is here to help you get your job done. In general, you may use the code in this book in your programs and documentation. You do not need to contact us for permission unless you're reproducing a significant portion of the code. For example, writing a program that uses several chunks of code from this book does not require permission. Selling or distributing a CD-ROM of examples from O'Reilly books does require permission. Answering a question by citing this book and quoting example code does not require permission. Incorporating a significant amount of example code from this book into your product's documentation does require permission.

We appreciate, but do not require, attribution. An attribution usually includes the title, author, publisher, and ISBN. For example: "*Programming Android, Second*

Edition by Zigurd Mednieks, Laird Dornin, G. Blake Meike, and Masumi Nakamura. Copyright 2012 O'Reilly Media, Inc., 978-1-449-31664-8."

If you feel your use of code examples falls outside fair use or the permission given here, feel free to contact us at *permissions@oreilly.com*.

Safari® Books Online

Safari Books Online (*www.safaribooksonline.com*) is an on-demand digital library that delivers expert content in both book and video form from the world's leading authors in technology and business.

Technology professionals, software developers, web designers, and business and creative professionals use Safari Books Online as their primary resource for research, problem solving, learning, and certification training.

Safari Books Online offers a range of product mixes and pricing programs for organizations, government agencies, and individuals. Subscribers have access to thousands of books, training videos, and prepublication manuscripts in one fully searchable database from publishers like O'Reilly Media, Prentice Hall Professional, Addison-Wesley Professional, Microsoft Press, Sams, Que, Peachpit Press, Focal Press, Cisco Press, John Wiley & Sons, Syngress, Morgan Kaufmann, IBM Redbooks, Packt, Adobe Press, FT Press, Apress, Manning, New Riders, McGraw-Hill, Jones & Bartlett, Course Technology, and dozens more. For more information about Safari Books Online, please visit us online.

How to Contact Us

Please address comments and questions concerning this book to the publisher:

O'Reilly Media, Inc.
1005 Gravenstein Highway North
Sebastopol, CA 95472
800-998-9938 (in the United States or Canada)
707-829-0515 (international or local)
707-829-0104 (fax)

We have a web page for this book, where we list errata, examples, and any additional information. You can access this page at *http://oreil.ly/prog_android_2e*.

To comment or ask technical questions about this book, send email to *bookquestions@oreilly.com*.

For more information about our books, courses, conferences, and news, see our website at *http://www.oreilly.com*.

Find us on Facebook: *http://facebook.com/oreilly*

Follow us on Twitter: *http://twitter.com/oreillymedia*

Watch us on YouTube: *http://www.youtube.com/oreillymedia*

Acknowledgments

The authors have adapted portions of this book from their previously released title, *Android Application Development* (O'Reilly).

Drafts of this book were released on the O'Reilly Open Feedback Publishing System (OFPS) in order to get your feedback on whether and how we are meeting the goals for this book. We are very grateful for the readers who participated in OFPS, and we owe them much in correcting our errors and improving our writing. Open review of drafts will be part of future editions, and we welcome your views on every aspect of this book.

Zigurd Mednieks

I am eternally grateful to Terry, my wife, and Maija and Charles, my children, who gave me the time to do this. This book exists because our agent, Carole Jelen, at Waterside Productions, whipped our proposal material into shape, and because Mike Hendrickson kicked off the project within O'Reilly. Brian Jepson and Andy Oram, our editors, kept this large troupe of authors unified in purpose and result. Thanks to Johan van der Hoeven, who provided review comments that contributed much to accuracy and clarity. Thanks to all the reviewers who used the Open Feedback Publishing System to help make this a better book.

Laird Dornin

Thanks to my wonderful Norah for encouraging me to take part in this project, even though you had no idea of the amount of effort involved in writing a book. Cheers to trips to Acadia, trips to New Hampshire, and late nights writing. I'm glad this book did not stall our truly important project, the arrival of our beautiful daughter Claire. Thanks to Andy our editor, and my coauthors for giving me this opportunity. Thanks to Larry for reviewing and enabling me to work on this project. I'm glad that ideas I developed at SavaJe could find a voice in this book. Finally, thanks to our main reviewers Vijay and Johan, you both found solid ways to improve the content.

G. Blake Meike

My thanks to our agent, Carole Jelen, Waterside Productions, without whom this book would never have been more than a good idea. Thanks, also, to editors Brian Jepson and Andy Oram, masters of the "gentle way." Everyone who reads this book benefits from the efforts of Johan van der Hoeven and Vijay Yellapragada, technical reviewers; Sumita Mukherji, Adam Zaremba, and the rest of the O'Reilly production team; and all those who used O'Reilly's OFPS to wade through early and nearly incomprehensible drafts, to produce salient comments and catch egregious errors. Thanks guys! Speaking of "thanks guys," it was quite an honor and certainly a pleasure to collaborate with my coauthors, Zigurd, Laird, and Masumi. Of course, last, best, and as ever, thanks and love to my wife Catherine, who challenges me in the good times and provides support when it's dark. Yeah, I know, the bookcase still isn't done.

Masumi Nakamura

I would like to thank my friends and family for bearing with me as I worked on this and other projects. An especially big thank you to Jessamyn for dealing with me all these years. I also would like to thank Brian and Andy for getting us through the fine points of writing and publishing, as well as my coauthors for bringing me in to work on this piece. Also, a quick shout out to all the people at WHERE, Inc. who have been very supportive in my technological wanderings. Finally, a thank you to you, the readers, and all you developers working tirelessly to make Android a great platform to work on and enjoy using.

PART I

Tools and Basics

Part I shows you how to install and use your tools, what you need to know about Java to write good Android code, and how to design and use SQL databases, which are central to the Android application model, persistence system, and implementation of key design patterns in Android programs.

## CHAPTER 1

Installing the Android SDK and Prerequisites

This chapter shows you how to install the Android software development kit (SDK) and all the related software you're likely to need. By the end, you'll be able to run a simple "Hello World" program on an emulator. Windows, Mac OS X, and Linux systems can all be used for Android application development. We will load the software, introduce you to the tools in the SDK, and point you to sources of example code.

Throughout this book, and especially in this chapter, we refer to instructions available on various websites for installing and updating the tools you will use for creating Android programs. The most important place to find information and links to tools is the Android Developers site:

http://developer.android.com

Our focus is on guiding you through installation, with explanations that will help you understand how the parts of Android and its developer tools fit together, even as the details of each part change.

Installing the Android SDK and Prerequisites

Successfully installing the Android SDK requires two other software systems that are not part of the Android SDK: the Java Development Kit (JDK) and the Eclipse integrated development environment (IDE). These two systems are not delivered as part of the Android SDK because you may be using them for purposes outside of Android software development, or because they may already be installed on your system, and redundant installations of these systems can cause version clashes.

The Android SDK is compatible with a range of recent releases of the JDK and the Eclipse IDE. Installing the current release of each of these tools will usually be the right choice. The exact requirements are specified on the "System requirements" page of the Android Developers site: *http://developer.android.com/sdk/requirements.html*.

One can use IDEs other than Eclipse in Android software development, and information on using other IDEs is provided in the Android documentation at *http://developer .android.com/guide/developing/other-ide.html*. We chose Eclipse as the IDE covered in this book because Eclipse supports the greatest number of Android SDK tools and other plug-ins, and Eclipse is the most widely used Java IDE, but IntelliJ IDEA is an alternative many Java coders prefer.

The Java Development Kit (JDK)

If your system has an up-to-date JDK installed, you won't need to install it again. The JDK provides tools, such as the Java compiler, used by IDEs and SDKs for developing Java programs. The JDK also contains a Java Runtime Environment (JRE), which enables Java programs, such as Eclipse, to run on your system.

If you are using a Macintosh running a version of Mac OS X supported by the Android SDK, the JDK is already installed.

If you are a Linux or Windows user, or you need to install the JDK from Oracle's site for some other reason, you can find the JDK at *http://www.oracle.com/technetwork/ java/javase/downloads/index.html*.

The Windows installer you download is an executable file. Run the executable installer file to install the JDK.

Linux users will need to extract the JDK folder they downloaded into their home directory, and perform the following steps to install the JDK. These steps assume you want to use the current Oracle JDK as your default Java runtime:

Download the archive or package corresponding to your system. (If it is a package, use the package manager to complete the installation; otherwise, follow these steps.)

```
tar -xvf archive-name.tar.gz
```

The JDK archive will be extracted into the *./jdk-name* directory. Now move the JDK directory to */usr/lib*:

```
sudo mv ./jdk-name /usr/lib/jvm/jdk-name
```

Moving the JDK to that location makes it a configurable alternative in your Linux environment, which is useful if you have projects or programs that require other versions of the JRE or JDK. Now run:

```
sudo update-alternatives --install "/usr/bin/java" "java" \
                                   "/usr/lib/jvm/jdk-name/bin/java" 1
sudo update-alternatives --install "/usr/bin/javac" "javac" \
                                   "/usr/lib/jvm/jdk-name.0/bin/javac" 1
sudo update-alternatives --install "/usr/bin/javaws" "javaws" \
                                   "/usr/lib/jvm/jdk-name/bin/javaws" 1
sudo update-alternatives --config java
```

You will see output similar to that shown here:

```
There are 3 choices for the alternative java (providing /usr/bin/java).

Selection  Path                                        Priority   Status
------------------------------------------------------------------------
* 0        /usr/lib/jvm/java-6-openjdk/jre/bin/java     63         auto mode
  1        /usr/lib/jvm/java-6-openjdk/jre/bin/java     63         manual mode
  2        /usr/lib/jvm/java-6-sun/jre/bin/java         63         manual mode
  3        /usr/lib/jvm/jdk1.7.0/jre/bin/java           1          manual mode

Press enter to keep the current choice[*], or type selection number:
```

When you select the JDK you are installing, you will see output like this:

```
update-alternatives: using /usr/lib/jvm/jdk1.7.0/jre/bin/java to provide
                           /usr/bin/java (java) in manual mode.
```

Repeat the preceding selection process for **javac**:

```
sudo update-alternatives --config javac
```

And for **javaws**:

```
sudo update-alternatives --config javaws
```

Depending on the different kinds of Java implementations installed on your system, and the current version of the JDK available when you read this, version numbers may differ from what you see in examples of command output here.

For every OS, you can now check the version of Java installed with this command:

```
java -version
```

The version reported should correspond to the version you installed. If not, repeat the installation steps, and make sure that no errors are reported during installation.

The Eclipse Integrated Development Environment (IDE)

Eclipse is a general-purpose technology platform. It has been applied to a variety of uses in creating IDEs for multiple languages and in creating customized IDEs for many specialized SDKs, as well as to uses outside of software development tools, such as providing a Rich Client Platform (RCP) for Lotus Notes and a few other applications.

Eclipse is usually used as an IDE for writing, testing, and debugging software, especially Java software. There are also several derivative IDEs and SDKs for various kinds of Java software development based on Eclipse. In this case, you will take a widely used Eclipse package and add a plug-in to it to make it usable for Android software development. Let's get that Eclipse package and install it.

Eclipse can be downloaded from *http://www.eclipse.org/downloads*.

You will see a selection of the most commonly used Eclipse packages on this page. An Eclipse "package" is a ready-made collection of Eclipse modules that make Eclipse better suited for certain kinds of software development. Usually, Eclipse users start with one of the Eclipse packages available for download on this page and customize it with plug-ins, which is what you will do when you add the Android Developer Tools (ADT) plug-in to your Eclipse installation. The System Requirements article on the Android Developers site lists three choices of Eclipse packages as a basis for an Eclipse installation for Android software development:

- Eclipse Classic (for Eclipse 3.5 or later)
- Eclipse IDE for Java Developers
- Eclipse for RCP/Plug-in Developers

Any of these will work, though unless you are also developing Eclipse plug-ins, choosing either Classic or the Java Developers package (EE or Standard) makes the most sense. The authors of this book started with the Java EE Developers package ("EE" stands for Enterprise Edition), and screenshots of Eclipse used in this book reflect that choice.

The Eclipse download site will automatically determine the available system-specific downloads for your system, though you may have to choose between 32 and 64 bits to match your operating system. The file you download is an archive. To install Eclipse, open the archive and copy the *eclipse* folder to your home folder. The executable file for launching Eclipse on your system will be found in the folder you just extracted from the archive.

 We really mean it about installing Eclipse in your home folder (or another folder you own), especially if you have multiple user accounts on your system. Do not use your system's package manager. Your Eclipse installation is one of a wide range of possible groupings of Eclipse plug-ins. In addition, you will probably further customize your installation of Eclipse. Eclipse plug-ins and updates are managed separately from other software in your system.

If you are using Ubuntu or another Linux distribution, you should not install Eclipse from your distribution's repositories, and if it is currently installed this way, you must remove it and install Eclipse as described here. The presence of an "eclipse" package in the Ubuntu repositories is an inheritance from the Debian repositories on which Ubuntu is based. It is not a widely used approach to installing and using Eclipse, because most of the time, your distribution's repositories will have older versions of Eclipse.

To confirm that Eclipse is correctly installed and that you have a JRE that supports Eclipse, launch the executable file in the Eclipse folder. You may want to make a shortcut to this executable file to launch Eclipse more conveniently. You should see the Welcome screen shown in Figure 1-1.

Eclipse is implemented in Java and requires a JRE. The JDK you previously installed provides a JRE. If Eclipse does not run, you should check that the JDK is correctly installed.

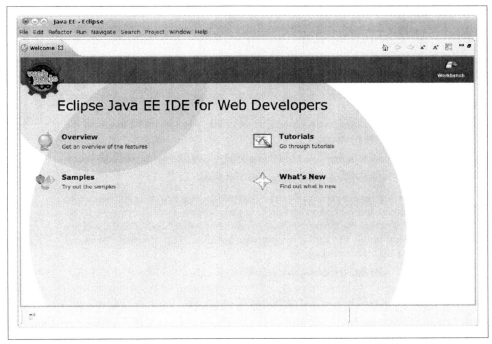

Figure 1-1. Welcome screen that you see the first time you run Eclipse

The Android SDK

With the JDK and Eclipse installed, you have the prerequisites for the Android SDK, and are ready to install the SDK. The Android SDK is a collection of files: libraries, executables, scripts, documentation, and tools. Installing the SDK means downloading the correct version of the SDK for your platform and putting the SDK files into a folder in your home directory. There is no installation script. Later, you will configure an Eclipse plug-in so it can find where you put the SDK. The appearance, requirements, and functionality of the Android toolkit are changing very rapidly. The following outlined process is a guideline that may not exactly reflect your experience. The most recent documentation can always be found at *http://developer.android.com/tools/index.html*.

To install the SDK, download the SDK package that corresponds to your system from *http://developer.android.com/sdk/index.html*.

The download is an archive. Open the archive and extract the folder at the top level of the archive to your home folder.

The SDK contains one or two folders for tools: one named *tools* and, starting in version 8 of the SDK, another called *platform-tools*. These folders need to be on your path, which is a list of folders your system searches for executable files when you invoke an executable from the command line. On Macintosh and Linux systems, setting the PATH environment variable is done in the *.profile* (Ubuntu) or *.bash_profile* (Mac OS X) file in your home directory. Add a line to that file that sets the PATH environment variable to include the *tools* directory in the SDK (individual entries in the list are separated by colons). For example, you could use the following line (but replace both instances of ~/android-sdk-*ARCH* with the full path to your Android SDK install):

```
export PATH=$PATH:~/android-sdk-ARCH/tools:~/android-sdk-ARCH/platform-tools
```

 If you are using a 64-bit version of Linux, you may need to install the ia32-libs package.

To check whether you need this package, try running the adb command:

```
~/android-sdk-linux_*/platform-tools/adb
```

If your system reports that the Android Debug Bridge (adb) cannot be found (despite being right there in the *platform-tools* directory) it likely means that the current version of adb, and possibly other tools, will not run without the ia32-libs package installed. The command to install the ia32-libs package is:

```
sudo apt-get install ia32-libs
```

On Windows systems, click Start→right-click Computer, and choose Properties. Then click Advanced System Settings, and click the Environment Variables button. Double-click the path system variable, and add the path to the folders by going to the end of this variable's value (do not change anything that's already there!) and adding the two paths to the end, separated by semicolons with no space before them. For example:

```
;C:\android-sdk-windows\tools;C:\android-sdk-windows\platform-tools
```

After you've edited your path on Windows, Mac, or Linux, close and reopen any Command Prompts or Terminals to pick up the new PATH setting (on Ubuntu, you may need to log out and log in unless your Terminal program is configured as a login shell).

Adding Build Targets to the SDK

Before you can build an Android application, or even create a project that would try to build an Android application, you must install one or more build targets. To do this, you will use the SDK and AVD Manager. This tool enables you to install packages in the SDK that will support multiple versions of the Android OS and multiple API levels.

Once the ADT plug-in is installed in Eclipse, which we describe in the next section, the SDK and AVD Manager can be invoked from within Eclipse. It can also be invoked from the command line, which is how we will do it here. To invoke the SDK and AVD Manager from the command line, issue this command:

```
android
```

The screenshot in Figure 1-2 shows the SDK and AVD Manager, with all the available SDK versions selected for installation.

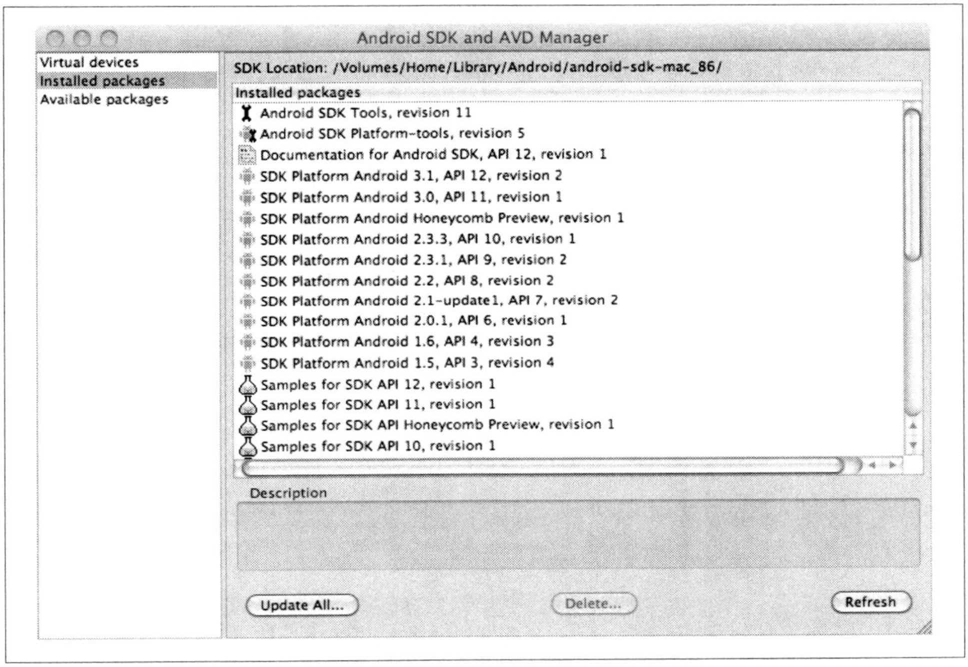

Figure 1-2. The SDK and AVD Manager, which enables installation of Android API levels

The packages labeled "SDK Platform" support building applications compatible with different Android API levels. You should install, at a minimum, the most recent (highest-numbered) version, but installing all the available API levels, and all the Google API add-on packages, is a good choice if you might someday want to build applications that run on older Android versions. You should also install, at a minimum, the most recent versions of the example applications package. You must also install the Android SDK Platform-Tools package.

The Android Developer Tools (ADT) Plug-in for Eclipse

Now that you have the SDK files installed, along with Eclipse and the JDK, there is one more critical part to install: the Android Developer Tools (ADT) plug-in. The ADT plug-in adds Android-specific functionality to Eclipse.

Software in the plug-in enables Eclipse to build Android applications, launch the Android emulator, connect to debugging services on the emulator, edit Android XML files, edit and compile Android Interface Definition Language (AIDL) files, create Android application packages (.*apk* files), and perform other Android-specific tasks.

Using the Install New Software Wizard to download and install the ADT plug-in

You start the Install New Software Wizard by selecting Help→Install New Software (Figure 1-3). To install the ADT plug-in, type this URL into the "Work with" field and press Return or Enter: **https://dl-ssl.google.com/android/eclipse/** (see Figure 1-4).

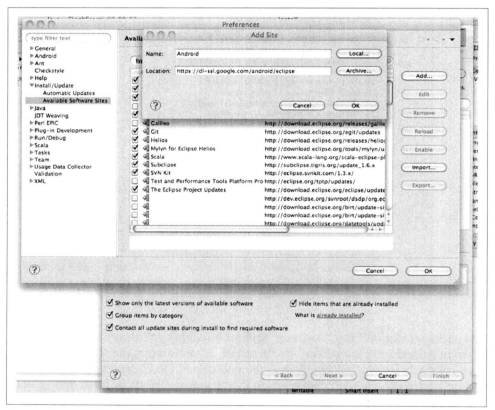

Figure 1-3. The Eclipse Add Site dialog

More information on installing the ADT plug-in using the Install New Software Wizard can be found on the Android Developers site, at *http: //developer.android.com/sdk/eclipse-adt.html#downloading.*

Eclipse documentation on this wizard can be found on the Eclipse documentation site, at *http://help.eclipse.org/galileo/index.jsp?topic=/org .eclipse.platform.doc.user/tasks/tasks-124.htm.*

Once you have added the URL to the list of sites for acquiring new plug-ins, you will see an entry called Developer Tools listed in the Available Software list.

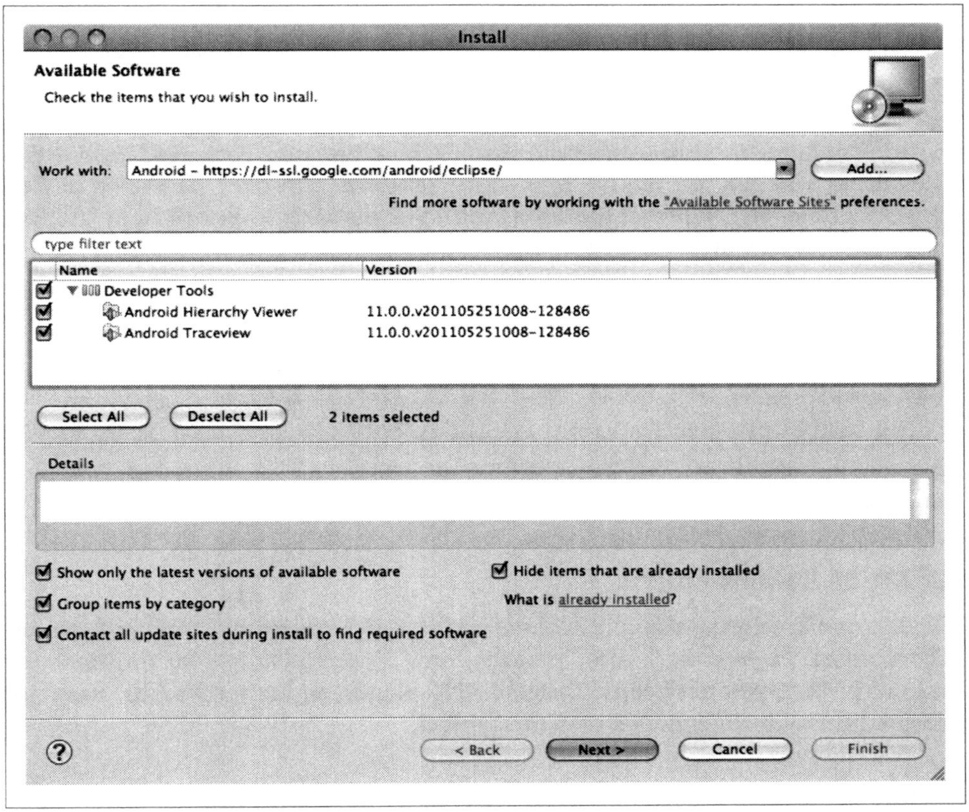

Figure 1-4. *The Eclipse Install dialog with the Android Hierarchy Viewer plug-in shown as available*

Select the Developer Tools item by clicking on the checkbox next to it, and click on the Next button. The next screen will ask you to accept the license for this software. After you accept and click Finish, the ADT will be installed. You will have to restart Eclipse to complete the installation.

Configuring the ADT plug-in

One more step, and you are done installing. Once you have installed the ADT plug-in, you will need to configure it. Installing the plug-in means that various parts of Eclipse now contain Android software development-specific dialogs, menu commands, and other tools, including the dialog you will now use to configure the ADT plug-in. Start the Preferences dialog using the Window→Preferences (Linux and Windows) or Eclipse→Preferences (Mac) menu option. Click the item labeled Android in the left pane of the Preferences dialog.

 The first time you visit this section of the preferences, you'll see a dialog asking if you want to send some usage statistics to Google. Make your choice and click Proceed.

A dialog with the Android settings is displayed next. In this dialog, a text entry field labeled SDK Location appears near the top. You must enter the path to where you put the SDK, or you can use the file browser to select the directory, as shown in Figure 1-5. Click Apply. Note that the build targets you installed, as described in "Adding Build Targets to the SDK" on page 8, are listed here as well.

Your Android SDK installation is now complete.

Test Drive: Confirm That Your Installation Works

If you have followed the steps in this chapter, and the online instructions referred to here, your installation of the Android SDK is now complete. To confirm that everything you installed so far works, let's create a simple Android application.

Making an Android Project

The first step in creating a simple Android application is to create an Android project. Eclipse organizes your work into "projects," and by designating your project as an Android project, you tell Eclipse that the ADT plug-in and other Android tools are going to be used in conjunction with this project.

 Reference information and detailed online instructions for creating an Android project can be found at *http://developer.android.com/guide/de veloping/eclipse-adt.html*.

Start your new project with the File→New→Android Project menu command. Locate the Android Project option in the New Android Project dialog (it should be under a

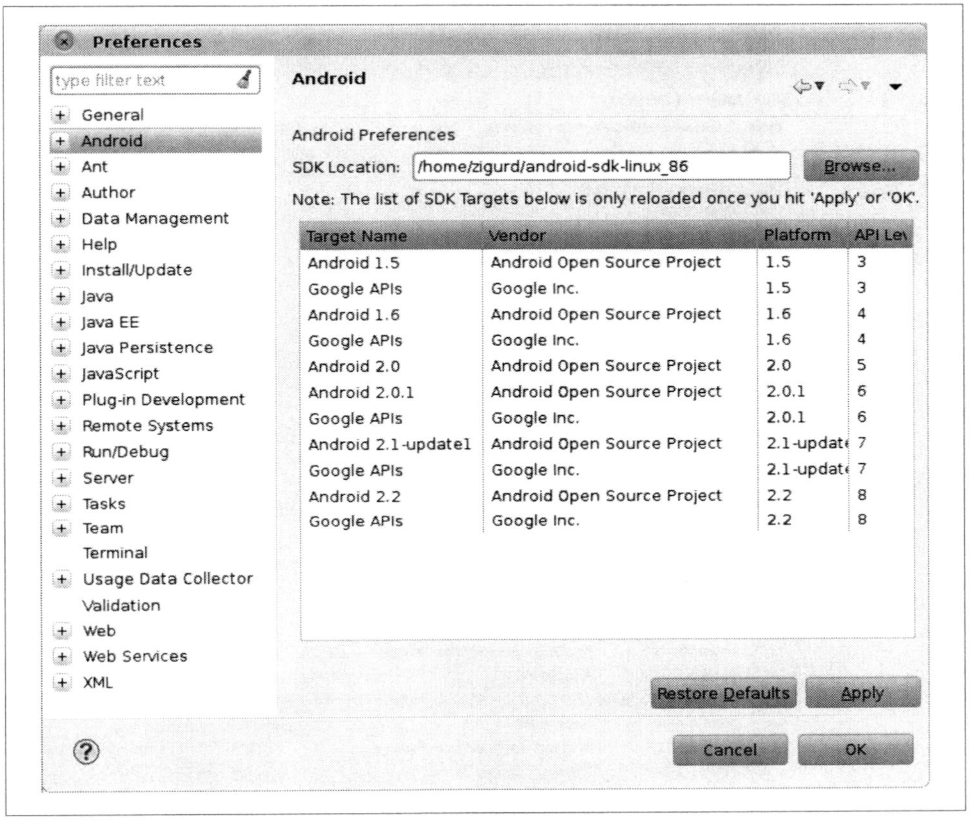

Preferences

type filter text

Android

General
Android
Ant
Author
Data Management
Help
Install/Update
Java
Java EE
Java Persistence
JavaScript
Plug-in Development
Remote Systems
Run/Debug
Server
Tasks
Team
Terminal
Usage Data Collector
Validation
Web
Web Services
XML

Android Preferences

SDK Location: /home/zigurd/android-sdk-linux_86   Browse...

Note: The list of SDK Targets below is only reloaded once you hit 'Apply' or 'OK'.

Target Name	Vendor	Platform	API Lev
Android 1.5	Android Open Source Project	1.5	3
Google APIs	Google Inc.	1.5	3
Android 1.6	Android Open Source Project	1.6	4
Google APIs	Google Inc.	1.6	4
Android 2.0	Android Open Source Project	2.0	5
Android 2.0.1	Android Open Source Project	2.0.1	6
Google APIs	Google Inc.	2.0.1	6
Android 2.1-update1	Android Open Source Project	2.1-update	7
Google APIs	Google Inc.	2.1-update	7
Android 2.2	Android Open Source Project	2.2	8
Google APIs	Google Inc.	2.2	8

Restore Defaults   Apply

Cancel   OK

Figure 1-5. Configuring the SDK location into the Eclipse ADT plug-in using the Android Preferences dialog

section named Android). Click Next, and the New Project dialog appears as shown in Figure 1-6.

To create your Android project, you will provide the following information:

Project name

This is the name of the project (not the application) that appears in Eclipse. Type **TestProject**, as shown in Figure 1-6.

Workspace

A workspace is a folder containing a set of Eclipse projects. In creating a new project, you have the choice of creating the project in your current workspace, or specifying a different location in the filesystem for your project. Unless you need to put this project in a specific location, use the defaults ("Create new project in workspace" and "Use default location").

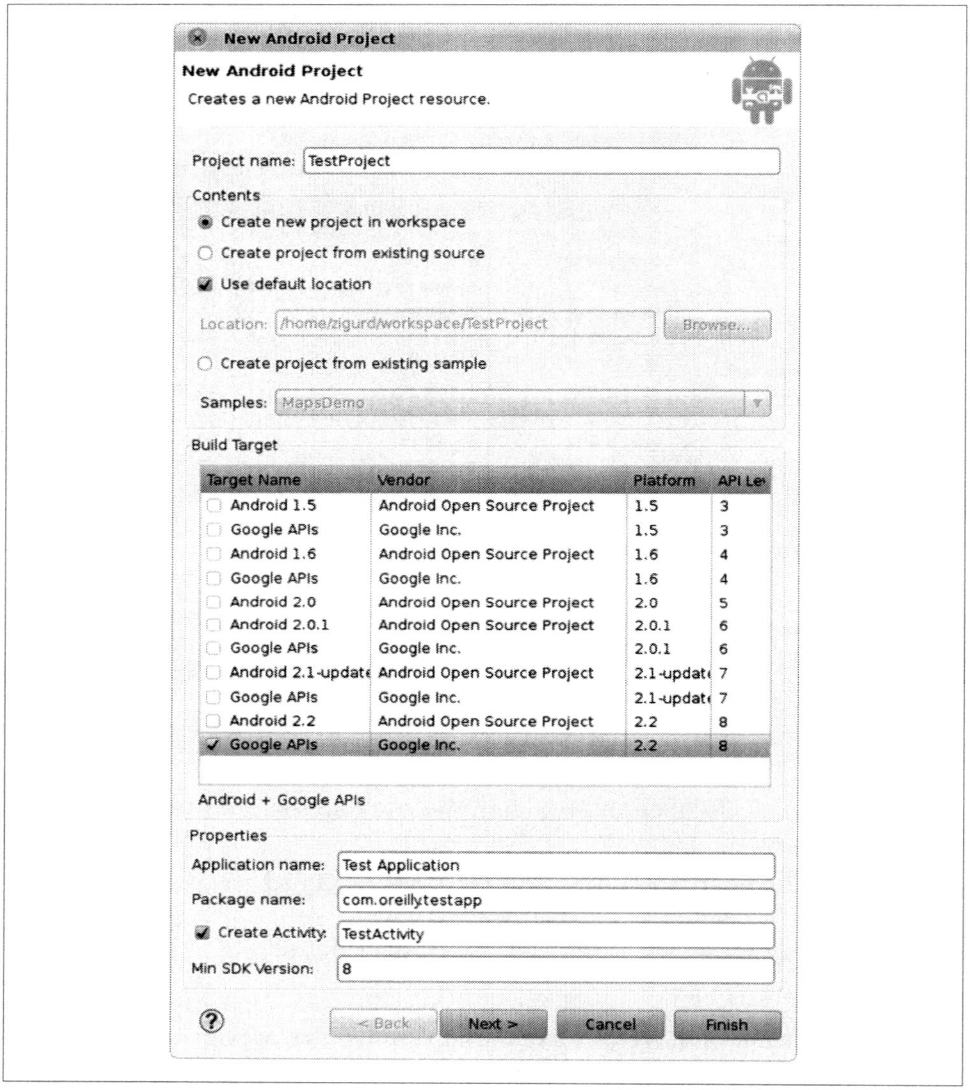

Figure 1-6. The New Android Project dialog

Target name

The Android system images you installed in the SDK are shown in the build target list. You can pick one of these system images, and the corresponding vendor, platform (Android OS version number), and API level as the target for which your application is built. The platform and API level are the most important parameters here: they govern the Android platform library that your application will be compiled with, and the API level supported—APIs with a higher API level than the one you select will not be available to your program. For now, pick the most recent Android OS version and API level you have installed.

Application name

This is the application name the user will see. Type **Test Application**.

Package name

The package name creates a Java package namespace that uniquely identifies packages in your application, and must also uniquely identify your whole Android application among all other installed applications. It consists of a unique domain name—the application publisher's domain name—plus a name specific to the application. Not all package namespaces are unique in Java, but the conventions used for Android applications make namespace conflicts less likely. In our example we used com.oreilly.testapp, but you can put something appropriate for your domain here (you can also use com.example.testapp, since example.com is a domain name reserved for examples such as this one).

Activity

An *activity* is a unit of interactive user interface in an Android application, usually corresponding to a group of user interface objects occupying the entire screen. Optionally, when you create a project you can have a skeleton activity created for you. If you are creating a visual application (in contrast with a service, which can be "headless"—without a visual UI), this is a convenient way to create the activity the application will start with. In this example, you should create an activity called TestActivity.

Minimum SDK version

The field labeled Min SDK Version should contain an integer corresponding to the minimum SDK version required by your application, and is used to initialize the uses-sdk attribute in the application's manifest, which is a file that stores application attributes. See "The Android Manifest Editor" on page 24. In most cases, this should be the same as the API level of the build target you selected, which is displayed in the rightmost column of the list of build targets, as shown in Figure 1-6.

Click Finish (not Next) to create your Android project, and you will see it listed in the left pane of the Eclipse IDE as shown in Figure 1-7.

If you expand the view of the project hierarchy by clicking the "+" (Windows) or triangle (Mac and Linux) next to the project name, you will see the various parts of an Android project. Expand the *src* folder and you will see a Java package with the name you entered in the wizard. Expand that package and you will see the **Activity** class created for you by the wizard. Double-click that, and you will see the Java code of your first Android program:

```
package com.oreilly.demo.pa.ch01.testapp;

import android.app.Activity;
import android.os.Bundle;
```

```
import com.oreilly.demo.pa.ch01.R;

public class TestActivity extends Activity {
    /** Called when the activity is first created. */
    @Override
    public void onCreate(Bundle savedInstanceState) {
        super.onCreate(savedInstanceState);
        setContentView(R.layout.main);
    }
}
```

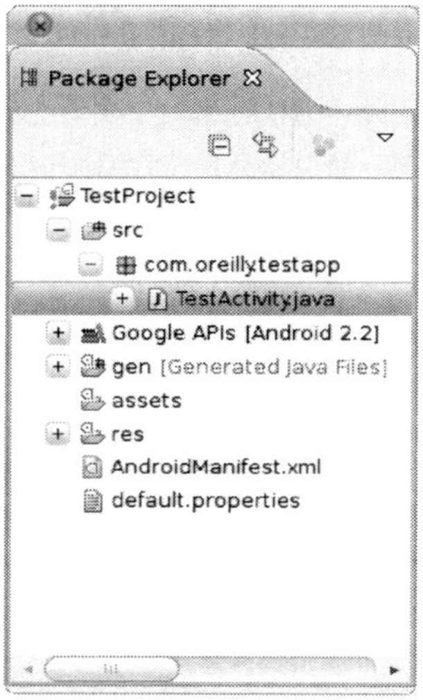

Figure 1-7. The Package Explorer view, showing the files, and their components, that are part of the project

If you've been following along and see the same thing on your computer, your SDK installation is probably working correctly. But let's make sure, and explore the SDK just a bit further, by running your first program in an emulator and on an Android device if you have one handy.

Making an Android Virtual Device (AVD)

The Android SDK provides an emulator, which emulates a device with an ARM CPU running an Android operating system (OS), for running Android programs on your PC. An Android Virtual Device (AVD) is a set of parameters for this emulator that configures it to use a particular system image—that is, a particular version of the Android operating system—and to set other parameters that govern screen size, memory size, and other emulated hardware characteristics. Detailed documentation on AVDs is available at *http://developer.android.com/guide/developing/tools/avd.html*, and detailed documentation on the emulator is found here: *http://developer.android.com/guide/developing/tools/emulator.html*.

Because we are just validating that your SDK installation works, we won't go into depth on AVDs, much less details of the emulator, just yet. Here, we will use the Android SDK and AVD Manager (see Figure 1-8) to set up an AVD for the purpose of running the program we just created with the New Android Project Wizard.

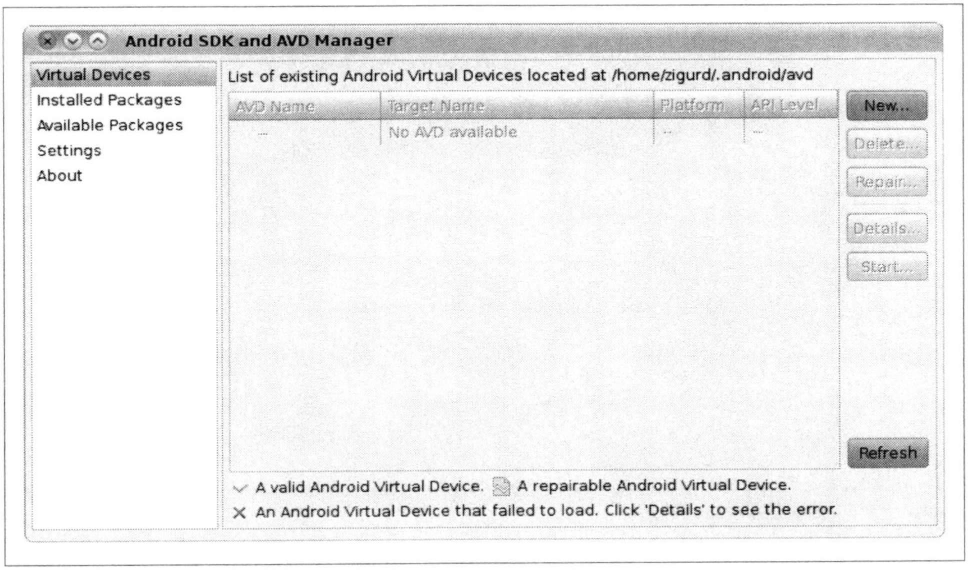

Figure 1-8. The SDK and AVD Manager

You will need to create an AVD with a system image that is no less recent than the target specified for the project you created. Click the New button. You will now see the "Create new Android Virtual Device (AVD)" dialog, shown in Figure 1-9, where you specify the parameters of your new AVD.

This screen enables you to set the parameters of your new AVD:

Name
> This is the name of the AVD. You can use any name for an AVD, but a name that indicates which system image it uses is helpful.

Target
> The Target parameter sets which system image will be used in this AVD. It should be the same as, or more recent than, the target you selected as the build target for your first Android project.

SD Card
> Some applications require an SD card that extends storage beyond the flash memory built into an Android device. Unless you plan to put a lot of data in SD card

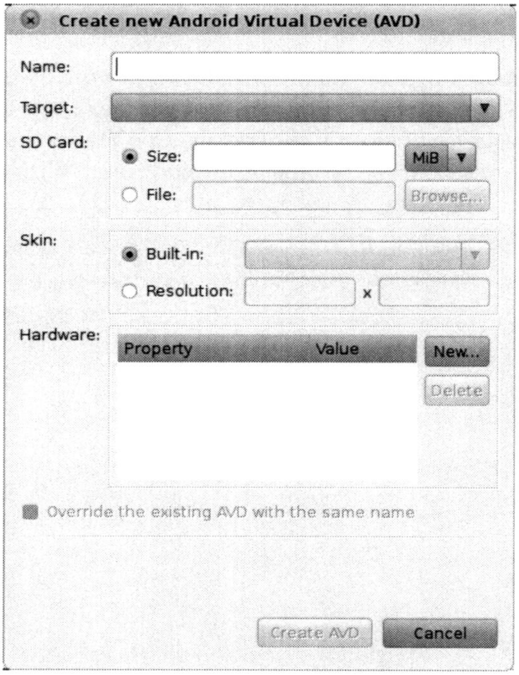

Figure 1-9. Creating a new AVD

storage (media files, for example) for applications you are developing, you can create a small virtual SD card of, say, 100 MB in size, even though most phones are equipped with SD cards holding several gigabytes.

Skin

The "skin" of an AVD mainly sets the screen size. You won't need to change the default for the purpose of verifying that your SDK installation works, but a variety of emulators with different screen sizes is useful to check that your layouts work across different devices.

Hardware

The Hardware field of an AVD configuration enables you to set parameters indicating which optional hardware is present. You won't need to change the defaults for this project.

Fill in the Name, Target, and SD Card fields, and create a new AVD by clicking the Create AVD button. If you have not created an AVD with a system image that matches or is more recent than the target you specified for an Android project, you won't be able to run your program.

Running a Program on an AVD

Now that you have a project that builds an application, and an AVD with a system image compatible with the application's build target and API level requirements, you can run your application and confirm that the SDK produced and is able to run an Android application.

To run your application, right-click on the project you created and, in the context menu that pops up, select Run As→Android Application.

If the AVD you created is compatible with the application you created, the AVD will start, the Android OS will boot on the AVD, and your application will start. You should see your application running in the AVD, similarly to what is shown in Figure 1-10.

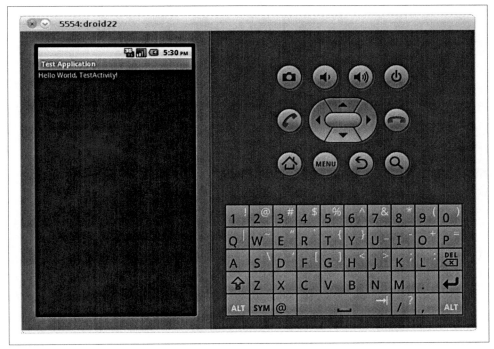

Figure 1-10. The application you just created, running in an AVD

If you have more than one compatible AVD configured, the Android Device Chooser dialog will appear and ask you to select among the AVDs that are already running, or among the Android devices attached to your system, if any, or to pick an AVD to start. Figure 1-11 shows the Android Device Chooser displaying one AVD that is running, and one that can be launched.

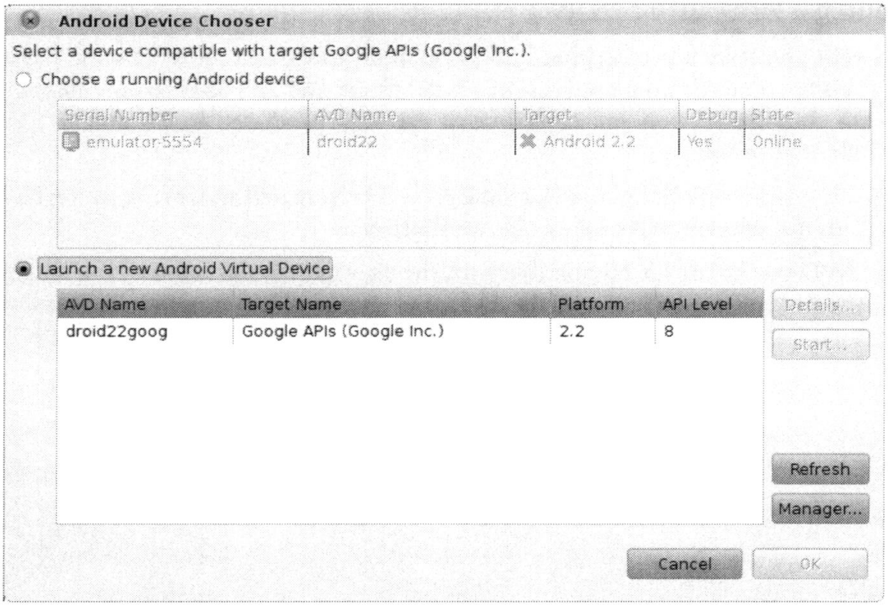

Figure 1-11. The Android Device Chooser

Running a Program on an Android Device

You can also run the program you just created on most Android devices.

You will need to connect your device to your PC with a USB cable, and, if needed, install a driver, or set permissions to access the device when connected via USB.

System-specific instructions for Windows, along with the needed driver, are available at *http://developer.android.com/sdk/win-usb.html*.

If you are running Linux, you will need to create a "rules" file for your Android device.

If you are running Mac OS X, no configuration is required.

Detailed reference information on USB debugging is available at *http://developer.an droid.com/guide/developing/device.html*.

You will also need to turn on USB debugging in your Android device. In most cases, you will start the Settings application, select Applications and then Development, and then see an option to turn USB debugging on or off.

If an AVD is configured or is running, the Android Device Chooser will appear, displaying both the Android device you have connected and the AVD.

Select the device, and the Android application will be loaded and run on the device.

Troubleshooting SDK Problems: No Build Targets

If you are unable to make a new project or import an example project from the SDK, you may have missed installing build targets into your SDK. Reread the instructions in "Adding Build Targets to the SDK" on page 8 and make sure the Android pane in the Preferences dialog lists build targets as installed in your SDK, as shown in Figure 1-5.

Components of the SDK

The Android SDK is made of mostly off-the-shelf components, plus some purpose-built components. In many cases, configurations, plug-ins, and extensions adapt these components to Android. The Android SDK is a study in the efficient development of a modern and complete SDK. Google took this approach to bring Android to market quickly. You will see this for yourself as you explore the components of the Android SDK. Eclipse, the Java language, QEMU, and other preexisting platforms, tools, and technologies comprise some of the most important parts of the Android SDK.

In creating the simple program that confirms that your SDK installation is correct, you have already used many of the components of the SDK. Here we will identify and describe the components of the SDK involved in creating your program, and other parts you have yet to use.

The Android Debug Bridge (adb)

The Android Debug Bridge (adb) is a program that enables you to control both emulators and devices, and to run a shell to execute commands in the environment of an emulator or device. Adb is especially handy for installing and removing programs from an emulator or device. Documentation on adb can be found at *http://developer.android .com/guide/developing/tools/adb.html*.

The Dalvik Debug Monitor Server (DDMS)

The Dalvik Debug Monitor Server (DDMS) is a traffic director between the single port that Eclipse (and other Java debuggers) looks for to connect to a Java Virtual Machine (JVM) and the several ports that exist for each Android device or virtual device; DDMS is also a traffic controller for each instance of the Dalvik virtual machine (VM) on each device. The DDMS also provides a collection of functionality that is accessible through a standalone user interface or through an interface embedded in Eclipse via the ADT plug-in.

When you invoke the DDMS from the command line, you will see something similar to the window shown in Figure 1-12.

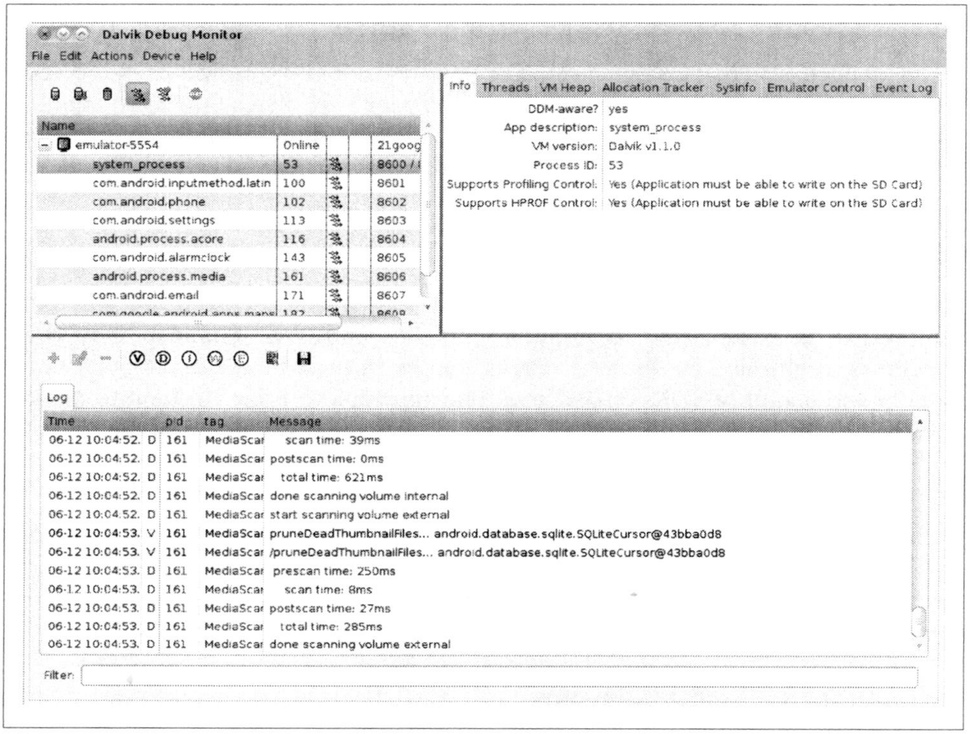

Figure 1-12. The Dalvik Debug Monitor running standalone

The DDMS's user interface provides access to the following:

A list of devices and virtual devices, and the VMs running on those devices
> In the upper-left pane of the DDMS window, you will see listed the Android devices you have connected to your PC, plus any AVDs you have running. Listed under each device or virtual device are the tasks running in Dalvik VMs.

VM information
> Selecting one of the Dalvik VMs running on a device or virtual device causes information about that VM to be displayed in the upper-right pane.

Thread information
> Information for threads within each process is accessed through the Threads tab in the upper-right pane of the DDMS window.

Filesystem explorer
> You can explore the filesystem on a device or virtual device using the DDMS filesystem explorer, accessible through the "File explorer" menu item in the Devices menu. It displays the file hierarchy in a window similar to the one shown in Figure 1-13.

Simulating phone calls

The Emulator Control tab in the upper-right pane of the DDMS window enables you to "fake" a phone call or text message in an emulator.

Screen capture

The "Screen capture" command in the Device menu fetches an image of the current screen from the selected Android device or virtual device.

Logging

The bottom pane of the DDMS window displays log output from processes on the selected device or virtual device. You can filter the log output by selecting a filter from among the buttons on the toolbar above the logging pane.

Dumping state for devices, apps, and the mobile radio

A set of commands in the Device menu enables you to command the device or virtual device to dump state for the whole device, an app, or the mobile radio.

Detailed documentation on the DDMS is available at *http://developer.android.com/guide/developing/tools/ddms.html.*

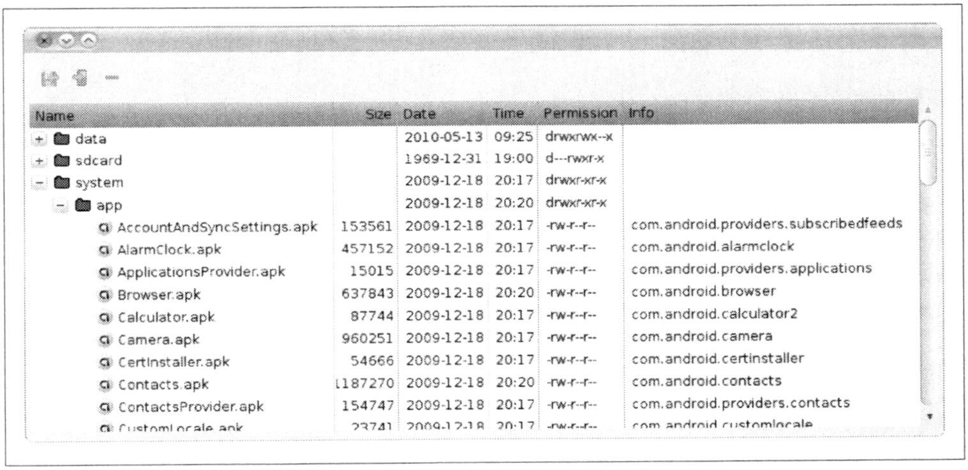

Figure 1-13. The DDMS filesystem explorer

Components of the ADT Eclipse Plug-in

Eclipse enables you to create specific project types, including several kinds of Java projects. The ADT plug-in adds the ability to make and use Android projects. When you make a new Android project, the ADT plug-in creates the project file hierarchy and all the required files for the minimal Android project to be correctly built. For Android projects, the ADT plug-in enables Eclipse to apply components of the ADT plug-in to editing, building, running, and debugging that project.

In some cases, components of the SDK can be used with Eclipse or in a standalone mode. But in most of the Android application development cases covered in this book, the way these components are used in or with Eclipse will be the most relevant.

The ADT plug-in has numerous separate components, and, despite the connotations of a "plug-in" as a modest enhancement, it's a substantial amount of software. Here we will describe each significant part of the ADT plug-in that you will encounter in using Eclipse for developing Android software.

The Android Layout Editor

Layouts for user interfaces in Android applications can be specified in XML. The ADT plug-in adds a visual editor that helps you to compose and preview Android layouts. When you open a layout file, the ADT plug-in automatically starts this editor to view and edit the file. Tabs along the bottom of the editing pane enable you to switch between the visual editor and an XML editor.

In earlier versions of the Android SDK, the Android Layout Editor was too limited to be of much use. Now, though, you should consider using visual editing of Android layouts as a preferred way of creating layouts. Automating the specification of layouts makes it more likely that your layouts will work on the widest range of Android devices.

The Android Manifest Editor

In Android projects, a manifest file is included with the project's software and resources when the project is built. This file tells the Android system how to install and use the software in the archive that contains the built project. The manifest file is in XML, and the ADT plug-in provides a specialized XML editor to edit the manifest.

Other components of the ADT Eclipse plug-in, such as the application builders, can also modify the manifest.

XML editors for other Android XML files

Other Android XML files that hold information such as specifications for menus or resources such as strings, or that organize graphical assets of an application, have specialized editors that are opened when you open these files.

Building Android apps

Eclipse projects are usually built automatically. That means you will normally not encounter a separate step for turning the source code and resources for a project into a deployable result. Android requires Android-specific steps to build a file you can deploy to an Android emulator or device, and the ADT plug-in provides the software that executes these steps. For Android projects, the result of building the project is an *.apk* file. You can find this file for the test project created earlier in this chapter in the *bin* subfolder of the project's file hierarchy in your Eclipse workspace.

The Android-specific builders provided in the ADT plug-in enable you to use Java as the language for creating Android software, while running that software on a Dalvik VM that processes its own bytecodes. That is, among other things these builders do, they turn the Java bytecode output of the Java compiler into Dalvik bytecodes. They also create *.apk* files, which have a different structure and content than *.jar* files.

Running and debugging Android apps

When you run or debug an Android project from within Eclipse, the *.apk* file for that project is deployed and started on an AVD or Android device, using the adb and DDMS to communicate with the AVD or device and the Dalvik runtime environment that runs the project's code. The ADT plug-in adds the components that enable Eclipse to do this.

The DDMS

In "The Dalvik Debug Monitor Server (DDMS)" on page 21 we described the Dalvik Debug Monitor and how to invoke the DDMS user interface from the command line. The DDMS user interface is also available from within Eclipse. You can access it by using the Window→Open Perspective→DDMS command in the Eclipse menu. You can also access each view that makes up the DDMS perspective separately by using the Window→Show View menu and selecting, for example, the LogCat view.

Android Virtual Devices

AVDs are made up of QEMU-based emulators that emulate the hardware of an Android device, plus Android system images, which consist of Android software built to run on the emulated hardware. AVDs are configured by the SDK and AVD Manager, which sets parameters such as the size of emulated storage devices and screen dimensions, and which enables you to specify which Android system image will be used with which emulated device.

AVDs enable you to test your software on a broader range of system characteristics than you are likely to be able to acquire and test on physical devices. Because QEMU-based hardware emulators, system images, and the parameters of AVDs are all inter-changeable parts, you can even test devices and system images before hardware is available to run them.

QEMU

QEMU is the basis of AVDs. But QEMU is a very general tool that is used in a wide range of emulation systems outside the Android SDK. While you will configure QEMU indirectly, through the SDK and AVD Manager, you may someday need to tweak emulation in ways unsupported by the SDK tools, or you may be curious about the capabilities and limitations of QEMU. Luckily, QEMU has a large and vibrant developer and user community, which you can find at *http://www.qemu.org*.

The SDK and AVD Manager

QEMU is a general-purpose emulator system. The Android SDK provides controls over the configuration of QEMU that make sense for creating emulators that run Android system images. The SDK and AVD Manager provides a user interface for you to control QEMU-based AVDs.

Other SDK Tools

In addition to the major tools you are likely to use in the normal course of most development projects, there are several other tools in the SDK, and those that are used or invoked directly by developers are described here. Still more components of the SDK are listed in the Tools overview article in the Android documentation found at *http://developer.android.com/guide/developing/tools/index.html*.

Hierarchy Viewer

The Hierarchy Viewer displays and enables analysis of the view hierarchy of the current activity of a selected Android device. This enables you to see and diagnose problems with your view hierarchies as your application is running, or to examine the view hierarchies of other applications to see how they are designed. It also lets you examine a magnified view of the screen with alignment guides that help identify problems with layouts.

Layoutopt

Layoutopt is a static analyzer that operates on XML layout files and can diagnose some problems with Android layouts. Detailed information on layoutopt is available at *http://developer.android.com/guide/developing/tools/layoutopt.html*.

Monkey

Monkey is a test automation tool that runs in your emulator or device. You invoke this tool using another tool in the SDK: adb. Adb enables you to start a shell on an emulator or device, and Monkey is invoked from a shell, like this:

```
adb shell monkey --wait-dbg -p your.package.name 500
```

This invocation of Monkey sends 500 random events to the specified application (specified by the package name) after waiting for a debugger to be attached. Detailed information on Monkey can be found at *http://developer.android.com/guide/developing/tools/monkey.html*.

sqlite3

Android uses SQLite as the database system for many system databases and provides APIs for applications to make use of SQLite, which is convenient for data storage and

---

presentation. SQLite also has a command-line interface, and the `sqlite3` command enables developers to dump database schemas and perform other operations on Android databases.

These databases are, of course, in an Android device, or they are contained in an AVD, and therefore the `sqlite3` command is available in the adb shell. Detailed directions for how to access the `sqlite3` command line from inside the adb shell are available at *http://developer.android.com/guide/developing/tools/adb.html#shellcommands*. We introduce `sqlite3` in "Example Database Manipulation Using sqlite3" on page 271.

keytool

`keytool` generates encryption keys, and is used by the ADT plug-in to create temporary debug keys with which it signs code for the purpose of debugging. In most cases, you will use this tool to create a signing certificate for releasing your applications, as described in "Creating a self-signed certificate" on page 131.

Zipalign

Zipalign enables optimized access to data for production releases of Android applications. This optimization must be performed after an application is signed for release, because the signature affects byte alignment. Detailed information on zipalign is available at *http://developer.android.com/guide/developing/tools/zipalign.html*.

Draw 9-patch

A *9-patch* is a special kind of Android resource, composed of nine images, and useful when you want, for example, buttons that can grow larger without changing the radius of their corners. Draw 9-patch is a specialized drawing program for creating and previewing these types of resources. Details on Draw 9-patch are available at *http://developer.android.com/guide/developing/tools/draw9patch.html*.

android

The command named `android` can be used to invoke the SDK and AVD Manager from the command line, as we described in the SDK installation instructions in "The Android SDK" on page 7. It can also be used to create an Android project from the command line. Used in this way, it causes all the project folders, the manifest, the build properties, and the ant script for building the project to be generated. Details on this use of the `android` command can be found at *http://developer.android.com/guide/developing/other -ide.html#CreatingAProject*.

Keeping Up-to-Date

The JDK, Eclipse, and the Android SDK each come from separate suppliers. The tools you use to develop Android software can change at a rapid pace. That is why, in this book, and especially in this chapter, we refer you to the Android Developers site for information on the latest compatible versions of your tools. Keeping your tools up-to-date and compatible is a task you are likely to have to perform even as you learn how to develop Android software.

Windows, Mac OS X, and Linux all have system update mechanisms that keep your software up-to-date. But one consequence of the way the Android SDK is put together is that you will need to keep separate software systems up-to-date through separate mechanisms.

Keeping the Android SDK Up-to-Date

The Android SDK isn't part of your desktop OS, nor is it part of the Eclipse plug-in, and therefore the contents of the SDK folder are not updated by the OS or Eclipse. The SDK has its own update mechanism, which has a user interface in the SDK and AVD Manager. As shown in Figure 1-14, select Installed Packages in the left pane to show a list of SDK components installed on your system. Click the Update All button to start the update process, which will show you a list of available updates.

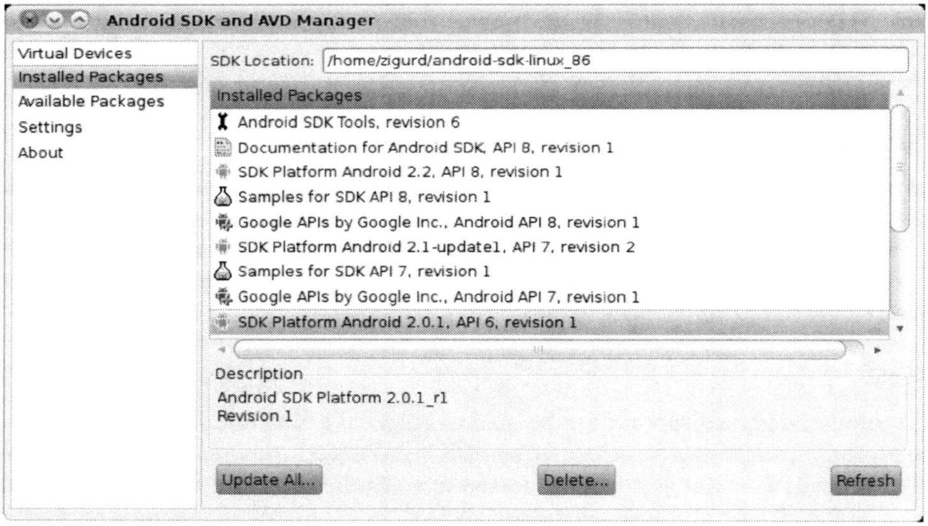

Figure 1-14. Updating the SDK with the SDK and AVD Manager

Usually, you will want to install all available updates.

Keeping Eclipse and the ADT Plug-in Up-to-Date

While the SDK has to be updated outside of both your operating system and Eclipse, the ADT plug-in, and all other components of Eclipse, are updated using Eclipse's own update management system. To update all the components you have in your Eclipse environment, including the ADT plug-in, use the Check for Updates command in the Help menu. This will cause the available updates to be displayed, as shown in Figure 1-15.

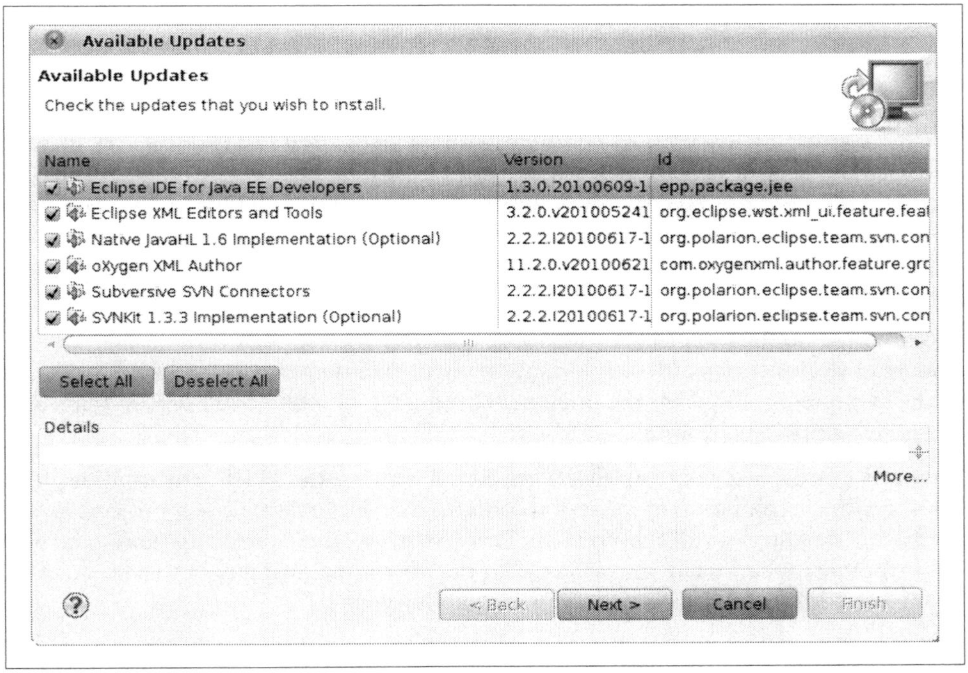

Figure 1-15. Updating Eclipse components and the ADT plug-in

Normally, you will want to use the Select All button to install all available updates. The updates you see listed on your system depend on what Eclipse modules you have installed and whether your Eclipse has been updated recently.

Keeping the JDK Up-to-Date

You won't be updating Java as much as the SDK, ADT plug-in, and other Eclipse plug-ins. Before choosing to update the JDK, first check the "System requirements" page of the Android Developers site at *http://developer.android.com/sdk/requirements.html*.

If an update is needed and you are using a Mac or Linux system, check the available updates for your system to see if a new version of the JDK is included. If the JDK was installed on your system by the vendor, or if you installed it from your Linux distribution's repositories, updates will be available through the updates mechanism on your system.

Example Code

Having installed the Android SDK and tested that it works, you are ready to explore. Even if you are unfamiliar with the Android Framework classes and are new to Java, exploring some example code now will give you further confidence in your SDK installation, before you move on to other parts of this book.

SDK Example Code

The most convenient sample code comes with the SDK. You can create a new project based on the SDK samples, as shown in Figure 1-16. The sample you select appears in the left pane of the Eclipse window, where you can browse the files comprising the sample and run it to see what it does. If you are familiar with using IDEs to debug code, you may want to set some breakpoints in the sample code to see when methods get executed.

Each sample application that comes with the SDK corresponds to an article on the Android Developers site. More information about each sample can be found there. All of the samples are listed on the documentation page at *http://developer.android.com/ resources/samples/index.html*.

There are more than a dozen applications, one of which—the API demos application— is a sprawling exploration of most of the Android APIs. Creating a few projects based on these code samples will give you familiarity with how these programs work, and will help you understand what you will read in the upcoming chapters of this book, even if you don't fully understand what you are looking at yet.

Example Code from This Book

Example code from this book can be downloaded from the book's website at *http:// oreil.ly/prog_android_2e*.

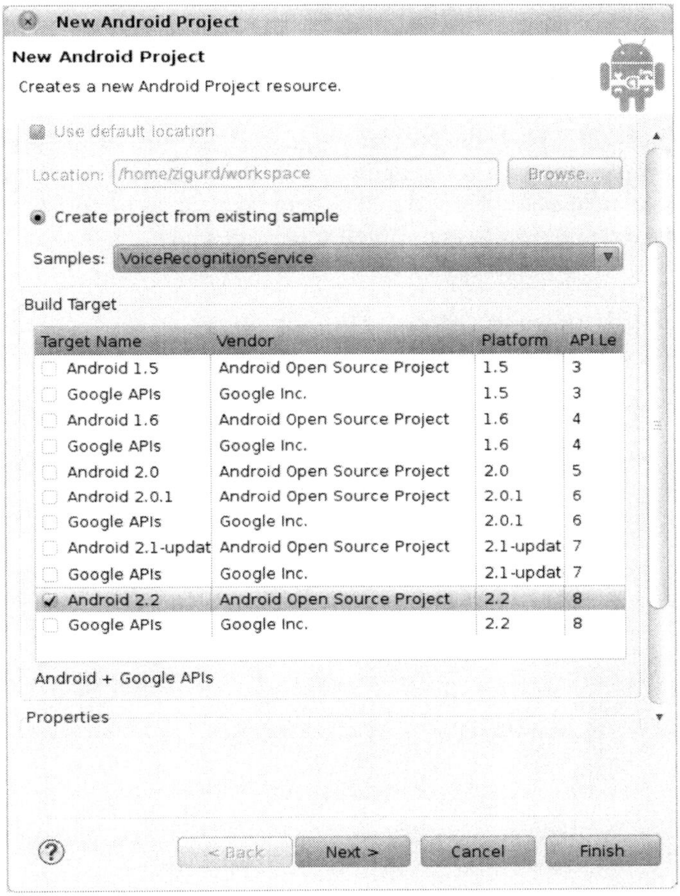

Figure 1-16. *Creating a new project using example code from the SDK*

In the dialog pictured in Figure 1-16, you must pick a build target before you pick a sample. Samples are organized by API level, and if you have not picked a build target, the drop-down list will be empty.

On Reading Code

Good coders read a lot of code. The example code provided by the authors of this book is intended to be both an example of good Java coding and an example of how to use capabilities of the Android platform.

Some examples you will read fall short of what you will need for creating the best possible extensible and maintainable commercial software. Many example applications make choices that make sense if the coder's goal is to create an example in a single Java class. In many cases, Android applications are overgrown versions of example code, and they end up unreadable and unmaintainable. But that does not mean you should avoid reading examples that are more expedient than a large application should be.

The next chapter will explore the Java language, with the goal of giving you the ability to evaluate example code with good engineering and design practices in mind. We want you to be able to take examples and make them better, and to apply the ideas in examples to code you engineer to create high-quality products.

## CHAPTER 2

Java for Android

We don't teach you Java in this book, but in this chapter we'll help you understand the special use of Java within Android. Many people can benefit from this chapter: students who have learned some Java but haven't yet stumbled over the real-life programming dilemmas it presents, programmers from other mobile environments who have used other versions of Java but need to relearn some aspects of the language in the context of Android programming, and Java programmers in general who are new to Android's particular conventions and requirements.

If you find this chapter too fast-paced, pick up an introductory book on Java. If you follow along all right but a particular concept described in this chapter remains unclear to you, you might refer to the Java tutorial at *http://download.oracle.com/docs/cd/E17409_01/javase/tutorial/index.html*.

Android Is Reshaping Client-Side Java

Android is already the most widely used way of creating interactive clients using the Java language. Although there have been several other user interface class libraries for Java (AWT, SWT, Swing, J2ME Canvas, and so on), none of them has been as widely accepted as Android. For any Java programmer, the Android UI is worth learning just to understand what the future of Java UIs might look like.

The Android toolkit doesn't gratuitously bend Java in unfamiliar directions. The mobile environment is simply different. There is a much wider variety of display sizes and shapes; there is no mouse (though there might be a touch screen); text input might be triple-tap; and so on. There are also likely to be many more peripheral devices: motion sensors, GPS units, cameras, multiple radios, and more. Finally, there is the ever-present concern about power. While Moore's law affects processors and memory (doubling their power approximately every two years), no such law affects battery life. When processors were slow, developers used to be concerned about CPU speed and efficiency. Mobile developers, on the other hand, need to be concerned about energy efficiency.

This chapter provides a refresher for generic Java; Android-specific libraries are discussed in detail in Chapter 3.

The Java Type System

There are two distinct, fundamental types in the Java language: objects and primitives. Java provides type safety by enforcing static typing, which requires that every variable must be declared with its type before it is used. For example, a variable named i declared as type int (a primitive 32-bit integer) looks like this:

```
int i;
```

This mechanism stands in contrast to nonstatically typed languages where variables are only optionally declared. Though explicit type declarations are more verbose, they enable the compiler to prevent a wide range of programming errors—accidental variable creation resulting from misspelled variable names, calls to nonexistent methods, and so on—from ever making it into running code. Details of the Java Type System can be found in the Java Language Specification (*http://java.sun.com/docs/books/jls/second _edition/html/j.title.doc.html*).

Primitive Types

Java primitive types are not objects and do not support the operations associated with objects described later in this chapter. You can modify a primitive type only with a limited number of predefined operators: "+", "-", "&", "|", "=", and so on. The Java primitive types are:

boolean
> The value true or false

byte
> An 8-bit 2's-complement integer

short
> A 16-bit 2's-complement integer

int
> A 32-bit 2's-complement integer

long
> A 64-bit 2's-complement integer

char
> A 16-bit unsigned integer representing a UTF-16 code unit

float
> A 32-bit IEEE 754 floating-point number

double
> A 64-bit IEEE 754 floating-point number

Objects and Classes

Java is an object-oriented language and focuses not on its primitives but on objects—combinations of data, and procedures for operating on that data. A *class* defines the fields (data) and methods (procedures) that comprise an object. In Java, this definition—the template from which objects are constructed—is, itself, a particular kind of object, a Class. In Java, classes form the basis of a type system that allows developers to describe arbitrarily complex objects with complex, specialized state and behavior.

In Java, as in most object-oriented languages, types may inherit from other types. A class that inherits from another is said to *subtype* or to be a *subclass* of its parent. The parent class, in turn, may be called the *supertype* or *superclass*. A class that has several different subclasses may be called the *base type* for those subclasses.

Both methods and fields have global scope within the class and may be visible from outside the object through a reference to an instance of the class.

Here is the definition of a very, very simple class with one field, ctr, and one method, incr:

```
public class Trivial {
    /** a field: its scope is the entire class */
    private long ctr;

    /** Modify the field. */
    public void incr() { ctr++; }
}
```

Object Creation

A new object, an instance of some class, is created by using the new keyword:

```
Trivial trivial = new Trivial();
```

On the left side of the assignment operator "=", this statement defines a variable, named trivial. The variable has a type, Trivial, so only objects of type Trivial can be assigned to it. The right side of the assignment allocates memory for a new instance of the Trivial class and initializes the instance. The assignment operator assigns a reference to the newly created object to the variable.

It may surprise you to know that the definition of ctr, in Trivial, is perfectly safe despite the fact that it is not explicitly initialized. Java guarantees that it will be initialized to have the value 0. Java guarantees that all fields are automatically initialized at object creation: boolean is initialized to false, numeric primitive types to 0, and all object types (including String) to null.

 This applies only to object fields. Local variables must be initialized before they are referenced!

You can take greater control over the initialization of an object by adding a *constructor* to its class definition. A constructor definition looks like a method except that it doesn't specify a return type. Its name must be exactly the name of the class that it constructs:

```
public class LessTrivial {
    /** a field: its scope is the entire class */
    private long ctr;

    /** Constructor: initialize the fields */
    public LessTrivial(long initCtr) { ctr = initCtr; }

    /** Modify the field. */
    public void incr() { ctr++; }
}
```

In fact, every class in Java has a constructor. The Java compiler automatically creates a constructor with no arguments, if no other constructor is specified. Further, if a constructor does not explicitly call some superclass constructor, the Java compiler will automatically add an implicit call to the superclass no-arg constructor as the very first statement. The definition of Trivial given earlier (which specifies no explicit constructor) actually has a constructor that looks like this:

```
public Trivial() { super(); }
```

Since the LessTrivial class explicitly defines a constructor, Java *does not* implicitly add a default. That means that trying to create a LessTrivial object, with no arguments, will cause an error:

```
LessTrivial fail = new LessTrivial(); // ERROR!!
LessTrivial ok = new LessTrivial(18); // ... works
```

There are two concepts that it is important to keep separate: *no-arg constructor* and *default constructor*. A default constructor is the constructor that Java adds to your class, implicitly, if you don't define any other constructors. It happens to be a no-arg constructor. A no-arg constructor, on the other hand, is simply a constructor with no parameters. There is no requirement that a class have a no-arg constructor. There is no obligation to define one, unless you have a specific need for it.

 One particular case in which no-arg constructors are necessary deserves special attention. Some libraries need the ability to create new objects, generically, on your behalf. The JUnit framework, for instance, needs to be able to create new test cases, regardless of what they test. Libraries that marshal and unmarshal code to a persistent store or a network connection also need this capability. Since it would be pretty hard for these libraries to figure out, at runtime, the exact calling protocol for your particular object, they typically require a no-arg constructor.

If a class has more than one constructor, it is wise to cascade them, to make sure only a single copy of the code actually initializes the instance and that all other constructors call it. For instance, as a convenience, we might add a no-arg constructor to the LessTrivial class, to accommodate a common case:

```
public class LessTrivial {
    /** a field: its scope is the entire class */
    private long ctr;

    /** Constructor: init counter to 0 */
    public LessTrivial() { this(0); }

    /** Constructor: initialize the fields */
    public LessTrivial(long initCtr) { ctr = initCtr; }

    /** Modify the field. */
    public void incr() { ctr++; }
}
```

Cascading methods is the standard Java idiom for defaulting the values of some arguments. All the code that actually initializes an object is in a single, complete method or constructor and all other methods or constructors simply call it. It is a particularly good idea to use this idiom with constructors that must make explicit calls to a superconstructor.

Constructors should be simple and should do no more work than is necessary to put an object into a consistent initial state. One can imagine, for instance, a design for an object that represents a database or network connection. It might create the connection, initialize it, and verify connectivity, all in the constructor. Although this might seem entirely reasonable, in practice it creates code that is insufficiently modular and difficult to debug and modify. In a better design, the constructor simply initializes the connection state as closed and leaves it to an explicit open method to set up the network.

The Object Class and Its Methods

The Java class Object—java.lang.Object—is the root ancestor of every class. Every Java object is an Object. If the definition of a class does not explicitly specify a superclass, it is a direct subclass of Object. The Object class defines the default implementations for several key behaviors that are common to every object. Unless they are overridden by the subclass, the behaviors are inherited directly from Object.

The methods wait, notify, and notifyAll in the Object class are part of Java's concurrency support. They are discussed in "Thread Control with wait() and notify() Methods" on page 71.

The toString method is the way an object creates a string representation of itself. One interesting use of toString is string concatenation: any object can be concatenated to a string. This example demonstrates two ways to print the same message: they both execute identically. In both, a new instance of the Foo class is created, its toString method is invoked, and the result is concatenated with a literal string.

The result is then printed:

```
System.out.println(
    "This is a new foo: " + new Foo());
System.out.println(
    "This is a new foo: ".concat((new Foo()).toString()));
```

The `Object` implementation of `toString` returns a not very useful string that is based on the location of the object in the heap. Overriding `toString` in your code is a good first step toward making it easier to debug.

The `clone` and `finalize` methods are historical leftovers. The Java runtime will call the `finalize` method only if it is overridden in a subclass. If a class explicitly defines `finalize`, though, it is called for an object of the class just before that object is garbage-collected. Not only does Java not guarantee when this might happen, it actually can't guarantee that it will happen at all. In addition, a call to `finalize` can resurrect an object! This is tricky: objects are garbage-collected when there are no live references to them. An implementation of `finalize`, however, could easily *create* a new live reference, for instance, by adding the object being finalized to some kind of list! Because of this, the existence of a `finalize` method precludes the defining class from many kinds of optimization. There is little to gain and lots to lose in attempting to use `finalize`.

The `clone` method creates objects, bypassing their constructors. Although `clone` is defined on `Object`, calling it on an object will cause an exception unless the object implements the `Cloneable` interface. The `clone` method is an optimization that can be useful when object creation has a significant cost. While clever uses of `clone` may be necessary in specific cases, a copy constructor—one that takes an existing instance as its only argument—is much more straightforward and, in most cases, has negligible cost.

The last two `Object` methods, `hashCode` and `equals`, are the methods by which a caller can tell whether one object is "the same as" another.

The definition of the `equals` method in the API documentation for the `Object` class stipulates the contract to which every implementation of `equals` must adhere. A correct implementation of the `equals` method has the following attributes, and the associated statements must always be true:

reflexive
    x.equals(x)

symmetric
    x.equals(y) == y.equals(x)

transitive
    (x.equals(y) && y.equals(z)) == x.equals(z)

consistent
    If x.equals(y) is true at any point in the life of a program, it is always true, provided x and y do not change.

Getting this right is subtle and can be surprisingly difficult. A common error—one that violates reflexivity—is defining a new class that is sometimes equal to an existing class. Suppose your program uses an existing library that defines the class EnglishWeekdays. Suppose, now, that you define a class FrenchWeekdays. There is an obvious temptation to define an equals method for FrenchWeekdays that returns true when it compares one of the EnglishWeekdays to its French equivalent. Don't do it! The existing English class has no awareness of your new class and so will never recognize instances of your class as being equal. You've broken reflexivity!

hashCode and equals should be considered a pair: if you override either, you should override both. Many library routines treat hashCode as an optimized rough guess as to whether two objects are equal or not. These libraries first compare the hash codes of the two objects. If the two codes are different, they assume there is no need to do any more expensive comparisons because the objects are definitely different. The point of hash code computation, then, is to compute something very quickly that is a good proxy for the equals method. Visiting every cell in a large array, in order to compute a hash code, is probably no faster than doing the actual comparison. At the other extreme, it would be very fast to return 0, always, from a hash code computation. It just wouldn't be very helpful.

Objects, Inheritance, and Polymorphism

Java supports *polymorphism*, one of the key concepts in object-oriented programming. A language is said to be polymorphic if objects of a single type can have different behavior. This happens when subtypes of a given class can be assigned to a variable of the base class type. An example will make this much clearer.

Subtypes in Java are declared through use of the extends keyword. Here is an example of inheritance in Java:

```java
public class Car {
    public void drive() {
        System.out.println("Going down the road!");
    }
}

public class Ragtop extends Car {
    // override the parent's definition.
    public void drive() {
        System.out.println("Top down!");

        // optionally use a superclass method
        super.drive();

        System.out.println("Got the radio on!");
    }
}
```

Ragtop is a subtype of Car. We noted previously that Car is, in turn, a subclass of Object. Ragtop changes the definition of Car's drive method. It is said to *override* drive. Car and Ragtop are both of type Car (they are not both of type Ragtop!) and have different behaviors for the method drive.

We can now demonstrate polymorphic behavior:

```
Car auto = new Car();
auto.drive();
auto = new Ragtop();
auto.drive();
```

This code fragment will compile without error (despite the assignment of a Ragtop to a variable whose type is Car). It will also run without error and will produce the following output:

```
Going down the road!
Top down!
Going down the road!
Got the radio on!
```

The variable auto holds, at different times in its life, references to two different objects of type Car. One of those objects, in addition to being of type Car, is also of subtype Ragtop. The exact behavior of the statement auto.drive() depends on whether the variable currently contains a reference to the former or the latter. This is polymorphic behavior.

Like many other object-oriented languages, Java supports type casting to allow coercion of the declared type of a variable to be any of the types with which the variable is polymorphic:

```
Ragtop funCar;

Car auto = new Car();
funCar = (Ragtop) auto; //ERROR! auto is a Car, not a Ragtop!
auto.drive();

auto = new Ragtop();
Ragtop funCar = (Ragtop) auto; //Works! auto is a Ragtop
auto.drive();
```

While occasionally necessary, excessive use of casting is an indication that the code is missing the point. Obviously, by the rules of polymorphism, all variables could be declared to be of type Object, and then cast as necessary. To do that, however, is to abandon the value of static typing.

Java limits a method's arguments (its actual parameters) to objects of types that are polymorphic with its formal parameters. Similarly, methods return values that are polymorphic with the declared return type. For instance, continuing our automotive example, the following code fragment will compile and run without error:

```
public class JoyRide {
    private Car myCar;
```

```
    public void park(Car auto) {
        myCar = auto;
    }

    public Car whatsInTheGarage() {
        return myCar;
    }

    public void letsGo() {
        park(new Ragtop());
        whatsInTheGarage().drive();
    }
}
```

The method park is declared to take an object of type Car as its only parameter. In the method letsGo, however, it is called with an object of type Ragtop, a subtype of type Car. Similarly, the variable myCar is assigned a value of type Ragtop, and the method whatsInTheGarage returns it. The object is a Ragtop: if you call its drive method, it will tell you about its top and its radio. On the other hand, because it is also a Car, it can be used anywhere that one would use a Car. This subtype replacement capability is a key example of the power of polymorphism and how it works with type safety. Even at compile time, it is clear whether an object is compatible with its use or not. Type safety enables the compiler to find errors, early, that might be much more difficult to find were they permitted to occur at runtime.

Final and Static Declarations

There are 11 modifier keywords that can be applied to a declaration in Java. These modifiers change the behavior of the declared object, sometimes in important ways. The earlier examples used a couple of them, public and private, without explanation: they are among the several modifiers that control scope and visibility. We'll revisit them in a minute. In this section, we consider two other modifiers that are essential to a complete understanding of the Java type system: final and static.

A final declaration is one that cannot be changed. Classes, methods, fields, parameters, and local variables can all be final.

When applied to a class, final means that any attempt to define a subclass will cause an error. The class String, for instance, is final because strings must be immutable (i.e., you can't change the content of one after you create it). If you think about it for a while, you will see that this can be *guaranteed* only if String cannot be subtyped. If it were possible to subtype the String class, a devious library could create a subclass of String, DeadlyString, pass an instance to your code, and change its value from fred to ; DROP TABLE contacts; (an attempt to inject rogue SQL into your system that might wipe out parts of your database) immediately after your code had validated its contents!

When applied to a method, final means that the method cannot be overridden in a subclass. Developers use final methods to design for inheritance, when the supertype needs to make a highly implementation-dependent behavior available to a subclass and cannot allow that behavior to be changed. A framework that implemented a generic cache might define a base class `CacheableObject`, for instance, which the programmer using the framework subtypes for each new cacheable object type. To maintain the integrity of the framework, however, `CacheableObject` might need to compute a cache key that was consistent across all object types. In this case, it might declare its `compu teCacheKey` method `final`.

When applied to a variable—a field, a parameter, or a local variable—`final` means that the value of the variable, once assigned, may not change. This restriction is enforced by the compiler: it is not enough that the value *does not* change, the compiler must be able to prove that it *cannot* change. For a field, this means that the value must be assigned either as part of the declaration or in every constructor. Failure to initialize a `final` field at its declaration or in the constructor—or an attempt to assign to it anywhere else—will cause an error.

For parameters, `final` means that, within the method, the parameter value always has the value passed in the call. An attempt to assign to a `final` parameter will cause an error. Of course, as the parameter value is most likely to be a reference to some kind of object, it is possible that the object might change. The application of the keyword `final` to a parameter simply means that the parameter cannot be assigned.

 In Java, parameters are passed by value: the method arguments are new copies of the values that were passed at the call. On the other hand, most things in Java are references to objects and Java only copies the reference, not the whole object! References are passed by value!

A `final` variable may be assigned no more than once. Because using a variable without initializing it is also an error, in Java a `final` variable must be assigned exactly once. The assignment may take place anywhere in the enclosing block, prior to use.

A `static` declaration belongs to the class in which it is described, not to an instance of that class. The opposite of `static` is `dynamic`. Any entity that is not declared static is implicitly dynamic. This example illustrates:

```
public class QuietStatic {
    public static int classMember;
    public int instanceMember;
}

public class StaticClient {
    public void test() {
        QuietStatic.classMember++;
        QuietStatic.instanceMember++; // ERROR!!

        QuietStatic ex = new QuietStatic();
        ex.classMember++; // WARNING!
        ex.instanceMember++;
```

```
        }
    }
```

In this example, `QuietStatic` is the name of a class, and `ex` is a reference to an instance of that class. The static member `classMember` is an attribute of the class; you can refer to it simply by qualifying it with the class name. On the other hand, `instanceMember` is a member of an *instance* of the class. An attempt to refer to it through the class reference causes an error. That makes sense. There are many different variables called `instance Member`, one belonging to each instance of `QuietStatic`. If you don't explicitly specify which one you are talking about, there's no way for Java to figure it out.

As the second pair of statements demonstrates, Java does actually allow references to class (static) variables through instance references. It is misleading, though, and considered a bad practice. Most compilers and IDEs will generate warnings if you do it.

The implications of static versus dynamic declarations can be subtle. It is easiest to understand the distinction for fields. Again, while there is exactly one copy of a static definition, there is one copy per instance of a dynamic definition. Static class members allow you to maintain information that is held in common by all members of a class. Here's some example code:

```
public class LoudStatic {
    private static int classMember;
    private int instanceMember;

    public void incr() {
        classMember++;
        instanceMember++;
    }

    @Override public String toString() {
        return "classMember: " + classMember
            + ", instanceMember: " + instanceMember;
    }

    public static void main(String[] args) {
        LoudStatic ex1 = new LoudStatic();
        LoudStatic ex2 = new LoudStatic();
        ex1.incr();
        ex2.incr();
        System.out.println(ex1);
        System.out.println(ex2);
    }
}
```

and its output:

```
classMember: 2, instanceMember: 1
classMember: 2, instanceMember: 1
```

The initial value of the variable `classMember` in the preceding example is 0. It is incremented by each of the two different instances. Both instances now see a new value, 2.

The value of the variable `instanceMember` also starts at 0, in each instance. Each instance increments its own copy and sees the value of its own variable, 1.

Static class and method definitions are similar in that, in both cases, a static object is visible using its qualified name, whereas a dynamic object is visible only through an instance reference. Beyond that, however, the differences are trickier.

One significant difference in behavior between statically and dynamically declared methods is that statically declared methods cannot be overridden in a subclass. The following, for instance, fails to compile:

```java
public class Star {
    public static void twinkle() { }
}

public class Arcturus extends Star {
    public void twinkle() { } // ERROR!!
}

public class Rigel {
    // this one works
    public void twinkle() { Star.twinkle(); }
}
```

There is very little reason to use static methods in Java. In early implementations of Java, dynamic method dispatch was significantly slower than static dispatch. Developers used to prefer static methods to "optimize" their code. In Android's just-in-time-compiled Dalvik environment, there is no need for this kind of optimization anymore. Excessive use of static methods is usually an indicator of bad architecture.

The difference between statically and dynamically declared classes is the subtlest. Most of the classes that comprise an application are static. A typical class is declared and defined at the *top level*—outside any enclosing block. Implicitly, all such declarations are static. Most other declarations, on the other hand, take place within the enclosing block of some class and are, by default, dynamic. Whereas most fields are dynamic by default and require a modifier to be static, most classes are static.

 A *block* is the code between two curly braces: { and }. Anything—variables, types, methods, and so on—defined within the block is visible within the block and within lexically nested blocks. Except within the special block defining a class, things defined within a block are not visible outside the block.

This is, actually, entirely consistent. According to our description of static—something that belongs to the class, not to an instance of that class—top-level declarations should be static (they belong to no class). When declared within an enclosing block, however—for example, inside the definition of a top-level class—a class definition is also dynamic by default. To create a dynamically declared class, just define it inside another class.

This brings us to the difference between a static and a dynamic class. A dynamic class has access to instance members of the enclosing class (because it belongs to the instance). A static class does not. Here's some code to demonstrate:

```
public class Outer {
    public int x;

    public class InnerOne {
        public int fn() { return x; }
    }

    public static class InnerTube {
        public int fn() {
            return x; // ERROR!!!
        }
    }
}

public class OuterTest {
    public void test() {
        new Outer.InnerOne(); // ERROR!!!
        new Outer.InnerTube();
    }
}
```

A moment's reflection will clarify what is happening here. The field x is a member of an instance of the class Outer. In other words, there are lots of variables named x, one for each runtime instance of Outer. The class InnerTube is a part of the class Outer, but not of any *instances* of Outer. It has no way of identifying an x. The class InnerOne, on the other hand, because it is dynamic, belongs to an instance of Outer. You might think of a separate class InnerOne for each instance of Outer (though this is not, actually, how it is implemented). Consequently, InnerOne has access to the members of the instance of Outer to which it belongs.

OuterTest demonstrates that, as with fields, we can use the static inner definition (in this case, create an instance of the class) simply by using its qualified name. The dynamic definition is useful, however, only in the context of an instance.

Abstract Classes

Java permits a class declaration to entirely omit the implementation of one or more methods by declaring the class and unimplemented methods to be abstract:

```
public abstract class TemplatedService {

    public final void service() {
        // subclasses prepare in their own ways
        prepareService();
        // ... but they all run the same service
        runService();
    }
```

```
    public abstract void prepareService();

    private final void runService() {
        // implementation of the service ...
    }
}

public class ConcreteService extends TemplatedService {
    void prepareService() {
        // set up for the service
    }
}
```

An abstract class cannot be instantiated. Subtypes of an abstract class either must provide definitions for all the abstract methods in the superclass or must, themselves, be declared abstract.

As hinted in the example, abstract classes are useful in implementing the common template pattern, which provides a reusable piece of code that allows customization at specific points during its execution. The reusable pieces are implemented as an abstract class. Subtypes customize the template by implementing the abstract methods.

For more information on abstract classes, see the Java tutorial at *http://download.oracle.com/javase/tutorial/java/IandI/abstract.html*.

Interfaces

Other languages (e.g., C++, Python, and Perl) permit a capability known as multiple implementation inheritance, whereby an object can inherit implementations of methods from more than one parent class. Such inheritance hierarchies can get pretty complicated and behave in unexpected ways (such as inheriting two field variables with the same name from two different superclasses). Java's developers chose to trade the power of multiple inheritance for simplicity. Unlike the mentioned languages, in Java a class may extend only a single superclass.

Instead of multiple implementation inheritance, however, Java provides the ability for a class to inherit from several types, using the concept of an *interface*. Interfaces provide a way to define a type without defining its implementation. You can think of interfaces as abstract classes with all abstract methods. There is no limit on the number of interfaces that a class may implement.

Here's an example of a Java interface and a class that implements it:

```
public interface Growable {
    // declare the signature but not the implementation
    void grow(Fertilizer food, Water water);
}

public interface Eatable {
    // another signature with no implementation
    void munch();
```

```
    }

/**
 * An implementing class must implement all interface methods
 */
public class Beans implements Growable, Eatable {

    @Override
    public void grow(Fertilizer food, Water water) {
        // ...
    }

    @Override
    public void munch() {
        // ...
    }
}
```

Again, interfaces provide a way to define a type distinct from the implementation of that type. This kind of separation is common even in everyday life. If you and a colleague are trying to mix mojitos, you might well divide tasks so that she goes to get the mint. When you start muddling things in the bottom of the glass, it is irrelevant whether she drove to the store to buy the mint or went out to the backyard and picked it from a shrub. What's important is that you have mint.

As another example of the power of interfaces, consider a program that needs to display a list of contacts, sorted by email address. As you would certainly expect, the Android runtime libraries contain generic routines to sort objects. Because they are generic, however, these routines have no intrinsic idea of what ordering means for the instances of any particular class. To use the library sorting routines, a class needs a way to define its own ordering. Classes do this in Java using the interface Comparable.

Objects of type Comparable implement the method compareTo. One object accepts another, similar object as an argument and returns an integer that indicates whether the argument object is greater than, equal to, or less than the target. The library routines can sort anything that is Comparable. A program's Contact type need only be Comparable and implement compareTo to allow contacts to be sorted:

```
public class Contact implements Comparable<Contact> {
    // ... other fields
    private String email;

    public Contact(
        // other params...
        String emailAddress)
    {
        // ... init other fields from corresponding params
        email = emailAddress;
    }

    public int compareTo(Contact c) {
        return email.compareTo(c.email);
```

```
    }
}

public class ContactView {
    // ...

    private List<Contact> getContactsSortedByEmail(
        List<Contact> contacts)
    {
        // getting the sorted list of contacts
        // is completely trivial
        return Collections.sort(contacts);
    }

    // ...
}
```

Internally, the `Collections.sort` routine knows only that `contacts` is a list of things of type `Comparable`. It invokes the class's `compareTo` method to decide how to order them.

As this example demonstrates, interfaces enable the developer to reuse generic routines that can sort any list of objects that implement `Comparable`. Beyond this simple example, Java interfaces enable a diverse set of programming patterns that are well described in other sources. We frequently and highly recommend the excellent *Effective Java* by Joshua Bloch (Prentice Hall).

Exceptions

The Java language uses *exceptions* as a convenient way to handle unusual conditions. Frequently these conditions are errors.

Code trying to parse a web page, for instance, cannot continue if it cannot read the page from the network. Certainly, it is possible to check the results of the attempt to read and proceed only if that attempt succeeds, as shown in this example:

```
public void getPage(URL url) {
    String smallPage = readPageFromNet(url);
    if (null != smallPage) {
        Document dom = parsePage(smallPage);
        if (null != dom) {
            NodeList actions = getActions(dom);
            if (null != action) {
                // process the action here...
            }
        }
    }
}
```

Exceptions make this more elegant and robust:

```
public void getPage(URL url)
    throws NetworkException, ParseException, ActionNotFoundException
{
    String smallPage = readPageFromNet(url);
```

```
        Document dom = parsePage(smallPage);
        NodeList actions = getActions(dom);
        // process the action here...
    }

    public String readPageFromNet(URL url) throws NetworkException {
    // ...
    public Document parsePage(String xml) throws ParseException {
    // ...
    public NodeList getActions(Document doc) throws ActionNotFoundException {
    // ...
```

In this version of the code, each method called from getPage uses an exception to immediately short-circuit all further processing if something goes wrong. The methods are said to *throw* exceptions. For instance, the getActions method might look something like this:

```
    public NodeList getActions(Document dom)
        throws ActionNotFoundException
    {
        Object actions = xPathFactory.newXPath().compile("//node/@action")
            .evaluate(dom, XPathConstants.NODESET);
        if (null == actions) {
            throw new ActionNotFoundException("Action not found");
        }
        return (NodeList) actions;
    }
```

When the throw statement is executed, processing is immediately interrupted and resumes at the nearest catch block. Here's an example of a try-catch block:

```
    for (int i = 0; i < MAX_RETRIES; i++) {
        try {
            getPage(theUrl);
            break;
        }
        catch (NetworkException e) {
            Log.d("ActionDecoder", "network error: " + e);
        }
    }
```

This code retries network failures. Note that it is not even in the same method, readPageFromNet, that threw the NetworkException. When we say that processing resumes at the "nearest" try-catch block, we're talking about an interesting way that Java delegates responsibility for exceptions.

If there is no try-catch block surrounding the throw statement within the method, a thrown exception makes it seem as though the method returns immediately. No further statements are executed and no value is returned. In the previous example, for instance, none of the code following the attempt to get the page from the network needs to concern itself with the possibility that the precondition—a page was read—was not met. The method is said to have been *terminated abruptly* and, in the example, control returns to `getActions`. Because `getActions` does not contain a `try-catch` block either, it is terminated abruptly, too. Control is passed back (up the stack) to the caller.

In the example, when a `NetworkException` is thrown, control returns to the first statement inside the example `catch` block, the call to log the network error. The exception is said to have been *caught* at the first `catch` statement with an argument type that is the same type, or a supertype, of the thrown exception. Processing resumes at the first statement in the `catch` block and continues normally afterward.

In the example, a network error while attempting to read a page from the network will cause both `ReadPageFromNet` and `getPage` to terminate abruptly. After the `catch` block logs the failure, the `for` loop will retry getting the page, up to `MAX_RETRIES` times.

It is useful to have a clear understanding of the root of the Java exception class tree, shown in Figure 2-1.

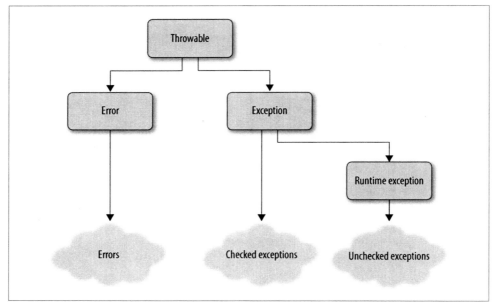

Figure 2-1. Exception base classes

All exceptions are subclasses of `Throwable`. There is almost never any reason to make reference to `Throwable` in your code. Think of it as just an abstract base class with two subclasses: `Error` and `Exception`. `Error` and its subclasses are reserved for problems with the Dalvik runtime environment itself. Although you can write code that appears to catch an `Error` (or a `Throwable`), you cannot, in fact, catch them. An obvious example of this, for instance, is the dreaded OOME, the `OutOfMemoryException` error. When the Dalvik system is out of memory, it may not be able to complete execution of even a single opcode! Writing tricky code that attempts to catch an OOME and then to release some block of preallocated memory might work—or it might not. Code that tries to catch `Throwable` or `Error` is absolutely whistling in the wind.

Java requires the signature of a method to include the exceptions that it throws. In the previous example, `getPage` declares that it throws three exceptions, because it uses three methods, each of which throws one. Methods that call `getPage` must, in turn, declare all three of the exceptions that `getPage` throws, along with any others thrown by any other methods that it calls.

As you can imagine, this can become onerous for methods far up the call tree. A top-level method might have to declare tens of different kinds of exceptions, just because it calls methods that throw them. This problem can be mitigated by creating an exception tree that is congruent to the application tree. Remember that a method needs only to declare supertypes for all the exceptions it throws. If you create a base class named `MyApplicationException` and then subclass it to create `MyNetworkException` and `MyUIException` for the networking and UI subsystems, respectively, your top-layer code need only handle `MyApplicationException`.

Really, though, this is only a partial solution. Suppose networking code somewhere way down in the bowels of your application fails, for instance, to open a network connection. As the exception bubbles up through retries and alternatives, at some point it loses any significance except to indicate that "something went wrong." A specific database exception, for instance, means nothing to code that is trying to prepopulate a phone number. Adding the exception to a method signature, at that point, is really just a nuisance: you might as well simply declare that all your methods throw `Exception`.

`RuntimeException` is a special subclass of `Exception`. Subclasses of `RuntimeException` are called *unchecked* exceptions and do not have to be declared. This code, for instance, will compile without error:

```
public void ThrowsRuntimeException() {
    throw new RuntimeException();
}
```

There is considerable debate in the Java community about when to use and when not to use unchecked exceptions. Obviously, you could use only unchecked exceptions in your application and never declare any exception in any of your method signatures. Some schools of Java programming even recommend this. Using checked exceptions, however, gives you the chance to use the compiler to verify your code and is very much in the spirit of static typing. Experience and taste will be your guide.

The Java Collections Framework

The Java Collections Framework is one of Java's most powerful and convenient tools. It provides objects that represent collections of objects: lists, sets, and maps. The interfaces and implementations that comprise the library are all to be found in the `java.util` package.

There are a few legacy classes in java.util that are historic relics and are not truly part of the framework. It's best to remember and avoid them. They are Vector, Hashtable, Enumeration, and Dictionary.

Collection interface types

Each of the five main types of object in the Collections Library is represented by an interface:

Collection

> This is the root type for all of the objects in the Collections Library. A Collection is a group of objects, not necessarily ordered, not necessarily addressable, possibly containing duplicates. You can add and remove things from it, get its size, and iterate over it (more on iteration in a moment).

List

> A List is an ordered collection. There is a mapping between the integers 0 and length −1 and the objects in the list. A List may contain duplicates. You can do anything to a List that you can do to a Collection. In addition, though, you can map an element to its index and an index to an element with the get and indexOf methods. You can also change the element at a specific index with the add(index, e) method. The iterator for a List returns the elements in order.

Set

> A Set is an unordered collection that does not contain duplicates. You can do anything to a Set that you can do to a Collection. Attempting to add an element to a Set that already contains it, though, does not change the size of the Set.

Map

> A Map is like a list except that instead of mapping integers to objects it maps a set of key objects to a collection of value objects. You can add and remove key–value pairs from the Map, get its size, and iterate over it, just like any other collection. Examples of maps might include mapping words to their definitions, dates to events, or URLs to cached content.

Iterator

> An Iterator returns the elements of the collection from which it is derived, each exactly once, in response to calls to its next method. It is the preferred means for processing all the elements of a collection. Instead of:

```
for (int i = 0; i < list.size(); i++) {
    String s = list.get(i)
    // ...
}
```

the following is preferred:

```
for (Iterator<String> i = list.iterator(); i.hasNext();) {
    String s = i.next();
    // ...
}
```

In fact, the latter may be abbreviated, simply, as:

```
for (String s: list) {
    // ...
}
```

Collection implementation types

These interface types have multiple implementations, each appropriate to its own use case. Among the most common of these are the following:

ArrayList
> An ArrayList is a list that is backed by an array. It is quick to index but slow to change size.

LinkedList
> A LinkedList is a list that can change size quickly but is slower to index.

HashSet
> A HashSet is a set that is implemented as a hash. add, remove, contains, and size all execute in constant time, assuming a well-behaved hash. A HashSet may contain (no more than one) null.

HashMap
> A HashMap is an implementation of the Map interface that uses a hash table as its index. add, remove, contains, and size all execute in constant time, assuming a well-behaved hash. It may contain a (single) null key, but any number of values may be null.

TreeMap
> A TreeMap is an ordered Map: objects in the map are sorted according to their natural order if they implement the Comparable interface, or according to a Comparator passed to the TreeMap constructor if they do not.

Idiomatic users of Java prefer to use declarations of interface types instead of declarations of implementation types, whenever possible. This is a general rule, but it is easiest to understand here in the context of the collection framework.

Consider a method that returns a new list of strings that is just like the list of strings passed as its second parameter, but in which each element is prefixed with the string passed as the first parameter. It might look like this:

```
public ArrayList<String> prefixList(
    String prefix,
    ArrayList<String> strs)
{
    ArrayList<String> ret
        = new ArrayList<String>(strs.size());
    for (String s: strs) { ret.add(prefix + s); }
    return ret;
}
```

There's a problem with this implementation, though: it won't work on just any list! It will only work on an ArrayList. If, at some point, the code that calls this method needs to be changed from using an ArrayList to a LinkedList, it can no longer use the method. There's no good reason for that, at all.

A better implementation might look like this:

```
public List<String> prefix(
    String prefix,
    List<String> strs)
{
    List<String> ret = new ArrayList<String>(strs.size());
    for (String s: strs) { ret.add(prefix + s); }
    return ret;
}
```

This version is more adaptable because it doesn't bind the method to a particular implementation of the list. The method depends only on the fact that the parameter implements a certain interface. It doesn't care how. By using the interface type as a parameter it requires exactly what it needs to do its job—no more, no less.

In fact, this could probably be further improved if its parameter and return type were Collection.

Java generics

Generics in Java are a large and fairly complex topic. Entire books have been written on the subject. This section introduces them in their most common setting, the Collections Library, but will not attempt to discuss them in detail.

Before the introduction of generics in Java, it wasn't possible to statically type the contents of a container. One frequently saw code that looked like this:

```
public List makeList() {
    // ...
}

public void useList(List l) {
    Thing t = (Thing) l.get(0);
    // ...
}

// ...
useList(makeList());
```

The problem is obvious: useList has no guarantee that makeList created a list of Thing. The compiler cannot verify that the cast in useList will work, and the code might explode at runtime.

Generics solve this problem—at the cost of some significant complexity. The syntax for a generic declaration was introduced, without comment, previously. Here's a version of the example, with the generics added:

```
public List<Thing> makeList() {
    // ...
}

public void useList(List<Thing> l) {
    Thing t = l.get(0);
    // ...
}

// ...
useList(makeList());
```

The type of the objects in a container is specified in the angle brackets (<>) that are part of the container type. Notice that the cast is no longer necessary in useList because the compiler can now tell that the parameter l is a list of Thing.

Generic type descriptions can get pretty verbose. Declarations like this are not uncommon:

```
Map<UUID, Map<String, Thing>> cache
    = new HashMap<UUID, Map<String, Thing>>();
```

Garbage Collection

Java is a garbage-collected language. That means your code does not manage memory. Instead, your code creates new objects, allocating memory, and then simply stops using those objects when it no longer needs them. The Dalvik runtime will delete them and compress memory, as appropriate.

In the not-so-distant past, developers had to worry about long and unpredictable periods of unresponsiveness in their applications when the garbage collector suspended all application processing to recover memory. Many developers, both those that used Java in its early days and those that used J2ME more recently, will remember the tricks, hacks, and unwritten rules necessary to avoid the long pauses and memory fragmentation caused by early garbage collectors. Garbage collection technology has come a long way since those days. Dalvik emphatically does not have these problems. Creating new objects has essentially no overhead. Only the most demandingly responsive of UIs—perhaps some games—will ever need to worry about garbage collection pauses.

Scope

Scope determines where variables, methods, and other symbols are visible in a program. Outside of a symbol's scope, the symbol is not visible at all and cannot be used. We'll go over the major aspects of scope in this section, starting with the highest level.

Java Packages

Java packages provide a mechanism for grouping related types together in a universally unique namespace. Such grouping prevents identifiers within the package namespace from colliding with those created and used by other developers in other namespaces.

A typical Java program is made up of code from a forest of packages. The standard Java Runtime Environment supplies packages like `java.lang` and `java.util`. In addition, the program may depend on other common libraries like those in the `org.apache` tree. By convention, application code—code you create—goes into a package with a name that is created by reversing your domain name and appending the name of the program. Thus, if your domain name is `androidhero.com`, the root of your package tree will be `com.androidhero` and you will put your code into packages like `com.androidhero.awesomeprogram` and `com.androidhero.geohottness.service`. A typical package layout for an Android application might have a package for persistence, a package for the UI, and a package for application logic or controller code.

In addition to providing a unique namespace, packages have implications on member (field and method) visibility for objects in the same package. Classes in the same package may be able to see one another's internals in ways that are not available to classes outside the package. We'll return to this topic in a moment.

To declare a class as part of a package, use the `package` keyword at the top of the file containing your class definition:

```
package your.qualifieddomainname.functionalgrouping
```

Don't be tempted to shortcut your package name! As surely as a quick, temporary implementation lasts for years, so the choice of a package name that is not guaranteed unique will come back to haunt you.

Some larger projects use completely different top-level domains to separate public API packages from the packages that implement those APIs. For example, the Android API uses the top-level package `android`, and implementation classes generally reside in the package `com.android`. Sun's Java source code follows a similar scheme. Public APIs reside in the `java` package, but the implementation code resides in the package `sun`. In either case, an application that imports an implementation package is clearly doing something fast and loose, depending on something that is not part of the public API.

Although it is possible to add code to existing packages, it is usually considered bad form to do so. In general, in addition to being a namespace, a package is usually a single source tree, at least up as far as the reversed domain name. It is only convention, but Java developers usually expect that when they look at the source for the package `com.brashandroid.coolapp.ui`, they will see all the source for the UI for CoolApp. Most will be surprised if they have to find another source tree somewhere with, for instance, page two of the UI.

The Android application framework also has the concept of a `Package`. It is different, and we'll consider it in Chapter 3. Don't confuse it with Java package names.

For more information on Java packages, see the Java tutorial at *http://download.oracle .com/javase/tutorial/java/package/packages.html*.

Access Modifiers and Encapsulation

We hinted earlier that members of a class have special visibility rules. Definitions in most Java blocks are lexically scoped: they are visible only within the block and its nested blocks. The definitions in a class, however, may be visible outside the block. Java supports publishing top-level members of a class—its methods and fields—to code in other classes, through the use of *access modifiers*. Access modifiers are keywords that modify the visibility of the declarations to which they are applied.

There are three access-modifying keywords in the Java language: `public`, `protected`, and `private`. Together they support four levels of access. While access modifiers affect the visibility of a declaration from outside the class containing it, within the class normal block scoping rules apply, regardless of access modification.

The `private` access modifier is the most restrictive. A declaration with `private` access is not visible outside the block that contains it. This is the safest kind of declaration because it guarantees that there are no references to the declaration, except within the containing class. The more `private` declarations there are in a class, the safer the class is.

The next most restrictive level of access is default or package access. Declarations that are not modified by any of the three access modifiers have default access and are visible only from other classes in the same package. Default access can be a very handy way to create state shared among objects, similar to the use of the `friend` declaration in C++.

The `protected` access modifier permits all the access rights that were permitted by default access but, in addition, allows access from within any subtype. Any class that extends a class with `protected` declarations has access to those declarations.

Finally, `public` access, the weakest of the modifiers, allows access from anywhere.

Here's an example that will make this more concrete. There are four classes in two different packages here, all of which refer to fields declared in one of the classes, `Accessible`:

```
package over.here;

public class Accessible {
    private String localAccess;
    String packageAccess;
```

```
        protected String subtypeAccess;
        public String allAccess;

        public void test() {
            // all of the assignments below work:
            // the fields are declared in an enclosing
            // block and are therefore visible.
            localAccess = "success!!";
            packageAccess = "success!!";
            subtypeAccess = "success!!";
            allAccess = "success!!";
        }
    }


    package over.here;
    import over.here.Accessible;

    // this class is in the same package as Accessible
    public class AccessibleFriend {

        public void test() {
            Accessible target = new Accessible();

            // private members are not visible
            // outside the declaring class
            target.localAccess = "fail!!"; // ERROR!!

            // default access visible within package
            target.packageAccess = "success!!";

            // protected access is superset of default
            target.subtypeAccess = "success!!";

            // visible everywhere
            target.allAccess = "success!!";
        }
    }


    package over.there;
    import over.here.Accessible;

    // a subtype of Accessible
    // in a different package
    public class AccessibleChild extends Accessible {

        // the visible fields from Accessible appear
        // as if declared in a surrounding block
        public void test() {
            localAccess = "fail!!"; // ERROR!!
            packageAccess = "fail!!"; // ERROR!!

            // protected declarations are
            // visible from subtypes
```

```
        subtypeAccess = "success!!";

        // visible everywhere
        allAccess = "success!!";
    }
}


package over.there;
import over.here.Accessible;

// a class completely unrelated to Accessible
public class AccessibleStranger {

    public void test() {
        Accessible target = new Accessible();
        target.localAccess = "fail!!"; // ERROR!!
        target.packageAccess = "fail!!"; // ERROR!!
        target.subtypeAccess = "success!!"; // ERROR!!

        // visible everywhere
        target.allAccess = "success!!";
    }
}
```

Idioms of Java Programming

Somewhere between getting the specifics of a programming language syntax right and good pattern-oriented design (which is language-agnostic), is idiomatic use of a language. An idiomatic programmer uses consistent code to express similar ideas and, by doing so, produces programs that are easy to understand, make optimal use of the runtime environment, and avoid the "gotchas" that exist in any language syntax.

Type Safety in Java

A primary design goal for the Java language was programming safety. Much of the frequently maligned verbosity and inflexibility of Java, which is not present in languages such as Ruby, Python, and Objective-C, is there to make sure a compiler can guarantee that entire classes of errors will never occur at runtime.

Java's static typing has proven to be valuable well beyond its own compiler. The ability for a machine to parse and recognize the semantics of Java code was a major force in the development of powerful tools like FindBugs and IDE refactoring tools.

Many developers argue that, especially with modern coding tools, these constraints are a small price to pay for being able to find problems immediately that might otherwise manifest themselves only when the code is actually deployed. Of course, there is also a huge community of developers who argue that they save so much time coding in a dynamic language that they can write extensive unit and integration tests and still come out ahead.

Whatever your position in this discussion, it makes a lot of sense to make the best possible use of your tools. Java's static binding absolutely is a constraint. On the other hand, Java is a pretty good statically bound language. It is a lousy dynamic language. It is actually possible to do fairly dynamic things with Java by using its reflection and introspection APIs and doing a lot of type casting. Doing so, except in very limited circumstances, is using the language and its runtime environment at cross-purposes. Your program is likely to run very slowly, and the Android tool chain won't be able to make heads or tails of it. Perhaps most important, if there are bugs in this seldom-used part of the platform, you'll be the first to find them. We suggest embracing Java's static nature—at least until there is a good, dynamic alternative—and taking every possible advantage of it.

Encapsulation

Developers limit the visibility of object members to create *encapsulation*. Encapsulation is the idea that an object should never reveal details about itself that it does not intend to support. To return to the mojito-making example, recall that, when it comes time to make the cocktail, you don't care at all how your colleague got the necessary mint. Suppose, though, that you had said to her, "Can you get the mint? And, oh, by the way, while you are out there, could you water the rosebush?" It is no longer true that you don't care how your colleague produces mint. You now depend on the exact way that she does it.

In the same way, the interface (sometimes abbreviated as API) of an object consists of the methods and types that are accessible from calling code. By careful encapsulation, a developer keeps implementation details of an object hidden from code that uses it. Such control and protection produce programs that are more flexible and allow the developer of an object to change object implementation over time without causing ripple-effect changes in calling code.

Getters and setters

A simple, but common, form of encapsulation in Java involves the use of getter and setter methods. Consider a naive definition of a Contact class:

```
public class Contact {
    public String name;
    public int age;
    public String email;
}
```

This definition makes it necessary for external objects to access the fields of the class directly. For example:

```
Contact c = new Contact();
c.name = "Alice";
```

```
        c.age = 13;
        c.email = "alice@mymail.com";
```

It will take only a tiny amount of use in the real world to discover that contacts actually have several email addresses. Unfortunately, adding a multiple-address feature to the naive implementation requires updating every single reference to Contact.email, in the entire program.

In contrast, consider the following class:

```
class Contact {
    private int age;
    private String name;
    private String email;

    Contact(int age, String name, String email) {
        this.age = age;
        this.name = name;
        this.email = email;
    }

    public int getAge() {
        return age;
    }

    public String getName() {
        return name;
    }

    public String getEmail() {
        return address;
    }
}
```

Use of the private access modifier prevents direct access to the fields of this version of the Contact class. Use of public getter methods provides the developer with the opportunity to change how the Contact object returns the name, age, or email address of the Contact. For example, the email address could be stored by itself, as in the preceding code, or concatenated from a username and a hostname if that happened to be more convenient for a given application. Internally, the age could be held as an int or as an Integer. The class can be extended to support multiple email addresses without any change to any client.

Java does allow direct reference to fields and does not, like some languages, automatically wrap references to the fields in getters and setters. To preserve encapsulation, you must define each and every access method yourself. Most IDEs provide code generation features that will do this quickly and accurately.

Wrapper getter and setter methods provide future flexibility, whereas direct field access means that all code that uses a field will have to change if the type of that field changes, or if it goes away. Getter and setter methods represent a simple form of object encapsulation. An excellent rule of thumb recommends that all fields be either private or final. Well-written Java programs use this and other, more sophisticated forms of encapsulation to preserve adaptability in more complex programs.

Using Anonymous Classes

Developers who have experience working with UI development will be familiar with the concept of a callback: your code needs to be notified when something in the UI changes. Perhaps a button is pushed and your model needs to make a corresponding change in state. Perhaps new data has arrived from the network and it needs to be displayed. You need a way to add a block of code to a framework, for later execution on your behalf.

Although the Java language does provide an idiom for passing blocks of code, it is slightly awkward because neither code blocks nor methods are first-class objects in the language. There is no way, in the language, to obtain a reference to either.

You can have a reference to an instance of a class. In Java, instead of passing blocks or functions, you pass an entire class that defines the code you need as one of its methods. A service that provides a callback API will define its protocol using an interface. The service client defines an implementation of this interface and passes it to the framework.

Consider, for instance, the Android mechanism for implementing the response to a user keypress. The Android View class defines an interface, OnKeyListener, which, in turn, defines an onKey method. If your code passes an implementation of OnKeyListener to a View, its onKey method will be called each time the View processes a new key event.

The code might look something like this:

```
public class MyDataModel {
    // Callback class
    private class KeyHandler implements View.OnKeyListener {
        public boolean onKey(View v, int keyCode, KeyEvent event) {
            handleKey(v, keyCode, event)
        }
    }

    /** @param view the view we model */
    public MyDataModel(View view) { view.setOnKeyListener(new KeyHandler()) }

    /** Handle a key event */
    void handleKey(View v, int keyCode, KeyEvent event) {
        // key handling code goes here...
    }
}
```

When a new MyDataModel is created, it is informed about the view to which it is attached by an argument to the constructor. The constructor creates a new instance of the trivial callback class, KeyHandler, and installs it in the view. Any subsequent key events will be relayed to the model instance's handleKey method.

Although this certainly gets the job done, it can get pretty ugly, especially if your model class needs to handle multiple kinds of events from multiple views! After a while, all those type definitions clutter up the top of your program. The definitions can be a long way from their use and, if you think about it, they really serve no purpose at all.

Java provides a way to simplify this somewhat, using an *anonymous class*. Here is a code fragment similar to the one shown earlier, except that it is implemented using an anonymous class:

```
public class MyDataModel {
    /** @param view the view we model */
    public MyDataModel(View view) {
        view.setOnKeyListener(
            // this is an anonymous class!!
            new View.OnKeyListener() {
                public boolean onKey(View v, int keyCode, KeyEvent event) {
                    handleKey(v, keyCode, event)
                } } );
    }

    /** Handle a key event */
    void handleKey(View v, int keyCode, KeyEvent event) {
        // key handling code goes here...
    }
}
```

Although it might take a minute to parse, this code is almost identical to the previous example. It passes a newly created instance of a subtype of View.OnKeyListener as an argument in the call to view.setOnKeyListener. In this example, though, the argument to the call to view.setOnKeyListener is special syntax that defines a new subclass of the interface View.OnKeyListener and instantiates it in a single statement. The new instance is an instance of a class that has no name: it is anonymous. Its definition exists only in the statement that instantiates it.

Anonymous classes are a very handy tool and are the Java idiom for expressing many kinds of code blocks. Objects created using an anonymous class are first-class objects of the language and can be used anywhere any other object of the same type would be legal. For instance, they can be assigned:

```
public class MyDataModel {
    /** @param view the view we model */
    public MyDataModel(View view1, View view2) {
        // get a reference to the anonymous class
        View.OnKeyListener keyHdlr = new View.OnKeyListener() {
            public boolean onKey(View v, int keyCode, KeyEvent event) {
                handleKey(v, keyCode, event)
            } };

        // use the class to relay for two views
        view1.setOnKeyListener(keyHdlr);
        view2.setOnKeyListener(keyHdlr);
    }
```

```
/** Handle a key event */
void handleKey(View v, int keyCode, KeyEvent event) {
    // key handling code goes here...
}
}
```

You might wonder why the anonymous class in this example delegates its actual implementation (the handleKey method) to the containing class. There's certainly no rule that constrains the content of the anonymous class: it absolutely could contain the complete implementation. On the other hand, good, idiomatic taste suggests putting the code that changes an object's state into the object class. If the implementation is in the containing class, it can be used from other methods and callbacks. The anonymous class is simply a relay and that is all it should do.

Java does have some fairly strong constraints concerning the use of the variables that are in scope—anything defined in any surrounding block—within an anonymous class. In particular, an anonymous class can only refer to a variable inherited from the surrounding scope if that variable is declared final. For example, the following code fragment will not compile:

```
/** Create a key handler that matches the passed key */
public View.OnKeyListener curry(int keyToMatch) {
    return new View.OnKeyListener() {
        public boolean onKey(View v, int keyCode, KeyEvent event) {
            if (keyToMatch == keyCode) { foundMatch(); } // ERROR!!
        } };
}
```

The remedy is to make the argument to curry final. Making it final, of course, means that it cannot be changed in the anonymous class. But there is an easy, idiomatic way around that:

```
/** Create a key handler that increments and matches the passed key */
public View.OnKeyListener curry(final int keyToMatch) {
    return new View.OnKeyListener() {
        private int matchTarget = keyToMatch;
        public boolean onKey(View v, int keyCode, KeyEvent event) {
            matchTarget++;
            if (matchTarget == keyCode) { foundMatch(); }
        } };
}
```

Modular Programming in Java

Although class extension in Java offers developers significant flexibility in being able to redefine aspects of objects as they are used in different contexts, it actually takes a reasonable amount of experience to make judicious use of classes and interfaces. Ideally, developers aim to create sections of code that are tolerant of change over time and that can be reused in as many different contexts as possible, in multiple applications or perhaps even as libraries. Programming in this way can reduce bugs and the application's time to market. Modular programming, encapsulation, and separation of concerns are all key strategies for maximizing code reuse and stability.

A fundamental design consideration in object-oriented development concerns the decision to delegate or inherit as a means of reusing preexisting code. The following series of examples contains different object hierarchies for representing automotive vehicles that might be used in a car gaming application. Each example presents a different approach to modularity.

A developer starts by creating a vehicle class that contains all vehicle logic and all logic for each different type of engine, as follows:

```java
// Naive code!
public class MonolithicVehicle {
    private int vehicleType;

    // fields for an electric engine
    // fields for a gas engine
    // fields for a hybrid engine
    // fields for a steam engine

    public MonolithicVehicle(int vehicleType) {
        vehicleType = vehicleType;
    }

    // other methods for implementing vehicles and engine types.

    void start() {
        // code for an electric engine
        // code for a gas engine
        // code for a hybrid engine
        // code for a steam engine
    }
}
```

This is naive code. Although it may be functional, it mixes together unrelated bits of implementation (e.g., all types of vehicle engines) and will be hard to extend. For instance, consider modifying the implementation to accommodate a new engine type (nuclear). The code for each kind of car engine has unrestricted access to the code for every other engine. A bug in one engine implementation might end up causing a bug in another, unrelated engine. A change in one might result in an unexpected change to another. And, of course, a car that has an electric engine must drag along representations of all existing engine types. Future developers working on the monolithic vehicle must understand all the complex interactions to modify the code. This just doesn't scale.

How might we improve on this implementation? An obvious idea is to use subclassing. We might use the class hierarchy shown in the following code to implement different types of automotive vehicles, each tightly bound to its engine type:

```java
public abstract class TightlyBoundVehicle {
    // has no engine field
```

```
    // each subclass must override this method to
    // implement its own way of starting the vehicle
    protected abstract void startEngine();

    public final void start() { startEngine(); }
}

public class ElectricVehicle extends TightlyBoundVehicle {
    protected void startEngine() {
        // implementation for engine start electric
    }
}

public class GasVehicle extends TightlyBoundVehicle {
    protected void startEngine() {
        // implementation for engine start gas
    }
}

public void anInstantiatingMethod() {
    TightlyBoundVehicle vehicle = new ElectricVehicle();
    TightlyBoundVehicle vehicle = new GasVehicle();
    TightlyBoundVehicle vehicle = new HybridVehicle();
    TightlyBoundVehicle vehicle = new SteamVehicle();
}
```

This is clearly an improvement. The code for each engine type is now encapsulated within its own class and cannot interfere with any others. You can extend individual types of vehicles without affecting any other type. In many circumstances, this is an ideal implementation.

On the other hand, what happens when you want to convert your tightly bound gas vehicle to biodiesel? In this implementation, cars and engines are the same object. They cannot be separated. If the real-world situation that you are modeling requires you to consider the objects separately, your architecture will have to be more loosely coupled:

```
interface Engine {
    void start();
}

class GasEngine implements Engine {
    void start() {
        // spark plugs ignite gas
    }
}

class ElectricEngine implements Engine {
    void start() {
        // run power to battery
    }
}

class DelegatingVehicle {
    // has an engine field
```

```
    private Engine mEngine;

    public DelegatingVehicle(Engine engine) {
        mEngine = engine;
    }

    public void start() {
        // delegating vehicle can use a gas or electric engine
        mEngine.start();
    }
}

void anInstantiatingMethod() {
    // new vehicle types are easily created by just
    // plugging in different kinds of engines.
    DelegatingVehicle electricVehicle =
      new DelegatingVehicle(new ElectricEngine());
    DelegatingVehicle gasVehicle = new DelegatingVehicle(new GasEngine());
    //DelegatingVehicle hybridVehicle = new DelegatingVehicle(new HybridEngine());
    //DelegatingVehicle steamVehicle = new DelegatingVehicle(new SteamEngine());
}
```

In this architecture, the vehicle class delegates all engine-related behaviors to an engine object that it owns. This is sometimes called *has-a*, as opposed to the previous, subclassed example, called *is-a*. It can be even more flexible because it separates the knowledge of how an engine actually works from the car that contains it. Each vehicle delegates to a loosely coupled engine type and has no idea how that engine implements its behavior. The earlier example makes use of a reusable `DelegatingVehicle` class that does not change at all when it is given a new kind of engine. A vehicle can use any implementation of the `Engine` interface. In addition, it's possible to create different types of vehicle—SUV, compact, or luxury, for instance—that each make use of any of the different types of `Engine`.

Using delegation minimizes the interdependence between the two objects and maximizes the flexibility to change them later. By preferring delegation over inheritance, a developer makes it easier to extend and improve the code. By using interfaces to define the contract between an object and its delegates, a developer guarantees that the delegates will have the expected behavior.

Basic Multithreaded Concurrent Programming in Java

The Java language supports concurrent threads of execution. Statements in different threads are executed in program order, but there is no ordering relationship between the statements in different threads. The basic unit of concurrent execution in Java is encapsulated in the class `java.lang.Thread`. The recommended method of spawning a thread uses an implementation of the interface `java.lang.Runnable`, as demonstrated in the following example:

```
// program that interleaves messages from two threads
public class ConcurrentTask implements Runnable {
```

```
    public void run() {
        while (true) {
            System.out.println("Message from spawned thread");
        }
    }
}

public void spawnThread() {
    (new Thread(new ConcurrentTask())).start();

    while (true) {
        System.out.println("Message from main thread");
    }
}
```

In the preceding example, the method spawnThread creates a new thread, passing a new instance of ConcurrentTask to the thread's constructor. The method then calls start on the new thread. When the start method of the thread is called, the underlying virtual machine (VM) will create a new concurrent thread of execution, which will, in turn, call the run method of the passed Runnable, executing it in parallel with the spawning thread. At this point, the VM is running two independent processes: order of execution and timing in one thread are unrelated to order and timing in the other.

The class Thread is not final. It is possible to define a new, concurrent task by subclassing Thread and overriding its run method. There is no advantage to that approach, however. In fact, using a Runnable is more adaptable. Because Runnable is an interface, the Runnable that you pass in to the Thread constructor may extend some other, useful class.

Synchronization and Thread Safety

When two or more running threads have access to the same set of variables, it's possible for the threads to modify those variables in a way that can produce data corruption and break the logic in one or more of those threads. These kinds of unintended concurrent access bugs are called *thread safety violations*. They are difficult to reproduce, difficult to find, and difficult to test.

Java does not explicitly enforce restrictions on access to variables by multiple threads. Instead, the primary mechanism Java provides to support thread safety is the synchronized keyword. This keyword serializes access to the block it controls and, more important, synchronizes visible state between two threads. It is very easy to forget, when trying to reason about concurrency in Java, that synchronization controls both access and visibility. Consider the following program:

```
// This code is seriously broken!!!
public class BrokenVisibility {
    public static boolean shouldStop;

    public static void main(String[] args) {
        new Thread(
```

```
        new Runnable() {
            @Override public void run() {
                // this code runs in the spawned thread
                final long stopTime
                    = System.currentTimeMillis() + 1000;
                for (;;) {
                    shouldStop
                        = System.currentTimeMillis() > stopTime;
                }
            }
        }
    ).start();

    // this runs in the main thread
    for (;;) {
        if (shouldStop) { System.exit(0); }
    }
}
}
```

One might think, "Well, there's no need to synchronize the variable shouldStop. Sure, the main thread and the spawned thread might collide when accessing it. So what? The spawned thread will, after one second, always set it to true. Boolean writes are atomic. If the main thread doesn't see it as true this time, surely it will see it as true the next time." This reasoning is dangerously flawed. It does not take into account optimizing compilers and caching processors! In fact, this program may well never terminate. The two threads might very easily each use their own copy of shouldStop, existing only in some local processor hardware cache. Because there is no synchronization between the two threads, the cache copy might never be published so that the spawned thread's value is visible from the main thread.

There is a simple rule for avoiding thread safety violations in Java: when two different threads access the same mutable state (variable) *all* access to that state must be performed holding a single lock.

Some developers may violate this rule, after reasoning about the behavior of shared state in their program, in an attempt to optimize code. Because many of the devices on which the Android platform is currently implemented cannot actually provide concurrent execution (instead, a single processor is shared, serially, across the threads), it is possible that these programs will appear to run correctly. However, when, inevitably, mobile devices have processors with multiple cores and large, multilayered processor caches, incorrect programs are likely to fail with bugs that are serious, intermittent, and extremely hard to find.

When implementing concurrent processes in Java, the best approach is to turn to the powerful java.util.concurrent libraries. Here you will find nearly any concurrent structure you might require, optimally implemented and well tested. In Java, there is seldom more reason for a developer to use the low-level concurrency constructs than there is for him to implement his own version of a doubly linked list.

The synchronized keyword can be used in three contexts: to create a block, on a dynamic method, or on a static method. When used to define a block, the keyword takes as an argument a reference to an object to be used as a semaphore. Primitive types cannot be used as semaphores, but any object can.

When used as a modifier on a dynamic method, the keyword behaves as though the contents of the method were wrapped in a synchronized block that used the instance itself as the lock. The following example demonstrates this:

```java
class SynchronizationExample {

    public synchronized void aSynchronizedMethod() {
        // a thread executing this method holds
        // the lock on "this".  Any other thread attempting
        // to use this or any other method synchronized on
        // "this" will be queued until this thread
        // releases the lock
    }

    public void equivalentSynchronization() {
        synchronized (this) {
            // this is exactly equivalent to using the
            // synchronized keyword in the method def.
        }
    }

    private Object lock = new Object();

    public void containsSynchronizedBlock() {
        synchronized (lock) {
            // A thread executing this method holds
            // the lock on "lock", not "this".
            // Threads attempting to seize "this"
            // may succeed.  Only those attempting to
            // seize "lock" will be blocked
        }
    }
}
```

This is very convenient but must be used with caution. A complex class that has multiple high-use methods and synchronizes them in this way may be setting itself up for lock contention. If several external threads are attempting to access unrelated pieces of data simultaneously, it is best to protect those pieces of data with separate locks.

If the synchronized keyword is used on a static method, it is as though the contents of the method were wrapped in a block synchronized on the object's class. All static synchronized methods for all instances of a given class will contend for the single lock on the class object itself.

Finally, it is worth noting that object locks in Java are reentrant. The following code is perfectly safe and does not cause a deadlock:

```java
class SafeSeizure {
    private Object lock = new Object();
```

```
    public void method1() {
        synchronized (lock) {
            // do stuff
            method2();
        }
    }

    public void method2() {
        synchronized (lock) {
            // do stuff
        }
    }
}
```

Thread Control with wait() and notify() Methods

The class `java.lang.Object` defines the methods `wait()` and `notify()` as part of the lock protocol that is part of every object. Because all classes in Java extend `Object`, all object instances support these methods for controlling the lock associated with the instance.

A complete discussion of Java's low-level concurrency tools is well beyond the scope of this book. Interested developers should turn to Brian Goetz's excellent *Java Concurrency in Practice* (Addison-Wesley Professional). This example, however, illustrates the essential element necessary to allow two threads to cooperate. One thread pauses while the other completes a task that it requires:

```
/**
 * Task that slowly fills a list and notifies the
 * lock on "this" when finished.  Filling the
 * list is thread safe.
 */
public class FillListTask implements Runnable {
    private final int size;
    private List<String> strings;

    public FillListTask(int size) {
        this.size = size;
    }

    public synchronized boolean isFinished() {
        return null != strings;
    }

    public synchronized List<String> getList() {
        return strings;
    }

    @Override
    public void run() {
        List<String> strs = new ArrayList<String>(size);
        try {
            for (int i = 0; i < size; i++ ) {
```

```
            Thread.sleep(2000);
            strs.add("element " + String.valueOf(i));
        }

        synchronized (this) {
            strings = strs;
            this.notifyAll();
        }
    }
    catch (InterruptedException e) {
        // catch interrupted exception outside loop,
        // since interrupted exception is a sign that
        // the thread should quit.
    }
}

/**
 * Waits for the fill list task to complete
 */
public static void main(String[] args)
    throws InterruptedException
{
    FillListTask task = new FillListTask(7);

    new Thread(task).start();

    // The call to wait() releases the lock
    // on task and suspends the thread until
    // it receives a notification
    synchronized (task) {
        while (!task.isFinished()) {
            task.wait();
        }
    }

    System.out.println("Array full: " + task.getList());
}
}
```

In fact, most developers will never use low-level tools like `wait` and `notify`, turning instead to the `java.util.concurrent` package for higher-level tools.

Synchronization and Data Structures

Android supports the feature-rich Java Collections Library from Standard Edition Java. If you peruse the library, you'll find that there are two versions of most kinds of collections: `List` and `Vector`, `HashMap` and `Hashtable`, and so on. Java introduced an entirely new collections framework in version 1.3. The new framework completely replaces the old collections. To maintain backward compatibility, however, the old versions were not deprecated.

The new collections should be preferred over their legacy counterparts. They have a more uniform API, there are better tools to support them, and so on. Perhaps most important, however, the legacy collections are all synchronized. That might sound like a great idea, but as the following example shows, it is not necessarily sufficient:

```java
public class SharedListTask implements Runnable {
    private final Vector<String> list;

    public SharedListTask(Vector<String> l) {
        this.list = l;
    }

    @Override
    public void run() {
        // the size of the list is obtained early
        int s = list.size();

        while (true) {
            for (int i = 0; i < s; i++ ) {
                // throws IndexOutOfBoundsException!!
                // when the list is size 3, and s is 4.
                System.out.println(list.get(i));
            }
        }
    }

    public static void main(String[] args) {
        Vector<String> list = new Vector<String>();
        list.add("one");
        list.add("two");
        list.add("three");
        list.add("four");

        new Thread(new SharedListTask(list)).start();

        try { Thread.sleep(2000); }
        catch (InterruptedException e) { /* ignore */ }

        // the data structure is fully synchronized,
        // but that only protects the individual methods!
        list.remove("three");
    }
}
```

Even though every use of the Vector is fully synchronized and each call to one of its methods is guaranteed to be atomic, this program breaks. The complete synchronization of the Vector is not sufficient, of course, because the code makes a copy of its size and uses it even while another thread changes that size.

Because simply synchronizing the methods of a collection object itself is so often insufficient, the collections in the new framework are not synchronized at all. If the code handling the collection is going to have to synchronize anyway, synchronizing the collection itself is redundant and wasteful.

## CHAPTER 3

The Ingredients of an Android Application

Based on the foundation laid in the preceding chapter for writing robust Java code, this chapter introduces the major high-level concepts involved in programming for the Android platform.

Traditional Programming Models Compared to Android

Operating systems traditionally use a single entry point, often called `main`, which might parse some command-line arguments and then proceed to execute a loop that reads user input and produces output. The OS would load the program code into a process and then start executing it. Conceptually, this kind of process might look something like Figure 3-1.

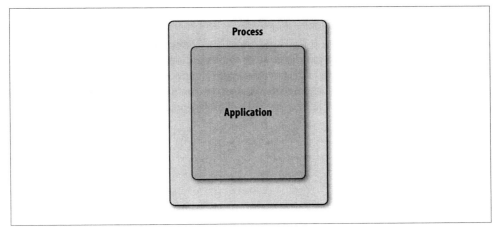

Figure 3-1. A simple application in a process

With programs written in Java, it gets a little more complex: a Java virtual machine (VM) in a process loads bytecode to which it creates instances of Java classes as the program uses them. This process looks something like Figure 3-2. If you use a rich graphical user interface system like Swing, you might start a UI system on a second thread. It might use callbacks into the mainline code to process events.

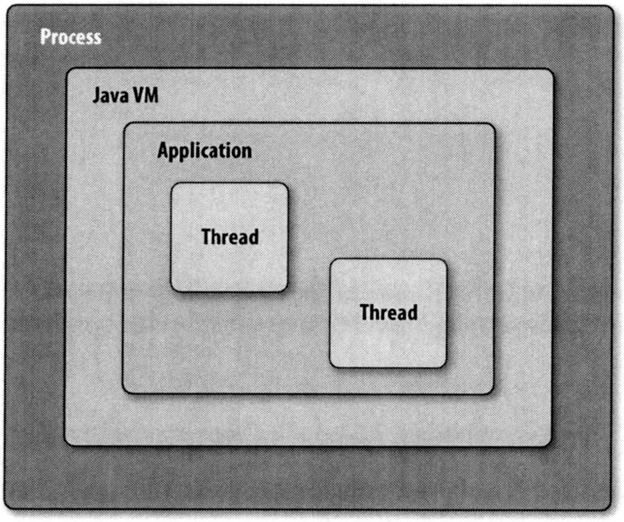

Figure 3-2. A Java application, running in a Java virtual machine, in a process

Android introduces a richer approach by supporting multiple application entry points. Android programs should expect the system to start them in different places, depending on where the user is coming from and what the user wants to do next.

Instead of a hierarchy of places, your program is a cooperating group of components that may be started from outside the flow of your application. For example, a component to scan a bar code provides a discrete function that many applications can integrate into their UI flow. Instead of relying on the user to directly start each application, the components themselves invoke one another to perform interactions on behalf of the user.

Activities, Intents, and Tasks

An Android activity is both a unit of user interaction—typically filling the whole screen of an Android mobile device—and a unit of execution. When you make an interactive Android program, you start by subclassing the `Activity` class. Activities provide the reusable, interchangeable parts of the flow of UI components across Android applications.

How does one activity invoke another, and pass information about what the user wants to do? The unit of communication is the `Intent` class. An intent represents an abstract description of an operation that one activity requires another activity to perform, such as taking a picture. Intents form the basis of a system of loose coupling that allows activities to launch one another, and provide results. When an application dispatches an intent, it's possible that several different activities might be registered to provide the desired operation.

At one layer of abstraction, Android applications look a lot like web applications. Activities are analogous to the servlets in web applications. A well-designed activity is responsible for managing a single UI page and each has its own unique name. Users move from page to page in a web application by following the links, while in Android applications users may find their interaction invoked by an intent. New pages can leverage old pages, simply by linking to them. Just as in the world of web applications, some servlets provide UIs and others provide APIs for services, so, in the Android world, activities provide UIs and the `Service` and `ContentProvider` classes, introduced in a moment, provide programmatic access to services. Understanding this architectural similarity will help you design Android applications that effectively use the Android Framework.

You have already "written" the code for an activity in the test application you created to verify that your Android SDK is correctly installed. Let's take a look at that code again:

```
public class TestActivity extends Activity {
    /** Called when the activity is first created. */
    @Override
    public void onCreate(Bundle savedInstanceState) {
        super.onCreate(savedInstanceState);
        setContentView(R.layout.main);
    }
}
```

When the system starts this activity it calls the constructor for `TestActivity`, a subclass of `Activity`, and then calls its `onCreate` method. This causes the view hierarchy described in the *main.xml* file to load and display. The `onCreate` method kicks off the life cycle of the `Activity`, which Chapter 10 covers in detail.

The `Activity` class is one of the most important classes in the Android system, promoting apps' modularity and allowing functionality to be shared. An activity interacts with the Android runtime to implement key aspects of the application life cycle. Each activity can also be independently configured, through a `Context` class.

 We use the word *activity* to refer to instances of the `Activity` class, much in the way that *object* is used to refer to instances of classes.

Each activity in an Android application is largely separate from other activities. The code that implements one activity does not directly call methods in the code that implements another activity. Other elements in the Android Framework—usually the intent mentioned earlier—are used to manage communication instead. You are very strongly discouraged from keeping references to `Activity` objects. The Android Runtime Environment, which creates and manages activities and other application components, often reclaims the memory they use to restrict individual tasks to relatively small amounts of memory.

 It is very common to find novice Android programmers trying to prevent Android's component life cycle from operating on a program's `Activity` instances. You will find ad hoc attempts to control Android memory management by keeping references to `Activity` objects to be futile and counterproductive.

Instead of a user interface flow control based on method calls, applications describe an intent that they want to execute and ask the system to find one that matches. The Android Home Screen application starts your program using these descriptions, and every app can do the same using its own choice of intents. The resultant flow is a "task": a chain of activities that often span more than one application, and, often, more than one process. Figure 3-3 shows a task spanning three applications and multiple activities (Table 3-1 gives an example). The chain of activities comprising this task spans three separate processes and heaps, and can exist independent of other tasks that may have started other instances of the same `Activity` subclasses.

Table 3-1. Examples of a single task, made up of activities across applications

App	Activity	User's next action
Messaging	View list of messages	User taps on a message in the list
Messaging	View a message	User taps Menu→View Contact
Contacts	View a contact	User taps Call Mobile
Phone	Call the contact's mobile number	

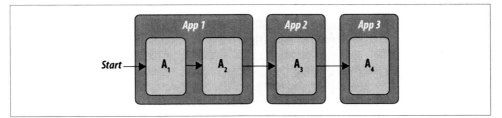

Figure 3-3. Activities in a single task, spanning multiple applications

Other Android Components

Three other components in Android contribute to applications: services, content providers, and broadcast receivers. The `Service` class supports background functions. The `ContentProvider` class provides access to a data store for multiple applications, and the `Broadcast Receiver` allows multiple parties to listen for intents broadcast by applications.

There is also an `Application` class, but you will find that, compared to its components, the application itself is a relatively unimportant unit. Well-designed applications "dissolve" into the Android environment, where they can start activities in other applications to borrow their functions, and provide or augment their own functionality through the use of supporting Android components.

Information about the constants used to match intents for the standard suite of Android apps can be found at *http://developer.android.com/guide/topics/intents/intents-filters .html* and at *http://developer.android.com/guide/appendix/g-app-intents.html*. You can think of Android's content providers and intents as a secondary API that you should learn to use in order to take advantage of Android's strongest features and integrate seamlessly with the Android platform.

Service

The Android `Service` class is for background tasks that may be active but not visible on the screen. A music-playing application would likely be implemented as a service to continue to play music while a user might be viewing web pages. Services also allow applications to share functions through long-term connections. This practice is reminiscent of Internet services such as FTP and HTTP, which wait until a request from a client triggers them. The Android platform avoids reclaiming service resources, so once a service starts, it is likely to be available unless memory gets extremely constrained.

Like `Activity`, the `Service` class offers methods that control its life cycle, such as stopping and restarting the service.

Content Providers

Content provider components are roughly analogous to a RESTful web service: you find them using a URI, and the operations of a `ContentProvider` subclass parallel RESTful web operations such as putting and getting data. A special URI starting with `content://`, which is recognized across the local device, gives you access to the content provider data. To use a `ContentProvider`, you specify a URI and how to act on referenced data. Here is a list of content provider operations, which provide the well-known quartet of basic data handling activities: create (insert), read (query), update, and delete:

Insert
> The `insert` method of the `ContentProvider` class is analogous to the REST `POST` operation. It inserts new records into the database.

Query
> The `query` method of the `ContentProvider` class is analogous to the REST `GET` operation. It returns a set of records in a specialized collection class called `Cursor`.

Update
> The `update` method of the `ContentProvider` class is analogous to the REST `UPDATE` operation. It replaces records in the database with updated records.

Delete
> The `delete` method of the `ContentProvider` class is analogous to the REST `DELETE` operation. It removes matching records from the database.

 REST stands for "Representational State Transfer." It isn't a formal protocol the way that HTTP is. It is more of a conceptual framework for using HTTP as a basis for easy access to data. REST implementations may differ, but they all strive for simplicity. Android's content provider API formalizes REST-like operations into an API and is designed in the spirit of REST's simplicity. You can find more information on REST on Wikipedia: *http://en.wikipedia.org/wiki/REST*.

Content provider components are the heart of the Android content model: by providing a `ContentProvider`, your application can share data with other applications and manage the data model of an application. A companion class, `ContentResolver`, enables other components in an Android system to find content providers. You will find content providers throughout the platform, used both in the operating system and in applications from other developers. Notably, the core Android applications make use of content providers that can provide quick and sophisticated functions for new Android applications, including providers for Browser, Calendar, Contacts, Call Log, Media, and Settings.

Content providers are unique among the IPC systems found on other platforms, such as CORBA, RMI, and DCOM, which focus on remote procedure calls. Content providers operate both as a persistence mechanism and as a form of interprocess communication. Instead of just enabling interprocess method calls, content providers allow developers to efficiently share entire SQL databases across processes: instead of sharing just objects, content providers manage entire SQL tables.

Using a content provider

When building a server-based web application, a developer typically has access to two different kinds of APIs. First are the code, libraries, and data model that comprise her own program. Second, though, she is likely to make calls to other web applications, using their well-defined APIs to obtain the data and services they provide. Similarly, Android provides two levels of API: the libraries and services that your code accesses directly and—at least as important—the variety of services available through content providers. Due to its importance in Android, we provide a brief introduction here to writing a client that uses a content provider.

This example, which uses one of the most important content providers—the Contacts database—should give you a better understanding of how a content provider can fit into your application. The ContentProvider class provides the central content provider API, which you can subtype to manipulate specific types of data. Activities access specific content provider instances using the ContentResolver class and associated URLs as follows:

```
Cursor c = getContentResolver().query(
    android.provider.ContactsContract.Data.CONTENT_URI,
    new String[] {
        android.provider.ContactsContract.Data._ID,
        android.provider.ContactsContract.Phone.NUMBER},
    null,
    null,
    null);;
```

The Contacts database is a separate application running in a different process. Using a content provider involves calling its data operations with REST-style URIs. Content provider URLs always take the following form:

```
content://authority/path/id
```

where *authority* is the content provider namespace (often the Java namespace of the content provider implementation and its root Java package). Here are some example content provider URIs:

```
// references a person
content://contacts/people/25

// this URI designates the phone numbers of the person whose ID is "25"
content://contacts/people/25/phones
```

When a developer calls the query method on a content provider, the call will return a Cursor object that implements the android.database.Cursor interface. This interface lets you retrieve one result (such as a row from a database) at a time using an index that is automatically updated as you retrieve each result. Developers familiar with JDBC can compare this to `java.sql.ResultSet`. In most cases, `Cursor` objects represent the results of queries on SQLite tables. Developers can access cursor fields using the indexes of the underlying SQLite table. Here is an example of iterating an Android cursor and accessing its fields:

```
// code from an activity method
Cursor contactsCursor = getContentResolver().query(
    ContactsContract.Contacts.CONTENT_URI,
    null,
    null,
    null,
    null);

if (contactsCursor.moveToFirst()) {
    int idx = contactsCursor.getColumnIndex(Contacts.People.DISPLAY_NAME);

    do { name = contactsCursor.getString(idx); }
    while (contactsCursor.moveToNext());
}
```

Note here that whenever a client uses a cursor from a provider, it is critical that it closes the cursor when it is done using it. Failure to do so will result in a serious memory leak that can crash your application. Android provides two ways to ensure that provider cursors get closed when not in use:

- The activity calls `Cursor.close` directly.
- The activity uses a Loader and relies on the system to watch cursor references to know when a given reference has no more active clients. When reference counts indicate that all clients have finished, the system will itself call `Cursor.close`.

We'll spend more time covering data and content providers in detail in Chapters 12 and 13.

Content providers and the Internet

Together with the activity component of an Android application, content providers provide the necessary parts of a Model-View-Controller (MVC) architecture. In addition to supporting REST-like operations, they implement the observer pattern that supports MVC. The `ContentResolver` class provides a `notifyChange` method that client code calls whenever there is a change in the underlying database. This call causes a broadcast notification to be sent to all `Cursor` objects that have registered as observers, using the `registerContentObserver` method.

You may be thinking, "That's nice, but the data I'm interested in is out there on the Internet." As it happens, Android provides plenty of tools to make accessing networked data relatively easy. You may well have used some applications that access Internet-based data using Android's network classes. Unfortunately, you can often recognize these applications because they take a noticeable amount of time to access and retrieve data from some server on the Internet. They might even show a progress indicator while you wait.

Wouldn't it be nicer if you could harness the power of content providers to cache data locally, and the power of Android's database-centric MVC architecture support to make fresh data appear on the user's screen as it arrives? That's what Chapter 13 is about. There you will learn how to combine user interfaces, content providers and related classes, Android's network APIs, and MVC support in Android to create a REST client that takes advantage of the similarity of the REST content provider architecture to free the user from staring at a progress indicator while your application fetches data.

BroadcastReceiver

The `BroadcastReceiver` class implements another variant of Android's high-level inter-process communication mechanism using `Intent` objects. `BroadcastReceiver` has a simpler life cycle than the other components we've covered. It is similar to an activity but does not have its own user interface. All of the broadcast receivers registered for a given intent receive that intent whenever it is broadcast. A typical use for a broadcast receiver might be to receive an alarm that causes an app to become active at a particular time.

Component Life Cycles

As described earlier, Android applications are not like applications on most operating systems. Instead of a bit of code that is started and left to fend for itself, Android applications are managed components, with complete life cycles. For instance, the `Activity` method `onCreate` is called when an application starts, and `onDestroy` is called when it is terminated. Component life cycles facilitate efficient use of application memory (heap space): they enable the state of entire processes to be preserved and restored so that the Android system can run more applications than can fit in memory.

The Activity Life Cycle

The most complex component life cycle is that of the activity. Here we will diagram it and take a look at how these state transitions are handled in code. In Figure 3-4, you see the states and state transitions in the activity life cycle. The key elements of handling life cycle state transitions are selecting which life cycle callbacks you need to implement, and knowing when they are called.

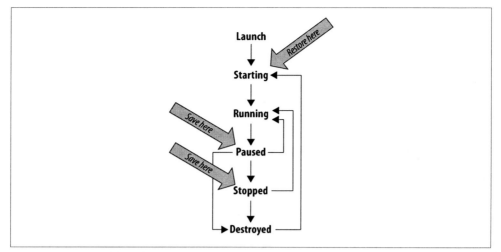

Figure 3-4. Activity life cycle states

In Chapter 10, we will revisit this topic in detail. For now, let's look at two methods of the `Activity` class: `onSaveInstanceState` and `onCreate`. The runtime calls the first to warn your application to save its state. It calls the second to allow a new `Activity` instance to restore the state of one that has been destroyed. The method implementations in the following code snippets are taken from Chapter 10, where you can see the full program listing, including the member variables to which the code refers:

```
@Override
protected void onSaveInstanceState(Bundle outState) {
// Save instance-specific state
outState.putString("answer", state);
super.onSaveInstanceState(outState);
Log.i(TAG, "onSaveInstanceState");
}
```

The runtime calls the `onSaveInstanceState` method when it determines that it might have to destroy the activity, but wants to be able to restore it later. That's an important distinction from other life cycle methods that are called on state transitions. For example, when an activity is explicitly ending, there may be no need to restore state, even though it will pass through the paused state, and have its `onPause` method called. As the previous code snippet shows, the work you need to do in your `onSaveInstanceS tate` method is to save any state that will let the user continue using the application later, hopefully unaware that it might have been destroyed and restored since the previous use:

```
@Override
    protected void onRestoreInstanceState(Bundle savedState) {
        super.onRestoreInstanceState(savedState);
        // Restore state; we know savedState is not null
        String answer = savedState.getString("answer");
```

```
        // ...
        Log.i(TAG, "onRestoreInstanceState"
                + (null == savedState ? "" : RESTORE) + " " + answer);
    }
```

The onRestoreInstanceState method is called when an activity that was destroyed is being re-created. A new instance of your application's activity is therefore running. The data you stored in the previous instance of the activity, through onSaveInstance State, is passed to the new instance via the onRestoreInstanceState method.

You might think that, with such a complex life cycle and stringent requirements to adhere to heap utilization limitations, the Android activity life cycle would be readily apparent in Android application code, and that you will spend a lot of time and effort catering to activity life cycle requirements. Yet this is not the case.

In a lot of Android code, especially in small examples, very few life cycle callbacks are implemented. That is because the Activity parent class handles life cycle callbacks, the View class, and the children of the View class, and also saves their state, as shown in Figure 3-5. This means that in many situations the Android View classes provide all the necessary user interface functionality, and that Android applications do not need to explicitly handle most life cycle callbacks.

This is essentially good, because it makes Android programming a lot more convenient. All of what you see diagrammed in Figure 3-5 happens without you writing any code. But it has a bad side too, because it leads programmers down the path of ignoring the activity life cycle until they have coded themselves into a buggy mess. This is why we emphasize understanding life cycles here, and why, in Chapter 10, we show how to handle all life cycle callbacks and log them. Starting with complete awareness of the activity life cycle is probably the most important thing you can do to prevent bugs that are difficult to diagnose.

On Porting Software to Android

Thus far, you've learned that Android has an application architecture that is radically different from the typical desktop application architecture and even quite different from most other systems on small devices (including the iOS operating system used in the iPhone, iPod Touch, and iPad). If you attempt to port software by subverting the Android application architecture and force-fitting a conventional application architecture into an Android application, to facilitate a method-by-method transliteration from Objective-C, C++, or C#, odds are the effort will come to grief.

If you want to port existing software to Android, first take it apart: the data model, the user interface, and major noninteractive modules and libraries should be ported or reimplemented in the Android application model depending on how they fit. Android does have similarities to other modern managed application runtime environments and language systems. Once you understand Android in greater depth, you will be equipped

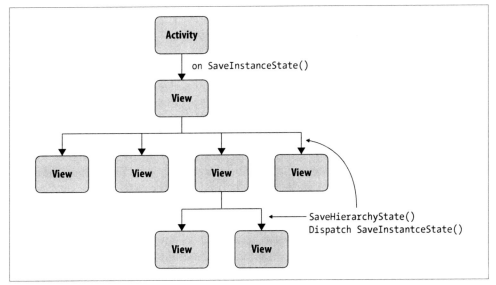

Figure 3-5. Saving the state of the user interface

to see architectural analogies with other platforms and make better implementation choices when porting.

Static Application Resources and Context

Having visited some of the basic architectural constructs from which an Android application is built, it is time to turn to the physical artifacts involved.

Chapter 1 introduced the basics of the Android SDK. In Chapter 5 we will look in detail at how to manage a project using one of the most common tools for Android development, the Eclipse IDE. For the moment, though, let's look at the basic organization of a project.

To reiterate, a *project* is a workspace devoted to producing a single deployable artifact. In the wider world of Java, that artifact might be a library (a *.jar* file that cannot be run by itself but that implements some specific functionality). It might, on the other hand, be a deployable web application or a double-clickable desktop application. In the Android space, the artifact is most likely to be a single runnable service: a content provider, a service, or an activity. A content provider that is used by a single activity certainly might start its life as a part of the activity project. As soon as an external activity needs to use it, though, it is time to consider refactoring it into its own project.

An Android application's project directory nearly always looks like this:

```
AndroidManifest.xml
bin/
        ... compiled classes ...
```

```
gen/
        ... code automatically generated by the android build system ...
res/
    layout/
        ... contains application layout files ...
    drawable/
        ...contains images, patches, drawable xml ...
    raw/
        ... contains data files that can be loaded as streams ...
    values/
        ... contains xml files that contain strings, number values used in code ...
src/
    java/package/directories/
```

Traditionally, the Java compiler expects directory trees to hold the source (*.java*) files that it parses and the binary (*.class*) files that it produces as output. Although it's not necessary, it's much easier to manage a project if those trees have different roots, commonly directories named *src* and *bin*, respectively.

In an Android project, there are two other important directory trees, *res* and *gen*. The first of these, *res*, contains definitions for static resources: colors, constant strings, layouts, and so on. Android tools preprocess these definitions, and turn them into highly optimized representations and the Java source through which application code refers to them. The autogenerated code, along with code created for AIDL objects (see "AIDL and Remote Procedure Calls" on page 125), is put into the *gen* directory. The compiler compiles the code from both directories to produce the contents of *bin*. We'll see in a minute how the *res* directory is particularly important for making application data accessible using a **Context** object.

 When you add your project to a revision control system like Git, Subversion, or Perforce, be sure to exclude the *bin* and *gen* directories!

Organizing Java Source

Your application source code goes in the *src* directory. As noted in Chapter 2, you should put all your code into a package with a name derived from the domain name of the owner of the code. Suppose, for instance, that you are a developer at large, doing business as `awesome-android.net`. You are under contract to develop a weather-prediction application for `voracious-carrier.com`. You will probably choose to put all your code into the package `com.voraciouscarrier.weatherprediction`, or possibly `com.voracious_carrier.weather-prediction`. Although the character "-" is perfectly legal in a DNS domain name, it is not legal in a Java package name. The UI for this ambitious application might go in `com.voraciouscarrier.weatherprediction.ui` and the model in `com.voraciouscarrier.weatherprediction.futureweather`.

If you look inside the *src* directory in your project, you will see that it contains a single directory, *com*; *com* in turn contains the directory *voraciouscarrier*, and so on. The source directory tree mirrors the package tree. The Java compiler expects this organization and may be unable to compile your code if it is violated.

Eventually, when the FutureWeather content provider becomes valuable on its own, you'll want to factor it out into a new project with a package namespace that is not restricted by the name of the application in which it was originally created. Doing this by hand is a nightmare. You have to create a new directory structure, correctly place the files within that structure, correct the package names that are at the head of each source file, and, finally, correct any references to things that have moved.

Eclipse refactoring tools are your best friend. With just a few clicks you can create a new project for the now standalone subtree, cut and paste the content provider code into it, and then rename the packages as appropriate. Eclipse will fix most things, including the changed references. We present more on this when we discuss Eclipse in detail in Chapter 5.

It's worth a reminder that shortcutting package names—using a package named just `weatherprediction`, for instance—is a bad idea. Even if you are pretty sure the code you are creating will never be used outside its current context, you may want to use externally produced code in that context. Don't set yourself up for a name collision.

Resources

In addition to their code, applications may need to store significant amounts of data to control their runtime behavior. This data might consist of images to display or simple text strings, the color for a background or the name of a font to be used. This data is called *resources* and, in keeping with software best practices, is kept separate from the code. Together, all this information forms the *context* of the application, and Android provides access to it through the `Context` class. Both `Activity` and `Service` extend the `Context` class: all activities and services have access to `Context` data through the `this` pointer. In subsequent sections, we will describe how to use a `Context` object to access application resources at runtime.

Android applications place images, icons, and user interface layout files into a directory named *res*. The *res* directory usually will contain at least four subdirectories, as follows:

layout
Contains Android user interface XML files, described in Chapter 6.

drawable
Contains drawing artifacts such as the application icon noted in the previous section.

raw

Holds files that may be read as streams during the execution of an application. Raw files are a great way to provide debug information to a running application without having to access the network to retrieve data.

values

Contains values that the application will read during its execution, or static data an application will use for such purposes as internationalization of UI strings.

Applications access resources in these directories using the method `Context.getResour` `ces()` and the R class.

To access the data in the *res* directory, a traditional Java developer might think about writing code to build relative resource file paths and then using the file API to open the resources. After loading resource bytes, the application developer might expect to parse an application-specific format to finally get access to the same items every app needs: images, strings, and data files. Anticipating each application's need to load similar information, Android instead includes a precompiler utility that converts resources into programmatically accessible data objects. The tool integrates with IDEs and makes it easy to create and maintain resource data.

The tool creates a directory called *gen*, which contains a class (always named R) in the Java application package named in the Android manifest. The R class file contains fields that uniquely identify all resources in the application package structure. A developer calls the `Context.getResources` method to obtain an instance of `android.` `content.res.Resources` that directly contains application resources. (Methods in the `Context` class can be called directly because `Activity`—and `Service` as well—extend `Context`.) Developers then call methods of the `Resources` object to obtain resources of the desired type as follows:

```
// code inside an Activity method
String helloWorld = this.getResources().getString(R.string.hello_world);
int anInt = this.getResources().getInteger(R.integer.an_int);
```

You will see that the R class is ubiquitous in Android, enabling easy access to resources such as the components in UI layout files.

 Java scoping rules dictate that classes in the same package are visible to one another, even if they have not been explicitly imported (with an `import` statement). This is true even if the classes are not in the same directory on the filesystem. Because the Android tooling automatically puts the R class into the Java package named in the manifest `package` attribute, it is very convenient if that package is also the package that contains most of your code. The `package` attribute in the manifest is a unique namespace for your application. There is no requirement that it be the same as the unique namespace that you use as the root package for your code, but it is a good idea.

Application Manifests

In addition to data that is used by a running application, an application also needs a way to describe the environment it expects: its name, the intents it registers, the permissions it needs, and other information that describes the app to the Android system. This data is stored in a file called the *manifest*. Android requires applications to explicitly describe these things in an XML file called *AndroidManifest.xml*. Here, applications declare the presence of content providers, services, required permissions, and other elements. Manifest data is also available to a running application through its context. The manifest file organizes an Android application into a well-defined structure that is shared by all applications and enables the Android operating system to load and execute them in a managed environment. The structure encompasses a common directory layout and common file types in those directories.

As we've seen, the four components of Android applications—`Activity`, `Service`, `ContentProvider`, and `BroadcastReceiver`—provide the foundation of Android application development (see Figure 3-6). To make use of any of them, an application must include corresponding declarations in its *AndroidManifest.xml* file.

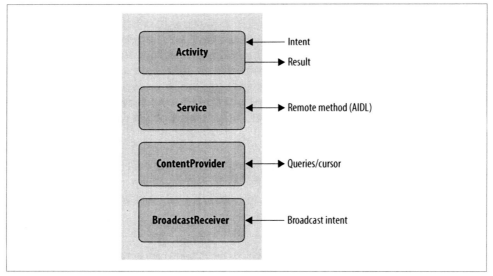

Figure 3-6. The four kinds of Android components

The Application Class

There is a "fifth Beatle" of Android components: the `Application` class. But many Android applications do not subclass `Application`. In most cases, subclassing `Application` is unnecessary: the Android Project Wizard doesn't create one for you automatically.

Initialization Parameters in AndroidManifest.xml

The following code shows the Android manifest from the test application that we introduced in Chapter 1. The test application does not do anything beyond demonstrating the basic layout of an Android application. This manifest file contains only a few, very basic elements:

```xml
<?xml version="1.0" encoding="utf-8"?>
<manifest xmlns:android="http://schemas.android.com/apk/res/android"
          package="com.oreilly.demo.pa.ch01.testapp"
          android:versionCode="1"
          android:versionName="1.0">

    <uses-permission android:name="android.permission.ACCESS_FINE_LOCATION" />
    <uses-permission android:name="android.permission.CALL_PHONE" />
    <uses-permission android:name="android.permission.ACCESS_MOCK_LOCATION" />
    <uses-permission android:name="android.permission.INTERNET" />

    <application android:icon="@drawable/icon"
                 android:label="@string/app_name"
                 android:debuggable="true">

        <activity android:name=".TestActivity"
                  android:label="Test Activity">
            <intent-filter>
                <action android:name="android.intent.action.MAIN"/>
                <category android:name="android.intent.category.LAUNCHER"/>
            </intent-filter>
        </activity>

        <provider android:name=".TestProvider"
                  android:authorities= "com.oreilly.demo.pa.ch11.video.FinchVideo"
                  />

        <service android:name=".TestService"
                 android:label="Test Service"/>

        <receiver
                android:name=".TestBroadcastReceiver"
                android:label="Test Broadcast Receiver"/>
    </application>
    <uses-sdk android:minSdkVersion="7" />
</manifest>
```

Like all good XML files, line 1 has the standard declaration of the version of XML and the character encoding used. The following lines define some parameters and declare some permissions that the application requires. Here are detailed explanations for each:

manifest

  package="com.oreilly.demo.pa.ch01.testapp"
      This is the default package where modules in the application can be found.

android:versionCode

This is an arbitrary integer denoting versions of the application. Every application should include a version code, and it should always increase for each version released to customers. This lets other programs (such as the Android Market, installers, and launchers) easily figure out which version of an application is later than another. The filename of your .*apk* file should include this same version number so that it is obvious which version is contained in it.

android:versionName

This is a string intended to be more like the version numbers you usually see for applications, such as 1.0.3. This is the version identifier that will be displayed to a user (either by your application or by another application). The naming convention is up to you, but in general, the idea is to use a scheme such as *m.n.o* (for as many numbers as you want to use), to identify successive levels of change to the application.

uses-permission android:name=...

Four declarations in the TestApp manifest declare that the application intends to use features of Android that require explicit permission from the user of the device running the application. The permission is requested when the application is installed. From then on, Android remembers that the user said it was OK to run this application and allow access to the secure features. If the user does not allow the requested permissions, Android will not install the application. Many permissions are already defined in Android, and all are described in the Android documentation (search for android.Manifest.permission). What's more, you can define your own permissions and use them to restrict other applications' access to functions in your application, unless the user grants the other application that permission. We have requested the following commonly used permissions as an example:

ACCESS_FINE_LOCATION

Required to obtain location information from a GPS sensor

CALL_PHONE

Allows a phone call on behalf of the user

ACCESS_MOCK_LOCATION

Allows us to get fake location information when we're running under the emulator

INTERNET

Allows us to open Internet connections to retrieve data

application

label

This provides a human-readable application label.

`icon="@drawable/icon"`

> This is the filename for a PNG file that contains the icon you'd like to use for your application. In this case, we're telling the Android SDK to look for the icon file in the *drawable* subdirectory of the *res* (resources) directory under *TestApp*. Android will use this icon for your application in the Android Desktop.

`activity`

Turning our attention to the definition of `TestActivity`, we first define a few attributes. The most important are:

`android:name`

> This is the name of the class for the activity. The full name of the activity includes the package name (which in this application is `com.oreilly.demo.pa.ch01.testapp`), but because this file is always used in the context of the package's namespace, we don't need to include the leading package names: we strip the name down to just `.TestActivity`. Actually, even the leading period is optional.

`android:label`

> This is the label that we want to appear at the top of the Android screen when the activity is visible. We've defined this in *strings.xml* to match our application.

`intent-filter`

Here we declare an intent filter that tells Android when this `Activity` should be run. When an app asks Android to fulfill an `Intent`, the runtime looks among the available activities and services to find something that can service it. We set two attributes:

`action`

> This tells Android how to launch this application once the runtime has decided this is the application to run. Android looks for an activity that declares itself ready to resolve the MAIN action. Any application that is going to be launched by the Launcher needs to have exactly one activity or service that makes this assertion.

`category`

> The `Intent` resolver in Android uses this attribute to further qualify the `Intent` that it's looking for. In this case, the qualification is that we'd like this `Activity` to be displayed in the User menu so that the user can select it to start this application. Specifying the LAUNCHER category accomplishes this. You can have a perfectly valid application without this attribute— you just won't be able to launch it from the Android desktop. Normally, again, you'll have exactly one LAUNCHER per application, and it will appear in the same intent filter as the opening `Activity` of your application.

`provider`

> This enables the declaration of a content provider. `name` specifies the name of the provider class and `authorities` specifies the URI authorities that the content provider should handle. A URI authority provides the domain section of a content provider URI and enables the Android content resolution system to locate a provider that should handle a particular type of URI. We'll provide more detail on how clients use content providers a bit later in the chapter. We've declared a provider with the name `TestProvider`.

`service`

> This enables the app to declare that it supports a given service, where `name` specifies the service class and `label` provides a human-readable label for the service. We've declared a service with the name `.TestService`.

`receiver`

> This provides a way to declare an app's support for a broadcast receiver. `name` again specifies the receiving class and `label` provides a human-readable label for the receiver. We've declared a receiver with the name `TestBroadcastReceiver`.

Packaging an Android Application: The .apk File

The final static component of an application is, of course, the packaged application itself. Android provides an application called `apkbuilder` for generating installable Android application files, which have the extension *.apk*. An *.apk* file is in ZIP file format, just like many other Java-oriented application formats, and contains the application manifest, compiled application classes, and all of the resources. The Android SDK also provides the utility `aapt` for converting the contents of the *res* directory into a packaged resource file and the accompanying `R` class. Most developers typically prefer to allow their development environment to build their applications for them. Most users simply rely on their IDE to keep the resource files up-to-date, and to build their *.apk*.

Once the *.apk* file has been created, it can be installed onto a device (or emulator) in one of several ways:

- Using the *adb* interface directory, or more commonly by using an IDE
- Using an SD card
- Making the file available on a web server
- Uploading the file to the Android Market, and then selecting Install

The Android Application Runtime Environment

Android's unique application component architecture is, in part, a product of the way Android implements a multiprocessing environment. To make that environment suitable for multiple applications from multiple vendors with a minimal requirement to trust each vendor, Android executes multiple instances of the Dalvik VM, one for each task. In "Component Life Cycles" on page 83, and in later chapters, we will explore in greater depth how component life cycles enable Android to enhance the way garbage collection works within application heaps, and how it enables a memory recovery strategy across multiple heaps.

As a result of this simple and reliable approach to multiprocessing, Android must efficiently enable multiple virtual machine heaps. Each heap should be relatively small so that many applications can fit in memory at the same time. Within each heap, the component life cycle enables components not in use—especially currently inactive user interface components—to be garbage-collected when heap space is tight, and then restored when needed. This, in turn, motivates a database-centric approach to data models where most data is inherently persistent at all times, something you will read a lot more about throughout this book, and especially in Chapter 10.

The Dalvik VM

Android's approach to multiprocessing, using multiple processes and multiple instances of a VM, requires that each instance of the VM be space-efficient. This is achieved partly through the component life cycle, which enables objects to be garbage-collected and re-created, and partly by the VM itself. Android uses the Dalvik VM to run a bytecode system developed specifically for Android, called dex. Dex bytecodes are approximately twice as space-efficient as Java bytecodes, inherently halving the memory overhead of Java classes for each process. Android systems also use copy-on-write memory management to share heap memory among multiple instances of the same Dalvik executable.

Zygote: Forking a New Process

It would also be inefficient for each new process to load all the necessary base classes each time it started a new instance of the VM. Because Android puts each application in a separate process, it can take advantage of the fork operation in the underlying Linux operating system to spawn new processes from a template process that is in the optimal state for launching a new VM instance. This template process is called Zygote. It is an instance of the Dalvik VM that contains a set of preloaded classes that, along with the rest of the state of the Zygote process, are duplicated into copies of Zygote created by forking. Forking the Zygote makes launching Android applications fast. The ability to preload classes works with the copy-on-write memory management used in the Dalvik heap to drastically cut memory footprint.

Sandboxing: Processes and Users

Android security relies heavily on security restrictions at the level of the Linux operating system, specifically on process and user-level boundaries. Because Android is designed for personal devices—that is, devices that are owned and used by one person—Android makes an interesting use of Linux's inherent multiuser support: Android creates a new user, and group, for each application vendor. This means each application runs with different user privileges (except for those signed by the same vendor). Files owned by one vendor's application are, by default, inaccessible by other vendors' applications.

The equivalent behavior on Windows would be as though you were running your word processor as one user and your web browser as another user, but you could see and use the user interface to both. The net effect is increased security as a result of each vendor's application running in its own filesystem "silo."

Desktop operating systems have typically not taken application sandboxing to this extent—once an application is installed, it is trusted with all of a user's data. Android's designers envisioned a world of numerous small applications from numerous vendors who cannot all be vetted for trustworthiness. Hence applications don't have direct access to other applications' data.

A complete description of Android security can be found in the Android documentation at *http://developer.android.com/guide/topics/security/security.html*.

The Android Libraries

Android introduces several new packages that, together with a handful of package trees from the forest of traditional Java (J2SE) packages, make up the API for the Android Runtime Environment. Let's take a minute to see what's in this combined API:

android *and* dalvik

>   These package trees contain the entire Android-specific portion of the Android Runtime Environment. These libraries are the subject of much of this book, as they contain the Android GUI and text handling libraries (named android.graphics, android.view, android.widget, and android.text), as well as the application framework libraries called android.app, android.content, and android.database. They also contain several other key, mobile-oriented frameworks such as android.tel ephony and android.webkit. A fluent Android programmer will have to be very familiar with at least the first few of these packages. To navigate the Android documentation from a package tree perspective, you can start at the top of the Android developer documentation, at *http://developer.android.com/reference/packages .html*.

java

>   This package contains the implementations of the core Java runtime libraries: all the things that every Java programmer knows like the back of his hand. The java.lang package contains the definition of the class Object, the base class for all Java objects. java also contains the util package, which contains the Java Collections Framework: Array, Lists, Map, Set, and Iterator and their implementations. The Java Collections Library provides a well-designed set of data structures for the Java language—they relieve you of the need to write your own linked lists and so on.

As mentioned in Chapter 2, the util package contains collections from two different lineages. Some originate from Java 1.1 and some from a more recent, re-engineered idea of collections. The 1.1 collections (e.g., Vector and Hashtable) are fully synchronized and are less consistent in their interfaces. The newer versions, (e.g., HashMap and ArrayList) are not synchronized, are more consistent, and are preferred.

To maintain compatibility with the Java language, the Android library also contains implementations of some legacy classes that you should avoid altogether. The Collections Framework, for instance, contains the Dictionary class, which has been explicitly deprecated. The Enumeration interface has been superceded by Iterator, and TimerTask has been replaced by ScheduledThreadPoolExecutor from the Concurrency Framework. The Android reference documentation does a good job of identifying these legacy types.

java also contains base types for several other frequently used objects such as Currency, Date, TimeZone, and UUID, as well as basic frameworks for I/O and networking, concurrency, and security.

The awt and rmi packages are absent in the Android version of the java package hierarchy. The awt package has been replaced by Android GUI libraries (android.view and android.widget). Remote messaging has no single replacement, but internal ServiceProviders using Parcelables, described in "Serialization" on page 118, provide similar functionality.

javax

This package is very similar to the java package. It contains parts of the Java language that are officially optional. These are libraries with behavior that is fully defined but that are not required as part of a complete implementation of the Java language. Because the Android Runtime Environment doesn't include some of the parts that are required (a reason it is not and cannot be called "Java"), the distinction exists in Android only to keep the Android packages looking as much like the Java packages as possible. Both package trees contain implementations of libraries described as part of the Java language.

The most important thing to be found in javax is the XML framework. There are both SAX and DOM parsers, an implementation of XPath, and an implementation of XSLT.

In addition, the javax package contains some important security extensions and the OpenGL API. A seasoned Java developer will notice that the Android Runtime Environment implementation of the javax package is missing several important sections, notably those that have to do with UI and media. javax.swing, javax.sound, and other similar sections are all missing. There are Android-specific packages that replace them.

org.apache.http

This package tree contains the standard Apache implementation of an HTTP client and server, HttpCore. This package provides everything you need to communicate using HTTP, including classes that represent messages, headers, connections, requests, and responses.

The Apache HttpCore project can be found online at *http://hc.apache.org/httpcomponents-core/index.html.*

org.w3c.dom, org.xml.sax, org.xmlpull, *and* org.json

These packages are the public API definitions for some common data formats: XML (*http://www.w3.org/standards/xml/*), XML Pull (*http://www.xmlpull.org/index.shtml*), and JSON (*http://www.json.org/*).

Extending Android

Now that you have a basic road map to the Android Framework, the obvious question is: "How do I use it to build my application?" How do you extend the framework—which we've characterized as very complex, but a zombie—to turn it into a useful application?

As you would expect, this question has several answers. The Android libraries are organized to allow applications to obtain access into the framework at various levels. The concepts described here, though, run deep in Android. Becoming familiar with them will improve your instincts for how to interact easily with the Android APIs.

The Android Application Template

Twenty years ago, an application probably ran from the command line and the bulk of its code was unique program logic. These days, though, applications need very complex support for interactive UIs, network management, call handling, and so on. This support logic is the same for all applications. As we've seen already, the Android Framework addresses this in a way that has become fairly common as application environments have become increasingly complex: the *skeleton application*, or *application template*.

When you built the simple demo application that verified your Android SDK installation back in Chapter 1, you created a complete running application. It was able to make network requests and display data on and handle input from the screen. It could handle incoming calls and, although there was no way to use it, check your location. The only thing missing was something for the application to do. That is the skeleton application.

Within the Android Framework, a developer's task is not so much to build a complete program as it is to implement specific behaviors and then inject them into the skeleton at the correct extension points. The motto of MacApp, one of the original skeleton application frameworks, was: "Don't call us, we'll call you." If creating Android applications is largely about understanding how to extend the framework, it makes sense to consider some generic best practices for making those extensions.

Overrides and Callbacks

The simplest and easiest to implement—and a developer's first choice for adding new behaviors to the framework—should be the callback. The basic idea of a callback, a pattern quite common in the Android libraries, was already illustrated in Chapter 2. To create a callback extension point, a class defines two things. First it defines a Java interface (typically with a name ending in "Handler", "Callback", or "Listener") that describes, but does not implement, the callback action. Second, it defines a setter method that takes, as an argument, an object implementing that interface.

Consider an application that needs a way to use text input from a user. Text entry, editing, and display, of course, require a large and complex set of user interface classes. An application need not concern itself with most of that, however. Instead, it adds a library widget—say, an EditText—to its layout (layouts and widgets are described in "Assembling a Graphical Interface" on page 175). The framework handles instantiating the widget, displaying it on the screen, updating its contents when the user types, and so on. In fact, it does everything except the part your application actually cares about: doing something when the text changes. That is done with a callback.

The Android documentation shows that the EditText object defines the method addTextChangedListener that takes, as an argument, a TextWatcher object. The TextWatcher defines methods that are invoked when the EditText widget's content text changes. Sample application code might look like this:

```java
public class MyModel {
    public MyModel(TextView textBox) {
        textBox.addTextChangedListener(
            new TextWatcher() {
                public void afterTextChanged(Editable s) {
                    handleTextChange(s);
                }
                public void beforeTextChanged(
                        CharSequence s,
                        int start,
                        int count,
                        int after)
                { }
                public void onTextChanged(
                        CharSequence s,
                        int start,
                        int count,
                        int after)
                { }
            });
    }

    void handleTextChange(Editable s) {
        // do something with s, the changed text.
    }
}
```

`MyModel` might be the heart of your application. It is going to take the text that the user types and do something useful with it. When it is created, it is passed a `TextBox`, from which it will get the text that the user types. By now, you are an old hand at parsing code like this: in its constructor, `MyModel` creates a new anonymous implementation of the interface `TextWatcher`. It implements the three methods that the interface requires. Two of them, `onTextChanged` and `beforeTextChanged`, do nothing. The third, though, `afterTextChanged`, calls the `MyModel` method `handleTextChange`.

This all works very nicely. Perhaps the two required methods that this particular application doesn't happen to use, `beforeTextChanged` and `onTextChanged`, clutter things a bit. Aside from that, though, the code separates concerns beautifully. `MyModel` has no idea how a `TextView` displays text, where it appears on the screen, or how it gets the text that it contains. The tiny relay class, an anonymous instance of `TextWatcher`, simply passes the changed text between the view and `MyModel`. `MyModel`, the model implementation, is concerned only with what happens when the text changes.

This process, attaching the UI to its behaviors, is often called *wiring up*. Although it is quite powerful, it is also quite restrictive. The client code—the code that registers to receive the callback—cannot change the behavior of the caller. Neither does the client receive any state information beyond the parameters passed in the call. The interface type—`TextWatcher` in this case—represents an explicit contract between the callback provider and the client.

Actually, there is one thing that a callback client can do that will affect the calling service: it can refuse to return. Client code should treat the callback as a notification only and not attempt to do any lengthy inline processing. If there is any significant work to be done—more than a few hundred instructions or any calls to slow services such as the filesystem or the network—they should be queued up for later execution, probably on another thread. We'll discuss how to do this, in depth, in "AsyncTask and the UI Thread" on page 105.

By the same token, a service that attempts to support multiple callback clients may find itself starved for CPU resources, even if all the clients are relatively well behaved. Whereas `addTextChangedListener` supports the subscription of multiple clients, many of the callbacks in the Android library support only one. With these callbacks (`setOn KeyListener`, for instance), setting a new client for a particular callback on a particular object replaces any previous client. The previously registered client will no longer receive any callback notifications. In fact, it won't even be notified that it is no longer the client. The newly registered client will, thenceforward, receive all notifications. This restriction in the code reflects the very real constraint that a callback cannot actually support an unlimited number of clients. If your code must fan notifications out to multiple recipients, you will have to do it in a way that is safe in the context of your application.

The callback pattern appears throughout the Android libraries. Because the idiom is familiar to all Android developers, it makes a lot of sense to design your own application code this way too. Whenever one class might need notifications of changes in another—especially if the association changes dynamically, at runtime—consider implementing the relationship as a callback. If the relationship is not dynamic, consider using dependency injection—a constructor parameter and a final field—to make the required relationship permanent.

Polymorphism and Composition

In Android development, as in other object-oriented environments, polymorphism and composition are compelling tools for extending the environment. By design, the previous example demonstrates both. Let's pause for a second to reinforce the concepts and restate their value as design goals.

The anonymous instance of `TextWatcher` that is passed to `addTextChangedListener` as a callback object uses composition to implement its behavior. The instance does not, itself, implement any behavior. Instead, it delegates to the `handleTextChange` method in `MyModel`, preferring has-a implementation to is-a implementation. This keeps concerns clear and separate. If `MyModel` is ever extended, for example, to use text that comes from another source, the new source will also use `handleTextChange`. It won't be necessary to track down code in several anonymous classes.

The example also demonstrates the use of polymorphism. The instance passed in to the `addTextChangedListener` method is strongly and statically typed. It is an anonymous subtype of `TextWatcher`. Its particular implementation—in this case, delegation to the `handleTextChange` in `MyModel`—is nearly certain to be unlike any other implementation of that interface. Because it is an implementation of the `TextWatcher` interface, though, it is statically typed, no matter how it does its job. The compiler can guarantee that the `addTextChangedListener` in `EditText` is passed only objects that are, at least, intended to do the right thing. The implementation might have bugs, but at least `addTextChangedListener` will never be passed, say, an object intended to respond to network events. That is what polymorphism is all about.

It is worth mentioning one particular antipattern in this context, because it is so common. Many developers find anonymous classes to be a verbose and clumsy way of essentially passing a pointer to a function. To avoid using them, they skip the messenger object altogether, like this:

```
// !!! Anti-pattern warning
public class MyModel implements TextWatcher {
    public MyModel(TextView textBox) {
        textBox.addTextChangedListener(this);
    }

    public void afterTextChanged(Editable s) {
        handleTextChange(s);
    }

    public void beforeTextChanged(
```

```
        CharSequence s,
        int start,
        int count,
        int after)
    { }

    public void onTextChanged(
        CharSequence s,
        int start,
        int count,
        int after)
    { }

    void handleTextChange(Editable s) {
        // do something with s, the changed text.
    }
}
```

Sometimes this approach makes sense. If the callback client, MyModel in this case, is small, simple, and used in only one or two contexts, this code is clear and to the point.

On the other hand, if (as the name MyModel suggests) the class will be used broadly and in a wide variety of circumstances, eliminating the messenger classes breaks encapsulation and limits extension. Obviously, it's going to be messy to extend this implementation to handle input from a second TextBox that requires different behavior.

Nearly as bad, though, is something called *interface pollution*, which happens when this idea is taken to an extreme. It looks like this:

```
// !!! Anti-pattern ALERT!
public class MyModel
    implements TextWatcher, OnKeyListener, View.OnTouchListener,
        OnFocusChangeListener, Button.OnClickListener
{
    // ....
}
```

Code like this is seductively elegant, in a certain way, and fairly common. Unfortunately, though, MyModel is now very tightly coupled to every one of the events it handles.

As usual, there are no hard-and-fast rules about interface pollution. There is, as already noted, lots of working code that looks just like this. Still, smaller interfaces are less fragile and easier to change. When an object's interface expands beyond good taste, consider using composition to split it up into manageable pieces.

Extending Android Classes

Although callbacks provide a clear, well-defined means of extending class behavior, there are circumstances in which they do not provide sufficient flexibility. An obvious problem with the callback pattern is that sometimes your code needs to seize control at some point not foreseen by the library designers. If the service doesn't define a callback, you'll need some other way to inject your code into the flow of control. One solution is to create a subclass.

Some classes in the Android library were specifically designed to be subclassed (for example, the `BaseAdapter` class from `android.widgets`, and `AsyncTask`, described shortly). In general, however, subclassing is not something that a designer should do lightly.

A subclass can completely replace the behavior of any nonfinal method in its superclass and, thus, completely violate the class architectural contract. Nothing in the Java typing system will prevent a subclass of `TextBox`, for example, from overriding the `addText ChangedListener` method so that it ignores its argument and does not notify callback clients of changes in text box content. (You might imagine, for example, an implementation of a "safe" text box that does not reveal its content.)

Such a violation of contract—and it isn't always easy to recognize the details of the contract—can give rise to two classes of bugs, both quite difficult to find. The first and more obvious problem occurs when a developer uses a rogue subclass such as the safe text box described earlier. Imagine that a developer builds a view containing several widgets that uses the `addTextChangedListener` method on each to register for its callbacks. During testing, though, she discovers that some widgets aren't working as expected. She examines her code for hours before it occurs to her that "it's as though that method isn't *doing* anything!" Suddenly, dawn breaks and, presuming it is available, she looks at the source for the widget to confirm that it has broken the class semantic contract. Grrr!

More insidious than this, though, is that the Android Framework itself might change between releases of the SDK. Perhaps the implementation of the `addTextChangedLis tener` method changes. Maybe code in some other part of the Android Framework starts to call `addTextChangedListener`, expecting normal behavior. Suddenly, because the subclass overrides the method, the entire application fails in spectacular ways!

You can minimize the danger of this kind of problem by calling `super` in the implementation of an overridden method, like this:

```
public void addTextChangedListener(TextWatcher watcher) {
    // your code here...
    super.addTextChangedListener(watcher)
    // more of your code here...
}
```

This guarantees that your implementation augments but does not replace existing behavior, even as, over time, the superclass implementation changes. There is a coding rule, enforced in some developer communities, called "Design for Extension." The rule mandates that all methods be either abstract or final. Although this may seem draconian, consider that an overriding method, by definition, breaks a base class's semantic contract unless it at least calls `super`.

Concurrency in Android

As mentioned in Chapter 2, writing correct concurrent programs can be very difficult. The Android libraries provide some convenient tools to make concurrency both easier and safer.

When discussing concurrent programs, developers get into the habit of talking as though writing code with multiple threads actually causes those threads to execute at the same time—as though threading actually makes the program run faster. Of course, it isn't quite that simple. Unless there are multiple processors to execute the threads, a program that needs to perform multiple, unrelated, compute-bound tasks will complete those tasks no more quickly if they are implemented as separate threads than it will if they are on the same thread. In fact, on a single processor, the concurrent version may actually run somewhat more slowly because of the overhead due to context switching.

Multithreaded Java applications were around for a long time before most people could afford machines with more than one processor on which to run them. In the Android world, multithreading is an essential tool, even though the majority of devices have only very recently gotten more than one core. So what is the point of concurrency if not to make a program run faster?

If you've been programming for any length of time at all, you probably don't even think about how absolutely essential it is that the statements in your code are executed in a rigid sequential order. The execution of any given statement must, unconditionally, happen before the execution of the next statement. Threads are no more than an explicit way of relaxing this constraint. They are the abstraction that developers use to make it possible to write code that is still ordered, logical, and easy to read, even when tasks embodied by the code are not related by ordering.

Executing independent threads concurrently doesn't introduce any intrinsic complexity when the threads are completely independent (e.g., if one is running on your computer and the other is running on mine). When two concurrent processes need to collaborate, however, they have to rendezvous. For instance, data from the network might have to be displayed on the screen or user input pushed to a data store. Arranging the rendezvous, especially in the context of code optimizers, pipelined processors, and multilayered memory cache, can be quite complex. This can become painfully apparent when a program that has run, apparently without problem, on a single processor, suddenly fails in strange and difficult-to-debug ways when run in a multiprocessor environment.

The rendezvous process, making data or state from one thread visible to another, is usually called *publishing* a reference. Whenever one thread stores state in a way that makes it visible from another thread, it is said to be publishing a reference to that state. As mentioned in Chapter 2, the only way that a reference can be published safely is if all threads that refer to the data synchronize on the same object during use. Anything else is incorrect and unsafe.

AsyncTask and the UI Thread

If you've worked with any modern GUI framework, the Android UI will look entirely familiar. It is event-driven, built on a library of nestable components, and, most relevant here, single-threaded. Designers discovered years ago that, because a GUI must respond to asynchronous events from multiple sources, it is nearly impossible to avoid deadlock if the UI is multithreaded. Instead, a single thread owns both the input (touch screen, keypad, etc.) and output devices (display, etc.) and executes requests from each, sequentially, usually in the order they were received.

While the UI runs on a single thread, nearly any nontrivial Android application will be multithreaded. The UI must, for instance, respond to the user and animate the display regardless of whether the code that retrieves data from the network is currently processing incoming data. The UI must be quick and responsive and cannot, fundamentally, be ordered with respect to other, long-running processes. The long-running processes must be run asynchronously.

One convenient tool for implementing an asynchronous task in the Android system is, in fact, called `AsyncTask`. It completely hides many of the details of the threads used to run the task.

Let's consider a very simplistic application that initializes a game engine, displaying some interstitial graphic while the content loads. Figure 3-7 shows a very basic example of such an application. When you press the button, it initializes the game level and then displays a welcome message in a text box.

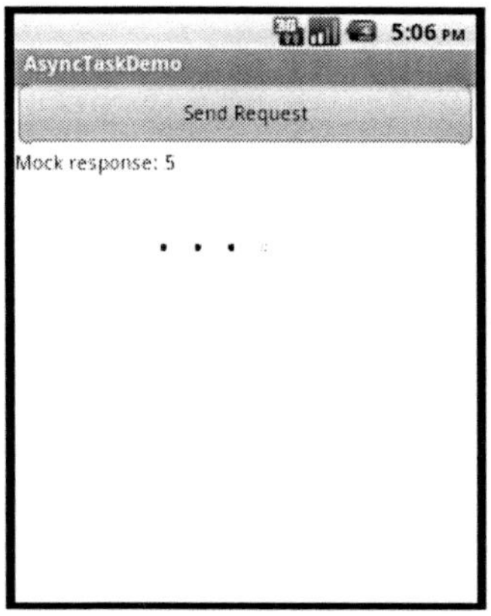

Figure 3-7. Simple application to initialize a game

Here is the boilerplate code for the application. All that is missing is the code that actually initializes the game and updates the text box.

```
/** AsyncTaskDemo */
public class AsyncTaskDemo extends Activity {

    int mInFlight;

    /** @see android.app.Activity#onCreate(android.os.Bundle) */
    @Override
    public void onCreate(Bundle state) {
        super.onCreate(state);

        setContentView(R.layout.asyncdemo);

        final View root = findViewById(R.id.root);
        final Drawable bg = root.getBackground();

        final TextView msg = ((TextView) findViewById(R.id.msg));

        final Game game = Game.newGame();

        ((Button) findViewById(R.id.start)).setOnClickListener(
            new View.OnClickListener() {
                @Override public void onClick(View v) {
                    // !!! initialize the game here!
                } });
    }
```

Now, let's suppose, for this example, that we simply want to display an animated background (the crawling dots in Figure 3-7) while the user waits for the game to initialize. Here's a sketch of the necessary code:

```
/**
 * Synchronous request to remote service
 * DO NOT USE!!!
 */
void initGame(
    View root,
    Drawable bg,
    Game game,
    TextView resp,
    String level)
{
    // if the animation hasn't been started yet,
    // do so now
    if (0 >= mInFlight++ ) {
        root.setBackgroundResource(R.anim.dots);
        ((AnimationDrawable) root.getBackground()).start();
    }

    // initialize the game and get the welcome message
    String msg = game.initialize(level);

    // if this is the last running initialization
```

```
// remove and clean up the animation
if (0 >= --mInFlight) {
    ((AnimationDrawable) root.getBackground()).stop();
    root.setBackgroundDrawable(bg);
}

resp.setText(msg);
}
```

This code is pretty straightforward. The user might mash the start button, so there might be multiple initializations in flight. If the interstitial background is not already showing, the code shows it and remembers that there is one more game starting up. Next, it makes the slow call to the game engine initializer. Once the game completes its initialization, it cleans up. If this is the last game to complete initialization, it clears the interstitial animation. Finally, it displays the greeting message in the text box.

This code is very nearly what is needed to make the example application work as specified, but it breaks down in one very important way: it blocks the UI thread for the entire duration of the call to game.initialize. That has all sorts of unpleasant effects.

The most apparent of these is that the background animation won't work. Even though the logic for setting up and running the animation is very nearly correct, the code specifies quite clearly that nothing else can happen in the UI until the call to the remote service is complete.

It gets worse. The Android Framework actually monitors application UI threads to prevent broken or malicious programs from hanging a device. If an application takes too long to respond to input, the framework will suspend it, alert the user that there is a problem, and offer her a chance to force it to close. If you build and run this example application, with initGame implemented as shown in the example (try it; it's actually somewhat instructive), the first time you click the Send Request button the UI will freeze. If you click a couple more times, you will see an alert similar to the one shown in Figure 3-8.

Figure 3-8. Unresponsive application

AsyncTask to the rescue! Android provides this class as a relatively safe, powerful, and easy-to-use way to run background tasks correctly. Here is a reimplementation of initGame as an AsyncTask:

```
private static final class AsyncInitGame
    extends AsyncTask<String, Void, String>
{
    private final View root;
    private final Game game;
    private final TextView message;
    private final Drawable bg;

    public AsyncInitGame(
        View root,
        Drawable bg,
        Game game,
        TextView msg)
    {
        this.root = root;
        this.bg = bg;
        this.game = game;
        this.message = msg;
    }

    // runs on the UI thread
    @Override protected void onPreExecute() {
        if (0 >= mInFlight++) {
            root.setBackgroundResource(R.anim.dots);
            ((AnimationDrawable) root.getBackground()).start();
        }
    }

    // runs on the UI thread
    @Override protected void onPostExecute(String msg) {
```

```
        if (0 >= --mInFlight) {
            ((AnimationDrawable) root.getBackground()).stop();
            root.setBackgroundDrawable(bg);
        }

        message.setText(msg);
    }

    // runs on a background thread
    @Override protected String doInBackground(String... args) {
        return ((1 != args.length) || (null == args[0]))
            ? null
            : game.initialize(args[0]);
    }
}
```

This code is nearly identical to the first example. It has been divided into three methods that execute nearly the same code, in the same order, as in `initGame`.

This `AsyncTask` is created on the UI thread. When the UI thread invokes the task's `execute` method, first the `onPreExecute` method is called on the UI thread. This allows the task to initialize itself and its environment—in this case, installing the background animation. Next the `AsyncTask` enqueues itself to run the `doInBackground` method concurrently. When, eventually, `doInBackground` completes, the `onPostExecute` method is invoked, once again in the UI thread.

Assuming that this implementation of an `AsyncTask` is correct, the click listener need only create an instance and invoke it, like this:

```
((Button) findViewById(R.id.start)).setOnClickListener(
    new View.OnClickListener() {
        @Override public void onClick(View v) {
            new AsyncInitGame(
                root,
                bg,
                game,
                msg)
            .execute("basic");
        } });
```

In fact, `AsyncInitGame` is very nearly complete, correct, and reliable. Let's examine it in more detail.

First, notice that the base class `AsyncTask` is abstract. The only way to use it is to create a subclass specialized to perform some specific job (an is-a relationship, not a has-a relationship). Typically, the subclass will be simple, and will define only a few methods. A regard for good style and separation of concerns, analogous to the issues mentioned in Chapter 2, suggests keeping the subclass small and delegating implementation to the classes that own the UI and the asynchronous task, respectively. In the example, for instance, `doInBackground` is simply a proxy to the `Game` class.

In general, an `AsyncTask` takes a set of parameters and returns a result. Because the parameters have to be passed between threads and the result returned between threads, some handshaking is necessary to ensure thread safety. An `AsyncTask` is invoked by calling its `execute` method with some parameters. Those parameters are eventually passed on, by the `AsyncTask` mechanism, to the `doInBackground` method, when it runs on a background thread. In turn, `doInBackground` produces a result. The `AsyncTask` mechanism returns that result by passing it as the argument to `doPostExecute`, run in the same thread as the original `execute`. Figure 3-9 shows the data flow.

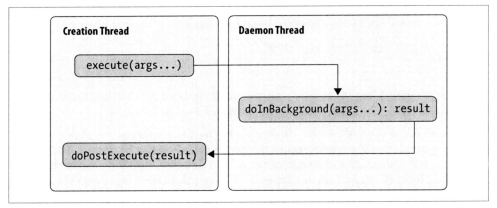

Figure 3-9. Data flow in AsyncTask

In addition to making this data flow thread-safe, `AsyncTask` also makes it type-safe. `AsyncTask` is a classic example of a type-safe template pattern. The abstract base class (`AsyncTask`) uses Java generics to allow implementations to specify the types of the task parameters and result.

When defining a concrete subclass of `AsyncTask`, you provide actual types for the type variables `Params`, `Progress`, and `Result`, in the definition of `AsyncTask`. The first and last of these type variables (`Params` and `Result`) are the types of the task parameters and the result, respectively. We'll get to that middle type variable in a minute.

The concrete type bound to `Params` is the type of the parameters to `execute`, and thus the type of the parameters to `doInBackground`. Similarly, the concrete type bound to `Result` is the type of the return value from `doInBackground`, and thus the type of the parameter to `onPostExecute`.

This is all a bit hard to parse, and the first example, `AsyncInitGame`, didn't help much because the input parameter and the result are both of the same type, `String`. Here are a couple of examples in which the parameter and result types are different. They provide a better illustration of the use of the generic type variables.

```
public class AsyncDBReq
    extends AsyncTask<PreparedStatement, Void, ResultSet>
{
    @Override
    protected ResultSet doInBackground(PreparedStatement... q) {
```

```
            // implementation...
        }

        @Override
        protected void onPostExecute(ResultSet result) {
            // implementation...
        }
    }

    public class AsyncHttpReq
        extends AsyncTask<HttpRequest, Void, HttpResponse>
    {
        @Override
        protected HttpResponse doInBackground(HttpRequest... req) {
            // implementation...
        }

        @Override
        protected void onPostExecute(HttpResponse result) {
            // implementation...
        }
    }
```

In the first example, the argument to the execute method of an AsyncDBReq instance will be one or more PreparedStatement variables. The implementation of doInBackground for an instance of AsyncDBReq will take those PreparedStatement parameters as its arguments and will return a ResultSet. The instance to the onPostExecute method will take that ResultSet as a parameter and use it appropriately.

Similarly, in the second example, the call to the execute method of an AsyncHttpReq instance will take one or more HttpRequest variables. doInBackground takes those requests as its parameters and returns an HttpResponse. onPostExecute handles the HttpResponse.

 Note that an instance of an AsyncTask can be run only once. Calling execute on a task a second time will cause it to throw an Illegal StateException. Each task invocation requires a new instance.

As much as AsyncTask simplifies concurrent processing, its contract imposes strong constraints that cannot be verified automatically. It is absolutely essential to take great care not to violate these constraints! Violations will cause exactly the sort of bugs described at the beginning of this section: failures that are intermittent and very difficult to find.

The most obvious of these constraints is that the doInBackground method, as it is run on a different thread, must make only thread-safe references to variables inherited into its scope. Here, for example, is a mistake that is easy to make:

```
// ... some class

int mCount;
```

```
public void initButton1( Button button) {
    mCount = 0;
    button.setOnClickListener(
        new View.OnClickListener() {
            @SuppressWarnings("unchecked")
            @Override public void onClick(View v) {
                new AsyncTask<Void, Void, Void>() {
                    @Override
                    protected Void doInBackground(Void... args) {
                        mCount++; // !!! NOT THREAD SAFE!
                        return null;
                    }
                }.execute();
            } });
}
```

Although there is nothing to alert you to the problem—no compiler error, no runtime warning, probably not even an immediate failure when the bug is driven—this code is absolutely incorrect. The variable mCount is being accessed from two different threads, without synchronization.

In light of this, it may be a surprise to see that access to mInFlight is not synchronized in AsyncTaskDemo. This is actually OK. The AsyncTask contract guarantees that onPreExecute and onPostExecute will be run on the same thread, the thread from which execute was called. Unlike mCount, mInFlight is accessed from only a single thread and has no need for synchronization.

Probably the most pernicious way to cause the kind of concurrency problem we've just warned you about is by holding a reference to a parameter. The following code, for instance, is incorrect. Can you see why?

```
public void initButton(
    Button button,
    final Map<String, String> vals)
{
    button.setOnClickListener(
        new View.OnClickListener() {
            @Override public void onClick(View v) {
                new AsyncTask<Map<String, String>, Void, Void>() {
                    @Override
                    protected Void doInBackground(
                        Map<String, String>... params)
                    {
                        // implementation, uses the params Map
                    }
                }.execute(vals);
                vals.clear();  // !!! THIS IS NOT THREAD SAFE !!!
            } });
}
```

The problem is pretty subtle. If you noticed that the argument to initButton, vals, is being referenced concurrently, without synchronization, you are correct! It is passed into the `AsyncTask`, as the argument to `execute`, when the task is invoked. The `AsyncTask` framework can guarantee that this reference is published correctly onto the background thread when `doInBackground` is called. It *cannot*, however, do anything about the reference to `vals` that is retained and used later, in the `initButton` method. The call to `vals.clear` modifies state that is being used on another thread, without synchronization. It is, therefore, not thread-safe.

The best solution to this problem is to make sure the arguments to `AsyncTask` are immutable. If they can't be changed—like a `String`, an `Integer`, or a POJO with only final fields—they are thread-safe and need no further care. The only way to be certain that a mutable object passed to an `AsyncTask` is thread-safe is to make sure that only the `AsyncTask` holds a reference. Because the parameter `vals` is passed into the `initButton` method in the previous example (Figure 3-7), it is completely impossible to guarantee that there are no dangling references to it. Even removing the call to `vals.clear` would not guarantee that this code was correct, because the caller of `initButton` might hold a reference to the map that is eventually passed as the parameter `vals`. The *only* way to make this code correct is to make a complete (deep) copy of the map and all the objects it contains!

Developers familiar with the Java Collections package might argue that an alternative to making a complete, deep copy of the map parameter would be to wrap it in an `unmodifiableMap`, like this:

```
public void initButton(
    Button button,
    final Map<String, String> vals)
{
    button.setOnClickListener(
        new View.OnClickListener() {
            @Override public void onClick(View v) {
                new AsyncTask<Map<String, String>, Void, Void>() {
                    @Override
                    protected Void doInBackground(
                        Map<String, String>... params)
                    {
                        // implementation, uses the params Map
                    }
                }.execute(Collections.unmodifiableMap(vals));
                vals.clear();  // !!! STILL NOT THREAD SAFE !!!
            } });
}
```

Unfortunately, this is *still* not correct. `Collections.unmodifiableMap` provides an immutable view of the map it wraps. It does not, however, prevent processes with access to a reference to the original, mutable object from changing that object at any time. In the preceding example, although the `AsyncTask` cannot change the map value passed to it in the `execute` method, the `onClickListener` method still changes the map referenced by `vals` at the same time the background thread uses it, without synchronization. Boom!

There is yet one more way that you can get bitten in the AsyncTask. Remember that the activity that spawns the task has a life cycle. If a task retains a pointer to the activity that created it, and the user takes a phone call while it is running, the task may find itself with a pointer to an activity that has been destroyed. This is especially easy to do with anonymous subclasses that retain an implicit pointer to the creating class. The AsyncTask is most suitable for running fairly short-lived tasks, maybe a few seconds. It should not be used for processes that will take minutes or longer.

To close this section, note that AsyncTask has one more method, not used in the example: onProgressUpdate. It is there to allow the long-running tasks to publish periodic status safely back into the UI thread. Here is how you might use it to implement a progress bar showing the user how much longer the game initialization process will take:

```
public class AsyncTaskDemoWithProgress extends Activity {

    private final class AsyncInit
        extends AsyncTask<String, Integer, String>
        implements Game.InitProgressListener
    {
        private final View root;
        private final Game game;
        private final TextView message;
        private final Drawable bg;

        public AsyncInit(
            View root,
            Drawable bg,
            Game game,
            TextView msg)
        {
            this.root = root;
            this.bg = bg;
            this.game = game;
            this.message = msg;
        }

        // runs on the UI thread
        @Override protected void onPreExecute() {
            if (0 >= mInFlight++) {
                root.setBackgroundResource(R.anim.dots);
                ((AnimationDrawable) root.getBackground()).start();
            }
        }

        // runs on the UI thread
        @Override protected void onPostExecute(String msg) {
            if (0 >= --mInFlight) {
                ((AnimationDrawable) root.getBackground()).stop();
                root.setBackgroundDrawable(bg);
            }

            message.setText(msg);
```

```
    }

    // runs on its own thread
    @Override protected String doInBackground(String... args) {
        return ((1 != args.length) || (null == args[0]))
            ? null
            : game.initialize(args[0], this);
    }

    // runs on the UI thread
    @Override protected void onProgressUpdate(Integer... vals) {
        updateProgressBar(vals[0].intValue());
    }

    // runs on the UI thread
    @Override public void onInitProgress(int pctComplete) {
        publishProgress(Integer.valueOf(pctComplete));
    }
}

int mInFlight;
int mComplete;

/** @see android.app.Activity#onCreate(android.os.Bundle) */
@Override
public void onCreate(Bundle state) {
    super.onCreate(state);

    setContentView(R.layout.asyncdemoprogress);

    final View root = findViewById(R.id.root);
    final Drawable bg = root.getBackground();

    final TextView msg = ((TextView) findViewById(R.id.msg));

    final Game game = Game.newGame();

    ((Button) findViewById(R.id.start)).setOnClickListener(
        new View.OnClickListener() {
            @Override public void onClick(View v) {
                mComplete = 0;
                new AsyncInit(
                    root,
                    bg,
                    game,
                    msg)
                .execute("basic");
            } });
}

void updateProgressBar(int progress) {
    int p = progress;
    if (mComplete < p) {
        mComplete = p;
        ((ProgressBar) findViewById(R.id.progress))
```

```
                    .setProgress(p);
            }
        }
    }
```

This example presumes that game initialization takes, as an argument, a Game.Init ProgressListener. The initialization process periodically calls the listener's onInitPro gress method to notify it of how much work has been completed. In this example, then, onInitProgress will be called from beneath doInBackground in the call tree, and therefore on the background thread. If onInitProgress were to call AsyncTaskDemoWithPro gress.updateProgressBar directly, the subsequent call to setProgress would also take place on the background thread, violating the rule that only the UI thread can modify View objects. It would cause an exception such as this:

```
11-30 02:42:37.471: ERROR/AndroidRuntime(162):
    android.view.ViewRoot$CalledFromWrongThreadException:
    Only the original thread that created a view hierarchy can touch its views.
```

To correctly publish the progress back to the UI thread, onInitProgress instead calls the AsyncTask method publishProgress. The AsyncTask handles the details of scheduling publishProgress on the UI thread so that onProgressUpdate can safely use View methods.

Let's leave this detailed look into the AsyncTask by summarizing some of the key points it illustrated:

- The Android UI is single-threaded. To use it well a developer must be comfortable with the task queue idiom.

- To retain UI liveness, tasks that take more than a couple of milliseconds, or a few hundred instructions, should not be run on the UI thread.

- Concurrent programming is really tricky. It's amazingly easy to get it wrong and very hard to check for mistakes.

- AsyncTask is a convenient tool for running small, asynchronous tasks. Just remember that the doInBackground method runs on a different thread! It must not write any state visible from another thread or read any state writable from another thread. This includes its parameters and, possibly, the implicit pointer to its creator.

- Immutable objects are an essential tool for passing information between concurrent threads.

Threads in an Android Process

Together, AsyncTask and ContentProvider form a very powerful idiom and can be adapted to a wide variety of common application architectures. Nearly any MVC pattern in which the View polls the Model can (and probably should) be implemented this way. In an application with an architecture that requires the Model to push changes to the View or in which the Model is long-lived and continuously running, AsyncTask may not be sufficient.

Recall that cardinal rule for sharing data among threads that we introduced back in "Synchronization and Thread Safety" on page 68. In its full generality, that rule is pretty onerous. The investigation of AsyncTask in the preceding section, however, illustrated one idiom that simplifies correct coordination of concurrent tasks in Android: the heavy lifting of publishing state from one thread into another was completely hidden in the implementation of a template class. At the same time, the discussion also reinforced some of the pitfalls of concurrency that lie in wait to entrap the incautious coder. There are other idioms that are safe and that can simplify specific classes of concurrent problems. One of them—a common idiom in Java programming in general—is baked into the Android Framework. It is sometimes called *thread confinement*.

Suppose that a thread, the DBMinder, creates an object and modifies it over a period of time. After it has completed its work, it must pass the object to another thread, DBViewer, for further processing. In order to do this, using thread confinement, DBMinder and DBViewer must share a drop point and an associated lock. The process looks like this:

1. DBMinder seizes the lock and stores a reference to the object in the drop.
2. DBMinder *destroys all its references to the object!*
3. DBMinder releases the lock.
4. DBViewer seizes the lock and notices that there is an object reference in the drop.
5. DBViewer recovers the reference from the drop and then clears the drop.
6. DBViewer releases the lock.

This process works for any object regardless of whether that object itself is thread-safe. This is because the only state that is ever shared among multiple threads is the drop box. Both threads correctly seize a single lock before accessing it. When DBMinder is done with an object, it passes it to DBViewer and retains no references: the state of the passed object is never shared by multiple threads.

Thread confinement is a surprisingly powerful trick. Implementations usually make the shared drop an ordered task queue. Multiple threads may contend for the lock, but each holds it only long enough to enqueue a task. One or more worker threads seize the queue to remove tasks for execution. This is a pattern that is also sometimes called the *producer/consumer model*. As long as a unit of work can proceed entirely in the context of the worker thread that claims it, there is no need for further synchronization. If you look into the implementation of AsyncTask you will discover that this is exactly how it works.

Thread confinement is so useful that Android has baked it into its framework in the class called Looper. When initialized as a Looper, a Java thread turns into a task queue. It spends its entire life removing things from a local queue and executing them. Other threads enqueue work, as described earlier, for the initialized thread to process. As long as the enqueueing thread deletes all references to the object it enqueues, both threads can be coded without further concern for concurrency. In addition to making it dramatically easier to make programs that are correct, this also removes any inefficiency that might be caused by extensive synchronization.

Does this description of a task queue bring to mind a construct to which we alluded earlier in this chapter? Android's single-threaded, event-driven UI is, simply, a `Looper`. When it launches a `Context` the system does some bookkeeping and then initializes the launch thread as a `Looper`. That thread becomes the main thread for the service or activity. In an activity, the UI framework preserves a reference to this thread, and its task queue becomes the UI event queue: all the external drivers, the screen, the keyboard, the call handler, and so on, enqueue actions on this queue.

The other half of `Looper` is `Handler`. A `Handler`, created on a `Looper` thread, provides a portal to the `Looper` queue. When a `Looper` thread wishes to allow some other thread access to its task queue, it creates a new `Handler` and passes it to that other thread. There are several shortcuts that make it even easier to use a `Handler`: `View.post(Runnable)`, `View.postDelayed(Runnable, long)`, and `Activity.runOnUiThread(Runnable)`.

There is one more convenient and powerful paradigm in the Android toolkit for interprocess communication and work sharing: the `ContentProvider`, which we'll discuss in Chapter 12. Consider whether a content provider can fit your needs before you build your own architecture on the low-level components discussed in this section. Content providers are flexible and extensible, and handle concurrent processing in a way that is fast enough for all but the most time-sensitive applications.

Serialization

Serialization is converting data from a fast, efficient, internal representation to something that can be kept in a persistent store or transmitted over a network. Converting data to its serialized form is often referred to as *marshaling* it. Converting it back to its live, in-memory representation is referred to as *deserializing* or *unmarshaling* it.

Exactly how data is serialized depends on the reason for serializing it. Data serialized for transmission over a network, for instance, may not need to be legible in flight. Data serialized for storage in a database, however, will be far more useful if the representation permits SQL queries that are easy to construct and make sense. In the former case the serialization format might be binary. In the latter it is likely to be labeled text.

The Android environment addresses four common uses for serialization:

Life cycle management
Unlike larger devices—laptop and desktop machines, for instance—Android devices cannot count on being able to swap an application to a fast backing store when that application becomes inactive. Instead, the framework provides an object called a `Bundle`. When an application is suspended it writes its state into the `Bundle`. When the application is re-created the Android Framework promises to supply a copy of the same `Bundle` during its initialization. An application must be

able to serialize anything it wants to keep across its suspension and to store the serialized version in the `Bundle`.

Persistence

In addition to the immediate application state kept in a `Bundle`, most applications manage some kind of persistent data store. This data store is most likely an SQLite database wrapped in a `ContentProvider`. Applications must convert back and forth between the internal representation of object data and the representations of those same objects in the database. In larger systems, this process—called *object-relational mapping* or just *ORM*—is supported by frameworks such as Hibernate and iBATIS. Android's local data store is simpler and lighter weight. It is described in Chapter 9.

Local interprocess communication

The Android Framework promotes an architecture that breaks larger, monolithic applications into smaller components: UIs, content providers, and services. These components do not have access to one another's memory space and must pass information across process boundaries as serialized messages. Android provides a highly optimized tool for this, AIDL.

Network communication

This is the part that makes mobile devices exciting. The ability to connect to the Internet and to use the incredible variety of services available there is what Android is all about. Applications need to be able to handle the protocols imposed by any external service, which includes translating internal information into queries to those services, and retranslating the response.

The following sections describe the various classes at your disposal for achieving these goals.

Java Serialization

Java defines a serialization framework through the `Serializable` marker interface and the pair of serialization types called `ObjectOutputStream` and `ObjectInputStream`. Because Java serialization mostly just works, even experienced Java programmers may not recognize its complexity. It is certainly outside the scope of this book. Josh Bloch devotes nearly 10% of his seminal book *Effective Java* (Prentice Hall) to a discussion of Java's serialization framework and how to use it correctly. The discussion is worthwhile reading as a way to understand the issues, even if you don't expect to use Java's framework.

Android does support Java serialization. The `Bundle` type, for instance, has the pair of methods `putSerializable` and `getSerializable`, which, respectively, add a Java `Serializable` to and recover it from a `Bundle`. For example:

```
public class JSerialize extends Activity {
    public static final String APP_STATE
        = "com.oreilly.android.app.state";
```

```
private static class AppState implements Serializable {
    // definitions, getters and setters
    // for application state parameters here.
    // ...
}

private AppState applicationState;

/** Called when the activity is first created. */
@Override
public void onCreate(Bundle savedAppState) {
    super.onCreate(savedAppState);

    applicationState = (null == savedAppState)
        ? new AppState(/* ... */)
        : (AppState) savedAppState.getSerializable(APP_STATE);

    setContentView(R.layout.main);

    // ...
}

/**
 * @see android.app.Activity#onSaveInstanceState(android.os.Bundle)
 */
@Override
protected void onSaveInstanceState(Bundle outState) {
    super.onSaveInstanceState(outState);
    outState.putSerializable(APP_STATE, applicationState);
}
}
```

In this example, the application keeps some global state information—perhaps a list of recently used items—as a `Serializable` object. When a `JSerialize` activity is paused so that another activity can replace it in memory, the Android Framework invokes the `JSerialize` callback method `onSaveInstanceState`, passing a `Bundle` object. The callback method uses `Bundle.putSerializable` to save the state of the object into the `Bundle`. When `JSerialize` is resumed, the `onCreate` method retrieves the state from the `Bundle` using `getSerializable`.

Parcelable

Although the Android Framework supports Java serialization, it is definitely not the best choice as a way to marshal program state. Android's own internal serialization protocol, `Parcelable`, is lightweight, highly optimized, and only slightly more difficult to use. It is the best choice for local interprocess communication. For reasons that will become apparent when we revisit `Parcelable` objects in "Classes That Support Serialization" on page 124, they cannot be used to store objects beyond the lifetime of an application. They are not an appropriate choice for marshaling state to, say, a database or a file.

Here's a very simple object that holds some state. Let's see what it takes to make it "parcelable."

```
public class SimpleParcelable {
    public enum State { BEGIN, MIDDLE, END; }

    private State state;
    private Date date;

    State getState() { return state; }
    void setState(State state) { this.state = state; }

    Date getDate() { return date; }
    void setDate(Date date) { this.date = date; }
}
```

An object must meet three requirements to be parcelable:

- It must implement the Parcelable interface.
- It must have a marshaler, an implementation of the interface method writeToParcel.
- It must have an unmarshaler, a public static final variable named CREATOR, containing a reference to an implementation of Parcelable.Creator.

The interface method writeToParcel is the marshaler. It is called for an object when it is necessary to serialize that object to a Parcel. The marshaler's job is to write everything necessary to reconstruct the object state to the passed Parcel. Typically, this will mean expressing the object state in terms of the six primitive data types: byte, double, int, float, long, and String. Here's the same simple object, but this time with the marshaler added:

```
public class SimpleParcelable implements Parcelable {
    public enum State { BEGIN, MIDDLE, END; }

    private static final Map<State, String> marshalState;
    static {
        Map<State, String> m = new HashMap<State, String>();
        m.put(State.BEGIN, "begin");
        m.put(State.MIDDLE, "middle");
        m.put(State.END, "end");
        marshalState = Collections.unmodifiableMap(m);
    }

    private State state;
    private Date date;

    @Override
    public void writeToParcel(Parcel dest, int flags) {
        // translate the Date to a long
        dest.writeLong(
            (null == date)
            ? -1
            : date.getTime());
```

```
        dest.writeString(
            (null == state)
            ? ""
            : marshalState.get(state));
    }

    State getState() { return state; }
    void setState(State state) { this.state = state; }

    Date getDate() { return date; }
    void setDate(Date date) { this.date = date; }
}
```

Of course, the exact implementation of writeToParcel will depend on the contents of the object being serialized. In this case, the SimpleParcelable object has two pieces of state and writes both of them into the passed Parcel.

Choosing a representation for most simple data types usually won't require anything more than a little ingenuity. The Date in this example, for instance, is easily represented by its time since the millennium.

Be sure, though, to think about future changes to data when picking the serialized representation. Certainly, it would have been much easier in this example to represent state as an int with a value that was obtained by calling state.ordinal. Doing so, however, would make it much harder to maintain forward compatibility for the object. Suppose it becomes necessary at some point to add a new state, State.INIT, before State.BEGIN. This trivial change makes new versions of the object completely incompatible with earlier versions. A similar, if slightly weaker, argument applies to using state.toString to create the marshaled representation of the state.

The mapping between an object and its representation in a Parcel is part of the particular serialization process. It is not an inherent attribute of the object. It is entirely possible that a given object has completely different representations when serialized by different serializers. To illustrate this principle—though it is probably overkill, given that the type State is locally defined—the map used to marshal state is an independent and explicitly defined member of the parcelable class.

SimpleParcelable, as shown earlier, compiles without errors. It could even be marshaled to a parcel. As yet, though, there is no way to get it back out. For that, we need the unmarshaler:

```
public class SimpleParcelable implements Parcelable {

    // Code elided...

    private static final Map<String, State> unmarshalState;
    static {
        Map<String, State> m = new HashMap<String, State>();
        m.put("begin", State.BEGIN);
        m.put("middle", State.MIDDLE);
        m.put("end", State.END);
```

```
            unmarshalState = Collections.unmodifiableMap(m);
        }

        // Unmarshaler
        public static final Parcelable.Creator<SimpleParcelable> CREATOR
            = new Parcelable.Creator<SimpleParcelable>() {
                public SimpleParcelable createFromParcel(Parcel src) {
                    return new SimpleParcelable(
                        src.readLong(),
                        src.readString());
                }

                public SimpleParcelable[] newArray(int size) {
                    return new SimpleParcelable[size];
                }
            };

        private State state;
        private Date date;

        public SimpleParcelable(long date, String state) {
            if (0 <= date) { this.date = new Date(date); }
            if ((null != state) && (0 < state.length())) {
                this.state = unmarshalState.get(state);
            }
        }

        // Code elided...

}
```

This snippet shows only the newly added unmarshaler code: the public, static `final` field called `CREATOR` and its collaborators. The field is a reference to an implementation of `Parcelable.Creator<T>`, where T is the type of the parcelable object to be unmarshaled (in this case `SimpleParcelable`). It's important to get all these things exactly right! If `CREATOR` is protected instead of public, is not static, or is spelled "Creator", the framework will be unable to unmarshal the object.

The implementation of `Parcelable.Creator<T>` is an object with a single method, `createFromParcel`, which unmarshals a single instance from the `Parcel`. The idiomatic way to do this is to read each piece of state from the `Parcel`, in exactly the same order as it was written in `writeToParcel` (again, this is important), and then to call a constructor with the unmarshaled state. Because the unmarshaling constructor is called from class scope, it can be package-protected, or even private.

Classes That Support Serialization

The Parcel API is not limited to the six primitive types mentioned in the previous section. The Android documentation gives the complete list of parcelable types, but it is helpful to think of them as divided into four groups.

The first group, simple types, consists of null, the six primitives (int, float, etc.), and the boxed versions of the six primitives (Integer, Float, etc.).

The next group consists of object types implementing Serializable or Parcelable. These objects are not simple, but they know how to serialize themselves.

Another group, collection types, covers arrays, lists, maps, bundles, and sparse arrays of the preceding two types (int[], float[], ArrayList<?>, HashMap<String, ?>, Bundle<?>, SparseArray<?>, etc.).

Finally, there are some special cases: CharSequence and active objects (IBinder).

Although all these types can be marshaled into a Parcel, there are two to avoid if possible: Serializable and Map. As mentioned earlier, Android supports native Java serialization. Its implementation is not nearly as efficient as the rest of Parcelable. Implementing Serializable in an object is not an effective way to make it parcelable. Instead, objects should implement Parcelable and add a CREATOR object and a writeToParcel method as described in "Parcelable" on page 120. This can be a tedious task if the object hierarchy is complex, but the performance gains are usually well worth it.

The other parcelable type to avoid is the Map. The Android-specific Bundle type provides the same functionality—a map with string keys—but is, in addition, type-safe. Objects are added to a Bundle with methods such as putDouble and putSparseParcelableArray, one for each parcelable type. Corresponding methods such as getDouble and get SparseParcelableArray get the objects back out. A Bundle is just like a map except that it can hold different types of objects for different keys in a way that is perfectly type-safe. Using a Bundle eliminates the entire class of hard-to-find errors that arise when, say, a serialized float is mistakenly interpreted as an int.

Type safety is also a reason to prefer the methods writeTypedArray and writeTyped List to their untyped analogs writeArray and writeList.

AIDL and Remote Procedure Calls

Android supports fairly complex interprocess communication with a tool called AIDL. To declare an AIDL interface, you'll need several things:

- An AIDL file that describes the API.

- For every nonsimple type used in the API, a subclass of `Parcelable` defining the type, and an AIDL file naming the type as parcelable. One caution when doing this: you must be willing to distribute the source for those classes to all clients that serialize them.

- A service that returns an implementation of the API stub, in response to `onBind`. `onBind` must be prepared to return the correct implementation for each intent with which it might be called. The returned instance provides the actual implementations of the API methods.

- On the client, an implementation of `ServiceConnection`. `onServiceConnected` should cast the passed binder, using `API.Stub.asInterface(binder)`, and save the result as a reference to the service API. `onServiceDisconnected` must null the reference. It calls `bindService` with an `Intent` that the API service provides, the `ServiceConnection`, and flags that control service creation.

- Binding that is asynchronous. Just because `bindService` returns `true` does not mean that you have a reference to the service yet. You must release the thread and wait for the invocation of `onServiceConnected` to use the service.

Serialization and the Application Life Cycle

As mentioned earlier, an Android application may not have the luxury of virtual memory. On a small device, there is no secondary store to which a running but hidden application can be pushed to make room for a new, visible application. Still, a good user experience demands that when the user returns to an application, it looks the way it did when he left it. The responsibility for preserving state across suspension falls to the application itself. Fortunately, the Android Framework makes preserving state straightforward.

The example in "Java Serialization" on page 119 showed the general framework mechanism that allows an application to preserve state across suspensions. Whenever the application is evicted from memory, its `onSaveInstanceState` method is called with a `Bundle` to which the application can write any necessary state. When the application is restarted, the framework passes the same `Bundle` to the `onCreate` method so that the application can restore its state. By sensibly caching content data in a `Content Provider` and saving lightweight state (e.g., the currently visible page) to the `onSaveInstance Bundle`, an application can resume, without interruption.

The framework provides one more tool for preserving application state. The `View` class—the base type for everything visible on the screen—has a hook method, onSaveInstanceState, that is called as part of the process of evicting an application from memory. In fact, it is called from `Activity.onSaveInstanceState`, which is why your application's implementation of that method should always call `super.onSave InstanceState`.

This method allows state preservation at the very finest level. An email application, for instance, might use it to preserve the exact location of the cursor in the text of an unsent mail message.

## CHAPTER 4

Getting Your Application into Users' Hands

This chapter covers everything it takes to get your application into users' hands. Earlier in this book, we told you everything you needed to get started reading example code and creating simple programs. Here, we complete the picture, with all the other operations you need to perform to widely distribute your applications, sell them (if that is your aim), and subsequently get paid by Google, which operates the Android Market.

You may not be ready to put your application into the Android Market, but keeping this process in mind will shape the way you design and implement your application. Commerce has considerations that are distinct from most other aspects of software development, including identifying yourself to the Android Market and to your customers, obtaining permission to use certain APIs, protecting your identity, and preparing your app to be run on a variety of hardware as well as to be updated over time.

Application Signing

Application signing, or code signing, enables Android devices, the Android Market, and alternative means of distribution to know which applications originate with the owner of a signing certificate, and to be certain the code has not been modified since it was signed.

Public Key Encryption and Cryptographic Signing

Public key cryptography depends on this mathematical principle: it is easy to multiply large prime numbers together, but it is extremely difficult to factor the resultant product. The multiplication might take milliseconds, while factoring would take from hundreds to millions of years and would require an astronomically powerful computer.

This asymmetry between multiplication and factoring means that a key made with the product of two large prime numbers can be made public. The knowledge that enables encrypted messages to be decrypted is the pair of large primes that are part of the private key. That means that documents encrypted with the public key are secure, and only the possessor of the private key can decrypt them.

Signing, which is what we will do to Android applications, depends on related properties of public key encryption.

The steps to sign a document are:

1. Compute a unique number—a hash—from the document. This is also known as a *message digest*.
2. "Encrypt" the message digest with the signer's private key. This is the signature.

Voilà! You now have a number—a signature—that is tied to the document by the hashing algorithm, and tied to the signer's private key.

The steps to verify a signed document are:

1. Compute a unique number—a hash—from the document.
2. "Decrypt" the signature using the public key, which should also result in the same number as the hash.

Now you know some interesting facts: the document—in our case, an application—came from the person with the private key corresponding to the public key you used in the verification. And you know that the document was not altered; otherwise, the hash decrypted from the signature would not be the same as the one computed from the document.

Verifying a signature also verifies that the signature was not copied to a different document. Signatures are unalterably tied to the document from which they were created.

You may have noticed we put the words *encrypt* and *decrypt* in quotes when we said the message digest, or hash, is encrypted. This is because it's not encryption in the way you normally use a public-private key system—to keep prying eyes away from a message by encrypting it with the public key so that only the person with the private key can read the message.

Here, "encrypt" just means "compute a number." You are not hiding information when you "encrypt" a hash or message digest with a signer's private key. The reason you use the words *encrypt* and *decrypt* is that you get the same hash or message digest when you decrypt with the public key.

Anyone with the public key and a published algorithm can "decrypt"—which is the point in verification: to see that you got the same hash the sender signed, which also *proves* that the sender is in possession of a private key corresponding to the public key, and *proves* that the document is what the sender signed.

Because verification can be computed using a public key, your Android system—and any other interested party—can verify that an application was signed with a particular key and that it was not modified since it was signed.

More generally, any electronic document—any set of bits—can be cryptographically signed, and cryptographic signatures, or "digital signatures," can be used to sign documents in a way that can legally substitute for a person's handwritten signature.

How Signatures Protect Software Users, Publishers, and Secure Communications

As a user of computer software, you may already have been thinking, "It would be nice to know where my software comes from and that it has not been modified en route to my device." Signed applications enable you to have this confidence. This is a form of confidence based on cryptographic signatures similar to one you already use. When you browse the Web you already rely on cryptographic signatures to trust that the ecommerce site you are communicating with is authentic, and not a rogue impostor set up to take your money and run. In the case of ecommerce, the client verifies a signature of the server's certificate using a public key from a certificate authority. Your browser comes with keys from several certificate authorities used for this purpose.

The role of the certificate authority is to consolidate the number of parties you need to trust: you trust your browser vendor to use only keys from reputable certificate authorities, and ecommerce vendors obtain certificates from authorities browser vendors trust. The certificate authorities have a responsibility to verify that the people claiming to be, for example, Amazon.com are, in fact, Amazon.com. Now, when your browser initiates a secure session with Amazon.com, you know two things: your data is secured from eavesdropping by encryption that only the ecommerce vendor's server can decrypt, and you are reasonably sure that the server you are connecting to is using a certificate issued by a certificate authority to the company you want to communicate with, because the certificate authority has taken steps to assure itself that it issues certificates to known parties.

Self-signed certificates for Android software

In signing Android software, the signing certificate does not have to come from a certificate authority. It can be created by the software publisher—in this case, you. Unlike ecommerce transactions, where you have the additional requirement that you want to ensure that each and every connection your browser makes is to the authentic Amazon.com, perhaps through a link of unknown provenance, the act of using software does not depend as critically on knowing the identity of the signing party.

For organizations considering using a signature issued by a certificate authority, the Google documentation explicitly mentions that there is no need to have your application signed using a certificate authority, and that self-certification is the informal standard for Android applications.

In addition to initially verifying application developer identity, digital signatures on Android are also used during application upgrades to ensure that an application upgrade should be permitted to access files created by an earlier version of the application, and that the upgrading application is not actually a malicious application trying to steal user data.

As long as you are confident that updates to the software come from the same party you obtained the software from in the first place, you can be reasonably sure the programs you are using are safe, and that the publisher of that software is known to the distributor of the software, which is the Android Market.

In addition to the assurance of updates from the original publisher, Android applications are sandboxed and require permissions, as described at *http://developer.android .com/guide/topics/security/security.html*, to access functionality that could compromise your data or cause chargeable events on your mobile service.

Signing an Application

The concepts behind cryptographic signing are subtle and complex. But the complexity is managed by the SDK tools. When you compile and run Android code on a device or on an emulator, you are running signed code.

Debug certificates

If you have been following the examples in this book and have created an Android project and run it in an emulator or device, you may have noticed you didn't need to create a certificate and that your application is installable on an Android handset, despite the fact that all Android code must be signed. This convenience is achieved through the use of an automatically created debug certificate. Let's take a look at the debug certificate.

Look in the *.android* folder in your home folder. There you will find a file named *debug.keystore*. Using the keytool command, you can find out what is inside this file:

```
keytool -list -keystore debug.keystore
```

When you are prompted for a password, enter **android**. You will see output that looks like this:

```
Keystore type: JKS
Keystore provider: SUN

Your keystore contains 1 entry

androiddebugkey, May 13, 2010, PrivateKeyEntry,
Certificate fingerprint (MD5): 95:04:04:F4:51:0B:98:46:14:74:58:15:D3:CA:73:CE
```

The keystore type and provider indicate the keystore is a Java keystore, compatible with the Java Cryptography Architecture and Java classes that enable Android to use code signing and other cryptography tools. More information on the Java Cryptography Architecture is available at *http://download.oracle.com/javase/6/docs/technotes/tools/solaris/keytool.html*.

The `keytool` command is part of the JDK, and is described briefly in "keytool" on page 27 and in greater detail at *http://developer.android.com/guide/publishing/app-signing.html#cert*. Detailed documentation on `keytool` can also be found at *http://download.oracle.com/javase/6/docs/technotes/tools/solaris/keytool.html*.

The last line produced by the `list` option in `keytool` is a certificate fingerprint. This is a unique number generated from a key. You've seen one way in which this number is used in "Application Signing" on page 127, where you used it to get an API key.

This certificate expires in a short enough interval that it cannot be used to distribute Android software other than for testing. Do not mistake the convenience of using a debug certificate for signing software as an indication that you can do without a signing certificate for distributing your applications!

Creating a self-signed certificate

Ready to sign some code for release? First, create a private key using the `keytool` command:

```
keytool -genkey -v -keystore my-release-key.keystore -alias alias_name \
  -keyalg RSA -keysize 2048 -validity 50000
```

 The \ character indicates a line break, and is valid for multiline commands on Unix and Mac OS X. However, you will need to type this all on one line without the \ on Windows.

You can substitute a name of your choice for *my-release-key* and an alias of your choice for *alias_name*. The `-keysize` and `-validity` parameters should remain as shown in the preceding code.

As shown in the following code, `keytool` will ask you for a password for the keystore, which you will need to remember when accessing it, and a series of questions about you, your organizational structure, and your location. `keytool` generates a private key, usable as a signing certificate with a valid life span of about 150 years, and puts it in the file named *<my-release_key>.keystore*.

```
example-user@default-hostname:~$ keytool -genkey -v \
  -keystore example-release-key.keystore -alias example_alias_name \
  -keyalg RSA -keysize 2048 -validity 50000
Enter keystore password:
Re-enter new password:
What is your first and last name?
```

```
  [Unknown]:  Example Examplenik
What is the name of your organizational unit?
  [Unknown]:  Example
What is the name of your organization?
  [Unknown]:  Example
What is the name of your City or Locality?
  [Unknown]:  Example
What is the name of your State or Province?
  [Unknown]:  Massachusetts
What is the two-letter country code for this unit?
  [Unknown]:  US
Is CN=Example Examplenik, OU=Example, O=Example, L=Example, ST=Massachusetts,
   C=US correct?
  [no]:  yes

Generating 2,048 bit RSA key pair and self-signed certificate (SHA1withRSA) with a
   validity of 50,000 days for: CN=Example Examplenik, OU=Example, O=Example,
   L=Example, ST=Massachusetts, C=US
Enter key password for <example_alias_name>
   (RETURN if same as keystore password):
Re-enter new password:
[Storing example-release-key.keystore]
```

You now have a valid key in a keystore.

Don't lose it!

While cryptographic digital signatures are, in many ways, more reliable and secure than a handwritten signature, there is one way in which they differ: you can lose your ability to sign a document digitally.

If you lose your signing certificate, you lose your identity to Android devices and the Android Market. This means that, despite the fact that you compile and release the same code as before, you cannot use these newly compiled applications to update applications in the field, as neither Android devices nor the Android Market will recognize you as the same publisher.

Keep multiple backup copies of your signing certificate on multiple types of media, including paper, in multiple locations. And keep those backups secure. If your signing certificate is used by people other than you, they can replace your programs on your customers' Android devices.

Detailed recommendations from the Android Developers site regarding securing your signing certificate are available at *http://developer.android.com/guide/publishing/app -signing.html#secure-key*.

 Conversely, your cryptographic signature is your signature solely because it is in your possession. Up to the time you want to publish an Android application and continue to be identified as the publisher, you can generate, use, and discard signatures as much as you like. Don't be afraid to experiment and learn!

Using a self-signed certificate to sign an application

Now it's time to sign an application. In Eclipse, select the project of the application you want to sign for release, and select the File→Export command. "Why the 'export' command?" you may ask. After all, if you want to give someone your app to try out, you can just give her a copy of the *.apk* file in the *bin* directory of the project file hierarchy. It is as arbitrary as it seems: the "export" dialog is a grab bag of functionality, and it was a convenient place to put a procedure that isn't quite the same as "deploying."

In this example we use the TestActivity project, but you can use any application—your own, or any project from the examples in this book.

You will be presented with a list of options for exporting, organized into folders. Select the *Android* folder and select Export Android Application (as shown in Figure 4-1), and then click the Next button.

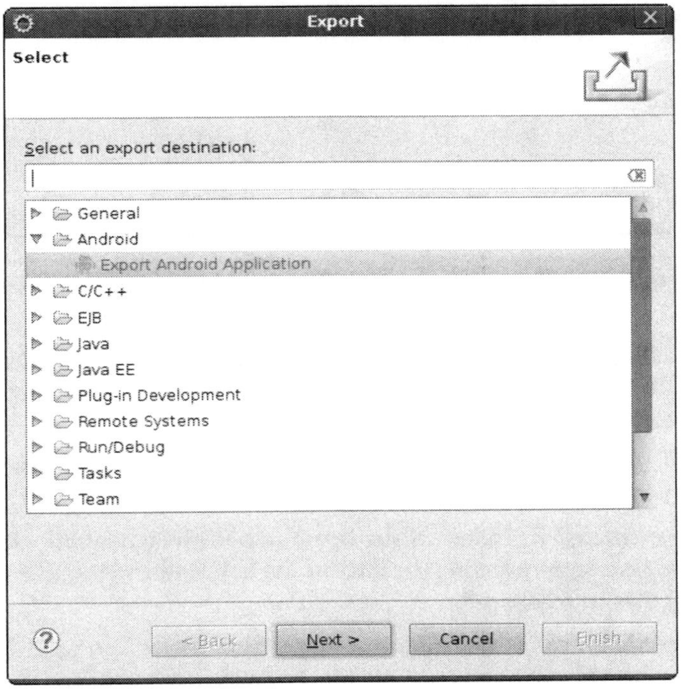

Figure 4-1. "Exporting" an Android application

First, you will see whether your application has any errors in configuration that might prevent it from being ready to publish, such as having the `debuggable` attribute set to `true` in the manifest. If your app is ready to go, you will see the dialog in Figure 4-2, which displays no errors.

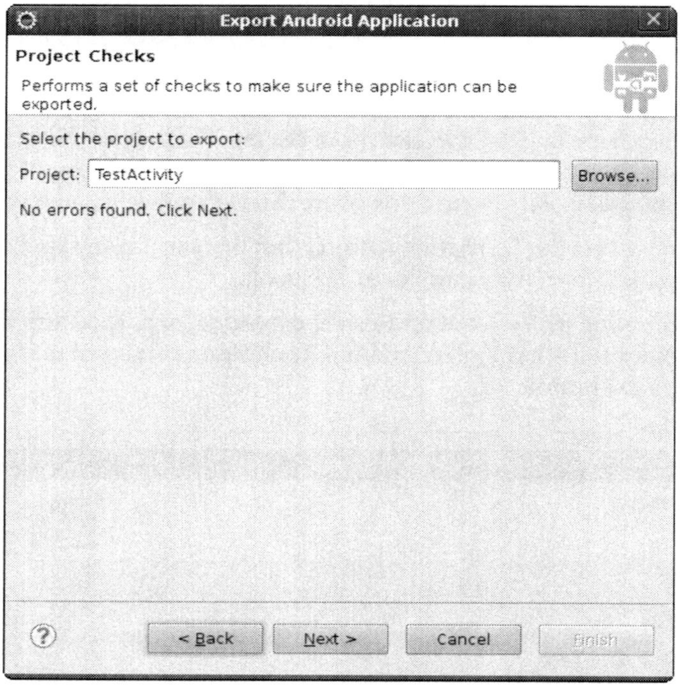

Figure 4-2. An Android application that has no problems preventing signing and publishing

Subsequent dialog boxes in this multistep sequence focus on signing. The information requested mirrors the information you entered to create your release key in "Creating a self-signed certificate" on page 131.

Next, you will select your keystore, as shown in Figure 4-3. The keystore is the file holding your key.

Once you have entered the name of the keystore and the password, click Next and proceed to the next step: selecting the alias of the key, and entering the password for the alias, as shown in Figure 4-4.

If you followed the steps in "Creating a self-signed certificate" on page 131, you have only one key, with one alias, in your keystore. Enter the password and click Next. The next step is to specify the destination *.apk* file and pass some checks to determine if anything else might be wrong with your app. If everything is in order, you will see a screen resembling that shown in Figure 4-5.

When you click Finish you will get a signed *.apk* file in the specified location.

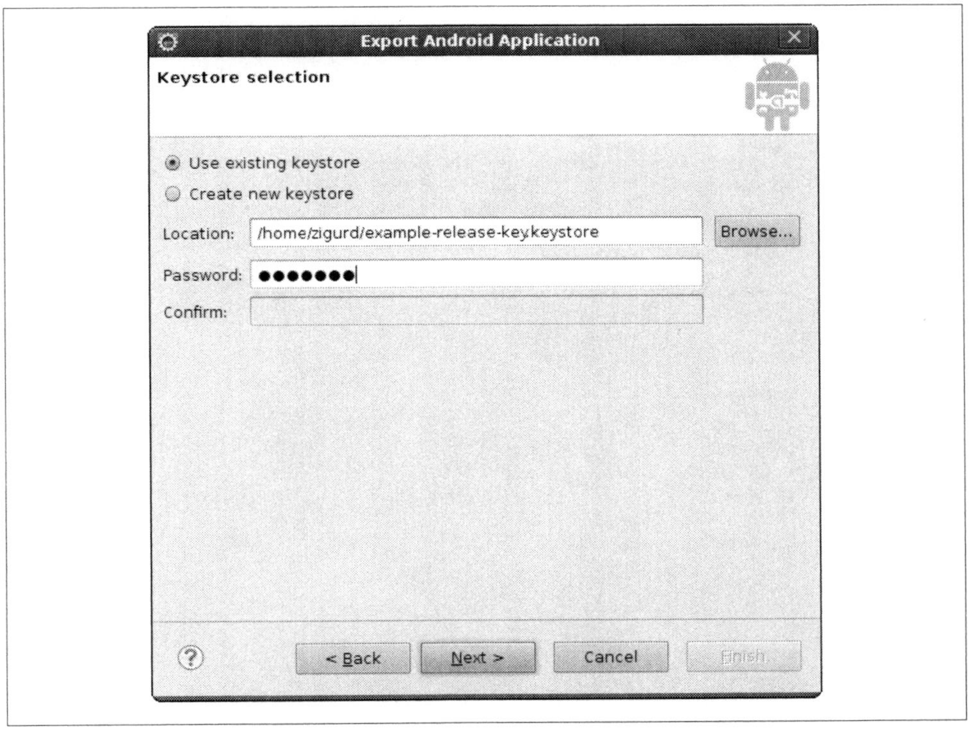

Figure 4-3. Selecting the keystore

Placing an Application for Distribution in the Android Market

Putting an application on the Android Market is remarkably easy, especially if you are comparing it to your experience with the Apple iTunes App Store. The only prerequisite is that you have a Google account such as a Gmail account. A $25 credit card transaction and some information about yourself are all you need to start uploading applications to the Android Market. Charging for applications and getting paid takes only slightly more information and effort—you don't even need a website or a corporate entity. (Consulting a lawyer before selling products is a good idea. A lawyer may suggest setting up a corporation and other ways to protect your personal assets from liabilities resulting from commercial activities.)

Becoming an Official Android Developer

The Android Market site is where you become an official Android developer. You can sign up at *http://market.android.com/publish/signup*.

This site will ask you for identifying information, and will ask you to pay a $25 fee using Google Checkout. This transaction confirms that you have a method of payment, such

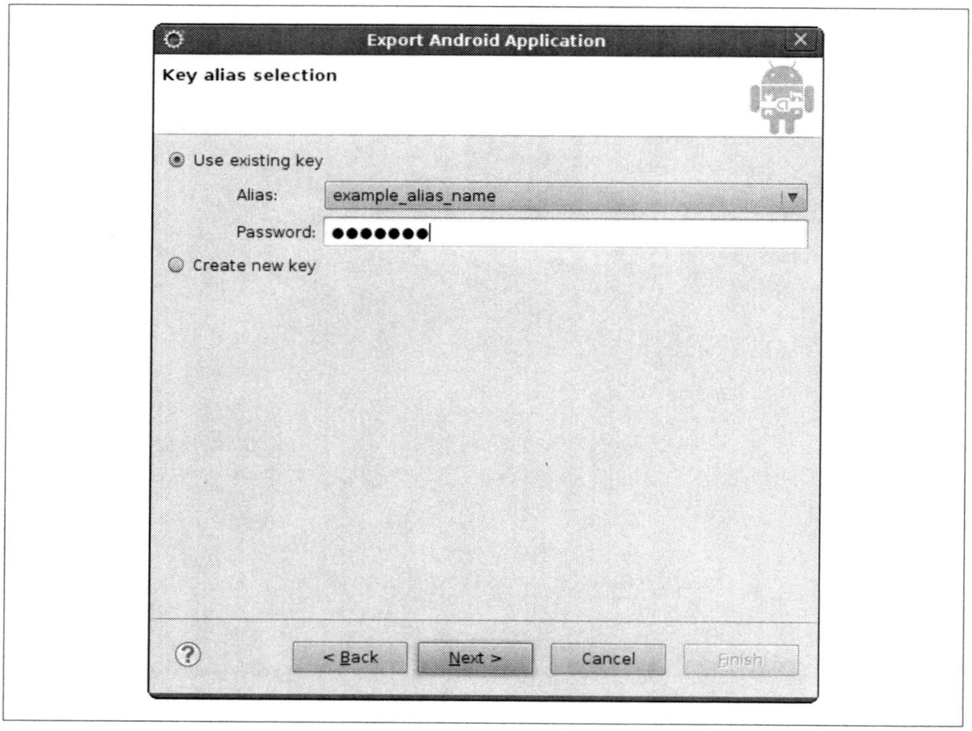

Figure 4-4. Selecting the key alias

as a credit card, accepted by Google Checkout. Once you are signed up as a developer, you can use your Google account to log in to the Android Market site.

At this point, Google has reasonable assurance that you are who you say you are: a financial transaction linked to some entity that can pay off a credit card bill. This, combined with the fact that your applications are signed, means Google is also confident that the key you created to sign your applications is in the possession of the person who created the Android Market account for the purpose of uploading applications to the Android Market. If you turn out to be a spammer or a source of badware, you will be shut down, and you will need to find another identity with which to create another Google Checkout account and Android Market account.

Uploading Applications in the Market

The page at *https://market.android.com/publish/Home#AppEditorPlace* is where you upload applications. On it, you will see the latest requirements, and options, for providing information about your application. The page has upload buttons for the application's *.apk* file, plus screenshots, videos, and similar content, most of which is optional. When you have an application you would like to leave up on the Market for

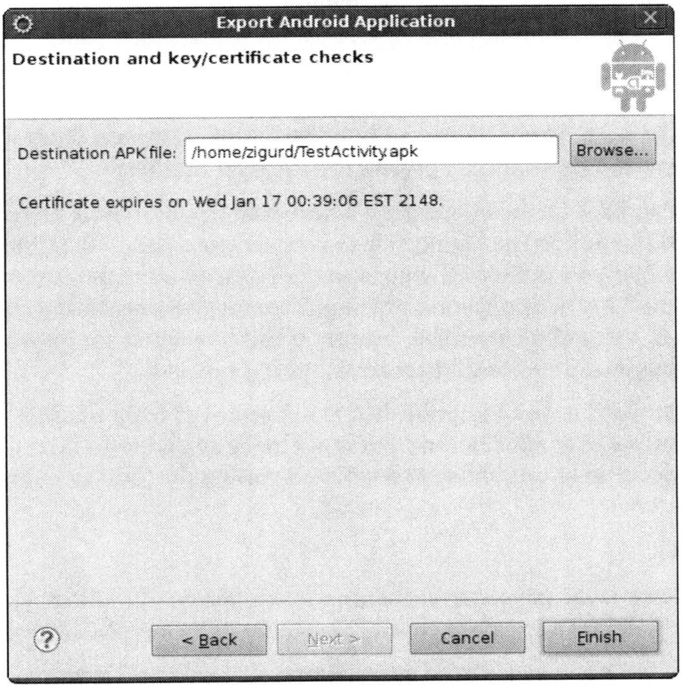

Figure 4-5. Selecting the destination, and final checks

others to download, you should read the descriptions of the kinds of promotional and explanatory material you can upload, and make use of them. For now, let's get our app up with the minimum requirements met.

The first thing to do is to upload an *.apk* file. To try it out, you can use the *.apk* file you created if you followed along in "Using a self-signed certificate to sign an application" on page 133. Don't worry that this is not your application, and that it is just an example. You can publish it and then unpublish it right away, as you will see from the instructions in the rest of this section.

Most required information is either part of your profile as an Android developer, or part of the application manifest. As of this writing, the required uploads are two screenshots and an icon image. You will find usable images in the *doc* folder of the example project. If these requirements change—and the Android Market has changed substantially since it was first introduced—you will find out if you have skipped any required fields or uploads when you click the Publish button at the bottom of the page. Anything you missed will be highlighted, and you can go back and fill in fields or perform uploads as needed to make your application ready for publication.

Click the Publish button.

Congratulations, you have published an Android application. If you go back to *https: //market.android.com/publish/Home*, you will see from the listing of applications that you have one published application (if you have not previously published an application). If you go to *https://market.android.com* and search for, say, your name, the search function should find the application you just published and list it the way a potential customer might see it if he were to find it in the Android Market. From there, you can click through to the application's page in the Android Market.

Now you can go back to the Home page where your application is listed and select it by clicking on the link in the listing. This takes you to a page where the information you entered when you published your app is displayed in such a way that you can modify it and update the application's listing. You can also unpublish your application from this page, using the Unpublish button at the bottom of the page. Whew! You thought you might start getting customer support inquiries!

An application that has been unpublished is not removed from the Market system. It is still listed among your applications, but is not made available for download. You can reverse your decision to unpublish at any time by using the Publish button.

Getting Paid

Google Checkout is the payment mechanism for the Android Market. That is, the Android Market provides a streamlined way to sign up as a Google Checkout merchant.

If you elect to be a publisher of paid applications, you will be directed to a page where you can create a "merchant account." This may sound a bit intimidating, but Google has made it easy to get paid. You don't need to form a corporation or get a business bank account.

 You should consult a lawyer about forming a corporate entity for your business and you should segregate your business finances from your personal accounts.

The process of getting a merchant account amounts to entering some more information —most importantly your tax ID, which can be your Social Security number—so that income from your sales can be reported.

Getting paid involves linking a bank account to your Google Checkout merchant account. Payments to Google Checkout for sales of your app will be deposited in your bank account. A full description of terms of service, payment terms, and similar information can be found in the sellers' section of the Google Checkout site, at *http://check out.google.com/support/sell/bin/answer.py?hl=en&answer=113730*.

Alternative Distribution

Another attribute that distinguishes the Android marketplace from the Apple marketplace is that, in the Android marketplace, many sales channels are available for your iOS application. Google does not prevent third-party entrepreneurs from creating their own markets with their own rules. Indeed, several other companies have set up their own application storefronts that serve specific markets. These markets vary dramatically in their target, their app submission procedures, and how they structure relationships with developers and customers. Two significant Android application stores spring to mind: Verizon's Verizon Apps and Amazon.com's Appstore.

Although deploying an application to several stores may seem like a slam dunk—more stores mean more exposure—there are drawbacks. Each marketplace has its own requirements for promotion, release, and customer support and each of these takes time away from development. A reasonable, practical plan might be to start with one marketplace, expanding into new ones as you get comfortable with the demands of those you are already in.

Verizon Applications for Android

The Verizon Apps store for Android provides some significant differences and potential advantages in comparison to the Android Market. The key distinction is that applications are reviewed before they are deployed to the store. This provides Verizon an opportunity to filter out low-quality or malicious applications before they find their way onto users' handsets. The approval process also enables Verizon to screen applications for appropriate network behavior.

The Verizon Apps store also provides developers with a streamlined mechanism for receiving payment and for billing users, called "carrier billing." The store is integrated with each user's account. When a user downloads an application, she automatically incurs charges for the cost of the application without having to register with an external payment service. Verizon shares application revenue with developers: 70% for the developer and 30% for Verizon.

Verizon also provides an API that enables "in-application" carrier billing, which enables applications to charge users for in-application items, such as opening additional levels in a game, and have the charges appear on the subscriber's wireless bill.

How to submit to the Verizon Apps store for Android

To submit an application to the Verizon Apps for Android store, follow these steps:

1. Create an account at *http://developer.verizon.com*.
2. Submit your application, which involves the following:
   a. Provide basic application information.
   b. Review and accept the Verizon Developer Community App License Agreement.
   c. Fill out setup and network usage questionnaires, which includes picking an appropriate application descriptor.
   d. Select up to four application screenshots and/or preview video.
   e. Select up to four application banners for merchandising opportunities.
   f. Select a pricing model, which can be "Always Free."
   g. Select an application rating that is appropriate for your application content.
   h. Upload your binary application and select the handset devices and operating system that your application supports.
   i. Wait for Verizon to send notification regarding the approval of your submission.
3. Get financially certified. This ensures faster, easier payment by validating that Verizon Wireless has accurate information to pay you for sales of your apps, and to ensure that all legal and other requirements are satisfied.
4. Get paid when developers install your application through the Verizon Apps store for Android.

Technical tips for Verizon Android development

When you develop for the Verizon Apps store, you should investigate some of the helpful tools that Verizon provides.

Deep linking

The Verizon Apps store for Android supports deep linking, an Android-based programming mechanism in which one Android application can invoke the Verizon Apps store user interface to install another application. This is useful for application developers who wish to encourage the installation of a "pay" version of an application as an upgrade from a free version of the same application. It also assists with application co-marketing, where one application can encourage the installation of another. Verizon provides code examples of this procedure on its developer site.

NAVBuilder Inside

Verizon supports a product called NAVBuilder Inside (NBI). NBI is mapping software similar to the Google Maps navigation system that is installed by default on most Android handsets. Many handsets that ship with Verizon also have a version of NBI preinstalled. The Verizon developer site provides an Android SDK and documentation dedicated to helping developers create applications for its NBI product. NBI is free, is cross-platform, and supports coupon-based revenue.

Network API

Verizon has opened its carrier network for web service development using SOAP-based and REST-based APIs. Although these APIs are not directly accessible from handset applications, it's possible to set up a web service proxy that can support indirect handset invocations. These APIs support the following services:

SMS- and MMS-based messaging
Enables sending and receiving SMS and MMS messages.

Location as a service
Provides locations to callers of the API.

Carrier information
Enables a caller to obtain the carrier that services a given mobile phone number. Works for numbers not directly subscribed to Verizon.

All Verizon Network APIs make use of a single, secure, and consistent gateway interface. Handset users must opt-in before any information, such as location fixes, becomes available through the API.

Related links

For more details, see the following Verizon Developer Community website locations:

- Verizon Apps for Android Submission Guide (*http://developer.verizon.com/content/vdc/en/verizon-app-submit.html*)
- NAVBuilder Inside SDK (*http://developer.verizon.com/content/vdc/en/verizon-tools-apis/verizon_apis/navbuilder-inside-sdk.html*)
- The Verizon Network API (*http://developer.verizon.com/content/vdc/en/verizon-tools-apis/verizon_apis/network-api.html*)

Amazon Applications for Android

The Amazon Appstore is an extremely visible marketplace and gives you instant access to the Kindle Fire, which at the time of this writing, is by far the most popular Android tablet. The submission process is web-based, straightforward, and pretty well documented at the developer portal located at *https://developer.amazon.com/welcome.html*. To get started, simply register yourself as a developer. Amazon is, at the moment, waiving the first $99 yearly developer fee. Once you have registered, you may submit as many applications as you choose: just follow the instructions at the portal.

As in most other markets, you will be asked, during the submission process, to provide various promotional assets. You will need, at the very least, an icon, a thumbnail, and three screenshots. You may additionally supply larger promotional images and even up to five short video clips, which Amazon may use to advertise your application.

Amazon pays you a royalty for your application that is the greater of 70% of the purchase price or 20% of the list price. When you list your application, you are entering into a legal relationship—with Amazon. As always, you should take care to understand the terms of the agreement, in this case, Amazon's Distribution Agreement (*https://developer.amazon.com/settings/docs.html*). You must be registered and logged in to see it. There are a few points of which you should be aware:

- Amazon expects you to support your application as long as it is in the Appstore. If Amazon determines that a problem with your application is "critical," you are expected to respond within 24 hours. You are expected to respond to all other customer requests within five days.

- Amazon sets the price of your application. Typical prices are just what you'd expect: $.99 or $1.99. On the other hand, Amazon runs a frequent promotion during which it gives applications away at no cost. It might choose to include your app in this promotion. You should consider whether you expect the app sale price to cover the cost of backend services that will support such promotions.

- In most marketplaces, you sign your application with a key that only you have. When customers install your application, they are assured that they are getting the exact bits that you, the developer, posted. For better or worse, you are solely responsible. This is not the case with the Amazon Appstore. Amazon wraps your code, and uses keys associated with your developer account to sign applications you sell through its store. Amazon requires this so that it can change your application's code to collect and report analytic usage data. It does provide a service that allows you to sign an application with your own, private key—but only after Amazon has modified it.

Amazon also provides a Digital Rights Management service. You can, at no charge, by checking a box during the submissions process, protect your application with Amazon's DRM system. Amazon claims that a protected application will run only on devices that also have the Amazon Appstore installed and then only if the Appstore can verify a valid license for the application.

Once you have submitted your app, Amazon will review it for quality and content. Its standards with respect to content are, again, probably about what you'd expect: it may choose to apply an appropriate rating to your app, or refuse it completely if its content is illegal, pornographic, or malicious. When the review process is complete, your app will become available to Amazon's enormous customer base.

Google Maps API Keys

A Google Maps API key, combined with the keys you use for signing applications, identifies you to Google and enables Google to enforce the terms of service for Google Maps. Google Maps relies on information Google collects and buys at significant expense, and must be protected from misappropriation and other misuse.

If you have been developing an application using the Google Maps API, you will have obtained an API key linked to the debug signature for your application. You can't use this API key when you ship your application. The Google Maps API, and the requirements for using it, are described at *http://code.google.com/android/maps-api-signup .html*.

When you ship your application, you will need a Google Maps API key linked to the signing key you used for distributing your application. That is, you will need a new API key that is made using an MD5 fingerprint of your signing key. Using the `keytool` command's `list` option, you can get the MD5 fingerprint of your signing key thusly:

```
keytool -list -keystore my-release-key.keystore
```

You will get this key the same way you got the API key for use with your debug signature, by visiting the Android Maps API Key Signup page at *http://code.google.com/android/ maps-api-signup.html* and using the MD5 fingerprint of your signing key in the form, as shown in Figure 4-6.

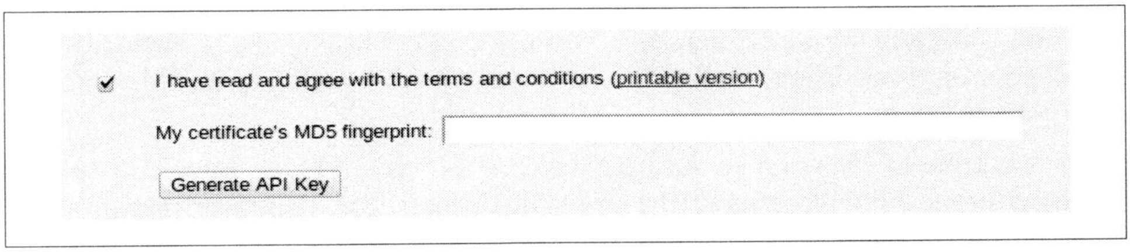

☑ I have read and agree with the terms and conditions (printable version)

My certificate's MD5 fingerprint:

    Generate API Key

Figure 4-6. Getting a Google Maps API key

When you click the Generate API Key button, you will get a web page showing the API key generated from your signing certificate's fingerprint, as shown in Figure 4-7.

 You really have to create your self-signing certificate and Google Maps API keys yourself. You cannot copy them from the screenshots here, you cannot use keys from example code you download, and you cannot use debug keys when releasing a product.

Figure 4-7. The Android Maps API key generated from your self-signing certificate

Specifying API-Level Compatibility

At any one time, multiple versions of Android can be available, and not all the prospective users of your application will have the most recent version. By specifying application compatibility in the manifest, you can control which Android systems can install your application, preventing its use in systems that are incompatible with the APIs you are using.

In the example in "Making an Android Project" on page 12, the same API level is specified for the build target as for the Min SDK Version field. This means the program will run only on systems with the specified API level or higher.

Because you can detect the API level at runtime, there may be cases where you want to ship one application for systems with a lower API level than you use, and to test for the API level and only use methods and classes of higher API levels if they are available. In these cases, you would specify a higher build target API level than the Min SDK Version.

Compatibility with Many Kinds of Screens

Android was built to accommodate multiple screen sizes and changes in screen orientation. The best way to accommodate screen size differences among Android devices is to enable your layouts to be as flexible as possible. The images your application uses may not look optimal in very large or unusually small configurations, but it is possible to specify layouts that are usable at screen sizes ranging from the smallest screen of moderate resolution up to a 1920 × 1080 HD display.

In other words, don't handle screen differences by trying to design a specific layout for each individual screen size. Instead, design a couple of layouts, each of which is flexible enough to cover a reasonable range of screens. By designing in this way, you prepare you application for any new device that might appear on the market.

Testing for Screen Size Compatibility

Testing is key to ensuring screen compatibility. The SDK and AVD Manager provides configurations for a range of screen sizes that cover all the smartphones on which Android runs. As described in "Making an Android Virtual Device (AVD)" on page 16, you can specify preset and custom screen sizes when creating an AVD.

Resource Qualifiers and Screen Sizes

Once you have layouts that can handle the majority of cases, you may want to improve the way your application looks on specific displays. You may need to use separate layouts in cases where you want to take advantage of greater screen real estate other than by just spreading a layout across the screen (a separate preview pane, for example). In these cases, or in cases of specialized apps that might be used for unusually small displays, you can design layouts for specific situations using resource qualifiers.

Resource qualifiers are a set of naming rules for resource directories that enable you to provide alternative resources for the conditions specified by the qualifier, such as high or low, pixel density, language, country, and certain hardware resource availability. The full range of resource qualifiers is described at *http://developer.android.com/guide/topics/resources/providing-resources.html#AlternativeResources*.

## CHAPTER 5

Eclipse for Android Software Development

Eclipse is a controversial topic. It is a great open source success story, it is the most widely used Java IDE, it is powerful, and it is the center of the largest ecosystem of add-ons and derivative products available for software development. These are the reasons Eclipse was chosen as the development target for plug-ins that customize it for Android software development. But Eclipse has been criticized for being unfriendly and difficult to learn.

Eclipse isn't like most GUI software that takes pains to protect the user from invoking operations that cannot succeed. Eclipse's developers favor modularity and power over smoothing the sharp edges. For example, one of the first things you may have noticed in running an example program is that Eclipse offers to do things with your Android program that don't make much sense, such as running it on a server, or as an applet, as shown in Figure 5-1.

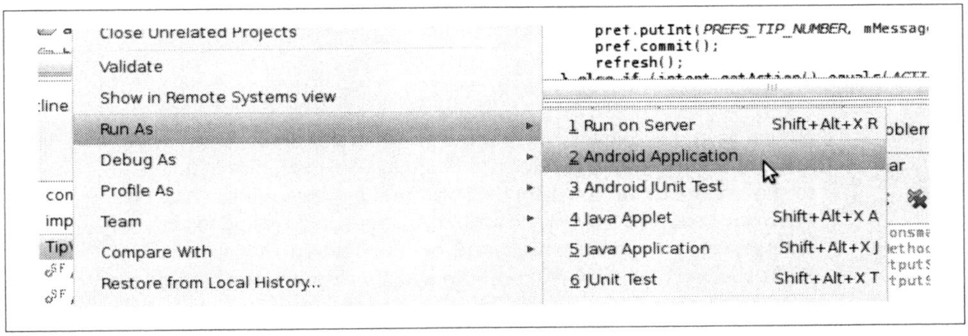

Figure 5-1. Running Eclipse as an applet, a task that is bound to fail

We are not here to criticize Eclipse, nor rationalize on its behalf. But we will explain why Eclipse does things like this. We will explain how Eclipse components fit together and work together. We will familiarize you with what you are looking at when you launch Eclipse and start coding. With this knowledge you will be better equipped to make effective use of Eclipse and less likely to find it frustrating.

Documentation for Eclipse is available at *http://www.eclipse.org/documentation.*

Eclipse Concepts and Terminology

Eclipse has its own nomenclature, behind which are the concepts that are key to understanding it. These concepts developed over a very long product life span, originating with VisualAge—a software development tool written in the SmallTalk language in the mid-1980s. The current implementation of Eclipse is written in the Java language, based on a framework called Equinox, which implements a specification for modular Java software systems called OSGi. OSGi is a way of specifying, in a manifest, the life cycle and dependencies of dynamically loaded modules, called bundles. That is, Eclipse is a collection of modules in a framework. When modules are added or removed, if they have dependencies on other modules, those dependencies will be satisfied automatically, if possible.

Further information on the Equinox OSGi implementation, including a detailed explanation of what happens when Eclipse starts up, is available at *http://eclipse.org/equinox/documents/quickstart.php.*

Plug-ins

When you set up your Android software development tools, you added plug-ins to Eclipse: the Android Development Tools (ADT) plug-ins. Plug-ins are OSGi bundles.

The Android SDK adds two plug-ins to Eclipse. You can find them by showing the Plug-ins view, by selecting Window→Show View→Other and expanding the "Plug-in development" item. Then select Plug-ins from the list of views. You will see the list shown in Figure 5-2.

 Note that in this chapter and in other places in this book, Eclipse view screenshots are shown in "detached" mode—in a separate window—so that we do not need to trim the surrounding views and toolbars out of screenshots. The way a view appears on your screen depends on the Eclipse perspective you are using and the other views in that perspective. Right-clicking on a view title pops up a menu with options for how to display the view, including the Detached option.

Plug-ins are listed alphabetically, so, near the top of the list you will see the two plug-ins required for working with the Android SDK: com.android.ide.eclipse.adt and com.android.ide.eclipse.ddms. Keep the Plug-ins view open. Later in this chapter we

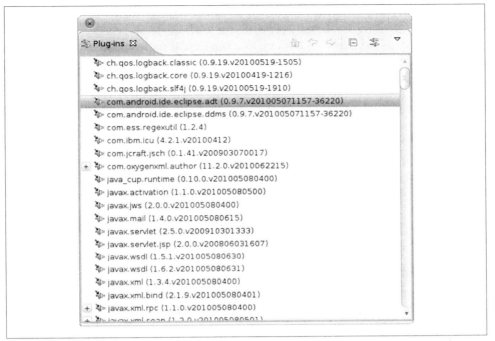

Figure 5-2. A list of all the plug-ins in an Eclipse environment

will look at some information about those plug-ins to see how they modify the Eclipse environment. You can also look at this list of plug-ins and see that Eclipse is, in fact, made of plug-ins, all the way down to the Equinox OSGi implementation.

Workspaces

Eclipse keeps a lot of state, and workspaces are where it is kept. When you first run Eclipse, it will ask if you want to create a workspace. Thereafter, when you start Eclipse, it picks up right where you left off, with all the projects, files, and views as you left them, by reading its previous state from a workspace. Eclipse implements workspaces using directories.

Every project belongs to a workspace. By default, new projects are directories created inside the workspace directory. Even if you create a project from a source that is not in the workspace directory, most of the meta information about that project is kept in the workspace.

Workspaces are independent. Settings that you set up in one workspace stay in that workspace. You can use multiple workspaces to separate projects that target different platforms, and that may use markedly different environments—for example, Rails projects and Android projects. You can use multiple workspaces to run more than one instance of Eclipse. Suppose you have Eclipse-based tools for some web application framework that are not compatible with the version of Eclipse you are using for Android development. By using a separate workspace for Android development, you can maintain separate state and even run both Eclipse versions at the same time.

Java Environments

Three distinct Java environments are used in Java software development in Eclipse.

Eclipse's Java Runtime Environment

The first environment is that in which Eclipse itself is running. In "The Eclipse Integrated Development Environment (IDE)" on page 5 we covered installing Java development tools and runtime environments, if your system does not already have one installed. If you need to use a different Java runtime for Eclipse, you can configure this choice in your *eclipse.ini* file in the folder where Eclipse is installed. If Eclipse is running out of memory, for instance, this is the environment you will want to adjust.

The Java compiler

The second environment is used to compile your code. Eclipse comes with its own incremental Java compiler. In addition to producing the compiled Java *.class* files, it creates the error messages displayed in the Java editor and produces the typing information Eclipse uses for suggestions, autocompletion, and so on. This environment is configured using the Java→Compiler node in the Preferences pane, but you can override the defaults for a specific project from the project's preferences.

In addition, this environment contains a description of the libraries against which the application is compiled. If you look at the Preferences→Build Path for an Android application, you will find that there is no Java runtime included in the list of libraries on which the project depends. Instead, an Android project depends on a version of the Android libraries. Because the Android tools are bolted onto Eclipse, though, you can't directly change the Android library version from the Build Path pane. If you need to do that, you'll have to open the Android Preferences pane.

The application runtime

The third environment is the one in which your application runs—in this case, one of the Android emulators. In setting up your development environment—either when you installed the SDK or when you set up the ADT plug-in—you set up one or more Android Virtual Devices (AVDs). When you create a new Android project you associate it with one of the AVDs. The plug-in uses the appropriate profile to set up both the compilation environment and the emulator used for running the application, reducing the chance for a mismatch between the runtime environment: an application compiled against the Android 2.2 libraries may not run on a 1.5 platform.

Projects

For software developers, Eclipse projects correspond to programs they are developing. For Android software developers, they correspond to Android applications. Within Eclipse, projects are how Eclipse plug-ins know which software to operate on: when you create an Android project, the project data includes information that Eclipse uses to select code from various plug-ins to perform various operations. The ADT plug-ins are invoked to help create a project with the right set of files and directory structure for an Android application. When you work on the files in an Android project, the right editors are used when you open XML files such as layouts and the manifest. When you modify files in a project, the right builders are called to build the application.

Builders and Artifacts

The Eclipse framework defines the concept of a "builder," used to generate project artifacts from their sources. Artifacts are files built from source files. The Android Eclipse plug-in defines several new builders that create *.dex* files from *.class* files, create Java constants that identify resources specified in XML, create *.apk* files, and perform other Android-specific operations that are part of turning code into an installable package. Eclipse will regenerate the installable application whenever you make changes. You should always be able to run it or debug it.

The transformation of *.class* files, which are the output of the Java compiler, to *.dex* files, which are bytecode interpreted by the Dalvik VM, is a neat trick: it enables you to program in Java, using the very highly developed editing and refactoring tools, as well as numerous other tools created to enhance the productivity and reliability of Java coding.

Extensions

Extensions are all the places where a plug-in extends Eclipse functionality. You won't manipulate or change extensions as an Android software developer, but while we have that Plug-ins view open, let's take a brief look at some of the extensions the Android plug-ins add. This will give you a more concrete idea of the relationship of the ADT plug-ins and the rest of the Eclipse system. In the Plug-ins view, as shown in Figure 5-2, double-click on the plug-in named com.android.ide.eclipse.adt and you will see an Extensions view, listing the extensions in the plug-in, as shown in Figure 5-3.

For example, you can select each extension named org.eclipse.core.resources .builders and, on the right side of the Extensions view, it will show you the extension names: Android Resource Manager, Android Pre Compiler, and Android Package Builder. These are the extensions needed to process Android resources; precompile AIDL (Android Interface Definition Language), which is described in Chapter 3, into Java code; and turn *.class* files, which are created using the Java builder, into *.dex* files as well as build the *.apk* file, which can be deployed to an Android device or AVD.

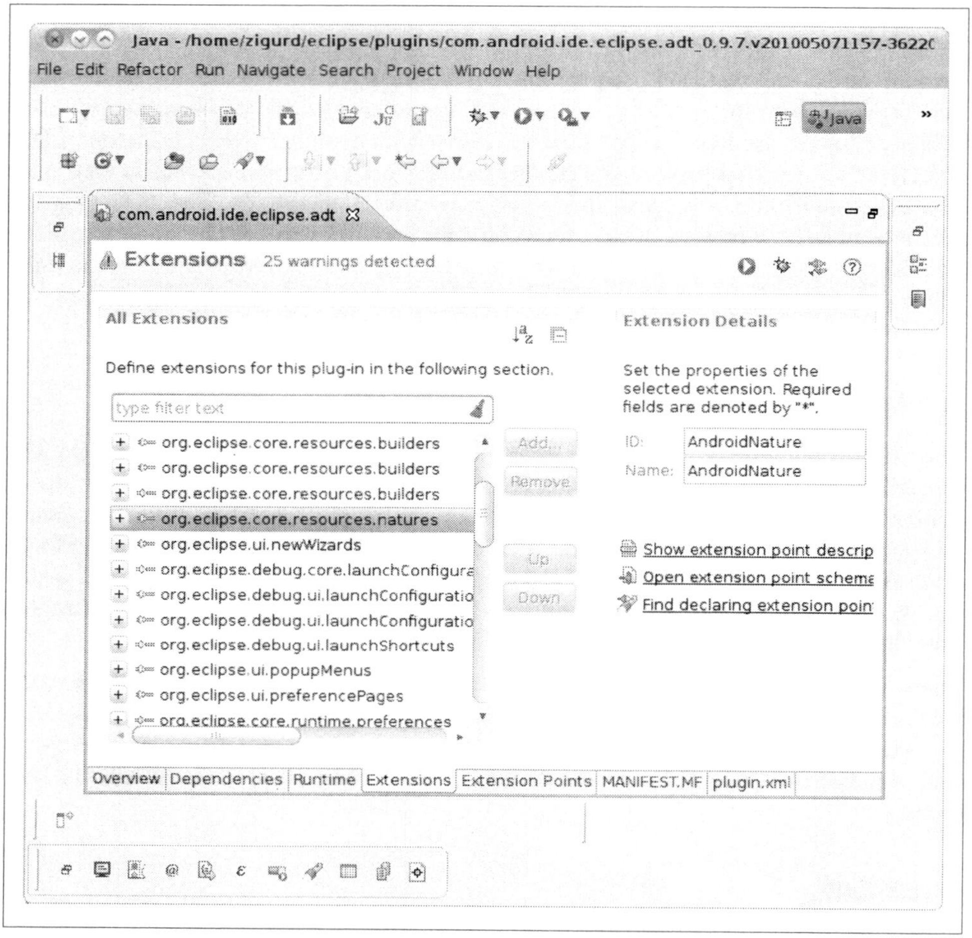

Figure 5-3. A list of extensions in the ADT plug-in

If you expand the `org.eclipse.ui.editors` item, you will see a list of the editors the ADT plug-in adds to the Eclipse system: the Android Manifest Editor, Resources Editor, Graphical Layout Editor, Menu Editor, and XML Resources Editor. There are many other extensions in this list, and this should give you an idea of the amount of code that is required to turn Eclipse into a tool for Android software development. The ones we've explored here are enough to reveal some of the most important aspects: how Android programs get built, and what is added to the Eclipse environment to help you edit Android-specific files—including the XML files that comprise the manifest, layouts, and other resources.

If you explore the other ADT plug-in similarly, you will see how Dalvik Debug Monitor Server (DDMS) features are added to Eclipse.

Associations

Associations are how files within a project are associated with, among other things, the editors that operate on them. For example, Java files within an Android project are edited with the Java editor, the same as any Java project, but XML files are edited with an Android-specific XML editor, which could be the Android Manifest Editor or the Resources Editor. These editors know how to edit specific structures in these files, but they fall short in other areas, such as general-purpose structure editing with the Outline view. If you wanted to open an Android XML file with an XML editor other than the one the association for the file calls for, you can override associations with the Open With command in the context menu for a source file, which pops up when you right-click on the file in the Package Explorer view.

The Open With command shows you a choice of editors that are likely to work on the file you selected. If you select the Other option, you will see a list of all editors in your Eclipse configuration and be offered the option of opening the selected file with an external program.

Eclipse Views and Perspectives

In addition to understanding the way the ADT plug-ins modify Eclipse, some familiarity with Eclipse's system of views and perspectives will help you recognize what you are looking at when you use Eclipse in Android software development. An Eclipse view is a part of the Eclipse window that displays information of a certain type, or in a certain way: a list of projects and project files, a list of errors in code, a hierarchical view of entities in a class, and so on. A perspective is an arrangement of views designed for a particular purpose, such as editing Java, or debugging.

If your Eclipse environment does not result in the same set of views shown in the examples here or listed among the main views, don't be alarmed. Different sets of plug-ins can result in different behavior, including the set of default views in some perspectives. The most important perspectives for Java coding are the Package Explorer, Editor, and Outline views, and those should be present in your Eclipse environment.

When you first start Eclipse (after you get past the Welcome screen) but before you have created any projects, you should see something similar to Figure 5-4.

The workspace pictured here is a little more cramped than what you will probably experience. Most coders use larger screens to see the information in the views surrounding the editor that goes in the middle of an Eclipse perspective, and leave enough room to see an adequate amount of code. We left these perspectives at the default minimum size to fit the screenshots on the page.

A typical Java editing perspective in Eclipse looks like the one in Figure 5-5, with views for exploring the contents of projects, a list of tasks, the output of builders and other operations, and so on. You can see that some changes from the default set of views

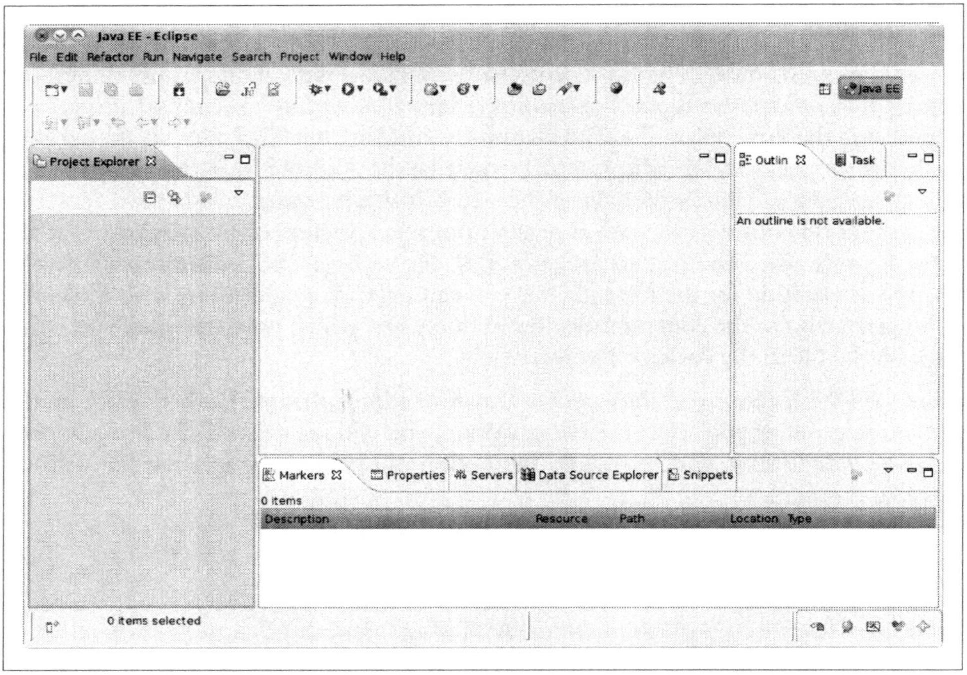

Figure 5-4. An empty workspace, with the ADT plug-in configured

were made in creating an Android project and editing a Java source file in an Android project. Let's take a look at the views that are displayed by default here.

The Package Explorer View

Eclipse is more than just an editor with a lot of chrome around the editing window. Most of the views displayed around the editor in an Eclipse perspective have the goal of speeding navigation in the project and in the project's files. The Package Explorer view will often be your starting point when editing source files and running and debugging your projects.

The Task List View

The Task List view lists tasks that you may have created using the New Task command in the view's toolbar, or by turning an item in the Problems view into a task. You can link the task list with a source code repository or bug tracker to share it with other people working on a project with you. Curiously, the Task List view does not list the TODO items many coders use to insert task reminders into code. These are parsed by the Java editor and are marked with icons in the left margin. There may be something about

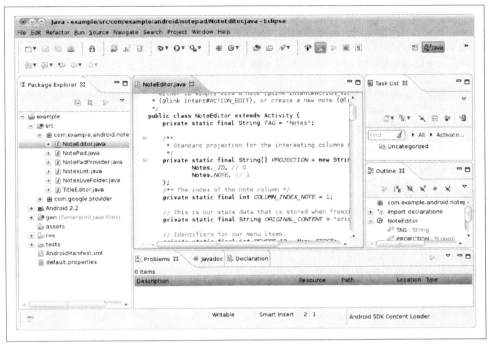

Figure 5-5. The Java editing perspective with an Android project, and an Android source file in the Java editor

the implementation of the plug-ins that implement these features that makes it difficult to present all tasks in one place.

The Outline View

A program is both its source code—which is usually ordinary text—and the structure into which it is parsed, which consists, in the case of Java, of fields and methods. The Outline view shows the structure of a Java class, and enables you to operate on that structure with many of the same commands you would apply to the selection in an Editor view. The Java editor relies on knowing the underlying structure, too. But the Outline view enables you to see that structure explicitly laid out in a hierarchy, with icons that indicate type and scope information to the left of the name of each item in this structured view. More information on the Outline view is available at *http://help .eclipse.org/helios/topic/org.eclipse.jdt.doc.user/reference/views/ref-view-outline.htm.*

The Problems View

The Eclipse concept of "builders" generalizes the idea of compiling source files into objects or, more generally in Eclipse parlance, artifacts. Problems are what prevent this from happening smoothly. Problems can be compiler errors, or any other error from a builder. Sometimes problems prevent a builder from completing an artifact, and sometimes they are warnings that do not prevent an artifact from being generated. The Problems view displays problems and enables fast navigation to them. Right-click on a problem to see the context menu: if you want to fix the problem right away, the Go To command opens the file and navigates to the line associated with the problem. If it is a warning that should eventually be fixed, you can track the problem by using the New Task From Marker command. Double-clicking on a problem also navigates to the source of the problem.

Java Coding in Eclipse

If you are new to Java and Eclipse, your first concern will be getting things right. But soon enough, your primary concern will be making coding fast and easy. Of all programming languages, Java has likely had the most effort applied to boosting programmer productivity through tools such as Eclipse. For this reason, the story of Java coding in Eclipse is a story driven by the desire for the highest possible level of productivity. Productivity has three key aspects: creating new code efficiently, finding code you need to read or modify, and making changes to code that affect more than just the line of code you are editing.

Editing Java Code and Code Completion

The central productivity feature for editing Java code in any Java-oriented IDE is code completion or, in Eclipse parlance, "content assist." Nearly anywhere in a Java source file you can press the keyboard shortcut Ctrl+spacebar to display a pop up that "proposes" to complete what you are currently doing. For example, if you know there is a method to find something, but you forget exactly how that goes, type **fi** and press Ctrl-space bar. You will then see something similar to Figure 5-6.

In this case, content assist is offering to insert the signature of a method, with a parameter list for you to fill in. You can see that the method `findViewById` is listed, and you can select this choice to avoid having to type the whole method name and argument list.

Had you pressed Ctrl-space bar before having typed anything, all the constants and methods of the class would have been offered as possible completions by content assist.

Refactoring

Java is statically typed, which requires every object and every reference to be explicitly declared before it is used. This can make Java look bureaucratic and inelegant, and make it seem as though coding in Java is needlessly wordy. IDEs such as Eclipse compensate for the verbosity of Java syntax by providing code completion and other

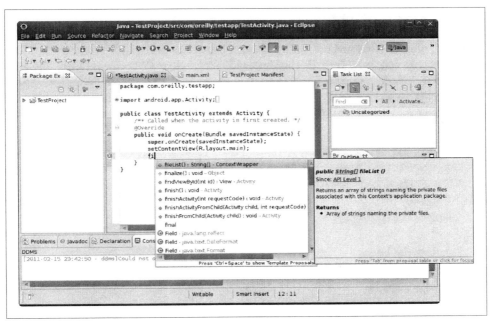

Figure 5-6. Offering a completion in the content assist pop up

speedups for coders. There is one aspect of coding productivity that works far better in statically typed languages: refactoring.

Refactoring means making changes that preserve program behavior. That is, refactoring does not change what the program does. It changes how the program is organized. Ensuring that behavior does not change while code is reorganized enables powerful transformations: even renaming a reference or type name can be perilous if you have to do it with text substitution. But with refactoring, you are assured that all and only the right names are modified.

Two factors greatly improve the kinds of refactorings that can be performed: the language should be statically typed, and the IDE should have a compiled model of the program. By "model of the program," we mean a data structure that represents compiled code, such that all the types and references in the program can be found within their scope. By knowing exact types, and the exact scope of a type or reference, the IDE can locate every use of that type or reference without any ambiguity.

Refactoring is the prime example of how languages can no longer be compared only by syntax, aesthetics, and expressive power. Conservatively designed languages such as Java can be both as safe as possible and highly productive in the context of the typical set of tools a coder has at her fingertips.

Eclipse and Android

The ADT plug-in adds several Android-specific tools to the Eclipse workbench. Most of these tools can be found in the Android perspective (Window→Open Perspective→Other, select DDMS). Each tool is a separate Eclipse view (Window→Show View→Other, select DDMS), though, and can be added to any other perspective, as convenience and screen real estate dictate. Here are a few of the most useful:

LogCat
> Displays the device logs in a scrolling pane. You can adjust filtering so that only the logs you are interested in are visible, or so that you can see everything down to the garbage collections and library loading.

File Explorer
> Displays the file explorer.

Heap
> Displays the heap.

Threads
> Displays threads.

Pixel Perfect
> Displays the Pixel Perfect view.

Layout View
> Displays the Layout view.

avdmgr
> Displays the Android SDK and AVD Manager.

Preventing Bugs and Keeping Your Code Clean

You can think of Eclipse as a specialized operating system: it is made up of thousands of files, has its own filesystem, and runs a web server. Eclipse is open and very extensible. Plug-ins—the Eclipse analog of an operating system's applications—are relatively easy to write, and the Eclipse ecosystem has many more extensions than any one Eclipse user could ever install and use. Because Android code is written in Java, you can apply all kinds of plug-ins to Android software development.

Here we will explore an often very valuable category of Eclipse extensions: static analyzers, or source code analyzers.

Static Analyzers

An informal definition of static analysis is that it picks up where compiler warnings leave off. In Eclipse, compiler warnings are, in general, very good. While a good compiler can provide you with warning messages that are helpful in catching potential runtime problems, it isn't a compiler's job to go hunting for hidden problems. Static analyzers cover that territory.

Static analyzers are called "static" because the analysis is performed on code that isn't running. While the compiler performs some functions that might come under the heading of static analysis—and the Java compiler in Eclipse does a very good job of cleaning up after the detritus of programming, such as variables and methods that are not used—static analyzers are more ambitious. Static analyzers attempt to find bugs, rather than just loose ends.

FindBugs

We will start exploring static analyzers by installing and using FindBugs. You can find documentation, as well as the source code for FindBugs, at *http://findbugs.sourceforge .net*. We will go into the installation process in some detail because it is similar to the installation process for most kinds of Eclipse plug-ins. To install FindBugs, you must first add the FindBugs repository to Eclipse's list of sites from which to install packages. You do this by using the Help→Install New Software Menu command, and clicking the Add button in the Install dialog. This opens the Add Repository dialog that allows you to add the FindBugs repository located at *http://findbugs.cs.umd.edu/eclipse*, as shown in Figure 5-7.

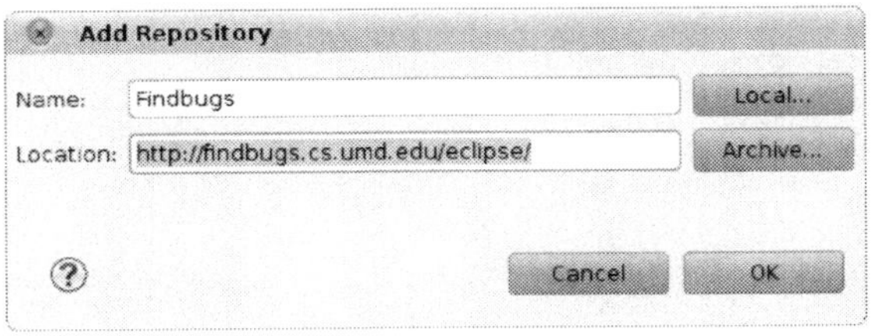

Figure 5-7. Adding a repository for the purpose of adding a plug-in to your Eclipse environment

The next step in installing FindBugs is to select the package from the repository, as shown in Figure 5-8. In this case, there is only one package to select.

Figure 5-8. Selecting the only available package in the FindBugs repository

Once the package has been selected, you can advance to the next dialog, which shows the list of packages to be installed. In this case, there's only one, as shown in Figure 5-9.

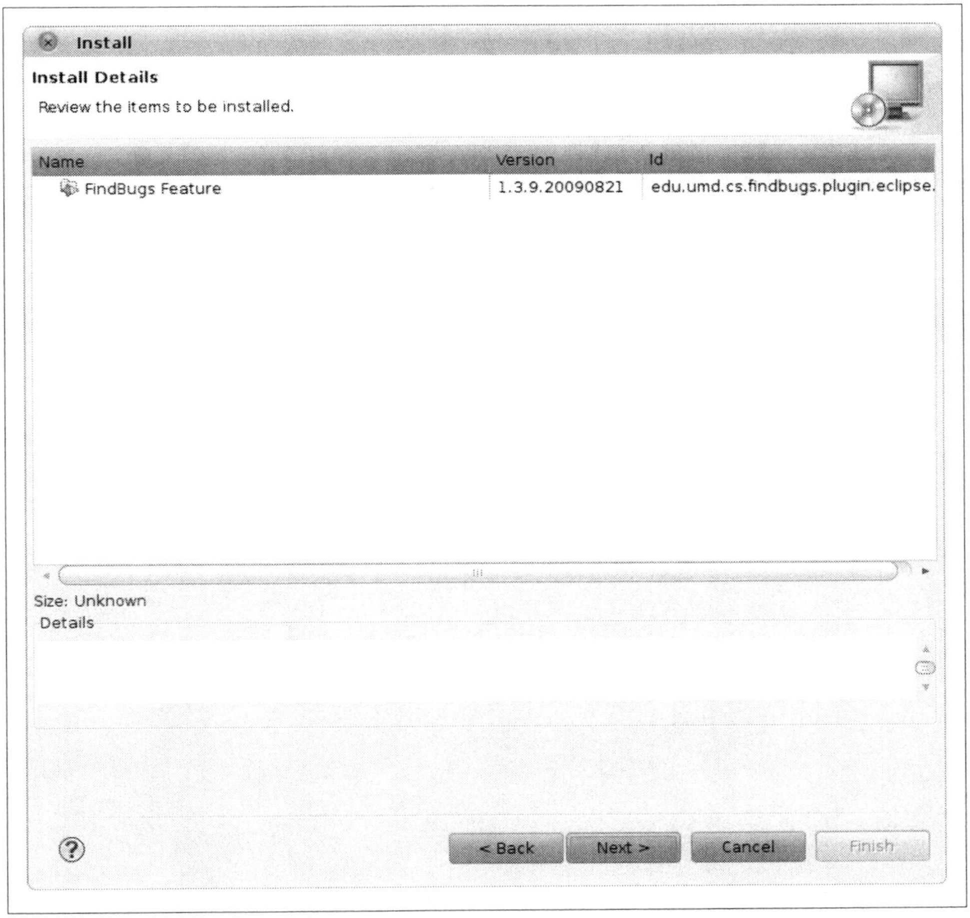

Figure 5-9. Reviewing that you have selected the only available package in the FindBugs repository

And there's more: the next dialog in the installation sequence enables you to read and accept, or not accept, the license agreement that accompanies this package, as shown in Figure 5-10.

Figure 5-10. Accepting the FindBugs license agreement

There may be one more hurdle to cross in installing this Eclipse plug-in. Because the package is not signed, you get a security warning, as shown in Figure 5-11.

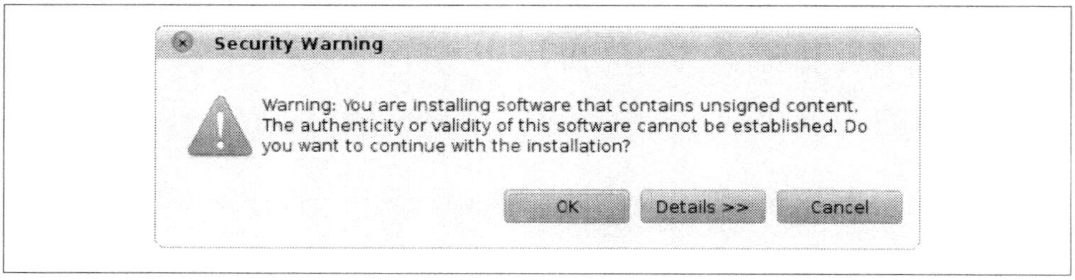

Figure 5-11. The security warning displayed when installing unsigned packages

And finally, you are prompted to restart Eclipse, as shown in Figure 5-12.

Figure 5-12. Restarting Eclipse after installing FindBugs

Applying Static Analysis to Android Code

FindBugs has a menu command, a perspective, and some views you will find useful in finding bugs. To start FindBugs, use the menu command in the context menu of a project, as shown in Figure 5-13.

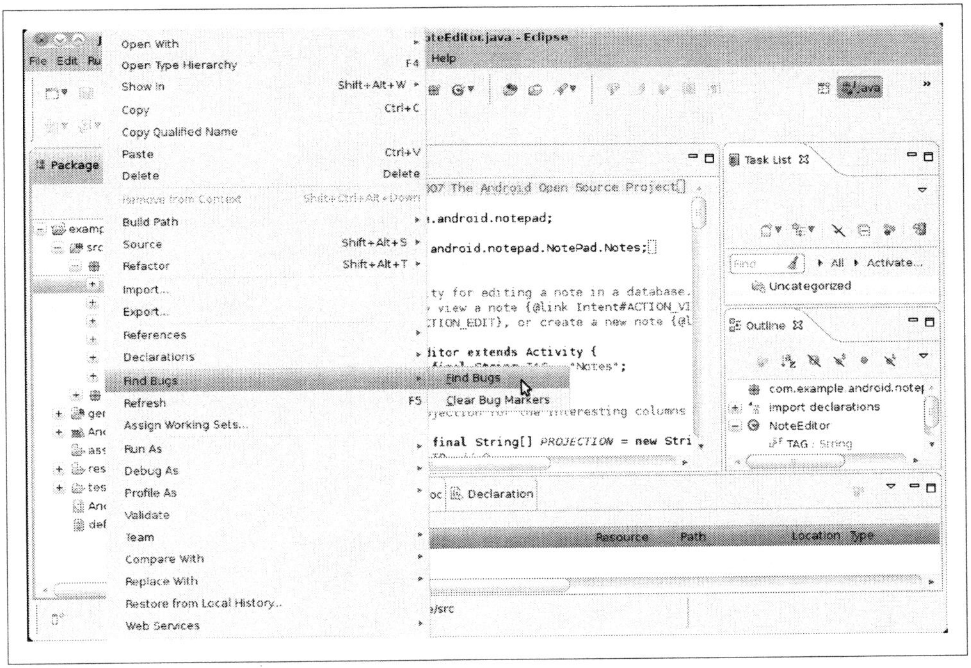

Figure 5-13. Invoking FindBugs

Once you have run FindBugs, you can change to the FindBugs perspective, as shown in Figure 5-14. The FindBugs perspective includes views that display a hierarchical list of potential problems FindBugs has found, organized by type of problem; an Editor view that includes markers for the problems; and, if you open the properties for a problem, a detailed explanation of the problem, including an explanation of why Find-Bugs can raise "false positives."

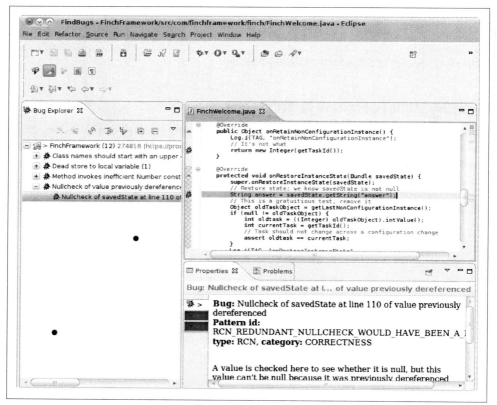

Figure 5-14. The FindBugs perspective

In this case, we will take a look at the "Nullcheck of value previously dereferenced (1)" problem, as shown in the Bug Explorer view in Figure 5-15.

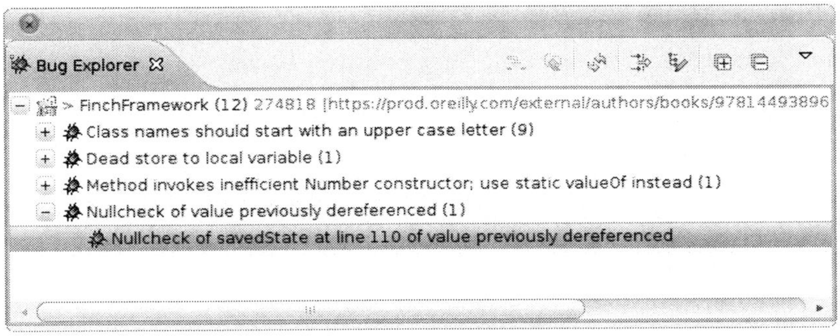

Figure 5-15. The FindBugs Bug Explorer

Verifying that a field has a non-null value field after already having dereferenced it isn't syntactically incorrect Java, but it is almost certainly either useless or an outright error. In the following code, you can see that the field savedState is used with the assumption that it is never null, but a null check occurs in the logging call:

```java
protected void onRestoreInstanceState(Bundle savedState) {
    super.onRestoreInstanceState(savedState);
    // Restore state; we know savedState is not null
    String answer = savedState.getString("answer");
    // This is a gratuitous test, remove it
    Object oldTaskObject = getLastNonConfigurationInstance();
    if (null != oldTaskObject) {
        int oldtask = ((Integer) oldTaskObject).intValue();
        int currentTask = getTaskId();
        // Task should not change across a configuration change
        assert oldtask == currentTask;
    }
    Log.i(TAG, "onRestoreInstanceState"
            + (null == savedState ? "" : RESTORE) + " " + answer);
}
```

In fact, savedState should be null-checked before it is used, because the value of saved State is not specified to be non-null. We will change the assignment that did not null-test savedState to the following:

```java
String answer = null != savedState ? savedState.getString("answer") : "";
```

Running FindBugs again confirms that this change eliminates the possible problem.

This is a good example of the kind of bug static analysis can find. It is outside the realm of compiler warnings because there are cases where this is exactly what the programmer intended, but a simple inference enables a static analyzer to suggest that this might be a bug, and it very often is a bug.

Limitations of Static Analysis

Static analyzers suffer from detecting false positives, because of the approaches they take to finding weaknesses in code. This is one thing that differentiates static analysis from compiler warnings. It would be considered a bug if a compiler error message indicated a problem that wasn't really a problem.

One of the weaker aspects of static analyzers is in finding code where coding conventions have not been observed. For example, the "Class names should start with an upper case letter" warning, shown in Figure 5-15, was provoked by autogenerated code, which coders should not have to inspect unless they suspect bugs in the code generator.

Highly experienced coders often question the usefulness of static analyzers, as their code contains relatively few problems that static analyzers can catch, and therefore the results have a higher proportion of false positives. It is an accepted fact that static analysis of code written by highly experienced coders finds only a fraction of the bugs in that code, and that it is no substitute for module tests and good debugging skills. However, if you are a relative newcomer to Java as well as to Android, you may find static analyzers are a very useful adjunct to compiler warnings.

Eclipse Idiosyncrasies and Alternatives

Now that you know that the Android SDK has many capabilities built on Eclipse, and how the Eclipse plug-in and extension architecture enables Android tools to "hook" so many aspects of an IDE's functionality, you may be wondering why it offers to run your Android application on a server, or as an applet. It is particularly troubling to have a tool that is supposed to enhance your productivity lay a red herring across your path in this way, because Eclipse expects you to find the right commands in a set of exceptionally lengthy menus.

Go ahead, see what happens: pick any Android project in your Eclipse workspace, right-click on the project name, and select Run As→Java Applet. You will see the dialog shown in Figure 5-16.

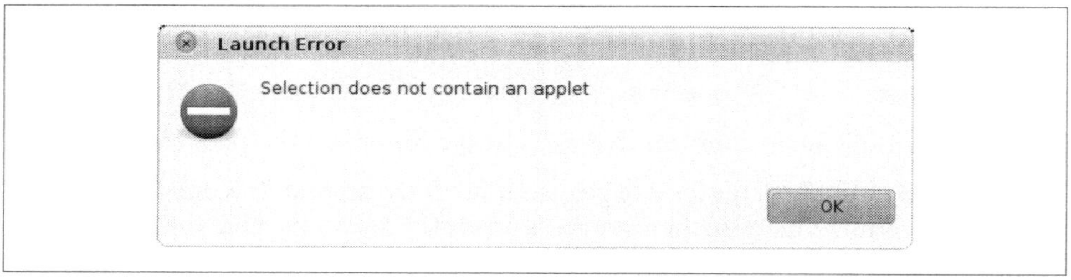

Figure 5-16. Dialog shown when the selection does not contain an applet

No harm done, but it is appalling: Eclipse, plus whatever plug-ins are in play at that moment, should know not to offer you an action that fails, guaranteed, 100% of the time. Eclipse is a bad example: don't treat the users of your Android programs this way! If the selection does not contain an applet, don't offer the user a command to run the selection as an applet. This is a fundamental precept of graphical user interfaces and foundational to the idea of generic operations on a selection: once the user has selected something, the program should know all the valid operations on that selection and present only valid operations. A good interface—especially a big, complex interface—should encourage safe exploration.

Why does Eclipse fail to be a good GUI application in such seemingly trivial ways? Such failure is baffling in light of the impressive power and ease of use of Eclipse refactoring and other features. There is no one fault to point to. Our conjecture is that the fine-grained modularity of Eclipse, which results in an explosion of extension interfaces, causes this combination of powerful features and niggling annoyances. At best, plug-in authors are faced with too many interfaces to hook to accomplish a highly polished user experience. At worst, Eclipse's architecture may make it practically impossible to do the right thing in some cases. This is why some people seek alternatives.

## PART II

About the Android Framework

The Android Framework is the set of base classes that underlie Android applications and the parts of Android system software that comprise the Android userland. Here we organize our presentation of the Android APIs around the goal of enabling you to implement applications that take maximum advantage of the Android system architecture.

## CHAPTER 6

Building a View

Android comes with many requirements that herald complexity in the user interface; it's a multiprocessing system that supports multiple concurrent applications, accepts multiple forms of input, is highly interactive, and is flexible enough to support a wide range of devices now and in the future. The user interface is both rich and easy to use.

This chapter provides you with the techniques for implementing a graphical interface on Android. It explains the architecture of the Android UI toolkit, while showing you in practical terms how to use basic interface elements such as buttons and text boxes. It also covers event handling, using multiple threads to offload long-running tasks so that the UI doesn't freeze, and other topics that make user interfaces pleasant and performant.

Android GUI Architecture

The Android environment adds yet another GUI toolkit to the Java ecosystem, joining AWT, Swing, SWT, LWUIT, and others. If you have worked with any of these, the Android UI framework will look familiar. Like them, it is single-threaded, event-driven, and built on a library of nestable components.

The Android UI framework is, like other Java UI frameworks, organized around the common Model-View-Controller (MVC) pattern illustrated in Figure 6-1. It provides structure and tools for building a Controller that handles user input (such as keystrokes and screen taps) and a View that renders graphical information to the screen.

The Model

The Model is the guts of your application—what it actually does. It might be, for instance, the database of music on your device and the code for playing the music. It might be your list of contacts and the code that places phone calls or sends IMs to them. It is the subject of a large part of the rest of this book.

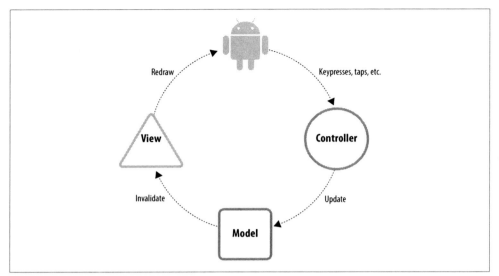

Figure 6-1. Model-View-Controller concept

While a particular application's View and Controller will necessarily reflect the Model they manipulate, a single Model might be used by several different applications. Consider, for instance, an MP3 player and another application that converts MP3 files into WAV files. For both applications, the Model includes the MP3 file format. The former application, however, has the familiar Stop, Start, and Pause controls, and plays tunes. The latter may not produce any sound at all. Instead, it will have controls for things such as sample rate and bit rate. The Model is all about the data.

The View

The View is the visualization of the Model. More generally, a view is the portion of the application responsible for rendering the display, sending audio to the speakers, generating tactile feedback, and so on. The graphical portion of the Android UI framework, described in detail in Chapter 8, is implemented as a tree of subclasses of the View class. Graphically, each object represents a rectangular area on the screen that is completely within the rectangular area represented by its parent in the tree. The root of this tree is the application window.

As an example, the display in our hypothetical MP3 player might contain a component that shows the album cover for the currently playing tune. Another View might display the name of the currently playing song while a third contains subviews such as the Play, Pause, and Stop buttons.

The UI framework paints the screen by walking the view tree, asking each component to draw itself in a *preorder traversal*. In other words, each View draws itself and then asks each of its children to do the same. When the whole tree has been rendered, the smaller, nested components that are the leaves of the tree—and that were therefore painted later—appear to be painted on top of the components that are nearer to the root and that were painted first.

The Android UI framework is actually more efficient than this simplified description. It does not paint an area of a parent view if it can be certain that some child will later paint the same area. It would be a waste of time to paint the background underneath an opaque object. It would also be a waste of time to repaint portions of a view that have not changed.

The Controller

The Controller is the portion of an application that responds to external actions: a keystroke, a screen tap, an incoming call, and so forth. It is implemented as an *event queue*. Each external action is represented as a unique event in the queue. The framework removes each event from the queue in order and dispatches it.

For example, when a user presses a key on her phone, the Android system generates a KeyEvent and adds it to the event queue. Eventually, after previously enqueued events have been processed, the KeyEvent is removed from the queue and passed as the parameter of a call to the dispatchKeyEvent method of the View that is currently selected.

Once an event is dispatched to the in-focus component, the component may take appropriate action to change the internal state of the program. In an MP3 player application, for instance, when the user taps a Play/Pause button on the screen and the event is dispatched to that button's target, the handler method might update the Model to resume playing some previously selected tune.

This chapter describes the construction of the Controller for an Android application.

Putting It Together

We now have all the concepts necessary to describe the complete UI system. When an external action occurs—when the user scrolls, drags, or presses a button; a call comes in; or an MP3 player arrives at the end of its playlist—the Android system enqueues an event representing the action on the event queue. Eventually, the event is dequeued— first in, first out—and dispatched to an appropriate event handler. The handler, which is often code you write as part of your application, responds to the event by notifying the Model that there has been a change in state. The Model takes the appropriate action.

Nearly any change in Model state will require a corresponding change in the View. In response to a keypress, for instance, an EditText component must show the newly typed character at the insert point. Similarly, in a phone book application, clicking on a contact will cause that contact to be highlighted and the previously highlighted contact to have its highlighting removed.

When the Model updates its own state it almost certainly will change the current display to reflect the internal change. To update the display, the Model must notify the UI framework that some portion of the display is now stale and has to be redrawn. The redraw request is actually nothing more than another event enqueued in the same framework event queue that held the Controller event a moment ago. The redraw event is processed, in order, like any other UI event.

Eventually, the redraw event is removed from the queue and dispatched. The event handler for a redraw event is the View. The tree of views is redrawn; each view is responsible, exactly, for rendering its current state at the time it is drawn.

To make this concrete, we can trace the cycle through a hypothetical MP3 player application:

1. When the user taps the screen image of the Play/Pause button, the framework creates a new MotionEvent containing, among other things, the screen coordinates of the tap. The framework enqueues the new event at the end of the event queue.

2. As described in "The Controller" on page 173, when the event percolates through the queue, the framework removes it and passes it down the view tree to the leaf widget within whose bounding rectangle the tap occurred.

3. Because the button widget represents the Play/Pause button, the application button handling code tells the core (the Model) that it should resume playing a tune.

4. The application model code starts playing the selected tune. In addition, it sends a redraw request to the UI framework.

5. The redraw request is added to the event queue and eventually processed as described in "The View" on page 172.

6. The screen gets redrawn with the Play button in its playing state and everything is again in sync.

UI component objects such as buttons and text boxes actually implement both View and Controller methods. This only makes sense. When you add a Button to your application's UI, you want it to appear on the screen as well as do something when the user pushes it. Even though the two logical elements of the UI, the View and the Controller, are implemented in the same object, you should take care that they do not directly interact. Controller methods, for instance, should never directly change the display. Leave it to the code that actually changes state to request a redraw and trust that, later, calls to rendering methods will allow the component to reflect the new state. Coding in this way minimizes synchronization problems and helps to keep your program robust and bug-free.

There is one more aspect of the Android UI framework that is important to recall: it is single-threaded. A single thread removes events from the event queue to make Controller callbacks and to render the view. This is significant for several reasons.

The simplest consequence of a single-threaded UI is that it is not necessary to use synchronized blocks to coordinate state between the View and the Controller. This is a valuable optimization.

Another advantage of a single-threaded UI is that the application is guaranteed that each event on the event queue is processed completely and in the order in which it was enqueued. That may seem fairly obvious, but its implications make coding the UI much easier. When a UI component is called to handle an event, it is guaranteed that no other UI processing will take place until it returns. That means, for instance, that a component that requests multiple changes in the program state—each of which causes a corresponding request that the screen be repainted—is guaranteed that the repaint will *not* start until it has completed processing, performed all its updates, and returned. In short, UI callbacks are atomic.

The third reason to remember that only a single thread is dequeuing and dispatching events from the UI event queue is that if your code stalls that thread for any reason, your UI will freeze! If a component's response to an event is simple—changing the state of variables, creating new objects, and so on—it is perfectly correct to do that processing on the main event thread. If, on the other hand, the handler must retrieve a response from some distant network service or run a complex database query, the entire UI will become unresponsive until the request completes. That definitely does not make for a great user experience! Long-running tasks must be delegated to another thread, as described in "Advanced Wiring: Focus and Threading" on page 195.

Assembling a Graphical Interface

The Android UI framework provides both a complete set of drawing tools with which to build a UI, and a rich collection of prebuilt components based on these tools. As we will see in Chapter 8, the framework graphics tools provide plenty of support for applications that need to create their own controls or to render special views. On the other hand, many applications may work very well using only canned views from the toolkit. Classes such as ListView, MapActivity, and MyLocationOverlay make it possible to create extremely sophisticated applications without doing any custom drawing at all.

We've already used the term *widget* once or twice, without explicitly defining it. Recall that the screen is rendered by a tree of components. In the Android UI framework, these components are all subclasses of android.view.View. The views that are leaves or nearly leaves do most of the actual drawing and are, in the context of an application UI, commonly called widgets. As mentioned earlier, a widget typically implements both Controller and View functionality.

The internal nodes, sometimes called *container views*, are special components that can have other components as children. In the Android UI framework, container views are subclasses of android.view.ViewGroup, which, of course, is in turn a subclass of View. They typically do very little drawing. Instead, they are responsible for arranging their child views on the screen and keeping them arranged as the View changes shape, orientation, and so on. Doing this can be complex.

To create complex displays, you need to assemble a tree of containers for the views you want to use in your application. Example 6-1 shows an application with a view tree that is three layers deep. A vertical linear layout contains two horizontal linear layouts. Each horizontal layout, in turn, contains two widgets.

Example 6-1. A complex View tree

```
package com.oreilly.android.intro;

import android.app.Activity;
import android.graphics.Color;
import android.os.Bundle;
import android.view.Gravity;
import android.view.ViewGroup;
import android.widget.Button;
import android.widget.EditText;
import android.widget.LinearLayout;


public class AndroidDemo extends Activity {
    private LinearLayout root;

    @Override
    public void onCreate(Bundle state) {
        super.onCreate(state);

        LinearLayout.LayoutParams containerParams
            = new LinearLayout.LayoutParams(
                ViewGroup.LayoutParams.FILL_PARENT,
                ViewGroup.LayoutParams.WRAP_CONTENT,
                0.0F);

        LinearLayout.LayoutParams widgetParams
            = new LinearLayout.LayoutParams(
                ViewGroup.LayoutParams.FILL_PARENT,
                ViewGroup.LayoutParams.FILL_PARENT,
                1.0F);

        root = new LinearLayout(this);
        root.setOrientation(LinearLayout.VERTICAL);
        root.setBackgroundColor(Color.LTGRAY);
        root.setLayoutParams(containerParams);

        LinearLayout l1 = new LinearLayout(this);
        l1.setOrientation(LinearLayout.HORIZONTAL);
        l1.setBackgroundColor(Color.GRAY);
        l1.setLayoutParams(containerParams);
        root.addView(l1);

        EditText tb = new EditText(this);
        tb.setText(R.string.defaultLeftText);
```

```
            tb.setFocusable(false);
            tb.setLayoutParams(widgetParams);
            ll.addView(tb);

            tb = new EditText(this);
            tb.setText(R.string.defaultRightText);
            tb.setFocusable(false);
            tb.setLayoutParams(widgetParams);
            ll.addView(tb);

            ll = new LinearLayout(this);
            ll.setOrientation(LinearLayout.HORIZONTAL);
            ll.setBackgroundColor(Color.DKGRAY);
            ll.setLayoutParams(containerParams);
            root.addView(ll);

            Button b = new Button(this);
            b.setText(R.string.labelRed);
            b.setTextColor(Color.RED);
            b.setLayoutParams(widgetParams);
            ll.addView(b);

            b = new Button(this);
            b.setText(R.string.labelGreen);
            b.setTextColor(Color.GREEN);
            b.setLayoutParams(widgetParams);
            ll.addView(b);

            setContentView(root);
    }
}
```

Note that the code preserves a reference to the root of the view tree for later use.

This example uses three LinearLayout views. A LinearLayout, just as its name implies, is a view that displays its children in a row or column, as determined by its orientation property. The child views are displayed in the order in which they are *added* to the LinearLayout (regardless of the order in which they were *created*), in the directions common for Western readers: left to right and top to bottom. The button labeled "Green", for instance, is in the lower-right corner of this layout, because it is the second thing added to the horizontal LinearLayout view, which was, in turn, the second thing added to the root, vertical LinearLayout.

Figure 6-2 shows what the results might look like to the user. The seven views in the tree are structured as shown in Figure 6-3.

The Android Framework provides a convenient capability for separating data resources from code. This is particularly useful in building View layouts. The previous example can be replaced with the dramatically simpler code in Example 6-2 and the XML definition of the View layout in Example 6-3.

Figure 6-2. How panels appear to the viewer

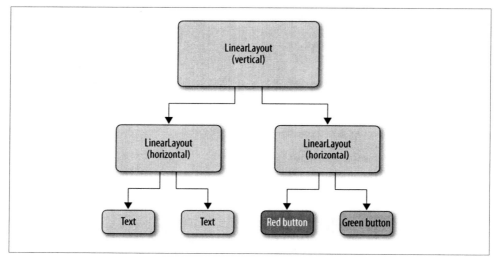

Figure 6-3. Hierarchy of panels in the View

Example 6-2. A complex View using a layout resource

```
package com.oreilly.android.intro;

import android.app.Activity;
import android.os.Bundle;


/**
 * Android UI demo program
 */
public class AndroidDemo extends Activity {
    private LinearLayout root;

    @Override public void onCreate(Bundle state) {
        super.onCreate(state);
        setContentView(R.layout.main);
        root = (LinearLayout) findViewById(R.id.root);
    }
}
```

Example 6-3. XML definition of a complex View layout resource

```xml
<LinearLayout xmlns:android="http://schemas.android.com/apk/res/android"
    android:id="@+id/root"
    android:orientation="vertical"
    android:background="@drawable/lt_gray"
    android:layout_width="match_parent"
    android:layout_height="wrap_content">

  <LinearLayout
      android:orientation="horizontal"
      android:background="@drawable/gray"
      android:layout_width="match_parent"
      android:layout_height="wrap_content">

    <EditText
        android:id="@+id/text1"
        android:text="@string/defaultLeftText"
        android:focusable="false"
        android:layout_width="match_parent"
        android:layout_height="match_parent"
        android:layout_weight="1"/>

    <EditText
        android:id="@+id/text2"
        android:text="@string/defaultRightText"
        android:focusable="false"
        android:layout_width="match_parent"
        android:layout_height="match_parent"
        android:layout_weight="1"/>
  </LinearLayout>

  <LinearLayout
      android:orientation="horizontal"
      android:background="@drawable/dk_gray"
      android:layout_width="match_parent"
      android:layout_height="wrap_content">

    <Button
        android:id="@+id/button1"
        android:text="@string/labelRed"
        android:textColor="@drawable/red"
        android:layout_width="match_parent"
        android:layout_height="match_parent"
        android:layout_weight="1"/>

    <Button
        android:id="@+id/button2"
        android:text="@string/labelGreen"
        android:textColor="@drawable/green"
        android:layout_width="match_parent"
        android:layout_height="match_parent"
        android:layout_weight="1"/>
  </LinearLayout>
</LinearLayout>
```

This version of the code, like the first one, also preserves a reference to the root of the view tree. It does this by tagging a widget in the XML layout (the root LinearLayout, in this case) with an android:id tag, and then using the findViewById method from the Activity class to recover the reference.

It is a very good idea to get into the habit of using a resource to define your view tree layout. Doing so allows you to separate the visual layout of a view from the code that brings it to life. You can tinker with the layout of a screen without recompiling. Most importantly, though, you can build your UI using tools that allow you to compose screens using a visual UI editor.

 At Google I/O 2011, the Android Tools team introduced a new layout editor that is really exciting. It can even preview animations and developer-created views; most developers should never need to look at XML, let alone inline code, for laying out views ever again.

Wiring Up the Controller

"Assembling a Graphical Interface" on page 175 demonstrated a view with two buttons. Although the buttons look nice—they even become highlighted when clicked—they aren't very useful. Clicking them doesn't actually do anything.

"The Controller" on page 173 described how the Android Framework translates external actions (screen taps, keypresses, etc.) into events that are enqueued and then passed into the application. Example 6-4 shows how to add an event handler to one of the buttons in the demo so that it does something when it is clicked.

Example 6-4. Wiring up a button

```
@Override public void onCreate(Bundle state) {
    super.onCreate(state);
    setContentView(R.layout.main);

    final EditText tb1 = (EditText) findViewById(R.id.text1);
    final EditText tb2 = (EditText) findViewById(R.id.text2);

    ((Button) findViewById(R.id.button2)).setOnClickListener(
        new Button.OnClickListener() {
            // mRand is a class data member
            @Override public void onClick(View arg0) {
                tb1.setText(String.valueOf(mRand.nextInt(200)));
                tb2.setText(String.valueOf(mRand.nextInt(200)));
            }
        }
    );
}
```

When run, this version of the application still looks a lot like Figure 6-2. Unlike the earlier example, though, in this version, every time a user clicks the button labeled "Green" the numbers in the EditText boxes change. This is illustrated in Figure 6-4.

Figure 6-4. Working button

Although simply changing numbers isn't very interesting, this small example demonstrates the standard mechanism that an application uses to respond to UI events. It is important to note that, appearances notwithstanding, this example does not violate the MVC separation of concerns! In response to the call to setText, in this implementation of OnClickListener, the EditText object updates an internal representation of the text it should display, and then calls its own invalidate method. It does not immediately draw on the screen. Very few rules in programming are absolute. The admonition to separate the Model, the View, and the Controller comes pretty close.

In the example, an instance of the Button class is wired to its behavior using a callback, as described in "Overrides and Callbacks" on page 99. Button is a subclass of View, which defines an interface named OnClickListener and a method named setOnClick Listener with which to register the listener. The OnClickListener interface defines a single method, onClick. When a Button receives an event from the framework, in addition to any other processing it might do, it examines the event to see if it qualifies as a "click." (The button in our first example would become highlighted when pressed, even before the listener was added.) If the event does qualify as a click, and if a click listener has been installed, that listener's onClick method is invoked.

The click listener is free to implement any custom behavior needed. In the example, the custom behavior creates two random numbers between 0 and 200 and puts one into each of the two text boxes. Instead of subclassing Button and overriding its event processing methods, all that is necessary to extend its behavior is to register a click listener that implements the desired behavior. Certainly a lot easier!

The click handler is especially interesting because, at the heart of the Android system—the framework event queue—there is no such thing as a click event! Instead, View event processing synthesizes the concept of a "click" from other events. If the device has a touch-sensitive screen, for instance, a single tap is considered a click. If the device has a center key in its D-pad, or an Enter key, pressing and releasing either will also register as a click. View clients need not concern themselves with what exactly a click is, or how it is generated on a particular device. They need only handle the higher-level concept, leaving the details to the framework.

A `View` can have only one `onClickListener`. Calling `setOnClickListener` a second time, on a given `View`, will remove the old listener and install the new one. On the other hand, a single listener can listen to more than one `View`. The code in Example 6-5, for instance, is part of another application that looks exactly like Example 6-2. In this version, though, pushing *either* of the buttons will update the text box.

This capability can be very convenient in an application in which several actions produce the same behavior. Do not be tempted, though, to create a single, enormous listener for all of your widgets! Your code will be easier to maintain and modify if it contains multiple smaller listeners, each implementing a single, clear behavior.

Example 6-5. Listening to multiple buttons

```
@Override public void onCreate(Bundle state) {
    super.onCreate(state);
    setContentView(R.layout.main);

    final EditText tb1 = (EditText) findViewById(R.id.text1);
    final EditText tb2 = (EditText) findViewById(R.id.text2);

    Button.OnClickListener listener = new Button.OnClickListener() {
        @Override public void onClick(View arg0) {
            tb1.setText(String.valueOf(rand.nextInt(200)));
            tb2.setText(String.valueOf(rand.nextInt(200)));
        } };

    ((Button) findViewById(R.id.button1)).setOnClickListener(listener);
    ((Button) findViewById(R.id.button2)).setOnClickListener(listener);
}
```

Listening to the Model

The Android UI framework uses the handler installation pattern pervasively. Although our earlier examples were all `Button` views, many other Android widgets define listeners. The `View` class defines several events and listeners that are ubiquitous, and which we will explore in further detail in a moment. Other classes, however, define other, specialized types of events and provide handlers for those events that are meaningful only for those classes. This is a standard idiom that allows clients to customize the behavior of a widget without having to subclass it.

This pattern is also an excellent way for your program to handle its own external, asynchronous actions. Whether responding to a change in state on a remote server or an update from a location-based service, your application can define its own events and listeners to allow its clients to react.

The examples so far have been elementary and have cut several corners. While they demonstrate connecting a View and a Controller, they have not had real Models.

(Example 6-4 actually used a `String` owned by the implementation of `EditText` as a model). To continue, we're going to have to take a brief detour to build a real, usable Model.

The following two classes shown in Example 6-6 comprise a Model that will support extensions to the demo application. They provide a facility for storing a list of objects, each of which has *x* and *y* coordinates, a color, and a size. They also provide a way to register a listener, and an interface that the listener must implement. The common Listener model underlies these examples, so they are fairly straightforward.

Example 6-6. The Dots model

```
package com.oreilly.android.intro.model;


/** A dot: the coordinates, color and size. */
public final class Dot {
    private final float x, y;
    private final int color;
    private final int diameter;

    /**
     * @param x horizontal coordinate.
     * @param y vertical coordinate.
     * @param color the color.
     * @param diameter dot diameter.
     */
    public Dot(float x, float y, int color, int diameter) {
        this.x = x;
        this.y = y;
        this.color = color;
        this.diameter = diameter;
    }

    /** @return the horizontal coordinate. */
    public float getX() { return x; }

    /** @return the vertical coordinate. */
    public float getY() { return y; }

    /** @return the color. */
    public int getColor() { return color; }

    /** @return the dot diameter. */
    public int getDiameter() { return diameter; }
}


package com.oreilly.android.intro.model;

import java.util.Collections;
import java.util.LinkedList;
import java.util.List;
```

```java
/** A list of dots. */
public class Dots {
    /** DotChangeListener. */
    public interface DotsChangeListener {
        /** @param dots the dots that changed. */
        void onDotsChange(Dots dots);
    }

    private final LinkedList<Dot> dots = new LinkedList<Dot>();
    private final List<Dot> safeDots = Collections.unmodifiableList(dots);

    private DotsChangeListener dotsChangeListener;

    /** @param l the new change listener. */
    public void setDotsChangeListener(DotsChangeListener l) {
        dotsChangeListener = l;
    }

    /** @return the most recently added dot, or null. */
    public Dot getLastDot() {
        return (dots.size() <= 0) ? null : dots.getLast();
    }

    /** @return the list of dots. */
    public List<Dot> getDots() { return safeDots; }

    /**
     * @param x dot horizontal coordinate.
     * @param y dot vertical coordinate.
     * @param color dot color.
     * @param diameter dot size.
     */
    public void addDot(float x, float y, int color, int diameter) {
        dots.add(new Dot(x, y, color, diameter));
        notifyListener();
    }

    /** Delete all the dots. */
    public void clearDots() {
        dots.clear();
        notifyListener();
    }

    private void notifyListener() {
        if (null != dotsChangeListener) {
            dotsChangeListener.onDotsChange(this);
        }
    }
}
```

In addition to using this model, the next example also introduces a library widget used to view it, the DotView. Its job is to draw the dots represented in the model, in the correct color, at the correct coordinates. The complete source for the application is on the website for this book.

Example 6-7 shows the new demo application, after adding the new Model and View.

Example 6-7. The Dots demo

```
package com.oreilly.android.intro;

import java.util.Random;

import android.app.Activity;
import android.graphics.Color;
import android.os.Bundle;
import android.view.View;
import android.widget.Button;
import android.widget.EditText;
import android.widget.LinearLayout;

import com.oreilly.android.intro.model.Dot;
import com.oreilly.android.intro.model.Dots;
import com.oreilly.android.intro.view.DotView;


/** Android UI demo program */
public class TouchMe extends Activity {
    public static final int DOT_DIAMETER = 6;

    private final Random rand = new Random();

    final Dots dotModel = new Dots();

    DotView dotView;

    /** Called when the activity is first created. */
    @Override public void onCreate(Bundle state) {
        super.onCreate(state);

        dotView = new DotView(this, dotModel);

        // install the View
        setContentView(R.layout.main);
        ((LinearLayout) findViewById(R.id.root)).addView(dotView, 0);❶

        // wire up the Controller
        ((Button) findViewById(R.id.button1)).setOnClickListener(
            new Button.OnClickListener() {❷
                @Override public void onClick(View v) {
                    makeDot(dots, dotView, Color.RED);❸
                } });
        ((Button) findViewById(R.id.button2)).setOnClickListener(
            new Button.OnClickListener() {❷
                @Override public void onClick(View v) {
                    makeDot(dots, dotView, Color.GREEN);❸
                } });
```

```
        final EditText tb1 = (EditText) findViewById(R.id.text1);
        final EditText tb2 = (EditText) findViewById(R.id.text2);
        dots.setDotsChangeListener(new Dots.DotsChangeListener() {❹
            @Override public void onDotsChange(Dots dots) {
                Dot d = dots.getLastDot();
                tb1.setText((null == d) ? "" : String.valueOf(d.getX()));
                tb2.setText((null == d) ? "" : String.valueOf(d.getY()));
                dotView.invalidate();
            } });
    }


    /**
     * @param dots the dots we're drawing
     * @param view the view in which we're drawing dots
     * @param color the color of the dot
     */
    void makeDot(Dots dots, DotView view, int color) {❺
        int pad = (DOT_DIAMETER + 2) * 2;
        dots.addDot(
            DOT_DIAMETER + (rand.nextFloat() * (view.getWidth() - pad)),
            DOT_DIAMETER + (rand.nextFloat() * (view.getHeight() - pad)),
            color,
            DOT_DIAMETER);
    }
}
```

Here are some of the highlights of the code:

❶ The new DotView is added to the top of the layout obtained from the XML definition.

❷ onClickListener callbacks are added to the "Red" and "Green" buttons. These event handlers differ from those in the previous example only in that, here, their behavior is proxied to the local method makeDot. This new method creates a single dot (item 5).

❸ A call to makeDot is made within onClick (to take place when the button is clicked).

❹ The most substantial change to the example, this is where the Model is wired to the View, using a callback to install a dotsChangeListener. When the Model changes, this new listener is called. It installs the x and y coordinates of the last dot into the left and right text boxes, respectively, and requests that the DotView redraw itself (the invalidate call).

❺ This is the definition of makeDot. This new method creates a dot, checking to make sure it is within the DotView's borders, and adds it to the model. It also allows the dot's color to be specified as a parameter.

Figure 6-5 shows what the application looks like when run.

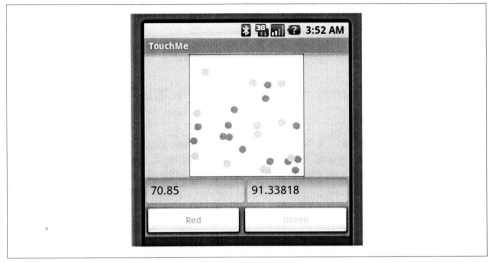

Figure 6-5. Running the Dots demo

Pushing the button labeled "Red" adds a new red dot to the `DotView`. Pushing the "Green" button adds a green one. The text fields contain the coordinates of the last dot added.

The basic structure of Example 6-2 is still recognizable, with some extensions.

Here is the chain of events that results from clicking, for instance, the "Green" button:

1. When the button is clicked, its `onClickHandler` is called.
2. This causes a call to `makeDot` with the color argument `Color.GREEN`. The `makeDot` method generates random coordinates and adds a new, green `Dot` to the Model at those coordinates.
3. When the Model is updated, it calls its `onDotsChangeListener`.
4. The listener updates the values in the text views and requests that the `DotView` be redrawn.

Listening for Touch Events

Modifying the demo application to handle taps, as you have surely guessed, is just a matter of adding a tap handler. The code in Example 6-8 extends the demo application to place a cyan dot in the `DotView` at the point at which the screen is tapped. This code would be added to the demo application (Example 6-7) at the beginning of the `onCreate` function right after the call to its parent method. Notice that, because the code that displays the *x* and *y* coordinates of the most recently added dot is wired only to the Model, it continues to work correctly, no matter how the View adds the dot.

Example 6-8. Touchable dots

```
dotView.setOnTouchListener(new View.OnTouchListener() {
    @Override public boolean onTouch(View v, MotionEvent event) {
        if (MotionEvent.ACTION_DOWN != event.getAction()) {
            return false;
        }
        dots.addDot(event.getX(), event.getY(), Color.CYAN, DOT_DIAMETER);
        return true;
    } });
```

The `MotionEvent` passed to the handler has several other properties in addition to the location of the tap that caused it. As the example indicates, it also contains the event type, one of DOWN, UP, MOVE, or CANCEL. A simple tap actually generates one DOWN and one UP event. Touching and dragging generates a DOWN event, a series of MOVE events, and a final UP event.

The gesture handling facilities provided by the `MotionEvent` are very interesting. The event contains the size of the touched area and the amount of pressure applied. That means that, on devices that support it, an application might be able to distinguish between a tap with one finger and a tap with two fingers, or between a very light brush and a firm push.

Efficiency is still important in the mobile world. A UI framework confronts the horns of a dilemma when tracking and reporting touch-screen events. Reporting too few events might make it impossible to follow motion with sufficient accuracy to do, for instance, handwriting recognition. On the other hand, reporting too many touch samples, each in its own event, could load a system unacceptably. The Android UI framework addresses this problem by bundling groups of samples together, reducing the load while still maintaining accuracy. To see all the samples associated with an event, use the history facility implemented with the methods `getHistoricalX`, `getHistoricalY`, and so on.

Example 6-9 shows how to use the history facility. It extends the demo program to track a user's gestures when he touches the screen. The framework delivers sampled *x* and *y* coordinates to the `onTouch` method of an object installed as the `OnTouch Listener` for the `DotView`. The method displays a cyan dot for each sample.

Example 6-9. Tracking motion

```
private static final class TrackingTouchListener
    implements View.OnTouchListener
{
    private final Dots mDots;

    TrackingTouchListener(Dots dots) { mDots = dots; }

    @Override public boolean onTouch(View v, MotionEvent evt) {
        switch (evt.getAction()) {
            case MotionEvent.ACTION_DOWN:
                break;
```

```
case MotionEvent.ACTION_MOVE:
    for (int i = 0, n = evt.getHistorySize(); i < n; i++) {
        addDot(
            mDots,
            evt.getHistoricalX(i),
            evt.getHistoricalY(i),
            evt.getHistoricalPressure(i),
            evt.getHistoricalSize(i));
    }
    break;

default:
    return false;
}

addDot(
    mDots,
    evt.getX(),
    evt.getY(),
    evt.getPressure(),
    evt.getSize());

return true;
}

private void addDot(Dots dots, float x, float y, float p, float s) {
    dots.addDot(
        x,
        y,
        Color.CYAN,
        (int) ((p * s * Dot.DIAMETER) + 1));
}
}
```

Figure 6-6 shows what the extended version of the application might look like after a few clicks and drags.

The implementation uses the size and pressure values from a given location's sample to determine the diameter of the dot drawn there. Unfortunately, the Android emulator does not emulate touch pressure and size, so all the dots have the same diameter. Size and pressure values are normalized across devices, as floating-point values between 0.0 and 1.0. It is possible, however, depending on the calibration of the screen, that either value may actually be larger than 1.0. The emulator always reports the event pressure and size as zero, their minimum value.

The loop that handles ACTION_MOVE events processes batched historical events. When touch samples change more quickly than the framework can deliver them, the framework bundles them into a single event. The MotionEvent method getHistorySize returns the number of samples in the batch, and the various getHistory methods get the subevent specifics.

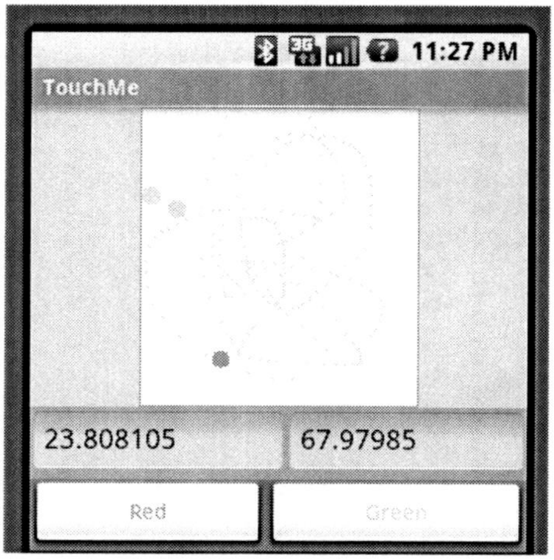

Figure 6-6. Running the Dots demo for an extended time

Devices with trackballs also generate MotionEvents when the trackball is moved. These events are similar to those generated by taps on a touch-sensitive screen, but they are handled differently. Trackball MotionEvents are passed into the View through a call to dispatchTrackballEvent, not to dispatchTouchEvent, which delivered taps. While dispatchTrackballEvent does pass the event to onTrackballEvent, it does not first pass the event to a listener! Trackball-generated MotionEvents are not visible through the normal tap handling machinery. To respond to them, a widget may have to subclass View and override the onTrackballEvent method.

MotionEvents generated by the trackball actually are available through a callback mechanism. If they are not *consumed* (to be defined shortly) in onTrackballEvent, they are converted into D-pad key events. This makes sense when you consider that devices typically have either a D-pad or a trackball, but not both. Without this conversion, it wouldn't be possible to generate D-pad events on a device with only a trackball. Of course, it also implies that an application that handles trackball events by overriding onTrackballEvent must do so carefully, lest it break the translation.

After the translation, trackball movement is visible to the applications as a series of D-pad keystrokes.

Multiple Pointers and Gestures

Many devices support tracking more than one pointer simultaneously, a feature sometimes called "multitouch." When users touch the screen in more than one place, the track of each contact is reported separately. These separate tracks can be used to discern complex gestures with specific meanings, such as scroll, zoom, next page, and so on.

All of the event methods introduced earlier, that return the information about a MOVE event—getX, getY, getHistoricalX, getHistoricalY, and so on—support multitouch by taking an additional argument that indicates the specific track to which the call refers. In addition to getX(), for instance, there is also the method getX(int pointer Index). The pointer index allows the caller access to each of the several separate tracks, and the method getPointerCount returns the number of separate tracks recorded in the event. Unfortunately, the index of a particular track within an event does not stay constant. In other words, if the user is touching the screen with her thumb and index finger, the track for the thumb may show up in successive motion events first at index 0, then at index 1, then at index 0. To follow a single track through several events, it is necessary to use the track *ID*, instead of its index. To do this, use the methods getPoin terId and findPointerIndex to convert between the ID and the index.

The code in Example 6-10 extends the onTouch method from the preceding example to follow multiple tracks.

Example 6-10. Tracking motion

```
@Override public boolean onTouch(View v, MotionEvent evt) {
    int n;
    int idx;
    int action = evt.getAction();
    switch (action & MotionEvent.ACTION_MASK) {
        case MotionEvent.ACTION_DOWN:
        case MotionEvent.ACTION_POINTER_DOWN:
            idx = (action & MotionEvent.ACTION_POINTER_INDEX_MASK)
                >> MotionEvent.ACTION_POINTER_INDEX_SHIFT;
            tracks.add(Integer.valueOf(evt.getPointerId(idx)));
            break;

        case MotionEvent.ACTION_POINTER_UP:
            idx = (action & MotionEvent.ACTION_POINTER_INDEX_MASK)
                >> MotionEvent.ACTION_POINTER_INDEX_SHIFT;
            tracks.remove(Integer.valueOf(evt.getPointerId(idx)));
            break;

        case MotionEvent.ACTION_MOVE:
            n = evt.getHistorySize();
            for (Integer i: tracks) {
                idx = evt.findPointerIndex(i.intValue());
                for (int j = 0; j < n; j++) {
                    addDot(
                        mDots,
                        evt.getHistoricalX(idx, j),
                        evt.getHistoricalY(idx, j),
                        evt.getHistoricalPressure(idx, j),
                        evt.getHistoricalSize(idx, j));
                }
            }
            break;

        default:
```

```
            return false;
    }

    for (Integer i: tracks) {
        idx = evt.findPointerIndex(i.intValue());
        addDot(
            mDots,
            evt.getX(idx),
            evt.getY(idx),
            evt.getPressure(idx),
            evt.getSize(idx));
    }

    return true;
}
```

There are several things to consider in this code. First of all, notice that the case statement now switches, not on the event's action but on a masked version of that action. This kind of bit banging is definitely a tad archaic. It's necessary to keep the calls backward-compatible. To ignore multiple tracks, don't do the masking and be sure to include a default case in the switch.

Next, notice the two new cases in the switch: MotionEvent.ACTION_POINTER_DOWN and MotionEvent.ACTION_POINTER_UP. In this simple example they are used to indicate the beginning and end of a new track. Because a contiguous track is identified by its ID, the code simply adds a new ID, when a new track begins, and removes it when it ends.

Finally, notice that if there is historical information in an event, there are the same number of historical records for all tracks.

In the very special but fairly common case where multiple traces comprise a gesture with a specific meaning (maybe pinch-zoom in or out), the Android libraries hint at support in the form of gesture detectors. The official documentation acknowledges that the two provided gesture detectors are meant more as a suggestion for implementations than as a complete solution. Indeed, the two existing detectors, GestureDetector and ScaleGestureDetector, somewhat haphazardly support a few common gestures: single-tap, double-tap, long-touch, and pinch.

In general, using a gesture detector requires creating an instance, registering a listener, adding the detector to your onTouch handler, and passing it each new event. It will notify its listener when a gesture occurs. The details of the behaviors of the detectors—including the types of the listeners—are specific to the particular detector.

Listening for Key Events

Handling keystroke input across multiple platforms can be very tricky. Some devices have many more keys than others, some require triple-tapping for character input, and so on. This is a great example of something that should be left to the framework—EditText or one of its subclasses—whenever possible.

To extend a widget's `KeyEvent` handling, use the `View` method `setOnKeyListener` to install an `OnKeyListener`. The listener will be called with multiple `KeyEvents` for each user keystroke, one for each action type: `DOWN`, `UP`, and `MULTIPLE`. The action types `DOWN` and `UP` indicate a key was pressed or released, just as they did for the `MotionEvent` class. A key action of `MULTIPLE` indicates that a key is being held down (autorepeating). The `KeyEvent` method `getRepeatCount` gives the number of keystrokes that a `MULTIPLE` event represents.

Example 6-11 shows a sample key handler. When added to the demo program, it causes dots to be added to the display, at randomly chosen coordinates, when keys are pressed and released. A magenta dot is added when the space bar is pressed and released, a yellow dot when the Enter key is pressed and released, and a blue dot when any other key is pressed and released. Though it works as described, this key handler is naive. It has problems that will come to light shortly!

Example 6-11. Handling keys

```
dotView.setOnKeyListener(new OnKeyListener() {
    @Override public boolean onKey(View v, int keyCode, KeyEvent event) {
        if (KeyEvent.ACTION_UP != event.getAction()) {
            int color = Color.BLUE;
            switch (keyCode) {
                case KeyEvent.KEYCODE_SPACE:
                    color = Color.MAGENTA;
                    break;
                case KeyEvent.KEYCODE_ENTER:
                    color = Color.YELLOW;
                    break;
                default: ;
            }

            makeDot(dots, dotView, color);
        }

        return true;
    } });
```

Choosing an Event Handler

You've probably noticed that the `on...` methods of all the listeners introduced thus far—including `onKey`—return a `boolean` value. This is a pattern for listeners that allows them to control subsequent event processing by their caller.

When a Controller event is handed to a widget, the framework code in the widget dispatches it, depending on its type, to an appropriate method: `onKeyDown`, `onTouchEvent`, and so on. These methods, either in `View` or in one of its subclasses, implement the widget's behavior. As described earlier, though, the framework first offers the event to an appropriate listener (`onTouchListener`, `onKeyListener`, etc.) if one exists. The listener's return value determines whether the event is then dispatched to the `View` methods.

If the listener returns `false`, the event is dispatched to the `View` methods as though the handler did not exist. If, on the other hand, a listener returns `true`, the event is said to have been *consumed*. The `View` aborts any further processing for it. The `View` methods are never called and have no opportunity to process or respond to the event. As far as the `View` methods are concerned, it is as though the event did not exist.

There are, then, three ways that an event might be processed:

There is no listener
> The event is dispatched to the `View` methods for normal handling. A widget implementation may, of course, override these methods.

A listener exists and returns `true`
> Listener event handling completely replaces normal widget event handling. The event is never dispatched to the `View`.

A listener exists and returns `false`
> The event is processed by the listener and then by the `View`. After listener event handling is completed the event is dispatched to the `View` for normal handling.

Consider, for instance, what would happen if the key listener from Example 6-11 were added to an `EditText` widget. Because the `onKey` method nearly always returns `true`, the framework will abort any further `KeyEvent` processing as soon as the method returns. That would prevent the `EditText` key handling mechanism from ever seeing the key events, and no text would ever appear in the text box. That is probably not the intended behavior!

If the `onKey` method instead returns `false` for some key events, the framework will dispatch those events to the `EditText` widget for continued processing. The `EditText` mechanism will see the events, and the associated characters will be appended to the `EditText` box, as expected. Example 6-12 shows an extension of Example 6-11 that, in addition to adding new dots to the model, also filters the characters passed to the hypothetical `EditText` box. This is still not a complete solution: it still hides important keystrokes such as the menu key. It does allow numeric characters to be processed normally.

Example 6-12. Extended key handling

```
new OnKeyListener() {
    @Override public boolean onKey(View v, int keyCode, KeyEvent event) {
        if (KeyEvent.ACTION_UP != event.getAction()) {
            int color = Color.BLUE;
            switch (keyCode) {
                case KeyEvent.KEYCODE_SPACE:
                    color = Color.MAGENTA;
                    break;
                case KeyEvent.KEYCODE_ENTER:
                    color = Color.YELLOW;
                    break;
                default: ;
            }
```

```
                makeDot(dotModel, dotView, color);
        }

        return (keyCode < KeyEvent.KEYCODE_0)
            || (keyCode > KeyEvent.KEYCODE_9);
    }
}
```

If your application needs to implement entirely new ways of handling events—something, for instance, that cannot be implemented reasonably by augmenting behavior and filtering, using an onKeyHandler—you will have to understand and override View key event handling. To sketch the process: events are dispatched to the View through the DispatchKeyEvent method. DispatchKeyEvent implements the behavior described previously, offering the event to the onKeyHandler first, and then, if the handler returns false, to the View methods implementing the KeyEvent.Callback interface: onKeyDown, onKeyUp, and onKeyMultiple.

Advanced Wiring: Focus and Threading

As demonstrated in Example 6-7 and "Listening for Touch Events" on page 187, Motio nEvents are delivered to the widget whose bounding rectangle contains the coordinates of the touch that generated them. It isn't quite so obvious how to determine which widget should receive a KeyEvent. To do this, the Android UI framework, like most other UI frameworks, supports the concept of selection, or *focus*.

To accept focus, a widget's focusable attribute must be set to true. This can be done using either an XML layout attribute (the EditText views in Example 6-3 have their focusable attribute set to false) or the setFocusable method, as shown in the first line of Example 6-11. A user changes which View has focus using D-pad keys or by tapping the screen when touch is supported.

When a widget is in focus, it usually renders itself with some kind of highlighting to provide feedback that it is the current target of keystrokes. For instance, when an EditText widget is in focus, it is drawn both highlighted and with a cursor at the text insert position.

To receive notification when a View enters or leaves focus, install an OnFocusChange Listener. Example 6-13 shows the listener needed to add a focus-related feature to the demo program. It causes a randomly positioned black dot to be added to the DotView automatically, at random intervals, whenever it is in focus.

Example 6-13. Handling focus

```
dotView.setOnFocusChangeListener(new OnFocusChangeListener() {
    @Override public void onFocusChange(View v, boolean hasFocus) {
        if (!hasFocus && (null != dotGenerator)) {
            dotGenerator.done();
            dotGenerator = null;
        }
```

```
            else if (hasFocus && (null == dotGenerator)) {
                dotGenerator = new DotGenerator(dots, dotView, Color.BLACK);
                new Thread(dotGenerator).start();
            }
    } });
```

There should be few surprises in the `OnFocusChangeListener`. When the `DotView` comes into focus, it creates the `DotGenerator` and spawns a thread to run it. When the widget leaves focus, the `DotGenerator` is stopped, and freed. The new data member `dot Generator` (the declaration of which is not shown in the example) is non-null only when the `DotView` is in focus. There is another important and powerful tool in the implementation of `DotGenerator`, and we'll return to it in a moment.

Focus is transferred to a particular widget by calling its `View` method, `requestFocus`. When `requestFocus` is called for a new target widget, the request is passed up the tree, parent by parent, to the tree root. The root remembers which widget is in focus and passes subsequent key events to it directly.

This is exactly how the UI framework changes focus to a new widget in response to D-pad keystrokes. The framework identifies the widget that will next be in focus and calls that widget's `requestFocus` method. This causes the previously focused widget to lose focus and the target to gain it.

The process of identifying the widget that will gain focus is complicated. To do it, the navigation algorithm has to perform some tricky calculations that may depend on the locations of every other widget on the screen!

Consider, for instance, what happens when the right D-pad button is pressed and the framework attempts to transfer focus to the widget immediately to the right of the one that is currently in focus. To a human looking at the screen, it may be completely obvious which widget that is. In the view tree, however, it is not nearly so obvious. The target widget may be at another level in the tree and several branches away. Identifying it depends on the exact dimensions of widgets in yet other, distant parts of the tree. Fortunately, despite the considerable complexity, the Android UI framework implementation usually just works as expected.

When it does not, there are four properties—set either by application method or by XML attribute—that can be used to force the desired focus navigation behavior. They are `nextFocusDown`, `nextFocusLeft`, `nextFocusRight`, and `nextFocusUp`. Setting one of these properties with a reference to a specific widget will ensure that D-pad navigation transfers focus directly to that widget, when navigating in the respective direction.

Another complexity of the focus mechanism is the distinction that the Android UI framework makes between D-pad focus and touch focus, for devices with touch-sensitive screens. To understand why this is necessary, recall that, on a screen that does not accept touch input, the only way to push a button is to focus on it, using D-pad navigation, and then to use the center D-pad key to generate a click. On a screen that does accept touch events, however, there is no reason, ever, to focus on a button.

Tapping the button clicks it, regardless of which widget happens to be in focus at the time. Even on a touch-sensitive screen, however, it is still necessary to be able to focus on a widget that accepts keystrokes—an EditText widget, for instance—to identify it as the target for subsequent key events. To handle both kinds of focus correctly, you will have to look into View handling of FOCUSABLE_IN_TOUCH_MODE, and the View methods isFocusableInTouchMode and isInTouchMode.

In an application with multiple windows, there is at least one more twist in the focus mechanism. It is possible for a window to lose focus without notifying the currently in-focus widget, in that window, that its focus has been lost. This makes sense when you think about it. If the out-of-focus window is brought back to the top, the widget that was in focus in that window will again be in focus, with no other action.

Consider entering a friend's phone number into an address book application. Suppose you momentarily switch back to a phone application to refresh your memory of the last few digits of her phone number. You'd be annoyed if, on returning to the address book, you had to again focus on the EditText box in which you'd been typing. You expect the state to be just as you left it.

On the other hand, this behavior can have surprising side effects. In particular, the implementation of the auto-dot feature presented in Example 6-13 continues to add dots to the DotView even when it is hidden by another window! If a background task should run only when a particular widget is visible, that task must be cleaned up when the widget loses focus, when the Window loses focus, and when the Activity is paused or stopped.

Most of the implementation of the focus mechanism is in the ViewGroup class, in methods such as requestFocus and requestChildFocus. Should it be necessary to implement an entirely new focus mechanism, you'll need to look carefully at these methods and override them appropriately.

Leaving the subject of focus and returning to the implementation of the newly added auto-dot feature, Example 6-14 shows the implementation of DotGenerator.

Example 6-14. Handling threads

```
private final class DotGenerator implements Runnable {
    final Dots dots;
    final DotView view;
    final int color;

    private final Handler hdlr = new Handler();①
    private final Runnable makeDots = new Runnable() {②
        public void run() { makeDot(dots, view, color); }
    };

    private volatile boolean done;

    // Runs on the main thread
    DotGenerator(Dots dots, DotView view, int color) {③
```

```
        this.dots = dots;
        this.view = view;
        this.color = color;
    }

    // Runs on the main thread
    public void done() { done = true; }

    // Runs on a different thread!
    public void run() {
        while (!done) {
            try { Thread.sleep(1000); }
            catch (InterruptedException e) { }
            hdlr.post(makeDots);❹
        }
    }
}
```

Here are some of the highlights of the code:

❶ An android.os.Handler object is created.

❷ A new thread that will run makeDot in item 4 is created.

❸ DotGenerator is run on the main thread.

❹ makeDot is run from the Handler created in item 1.

A naive implementation of DotGenerator would simply call makeDot directly within its run block. Doing this wouldn't be safe, however, unless makeDot was thread-safe—and the Dots and DotView classes, too, for that matter. This would be tricky to get correct and hard to maintain. In fact, the Android UI framework actually forbids access to a View from multiple threads. Running the naive implementation would cause the application to fail with a RuntimeException similar to this:

```
11-30 02:42:37.471: ERROR/AndroidRuntime(162):
android.view.ViewRoot$CalledFromWrongThreadException:
Only the original thread that created a view hierarchy can touch its views.
```

We met this problem and one solution, the Handler, in "Threads in an Android Process" on page 116. To get around the restriction, DotGenerator creates a Handler object within its constructor. A Handler object is associated with the thread on which it is created and provides safe, concurrent access to the canonical event queue for that thread.

Because DotGenerator creates a Handler during its own construction, the Handler is associated with the main thread. Now DotGenerator can use the Handler to enqueue from another thread a Runnable that calls makeDot from the UI thread. It turns out, as you might guess, that the canonical event queue to which the Handler points is exactly the same one that is used by the UI framework. The call to makeDot is dequeued and dispatched, like any other UI event, in its proper order. In this case, that causes its

Runnable to be run. `makeDot` is called from the main thread, and the UI stays single-threaded.

It is worth reiterating that this is an essential pattern for coding with the Android UI framework. Whenever processing that is started on behalf of the user might take more than a few milliseconds to complete, doing that processing on the main thread might cause the entire UI to become sluggish or, worse, to freeze for a long time. If the main application thread does not service its event queue for a couple of seconds, the Android OS will kill the application for being unresponsive! The `Fragment`, `AsyncTask`, and `Handler` classes all allow a developer to avoid this danger by delegating slow or long-running tasks to other threads so that the main thread can continue to service the UI. This example demonstrates the lowest level of the three choices: using a `Thread` with a `Handler` that periodically enqueues updates for the UI.

The demo application takes a slight shortcut here. It enqueues the creation of a new dot and its addition to the dot Model on the main thread. A more complex application might pass a main-thread `Handler` to the model, on creation, and provide a way for the UI to get a model-thread `Handler` from the model. The main thread would receive update events enqueued for it by the model, using its main-thread `Handler`. The model, running in its own thread, would use the `Looper` class to dequeue and dispatch incoming messages from the UI. Before architecting anything that complex, though, you should consider using a `Fragment`, a `Service`, or a `ContentProvider` (see Chapter 13).

Passing events between the UI and long-running threads in this way dramatically reduces the constraints required to maintain thread safety. In particular, recall from "Threads in an Android Process" on page 116 that if an enqueueing thread retains no references to an enqueued object, or if that object is immutable, no additional synchronization is necessary.

The Menu and the Action Bar

The final aspects of application control we'll cover in this chapter are the menu and the action bar. Example 6-15 shows how to implement a simple menu by overriding two `Activity` methods.

Example 6-15. Implementing a menu

```
@Override public boolean onCreateOptionsMenu(Menu menu) {
    getMenuInflater().inflate(R.menu.simple_menu, menu);
    return true;
}

@Override public boolean onOptionsItemSelected(MenuItem item) {
    switch (item.getItemId()) {
        case R.id.menu_clear:
            dotModel.clearDots();
            return true;
```

```
            default:
                return super.onOptionsItemSelected(item);
        }
    }
}
```

When this code is added to the `TouchMe` class, clicking the device's Menu key will cause the application to present a menu, as shown in Figure 6-7.

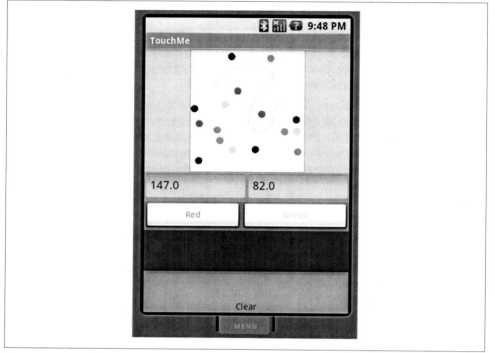

Figure 6-7. A simple menu

Clicking the Enter key, or tapping the menu item again, will clear the dot view.

As of Honeycomb (Android 3.0), Google has deprecated the dedicated menu button in favor of the *Action Bar*, discussed in more detail in Chapter 9. For the moment, though, it is important to know that the code shown previously is forward-compatible.

Google is encouraging developers to move away from the concept of a menu entirely. Instead, it encourages creating UIs in which objects are manipulated directly. The Action Bar provides a consistent interface for handling global behaviors that is adaptable to many screen sizes.

When the Dots application is updated to target Ice Cream Sandwich (`targetSdk Version="14"` in the application manifest), and run on a post-Honeycomb version of Android, this same code will cause the display of an action button in the Action Bar.

This button, the trashcan icon in the upper right of the display as shown in Figure 6-8, is the application's "Clear" action button. As in the previous version, tapping it will clear the dot view.

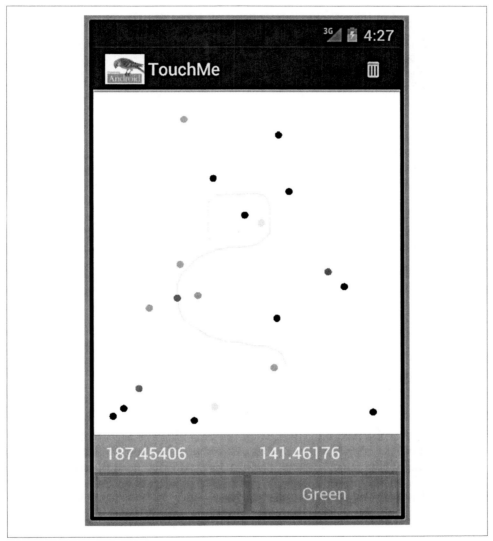

Figure 6-8. An action button

Interestingly, if you run this application on a pre-Honeycomb version of Android, you will find that while the added menu item works most of the time, it does not work when the DotView is in focus. Can you guess why?

If you guessed that the problem is caused by the `OnKeyListener` installed in the `Dot View`, you are correct! As implemented in Example 6-16, the listener swallows the menu key event by returning `true` when it is clicked. This prevents the standard `View` processing of the menu key keystroke. To make the menu work, the `OnKeyListener` needs a new case.

Example 6-16. Improved key handling

```
switch (keyCode) {
    case KeyEvent.KEYCODE_MENU:
        return false;
    // ...
```

The Android UI framework also supports contextual menus, through the `Context Menu` class. This type of menu appears in response to a long click in a widget that supports it. The code required to add a contextual menu to an application is entirely analogous to that for the options menu shown earlier, except that the respective methods are `onCreateContextMenu` and `onContextItemSelected`. One additional call is required. To support contextual menus, a widget must be assigned a `View.OnCreateContext MenuListener` by calling the `setOnCreateContextMenuListener` method on its `View` class. Fortunately, because `Activity` implements the `View.OnCreateContextMenuListener` interface, a common idiom looks like the code shown in Example 6-17.

Example 6-17. Installing a ContextMenuListener

```
findViewById(R.id.ctxtMenuView).setOnCreateContextMenuListener(this);
```

Simply overriding the default, empty `Activity` implementations of the contextual menu's listener methods will give your application a contextual menu.

View Debugging and Optimization

The Android SDK provides several tools to help you understand the behavior of your view tree. The first of these is a tool that was called `layoutopt` until recently. In more recent versions of the Android Tools, all of the capabilities of `layoutopt`—and many more as well—have been incorporated in a new tool called `Lint`. Whereas `layoutopt` was exclusively a command-line tool, `Lint` can be used either from the command line or, more conveniently, from Eclipse. It performs a number of ad hoc checks on the XML files that comprise an application's layout.

Anyone who has worked with Android for any length of time will be familiar with the very annoying consequences of having an XML resource (a layout or a menu) that is syntactically correct but contains semantic errors. If *aapt*, the tool that processes the *res* directory, fails to correctly build the *gen* directory, half the files in the project will suddenly fail to compile (because the class `R` is missing). If you are using Eclipse, for instance, your entire project will suddenly turn red with errors all over the place—

except, unfortunately, the location of the actual problem. The Lint tool may help to identify problems such as this.

In addition, Lint is useful for identifying potential problems in project resources. It performs a number of sanity checks and checks for best practices that grow with each release of the Android developer tools. In Eclipse, Lint is run whenever resource files are changed, and the problems that it finds appear both as standard Eclipse warnings and in a dedicated Lint Warnings window.

Sometimes Lint will identify issues that you may not even have known were issues. It will sometimes take research and refactoring to resolve them. While the tool is still being tuned and will occasionally complain about things that are working, it may well highlight potential problems. It is always worthwhile to understand the issue and verify that it is not significant.

Because Lint is a static analyzer that sifts through source code, there are classes of problems that it cannot find. It cannot, for instance, find widgets that are dynamically added to a view. Fortunately, the Android toolkit also includes a tool that can analyze the actual view tree of a running application: Hierarchy Viewer. This is a multipurpose tool with multiple modes. Although parts of it were integrated into Eclipse in the past, those views no longer work in recent versions of the toolkit. Hierarchy Viewer must be used from the command line. It is in the SDK folder *tools*, and it works best with version 9 (Gingerbread) or later of the Android OS.

Hierarchy Viewer works like a debugger to analyze a running application. It must be able to find a connected device or emulator. If the tools connect to a running device, a button at the top provides the ability to load the view hierarchy. Upon pushing that button, a screen similar to Figure 6-9 appears.

This window presents a lot of information and the toolkit documentation describes its use in some detail. The most important features, though, are the ability to see the entire view tree at once.

As you will see in Chapter 8, the cost of drawing a tree of views explodes as the tree gets deeper. Part of optimizing an application is keeping its view tree as shallow as possible. From this window it is easy to see how deep the tree for a particular window is and to determine how to reduce that depth.

The three colored dots give insight into the time taken by a view in each of the three phases of rendering: measure, layout, and draw. A view with a green dot is faster than the median time for views in the window. A view with a yellow dot takes more than the median time, and the red dot is awarded to the views with slowest time for the entire tree. This rough comparison among the members of a view tree can point out trouble spots in one of the drawing phases and may point you in the right direction for fixing a sluggish application.

This chapter showed how the Android Controller interface works overall, and gave you the tools to manipulate its basic components: windows, views, and events. The fol-

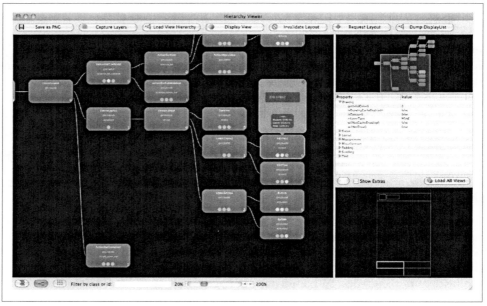

Figure 6-9. An Action Button

lowing several chapters expand on these ideas and provide further detail into how to build your user interface.

## CHAPTER 7

Fragments and Multiplatform Support

Now that you have written some Android code you know that `Activity`, `View`, and the layout and widget subclasses of `View` are among the most important classes in Android. Typically, an Android user interface is built from widget views organized in layouts: a `ListView` in a `LinearLayout`, for instance. A single hierarchy of view objects gets loaded from a resource (or created by code) when an `Activity` is started. It is initialized and displayed on the device screen.

For small screens, this is fine: users move from screen to screen to access different parts of a program's UI, and the `Activity` class (Android's concept of a task) supports a back stack that enables quick and intuitive traversal through the strictly tree-structured interface. This changes completely, however, when the UI is spread over the surface of a larger tablet screen. Some parts of the screen remain constant over longer durations than others. Some parts of the screen determine the contents of other parts. A card-stack metaphor just doesn't cut it.

It is entirely possible to implement UIs in which some parts of the screen change in response to activities in another part, simply by showing and hiding views. Android's developers decided, however, that they needed more than just convention to encourage great large-screen UIs with a consistent feel and behavior. To facilitate this new kind of interaction, they introduced a new feature based on the `Fragment` class, as part of the Android 3.0 SDK (API 11, Honeycomb).

A `Fragment` object is somewhere between a `View` and an `Activity`. Like a `View`, it can be added to a `ViewGroup` or be part of a layout. It isn't a subclass of `View`, however, and can only be added to a `ViewGroup` using a `FragmentTransaction`. Like an `Activity`, a `Fragment` has a life cycle and implements both the `ComponentCallbacks` and `View.OnCreateCon textMenuListener` interfaces. Unlike an `Activity`, though, a `Fragment` is not a `Context`, and its life cycle is dependent on that of the `Activity` to which it belongs.

Fragments constitute a major change in the Android API. To ease transition to the new API, Google provides a compatibility library that supports the feature in versions as far back as Android version 1.6 (API Level 4, Donut). We'll have a look at backward compatibility in a moment. First, though, let's look at fragments in their native environment, in systems running Android 3.0 and later.

Creating a Fragment

Like any other view object, a fragment can either be part of the XML definition of a layout, or be added to a view programmatically. In a layout, a fragment looks like this:

```
<LinearLayout
    xmlns:android="http://schemas.android.com/apk/res/android"
    android:orientation="horizontal"
    android:layout_width="fill_parent"
    android:layout_height="fill_parent"
    >

    <fragment
        class="com.oreilly.demo.android.contactviewer.DateTime"
        android:id="@+id/date_time"
        android:layout_width="fill_parent"
        android:layout_height="fill_parent"
        />

</LinearLayout>
```

An activity would use this layout in the normal way:

```
@Override
public void onCreate(Bundle state) {
    super.onCreate(state);
    setContentView(R.layout.main);
}
```

This should all look pretty familiar by now. The only thing that is new is the fragment tag in *main.xml*. The tag uses a class attribute to specify the fully qualified name of a class that implements the fragment. There are a couple of constraints on a fragment implementation class, which in this case is com.oreilly.demo.android.contactviewer.DateTime:

- A class with the exact name must exist and be visible from the application.
- The named class must be a subclass of Fragment.

Although it would be quite possible to verify both of these things statically, the current Android tools do not do so. You'll have to check both constraints by hand.

The Android framework creates a new instance of the named class when the layout is inflated. The implications of this can be surprising. To begin, it means the class must have a no-args constructor. This is the constructor that Java supplies by default. The Android Developer Documentation recommends—strongly, in fact—against defining any constructors at all in subclasses of Fragment because a newly created Fragment object may not be in a consistent state at creation. The documentation recommends that fragment initialization be postponed until later in the fragment life cycle.

No matter how you use the fragment elsewhere in the application, if you use it in a layout, the inflation process must be able to create it, without supplying any initialization parameters. As a corollary, a fragment that is created in this way must be prepared to do something sensible even without initialization. A fragment, for instance, that displays content from a passed URL must handle the case where the URL—and therefore the content—is empty.

Here, then, is a very simple fragment:

```
public class DateTime extends Fragment {
    private String time;

    public void onCreate(Bundle state) {
        super.onCreate(state);
        if (null == time) {
            time = new SimpleDateFormat("d MMM yyyy HH:mm:ss")
                .format(new Date());
        }
    }

    @Override
    public View onCreateView(
        LayoutInflater inflater,
        ViewGroup container,
        Bundle b)
    {
        View view = inflater.inflate(
            R.layout.date_time,
            container,
            false);  //!!! this is important

        ((TextView) view.findViewById(R.id.last_view_time))
            .setText(time);

        return view;
    }
}
```

This code demonstrates several essential points. First, just the existence of an onCreate life cycle method should bring to mind the Activity class and its life cycle methods. Although the life cycle of a Fragment is not identical to that of an Activity, it does have many of the same methods. As for an activity, a fragment's onCreate method is called when the fragment is initialized. This is a great place to do the initialization that was postponed from the constructor. The example guarantees that the value of the variable time, the thing the fragment will display, is correctly initialized.

Fragments have a few additional life cycle methods, including onCreateView, also used in this example. The onCreateView method is called when a fragment's view is initialized, in contrast with onCreate, which is called when the fragment itself is initialized. Notice that the fragment creates the view it manages by using the passed LayoutInflater to instantiate the view described in the layout R.layout.date_time. It is a simple view—just a pair of TextViews in a RelativeLayout. It is defined in its own file, *layout/ date_time.xml* (not shown here), much as was the main layout shown earlier.

Also notice (and this is a bit of a gotcha) that this is not the standard, two-argument version of the inflate method, which we've seen previously. There is a third parameter, the boolean false, in this call. It is important! The inflater must have access to container, the view that will eventually be the newly created shard's parent. It needs the parent view to handle layout correctly. Suppose, for instance, that container happens to be a RelativeLayout that specifies the position of the newly created shard using a layout_toRightOf directive.

On the other hand, the fragment framework owns and manages the view that is returned by the onCreateView method. The code in onCreateView must not attach the view hierarchy to its container, as it normally would during inflation. That third argument is the flag that tells the inflater that the fragment framework is in control and that it must not attach the view hierarchy to the container.

Once the fragment's view shard is created, its findViewById method can be used to find other widgets nested within. The example uses it to locate the TextView that will display the time, and to set its value from the variable time, initialized in onCreate.

When run, this application looks like Figure 7-1.

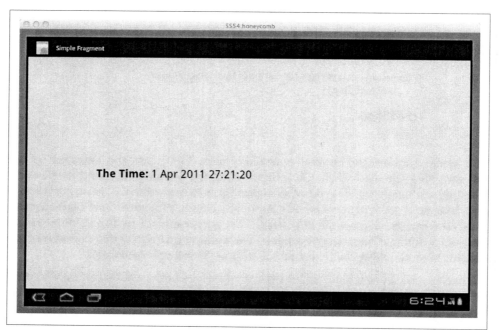

Figure 7-1. A simple fragment

Fragment Life Cycle

If you run this application as it is described so far, and rotate the screen while it is running, you'll notice that the displayed date changes each time the screen is rotated. Rotating the screen causes an application to be destroyed and re-created. This version of the example application loses all its state each time that happens.

 This is a great way to test your application. Pressing Ctrl-F11 rotates the emulator 90 degrees. In response to this rotation, Android steps an application through nearly its entire life cycle. With this one key-chord, you get coverage for most of your code!

In this trivial example application, losing state is not particularly significant. A real application, however, must not lose state. It would be annoying if, for instance, rotating your phone to landscape mode while looking at some web page caused the browser to return to a home page.

The application can be modified to keep its state with two small changes. First, override the `DateTime` fragment's life cycle method `onSaveInstanceState` to preserve its state. Second, change the `onCreate` method to recover the preserved state. As it did with activities (see "The Activity Life Cycle" on page 83), the Android framework provides a `Bundle` object to the former method when it suspends the fragment. It provides the same bundle to `onCreate` when reconstructing a clone of a suspended fragment.

Here are the two affected methods, changed to support state preservation:

```
@Override
public void onCreate(Bundle state) {
    super.onCreate(state);

    if (null != state) { time = state.getString(TAG_DATE_TIME); }

    if (null == time) {
        time = new SimpleDateFormat("d MMM yyyy HH:mm:ss")
            .format(new Date());
    }
}

@Override
public void onSaveInstanceState(Bundle state) {
    super.onSaveInstanceState(state);
    state.putString(TAG_DATE_TIME, time);
}
```

That's it. Running this version of the program through its life cycle will no longer cause it to lose its state. Notice, incidentally, that because the variable `time` (and, in general, any fragment state) is initialized in the `onCreate` method, it cannot be declared `final`. This reduces the value of using a constructor to set up the fragment state and is in keeping with the recommendation that `Fragment` subclasses not have any explicit constructors at all.

The Android Developer Documentation (*http://developer.android.com/guide/topics/fundamentals/fragments.html#Creating*) describes the complete fragment life cycle. One other life cycle callback method, though, deserves special notice: `onPause`. The `onPause` method is important for the same reason that it is important in an activity. For an application to play nicely in the Android environment, it should not be doing things (using the CPU, running down the battery, etc.) when it is not visible. The Android environment arranges to call a fragment's `onPause` method whenever the fragment becomes invisible. In this method, a fragment should release any resources it might be holding, terminate any long-running processes that it has started, and so on. The `onResume` method should reconstruct resources and restart appropriately.

The Fragment Manager

As mentioned earlier, fragments can be created programmatically as well as in layouts. Programmatic manipulation of fragments is accomplished using an instance of the class `FragmentManager` obtained from an `Activity` using its `getFragmentManager` method. The fragment manager handles three important groups of operations: fragment tagging and location, transactions, and the back stack. Let's extend the example program to investigate each in turn.

Adapting the example application to use programmatically created fragments requires only two changes: one in the layout *main.xml* and the other in the `SimpleFragment` activity. In the layout, the fragment element is replaced with a nearly identical `FrameLayout`:

```
<LinearLayout
    xmlns:android="http://schemas.android.com/apk/res/android"
    android:orientation="horizontal"
    android:layout_width="fill_parent"
    android:layout_height="fill_parent"
    >

    <FrameLayout
        android:id="@+id/date_time"
        android:layout_width="fill_parent"
        android:layout_height="fill_parent"
        android:background="@color/green"
        />

</LinearLayout>
```

`SimpleFragment` will still use this layout, just as it did before. Now, though, the layout does not automatically create a new fragment. Instead, the following code does that:

```
@Override
public void onCreate(Bundle state) {
    super.onCreate(state);
```

```
        setContentView(R.layout.main);

        FragmentManager fragMgr = getFragmentManager();

        FragmentTransaction xact = fragMgr.beginTransaction();
        if (null == fragMgr.findFragmentByTag(FRAG1_TAG)) {
            xact.add(R.id.date_time, new DateTime(), FRAG1_TAG);
        }
        xact.commit();
    }
```

This new code introduces the fragment transaction manager but no new application features. When run, this version of the example behaves exactly as did the original, layout-based version.

The important feature in this code snippet is the use of tagging. It is entirely possible that an activity's onCreate will be called while it is still associated with a previously created fragment. Simply adding a new fragment whenever onCreate method is called will leak fragments. To prevent that, the example code makes use of the fragment manager's tagging and location features.

The third argument to the add method is a unique tag, assigned to the fragment as it is added to the activity. Once the tag has been created, the fragment manager method findFragmentByTag can be used to recover the exact, single fragment that was added with the given tag. The example checks to see if the tagged fragment already exists before it creates a new fragment instance. If there is no such fragment, it creates it. If the fragment already exists, no action is necessary. This guarantees that there is only a single fragment in a given role, and prevents fragment leaking.

Tagging and location can be used for other purposes as well. Whenever an activity needs to communicate some change of state to an attached fragment, it will probably do so by tagging that fragment in advance, and then using the FragmentManager to look up the tag to obtain a reference to the fragment at the appropriate time.

Fragment Transactions

In addition to using fragment tagging, the new code also alludes to fragment transactions. Let's extend the application once again to demonstrate their value.

Before we take on transactions, though, we need to take a brief detour. We noted earlier that the Android Developer Documentation recommends that fragment subclasses not have explicit constructors. So, how does an external object supply initialization state for a new fragment? The Fragment class supports two methods, setArguments and get Arguments, that provide this capability. Respectively, they allow an external caller— probably the fragment creator—to store a Bundle in the fragment and the fragment to recover that bundle at some later time.

This elaborate combination of a new instance of the fragment, a `Bundle`, and a call to `setArguments` functions very much like a constructor. It makes sense, then, to combine them into a static factory method in the `Fragment` object, like this:

```
public static DateTime newInstance(Date time) {
    Bundle init = new Bundle();
    init.putString(
        DateTime.TAG_DATE_TIME,
        getDateTimeString(time));

    DateTime frag = new DateTime();
    frag.setArguments(init);
    return frag;
}

private static String getDateTimeString(Date time) {
    return new SimpleDateFormat("d MMM yyyy HH:mm:ss")
        .format(time);
}
```

Now we can use the static factory method from `SimpleFragment`'s `onCreate` method to create a new instance of the fragment with its argument bundle correctly initialized. This code is nearly identical to the preceding version, except that it now uses `Date Time`'s static factory method and passes it an argument:

```
@Override
public void onCreate(Bundle state) {
    super.onCreate(state);

    setContentView(R.layout.main);

    FragmentManager fragMgr = getFragmentManager();

    FragmentTransaction xact = fragMgr.beginTransaction();
    if (null == fragMgr.findFragmentByTag(FRAG1_TAG)) {
        xact.add(
            R.id.date_time,
            DateTime.newInstance(new Date()),
            FRAG1_TAG);
    }
    xact.commit();
}
```

Finally, the fragment `onCreate` method retrieves the initialization data from the passed argument bundle, unless there is state from a previous incarnation:

```
@Override
public void onCreate(Bundle state) {
    super.onCreate(state);

    if (null == state) { state = getArguments(); }

    if (null != state) { time = state.getString(TAG_DATE_TIME); }
```

```
    if (null == time) { time = getDateTimeString(new Date()); }
}
```

Once again, the application as modified to this point still behaves exactly as did the original. The implementation is quite different, though, and much more flexible. In particular, we now have a fragment that can be initialized externally and can be used to demonstrate transactions.

The idea of a fragment transaction is, as the name implies, that all changes take place as a single, atomic action. To demonstrate this, let's make one final extension to the example program: let's add the ability to create pairs of fragments.

Here's the new layout:

```
<LinearLayout
    xmlns:android="http://schemas.android.com/apk/res/android"
    android:orientation="vertical"
    android:layout_width="fill_parent"
    android:layout_height="fill_parent"
    >

    <Button
        android:id="@+id/new_fragments"
        android:layout_width="fill_parent"
        android:layout_height="0dp"
        android:layout_weight="1"
        android:textSize="24dp"
        android:text="@string/doit"
        />

    <FrameLayout
        android:id="@+id/date_time2"
        android:layout_width="fill_parent"
        android:layout_height="0dp"
        android:layout_weight="2"
        android:background="@color/blue"
        />

    <FrameLayout
        android:id="@+id/date_time"
        android:layout_width="fill_parent"
        android:layout_height="0dp"
        android:layout_weight="2"
        android:background="@color/green"
        />

</LinearLayout>
```

Here are the corresponding additions to the onCreate method in SimpleFragment:

```
public void onCreate(Bundle state) {
    super.onCreate(state);

    setContentView(R.layout.main);

    ((Button) findViewById(R.id.new_fragments))
```

```
        .setOnClickListener(
            new Button.OnClickListener() {
                @Override
                public void onClick(View v) { update(); }
            });

    Date time = new Date();

    FragmentManager fragMgr = getFragmentManager();

    FragmentTransaction xact = fragMgr.beginTransaction();
    if (null == fragMgr.findFragmentByTag(FRAG1_TAG)) {
        xact.add(
            R.id.date_time,
            DateTime.newInstance(time),
            FRAG1_TAG);
    }

    if (null == fragMgr.findFragmentByTag(FRAG2_TAG)) {
        xact.add(
            R.id.date_time2,
            DateTime.newInstance(time),
            FRAG2_TAG);
    }

    xact.commit();
}
```

Finally, the example application does something different. When run, it looks like Figure 7-2.

Both fragments display the exact same date and time because a single value is passed to both. Neither visiting other applications and returning to the demo nor rotating the display will cause this application to lose its state. It's pretty solid. So let's give the button an implementation. Here it is:

Example 7-1. Replacing a fragment

```
void update() {
    Date time = new Date();

    FragmentTransaction xact
        = getFragmentManager().beginTransaction();

    xact.replace(
        R.id.date_time,
        DateTime.newInstance(time),
        FRAG1_TAG);

    xact.replace(
        R.id.date_time2,
        DateTime.newInstance(time),
        FRAG2_TAG);

    xact.addToBackStack(null);
```

```
xact.setTransition(FragmentTransaction.TRANSIT_FRAGMENT_OPEN);

    xact.commit();
}
```

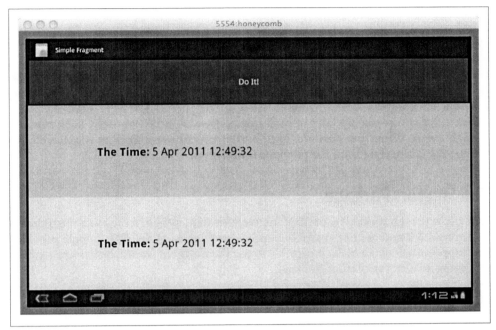

Figure 7-2. Fragment transactions

This method actually makes use of the atomicity of fragment transactions. It looks a lot like the fragment initialization code in `SimpleFragment`'s `onCreate` method. Instead of using the transaction to add new fragment instances, however, it replaces the current fragments. The call to `commit` at the end of the method causes both of the new fragments to become visible simultaneously. The times in the top and bottom views will always be in sync.

 A fragment created in a layout (using an XML fragment tag) must never be replaced with a dynamically created fragment. Although is it pretty hard to tell just by looking at them, the life cycle of one is much different from that of the other. There's no reason you can't use both in your application, but never replace one with the other. Attempting to use `setContentView`, for instance, with a layout that has had a layout fragment replaced with one that was programmatically created will cause bugs that can be difficult to find and fix. A frequent symptom of this kind of problem is an `IllegalStateException` with the message "Fragment did not create a view."

This brings us to the last essential feature of fragments, the back stack. If you run several activities in sequence, you can return to them in reverse order using the back button. This behavior also applies to fragment transactions.

If you run this application, the display will look something like Figure 7-2. When you push the button at the top of the display, the top and bottom fragments will update simultaneously. Better yet, though, if you push the back button (the left-facing arrow icon in the lower-right corner of the display), you will see, in reverse order, each update you generated by pushing the Do It! button. For instance, if both fragments display the time "5 Apr 2011 12:49:32" and you push the Do It! button, the display might be updated so that both regions show the date/time as "5 Apr 2011 13:02:43". If you now push the back button, both fragments will again display "5 Apr 2011 12:49:32". The entire transaction—the updates of both fragments—is pushed onto the back stack as a single event. When you push the back button, an entire transaction is removed, revealing the entire state from the previous transaction.

The Support Package

One of the most important aspects of fragments is that, although they were introduced in Android 3.0 and are not available in previous releases of the API, Google provides the Support Package to make it possible to use the fragment feature on devices that are still using an older version of Android.

The Support Package has limitations. An application that runs using the Support Package requires the Support Package, even when running on an Android 3.0 system. When choosing an implementation strategy for the Support Package, Google faced a conundrum. Even if it had been possible to implement the Support Package so that an application ported transparently, without change, from Android 3.0 to Android 2.0, there would have been a problem. The Support Package must be included, as a library, as part of each application that uses it. If the Support Package defined classes with names that are identical to those in Android 3.0, an application that contained the Support Package library would, without some serious class loader trickery, define classes that collided with Android base classes.

Instead, the Support Package uses a different package name, `android.support.v4`, in which to define the compatibility features. For this reason, a program developed for Android 3.0 will need code changes to use the Support Package. You will need to make, at least, the following changes:

- Copy the Support Package library to your project. Create a directory named *lib* at the top level of your project and copy *android-support-v4.jar* from the Android SDK folder *extras/android/compatibility/v4/* into it.

- Add the Support Package to your project build path. In Eclipse, select the library in the Package Explorer (you may have to refresh the project to see it: press F5 or left-click→Refresh). Once it is selected, you should be able to left-click→Build Path→Add to Build Path.

As a shortcut for these two steps you can—from the Package Explorer, in the context of your application—left-click→Android Tools→Add Compatibility Library...

- Change your project build target from Android 3.0 to Android 2.0.1 (Properties→Android). This will cause many errors to appear.

- Some imports that refer to *android.app* will have to be updated to refer to *android.support.v4.app*. Presuming your program had no errors before changing its build target, you need only find broken imports and update their base package.

- All the activities in the application that use fragments must be updated to the sub-class `FragmentActivity` instead of `Activity`.

- Change all calls to `getFragmentManager` into calls to `getSupportFragmentManager`.

- Fix any remaining errors and test your program.

Fragments and Layout

The preceding section described how to get a project that is designed to use fragments to compile on pre-Honeycomb versions of Android. For most applications, however, that's only the beginning. The mere fact that an application compiles for Froyo in no way guarantees that it looks good on a Froyo device. Actually, a guarantee of a nice UI is pretty hard to get under any circumstances. This section, though, will describe some of the issues and suggest a couple of ways to resolve them.

To be blunt, there's bad news here. An application that, during its lifetime, might be run on a 1080i large-screen television, in the back seat of a family automobile, and on a 12-inch tablet, all in landscape orientation, and also on a phone in portrait orientation, simply cannot have a single UI. The only way it will look great on each of those devices is if its UI is actually designed with each in mind. The customization necessary to port a UI to the next device may be as small as a couple of tweaks to graphics and fonts. It may, on the other hand, require significant changes to the UI workflow.

The simplest way to adapt a UI to multiple devices is to use a configuration qualifier. A configuration qualifier is simply a special suffix added to the name of a directory in the application resource directory tree. It allows an application to contain multiple versions of a resource, each appropriate to a specific context.

Consider, for instance, an activity with a screen that is described in a single layout resource, `main.xml`. This layout is referenced from code using the constant `R.lay out.main` and is defined in the project source in the single file *.../res/layout/main.xml*.

Using configuration qualifiers, the single constant, `R.layout.main`, might actually have multiple definitions, one in *.../res/layout-land/main.xml* and the other in *.../res/layout-port/main.xml*. The Android system, at runtime, resolves the single constant to either the landscape or the portrait version, according to the current orientation of the device display.

There are configuration qualifiers for screen orientation, pixel density, aspect ratio, and absolute size. There are others for language and region, docking mode, and night/day display. While it is unlikely that it would ever be necessary, it is possible that a single resource constant could have thousands of variants, one for each of the possible combinations of qualifier dimensions.

Configuration qualifiers don't make it easy to deal with a variety of contexts; they just make it possible. The Eclipse developer tool does have minimal support for qualifiers. The second page of the wizard that creates a new resource file (File→ New→Other→Android XML Values File; Next button, after the new resource file has been named) lists configuration qualifiers and allows adding as many or as few as are appropriate.

Configuration qualifiers are of particular interest to UIs that use fragments, because they allow natural adaptation between landscape and portrait orientations. For Western readers viewing a device in landscape orientation, the natural arrangement for a typical fragment UI puts context on the left side of the screen and details in a fragment to the right, as shown in Figure 7-3.

Figure 7-3. Typical fragment landscape layout

In portrait orientation, obviously this won't work at all. It is a simple matter, however, to create portrait and landscape variants of the layout, using configuration qualifiers, and to change the orientation of the LinearLayout that holds the two fragments from horizontal to vertical. Figure 7-4 demonstrates that, with a little tweaking, the UI can look pretty good again.

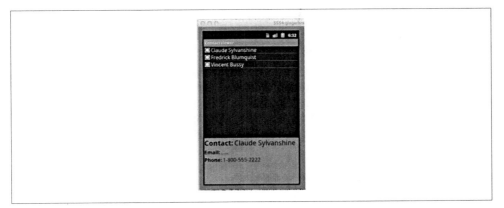

Figure 7-4. Fragments in a portrait layout

This still presumes that the screen has enough space so that it makes sense to divide a single screen into multiple regions. Remember that fragments are a way to effectively use large screens and are not a generally applicable improvement in UI design. Although some phones today have screens that are big enough to support fragments, there are lots of devices that cannot. On these devices you will want to smoothly revert from a new, fragment-oriented UI to Android's original, deck-of-cards UI.

There are several ways to select among UI styles. One possibility is to maintain multiple distinct versions of your application and to distinguish them in the Android Market using *market filters* in the manifest. For example, the manifest for the version customized for a small screen might include something like this:

```
<supports-screens
          android:largeScreens="false"
          android:xlargeScreens="false" />
```

The manifest for the version customized for large screens might instead look like this:

```
<supports-screens
          android:smallScreens="false"
          android:normalScreens="false"
          android:largeScreens="true"
          android:xlargeScreens="true" />
```

This idea really makes sense only if there are reasons other than screen size for distinguishing application versions. If, for instance, a version of the application is intended for use in a particular environment—perhaps the version targeted for use in an automobile has been extended to monitor gas consumption—and that environment includes a screen with specific dimensions, using the Market to select UI style might be effective.

It might occasionally work, but using market filters to match a UI style to a device is asking for trouble. Even a cursory look at the documentation for the market filter attributes that distinguish among screen sizes shows that they are in transition. As of API version 13 the ...Screens attributes used in the earlier examples have been replaced with the android:requiresSmallestWidthDp attribute. Unfortunately, the Market does not yet filter on this new attribute.

There is a standard idiom for selecting between fragment- and card-stack–based UIs at runtime, by using configuration qualifiers in a clever way. Consider the layout for the fragment-based UI introduced in Figure 7-3. This application is a simple Contacts viewer: clicking on the name of a contact in the lefthand list view shows details for that contact in the fragment on the right. The layout looks something like this:

```
<LinearLayout
        xmlns:android="http://schemas.android.com/apk/res/android"
        android:orientation="horizontal"
        android:layout_width="fill_parent"
        android:layout_height="fill_parent"
        >

        <ListView
            android:id="@+id/contacts"
            android:layout_width="fill_parent"
            android:layout_height="0dp"
            android:layout_weight="1"
        />

        <FrameLayout
            android:id="@+id/contact_detail"
            android:layout_width="fill_parent"
            android:layout_height="0dp"
            android:layout_weight="2"
            android:background="@color/blue"
        />

</LinearLayout>
```

We've already seen how configuration qualifiers can be used to create multiple versions of this layout in a single application. In the preceding example, we added a second, similar layout optimized for display in portrait mode and used the configuration qualifiers to tell the Android runtime when to use which.

The trick for reverting to the stack-of-cards UI style is to create a new layout that doesn't have the fragment component at all, like this:

```
<LinearLayout
        xmlns:android="http://schemas.android.com/apk/res/android"
        android:orientation="horizontal"
        android:layout_width="fill_parent"
        android:layout_height="fill_parent"
        >

        <ListView
            android:id="@+id/contacts"
            android:layout_width="fill_parent"
            android:layout_height="0dp"
            android:layout_weight="1"
```

```
                    />
    </LinearLayout>
```

All that remains is to modify the code so that it checks, before creating a fragment, to be sure that there is a place for it. If there is no place to put the fragment, it reverts to a stack-based UI.

```
    public void onCreate(Bundle state) {
        super.onCreate(state);

        setContentView(R.layout.main);

        final boolean useFrag
            = null != findViewById(R.id.contact_detail);

        if (useFrag) { installFragment(); }

        contacts = (ListView) findViewById(R.id.contacts);
        setAdapter(contacts);
        contacts.setOnItemClickListener(
            new AdapterView.OnItemClickListener() {
                @Override public void onItemClick(
                    AdapterView<?> parent,
                    View view,
                    int position,
                    long id)
            {
                    if (useFrag) { stackFragment(/*...*/); }
                    else { stackActivity(/*...*/); }
            } });
    }
```

The methods `stackFragment` and `stackActivity` implement the fragment and stack-of-cards UI styles, respectively. The `stackFragment` method uses the transaction manager to replace the current fragment, as shown in Example 7-1. The `stackActivity` method, on the other hand, launches a new activity in the standard way, using a new `Intent`. Abstracting the behavior of the contact details into a single class, used from both UI classes, `ContactDetailsActivity` and `ContactDetailsFragment`, is usually relatively straightforward.

There is a second way to select between fragment- and card-stack–based UIs at runtime: use the Activity method `startActivityFromFragment`. This method intercepts any attempt by a fragment to launch an intent.

To use this technique in our sample program, we need a slightly different strategy. The lefthand pane, the list view, will be a fragment, regardless of the UI style. It will *always* attempt to launch an intent, to display details. If the application is on a screen small enough to require the stack-of-cards UI style, this intent will launch the details activity. If, on the other hand, the application has space to use the fragment UI style, the root activity simply intercepts the launch attempt and instead displays a `Contact DetailsFragment`. The code looks very similar. Here are the layouts, card-stack and fragment, respectively. The first definition will be only in the directory *res/layout-small* (content qualifier "small") and the second will be in the layout directories with other qualifiers ("large," etc.).

```
<LinearLayout
    xmlns:android="http://schemas.android.com/apk/res/android"
    android:orientation="vertical"
    android:layout_width="fill_parent"
    android:layout_height="fill_parent"
    >

    <fragment
        class="com.oreilly.demo.android.contactviewer.ContactsFragment"
        android:id="@+id/contacts"
        android:layout_width="fill_parent"
        android:layout_height="fill_parent"
        />

</LinearLayout>

<LinearLayout
    xmlns:android="http://schemas.android.com/apk/res/android"
    android:orientation="horizontal"
    android:layout_width="fill_parent"
    android:layout_height="fill_parent"
    >

    <fragment
        class="com.oreilly.demo.android.contactviewer.ContactsFragment"
        android:id="@+id/contacts"
        android:layout_width="0dp"
        android:layout_height="fill_parent"
        android:layout_weight="1"
        />

    <FrameLayout
        android:id="@+id/contact_detail"
        android:layout_width="0dp"
        android:layout_height="fill_parent"
        android:layout_weight="2"
        android:background="@color/blue"
        />

</LinearLayout>
```

Here is the code for the root activity. The ContactsFragment will be inflated automatically from R.layout.main. StartActivityFromFragment decides whether or not to launch the DetailFragment based on whether or not there is a layout item to which to attach it. If there is none, it starts a new activity.

```
public class ContactViewer extends FragmentActivity {
    private static final String FRAG_TAG
        = ContactViewer.class.getCanonicalName() + ".fragment";

    private boolean useFrag;
```

```java
    @Override
    public void onCreate(Bundle state) {
        super.onCreate(state);

        setContentView(R.layout.main);

        useFrag = null != findViewById(R.id.contact_detail);

        if (useFrag) { installDetailsFragment(); }
    }

    @Override
    public void startActivityFromFragment(
        Fragment fragment,
        Intent intent,
        int requestCode)
    {
        if (!useFrag) { startActivity(intent); }
        else if (fragment instanceof ContactsFragment) {
            launchDetailFragment(intent.getExtras());
        }
    }

    // methods elided...
}
```

Finally, this is the ContactFragment. When there is a click in the list view, it is always forwarded as an intent. The root activity may choose to forward the intent or, instead, to represent the request as a new fragment.

```java
public class ContactsFragment extends ListFragment {

    @Override
    public View onCreateView(
        LayoutInflater inflater,
        ViewGroup container,
        Bundle b)
    {
        View view = super.onCreateView(inflater, container, b);

        installListAdapter(getActivity());

        return view;
    }

    @Override
    public void onListItemClick(ListView l, View v, int pos, long row){
        Cursor cursor = (Cursor) getListAdapter().getItem(pos);

        String id = cursor.getString(
            cursor.getColumnIndex(BaseColumns._ID));
        String name = cursor.getString(
            cursor.getColumnIndex(Contacts.DISPLAY_NAME));
```

```java
        Intent intent = new Intent();
        intent.setClass(getActivity(), ContactDetailActivity.class);
        intent.putExtra(ContactDetails.TAG_ID, id);
        intent.putExtra(ContactDetails.TAG_CONTACT, name);
        startActivity(intent);
    }

    // methods elided...
}
```

## CHAPTER 8

Drawing 2D and 3D Graphics

The Android menagerie of widgets and the tools for assembling them are convenient and powerful, and cover a broad variety of needs. What happens, though, when none of the existing widgets offer what you need? Maybe your application needs to represent playing cards, phases of the moon, or the power diverted to the main thrusters of a rocket ship. In that case, you'll have to know how to roll your own.

This chapter is an overview of graphics and animation on Android. It's directed at programmers with some background in graphics, and goes into quite a bit of depth about ways to twist and turn the display. You will definitely need to supplement the chapter with Android documentation, particularly because the framework is still changing. A major change in implementation, around the time of Honeycomb, for instance, takes better advantage of hardware acceleration. It also substantially affects the ways in which an application can optimize its drawing. Still, the techniques here will help you dazzle your users.

Rolling Your Own Widgets

As mentioned earlier, *widget* is just a convenient term for a subclass of `android.view.View`, typically a leaf node in the view tree, that implements both a view and its controller. Internal nodes in the view tree, though they may contain complex code, tend to have simpler user interactions. The term *widget*, although informal, is usually reserved for discussing the workhorse parts of the user interface: those that have the information and the behavior users care about.

You can accomplish a lot without creating a new widget. `TextView`, `Button`, and `Date Picker` are all examples of widgets provided by the Android UI toolkit. In this book, we have already constructed several applications consisting entirely of existing pre-packaged widgets or simple subclasses of existing widgets. The code in those applications just built trees of views, laying them out in code or through layout resources in XML files.

The nontrivial MicroJobs application, which we'll cover in Chapter 9, has a view that contains a list of names corresponding to locations on a map. As additional locations are added to the map, new name-displaying widgets are added dynamically to the list. Even this dynamically changing layout is just a use of preexisting widgets; it is not creating new ones. The techniques in MicroJobs are, figuratively, adding or removing boxes from a tree like the one illustrated in Figure 6-3 of Chapter 6.

A more complex widget—one that can nest other widgets—will have to subclass `View Group`, which is itself a subclass of `View`. A very complex widget, perhaps one that is used as an interface tool used in several places (even by multiple applications), might be an entire package of classes, only one of which is a descendant of `View`.

This chapter shows you how to roll your own widget, which involves looking under the `View` hood. It is about graphics, and therefore about the View part of the Model-View-Controller (MVC) pattern. As mentioned earlier, widgets also contain Controller code—which is good design because it keeps together all the code relevant to a behavior and its representation on the screen. This chapter discusses only the implementation of the View. The implementation of the Controller was discussed in Chapter 6.

Concentrating on graphics, then, we can break the tasks of this chapter into two essential parts: finding space on the screen and drawing in that space. The first task is known as *layout*. A leaf widget can assert its space needs by defining an `onMeasure` method that the Android UI framework will call at the right time. The second task, actually rendering the widget, is handled by the widget's `onDraw` method.

Layout

Most of the heavy lifting in the Android framework layout mechanism is implemented by *container views*. A container view is one that contains other views. It is an internal node in the view tree and is the subclasses of `ViewGroup`. The framework toolkit provides a variety of sophisticated container views that offer powerful and adaptable strategies for arranging a screen. `LinearLayout` and `RelativeLayout`, to name some common ones, are container views that are both relatively easy to use and not trivial to reimplement correctly. Because convenient, powerful container views already exist, you will probably never have to implement one or the layout algorithm discussed here. Understanding how it works, though—how the Android UI framework manages the layout process—will help you build correct, robust widgets.

Example 8-1 shows what is perhaps the simplest working widget one could design. If added to some `Activity`'s view tree, this widget will fill in the space allocated to it with the color cyan. Not very interesting, but before we move on to create anything more complex, let's look carefully at how this example fulfills the two basic tasks of layout and drawing. We'll start with the layout process; we'll describe drawing later in "Canvas Drawing" on page 231.

Example 8-1. A trivial widget

```java
public class TrivialWidget extends View {

    public TrivialWidget(Context context) {
        super(context);
        setMinimumWidth(100);
        setMinimumHeight(20);
    }

    @Override
    protected void onMeasure(int widthMeasureSpec, int heightMeasureSpec) {
        setMeasuredDimension(
            getSuggestedMinimumWidth(),
            getSuggestedMinimumHeight());
    }

    @Override
    protected void onDraw(Canvas canvas) {
        canvas.drawColor(Color.CYAN);
    }
}
```

Dynamic layout is necessary because the space requirements for widgets change dynamically. Suppose, for instance, that a widget in a GPS-enabled application displays the name of the city in which you are currently driving. As you go from "Ely" to "Post Mills," the widget receives notification of the change in location. When it prepares to redraw the city name, though, it notices that it doesn't have enough room for the whole name of the new town. It needs to ask the display to redraw the screen in a way that gives it more space, if that is possible.

Layout can be a surprisingly complex task and very difficult to get right. It is probably not very hard to make a particular leaf widget look right on a single device. It can be very tricky, on the other hand, to get a widget that must arrange children to look right on multiple devices, even when the dimensions of the screen change.

The layout process is initiated when the `requestLayout` method is invoked on some view in the view tree. Typically, a widget calls `requestLayout` on itself, when it needs more space. The method could be invoked, though, from any place in an application, to indicate that some view in the current screen no longer has the right amount of room.

The `requestLayout` method causes the Android UI framework to enqueue an event on the UI event queue. When the event is processed, in order, the framework gives every container view an opportunity to ask each of its child widgets how much space it would like for drawing. The process is separated into two phases: measuring child views and then arranging them in their new positions. All views must implement the first phase, but the second is necessary only in the implementations of container views that must manage the layout of child views.

Measurement

The goal of the measurement phase is to provide each view with an opportunity to dynamically request the space it would like, ideally, for drawing. The UI framework starts the process by invoking the measure method of the view at the root of the view tree. Starting there, each container view asks each of its children how much space it would prefer. The call is propagated to all descendants, depth first, so that every child gets a chance to compute its size before its parent. The parent computes its own size based on the sizes of its children and reports that to its parent, and so on, up the tree.

In "Assembling a Graphical Interface" on page 175, for instance, the topmost Linear Layout asks each nested LinearLayout widget for its preferred dimensions. They, in turn, ask the Button or EditText views they contain for theirs. Each child reports its desired size to its parent. The parents then add up the sizes of the children, along with any padding they insert themselves, and report the total to the topmost LinearLayout.

Because the framework must guarantee certain behaviors for all views during this process, the View method measure is final and cannot be overridden. Instead, measure calls onMeasure, which widgets may override to claim their space.

The arguments to the onMeasure method describe the space the parent is willing to make available: a width specification and a height specification, measured in pixels. The framework assumes that no view will ever be smaller than 0 or bigger than 2^{30} pixels in size and, therefore, uses the high-order bits of the passed int parameter to encode the *measurement specification mode*. It is as though onMeasure were actually called with four arguments: the width specification mode, the width, the height specification mode, and the height. Do not be tempted to do your own bit shifting to separate the pairs of arguments! Instead, use the static methods MeasureSpec.getMode and MeasureSpec.get Size.

The specification modes describe how the container view wants the child to interpret the associated size. There are three of them:

MeasureSpec.EXACTLY
> The calling container view has already determined the exact size of the child view.

MeasureSpec.AT_MOST
> The calling container view has set a maximum size for this dimension, but the child is free to request less.

MeasureSpec.UNSPECIFIED
> The calling container view has not imposed any limits on the child; the child may request anything it chooses.

A widget is always responsible for telling its parent in the view tree how much space it needs. It does this by calling setMeasuredDimensions to set its height and width properties. The parent can later retrieve these properties through the methods getMeasured Height and getMeasuredWidth. If your implementation overrides onMeasure but does not call setMeasuredDimensions, the measure method will throw IllegalStateException instead of completing normally.

The default implementation of onMeasure, inherited from View, calls setMeasured Dimensions with one of two values in each direction. If the parent specifies Measure Spec.UNSPECIFIED, the child calls setMeasuredDimensions with the default size of the view: the value supplied by either getSuggestedMinimumWidth or getSugges tedMinimumHeight. If, instead, the parent specifies either of the other two modes, the default implementation uses the size offered by the parent. This is a very reasonable strategy and allows a typical widget implementation to handle the measurement phase completely, without complex calculation, simply by using the values returned by get SuggestedMinimumWidth and getSuggestedMinimumHeight.

Your widget may not actually get the space it requests. Consider a view that is 100 pixels wide and that has three children. It is probably obvious how the parent should arrange its children if the sum of the pixel widths requested by the children is 100 or less. If, however, each child requests 50 pixels, the parent container view is not going to be able to satisfy them all.

A container view has complete control of how it arranges its children. It might, in the circumstances just described, decide to be "fair" and allocate 33 pixels to each child. It might, just as easily, decide to allocate 50 pixels to the leftmost child and 25 to each of the other two. In fact, it might decide to give one of the children the entire 100 pixels and nothing at all to the others. Whatever its method, though, in the end the parent determines a size and location for the bounding rectangle for each child.

Another example of a container view's control of the space allocated to a widget comes from the example widget in Example 8-1. The example demonstrates a minimal strategy that always requests the amount of space it prefers, regardless of what it is offered (unlike the default implementation). This strategy is handy to remember for widgets that will be added to toolkit containers, notably LinearLayout, that implement *gravity*. Gravity is a property that some views use to specify the alignment of their sub-elements. You may be surprised, the first time you use one of these containers, to find that, by default, only the first of your custom widgets gets drawn! You can fix this either by using the setGravity method to change the property to Gravity.FILL, or by making your widgets insistent about the amount of space they request.

It is also important to note that a container view may call a child's measure method several times during a single measurement phase. As part of its implementation of onMeasure, a clever container view, attempting to lay out a horizontal row of widgets, might, for instance, call each child widget's measure method with mode MEASURE_SPEC.UNSPECIFIED and a width of 0 to find out what size the widget would prefer. Once it has collected the preferred widths for each of its children, it could compare the sum to the actual width available (which was specified in its parent's call to its measure method). Now it might call each child widget's measure method again, this time with the mode MeasureSpec.AT_MOST and a width that is an appropriate proportion of the space actually available. Because `measure` may be called multiple times, an implementation of `onMeasure` must be idempotent and must not change the application state.

 An action is said to be "idempotent" if the effect of performing it once is the same as the effect of performing it multiple times. For instance, the statement x = 3 is idempotent because no matter how many times you do it, x always ends up as 3. The statement x = x + 1, however, is not idempotent because the value of x depends on how many times the statement is executed.

A container view's implementation of `onMeasure` is likely to be fairly complex. `View Group`, the superclass of all container views, does not supply a default implementation. Each Android UI framework container view has its own. If you contemplate implementing a container view, you might consider basing it on one of them. If, instead, you implement measurement from scratch, you are still likely to need to call `measure` for each child and should consider using the `ViewGroup` helper methods: `measureChild`, `measureChildren`, and `measureChildWithMargins`.

At the conclusion of the measurement phase, a container view, like any other widget, must report the space it needs by calling `setMeasuredDimensions`.

Arrangement

Once all the container views in a view tree have had a chance to negotiate the sizes of each of their children, the framework begins the second phase of layout, which consists of arranging the children. Again, unless you implement your own container view you will probably never have to implement your own arrangement code. This section describes the underlying process so that you can better understand how it might affect your widgets. The default method, implemented in `View`, will work for typical leaf widgets, as demonstrated by Example 8-1.

Because a view's `onMeasure` method might be called several times, the framework must use a different method to signal that the measurement phase is complete and that container views must fix the final locations of their children. Like the measurement phase, the arrangement phase is implemented with two methods. The framework invokes a final method, `layout`, at the top of the view tree. The `layout` method performs processing common to all views and then invokes `onLayout`, which custom widgets override to implement their own behaviors. A custom implementation of `onLayout` must, at least, calculate the bounding rectangle that it will supply to each child when it is drawn and, in turn, invoke the `layout` method for each child (because that child might, in turn, be a parent to other widgets). This process can be complex. If your widget needs to arrange child views, you might consider basing it on an existing container, such as `Linear Layout` or `RelativeLayout`.

It is worth reiterating that a widget is not guaranteed to receive the space it requests. It must be prepared to draw itself in whatever space is actually allocated to it. If it attempts to draw outside the space allocated to it by its parent, the drawing will be clipped by the clip rectangle (discussed later in this chapter). To exert fine control—to exactly fill the space allocated to it, for instance—a widget must either implement onLayout and record the dimensions of the allocated space, or inspect the clip rectangle of the Canvas that is the parameter to onDraw.

Canvas Drawing

Now that we've explored how widgets allocate the space on the screen in which they draw themselves, we can turn to coding some widgets that actually do some drawing.

The Android UI framework handles drawing in a way that should seem familiar, now that you've read about measurement and arrangement. When some part of the application determines that the current screen drawing is stale because some state has changed, it calls the View method invalidate. This call causes a redraw event to be added to the event queue.

When, eventually, that event is processed, it causes the framework to call the draw method at the top of the view tree. This time the call is propagated preorder, each view drawing itself before it calls its children. This means that leaf views are drawn after their parents, which are, in turn, drawn after their parents. Views that are lower in the tree appear to be drawn on top of those nearer the root of the tree. This is sometimes called the "painter's algorithm."

The View draw method calls onDraw, which each subclass overrides to implement its custom rendering. When your widget's onDraw method is called, it must render itself according to the current application state and return. It turns out, by the way, that neither View.draw nor ViewGroup.dispatchDraw (responsible for the traversal of the view tree) is final. But override them at your peril!

To prevent extra painting, the Android UI framework maintains some state information about the view, called the *clip rectangle*. A key concept in the framework, the clip rectangle is part of the state that is passed in calls to a component's graphical rendering methods. It has a location and size that can be retrieved and adjusted through methods on the Canvas (introduced in a moment). It acts like a stencil through which a component does all its drawing: the component can only draw on the portions of the canvas visible through the clip rectangle. By correctly setting the size, shape, and location of the clip rectangle aperture, the framework can prevent a component from drawing outside its boundaries or redrawing regions that are already correctly drawn.

Another important optimization tool arrived in Android API Level 7, Eclair. A view that is opaque—one that completely fills its clip rectangle with nontransparent objects —should consider overriding the view method isOpaque so that it returns the boolean value true. By doing so, the widget provides a clue to the drawing algorithm that it need not render any other views that the widget obscures. In even a moderately complex view tree, this might reduce the number of times a given pixel is painted from four or five to one. This can easily be the difference between, for instance, a list view that scrolls smoothly and one that stutters.

Before proceeding to the specifics of drawing, let's again put the discussion in the context of Android's single-threaded MVC design pattern. There are two essential rules:

- Drawing code should be inside the onDraw method. Your widget should draw itself completely, reflecting the program state, when onDraw is invoked.

- A widget should draw itself as quickly as possible when onDraw is invoked. The middle of the call to onDraw is no time to run a complex database query or to determine the status of some distant networked service. All the state you need to draw should be cached and ready for use, at drawing time. Long-running tasks should use a separate thread and one of the mechanisms described in "Advanced Wiring: Focus and Threading" on page 195. Model state information cached in the view is sometimes called the *view model*.

The Android UI framework uses four main classes in drawing. If you are going to implement custom widgets and do your own drawing you will want to become very familiar with them.

Canvas *(a subclass of* android.graphics.Canvas*)*
Perhaps surprisingly, the Canvas has no clear analog in real-life materials. You might think of it as a complex easel that can orient, bend, and even crumple the paper on which you are drawing, in interesting ways. It maintains the clip rectangle, the stencil through which you paint. It can also scale drawings as they are drawn, like a photographic enlarger. It can even perform other transformations for which material analogs are more difficult to find: mapping colors and drawing text along paths, and so on.

Paint *(a subclass of* android.graphics.Paint*)*
This is the medium with which you will draw. It controls the color, transparency, and brush size for objects painted on the canvas. It also controls font, size, and style when drawing text.

Bitmap *(a subclass of* android.graphics.Bitmap*)*
This is the paper you are drawing on. It holds the actual pixels that you draw.

Drawable *(likely a subclass of* android.graphics.drawable.Drawable*)*
This is the thing you want to draw: perhaps a rectangle or an image. Although not all the things that you draw are Drawables (text, for instance, is not), many, especially the more complex ones, are.

Example 8-1 accomplished its drawing by using only the Canvas, passed as a parameter to onDraw. To do anything more interesting, we will need, at the very least, Paint. Paint provides control over the color and transparency (alpha) of the graphics drawn with it. It also controls the width of the brush used for drawing. When used in connection with text drawing methods, it controls the font, size, and style of the text. Paint has many, many other capabilities, some of which are described in "Bling" on page 248. Example 8-2, however, is enough to get started. It sets two of the many parameters Paint controls (color and line width) before drawing a thick vertical line, followed by a series of horizontal lines. The alpha value (which plays the same role as the fourth value in RGB web colors) is reduced for each green line to make it more transparent than the previous one. Explore the class documentation for other useful attributes.

Example 8-2. Using Paint

```
@Override
protected void onDraw(Canvas canvas) {
    canvas.drawColor(Color.WHITE);

    Paint paint = new Paint();

    canvas.drawLine(33, 0, 33, 100, paint);

    paint.setColor(Color.RED);
    paint.setStrokeWidth(10);
    canvas.drawLine(56, 0, 56, 100, paint);

    paint.setColor(Color.GREEN);
    paint.setStrokeWidth(5);

    for (int y = 30, alpha = 255; alpha > 2; alpha >>= 1, y += 10) {
        paint.setAlpha(alpha);
        canvas.drawLine(0, y, 100, y, paint);
    }
}
```

The graphic created by the code in the example is shown in Figure 8-1.

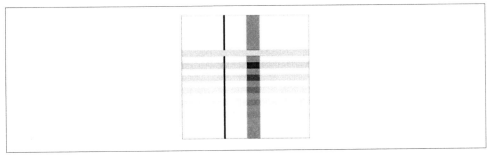

Figure 8-1. Output using Paint

With the addition of Paint, we are prepared to understand most of the other tools necessary to draw a useful widget. The code in Example 8-3, for instance, is the widget used in Example 6-7. Although still not very complex, it demonstrates all the pieces of a fully functional widget. It handles layout, uses highlighting (reflecting whether or not the view has the user's focus), and reflects the state of the model to which it is attached. The widget draws a series of dots for which information is stored in a private array. Each dot specifies its own *x* and *y* location as well as its diameter and color. The onDraw function resets the color of its Paint for each, and uses the other parameters to specify the circle being drawn by the canvas's drawCircle method.

Example 8-3. Dot widget

```
package com.oreilly.android.intro.view;

import android.content.Context;

import android.graphics.Canvas;
import android.graphics.Color;
import android.graphics.Paint;
import android.graphics.Paint.Style;

import android.view.View;

import com.oreilly.android.intro.model.Dot;
import com.oreilly.android.intro.model.Dots;

public class DotView extends View {
    private final Dots dots;

    /**
     * @param context the rest of the application
     * @param dots the dots we draw
     */
    public DotView(Context context, Dots dots) {
        super(context);
        this.dots = dots;
        setMinimumWidth(180);
        setMinimumHeight(200);
        setFocusable(true);
    }

    /** @see android.view.View#onMeasure(int, int) */
    @Override
    protected void onMeasure(int widthMeasureSpec, int heightMeasureSpec) {
        setMeasuredDimension(
            getSuggestedMinimumWidth(),
            getSuggestedMinimumHeight());
    }

    /** @see android.view.View#onDraw(android.graphics.Canvas) */
    @Override protected void onDraw(Canvas canvas) {
        canvas.drawColor(Color.WHITE);

        Paint paint = new Paint();
        paint.setStyle(Style.STROKE);
        paint.setColor(hasFocus() ? Color.BLUE : Color.GRAY);
        canvas.drawRect(0, 0, getWidth() - 1, getHeight() - 1, paint);
```

```
        paint.setStyle(Style.FILL);
        for (Dot dot : dots.getDots()) {
            paint.setColor(dot.getColor());
            canvas.drawCircle(
                dot.getX(),
                dot.getY(),
                dot.getDiameter(),
                paint);
        }
    }
}
```

As with Paint, we have only enough space to begin an exploration of Canvas methods. There are two groups of functionality, however, that are worth special mention.

Drawing text

Among the most important Canvas methods are those used to draw text. Although some Canvas functionality is duplicated in other places, text rendering capabilities are not. To put text in your widget, you will have to use Canvas (or, of course, subclass some other widget that uses it).

Canvas provides several methods for rendering text that give you various amounts of flexibility over the placement of each character in the text. The methods come in pairs: one taking a String and the other taking a char[] array. In some cases, there are additional convenience methods. The simplest way to draw text passes the x and y coordinates where the text starts and Paint that specifies its font, color, and other attributes (see Example 8-4).

Example 8-4. A pair of text drawing methods

```
public void drawText(String text, float x, float y, Paint paint)
public void drawText(char[] text, int index, int count, float x,
                     float y, Paint paint)
```

While the first method passes text as a single String parameter, the second method uses three parameters: an array of char, an index indicating the first character in that array to be drawn, and, last, the number of characters from the array, to be rendered.

If you want something fancier than a simple horizontal text, you can lay it out along a geometric path or even place each character precisely where you want. Example 8-5 contains an onDraw method that demonstrates the use of each of the three text rendering methods. The output is shown in Figure 8-2.

Example 8-5. Three ways to draw text

```
@Override
protected void onDraw(Canvas canvas) {
    canvas.drawColor(Color.WHITE);

    Paint paint = new Paint();
```

```
paint.setColor(Color.RED);
canvas.drawText("Android", 25, 30, paint);

Path path = new Path();
path.addArc(new RectF(10, 50, 90, 200), 240, 90);
paint.setColor(Color.CYAN);
canvas.drawTextOnPath("Android", path, 0, 0, paint);

float[] pos = new float[] {
    20, 80,
    29, 83,
    36, 80,
    46, 83,
    52, 80,
    62, 83,
    68, 80
};
paint.setColor(Color.GREEN);
canvas.drawPosText("Android", pos, paint);
}
```

Figure 8-2. Output from three ways of drawing text

As you can see, the most elementary of the pairs, drawText, simply starts text at the passed coordinates. With drawTextOnPath, on the other hand, you can draw text along any Path. The example path is just an arc. It could just as easily have been a line drawing or Bezier curve.

For those occasions on which even drawTextOnPath is insufficient, Canvas offers draw PosText, which lets you specify the exact position of each character in the text. Note that the character positions are specified by alternating elements in the array of float passed as the second argument: *x1,y1,x2,y2...*

Matrix transformations

The second interesting group of Canvas methods are the Matrix transformations and their related convenience methods, rotate, scale, and skew. These methods transform what you draw in ways that are immediately recognizable to those familiar with 3D graphics in other environments. The methods allow a single drawing to be rendered in ways that can make it appear as though the viewer were moving with respect to the objects in the drawing.

The small application in Example 8-6 demonstrates the Canvas's coordinate transformation capabilities.

Example 8-6. Using a transformation in a Canvas

```
import android.app.Activity;

import android.content.Context;

import android.graphics.Canvas;
import android.graphics.Color;
import android.graphics.Paint;
import android.graphics.Rect;

import android.os.Bundle;

import android.view.View;

import android.widget.LinearLayout;

public class TranformationalActivity extends Activity {

    private interface Transformation {
        void transform(Canvas canvas);
        String describe();
    }

    private static class TransformedViewWidget extends View {❶
        private final Transformation transformation;

        public TransformedViewWidget(Context context, Transformation xform) {
            super(context);

            transformation = xform;❷

            setMinimumWidth(160);
            setMinimumHeight(105);
        }

        @Override
        protected void onMeasure(int widthMeasureSpec, int heightMeasureSpec) {
            setMeasuredDimension(
                getSuggestedMinimumWidth(),
                getSuggestedMinimumHeight());
        }

        @Override
        protected void onDraw(Canvas canvas) {❸
            canvas.drawColor(Color.WHITE);

            Paint paint = new Paint();
```

```
            canvas.save();❹
            transformation.transform(canvas);❺

            paint.setTextSize(12);
            paint.setColor(Color.GREEN);
            canvas.drawText("Hello", 40, 55, paint);

            paint.setTextSize(16);
            paint.setColor(Color.RED);
            canvas.drawText("Android", 35, 65, paint);

            canvas.restore();❻

            paint.setColor(Color.BLACK);
            paint.setStyle(Paint.Style.STROKE);
            Rect r = canvas.getClipBounds();
            canvas.drawRect(r, paint);

            paint.setTextSize(10);
            paint.setColor(Color.BLUE);
            canvas.drawText(transformation.describe(), 5, 100, paint);
        }

    }

    @Override
    public void onCreate(Bundle savedInstanceState) {❼
        super.onCreate(savedInstanceState);
        setContentView(R.layout.transformed);

        LinearLayout v1 = (LinearLayout) findViewById(R.id.v_left);❽
        v1.addView(new TransformedViewWidget(❾
            this,
            new Transformation() {❿
                @Override public String describe() { return "identity"; }
                @Override public void transform(Canvas canvas) { }
            } ));
        v1.addView(new TransformedViewWidget(❾
            this,
            new Transformation() {❿
                @Override public String describe() { return "rotate(-30)"; }
                @Override public void transform(Canvas canvas) {
                    canvas.rotate(-30.0F);
                } }));
        v1.addView(new TransformedViewWidget(❾
            this,
            new Transformation() {❿
                @Override public String describe() { return "scale(.5,.8)"; }
                @Override public void transform(Canvas canvas) {
                    canvas.scale(0.5F, .8F);
                } }));
        v1.addView(new TransformedViewWidget(❾
            this,
            new Transformation() {❿
                @Override public String describe() { return "skew(.1,.3)"; }
```

```
        @Override public void transform(Canvas canvas) {
            canvas.skew(0.1F, 0.3F);
        } }));

    LinearLayout v2 = (LinearLayout) findViewById(R.id.v_right); ⓫
    v2.addView(new TransformedViewWidget( ⓬
        this,
        new Transformation() { ⓾
            @Override public String describe() { return "translate(30,10)"; }
            @Override public void transform(Canvas canvas) {
                canvas.translate(30.0F, 10.0F);
            } }));
    v2.addView(new TransformedViewWidget( ⓬
        this,
        new Transformation() { ⓾
            @Override public String describe() {
                return "translate(110,-20),rotate(85)";
            }
            @Override public void transform(Canvas canvas) {
                canvas.translate(110.0F, -20.0F);
                canvas.rotate(85.0F);
            } }));
    v2.addView(new TransformedViewWidget( ⓬
        this,
        new Transformation() { ⓾
            @Override public String describe() {
                return "translate(-50,-20),scale(2,1.2)";
            }
            @Override public void transform(Canvas canvas) {
                canvas.translate(-50.0F, -20.0F);
                canvas.scale(2F, 1.2F);
            } }));
    v2.addView(new TransformedViewWidget( ⓬
        this,
        new Transformation() { ⓾
            @Override public String describe() { return "complex"; }
            @Override public void transform(Canvas canvas) {
                canvas.translate(-100.0F, -100.0F);
                canvas.scale(2.5F, 2F);
                canvas.skew(0.1F, 0.3F);
            } }));
    }
}
```

The results of this protracted exercise are shown in Figure 8-3.

Here are some of the highlights of the code:

❶ This is the definition of the new widget, TransformedViewWidget.

❷ This gets the actual transformation to perform from the second argument of the constructor.

❸ This is the onDraw method of TransformedViewWidget.

❹ This pushes the current drawing state on the stack using **save** before performing any transformation.

❺ This performs the transformation passed as constructor argument 2.

❻ This restores the old state saved in item 4, in preparation for drawing the bound box and label.

❼ This is the **Activity**'s **onCreate** method.

❽ This creates the container view for the lefthand column of widgets.

❾ These are instantiations of **TransformedViewWidget**, added to the lefthand column.

❿ This creates a transformation as part of the parameter list to the constructor of **TransformedViewWidget**.

⓫ This creates the container view for the righthand column of widgets.

⓬ These are instantiations of **TransformedViewWidget**, added to the righthand column.

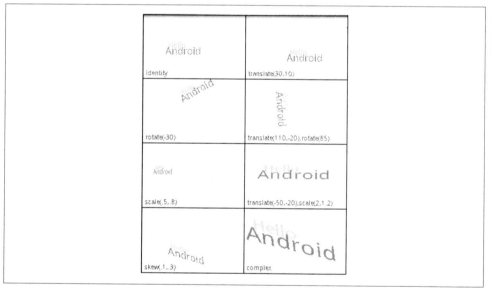

Figure 8-3. Transformed views

This small application introduces several new ideas. In terms of views and widgets, the application defines a single widget, **TransformedViewWidget**, of which it creates eight instances. For layout, the application creates two views named **v1** and **v2**, retrieving their parameters from resources. Then it adds four instances of **TransformedView Widget** to each **LinearLayout** view. This is an example of how applications combine resource-based and dynamic views. Note that the creation of the layout, views, and all eight widgets all takes place within the activity's **onCreate** method.

This application also makes the new widget flexible through a sophisticated division of labor between the widget and the parent view. Several simple objects are drawn directly within the definition of `TransformedViewWidget`, in its `onDraw` method:

- A white background
- The word `Hello` in 12-point green type
- The word `Android` in 16-point red type
- A black frame
- A blue label

In most cases a view's background is set up using the `View` method `setBackground`. This causes the view to draw the background automatically, as necessary. While the widget in this example has been coded to demonstrate, explicitly, all of the phases necessary for it to completely render itself, as we shall see shortly, using a view's built-in background provides some nifty additional functionality.

In the middle of this, the `onDraw` method performs a transformation that was specified at the widget's creation. The application defines its own interface called `Transformation`, and the constructor for `TransformedViewWidget` accepts a `Transformation` as a parameter. We'll see in a moment how the caller actually codes a transformation.

It's important first to see how `onDraw` preserves it own text while allowing the transformation. In this example, we want to make sure the frame and label are drawn last so that they are drawn over anything else drawn by the widget, even if they might overlap. We do not want the transformation to affect either the frame or the label.

Fortunately, the `Canvas` maintains an internal stack onto which we can record and recover the translation matrix, clip rectangle, and all other elements of mutable state in the `Canvas`. Taking advantage of this stack, `onDraw` calls `Canvas.save` to save its state before the transformation, and `Canvas.restore` afterward to restore the saved state.

The rest of the application controls the transformation applied to each of the eight instances of `TransformedViewWidget`. Each new instance of the widget is created with its own anonymous instance of `Transformation`. The image in the area labeled "identity" has no translation applied. The other seven areas are labeled with the transformations they demonstrate.

The base methods for `Canvas` transformations are `setMatrix` and `concatMatrix`. These two methods allow you to build any possible transformation. The methods introduced in the example—`translate`, `rotate`, `scale`, and `skew`—are convenience methods that compose specific, constrained matrices into the current `Canvas` state. Finally, the `getMatrix` method allows you to recover a matrix constructed dynamically—say, with multiple calls to translate and rotate—for later use.

Although it may not be obvious at first, these transformation functions can be tremendously useful. They allow your application to appear to change its point of view with respect to a 3D object! It doesn't take too much imagination, for instance, to see the scene in the square labeled "scale(.5,.8)" as the same as that seen in the square labeled "identity", but viewed from farther away. With a bit more imagination, the image in the box labeled "skew(.1,.3)" could be the untransformed image again, but this time viewed from above and slightly to the right. Scaling or translating an object can make it appear to a user as though the object has moved. Skewing and rotating can make it appear that the object has turned.

When you consider that these transform functions apply to everything drawn on a canvas—lines, text, and even images—their importance in applications becomes even more apparent. A view that displays thumbnails of photos could be implemented trivially, though perhaps not optimally, as a view that scales everything it displays to 10% of its actual size. An application that displays what you see as you look to your left while driving down the street might be implemented, in part, by scaling and skewing a small number of images. This is especially important because transformations can be very fast and are especially suited to hardware optimization.

Drawables

A `Drawable` is an object that knows how to render itself on a `Canvas`. Because a `Drawable` has complete control during rendering, even a very complex rendering process can be encapsulated in a way that makes it fairly easy to use.

Examples 8-7 and 8-8 show the changes necessary to implement the example shown in Figure 8-3, using a `Drawable`. The code that draws the red and green text has been refactored into a `HelloAndroidTextDrawable` class, used in rendering by the widget's `onDraw` method.

Example 8-7. Using a TextDrawable

```
private static class HelloAndroidTextDrawable extends Drawable {
    private ColorFilter filter;
    private int opacity;

    public HelloAndroidTextDrawable() {}

    @Override
    public void draw(Canvas canvas) {
        Paint paint = new Paint();

        paint.setColorFilter(filter);
        paint.setAlpha(opacity);

        paint.setTextSize(12);
        paint.setColor(Color.GREEN);
        canvas.drawText("Hello", 40, 55, paint);

        paint.setTextSize(16);
        paint.setColor(Color.RED);
        canvas.drawText("Android", 35, 65, paint);
}
```

```
    @Override
    public int getOpacity() { return PixelFormat.TRANSLUCENT; }

    @Override
    public void setAlpha(int alpha) { }

    @Override
    public void setColorFilter(ColorFilter cf) { }
}
```

Using the new `Drawable` implementation requires only a few small changes to the
`onDraw` method from our example.

Example 8-8. Using a Drawable widget

```
package com.oreilly.android.intro.widget;

import android.content.Context;
import android.graphics.Canvas;
import android.graphics.Color;
import android.graphics.Paint;
import android.graphics.Rect;
import android.graphics.drawable.Drawable;
import android.view.View;

/**A widget that renders a drawable with a transformation */
public class TransformedViewWidget extends View {

    /** A transformation */
    public interface Transformation {
        /** @param canvas */
        void transform(Canvas canvas);
        /** @return text description of the transform. */
        String describe();
    }

    private final Transformation transformation;
    private final Drawable drawable;

    /**
     * Render the passed drawable, transformed.
     *
     * @param context app context
     * @param draw the object to be drawn, in transform
     * @param xform the transformation
     */
    public TransformedViewWidget(
        Context context,
        Drawable draw,
        Transformation xform)
    {
        super(context);

        drawable = draw;
```

```
        transformation = xform;

        setMinimumWidth(160);
        setMinimumHeight(135);
    }

    /** @see android.view.View#onMeasure(int, int) */
    @Override
    protected void onMeasure(int widthMeasureSpec, int heightMeasureSpec) {
        setMeasuredDimension(
            getSuggestedMinimumWidth(),
            getSuggestedMinimumHeight());
    }

    /** @see android.view.View#onDraw(android.graphics.Canvas) */
    @Override
    protected void onDraw(Canvas canvas) {
        canvas.drawColor(Color.WHITE);

        canvas.save();
        transformation.transform(canvas);
        drawable.draw(canvas);
        canvas.restore();

        Paint paint = new Paint();
        paint.setColor(Color.BLACK);
        paint.setStyle(Paint.Style.STROKE);
        Rect r = canvas.getClipBounds();
        canvas.drawRect(r, paint);

        paint.setTextSize(10);
        paint.setColor(Color.BLUE);
        canvas.drawText(
            transformation.describe(),
            5,
            getMeasuredHeight() - 5,
            paint);
    }
}
```

This code begins to demonstrate the power of using a `Drawable`. This implementation of `TransformedViewWidget` will transform any `Drawable`, no matter what it happens to draw. It is no longer tied to rotating and scaling our original, hardcoded text. It can be reused to transform both the text from the previous example and a photo captured from the camera, as Figure 8-4 demonstrates. It could even be used to transform a `Drawable` animation.

`Drawable`s make complex graphical techniques like 9-patches and animation tractable. In addition, because they wrap the rendering process completely, `Drawable`s can be nested to compose complex rendering from small reusable pieces.

Consider for a moment how we might extend the previous example to make each of the six images fade to white over a period of a minute. Certainly, we might just change

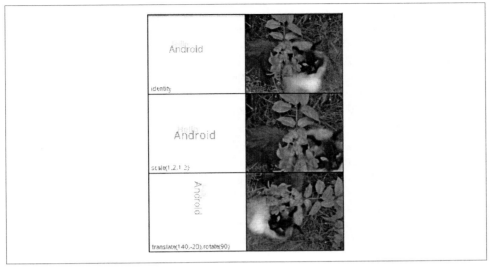

Figure 8-4. Transformed views with photos

the code in Example 8-8 to do the fade. A different—and very appealing—implementation involves writing one new Drawable.

The constructor of this new Drawable, which we'll call FaderDrawable, will take as an argument a reference to its target, the Drawable that it will fade to white. In addition, it must have some notion of time, probably an integer—let's call it t—that is incremented by a timer. Whenever the draw method of FaderDrawable is called, it first calls the draw method of its target. Next, however, it paints over exactly the same area with the color white, using the value of t to determine the transparency (alpha value) of the paint (as demonstrated in Example 8-2). As time passes, t gets larger, the white gets increasingly opaque, and the target Drawable fades to white.

This hypothetical FaderDrawable demonstrates some of the important features of Drawables. Note, first of all, that FaderDrawable is eminently reusable. It will fade just about any Drawable. Also note that, because FaderDrawable extends Drawable, we can use it anywhere we would have used its target, the Drawable that it fades to white. Any code that uses a Drawable in its rendering process can use a FaderDrawable, without change.

Of course, a FaderDrawable could, itself, be wrapped. In fact, it is possible to achieve very complex effects, simply by building a chain of Drawable wrappers. The Android toolkit provides several Drawable wrappers that support this strategy, including Clip Drawable, RotateDrawable, and ScaleDrawable.

At this point, you may be mentally redesigning your entire UI in terms of Drawables. They are a powerful tool, but they are not a panacea. There are several issues to keep in mind when considering the use of Drawables.

You may well have noticed that they share a lot of the functionality of the View class: location, dimensions, visibility, and so on. It's not always easy to decide when a View should draw directly on the Canvas, when it should delegate to a subview, and when it should delegate to one or more Drawable objects. There is even a DrawableContainer class that allows the grouping of several child Drawables within a parent. It is possible to build trees of Drawables that parallel the trees of Views we've been using so far. In dealing with the Android UI framework, you just have to accept that there is more than one way to scale a cat.

The most obvious difference between a View and a Drawable is that Drawables do not, directly, implement a controller to handle user input: they cannot be widgets as we are using the term. In addition, Drawables do not implement the View measure/layout protocol, which, you'll recall, allows a container view to negotiate the layout of its components in response to changing view size. If a renderable object needs to respond directly to the user, or to add, remove, or lay out internal components, it's a pretty good indication that it should be a full-fledged View instead of a Drawable.

A second issue to consider is that, because Drawables completely wrap the drawing process, they are not drawn in the same way as a String or a Rect. There are, in particular, no Canvas methods that will render a Drawable at specific coordinates. You may find yourself deliberating over whether, in order to render a certain image twice, a View's onDraw method should use two different, immutable Drawables or a single Drawable twice, resetting its coordinates.

Perhaps most important, though, is a more generic problem. The reason the idea of a chain of Drawables works is that the Drawable interface contains no information about the internal implementation of the Drawable. When your code is passed a Drawable, there is no way for it to know whether it is something that will render a simple image or a complex chain of effects that rotates, flashes, and bounces. Clearly this can be a big advantage. It can also be a problem, though.

Quite a bit of the drawing process is stateful. You set up Paint and then draw with it. You set up Canvas clip regions and transformations and then draw through them. When cooperating in a chain, Drawables must be very careful, if they change state, that those changes never collide. The problem is that, when constructing a Drawable chain, the possibility of collision cannot, by definition (they are all just Drawables), be explicit in the object's type. A seemingly small change might have an effect that is not desirable and is difficult to debug.

To illustrate, consider two Drawable wrapper classes, one that is meant to shrink its contents and another that is meant to rotate them by 90 degrees. If either is implemented by setting the transformation matrix to a specific value, composing the two may not have the desired effect. Worse, it might work perfectly if A wraps B, but not if B wraps A! Careful documentation of how a Drawable is implemented is essential.

Bitmaps

The `Bitmap` is the last member of the four essentials for drawing: something to draw (a `String`, `Rect`, etc.), a `Paint` with which to draw, a `Canvas` on which to draw, and the `Bitmap` to hold the bits. Most of the time, you don't have to deal directly with a `Bitmap`, because the `Canvas` provided as an argument to the `onDraw` method already has one behind it. There are circumstances, though, under which you may want to use a `Bitmap` directly.

A common use for a `Bitmap` is to cache a drawing that may be time-consuming to draw but unlikely to change frequently. Consider, for example, a drawing program that allows the user to draw in multiple layers. The layers act as transparent overlays on a base image, and the user turns them off and on at will. It might be very expensive to actually draw each individual layer every time `onDraw` gets called. Instead, it might be faster to render the entire drawing upon first appearance, with all visible layers, and then redraw the single layer that needs changing only when the user makes a visible change to it.

The implementation of such an application might look something like Example 8-9.

Example 8-9. Bitmap caching

```java
private class CachingWidget extends View {
    private Bitmap cache;

    public CachingWidget(Context context) {
        super(context);
        setMinimumWidth(200);
        setMinimumHeight(200);
    }

    public void invalidateCache() {
        cache = null;
        invalidate();
    }

    @Override
    protected void onDraw(Canvas canvas) {
        if (null == cache) {
            cache = Bitmap.createBitmap(
                getMeasuredWidth(),
                getMeasuredHeight(),
                Bitmap.Config.ARGB_8888);

            drawCachedBitmap(new Canvas(cache));
        }

        canvas.drawBitmap(cache, 0, 0, new Paint());
    }


    // ... definition of drawCachedBitmap
```

}

This widget normally just copies the cached `Bitmap`, `cache`, to the `Canvas` passed to `onDraw`. Only if the cache is marked stale, by calling `invalidateCache`, will `drawCached Bitmap` be called to actually render the widget.

The most common way to encounter a `Bitmap` is as the programmatic representation of a graphics resource. `Resources.getDrawable` returns a `BitmapDrawable` when the resource is an image.

Combining these two ideas, caching an image and wrapping it in a `Drawable`, opens yet another interesting window. It means anything that can be drawn can also be post-processed! An application that used all the techniques demonstrated in this chapter could allow a user to draw furniture in a room (creating a bitmap) and then to walk around it (using the matrix transforms).

 With Honeycomb, there have been substantial changes in Android's rendering architecture. These changes take advantage of the increasing power of GPUs and create a whole new set of rules for optimizing the way your UI is drawn. Caching bitmaps while using the new graphics pipeline may actually be slower than drawing them as needed. Consider `View.setLayerType` before doing your own bitmap caching.

Bling

The Android UI framework is a lot more than just an intelligent, well-put-together GUI toolkit. When it takes off its glasses and shakes out its hair, it can be downright sexy! The tools mentioned here certainly do not make an exhaustive catalog. They might get you started, though, on the path to making your application Filthy Rich.

 Several of the techniques discussed in this section are close to the edges of the Android landscape. As such, they are less well established than the classes we discussed earlier in the chapter: the documentation is not as thorough, some of the features are clearly in transition, and you may even find bugs. If you run into problems, the Android Developers Google Group is an invaluable resource. Questions about a particular aspect of the toolkit have sometimes been answered by the very person responsible for implementing that aspect.

Be careful about checking the dates on solutions you find by searching the Web. Some of these features are changing rapidly. Code that worked as recently as six months ago may no longer be correct. A corollary, of course, is that any application that gets wide distribution is likely to be run on platforms that have differing implementations of the features discussed here. By using these techniques, you may limit the lifetime of your application, and the number of devices that it will support.

The rest of this section considers a single application, much like the one used in Example 8-6: a couple of `LinearLayout` views that contain multiple instances of a single widget, each demonstrating a different graphics effect. Example 8-10 provides the key parts of the widget, with code discussed previously, elided for brevity. The widget simply draws a few graphical objects and defines an interface through which various graphics effects can be applied to the rendering.

Example 8-10. Effects widget

```
public class EffectsWidget extends View {

    /** The effect to apply to the drawing */
    public interface PaintEffect { void setEffect(Paint paint); }

    // ...

    // PaintWidget's widget rendering method
    protected void onDraw(Canvas canvas) {
        Paint paint = new Paint();
        paint.setAntiAlias(true);

        effect.setEffect(paint);
        paint.setColor(Color.DKGRAY);

        paint.setStrokeWidth(5);
        canvas.drawLine(10, 10, 140, 20, paint);

        paint.setTextSize(26);
        canvas.drawText("Android", 40, 50, paint);

        paint = new Paint();
        paint.setColor(Color.BLACK);
        canvas.drawText(String.valueOf(id), 2.0F, 12.0F, paint);
        paint.setStyle(Paint.Style.STROKE);
        paint.setStrokeWidth(2);
        canvas.drawRect(canvas.getClipBounds(), paint);
    }
}
```

The application that uses this widget (Example 8-11) should also feel familiar. It creates several copies of the `EffectsWidget`, each with its own effect. The widget at the bottom of the right column is special. It has an animated background.

Example 8-11. Effects application

```
private AnimationDrawable buildEfxView(LinearLayout lv, LinearLayout rv) {
    lv.addView(new EffectsWidget(
        this,
        1,
        new EffectsWidget.PaintEffect() {
            @Override public void setEffect(Paint paint) {
                paint.setShadowLayer(1, 3, 4, Color.BLUE);
            } }));
    lv.addView(new EffectsWidget(
```

```java
            this,
            3,
            new EffectsWidget.PaintEffect() {
                @Override public void setEffect(Paint paint) {
                    paint.setShader(
                        new LinearGradient(
                            0.0F,
                            0.0F,
                            100.0F,
                            10.0F,
                            new int[] {
                                Color.BLACK, Color.RED, Color.YELLOW },
                            new float[] { 0.0F, 0.5F, 0.95F },
                            Shader.TileMode.REPEAT));
                } }));
    lv.addView(new EffectsWidget(
        this,
        5,
        new EffectsWidget.PaintEffect() {
            @Override public void setEffect(Paint paint) {
                paint.setMaskFilter(
                    new BlurMaskFilter(2, BlurMaskFilter.Blur.NORMAL));
            } }));

    rv.addView(new EffectsWidget(
        this,
        2,
        new EffectsWidget.PaintEffect() {
            @Override public void setEffect(Paint paint) {
                paint.setShadowLayer(3, -8, 7, Color.GREEN);
            } }));
    rv.addView(new EffectsWidget(
        this,
        4,
        new EffectsWidget.PaintEffect() {
            @Override public void setEffect(Paint paint) {
                paint.setShader(
                    new LinearGradient(
                        0.0F,
                        40.0F,
                        15.0F,
                        40.0F,
                        Color.BLUE,
                        Color.GREEN,
                        Shader.TileMode.MIRROR));
            } }));
    View w = new EffectsWidget(
        this,
        6,
        new EffectsWidget.PaintEffect() {
            @Override public void setEffect(Paint paint) { }
        });
    rv.addView(w);
    w.setBackgroundResource(R.drawable.throbber);
```

```
        return (AnimationDrawable) w.getBackground();
}
```

Figure 8-5 shows the results of running the code. As mentioned, widget 6 is animated. As we'll see in a minute, it has a background that pulses red.

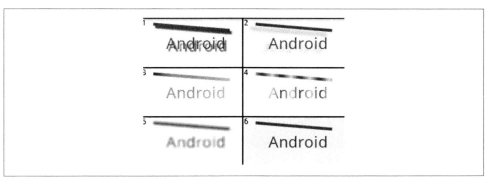

Figure 8-5. Graphics effects

We'll talk more about each effect in the following section.

Shadows, Gradients, Filters, and Hardware Acceleration

PathEffect, MaskFilter, ColorFilter, Shader, and ShadowLayer are all attributes of Paint. Anything drawn with Paint can be drawn under the influence of one or more of these transformations. The first five widgets in Figure 8-5 give examples of several of these effects.

Widgets 1 and 2 demonstrate shadows. Shadows are currently controlled by the set ShadowLayer method. The arguments, a blur radius and x and y displacements, control the apparent distance and position of the light source that creates the shadow, with respect to the shadowed object.

The second row of widgets demonstrate Shader effects. The Android toolkit contains several prebuilt shaders. Widgets 3 and 4 demonstrate one of them, the LinearGradi ent shader. A gradient is a regular transition between colors that can be used, for instance, to give a page background a bit more life without resorting to expensive bitmap resources.

A LinearGradient is specified with a vector that determines the direction and rate of the color transition, an array of colors through which to transition, and a mode. The final argument, the mode, determines what happens when a single complete transition through the gradient is insufficient to cover the entire painted object. For instance, in widget 4, the transition is only 15 pixels long, whereas the drawing is more than 100 pixels wide. Using the mode Shader.TileMode.Mirror causes the transition to repeat, alternating direction across the drawing. In the example, the gradient transitions from blue to green in 15 pixels, then from green to blue in the next 15, and so on, across the canvas.

One of the side effects of the reimplementation of the UI framework that took place with the release of Honeycomb is that several of the more esoteric drawing effects have either been constrained or disabled completely. Both `drawTextOnPath` and `drawText Pos`, mentioned previously, are casualties. The `setShadowLayer` method still works, but only for text. If widgets 1 and 2 are drawn using the new, hardware accelerated graphics pipeline, the text will appear with shadows but the line above it will not.

It is possible to force a Honeycomb device into a compatibility mode, in which these methods render in their pre-Honeycomb glory. The most dramatic way to force the use of the legacy rendering pipeline (software, as opposed to hardware rendering) is to add the attribute in Example 8-12 to the application manifest.

Example 8-12. Disabling hardware acceleration

```
<application
    ...
    android:hardwareAccelerated="false">
```

Actually, this is the default. To benefit from post-Honeycomb hardware accelerated graphics, you must specifically set the value of this attribute to `true` in your application. Were this not the case, no doubt hundreds of applications would stop working correctly when the device running them was upgraded to run Android v3 or later. It is very important to remember that unless you actively enable hardware acceleration for your app, it will not get it.

It is possible to exercise much more granular control over hardware acceleration. In addition to including the `android:hardwareAccelerated` attribute in the `application` element of the manifest, where it affects the entire application, it can also be applied to an individual activity. An activity that does not render correctly using the new pipeline might set the attribute to `false`, while the rest of the activities set it to `true`.

The following two code fragments shown in Example 8-12 demonstrate how to control hardware acceleration at an even finer granularity—the window and view levels, respectively.

Example 8-13. Fine-grained disabling of hardware acceleration

```
getWindow().setFlags(
    WindowManager.LayoutParams.FLAG_HARDWARE_ACCELERATED,
    WindowManager.LayoutParams.FLAG_HARDWARE_ACCELERATED);

myView.setLayerType(View.LAYER_TYPE_SOFTWARE, null);
```

Remember, though, that your goal should be to let your application run correctly with hardware acceleration turned on. There is no other optimization that you can make, especially for newer devices, that will provide anything like the speed and usability improvements that will come from using hardware-optimized rendering.

Animation

The Android UI toolkit offers several different animation tools. Transition animations—which the Google documentation calls *tweened animations*—are subclasses of `android.view.animation.Animation`: `RotateAnimation`, `TranslateAnima` `tion`, `ScaleAnimation`, and so on. These animations are used as transitions between pairs of
views. A second type of animation, subclasses of `android.graphics.drawable` `.AnimationDrawable.AnimationDrawable`, can be put into the background of any widget to provide a wide variety of effects. Finally, there is a full-on animation class on top of a `SurfaceView` that gives you complete control to do your own seat-of-the-pants animation.

Because both of the first two types of animation, transition and background, are supported by `View`, either can be used in nearly any widget.

Transition animation

A transition animation is started by calling the `View` method `startAnimation` with an instance of `Animation` (or, of course, your own subclass). Once installed, the animation runs to completion: transition animations have no pause state.

The heart of the animation is its `applyTransformation` method. This method is called to produce successive frames of the animation. Example 8-14 shows the implementation of one transformation. As you can see, it does not actually generate entire graphical frames for the animation. Instead, it generates successive transformations to be applied to a single image being animated. You will recall, from "Matrix transformations" on page 236, that matrix transformations can be used to make an object appear to move. Transition animations depend on exactly this trick.

Example 8-14. Transition animation

```
@Override
protected void applyTransformation(float t, Transformation xf) {
    Matrix xform = xf.getMatrix();

    float z = ((dir > 0) ? 0.0f : -Z_MAX) - (dir * t * Z_MAX);
    camera.save();
    camera.rotateZ(t * 360);
    camera.translate(0.0F, 0.0F, z);
    camera.getMatrix(xform);
    camera.restore();

    xform.preTranslate(-xCenter, -yCenter);
    xform.postTranslate(xCenter, yCenter);
}
```

This particular implementation makes its target appear to spin in the screen plane (the rotate method call) and, at the same time, to shrink into the distance (the `translate` method call). The matrix that will be applied to the target image is obtained from the `Transformation` object passed in that call.

This implementation uses `camera`, an instance of the utility class `Camera`. This `Camera` class—not to be confused with the camera in the phone—is a utility that makes it possible to record rendering state. It is used here to compose the rotation and translation transformations into a single matrix, which is then stored as the animation transformation.

The first parameter to `applyTransformation`, named `t`, is effectively the frame number. It is passed as a floating-point number between 0.0 and 1.0, and might also be understood as the percent of the animation that is complete. This example uses `t` to increase the apparent distance, along the z-axis (a line perpendicular to the plane of the screen), of the image being animated, and to set the proportion of one complete rotation through which the image has passed. As `t` increases, the animated image appears to rotate further and further counterclockwise and to move farther and farther away, along the z-axis, into the distance.

The `preTranslate` and `postTranslate` operations are necessary to translate the image around its center. By default, matrix operations transform their target around the origin (upper-left corner). If we did not perform these bracketing translations, the target image would appear to rotate around its upper-left corner. `preTranslate` effectively moves the origin to the center of the animation target for the translation, and `postTranslate` causes the default to be restored after the translation.

If you consider what a transition animation must do, you'll realize that it is actually likely to compose two animations: the previous screen must be animated out and the next one animated in. Example 8-14 supports this using the remaining, unexplained variable, `dir`. Its value is either 1 or −1, and controls whether the animated image seems to shrink into the distance or grow into the foreground. We need only find a way to compose a shrinking and a growing animation.

This is done using the familiar `Listener` pattern. The `Animation` class defines a listener named `Animation.AnimationListener`. Any instance of `Animation` with a non-null listener calls that listener once when it starts, once when it stops, and once for each iteration in between. A listener that notices when the shrinking animation completes and spawns a new growing animation will create exactly the effect we desire. Example 8-15 shows the rest of the implementation of the animation.

Example 8-15. Transition animation composition

```
public void runAnimation() {
    animateOnce(new AccelerateInterpolator(), this);
}

@Override
public void onAnimationEnd(Animation animation) {
    root.post(new Runnable() {
        public void run() {
```

```
                curView.setVisibility(View.GONE);
                nextView.setVisibility(View.VISIBLE);
                nextView.requestFocus();
                new RotationTransitionAnimation(-1, root, nextView, null)
                    .animateOnce(new DecelerateInterpolator(), null);
        } });
}

void animateOnce(
    Interpolator interpolator,
    Animation.AnimationListener listener)
{
    setDuration(700);
    setInterpolator(interpolator);
    setAnimationListener(listener);
    root.startAnimation(this);
}
```

The `runAnimation` method starts the transition. The overridden `AnimationListener` method, `onAnimationEnd`, spawns the second half. Called when the target image appears to be far in the distance, it hides the image being animated out (the `curView`) and replaces it with the newly visible image, `nextView`. It then creates a new animation that, running in reverse, spins and grows the new image into the foreground.

The `Interpolator` class represents a nifty attention to detail. The values for `t`, passed to `applyTransformation`, need not be linearly distributed over time. In this implementation the animation appears to speed up as it recedes, and then to slow again as the new image advances. This is accomplished by using the two interpolators, `AccelerateInterpolator` for the first half of the animation and `Decelerate Interpolator` for the second. Without the interpolator, the difference between successive values of `t`, passed to `applyTransformation`, would be constant. This would make the animation appear to have a constant speed. The `AccelerateInterpolator` converts those equally spaced values of `t` into values that are close together at the beginning of the animation and much farther apart toward the end. This makes the animation appear to speed up. `DecelerateInterpolator` has exactly the opposite effect. Android also provides a `CycleInterpolator` and `LinearInterpolator` for use as appropriate.

Animation composition is actually built into the toolkit, using the (perhaps confusingly named) `AnimationSet` class. This class provides a convenient way to specify a list— fortunately *not* a set: it is ordered and may refer to a given animation more than once—of animations to be played, in order. In addition, the toolkit provides several standard transitions: `AlphaAnimation`, `RotateAnimation`, `ScaleAnimation`, and `TranslateAnimation`. Certainly, there is no need for these transitional animations to be symmetric, as they are in the previous example. A new image might alpha-fade in as the old one shrinks into a corner, or slide up from the bottom as the old one fades out. The possibilities are endless.

Background animation

Frame-by-frame animation, as it is called in the Google documentation, is completely straightforward: a set of frames, played in order at regular intervals. This kind of animation is implemented by subclasses of `AnimationDrawable`.

As subclasses of `Drawable`, `AnimationDrawable` objects can be used in any context in which any other `Drawable` is used. The mechanism that animates them, however, is not a part of the `Drawable` itself. To animate, an `AnimationDrawable` relies on an external service provider—an implementation of the `Drawable.Callback` interface—to animate it.

The `View` class implements this interface and can be used to animate an `Animation Drawable`. Unfortunately, it will supply animation services *only* to the one `Drawable` object that is installed as its background.

The good news, however, is that this is probably sufficient. A background animation has access to the entire widget canvas. Everything it draws will appear to be behind anything drawn by the `View.onDraw` method, so it would be hard to use it to implement full-fledged sprites. Still, with clever use of the `DrawableContainer` class (which allows you to animate several different animations simultaneously), and because the background can be changed at any time, it is possible to accomplish quite a bit without resorting to implementing your own animation framework.

An `AnimationDrawable` in a view background is entirely sufficient to do anything from, say, indicating that some long-running activity is taking place—maybe winged packets flying across the screen from a phone to a tower—to simply making the background to a button pulse.

The pulsing button example in widget 6 is illustrative and surprisingly easy to implement. Examples 8-16 and 8-17 show everything you need. The animation is defined as a resource, and code applies it to the button. You can set a `Drawable` as a background using either `setBackgroundDrawable` or `setBackgroundResource`.

Example 8-16. Frame-by-frame animation (resource)

```
<animation-list
    xmlns:android="http://schemas.android.com/apk/res/android"
    android:oneshot="false">
  <item android:drawable="@drawable/throbber_f0" android:duration="160" />
  <item android:drawable="@drawable/throbber_f1" android:duration="140" />
  <item android:drawable="@drawable/throbber_f2" android:duration="130" />
  <item android:drawable="@drawable/throbber_f3" android:duration="100" />
  <item android:drawable="@drawable/throbber_f4" android:duration="130" />
  <item android:drawable="@drawable/throbber_f5" android:duration="140" />
  <item android:drawable="@drawable/throbber_f6" android:duration="160" />
</animation-list>
```

Example 8-17 shows the code that runs the animations. An `onClickListener` in the main view starts the transition animation and swaps views so that on the next click, it will again toggle between the views. In addition, it toggles the background animation so that it is not running when it is not visible.

 In early versions of Android there was no way to start a background animation from the `Activity` `onCreate` method and it was necessary to use trickery to get it going. This bug was fixed in API level 6 (Muffin), and simply `((AnimationBackground) view.getBackground()).start()` works fine.

Example 8-17. Frame-by-frame animation (code)

```
@Override
public void onCreate(Bundle savedInstanceState) {

    // .... code elided

    // install the animation click listener
    final View root = findViewById(R.id.main);
    findViewById(R.id.main).setOnClickListener(
        new OnClickListener() {
            @Override public void onClick(View v) {
                new RotationTransitionAnimation(1, root, cur, next)
                    .runAnimation();
                // exchange views
                View t = cur;
                cur = next;
                next = t;
                toggleThrobber();
        } });
}

// .... code elided

void toggleThrobber() {
    if (null != throbber) {
        if (efxView.equals(cur)) { throbber.start(); }
        else { throbber.stop(); }
    }
}
```

It's worth pointing out that if you have worked with other UI frameworks, especially mobile UI frameworks, you may be accustomed to painting the view background in the first couple of lines of the onDraw method (or equivalent). Notice that if you do that here, you will paint over your animation! It is, in general, a good idea to get into the habit of using setBackground to control the View background, whether it is a solid color, a gradient, an image, or an animation.

Specifying a DrawableAnimation by resource is very flexible. You can specify a list of drawable resources—any images you like—that comprise the animation. If your animation needs to be dynamic, `AnimationDrawable` is a straightforward recipe for creating a dynamic drawable that can be animated in the background of a `View`.

Surface view animation

Full-on animation requires a `SurfaceView`. The `SurfaceView` provides a node in the view tree—and, therefore, space on the display—on which any process at all can draw. After you lay out and size the `SurfaceView` node, it receives clicks and updates, just like any other widget. Instead of drawing, however, it simply reserves space on the screen, preventing other widgets from affecting any of the pixels within its frame.

Drawing on a `SurfaceView` requires implementing the `SurfaceHolder.Callback` interface. The two methods `surfaceCreated` and `surfaceDestroyed` inform the implementor that the drawing surface is available for drawing and that it has become unavailable, respectively. The argument to both calls is an instance of yet a third class, `Surface Holder`. In the interval between these two calls, a drawing routine can call the `Surface View` methods `lockCanvas` and `unlockCanvasAndPost` to edit the pixels there.

If this seems complex, even alongside some of the elaborate animation discussed previously—well, it is. As usual, concurrency increases the likelihood of nasty, hard-to-find bugs. The client of a `SurfaceView` must be sure, not only that access to any state shared across threads is properly synchronized, but also that it never touches the `SurfaceView`, `Surface`, or `Canvas` except in the interval between the calls to `surface Created` and `surfaceDestroyed`. The toolkit could, clearly, benefit from more complete framework support for `SurfaceView` animation.

If you are considering `SurfaceView` animation, you are probably also considering OpenGL graphics. As we'll see, an extension is available for OpenGL animation on a `SurfaceView`. It will turn up in a somewhat out-of-the-way place, though.

OpenGL Graphics

The Android platform supports OpenGL graphics in roughly the same way that a silk hat supports rabbits. While this is certainly among the most exciting technologies in Android, it is definitely at the edge of the map. The good news is that, as of the Honeycomb release, OpenGL has been fully integrated into Android graphics. Whereas early versions of Android supported OpenGL 1.0 and 1.1, according to the documentation, Honeycomb not only supports OpenGL 2.0, but also uses it as the basis for rendering `View` objects. OpenGL is essentially a domain-specific language embedded in Java. Someone who has been doing gaming UIs for a while is likely to be much more comfortable developing Android OpenGL programs than a Java programmer, even a Java UI expert.

Before discussing the OpenGL graphics library itself, we should take a minute to consider exactly how pixels drawn with OpenGL appear on the display. Thus far, this chapter has discussed the intricate `View` framework that Android uses to organize and represent objects on the screen. OpenGL is a language in which an application describes an entire scene that will be rendered by an engine that is not only outside the VM, but probably running on another processor altogether (the Graphics Processing Unit, or GPU). Coordinating the two processors' views of the screen is tricky.

The SurfaceView, discussed earlier, is nearly sufficient. Its purpose is to create a surface on which a thread other than the UI graphics thread can draw. The tool we'd like is an extension of SurfaceView that has a bit more support for concurrency combined with support for OpenGL. It turns out that there is exactly such a tool. All the demo applications in the Android SDK distribution that do OpenGL animation depend on the utility class GLSurfaceView. Because the demo applications, written by the creators of Android, use this class, considering it for your applications seems advisable.

GLSurfaceView defines an interface, GLSurfaceView.Renderer, which dramatically simplifies the otherwise overwhelming complexity of using OpenGL and GLSurfaceView. GLSurfaceView calls the getConfigSpec rendering method to get its OpenGL configuration information. Two other methods, sizeChanged and surfaceCreated, are called by the GLSurfaceView to inform the renderer that its size has changed or that it should prepare to draw, respectively. Finally, drawFrame, the heart of the interface, is called to render a new OpenGL frame.

Example 8-18 shows the important methods from the implementation of an OpenGL renderer.

Example 8-18. Frame-by-frame animation with OpenGL

```
// ... some state set up in the constructor

@Override
public void surfaceCreated(GL10 gl) {
    // set up the surface
    gl.glDisable(GL10.GL_DITHER);

    gl.glHint(
        GL10.GL_PERSPECTIVE_CORRECTION_HINT,
        GL10.GL_FASTEST);

    gl.glClearColor(0.2f, 0.1f, 0.8f, 0.1f);
    gl.glShadeModel(GL10.GL_SMOOTH);
    gl.glEnable(GL10.GL_DEPTH_TEST);

    // fetch the checkerboard
    initImage(gl);
}

@Override
public void drawFrame(GL10 gl) {
    gl.glClear(GL10.GL_COLOR_BUFFER_BIT | GL10.GL_DEPTH_BUFFER_BIT);

    gl.glMatrixMode(GL10.GL_MODELVIEW);
    gl.glLoadIdentity();
```

```
        GLU.gluLookAt(gl, 0, 0, -5, 0f, 0f, 0f, 0f, 1.0f, 0.0f);

        gl.glEnableClientState(GL10.GL_VERTEX_ARRAY);
        gl.glEnableClientState(GL10.GL_TEXTURE_COORD_ARRAY);

        // apply the checkerboard to the shape
        gl.glActiveTexture(GL10.GL_TEXTURE0);

        gl.glTexEnvx(
            GL10.GL_TEXTURE_ENV,
            GL10.GL_TEXTURE_ENV_MODE,
            GL10.GL_MODULATE);
        gl.glTexParameterx(
            GL10.GL_TEXTURE_2D,
            GL10.GL_TEXTURE_WRAP_S,
            GL10.GL_REPEAT);
        gl.glTexParameterx(
            GL10.GL_TEXTURE_2D,
            GL10.GL_TEXTURE_WRAP_T,
            GL10.GL_REPEAT);

        // animation
        int t = (int) (SystemClock.uptimeMillis() % (10 * 1000L));
        gl.glTranslatef(6.0f - (0.0013f * t), 0, 0);

        // draw
        gl.glFrontFace(GL10.GL_CCW);
        gl.glVertexPointer(3, GL10.GL_FLOAT, 0, vertexBuf);
        gl.glEnable(GL10.GL_TEXTURE_2D);
        gl.glTexCoordPointer(2, GL10.GL_FLOAT, 0, textureBuf);
        gl.glDrawElements(
            GL10.GL_TRIANGLE_STRIP,
            5,
            GL10.GL_UNSIGNED_SHORT, indexBuf);
    }

    private void initImage(GL10 gl) {
        int[] textures = new int[1];
        gl.glGenTextures(1, textures, 0);
        gl.glBindTexture(GL10.GL_TEXTURE_2D, textures[0]);

        gl.glTexParameterf(
            GL10.GL_TEXTURE_2D,
            GL10.GL_TEXTURE_MIN_FILTER,
            GL10.GL_NEAREST);
        gl.glTexParameterf(
            GL10.GL_TEXTURE_2D,
            GL10.GL_TEXTURE_MAG_FILTER,
            GL10.GL_LINEAR);
        gl.glTexParameterf(
            GL10.GL_TEXTURE_2D,
            GL10.GL_TEXTURE_WRAP_S,
            GL10.GL_CLAMP_TO_EDGE);
        gl.glTexParameterf(
            GL10.GL_TEXTURE_2D,
```

```
        GL10.GL_TEXTURE_WRAP_T,
        GL10.GL_CLAMP_TO_EDGE);
    gl.glTexEnvf(
        GL10.GL_TEXTURE_ENV,
        GL10.GL_TEXTURE_ENV_MODE,
        GL10.GL_REPLACE);

    InputStream in
        = context.getResources().openRawResource(R.drawable.cb);
    Bitmap image;
    try { image = BitmapFactory.decodeStream(in); }
    finally {
        try { in.close(); } catch(IOException e) {   }
    }

    GLUtils.texImage2D(GL10.GL_TEXTURE_2D, 0, image, 0);

    image.recycle();
}
```

The method surfaceCreated prepares the scene. It sets several OpenGL attributes that need to be initialized only when the widget gets a new drawing surface. In addition, it calls initImage, which reads in a bitmap resource and stores it as a 2D texture. When, finally, drawFrame is called, everything is ready for drawing. The texture is applied to a plane, whose vertices were set up in vertexBuf by the constructor; the animation phase is chosen; and the scene is redrawn. Figure 8-6 shows the running OpenGL example.

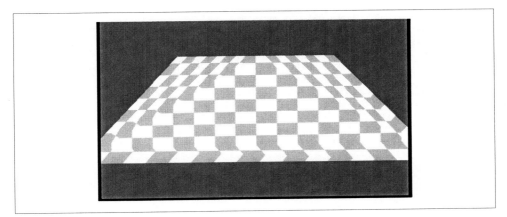

Figure 8-6. OpenGL drawing

As always, you must remember that your view is embedded in an activity with a life cycle! If you are using OpenGL, be sure to turn off long-running animation processes when the activity is not visible.

## CHAPTER 9

Handling and Persisting Data

To accomplish many of the activities offered by modern mobile phones, such as tracking contacts, events, and tasks, a mobile operating system and its applications must be adept at storing and keeping track of large quantities of data. This data is usually structured in rows and columns, similar to a spreadsheet or a very simple database. Beyond a traditional application's requirements for storing data, the Android application life cycle demands rapid and consistent persistence of data for it to survive the volatility of the mobile environment, where devices can suddenly lose power or the Android operating system can arbitrarily decide to remove your application from memory.

Android provides the lightweight but powerful SQLite relational database engine for persisting data. Furthermore, as described in Chapter 3, the content provider feature lets applications expose their data to other applications.

In this chapter, we provide a simple SQL tutorial so that you can learn to work with Android SQLite persistence. We also walk you through an interesting application—MJAndroid—that provides a real-world look at how to manipulate a database in Android. Later, in Chapter 15, we'll reference the same example to demonstrate the use of the mapping API in Android. Chapter 12 will show you how to implement a content provider.

Relational Database Overview

A relational database provides an efficient, structured, and generic system for managing persistent information. With a database, applications use structured queries to modify information in persistent two-dimensional matrices called *tables* (or in the original theoretical papers, *relations*). Developers write queries in a high-level language called the Structured Query Language, or more commonly, SQL. SQL is the common language for relational database management systems (RDBMS) that have been a popular tool for data management since the late 1970s. SQL became an industry-wide standard when it was adopted by NIST in 1986 and ISO in 1987. It is used for everything from terabyte Oracle and SQL Server installations to, as we shall see, storing email on your phone.

Database tables are a natural fit for data that includes many instances of the same kind of thing—a typical occurrence in software development. For example, a contact list has many contacts, all of which potentially have the same type of information (i.e., address, phone number, etc.). Each "row" of data in a table stores information about a different person, while each "column" stores a specific attribute of each person: names in one column, addresses in another column, and home phone numbers in a third. When someone is related to multiple things (such as multiple addresses), relational databases have ways of handling that too, but we won't go into such detail in this chapter.

SQLite

Android uses the SQLite database engine, a self-contained, transactional database engine that requires no separate server process. Many applications and environments beyond Android make use of it, and a large open source community actively develops SQLite. In contrast to desktop-oriented or enterprise databases, which provide a plethora of features related to fault tolerance and concurrent access to data, SQLite aggressively strips out features that are not absolutely necessary to achieve a small footprint. For example, many database systems use static typing, but SQLite does not store database type information. Instead, it pushes the responsibility of keeping type information into high-level languages, such as Java, that map database structures into high-level types.

SQLite is not a Google project, although Google has contributed to it. SQLite has an international team of software developers who are dedicated to enhancing the software's capabilities and reliability. Reliability is a key feature of SQLite. More than half of the code in the project is devoted to testing the library. The library is designed to handle many kinds of system failures, such as low memory, disk errors, and power failures. The database should never be left in an unrecoverable state, as this would be a showstopper on a mobile phone where critical data is often stored in a database. Fortunately, the SQLite database is not susceptible to easy corruption—if it were, an inopportune battery failure could turn a mobile phone into an expensive paperweight.

The SQLite project provides comprehensive and detailed documentation at *http://www.sqlite.org/docs.html*.

The SQL Language

Writing Android applications usually requires a basic ability to program in the SQL language, although higher-level classes are provided for the most common data-related activities. This chapter provides a beginner's introduction to SQLite. Although this is not a book about SQL, we will provide you with enough detail about Android-oriented

SQL to let you implement data persistence in a wide variety of Android applications. For more comprehensive information pertaining to the SQLite language, see *http://www.sqlite.org/lang.html*. We'll use simple SQL commands to explain the SQLite language, and along the way, we'll demonstrate how to use the `sqlite3` command to see the effects those queries have on the tables they modify. You may also find the W3Schools tutorial useful: *http://www.w3schools.com/sql/sql_intro.asp*.

With SQLite, the database is a simple file in the Android filesystem, which could reside in flash or external card memory, but you will find that most applications' databases reside in a directory called *</data/data/com.example.yourAppPackage/databases>*. You can issue the `ls` command in the adb shell to list the databases that Android has created for you in that directory.

The database takes care of persistence—that is, it updates the SQLite file in the way specified by each SQL statement issued by an application. In the following text, we describe SQLite commands as they are used inside the `sqlite3` command-line utility. Later we will show ways to achieve the same effects using the Android API. Although command-line SQL will not be part of the application you ship, it can certainly help to debug applications as you're developing them. You will find that writing database code in Android is usually an iterative process of writing Java code to manipulate tables, and then peeking at created data using the command line.

SQL Data Definition Commands

Statements in the SQL language fall into two distinct categories: those used to create and modify tables—the locations where data is stored—and those used to create, read, update, and delete the data in those tables. In this section we'll look at the former, the data definition commands:

CREATE TABLE *(http://www.sqlite.org/lang_createtable.html)*
>   Developers start working with SQL by creating a table to store data. The CREATE TABLE command creates a new table in an SQLite database. It specifies a name, which must be unique among the tables in the database, and various *columns* to hold the data. Each column has a unique name within the table and a type (the types are defined by SQL, such as a date or text string). The column may also specify other attributes, such as whether values have to be unique, whether there is a default value when a row is inserted without specifying a value, and whether NULL is allowed in the column.

>   A table is similar to a spreadsheet. Returning to the example of a contact database, each row in the table contains the information for one contact. The columns in the table are the various bits of information you collect about each individual contact: first name, last name, birthday, and so on. We provide several examples in this chapter that will help you to begin using our job database.

The tables created by SQL `CREATE TABLE` statements and the attributes they contain are called a *database schema*.

DROP TABLE *(http://www.sqlite.org/lang_droptable.html)*
> This removes a table added with the `CREATE TABLE` statement. It takes the name of the table to be deleted. On completion, any data that was stored in the table may not be retrieved.

Here is some SQL code that will create and then delete a simple table for storing contacts:

```
CREATE TABLE contacts (
    first_name TEXT,
    last_name TEXT,
    phone_number TEXT,
    height_in_meters REAL);

DROP TABLE contacts;
```

When entering commands through `sqlite3`, you must terminate each command with a semicolon.

You may change a table's schema after you create it (which you may want to do to add a column or change the default value of a column) by entering the `ALTER TABLE` command.

SQLite types

You must specify a type for each column that you create in all tables that you define, as discussed in "SQL Data Definition Commands" on page 265. SQLite supports the following data types:

TEXT
> A text string, stored using the database encoding (UTF-8, UTF-16BE, or UTF-16LE). You will find that the TEXT type is the most common.

REAL
> A floating-point value, stored as an 8-byte IEEE floating-point number.

BLOB
> Arbitrary binary data, stored exactly as though it were input. You can use the BLOB data type to store any kind of variable-length data, such as an executable file or a downloaded image. Generally, blobs can add a large performance overhead to a mobile database and you should usually avoid using them. In Chapter 13, we present an alternate scheme to store images downloaded from the Internet.

```
INTEGER
```
A signed integer, stored in 1, 2, 3, 4, 6, or 8 bytes depending on the magnitude of the value.

Specific information regarding SQLite types is available at *http://www.sqlite.org/data type3.html*.

Database constraints

Database constraints mark a column with particular attributes. Some constraints enforce data-oriented limitations, such as requiring all values in a column to be unique (e.g., a column containing Social Security numbers). Other constraints exhibit more functional uses. Relational constraints, `PRIMARY KEY` and `FOREIGN KEY`, form the basis of intertable relationships.

Most tables should have a particular column that uniquely identifies each given row. Designated in SQL as a `PRIMARY KEY`, this column tends to be used only as an identifier for each row and (unlike a Social Security number) has no meaning to the rest of the world. Thus, you do not need to specify values for the column. Instead, you can let SQLite assign incrementing integer values as new rows are added. Other databases typically require you to specially mark the column as autoincrementing to achieve this result. SQLite also offers an explicit `AUTOINCREMENT` constraint, but autoincrements primary keys by default. The incrementing values in the column take on a role similar to an opaque object pointer in a high-level language such as Java or C: other database tables and code in a high-level language can use the column to reference that particular row.

When database rows have a unique primary key, it is possible to start thinking about dependencies between tables. For example, a table used as an employee database could define an integer column called `employer_id` that would contain the primary key values of rows in a different table called `employers`. If you perform a query and select one or more rows from the `employers` table, you can grab the employer IDs and determine, for each, the respective employees, using the `employees` table's `employer_id` column. This allows a program to find the employees of a given employer. The two tables (stripped down to a few columns relevant to this example) might look like this:

```
CREATE TABLE employers (
    _id INTEGER PRIMARY KEY,
    company_name TEXT);

CREATE TABLE employees (
    name TEXT,
    annual_salary REAL NOT NULL CHECK (annual_salary > 0),
    employer_id REFERENCES employers(_id));
```

The idea of a table referring to another table's primary key has formal support in SQL as the `FOREIGN KEY` column constraint, which enforces the validity of cross-table references. This constraint tells the database that integers in a column with a foreign key constraint must refer to valid primary keys of database rows in another table. Thus, if you insert a row into the employees table with an employer_id for a row that does not exist in the employers table, many flavors of SQL will raise a constraint violation. This may help you to avoid orphaned references, also known as enforcement of foreign keys. However, the foreign key constraint in SQLite is optional, and is turned off in Android. You cannot rely on a foreign key constraint to catch incorrect foreign key references, so you will need to take care when creating database schemas that use foreign keys.

There are several other constraints with less far-reaching effects:

UNIQUE

> Forces the value of the given column to be different from the values in that column in all existing rows, whenever a row is inserted or updated. Any insert or update operation that attempts to insert a duplicate value will result in an SQLite constraint violation.

NOT NULL

> Requires a value in the column; NULL cannot be assigned. Note that a primary key is both UNIQUE and NOT NULL.

CHECK

> Takes a Boolean-valued expression and requires that the expression return true for any value inserted in the column. An example is the CHECK (annual_salary > 0), attribute shown earlier in the employees table.

SQL Data Manipulation Commands

Once you have defined tables using data definition commands, you can then insert your data and query the database. The following data manipulation commands are the most commonly used SQL statements:

SELECT

> This statement provides the main tool for querying the database. The result of this statement is zero or more rows of data, where each row has a fixed number of columns. You can think of the SELECT statement as producing a new table with only the rows and columns that you choose in the statement. The SELECT statement is the most complicated command in the SQL language, and supports a broad number of ways to build relationships between data across one or more database tables. Clauses for SQL's SELECT command, which are all supported by the Android API, include the following:
>
> * FROM, which specifies the tables from which data will be pulled to fulfill the query.
> * WHERE, which specifies conditions that selected rows in the tables must match to be returned by the query.
> * GROUP BY, which orders results in clusters according to column name.

- HAVING, which further limits results by evaluating groups against expressions. You might remove groups from your query that do not have a minimum number of elements.
- ORDER BY, which sets the sort order of query results by specifying a column name that will define the sort, and a function (e.g., ASC for ascending, DSC for descending) that will sort the rows by elements in the specified column.
- LIMIT, which limits the number of rows in a query to the specified value (e.g., five rows).

Here are a few examples of SELECT statements:

```
SELECT * FROM contacts;

SELECT first_name, height_in_meters
    FROM contacts
    WHERE last_name = "Smith";

SELECT employees.name, employers.name
    FROM employees, employers
    WHERE employee.employer_id = employer._id
    ORDER BY employer.company_name ASC;
```

The first statement retrieves all the rows in the contacts table, because no WHERE clause filters results. All columns (indicated by the asterisk, *) of the rows are returned. The second statement gets the names and heights of the members of the Smith family. The last statement prints a list of employees and their employers, sorted by company name.

For more information, see *http://www.sqlite.org/lang_select.html*.

INSERT

This statement adds a new data row to a specified database table along with a set of specified values of the proper SQLite type for each column (e.g., 5 for an integer). The insert may specify a list of columns affected by the insert, which may be less than the number of columns in the table. If you don't specify values for all columns, SQLite will fill in a default value for each unspecified column, if you defined one for that column in your CREATE TABLE statement. If you don't provide a default, SQLite uses a default of NULL.

Here are a few examples of INSERT statements:

```
INSERT INTO contacts(first_name)
    VALUES("Thomas");

INSERT INTO employers VALUES(1, "Acme Balloons");
INSERT INTO employees VALUES("Wile E. Coyote", 100000.000, 1);
```

The first adds a new row to the contacts for someone whose first name is Thomas and whose last name, phone number, and height are unknown (NULL). The second adds Acme Balloons as a new employer, and the third adds Wile E. Coyote as an employee there.

For more information, see *http://www.sqlite.org/lang_insert.html*.

UPDATE

This statement modifies some rows in a given table with new values. Each assignment specifies a table name and a given function that should provide a new value for the column. Like SELECT, you can specify a WHERE clause that will identify the rows that should be updated during an invocation of the UPDATE command. Like INSERT, you can also specify a list of columns to be updated during command execution. The list of columns works in the same manner as it does with INSERT. The WHERE clause is critical; if it matches no rows, the UPDATE command will have no effect, but if the clause is omitted, the statement will affect every row in the table.

Here are a few examples of UPDATE statements:

```
UPDATE contacts
    SET height_in_meters = 10, last_name = "Jones";

UPDATE employees
    SET annual_salary = 200000.00
    WHERE employer_id = (
        SELECT _id
            FROM employers
            WHERE company_name = "Acme Balloons");
```

The first claims that all your friends are giants with the last name Jones. The second is a more complex query. It gives a substantial raise to all the employees of Acme Balloons.

For more information, see *http://www.sqlite.org/lang_update.html*.

Additional Database Concepts

You now know enough simple SQL to be able to start working with databases in Android. As the applications you write grow in sophistication, you are likely to make use of the following SQL constructs that we won't cover in detail in this book:

Inner join

An inner join selects data across two or more tables where data is related by a foreign key. This type of query is useful for assembling objects that need to be distributed across one or more tables. The employee/employer example earlier demonstrated an inner join. As we've noted, because Android does not enforce foreign keys, you can get into trouble here if a key for a join does not exist as a valid cross-table reference—that is, a foreign key column actually points to a primary key of a row in another table that actually exists.

Compound query

SQLite supports complex database manipulations through combinations of statements. One of the update examples shown earlier was a compound query with a SELECT embedded in an UPDATE.

Triggers

A database trigger allows a developer to write SQL statements that will receive a callback when particular database conditions occur.

For detailed information on these topics, we suggest you consult a book on SQL, such as *Learning SQL* (*http://oreilly.com/catalog/9780596520847*) by Alan Beaulieu or *SQL Pocket Guide* (*http://oreilly.com/catalog/0636920013471*) by Jonathan Gennick, both published by O'Reilly.

Database Transactions

Database transactions make sequences of SQL statements atomic: either all statements succeed or none of them have any effect on the database. This can be important, for instance, if your app encounters an unfortunate occurrence such as a system crash. A transaction will guarantee that if the device fails partway through a given sequence of operations, none of the operations will affect the database. In database jargon, SQLite transactions support the widely recited ACID transaction properties: *http://en.wikipe dia.org/wiki/ACID*.

With SQLite, every database operation that modifies a database runs in its own database transaction, which means a developer can be assured that all values of an insert will be written if the statement succeeds at all. You can also explicitly start and end a transaction so that it encompasses multiple statements. For a given transaction, SQLite does not modify the database until all statements in the transaction have completed successfully.

Given the volatility of the Android mobile environment, we recommend that in addition to meeting the needs for consistency in your app, you also make liberal use of transactions to support fault tolerance in your application.

Example Database Manipulation Using sqlite3

Now that you understand the basics of SQL as it pertains to SQLite, let's have a look at a simple database for storing video metadata using the `sqlite3` command-line tool and the Android debug shell, which you can start by using the `adb` command. Using the command line will allow us to view database changes right away, and will provide some simple examples of how to work with this useful database debugging tool. SQLite has more information on `sqlite3` at *http://www.sqlite.org/sqlite.html*. Note that it is likely easiest at first to run this example using the Android emulator, as you will need root access to run it on a device.

We'll get the example started by initializing the database:

```
$ adb shell
# cd /data/data/
# mkdir com.oreilly.demo.pa.ch10.sql
# cd com.oreilly.demo.pa.ch10.sql
```

```
# mkdir databases
# cd databases
#
# sqlite3 simple_video.db
SQLite version 3.6.22
Enter ".help" for instructions
Enter SQL statements terminated with a ";"
sqlite>
```

 Note that developers should not create these directories by hand, as we have done in this example, as Android will create them during installation of an application. Directory creation is merely useful for this particular example because we do not yet have an application in which the directories would have been automatically created.

The `sqlite3` command line accepts two kinds of commands: legal SQL, and single-word commands that begin with a period (.). You can see the first (and probably most important!) of these in the introduction message: `.help`. Try it out, just to get an idea of the options available to you:

```
sqlite> .help
.bail ON|OFF            Stop after hitting an error.  Default OFF
.databases             List names and files of attached databases
.dump ?TABLE? ...      Dump the database in a SQL text format
.echo ON|OFF           Turn command echo on or off
.exit                  Exit this program
.explain ON|OFF        Turn output mode suitable for EXPLAIN on or off.
.header(s) ON|OFF      Turn display of headers on or off
.help                  Show this message
.import FILE TABLE     Import data from FILE into TABLE
.indices TABLE         Show names of all indices on TABLE
.load FILE ?ENTRY?     Load an extension library
.mode MODE ?TABLE?     Set output mode where MODE is one of:
                         csv      Comma-separated values
                         column   Left-aligned columns.  (See .width)
                         html     HTML <table> code
                         insert   SQL insert statements for TABLE
                         line     One value per line
                         list     Values delimited by .separator string
                         tabs     Tab-separated values
                         tcl      TCL list elements
.nullvalue STRING      Print STRING in place of NULL values
.output FILENAME       Send output to FILENAME
.output stdout         Send output to the screen
.prompt MAIN CONTINUE  Replace the standard prompts
.quit                  Exit this program
.read FILENAME         Execute SQL in FILENAME
.schema ?TABLE?        Show the CREATE statements
.separator STRING      Change separator used by output mode and .import
.show                  Show the current values for various settings
.tables ?PATTERN?      List names of tables matching a LIKE pattern
.timeout MS            Try opening locked tables for MS milliseconds
```

```
.timer ON|OFF          Turn the CPU timer measurement on or off
.width NUM NUM ...     Set column widths for "column" mode
```

There's another important command in this list: .exit. Remember it! It's how you get out of here. Alternatively, you can quit with the Ctrl-D keystroke.

Another important thing to remember is that every SQL command needs to be terminated with a semicolon. If you see something like this:

```
sqlite> ls
...>
```

it just means SQLite thinks you've started to enter SQL, and it is waiting for the ; at the end. Note that the . commands do not need to be terminated by a semicolon.

 We've used ls as an example of a command a user might have absent-mindedly typed if he forgot he was using sqlite3. ls is not actually an sqlite3 command; if you type ; after ls, sqlite will complain with an error, and then you can enter correct dot commands or SQL statements.

Most of the "dot" commands aren't very interesting at this point, because this database is still empty. So let's add some data:

```
sqlite> create table video (
   ...> _id integer primary key,
   ...> title text,
   ...> description text,
   ...> url text);
```

These lines create a new table called video. The types of the columns are integer and text. The table contains a primary key called _id. This particular column name is not chosen accidentally. Android requires the use of this exact name in order for the table to work with its cursor system.

We can see the newly created tables using the "dot" command .table:

```
sqlite> .table
video
sqlite>
```

Next we'll go through a few different queries that illustrate the SQL concepts we introduced earlier, and then an application based on these tables. First, let's insert some data into our new tables so that our queries return some example results:

```
INSERT INTO video (_id, title, url)
   VALUES(1, "Epic Fail Car", "http://www.youtube.com/watch?v=O1ynapTnYVkeGE");
INSERT INTO video (_id, title, url)
   VALUES(2, "Epic Fail Bicycle", "http://www.youtube.com/watch?v=7n7apTnYVkeGE");
INSERT INTO video (_id, title, url)
   VALUES(3, "Epic Fail Wagon", "http://www.youtube.com/watch?v=mOiGn2c47LA");
INSERT INTO video (_id, title, url)
   VALUES(4, "Epic Fail Sidewalk", "http://www.youtube.com/watch?v=mOiGn2cNcNo");
INSERT INTO video (_id, title, url)
```

```
VALUES(5, "Epic Fail Motorcycle",
     "http://www.youtube.com/watch?v=7n7apBB8qkeGE");
```

Be careful to balance your quotes. If you enter a single quote, `sqlite3` will prompt you forever, until it gets the match.

In this example, we did not enter values for all the columns in the table. The contents of the parentheses after the `INTO` phrase in the statement list the columns into which the statement will put data. The parentheses after the `VALUES` phrase contain the values themselves, in the same order.

Now suppose you want to find the names of all the videos that have the word fragment *cycle* in them. Use a `SELECT` query:

```
sqlite> SELECT title FROM video WHERE title LIKE "%cycle%";
Epic Fail Bicycle
Epic Fail Motorcycle
```

`sqlite3` prints the rows one to a line. In the example, we capitalized SQL reserved words to help keep syntax clear. It is not necessary to do so. They can be uppercase, lowercase, or mixed case.

The example also shows the rudimentary pattern matching available in SQL. The keyword `LIKE`, combined with the wildcard percent sign character (%), allows you to match parts of strings.

Suppose now that we'd like all the videos, with their URLs, sorted in reverse alphabetical order by title:

```
sqlite> SELECT title, url FROM video ORDER BY title DESC;
Epic Fail Wagon|http://www.youtube.com/watch?v=mOiGn2c47LA
Epic Fail Sidewalk|http://www.youtube.com/watch?v=mOiGn2cNcNo
Epic Fail Motorcycle|http://www.youtube.com/watch?v=7n7apBB8qkeGE
Epic Fail Car|http://www.youtube.com/watch?v=O1ynapTnYVkeGE
Epic Fail Bicycle|http://www.youtube.com/watch?v=7n7apTnYVkeGE
```

You can see that `sqlite3` uses the pipe character (|) to separate the values in different columns.

We didn't add descriptions for our videos. Let's add just one, now:

```
sqlite> UPDATE video SET description="Crash!" WHERE title LIKE "%Car";
sqlite> UPDATE video SET description="Trip!" WHERE  title LIKE '%Sidewalk%';
sqlite> SELECT title, description FROM video WHERE NOT description IS NULL;
Epic Fail Car|Crash!
Epic Fail Sidewalk|Trip!
```

Finally, let's delete a record using its ID:

```
sqlite> DELETE FROM video WHERE _id = 1;
sqlite> SELECT _id, description FROM videos;
2|Epic Fail Bicycle
3|Epic Fail Wagon
4|Epic Fail Sidewalk
5|Epic Fail Motorcycle
```

SQL and the Database-Centric Data Model for Android Applications

Now that you have some basic SQL programming knowledge, we can start thinking about how to put it to use in an Android application. Our goal is to create robust applications based on the popular Model-View-Controller (MVC) pattern that underlies well-written UI programs, specifically in a way that works well for Android. Wikipedia has background information on MVC at *http://en.wikipedia.org/wiki/Model_view_controller*.

One fundamental difference between mobile phone apps and desktop apps is how they handle persistence. Traditional desktop-based applications—word processors, text editors, drawing programs, presentation programs, and so on—often use a document-centric form of the MVC pattern. They open a document, read it into memory, and turn it into objects in memory that form the data model. Such programs will make views for the data model, process user input through their controller, and then modify the data model (Figure 9-1). The key consequence of this design is that you explicitly open and save documents in order to make the data model persist between program invocations. We've seen how user interface components work in Android. Next we'll explore the Android APIs for database manipulation, which will prepare you to implement an application data model that works in a new way.

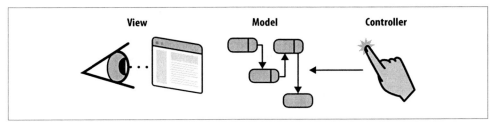

Figure 9-1. Document-centric applications, which implement a data model with in-memory objects

Robust use of Android combines data models and user interface elements in a different manner. Apps run on mobile devices with limited memory, which can run out of battery power at unpredictable and possibly inopportune times. Small mobile devices also place a premium on reducing the interactive burden on the user: reminding a user he ought to save a document when he is trying to answer a phone call is not a good user experience. The whole concept of a document is absent in Android. The user should always have the right data at hand and be confident his data is safe.

To make it easy to store and use application data incrementally, item by item, and always have it in persistent memory without explicitly saving the whole data model, Android provides support in its database, view, and activity classes for database-centric data (Figure 9-2). We'll explain how to use Android database classes to implement this kind of model.

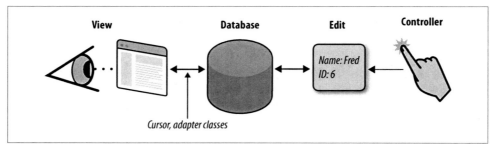

Figure 9-2. *Android support for a data model that mostly resides in a database*

The Android Database Classes

This section introduces the Java classes that give you access to the SQLite functions described earlier in the chapter, with the data-centric model we just described in mind:

SQLiteDatabase

Android's Java interface to its relational database, SQLite. It supports an SQL implementation rich enough for anything you're likely to need in a mobile application, including a cursor facility.

Cursor

A container for the results of a database query that supports an MVC-style observation system. Cursors are similar to JDBC result sets and are the return value of a database query in Android. A cursor can represent many objects without requiring an instance for each one. With a cursor, you can move to the start of query results and access each row one at a time as needed. To access cursor data, you call methods named as Cursor.getAs*(int columnNumber) (e.g., getAsString). The values the cursor will return depend on the current cursor index, which you can increment by calling Cursor.moveToNext, or decrement by calling Cursor.moveTo Previous, as needed. You can think of the current index of the cursor as a pointer to a result object.

Cursors are at the heart of the basis for Android MVC, which we will cover in detail in Chapter 12.

SQLiteOpenHelper

Provides a life cycle framework for creating and upgrading your application database. It's quite helpful to use this class to assist with the critical task of transitioning the data from one version of an application to a possible new set of database tables in a new version of an application.

SQLiteQueryBuilder

Provides a high-level abstraction for creating SQLite queries for use in Android applications. Using this class can simplify the task of writing a query because it saves you from having to fiddle with SQL syntax yourself.

Database Design for Android Applications

In the next section, we'll examine some code from Chapter 12 that deals with persistent storage of video-related metadata information: title, description, and video URL. This code resides inside an Android content provider, which we feel is an appropriate location for database code. Without explaining much about content providers, we'll discuss how to write a database for one. Chapter 12 explains in detail how to write a content provider. The following code will help us illustrate how to create and use an SQLite database in Android. This application will use roughly the same database that we just examined using the sqlite3 command-line tool. This time, though, we'll be writing code that uses the Android API to manipulate the data.

Basic Structure of the SimpleVideoDbHelper Class

In our example, the *SimpleFinchVideoContentProvider.java* file encapsulates all the SQL logic necessary to work with the *simple_video* database in Android. Applications that need access to the persistent data in this database interact with the provider and the cursors it supplies, as we'll explain in Chapter 12. Clients are completely insulated from the details of how the data is actually stored. This is good programming practice and should be emulated in all your Android applications that use databases.

For now, because we are focusing on how to use databases in Android, it's sufficient to know that SimpleVideoDbHelper is the model of the database in the provider: everything specific to the implementation of the database—its name, the names of its columns, the definitions of its tables—takes effect in this class. For a large, complex database, of course, the helper class may be much more complex and be composed of several components.

SimpleVideoDbHelper inherits from the abstract SQLiteOpenHelper class, and therefore must override the onCreate and onUpgrade methods. The onCreate method is automatically called when the application starts for the first time. Its job is to create the database. When new versions of the application ship, it may be necessary to update the database, perhaps adding tables, adding columns, or even changing the schema entirely. When this is necessary, the task falls to the onUpgrade method, which is called whenever the DATABASE_VERSION in the call to the constructor is different from the one stored with the database. When you ship a new version of a database, you must increment the version number:

```java
public static final String VIDEO_TABLE_NAME = "video";

public static final String DATABASE_NAME = SIMPLE_VIDEO + ".db";
private static int DATABASE_VERSION = 2;

public static final int ID_COLUMN = 0;
public static final int TITLE_COLUMN = 1;
public static final int DESCRIPTION_COLUMN = 2;
public static final int TIMESTAMP_COLUMN = 3;
```

```
public static final int QUERY_TEXT_COLUMN = 4;
public static final int MEDIA_ID_COLUMN = 5;

private static class SimpleVideoDbHelper extends SQLiteOpenHelper {
    private SimpleVideoDbHelper(Context context, String name,
                               SQLiteDatabase.CursorFactory factory)
    {
        super(context, name, factory, DATABASE_VERSION);
    }

    @Override
    public void onCreate(SQLiteDatabase sqLiteDatabase) {
        createTable(sqLiteDatabase);
    }

    private void createTable(SQLiteDatabase sqLiteDatabase) {
        String qs = "CREATE TABLE " + VIDEO_TABLE_NAME + " (" +
                FinchVideo.SimpleVideos._ID +
                " INTEGER PRIMARY KEY AUTOINCREMENT, " +
                FinchVideo.SimpleVideos.TITLE_NAME + " TEXT, " +
                FinchVideo.SimpleVideos.DESCRIPTION_NAME + " TEXT, " +
                FinchVideo.SimpleVideos.URI_NAME + " TEXT);";
        sqLiteDatabase.execSQL(qs);
    }

    @Override
    public void onUpgrade(SQLiteDatabase sqLiteDatabase,
                          int oldv, int newv)
    {
        sqLiteDatabase.execSQL("DROP TABLE IF EXISTS " +
                VIDEO_TABLE_NAME + ";");
        createTable(sqLiteDatabase);
    }
}
```

The general elements associated with SimpleVideoDbHelper code are:

Constants

The SimpleVideoDbHelper class defines four important constants:

DATABASE_NAME

This holds the filename of the database, *simple_video.db* in this case.
This names the actual SQLite database file. Recall that we mentioned this file
resides in the following path, and that Android will take care to create the
database file for you: */data/data/com.oreilly.demo.pa.finchvideo/databases/sim-
ple_video.db*.

DATABASE_VERSION

This defines the database version, which you choose arbitrarily and increment
whenever you change the database schema. If the version of the database on
the machine is less than DATABASE_VERSION, the system runs your onUpgrade
method to upgrade the database to the current level.

VIDEO_TABLE_NAME

This is the name of the only table in our simple database.

*_NAME

These are the names of the columns in the database. As mentioned earlier, it is essential to define a column named _id and use it as the primary key, for any table that you will access through a cursor.

Constructor

The constructor for the database in this provider, SimpleVideoDbHelper, uses the super function to call its parent's constructor. The parent does most of the work of creating the database object.

onCreate

When an Android application attempts to read or write data to a database that does not exist, the framework executes the onCreate method. The onCreate method in the YouTubeDbHelper class shows one way to create the database. If initializing the database required a substantial amount of SQL code, it might be preferable to keep the code in the *strings.xml* resource file. This might make the Java code much more readable. But it also forces a developer modifying the code to look in two separate files to see what's really going on. Of course, if a program has a simple database, it might be easier to just write the SQL in Java, as we have done in SimpleVideoDbHelper, or if you use a query builder, there may be no SQL at all.

 If you intend to load your SQL from a String resource, you must take care of a change to the string mentioned only briefly in the Android documentation: escape all single quotes and double quotes with a backslash (changing " to \" and ' to \') within a resource string, or enclose the entire string in either single or double quotes. You should also turn off formatting in the string, using the formatted="false" attribute. For example:

```
<string name="sql_query" formatted="false">
    SELECT * FROM videos WHERE name LIKE \"%cycle%\"
</string>
```

The onCreate method doesn't actually have to create the database. It is passed a brand-new, empty database and must completely initialize it. In SimpleVideoDb Helper, this is a simple task and is accomplished with the call to createTable.

onUpgrade

The onUpgrade method for SimpleVideoDbHelper is very simple: it deletes the database. When the provider tries to use it later, Android will call the onCreate method because it does not exist. While such a crude approach might be acceptable in this extremely simple case, a provider intended only as a cache for network data, it would certainly not be acceptable for, say, a database of contacts! Your customers won't be very happy if they have to re-key their information each time they upgrade software versions. So our onUpgrade method won't work very well in real life. In general, the `onUpgrade` method will have to recognize all previous versions of databases used by an application and have a data-safe strategy for converting those databases to the most recent format. A larger application would have several upgrade scripts, one for each version that might be out in the wild. The application would then execute each upgrade script in turn until the database was completely up-to-date.

`createTable`

We created this function to encapsulate the SQL code that creates our table.

Using the Database API: MJAndroid

In this section, we present a more advanced example application, called MJAndroid, that demonstrates the use of a small database for a hypothetical job-searching application. In this chapter, we explore the data persistence aspects of this program. In Chapter 15, we take a look at how the application integrates mapping features to show job query results on a map. First we'll explain the application in a bit more detail.

Android and Social Networking

One of the great promises of Android mobile phones is their ability to run applications that enhance opportunities for social networking among users. This promise echoes the reality of the Internet—the first generation of Internet applications were about user access to information, and many of those applications have been very popular. The second wave of Internet applications were about connecting users to one another. Applications such as Facebook, YouTube, and many others enhance our ability to connect with people of similar interests, and allow the application users to provide some or all of the content that makes the application what it is. Android has the potential to take that concept and add a new dimension—mobility. It's expected that a whole new generation of applications will be built for users of mobile devices: social networking applications that are easy to use while walking down the street, applications that are aware of the user's location, applications that allow the easy sharing of content-rich information such as pictures and videos and so on. MJAndroid provides a concrete example of how Android can address this growing niche.

In the case of the MJAndroid MicroJobs application, the user is trying to locate a temporary job in her geographic vicinity, where she can work for a few hours to earn some extra money. The premise is that employers looking for temporary help have entered available jobs, descriptions, hours, and offered wages in a web-based database that is accessible from Android mobile phones. People looking for a few hours' work can use the MicroJobs application to access that database, look for jobs in their immediate area, communicate with friends about potential employers and potential jobs, and call the employer directly if they are interested in the position. For our purposes here, we won't create an online service, we'll just have some canned data on the phone. The application has a number of features that extend that central idea in ways that are unique to mobile handsets:

Mapping

The Android mobile phone environment provides support for dynamic, interactive maps, and we're going to take full advantage of its capabilities. In "The MapView and MapActivity" on page 414 you'll see that with very little code, we'll be able to show dynamic maps of our local neighborhood, getting location updates from the internal GPS to automatically scroll the map as we move. We'll be able to scroll the map in two directions, zoom in and out, and even switch to satellite views.

Finding friends and events

Again in Chapter 15, we'll see a graphic overlay on the map that will show us where jobs are located in the area, and will allow us to get more information about a job by just touching its symbol on the map. We will access Android's contact manager application to get address information for our friends (telephone numbers, instant messaging addresses, etc.), and the MicroJobs database to get more information about posted jobs.

Instant messaging

When we find friends we want to chat with, we will be able to contact them via instant messages, by trading SMS messages with our friends' mobile phones.

Talking with friends or employers

If IMing is too slow or cumbersome, we'll be able to easily place a cellular call to our friends, or call the employer offering a job.

Browsing the Web

Most employers have an associated website that provides more detailed information. We'll be able to select an employer off a list or off the map and quickly zero in on their website to find out, for example, what the place looks like.

This is a fun application that could easily be developed further into a full-blown service, but our intent in this book is to show you just how easy it is to develop and combine these powerful capabilities in your own application. Like all the code in this book, the complete code is available for download. Although it's not absolutely required to understand the material in the book, you are strongly encouraged to download the source to your own computer. That way you'll have it readily available for reference, and it will be easy to cut sections of code and paste them into your own applications as you move on. For now, we'll use the MJAndroid example to provide a "close to real world" example to dig into the Android database API.

Figure 9-3 shows the screen displayed by MJAndroid when you first run it. It's a map of your local area, overlaid with a few buttons and pins.

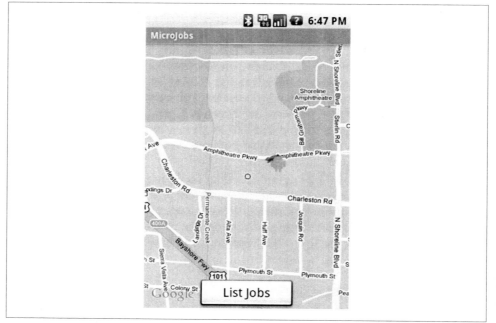

Figure 9-3. MJAndroid opening screenshot

The Source Folder (src)

The package name for MJAndroid is com.microjobsinc.mjandroid. Eclipse lays out the equivalent directory structure, just as it would for any Java project, and shows you the whole thing when you open the *src* folders. In addition to these package folders there is a folder named for the package that contains all the Java files for the project. These include the following files:

MicroJobs.java
> The main source file for the application—the activity that starts first, displays the map that is the centerpiece of the application, and calls other activities or services as necessary to implement different features in the user interface.

MicroJobsDatabase.java
> A database helper that provides easy access to the local MJAndroid database. This is where all the employer, user, and job information is stored, using SQLite.

AddJob.java and EditJob.java
> Part of the database portion of MJAndroid. They provide screens that the user can use to add or edit job entries in the database.

MicroJobsDetail.java
> The `Activity` that displays all the detail information about a particular job opportunity.

MicroJobsEmpDetail.java

The `Activity` that displays information about an employer, including name, address, reputation, email address, phone number, and so forth.

MicroJobsList.java

The `Activity` that displays a list of jobs (as opposed to the map view in *Micro-Jobs.java*). It shows a simple list of employers and jobs, and allows the user to sort the list by either field, as well as to call up specifics about the job or employer by touching the name on the list.

Loading and Starting the Application

Running MJAndroid from the SDK is complicated by the fact that the application uses a `MapView`. Android requires a special Maps API key whenever you use a `MapView`, and the key is tied to your particular development machine. We learned in "Google Maps API Keys" on page 143 about the requirements for signing and starting your application, and because this application relies on the Maps API, you will need to have set up your API key for the example to work properly. To start MJAndroid, just open and run the Eclipse project for this chapter, as you have done for other chapters.

Database Queries and Reading Data from the Database

There are many ways to read data from an SQL database, but they all come down to a basic sequence of operations:

1. Create an SQL statement that describes the data you need to retrieve.
2. Execute that statement against the database.
3. Map the resultant SQL data into data structures that the language you're working in can understand.

This process can be very complex in the case of object-relational mapping software, or relatively simple but labor-intensive when writing the queries directly into your application. Object-relational mapping (ORM, at *http://en.wikipedia.org/wiki/Object_rela tional_mapping*) tools shield your code from the complexities of database programming and object mapping by moving that complexity out of your immediate field of vision. Your code may be more robust in the face of database changes, but at the cost of complex ORM setup and maintenance. It is not typical to use an ORM in an Android application.

The simple approach of writing queries directly into your application works well only for very small projects that will not change much over time. Applications directly containing database code have some added risk of fragility, because when the database schema changes, any code that references the schema must be examined and potentially rewritten.

A common middle-ground approach is to sequester all the database logic into a set of objects that have as their sole purpose to translate application requests into database requests and deliver the results back to the application. This is the approach we have taken with the MJAndroid application; all the database code is contained in the single class MicroJobsDatabase, which also extends SQLiteOpenHelper. But with SimpleFinch VideoContentProvider the database is simple enough that we don't bother to use external strings.

When not used with a content provider, Android gives us the ability to customize cursors, and we use that ability to further reduce code dependencies by hiding all the information about each specific database operation inside a custom cursor. The interface to the caller in the getJobs method of MicroJobsDatabase appears first in the code that follows. The method's job is to return a JobsCursor filled with jobs from the database. The user can choose (through the single parameter passed to the getJobs method) to sort jobs by either the title column or the employer_name column.

```
public class MicroJobsDatabase extends SQLiteOpenHelper {
...
    /** Return a sorted JobsCursor
     * @param sortBy the sort criteria
     */
    public JobsCursor getJobs(JobsCursor.SortBy sortBy) {❶
        String sql = JobsCursor.QUERY + sortBy.toString();❷
        SQLiteDatabase d = getReadableDatabase();❸
        JobsCursor c = (JobsCursor) d.rawQueryWithFactory(❹
            new JobsCursor.Factory(),
            sql,
            null,
            null);
        c.moveToFirst();❺
        return c;❻
    }
...
    public static class JobsCursor extends SQLiteCursor{❼
        public static enum SortBy{❽
            title,
            employer_name
        }
        private static final String QUERY =
            "SELECT jobs._id, title, employer_name, latitude, longitude, status "+
            "FROM jobs, employers "+
            "WHERE jobs.employer_id = employers._id "+
            "ORDER BY ";
        private JobsCursor(SQLiteDatabase db, SQLiteCursorDriver driver,
            String editTable, SQLiteQuery query) {❾
            super(db, driver, editTable, query);
        }
        private static class Factory implements SQLiteDatabase.CursorFactory{❿
            @Override
            public Cursor newCursor(SQLiteDatabase db,
                    SQLiteCursorDriver driver, String editTable,
                    SQLiteQuery query) {⓫
```

```
                return new JobsCursor(db, driver, editTable, query);❷
            }
        }
        public long getColJobsId(){❸
            return getLong(getColumnIndexOrThrow("jobs._id"));
        }
        public String getColTitle(){
            return getString(getColumnIndexOrThrow("title"));
        }
        public String getColEmployerName(){
            return getString(getColumnIndexOrThrow("employer_name"));
        }
        public long getColLatitude(){
            return getLong(getColumnIndexOrThrow("latitude"));
        }
        public long getColLongitude(){
            return getLong(getColumnIndexOrThrow("longitude"));
        }
        public long getColStatus(){
            return getLong(getColumnIndexOrThrow("status"));
        }
    }
}
```

Here are some of the highlights of the code:

❶ Function that fashions a query based on the user's requested sort column (the sortBy parameter) and returns results as a cursor.

❷ Creates the query string. Most of the string is static (the QUERY variable), but this line tacks on the sort column. Even though QUERY is private, it is still available to the enclosing class. This is because the getJobs method and the JobsCursor class are both within the MicroJobsDatabase class, which makes JobsCursor's private data members available to the getJobs method.

To get the text for the sort column, we just run toString on the enumerated parameter passed by the caller. We could have defined an associative array, which would give us more flexibility in naming variables, but this solution is simpler. Additionally, the names of the columns pop up quite nicely using your IDE's autocompletion.

❸ Retrieves a handle to the database.

❹ Creates the JobsCursor cursor using the SQLiteDatabase object's rawQueryWith Factory method. This method lets us pass a factory method that Android will use to create the exact type of cursor we need. If we had used the simpler rawQuery method, we would get back a generic Cursor lacking the special features of JobsCursor.

❺ As a convenience to the caller, moves to the first row in the result. This way, the cursor is returned ready to use. A common mistake is to forget the moveToFirst call and then pull your hair out trying to figure out why the Cursor object is throwing exceptions.

❻ The cursor is the return value.

❼ Class that creates the cursor returned by getJobs.

❽ Simple way to provide alternate sort criteria: store the names of columns in an enum. This type is used in item 2.

❾ Constructor for the customized cursor. The final argument is the query passed by the caller.

❿ Factory class to create the cursor, embedded in the JobsCursor class.

⓫ Creates the cursor from the query passed by the caller.

⓬ Returns the cursor to the enclosing JobsCursor class.

⓭ Convenience functions that extract particular columns from the row under the cursor. For instance, getColTitle returns the value of the title column in the row currently referenced by the cursor. This separates the database implementation from the calling code and makes that code easier to read.

 While subclassing a cursor is a nice trick for using a database within a single application, it won't work with the content provider API, because Android does not have a way for cursor subclasses to be shared across processes. Additionally, the MJAndroid application is a contrived example to demonstrate using a database: we present an application with a more robust architecture that you might see in a production application in Chapter 13.

A sample use of the database follows. The code gets a cursor, sorted by title, through a call to getJobs. It then iterates through the jobs.

```
MicroJobsDatabase db = new MicroJobsDatabase(this);❶
JobsCursor cursor = db.getJobs(JobsCursor.SortBy.title);❷

for (int rowNum = 0; rowNum < cursor.getCount(); rowNum++) {❸
    cursor.moveToPosition(rowNum);
    doSomethingWith(cursor.getColTitle());❹
}
```

Here are some of the highlights of the code:

❶ Creates a MicroJobsDatabase object. The argument, this, represents the context as discussed previously.

❷ Creates the JobsCursor cursor, referring to the SortBy enumeration discussed earlier.

❸ Uses generic Cursor methods to iterate through the cursor.

❹ Still within the loop, invokes one of the custom accessor methods provided by JobsCursor to "do something" chosen by the user with the value of each row's title column.

Using the query method

While it's helpful for applications that execute nontrivial database operations to isolate their SQL statements as shown previously, it's also convenient for applications with simple database operations, such as our `SimpleFinchVideoContentProvider`, to make use of the method `SQLiteDatabase.query`, as shown in the following video-related example:

```
videoCursor = mDb.query(VIDEO_TABLE_NAME, projection,
    where, whereArgs,
    null, null, sortOrder);
```

As with `SQLiteDatabase.rawQueryWithFactory` shown previously, the return value of the query method is a `Cursor` object. Here, we assign this cursor to the previously defined `videoCursor` variable.

The `query` method runs a `SELECT` on a given table name, in this case the constant `VIDEO_TABLE_NAME`. The method takes two parameters. The first parameter is a projection that names the columns that should only show up in the query—other column values will not show up in the cursor results. Many applications work just fine passing `null` for the projection, which will cause all column values to show up in the resultant cursor. Next, the `where` argument contains an SQL `where` clause, without the `WHERE` keyword. The `where` argument can also contain a number of '?' strings that will be replaced with the values of `whereArgs`. We'll discuss in more detail how these two values bind together when we discuss the `execSQL` method.

Modifying the Database

Android `Cursors` are great when you want to read data from the database, but the class `android.database.Cursor` does not provide methods for creating, updating, or deleting data. The `SQLiteDatabase` class provides two basic APIs that you can use for both reading and writing:

- A set of four methods called simply `insert`, `query`, `update`, and `delete`
- A more general `execSQL` method that takes any single SQL statement that does not return data and runs it against the database

We recommend using the first set of calls when your operations fit its capabilities. We'll show you both ways to use the MJAndroid operations.

Inserting data into the database

The SQL `INSERT` statement is used whenever you want to insert data into an SQL database. The `INSERT` statement maps to the "create" operation of the CRUD methodology.

In the MJAndroid application, the user can add jobs to the list by clicking on the Add Job menu item when looking at the Jobs list. The user can then fill out a form to input the employer, job title, and description. After the user clicks on the Add Job button on the form, the following line of code is executed:

```
db.addJob(employer.id, txtTitle.getText().toString(),
    txtDescription.getText().toString());
```

This code calls the addJob function, passing in the employer ID, the job title, and the job description. The addJob function does the actual work of writing the job out to the database.

Using the insert method. The following example demonstrates use of the insert method:

```
/**
 * Add a new job to the database.  The job will have a status of open.
 * @param employer_id    The employer offering the job
 * @param title          The job title
 * @param description     The job description
 */
public void addJob(long employer_id, String title, String description) {
    ContentValues map = new ContentValues();❶
    map.put("employer_id", employer_id);
    map.put("title", title);
    map.put("description", description);
    try{
        getWritableDatabase().insert("jobs", null, map);❷
    } catch (SQLException e) {
        Log.e("Error writing new job", e.toString());
    }
}
```

Here are some of the highlights of the code:

❶ The ContentValues object is a map of column names to column values. Internally, it's implemented as a HashMap<String,Object>. However, unlike a simple HashMap, ContentValues is strongly typed. You can specify the data type of each value stored in a ContentValues container. When you pull values back out, ContentValues will automatically convert values to the requested type if possible.

❷ The second parameter to the insert method is nullColumnHack. It's used only as a default value when the third parameter, the map, is null and therefore the row would otherwise be completely empty.

Using the execSQL method. This solution works at a lower level than the insert solution. It creates SQL and passes it to the library to execute. Although you could hardcode every statement, including the data passed by the user, this section shows a preferable method that employs bind parameters.

A bind parameter is a question mark that holds a place in an SQL statement, usually for a parameter passed by the user such as a value in a WHERE clause. After creating an SQL statement with bind parameters, you can reuse it repeatedly, setting the actual value of the bind parameters before executing it each time:

```
/**
 * Add a new job to the database.  The job will have a status of open.
 * @param employer_id    The employer offering the job
 * @param title          The job title
 * @param description     The job description
 */
public void addJob(long employer_id, String title, String description){
    String sql = ❶
        "INSERT INTO jobs " +
        "(_id,  employer_id, title, description, start_time, end_time, status) " +
        "VALUES " +
        "(NULL, ?,           ?,     ?,          0,          0,         3)";
    Object[] bindArgs = new Object[]{employer_id, title, description};
    try{
        getWritableDatabase().execSQL(sql, bindArgs);❷
    } catch (SQLException e) {
        Log.e("Error writing new job", e.toString());
    }
}
```

Here are some of the highlights of the code:

❶ Builds an SQL query template named `sql` that contains bindable parameters that will be filled in with user data. The bindable parameters are marked by question marks in the string. Next, we build an object array named `bindArgs` that contains one object per element in our SQL template. There are three question marks in the template, so there must be three elements in the object array.

❷ Executes the SQL command by passing the SQL template string and the bind arguments to `execSQL`.

Using an SQL template and bind arguments is much preferred over building up the SQL statement, complete with parameters, into a `String` or `StringBuilder`. By using a template with parameters, you protect your application from SQL injection attacks. These attacks occur when a malicious user enters information into a form that is deliberately meant to modify the database in a way that was not intended by the developer. Intruders normally do this by ending the current SQL command prematurely, using SQL syntax characters, and then adding new SQL commands directly in the form field. The template-plus-parameters approach also protects you from more run-of-the-mill errors, such as invalid characters in the parameters. It also leads to cleaner code as it avoids long sequences of manually appended strings by automatically replacing question marks.

Updating data already in the database

The MicroJobs application enables the user to edit a job by clicking on the job in the Jobs list and choosing the Edit Job menu item. The user can then modify the strings for employer, job title, and description in the editJob form. After the user clicks on the Update button on the form, the following line of code is executed:

```
db.editJob((long)job_id, employer.id, txtTitle.getText().toString(),
    txtDescription.getText().toString());
```

This code calls the editJob method, passing the job ID and the three items the user can change: employer ID, job title, and job description. The editJob method does the actual work of modifying the job in the database.

Using the update method. The following example demonstrates use of the update method:

```
/**
 * Update a job in the database.
 * @param job_id        The job id of the existing job
 * @param employer_id   The employer offering the job
 * @param title         The job title
 * @param description   The job description
 */
public void editJob(long job_id, long employer_id, String title, String description)
{
    ContentValues map = new ContentValues();
    map.put("employer_id", employer_id);
    map.put("title", title);
    map.put("description", description);
    String[] whereArgs = new String[]{Long.toString(job_id)};
    try{
        getWritableDatabase().update("jobs", map, "_id=?", whereArgs);❶
    } catch (SQLException e) {
        Log.e("Error writing new job", e.toString());
    }
}
```

Here are some of the highlights of the code:

❶ The first parameter to update is the name of the table to manipulate. The second is the map of column names to new values. The third is a small snippet of SQL. In this case, it's an SQL template with one parameter. The parameter is marked with a question mark, and is filled out with the contents of the fourth argument.

Using the execSQL method. The following example demonstrates use of the execSQL method:

```
/**
 * Update a job in the database.
 * @param job_id        The job id of the existing job
 * @param employer_id   The employer offering the job
 * @param title         The job title
 * @param description   The job description
 */
public void editJob(long job_id, long employer_id, String title, String description)
```

```
{
    String sql =
        "UPDATE jobs " +
        "SET employer_id = ?, "+
        " title = ?,  "+
        " description = ? "+
        "WHERE _id = ? ";
    Object[] bindArgs = new Object[]{employer_id, title, description, job_id};
    try{
        getWritableDatabase().execSQL(sql, bindArgs);
    } catch (SQLException e) {
        Log.e("Error writing new job", e.toString());
    }
}
```

For this example application, we show the simplest possible function. This makes it easy to understand in a book, but is not enough for a real application. In a real application you would want to check input strings for invalid characters, verify that the job exists before trying to update it, verify that the employer_id value is valid before using it, do a better job of catching errors, and so on. You would also probably authenticate the user for any application that is shared by multiple people.

Deleting data in the database

The MicroJobs application enables the user to delete a job as well as create and change it. From the main application interface, the user clicks on the List Jobs button to get a list of jobs and then clicks on a particular job to see the job detail. At this level, the user can click the "Delete this job" menu item to delete the job. The application asks the user whether he really wants to delete the job. When the user hits the Delete button in response, the following line of code in the *MicroJobsDetail.java* file is executed:

```
db.deleteJob(job_id);
```

This code calls the deleteJob method of the MicroJobsDatabase class, passing it the job ID to delete. The code is similar to the functions we've already seen and lacks the same real-world features.

Using the delete method. The following example demonstrates use of the delete method:

```
/**
 * Delete a job from the database.
 * @param job_id      The job id of the job to delete
 */
public void deleteJob(long job_id) {
    String[] whereArgs = new String[]{Long.toString(job_id)};
    try{
        getWritableDatabase().delete("jobs", "_id=?", whereArgs);
    } catch (SQLException e) {
        Log.e("Error deleting job", e.toString());
    }
}
```

Using the execSQL method. The following example demonstrates use of the execSQL method:

```
/**
 * Delete a job from the database.
 * @param job_id        The job id of the job to delete
 */
public void deleteJob(long job_id) {
    String sql = String.format(
            "DELETE FROM jobs " +
            "WHERE _id = '%d' ",
            job_id);
    try{
        getWritableDatabase().execSQL(sql);
    } catch (SQLException e) {
        Log.e("Error deleting job", e.toString());
    }
}
```

A Skeleton Application for Android

The first two parts of this book describe an approach to key architectural issues in Android applications. The skeleton applications described in Part III embody this approach. You can use the code as a starting point for your own applications.

A Framework for a
Well-Behaved Application

In this chapter and the next, we introduce framework, or skeleton, applications that exemplify many of the design and implementation approaches presented in this book, especially in Chapter 3 where we introduced the components of an application.

The framework application in this chapter can be used as a starting point for your own applications. We recommend this approach to creating applications over starting from scratch, or from smaller examples that do not implement all the aspects of the `Activity` object and activity life cycle.

The approach we take in this chapter enables you to visualize and understand the component life cycle before you know you need it. Retrofitting life cycle handling to an application that was written without understanding life cycles, or with the expectation that life cycle handling won't be needed, is one of the easiest ways to create an Android application that fails unexpectedly, in ways that are hard to reproduce consistently, and that has persistent bugs that can remain undiscovered across multiple attempts to eradicate them. In other words, it's best to learn this before it bites you in the ass.

This chapter isn't about user interfaces, but you should keep in mind that the Android user interface classes were designed with both the constraints of the Android architecture and the capabilities of the Android system in mind. Implementations of user interface and life cycle handling go hand in hand. Correctly handling the life cycles of an application, the process that contains the application, the `Activity` objects that contain the UI of the application, and the `Fragment` objects that might be contained in an `Activity` instance are key to a good user experience.

To get the application framework code as you read it here, you can download an archive from the Examples link on the book's website, *https://github.com/bmeike/Programming Android2Examples.git*, which may include more features and corrections of errata.

Visualizing Life Cycles

Earlier in this book, and in the Android developer documentation, you saw aspects of component life cycles diagrammed and you read about how life cycles work. The problem with these descriptions is that component life cycles are dynamic, and a state diagram is a static picture. Moreover, component and process life cycle transitions are driven by memory management: when you run out, things start to happen in component life cycles to recover memory. Memory allocation, garbage collection, and the way Android enables memory recovery to span processes are inherently not as deterministic as running a block of code, and are configuration-dependent. Here, by instrumenting and running code, we will see application life cycles as they happen, and you will be able to experiment with them in a running program.

Visualizing the Activity Life Cycle

We will make the `Activity` component life cycle more visible to you by running an instrumented program and observing the behavior of the `Activity` life cycle methods using the LogCat view in Eclipse. The following code is a listing of the `Activity` subclass with the life cycle methods implemented, and logging calls in each method. The callouts in the code refer to a method-by-method explanation of life cycle handling in "Life cycle methods of the Activity class" on page 304. Take a look at this listing to see what kind of information will be logged:

```
package com.oreilly.demo.pa.ch10.finchlifecycle;

import android.app.Activity;
import android.os.Bundle;
import android.util.Log;
import android.view.Menu;
import android.view.MenuItem;

public class FinchLifecycle extends Activity {

    // Make strings for logging
    private final String TAG = this.getClass().getSimpleName();
    private final String RESTORE = ", can restore state";

    // The string "fortytwo" is used as an example of state
    private final String state = "fortytwo";

    @Override
    public void onCreate(Bundle savedState) {❶
        super.onCreate(savedState);
        setContentView(R.layout.main);
        String answer = null;
        // savedState could be null
        if (null != savedState) {
            answer = savedState.getString("answer");
        }
        Log.i(TAG, "onCreate"
```

```
                    + (null == savedState ? "" : (RESTORE + " " + answer))));
}

@Override
protected void onRestart() {❷
    super.onRestart();
    // Notification that the activity will be started
    Log.i(TAG, "onRestart");
}

@Override
protected void onStart() {❸

    super.onStart();
    // Notification that the activity is starting
    Log.i(TAG, "onStart");
}

@Override
protected void onResume() {❹

    super.onResume();
    // Notification that the activity will interact with the user
    Log.i(TAG, "onResume");
}

protected void onPause() {❺

    super.onPause();
    // Notification that the activity will stop interacting with the user
    Log.i(TAG, "onPause" + (isFinishing() ? " Finishing" : ""));
}

@Override
protected void onStop() {❻

    super.onStop();
    // Notification that the activity is no longer visible
    Log.i(TAG, "onStop");
}

@Override
protected void onDestroy() {❼

    super.onDestroy();
    // Notification that the activity will be destroyed
    Log.i(TAG,
            "onDestroy "
                    // Log which, if any, configuration changed
                    + Integer.toString(getChangingConfigurations(), 16));
}

// /////////////////////////////////////////////////////////////////////////
// Called during the life cycle, when instance state should be saved/restored
// /////////////////////////////////////////////////////////////////////////
```

```
@Override
protected void onSaveInstanceState(Bundle outState) {❽
    // Save instance-specific state
    outState.putString("answer", state);
    super.onSaveInstanceState(outState);
    Log.i(TAG, "onSaveInstanceState");

}

@Override
public Object onRetainNonConfigurationInstance() { ❾

    Log.i(TAG, "onRetainNonConfigurationInstance");
    return new Integer(getTaskId());
}

@Override
protected void onRestoreInstanceState(Bundle savedState) {❿
    super.onRestoreInstanceState(savedState);
    // Restore state; we know savedState is not null
    String answer = null != savedState ? savedState.getString("answer") : "";
    Object oldTaskObject = getLastNonConfigurationInstance();
    if (null != oldTaskObject) {
        int oldtask = ((Integer) oldTaskObject).intValue();
        int currentTask = getTaskId();
        // Task should not change across a configuration change
        assert oldtask == currentTask;
    }
    Log.i(TAG, "onRestoreInstanceState"
            + (null == savedState ? "" : RESTORE) + " " + answer);
}


// //////////////////////////////////////////////////////////////////////////
// These are the minor life cycle methods, you probably won't need these
// //////////////////////////////////////////////////////////////////////////

@Override
protected void onPostCreate(Bundle savedState) { ⓫

    super.onPostCreate(savedState);
    String answer = null;
    // savedState could be null
    if (null != savedState) {
        answer = savedState.getString("answer");
    }
    Log.i(TAG, "onPostCreate"
            + (null == savedState ? "" : (RESTORE + " " + answer)));

}

@Override
protected void onPostResume() { ⓬

    super.onPostResume();
```

```
    Log.i(TAG, "onPostResume");
}

@Override
protected void onUserLeaveHint() { ⓭

    super.onUserLeaveHint();
    Log.i(TAG, "onUserLeaveHint");
}

}
```

When you are ready to run the application, first show the LogCat view by selecting
Window→Show View→Other and expanding the Android folder in the Show View dialog. Then select LogCat, as shown in Figure 10-1.

Figure 10-1. Selecting the LogCat view from the list shown

Now run the application in an emulator, or on a physical device. Because the example
in this chapter has been built with both the Fragment API in Android API level 11,
corresponding to Android version 3.0 Honeycomb, and the version of the Fragment
class in the Support Package, you can use either codebase to run the example.

You will start to see logging information in the LogCat view in Eclipse. To see only the
logging information from the code in the previous listing, you can filter the logging
information. Click the green plus sign in the toolbar of the logging window to bring up
a dialog for defining a logging filter, as shown in Figure 10-2.

In this case, you will want to filter the log based on the tag we use in the Finch Lifecycle class, which happens to be the name of the class: "FinchLifecycle". We name the filter "activity-lifecycle", as shown in Figure 10-2.

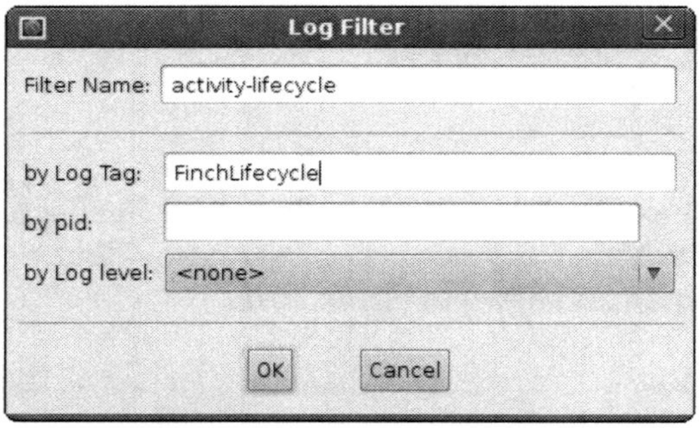

Log Filter	
Filter Name:	activity-lifecycle
by Log Tag:	FinchLifecycle
by pid:	
by Log level:	<none> ▾

OK   Cancel

Figure 10-2. Making a filter that will show only log data tagging with "FinchLifecycle"

Now, when you run the program, you will see only the logging output for the activity life cycle methods in the tab labeled "activity-lifecycle" in the LogCat view, as shown in Figure 10-4. If you want to see all the logging information, the Log tab will show an unfiltered log.

When you run the program, you will see, if you use an emulator running Android 3.0, something like the screenshot in Figure 10-3.

We use Android 3.0 here because this chapter includes coverage of life cycles and the Fragment class.

 If you want to run the example on a device or emulator that predates Android 3.0, you can use the "backported" version of the example that makes use of the Support Package, which enables the use of Fragment and other Android API level 11 classes in Android versions back to API level 4, corresponding to Android 1.6.

The first thing you will see in the "activity-lifecycle" tab of the LogCat view is the set of log messages in Figure 10-4.

To generate interesting logging information, you can start other applications and go back and forth, using the application switcher or the Launcher to return to the Finch application. Start enough other applications, and on returning to the Finch application, you will see that the process ID, or PID, has changed, but the application appears to be in the same state as you left it. This is because state was restored for this activity, and all other components of the application, from the saved state. The log information shown in the screenshot in Figure 10-5 shows just such a transition.

Figure 10-3. The example code of this chapter running in an Android 3.0 emulator

 If you find there is no output in the LogCat view, switch to the DDMS perspective (using the Window menu) and click on the device, or emulator, you are using in the Devices view.

By starting other applications that need memory, you have triggered some of the strategies Android uses to recover memory. Of course, because Android applications run in a virtual machine similar to a Java virtual machine, the first thing that happens is garbage collection, where the memory taken up by unused, unreferenced instances of objects is recovered. Android adds another strategy to garbage collection: activity components that are not visible to the user can have their state saved, and then they are "destroyed," which really just means the system deletes its references to those components and they can then be garbage-collected. Android has yet another strategy for memory recovery: by telling all the components in an application to save their state, whole processes can be deleted and their memory recovered. This is how Android enables a form of "garbage collection" that spans multiple processes.

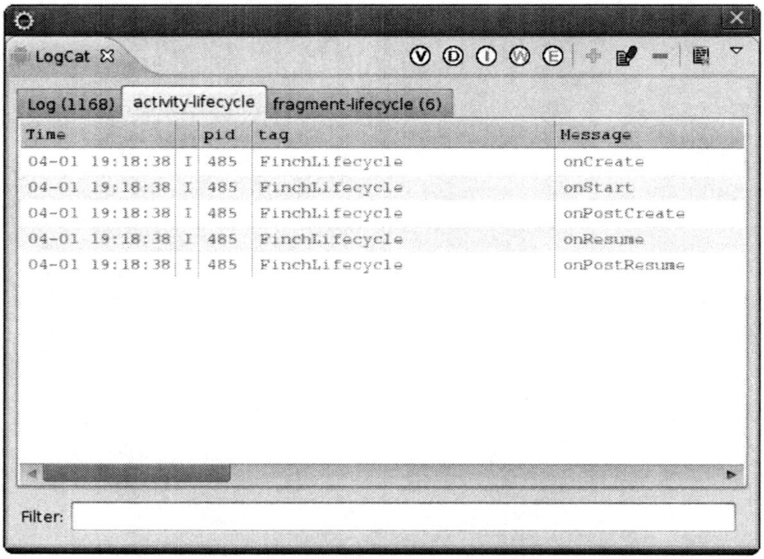

```
LogCat ⊠                                Ⓥ Ⓓ Ⓘ Ⓦ Ⓔ    ✎  —  📋  ▽

Log (1168)  activity-lifecycle   fragment-lifecycle (6)

Time            pid  tag              Message
04-01 19:18:38 I 485  FinchLifecycle   onCreate
04-01 19:18:38 I 485  FinchLifecycle   onStart
04-01 19:18:38 I 485  FinchLifecycle   onPostCreate
04-01 19:18:38 I 485  FinchLifecycle   onResume
04-01 19:18:38 I 485  FinchLifecycle   onPostResume



Filter:
```

Figure 10-4. Logging output showing a new process and activity state being restored

Memory recovery and life cycles

The life of an Android activity seems perilous and fleeting. An activity's process can be *killed* or the `Activity` object *destroyed*, seemingly at the system's whim. On top of that, you don't even get a guarantee that all your life cycle method overrides will get called when the process is killed.

A good basis for understanding life cycles in Android is to focus on what happens when an `Activity` instance is destroyed, and when a process is killed:

Destroying an activity

An activity is destroyed and the `onDestroy` method is called when Android wants to discard *this instance of the* `Activity` *class*. "Discard" means that the Android system will set its references to the `Activity` instance to `null`. And that means that, unless your code is holding a reference to this `Activity`, the `Activity` will, by and by, get garbage-collected. The word *destroy* is confusing to some—it implies actively wiping out something.

After the `onDestroy` method is called, you can be sure that this instance of your subclass of `Activity` will not be used again. But this does not necessarily mean that your application, or the process it is running in, is going to stop running. In fact, a new instance of the same `Activity` subclass could be instantiated and called. For example, this happens almost immediately after a configuration change (changing

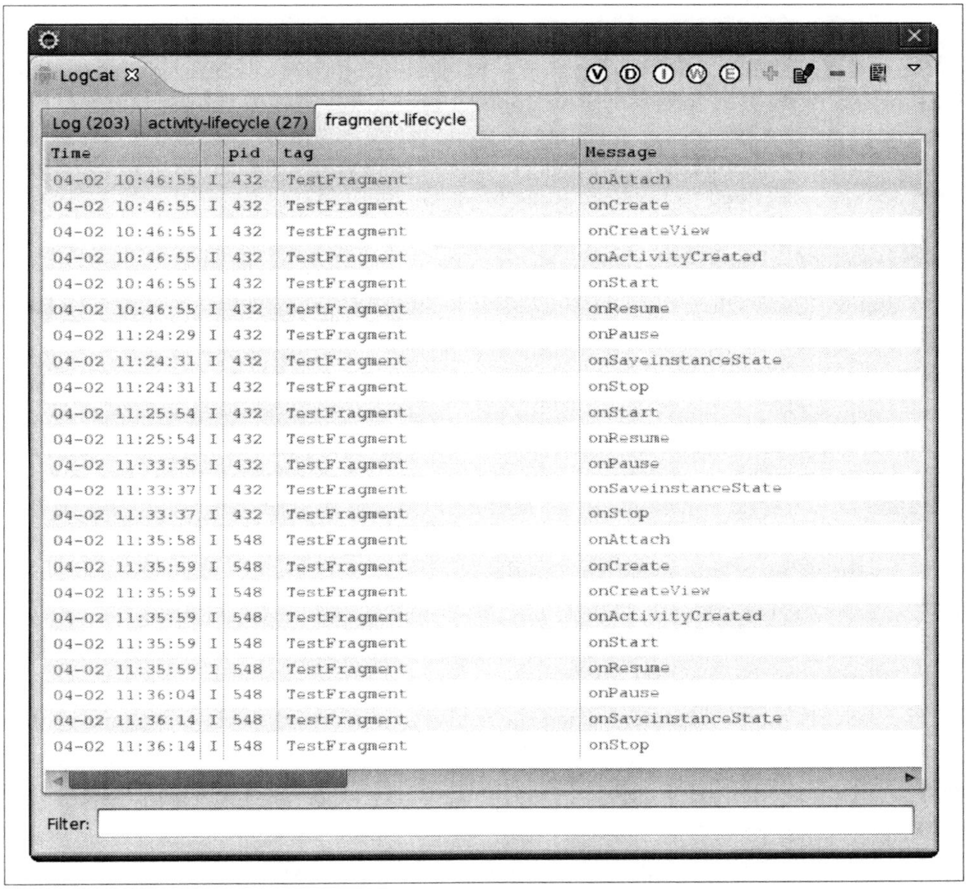

Figure 10-5. Logging output showing a new process and activity state being restored

the screen orientation, for example) causes the previously used `Activity` object to be destroyed so that resource loading can start afresh for the new configuration.

Killing a process

When an Android system starts running out of memory, it finds processes to kill. Typically, Android applications run in separate processes, so garbage collection in one process can't reach all the memory in an Android system. That means that in low-memory conditions, Android finds processes that do not have components that are in use and kills them. In extremis, Android will also kill processes that do have components that are being used. For simple applications, their process becomes a candidate for being killed after `onPause` has been called. That is, all the other `Activity` life cycle methods that can be called after `onPause` have no guarantee they will be called if the Android system needs to acquire some free memory by killing a process.

In both of these cases, your application is likely to need to save some state that exists temporarily in the user interface of an application: various inputs the user entered that have not yet been processed, the state of some visual indicator that is not part of the data model, and so on. This is why each component of your application, and especially each activity, will need to override some life cycle methods.

Life cycle methods of the Activity class

Now that we know when and why the life cycle methods are called in general, let's look at the individual methods in the previous program listing and see what they do:

❶ The onCreate method is called after an Activity instance has been created. This is where most applications perform most of their initialization: reading in the layouts and creating View instances, binding to data, and so on. Note that, if this Activity instance has not been destroyed, nor the process killed, this is not called again. It is called only if a new instance of an Activity class is created. The argument to this method is a Bundle object that contains saved application state. If there is no saved state, the value of this argument is null.

❷ The onRestart method is called only if an activity has been stopped. "Stopped" means the activity is not in the foreground, interacting with the user. This method is called before the onStart method.

❸ The onStart method is called when the Activity object and its views become visible to the user.

❹ The onResume method is called when the Activity object and its views become interactive with the user.

❺ The onPause method is called when a different Activity instance is going to be visible and the current Activity has stopped interacting with the user.

❻ The onStop method is called when an activity is no longer visible to, or interacting with, the user.

❼ The onDestroy method is called when an Activity instance is going to be destroyed— that is no longer used. Before this method is called, the activity has already stopped interacting with the user and is no longer visible on the screen. If this method is being called as the result of a call to finish, a call to isFinishing will return true.

Saving and restoring instance state

Memory recovery and the component life cycle is why your Activity subclasses need to save state. Here is how and when they should do it:

The Bundle class exists to hold serialized data in the form of key–value pairs. The data can be primitive types, or it can be any type that implements the Parcelable interface (see "Parcelable" on page 120). You can find out more about `Bundle` on the Android Developers site, at *http://developer.android.com/reference/android/os/Bundle.html.* In saving `Activity` instance state, you will use the "put" methods of the `Bundle` class.

In the call to onCreate, and in the call to onRestoreInstanceState, a `Bundle` object is passed to the method. It contains data that a previous instance of the same `Activity` class put there in order to store it across instantiations. That is, if an `Activity` instance has state, apart from what is persisted in a data model, it can be saved and restored across multiple instances of that `Activity` class. To the user, it looks like she has picked up right where she left off, but she may be looking at an entirely new instance of an `Activity` class, possibly in an entirely new process.

You may have noticed that the onPause life cycle method does not provide a `Bundle` object for storing state. So when is state stored? There are separate methods in the `Activity` class for saving state, and for being notified that state is being restored:

❽ This is where an application gets a chance to save instance state. Instance state should be state that is not persisted with an application's data model, such as the state of an indicator or other state that is only part of the `Activity` object. This method has an implementation in the parent class: it calls the onSaveInstance State method of each `View` object in this instance of `Activity`, which has the result of saving the state of these `View` objects, and this is often the only state you need to store this way. Data that your subclass needs to store is saved using the "put" methods of the `Bundle` class.

❿ The onRestoreInstanceState method is called when there is instance state to be restored. If this method is called, it is called after onStart and before onPostCreate, which is a minor life cycle method described in "Minor life cycle methods of the Activity class" on page 307.

Configuration changes and the activity life cycle

Previously, we covered how you can provoke the Android system into killing the process that your activity, and every other component of your application, is running in by launching enough applications that some processes are killed. The logs you would see, and the one in the screenshot in Figure 10-5, show that the process ID changes, and that a new instance of the `Activity` subclass that defines how this application interacts with the user is created. This new instance reloads all the resources for this activity, and if there were any application data to be loaded, that would be loaded anew, too. The net effect is that the user proceeds as though nothing has happened: the new instance looks like the old one because it has the same state.

There is another way to force Android to use a new `Activity` instance: change the configuration of the system. The most common configuration change applications encounter is a change in screen orientation. But there are many dimensions to what counts as a new configuration: changes in whether a hard keyboard is accessible or not, changes in locale, changes in font size, and more. The common factor in all changes to configuration is that they *can* require resources to be reloaded, usually because they need layouts to be recalculated.

The easiest way to make sure every resource used in an activity is loaded anew in light of the new configuration is for the current instance of the activity to be discarded, and a new instance created, so that it reloads all resources. To cause this to occur while running the application in an emulator, press the 9 key on the numeric keypad. This changes the screen orientation in the emulator. In the log, you will see something like what is in the screenshot in Figure 10-6. You will see in the log that the onDestroy method is called since the Activity instance is discarded as part of changing configurations, not when the system, running low on memory, kills the process. You will also notice that across new instances of the Activity object the process ID stays the same— the system has no need to recover the memory the application is using.

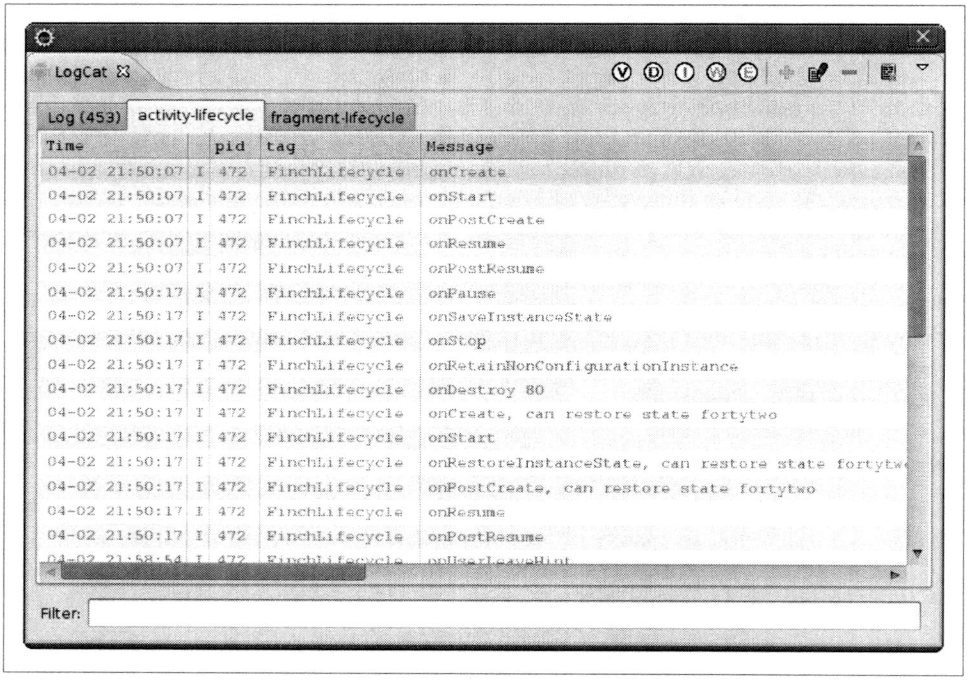

Figure 10-6. The PID remaining unchanged when the onDestroy method is called

This approach may seem profligate: a new instance of the Activity? What for? Why can't I preserve this instance? Isn't that going to be slow? In most cases, however, the resources loaded by an activity when it starts constitute most of the state of that Activity instance. In many cases, the largest amount of computation that takes place in an activity happens when it reads the XML file and calculates layouts. And, in most cases, a configuration change such as screen orientation or locale change requires nearly every resource to have its layout recalculated. So, turning a configuration change into what amounts to a restart of an activity is inevitable, as is the amount of processing that goes into that restart.

Keep in mind that the only thing going on when Android "destroys" an activity is that the reference to the activity is discarded, eventually to be garbage-collected. Every time the user moves from one activity to a new activity, all the computation that goes into creating that new activity is performed. Doing the same when a configuration change occurs is not an extraordinary amount of work for the system.

Minor life cycle methods of the Activity class

Several additional methods, other than the main life cycle methods used in the Android documentation to describe the activity life cycle, are also called as an activity moves through its life cycle:

⓫ The onPostCreate method is called after onRestoreInstanceState is called. It may be useful if your application requires that state be restored in two stages. It is passed a Bundle object containing instance state.

⓬ The onPostResume method is called after onResume, when the Activity instance should be visible and is interacting with the user.

⓭ The onUserLeaveHint method is called if an activity is going to stop being visible and interacting with the user due to the user's actions—for example, pressing the back or home hard key. This is a convenient place to clear alerts and dialogs.

You can see in the program listing in Figure 10-6 that we have implemented overrides of these methods to log when they are called. These methods exist for cases where, for example, you need an additional stage for restoring instance state.

However, if you really need to preserve some data across configuration changes, and it isn't part of the state that gets stored in the Bundle object between instances, and it isn't part of the data model that would get saved, you can use the onRetainNonConfi gurationInstance method to "stash" a reference to an object. This reference can then be requested by a new Activity instance using the getLastNonConfigurationInstance method:

❾ The onRetainNonConfigurationInstance method is called after onStop, which means there is no guarantee it will be called, nor even, if it is called, that the reference returned will be preserved and provided to the subsequent Activity instance. The getLastNonConfigurationInstance() method can be called in the onCreate method, or subsequently when restoring activity state.

To illustrate the use of these methods, we return an object containing the task ID of the activity when onRetainNonConfigurationInstance is called, and when onRestore InstanceState(Bundle) is called we check it to see that the task ID has not changed.

This confirms that, even if the instance of the component or even of the whole process is different to the user, it's the same task.

The most commonly cited use case for using these methods is to store the results of a web query: you could redo the query, but the latency of a query to a web server might be a few seconds. So, while the data can be re-created if the system cannot preserve it for the new `Activity` object instance to retrieve, there is a significant upside to caching it. However, in this book we show you, in Chapter 13, how to interpose a local database as a cache in RESTful applications, reducing the need for this kind of optimization.

Visualizing the Fragment Life Cycle

If you are developing for Android 3.0 Honeycomb, API level 11 or later, the Fragment API is available. If, however, you prefer to develop for a pre-Honeycomb version of Android and would like to use `Fragment` objects in your user interface, you can use the Support Package, as described in Chapter 7. The example code for this chapter is provided in two forms: one that is set up to work with API level 11 as the target API, and one that can be targeted to API levels as low as API level 4, corresponding to Android 1.6. You will find the following `Fragment` code identical except for the package declaration for the `Fragment` class, and you will find it behaves identically with respect to the `Fragment` life cycle.

This code, like the `Activity` class presented earlier, instruments the life cycle callbacks so that they can be observed as the program runs:

```
package com.oreilly.demo.pa.ch10.finchlifecycle;

import android.app.Activity;
import android.app.Fragment;
import android.os.Bundle;
import android.util.Log;
import android.view.LayoutInflater;
import android.view.View;
import android.view.ViewGroup;

public class TestFragment extends Fragment {

    // get a label for our log entries
    private final String TAG = this.getClass().getSimpleName();

    public TestFragment() {

    }

    @Override
    public void onAttach(Activity activity) {❶
        super.onAttach(activity);
        Log.i(TAG, "onAttach");
    }
```

```
@Override
public void onCreate(Bundle saved) {❷
    super.onCreate(saved);
    if (null != saved) {
        // Restore state here
    }
    Log.i(TAG, "onCreate");
}

@Override
public View onCreateView(LayoutInflater inflater, ViewGroup container,❸
        Bundle saved) {
    View v = inflater.inflate(R.layout.fragment_content, container, false);
    Log.i(TAG, "onCreateView");
    return v;
}

@Override
public void onActivityCreated(Bundle saved) {❹
    super.onActivityCreated(saved);
    Log.i(TAG, "onActivityCreated");
}

@Override
public void onStart() {❺
    super.onStart();
    Log.i(TAG, "onStart");
}

@Override
public void onResume() {❻
    super.onResume();
    Log.i(TAG, "onResume");
}

@Override
public void onPause() {❼
    super.onPause();
    Log.i(TAG, "onPause");
}

@Override
public void onStop() {❽
    super.onStop();
    Log.i(TAG, "onStop");
}

// ///////////////////////////////////////////////////////////////////
// Called during the life cycle, when instance state should be saved/restored
// ///////////////////////////////////////////////////////////////////

@Override
public void onSaveInstanceState(Bundle toSave) {❾
    super.onSaveInstanceState(toSave);
    Log.i(TAG, "onSaveinstanceState");
```

```
        }
    }
```

As you did with the LogCat filter for finding the log entries that show Activity component callbacks, you will set up a filter for Fragment callbacks.

If you repeat the steps you took—starting other applications until you see in the LogCat window that the Fragment life cycle methods are being called—you will see that each Fragment instance in an Activity instance behaves like the enclosing Activity with respect to the Views it contains. Similar life cycle transitions and states are called.

Let's take a look at each method that gets called, now that we know when they are called:

❶ The onAttach method is called when the Fragment instance is associated with an Activity instance. This does not mean the Activity is fully initialized.

❷ The onCreate method is called when the Fragment instance is being created, or re-created. If it is being re-created after the Fragment or the containing Activity component has been destroyed, the bundle argument will be non-null if any state had been saved.

❸ The onCreateView method is called when the Fragment instance should create the View object hierarchy it contains. Fragment has an unusual role in an Activity: it behaves somewhat like a ViewGroup, but it isn't part of the View class hierarchy. You can think of it as enabling the Activity to contain multiple sets of View instances. In our example, we load an extremely simple layout containing a TextView.

❹ The onActivityCreated method is called when the Activity containing the Fragment instance has been created, and the View objects contained by the Fragment have been created. At this point, it is safe to search for View objects by their ID, for example.

❺ The onStart method is called when the Fragment becomes visible, in a very similar way to the Activity method onStart.

❻ The onResume method is called when the Fragment becomes visible, and is running.

❼ The onPause method also is called under the same conditions as an Activity instance's onPause method when the Fragment is about to be taken out of the foreground.

❽ The onStop method is called when the Fragment is about to stop running.

❾ The onSaveInstanceState method is called when it is necessary to save instance state so that if the instance is destroyed (really, just dereferenced) any class-specific state that needs to be stored can be stored in the Bundle object passed to this call.

Fragment objects are not components. You can think of them as a way of breaking up an Activity object into multiple objects contained within an Activity, each with its own View hierarchy that behaves like it is inside an Activity.

The Activity Class and Well-Behaved Applications

Understanding application life cycles is key to implementing well-behaved applications, and it is also key to understanding misbehaving applications. Lagging performance, excessive resource use, and unexpected user interface behavior can often be diagnosed by observing the application's life cycle. Life cycle is difficult to understand just by looking at code or the documentation page for the `Activity` class. To enable you to observe life cycle as it is happening, we will put logging calls into our implementations of Android life cycle methods, run the programs, and observe how life cycle works in a running program. In using this framework, you can leave these logging calls in your application's code as you develop it because applications often come to need logging in these methods to diagnose problems.

Most of the methods called on changes in life cycle are implemented on a per-component basis, and some on a per-process basis. Each type of component—`Service`, `BroadcastReceiver`, `ContentProvider`, and `Activity`—has its own life cycle. Life cycles of components other than `Activity` are covered in Chapter 3. Most life cycles are simpler than the `Activity` life cycle. This is because the `Activity` class interacts with the user, and when an `Activity` is no longer a visible part of the user interface, it is likely that the memory occupied by resources associated with that `Activity` instance could be scavenged if needed. Managing memory occupied by resources related to components is one of the principal purposes of component life cycles.

The Activity Life Cycle and the User Experience

In fact, if your application is well designed for the mobile environment in general, it will need less code in application life cycle management:

- If the data used by an activity is always up-to-date and in a database, you will not have to explicitly store it in the code in an application life cycle method.
- If your user interface has minimal state, you won't have to save much, if any, state in an activity life cycle method.

These seem like stringent constraints, but in mobile and other appliance-like devices, they are not. The battery on a mobile phone can die at any time, and the less an application's data model and state are held in memory, the less the user will lose when the device shuts off unexpectedly. A mobile user may be interrupted by a phone call and the user will never get a chance to return to an application to perform operations that save data. Mobile applications are not intended to work like typical interactive applications on personal computers, with documents on filesystems that become in-memory data models, to be explicitly saved, or else the data is lost.

In this chapter and the next, you will see that application life cycle, the data model and other aspects of application architecture, and the user experience are all intertwined, and that the path of least resistance, and least implementation in life cycle methods, leads to application implementations that are robust, are easy to use, are good citizens of the Android environment, and perform well. If you treat a battery failure the same as the user no longer using an activity or the same as the system killing an activity to claw back memory and other system resources, you will simplify your implementation and unburden the user. Explicit actions such as "save" and "quit" should be avoided in the mobile user experience, and in the implementation of well-behaved applications.

Life Cycle Methods of the Application Class

The life cycle methods of the Application class are, and should be, infrequently used in simple applications. And they should be used with restraint even in complex applications. Is is easy to bloat Application class overrides with data that hangs around in memory across multiple activities. This defeats Android's ability to manage resources on a per-component basis. For example, if you move the reference to some data from an Activity object to the Application object, all you have done is extend the system's chase for resources in a low-memory situation to the application life cycle, and you must manage this data separately from the activity life cycle.

Here, we implement the life cycle methods of the Application class to show their place in the Android application life cycle, and because logging information from these methods may be useful:

```
package com.finchframework.finch;

import android.app.Application;
import android.content.res.Configuration;
import android.util.Log;

/**
 * @author zigurd
 *
 *          This is the framework's Application subclass. This illustrates what
 *          you may need to do in an Application subclass.
 *
 *          To get this class instantiated, you must refer to it in the
 *          application tag of the manifest.
 */
public class FinchApplication extends Application {
    private final String TAG = this.getClass().getSimpleName();

    @Override
    public void onCreate() {
        // First, call the parent class
        super.onCreate();

        // This is a good place to put code that must manage global data across
        // multiple activities, but it's better to keep most things in a
        // database, rather than in memory
        Log.i(TAG, "onCreate");
    }
```

```
@Override
public void onTerminate() {
    Log.i(TAG, "onTerminate");

}

@Override
public void onLowMemory() {
    // In-memory caches should be thrown overboard here
    Log.i(TAG, "onLowMemory");
}

@Override
public void onConfigurationChanged(Configuration newConfig) {
    Log.i(TAG, "onConfigurationChanged");
    if (Log.isLoggable(TAG, Log.VERBOSE)) {
        Log.v(TAG, newConfig.toString());
    }

}

}
```

Earlier we mentioned that many applications can do without subclassing Application. Because of this, the New Android Project Wizard does not create an Application subclass, nor does it add a reference to it in the manifest. Like the initial object that gets started when an interactive application starts, the Application subclass you create gets instantiated by the Android system as part of launching an application. In much the same way as Android handles Activity subclasses, it knows which class to make an instance of, and uses the android:name property of the application tag in the manifest. The easiest way to get this right is by using the Application tab of the manifest editor. The first field on that editing tab is labeled Name (see Figure 10-7). Clicking the Browse button next to that field shows the Application subclasses in your application.

As with the Activity class's life cycle methods, it is most revealing to know when life cycle methods get called. You can, of course, find this out by debugging an application and setting breakpoints in each method, but often the most informative information is found by looking at long-running applications' behavior, and filtering a log by the tags used in the Activity and Application subclasses, to get an idea of when life cycle methods have been called.

Two of the most interesting callbacks to track in the Application class are onLow Memory and onTerminate, which will tell you when, obviously enough, the system thinks it is in a low-memory condition and when your application terminates. The second situation is usually not obvious because most Android applications do not need to explicitly exit, as Android's memory management, in concert with component life cycles, is enough to sweep out unused code if it was correctly implemented with respect to life cycle and memory management.

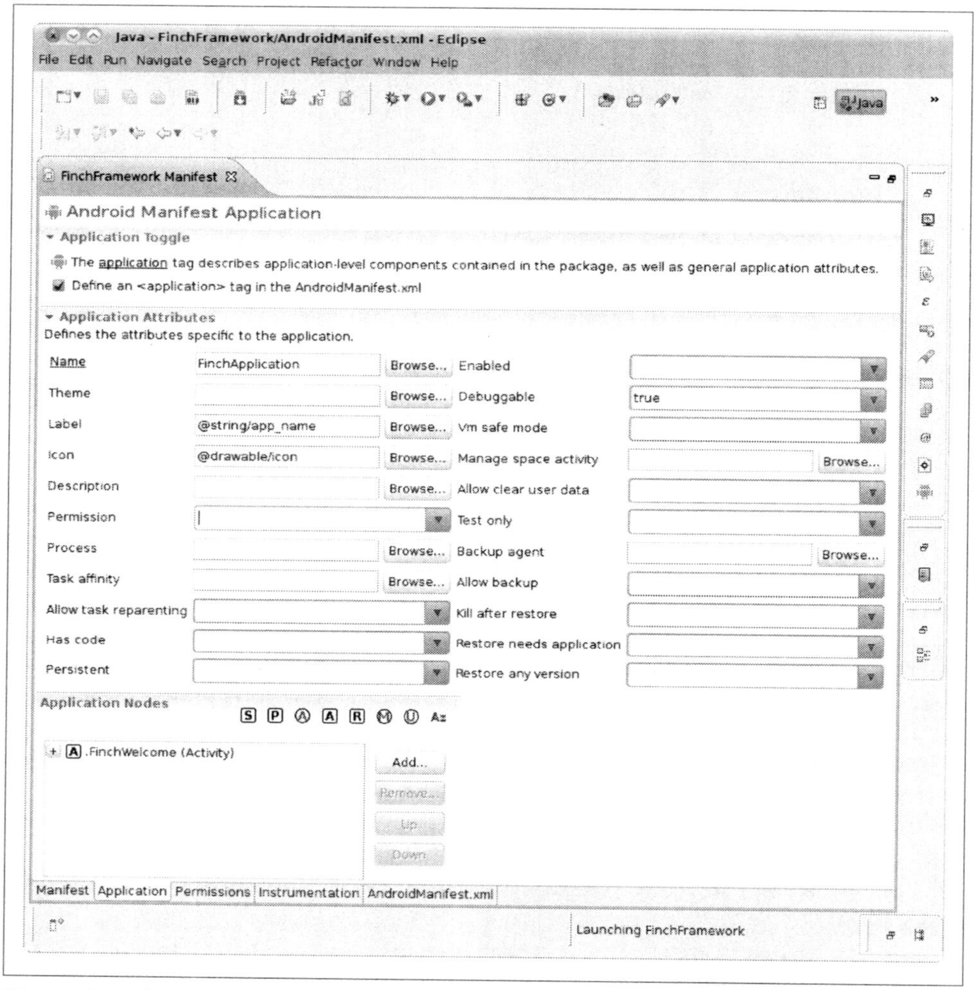

Figure 10-7. The Name field on the Application tab of the manifest editor, where you enter the name of the Application subclass you have defined

Building a User Interface

This chapter will enable you to connect APIs and tools with the user interface design process. Android's user interface classes and the tools in the SDK were designed to help you conveniently create easy-to-use Android applications.

The tools Android provides for creating user interfaces enable an infinite variety of combinations. The APIDemos example, and other example programs in the SDK, contain several examples of the different ways Android's user interface classes, especially `Activity` and `Fragment`, can be used. But it's up to you to combine these examples into an app.

The example code for this chapter will implement up-to-date user interfaces following best practices in user interface implementation, illustrate the most important user interface classes, and provide logging and instrumentation to help you understand what is behind what happens on the screen.

The visible result from this example will look like the screen in Figure 11-1 on a tablet.

On a handset, it will look like the screenshot in Figure 11-2.

The same code runs in both cases. That is, all the decisions about the look of the user interface that depend on screen size are made at runtime, and almost all of those decisions are made by the Android system.

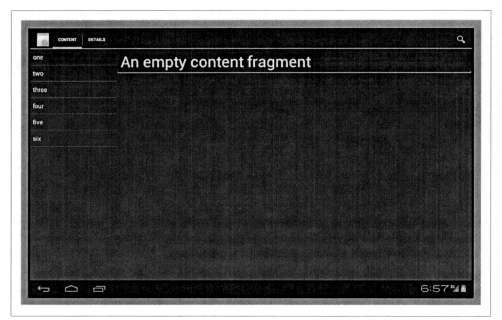

Figure 11-1. What your program will look like on a tablet screen

Top-Level Design

The "top-level" design of the user interface encompasses all the design elements that will be visible or readily accessible in the user interface. This is where you draw what you want it to look like.

We will show you a typical design for an Android user interface, and how to design it to create a single code-base that meets the following goals:

- It works on tablets and on handsets, by delegating as much of the user interface code as possible to Fragment classes, and by having the Activity classes respond to the way the Android system decides to use layout resources based on screen size and pixel density.
- It works in both orientations, using a different layout in landscape and portrait mode to maintain clarity in presentation
- It shows how Fragment objects can be added and removed from an Activity object, and how transitions and Fragment transactions work together.
- It shows how the Action Bar and the items in it can be combined or split up, and how to use tabs, to go along with the Fragment-based strategy for fitting the UI to tablet and handset screen sizes.

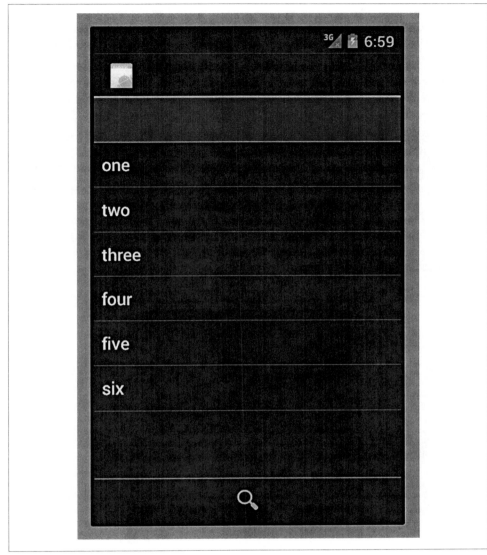

Figure 11-2. What your program will look like on a handset

Fragment, Activity, and Scalable Design

Here, we will be using fragments to create a good-looking and functional user experience. For an in-depth discussion of the `Fragment` class, `FragmentManager`, and the `Fragment` life cycle, see "Fragment Life Cycle" on page 209.

A `Fragment` instance, like an `Activity` instance, can add nested `View` objects to the View hierarchy. But a `Fragment` can be laid out, either by editing the layout specification in XML directly, or using the visual layout editor, inside an Activity as a View would be.

In Figures 11-1 and 11-2, you saw how the app in this chapter looks on large and small screens. Here we will plan out how to achieve that look. We will use "wireframe" drawings to plan our layouts, and how we will divide the user interface among activities for smaller screens.

We are starting with the design for a large tablet screen first. That way we consider how to present different kinds of information alongside one another *before* we consider how to divide this information up among smaller screens and create a navigation hierarchy.

`Fragment` is what makes this modularity possible. By containing the code that handles interaction with the `View` objects organized together in a `Fragment`, `Fragments` make it much easier to reuse code and layouts, even though the user interface organization and flow differs between large and small screens. The wireframe drawing in Figure 11-4 shows how we intend to divide the user interface in Figure 11-3 between two activities on a smaller, handset-sized screen.

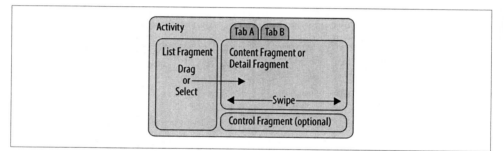

Figure 11-3. Wireframe drawing laying out fragments for large-screen devices

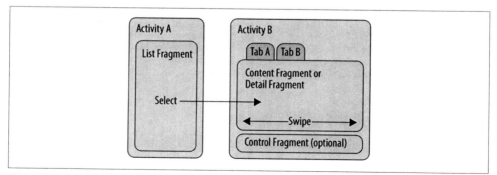

Figure 11-4. Wireframe drawing laying out fragments for small-screen devices

Visual Editing of User Interfaces

Android was born with primitive tools for visual editing of user interfaces. Most of the books on Android software development discourage reliance on the early UI editors and provide examples of specifying UIs in XML.

One of the biggest changes in Android software development in recent versions of the SDK is the replacement of these primitive tools with a full-featured visual UI editor. This editor is sufficiently powerful and expressive that developers should use it as their first approach to creating user interfaces. Doing so will help avoid XML syntax errors that can be difficult to diagnose and correct.

The new UI editor can even refactor user interface specifications through the visual editing interface, and it can find duplicate UI specifications and extract them into common code.

Because the Android SDK is a cross-development environment, making a visual GUI editor is more difficult than it is for a fully "self-hosted" development environment. For example, when Sun made the Matisse UI editor for Swing, it could take advantage of the fact that the NetBeans IDE is written using Swing. The same classes for rendering a UI and responding to input in applications are available in the IDE. So when it is time to show the developer what their UI looks like, the Swing classes are called to draw it.

Android's SDK has a harder problem, in more than one dimension: Eclipse is running in a Java VM, not the Dalvik VM, and Eclipse's UI is built using the SWT classes. So an Android UI editor has to build enough of the behavior of Android's UI classes into an Eclipse plug-in to render Android UIs, even though all the underlying graphics classes and UI classes are different from the classes in an actual Android runtime environment.

Starting with a Blank Slate

Here, we will design our user interface from the top down, starting with the `Activity` class that contains the main parts of the user interface as it would appear on a tablet device, and the `Fragment` objects that will be created inside the instances of this `Activity` class.

There is an important step to complete before we can get on with using the visual tools for editing layout files to turn our wireframes into XML code that specifies the user interface: because the `Fragment` class is always subclassed, we will create those classes before laying out our fragments.

Referring to the wireframe to keep track of what we need, we will create three subclasses of Fragment:

- ContentFragment
- DetailFragment
- QueryResultsListFragment

Many of the life cycle callbacks in our Fragment subclasses are implemented for the purpose of logging, to provide easy visualization of Fragment object life cycle, and to enable building the application-specific code around the code skeleton methods. Below is the source code for our QueryResultsListFragment class.

In this code you can see:

❷ Life cycle methods with logging code

❶ An implementation of onCreateView that inflates our layout and calls attachAdapter.

❸ The private method attachAdapter that enables the list in this fragment to display some test data.

❹ An implementation of the OnItemClickListener interface that responds to user interactions, which, in this case, executes some simple code that sends some test data to the Fragment objects on the right side of the screen, or on a subsequent activity if the screen is too small to display two fragments. Note that there is no code here for making that decision.

```java
package com.finchframework.uiframework;

import android.app.Activity;
import android.app.Fragment;
import android.content.res.Configuration;
import android.os.Bundle;
import android.util.Log;
import android.view.LayoutInflater;
import android.view.Menu;
import android.view.MenuInflater;
import android.view.View;
import android.view.ViewGroup;
import android.widget.AdapterView;
import android.widget.AdapterView.OnItemClickListener;
import android.widget.ArrayAdapter;
import android.widget.ListView;

public class QueryResultsListFragment extends Fragment implements OnItemClickListener{

    // String for logging the class name
    private final String TAG = getClass().getSimpleName();

    // Turn logging on or off
    private final boolean L = true;

    public void onAttach(Activity activity) {
```

```java
        super.onAttach(activity);
        // Notification that the fragment is associated with an Activity
        if (L)
            Log.i(TAG, "onAttach " + activity.getClass().getSimpleName());
    }

    public void onCreate(Bundle savedInstanceState) {
        super.onCreate(savedInstanceState);

        // Tell the system we have an options menu
        this.setHasOptionsMenu(true);

        if (null != savedInstanceState)
            restoreState(savedInstanceState);
        // Notification that
        if (L) Log.i(TAG, "onCreate");
    }

    // Factor this out of methods that get saved state
    private void restoreState(Bundle savedInstanceState) {
        // TODO Auto-generated method stub

    }

    @Override
    public View onCreateView(LayoutInflater inflater, ViewGroup container,
            Bundle savedInstanceState) {❶

        final ListView list = (ListView) inflater.inflate(
                R.layout.list_frag_list, container, false);
        if (L) Log.i(TAG, "onCreateView");

        attachAdapter(list);
        list.setOnItemClickListener(this);

        return list;
    }

    public void onStart() {❷
        super.onStart();
        if (L) Log.i(TAG, "onStart");
    }

    public void onresume() {
        super.onResume();
        if (L) Log.i(TAG, "onResume");
    }

    public void onPause() {
        super.onPause();
        if (L) Log.i(TAG, "onPause");
    }

    public void onStop() {
        super.onStop();
```

```java
        if (L) Log.i(TAG, "onStop");
    }

    public void onDestroyView() {
        super.onDestroyView();
        if (L) Log.i(TAG, "onDestroyView");
    }

    public void onDestroy() {
        super.onDestroy();
        if (L) Log.i(TAG, "onDestroy");
    }

    public void onDetach() {
        super.onDetach();
        if (L) Log.i(TAG, "onDetach");
    }

    // //////////////////////////////////////////////////////////////////////////
    // Minor lifecycle methods
    // //////////////////////////////////////////////////////////////////////////

    public void onActivityCreated() {
        // Notification that the containing activiy and its View hierarchy exist
        if (L) Log.i(TAG, "onActivityCreated");
    }

    // //////////////////////////////////////////////////////////////////////////
    // Overrides of the implementations ComponentCallbacks methods in Fragment
    // //////////////////////////////////////////////////////////////////////////

    @Override
    public void onConfigurationChanged(Configuration newConfiguration) {
        super.onConfigurationChanged(newConfiguration);

        // This won't happen unless we declare changes we handle in the manifest
        if (L)
            Log.i(TAG, "onConfigurationChanged");
    }

    @Override
    public void onLowMemory() {
        // No guarantee this is called before or after other callbacks
        if (L)
            Log.i(TAG, "onLowMemory");
    }


    //////////////////////////////////////////////////////////////////////////
    // Menu handling code
    //////////////////////////////////////////////////////////////////////////

    public void onCreateOptionsMenu(Menu menu, MenuInflater inflater) {
        inflater.inflate(R.menu.search_menu, menu);
    }
```

```
// ///////////////////////////////////////////////////////////////////////
// App-specific code
// ///////////////////////////////////////////////////////////////////////

/**
 * Attach an adapter that loads the data to the specified list
 * @param list
 */
private void attachAdapter(final ListView list) {❸

    // Make a trivial adapter that loads an array of strings
    ArrayAdapter<String> numbers = new ArrayAdapter<String>(
            list.getContext().getApplicationContext(),
            android.R.layout.simple_list_item_1,
            new String [] {
            "one", "two", "three", "four", "five", "six"
        });

    // tell the list to use it
    list.setAdapter(numbers);
    // l.setOnItemClickListener(this);
}

// ///////////////////////////////////////////////////////////////////////
// Implementation of the OnItemClickListener interface
// ///////////////////////////////////////////////////////////////////////

@Override
public void onItemClick(AdapterView<?> arg0, View view, int position, long id) {❹
    // As an example of sending data to our fragments, we will create a bundle
    // with an int and a string, based on which view was clicked
    Bundle b = new Bundle();
    int ordinal = position + 1;
    b.putInt("place", ordinal);
    b.putString("placeName", Integer.toString(ordinal));
    TabManager.loadTabFragments(getActivity(), b);

    }
}
```

The one thing our Fragment subclasses must do is to return a View from the onCreate
View method. So we will also define a simple layout for each Fragment class to load and
return the resulting View hierarchy.

Laying Out the Fragments

By creating skeletal Fragment classes that contain simple layouts, we can use Android's
visual UI editor as a tool for composing each screen in the application. Let's turn our
wireframes into the XML for the *main.xml* file our main activity will use using the visual
editor.

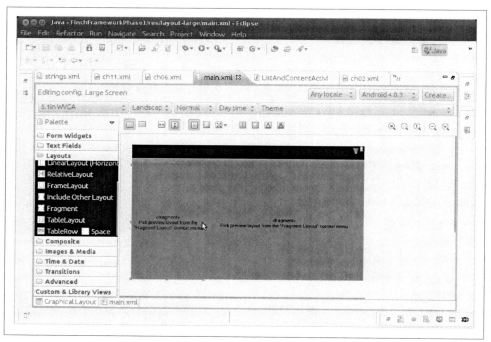

Figure 11-5. Laying out multiple fragments on a large tablet screen

Lay Out Fragments Using the Visual Editor

In the screen shot in Figure 11-5 you can see the results of dragging two Fragment items from the palette on the left into position, and adjusting their sizes by dragging the handles on the sides of the rectangles representing the fragments.

Some parameters are more conveniently edited in the XML view of the layout. In the following program listing, note that the class parameter is set to the fully qualified name of the Fragment subclass for that fragment.

```xml
<?xml version="1.0" encoding="utf-8"?>
<LinearLayout xmlns:android="http://schemas.android.com/apk/res/android"
    android:layout_width="fill_parent"
    android:layout_height="fill_parent"
    android:orientation="horizontal" >

    <fragment
        android:id="@+id/list_frag"
        android:name="com.finchframework.uiframework.QueryResultsListFragment"
        android:layout_width="250dp"
        android:layout_height="match_parent"
        class="com.finchframework.uiframework.QueryResultsListFragment" />

    <LinearLayout
        xmlns:android="http://schemas.android.com/apk/res/android"
        android:layout_width="match_parent"
```

```
            android:layout_height="match_parent"
            android:orientation="vertical" >

        <fragment
            android:id="@+id/content_frag"
            android:name="com.finchframework.uiframework.ContentFragment"
            android:layout_width="match_parent"
            android:layout_height="match_parent"
            class="com.finchframework.uiframework.ContentFragment" />

        <fragment
            android:id="@+id/detail_frag"
            android:name="com.finchframework.uiframework.DetailFragment"
            android:layout_width="match_parent"
            android:layout_height="match_parent"
            class="com.finchframework.uiframework.DetailFragment" />
    </LinearLayout>

</LinearLayout>
```

Multiple Layouts

Android enables developers to provide alternative resources for different screen sizes and pixel densities. You have probably already encountered the use of multiple variants on graphical assets in programs for lower and higher resolution screens, and all Android apps created with the new app wizard come with folders for low-, medium-, and high-resolution drawables.

In this example, we'll use the Android naming conventions to create multiple layout folders for normal-sized screens, large screens, and large screens in portrait mode. The layout in the preceding program listing will go into a folder named *layout large*.

Now let's create a layout file for handset-sized screens, which Android considers a normal size. The layout in the following program listing is also named *main.xml*, but it will go in the folder named *layout*.

```
    <?xml version="1.0" encoding="utf-8"?>
    <LinearLayout xmlns:android="http://schemas.android.com/apk/res/android"
        android:layout_width="fill_parent"
        android:layout_height="fill_parent"
        android:orientation="horizontal" >

        <fragment
            android:id="@+id/list_frag"
            android:name="com.finchframework.uiframework.QueryResultsListFragment"
            android:layout_width="match_parent"
            android:layout_height="match_parent"
            class="com.finchframework.uiframework.QueryResultsListFragment" />

    </LinearLayout>
```

This file has only one fragment. The system picks which layout to use based on screen size. What the code does is, for the most part, adapt; there isn't any code that asks, "Which layout am I using?" It doesn't need to. Code for responding to user interaction is in the `Fragment` classes, so the `Activity` class that loads these layouts doesn't need to do anything different.

In addition to the preceding two layouts, there is folder called *layout-large-port* in the example code containing yet another version of *main.xml*. This one is for large tablet devices in a portrait configuration. It stacks the fragments on top of each other rather than displaying them side by side. As with the other layouts, the code doesn't have to do anything conditioned on which layout is used.

Folding and Unfolding a Scalable UI

So far, you have seen that we have three fragments: one for the list on the left of the large screen layout, and two for the tabs on the right side of the screen, or, if there is no room for them, on the activity that gets started to display them. And, so far, you have seen no code that makes decisions about what to put where. You have also seen the use of a declarative UI to implement three distinctly different appearances on screen, using the same Java code for all three.

Decisions about Screen Size and Resolution

A key element of the implementation approach throughout this application is that the code never deals in screen size, pixel density, or orientation. Imagine the complexity if your application had to make decisions about whether fragments could fit side by side, or stacked on top of each other, on the screen. In fact we take this a step further: the code never actually decides about screen size. Instead it is written to run in any of the configurations specified in layout files.

The program reacts to what the *system* decided about layout. The following code is the main activity of this example app. As with the `Fragment` subclass described earlier, this code contains no explicit decisions about screen size, and whether one of two fragments fit on the screen. It can accommodate one fragment, or two, but it makes no decisions about whether one or two fragments end up in this activity.

```
package com.finchframework.uiframework;

import com.finchframework.uiframework.R;

import android.app.ActionBar;
import android.app.Activity;
import android.content.res.Configuration;
import android.os.Bundle;
import android.util.Log;

public class ListAndContentActivity extends Activity {
```

```java
// String for logging the class name
private final String TAG = getClass().getSimpleName();

// Turn logging on or off
private final boolean L = true;

@Override
protected void onCreate(Bundle savedState) {
    super.onCreate(savedState);

    // To keep this method simple
    doCreate(savedState);

    // If we had state to restore, we note that in the log message
    if (L) Log.i(TAG, "onCreate" +
            (null == savedState ? " Restored state" : ""));
}

@Override
protected void onRestart() {
    super.onRestart();
    // Notification that the activity will be started
    if (L) Log.i(TAG, "onRestart");
}

@Override
protected void onStart() {
    super.onStart();
    // Notification that the activity is starting
    if (L) Log.i(TAG, "onStart");
}

@Override
protected void onResume() {
    super.onResume();
    // Notification that the activity will interact with the user
    if (L) Log.i(TAG, "onResume");
}

protected void onPause() {
    super.onPause();
    // Notification that the activity will stop interacting with the user
    if (L) Log.i(TAG, "onPause" + (isFinishing() ? " Finishing" : ""));
}

@Override
protected void onStop() {
    super.onStop();
    // Notification that the activity is no longer visible
    if (L) Log.i(TAG, "onStop");
}

@Override
protected void onDestroy() {
```

```java
        super.onDestroy();
        // Notification the activity will be destroyed
        if (L) Log.i(TAG, "onDestroy"
                // Are we finishing?
                + (isFinishing() ? " Finishing" : ""));
    }

    @Override
    protected void onSaveInstanceState(Bundle outState) {
        super.onSaveInstanceState(outState);
        saveState(outState);

        // Called when state should be saved
        if (L) Log.i(TAG, "onSaveInstanceState");

    }

    @Override
    protected void onRestoreInstanceState(Bundle savedState) {
        super.onRestoreInstanceState(savedState);
        if (null != savedState) restoreState(savedState);

        // If we had state to restore, we note that in the log message
        if (L) Log.i(TAG, "onRestoreInstanceState" +
                (null == savedState ? " Restored state" : ""));
    }

    ////////////////////////////////////////////////////////////////////////////
    // The minor lifecycle methods - you probably won't need these
    ////////////////////////////////////////////////////////////////////////////

    @Override
    protected void onPostCreate(Bundle savedState) {
        super.onPostCreate(savedState);
        if (null != savedState) restoreState(savedState);

        // If we had state to restore, we note that in the log message
        if (L) Log.i(TAG, "onCreate" + (null == savedState ? " Restored state" : ""));

    }

    @Override
    protected void onPostResume() {
        super.onPostResume();
        // Notification that resuming the activity is complete
        if (L) Log.i(TAG, "onPostResume");
    }

    @Override
    protected void onUserLeaveHint() {
        super.onUserLeaveHint();
        // Notification that user navigated away from this activity
        if (L) Log.i(TAG, "onUserLeaveHint");
    }
```

```
//////////////////////////////////////////////////////////////////////////
// Overrides of the implementations ComponentCallbacks methods in Activity
//////////////////////////////////////////////////////////////////////////

@Override
public void onConfigurationChanged(Configuration newConfiguration) {
    super.onConfigurationChanged(newConfiguration);

    // This won't happen unless we declare changes we handle in the manifest
    if (L) Log.i(TAG, "onConfigurationChanged");
}

@Override
public void onLowMemory() {
    // No guarantee this is called before or after other callbacks
    if (L) Log.i(TAG, "onLowMemory");
}

//////////////////////////////////////////////////////////////////////////
// App-specific code here
//////////////////////////////////////////////////////////////////////////


/**
 * This is where we restore state we previously saved.
 * @param savedState the Bundle we got from the callback
 */
private void restoreState(Bundle savedState) {
    // Add your code to restore state here

}

/**
 * Add this activity's state to the bundle and/or commit pending data
 */
private void saveState(Bundle state) {
    // Add your code to add state to the bundle here
}

/**
 * Perform initializations on creation of this Activity instance
 * @param savedState
 */
private void doCreate(Bundle savedState) {
    setContentView(R.layout.main);

    if (null != savedState) restoreState(savedState);

    ActionBar bar = getActionBar();  ❶
    bar.setDisplayShowTitleEnabled(false);
    bar.setNavigationMode(ActionBar.NAVIGATION_MODE_TABS);

    // Initialize the tabs (Fails silently if the tab fragments don't exist) ❷
    int names[] = {R.string.content, R.string.detail };
    int fragments[] = { R.id.content_frag, R.id.detail_frag };
```

```
        TabManager.initialize(this, 0, names, fragments);
    }

}
```

The important lines of code in this class are:

❶ Code that finds the Action Bar and sets some options for the way we use it.

❷ Code that initializes tab management. `TabManager` is a utility class that is examined later in this chapter.

Delegating to Fragment Classes

Delegating user interaction to the `Fragment` subclasses in this example is one way in which how we organize code makes it unnecessary to make explicit decisions about screen size. We have fragments on the screen when they fit on the screen, and when we interact with widgets in those fragments, the code to handle those interactions is in the `Fragment` subclasses we created.

```
package com.finchframework.uiframework;

import com.finchframework.uiframework.TabManager.SetData;

import android.app.ActionBar.Tab;
import android.app.ActionBar.TabListener;
import android.app.Activity;
import android.app.Fragment;
import android.app.FragmentTransaction;
import android.content.res.Configuration;
import android.os.Bundle;
import android.util.Log;
import android.view.LayoutInflater;
import android.view.View;
import android.view.ViewGroup;
import android.widget.EditText;
import android.widget.FrameLayout;

public class ContentFragment extends Fragment implements
                             TabListener, SetData { ❶

    // String for logging the class name
    private final String TAG = getClass().getSimpleName();

    //Turn logging on or off
    private final boolean L = true;

    public void onAttach(Activity activity) {
        super.onAttach(activity);

        // Notification that the fragment is associated with an Activity
        if (L) Log.i(TAG, "onAttach " + activity.getClass().getSimpleName());
    }
```

```java
public void onCreate(Bundle savedInstanceState) {
    super.onCreate(savedInstanceState);

    // Notification that
    Log.i(TAG, "onCreate");
}

public View onCreateView(LayoutInflater inflater, ViewGroup container,
                                        Bundle savedInstanceState) {
    FrameLayout content = (FrameLayout) inflater.inflate(R.layout.content,
                                        container, false);
    if (L) Log.i(TAG, "onCreateView");
    return content;

}

public void onStart() {
    super.onStart();
    Log.i(TAG, "onStart");
}

public void onresume() {
    super.onResume();
    Log.i(TAG, "onResume");
}

public void onPause() {
    super.onPause();
    Log.i(TAG, "onPause");
}

public void onStop() {
    super.onStop();
    Log.i(TAG, "onStop");
}

public void onDestroyView() {
    super.onDestroyView();
    Log.i(TAG, "onDestroyView");
}

public void onDestroy() {
    super.onDestroy();
    Log.i(TAG, "onDestroy");
}

public void onDetach() {
    super.onDetach();
    Log.i(TAG, "onDetach");
}

/////////////////////////////////////////////////////////////////////
// Minor lifecycle methods
/////////////////////////////////////////////////////////////////////
```

```java
    public void onActivityCreated() {
        // Notification that the containing activiy and its View hierarchy exist
        Log.i(TAG, "onActivityCreated");
    }

    ////////////////////////////////////////////////////////////////////////
    // Overrides of the implementations ComponentCallbacks methods in Fragment
    ////////////////////////////////////////////////////////////////////////

    @Override
    public void onConfigurationChanged(Configuration newConfiguration) {
        super.onConfigurationChanged(newConfiguration);

        // This won't happen unless we declare changes we handle in the manifest
        if (L) Log.i(TAG, "onConfigurationChanged");
    }

    @Override
    public void onLowMemory() {
        // No guarantee this is called before or after other callbacks
        if (L) Log.i(TAG, "onLowMemory");
    }

    ////////////////////////////////////////////////////////////////////////
    // Implementation of TabListener
    ////////////////////////////////////////////////////////////////////////

    @Override
    public void onTabReselected(Tab tab, FragmentTransaction ft) {
        // TODO Auto-generated method stub

    }

    @Override
    public void onTabSelected(Tab tab, FragmentTransaction ft) {
        ft.show(this);

    }

    @Override
    public void onTabUnselected(Tab tab, FragmentTransaction ft) {
        ft.hide(this);

    }

    ////////////////////////////////////////////////////////////////////////
    // Implementation of SetData
    ////////////////////////////////////////////////////////////////////////

    @Override
    public void setData(Bundle data) { ❷
        // Display the number
        EditText t = (EditText) getActivity().findViewById(R.id.editText1);
        int i = data.getInt("place");
        t.setText(Integer.toString(i));
```

```
        }

    }
```

Here we will see a `Fragment` subclass that displays content on the right side of the screen. There are two such subclasses in our example app, but because they are not very different, we'll take a close look at only one of them here:

❶ First, note that the `Fragment` subclass implements two interfaces: `TabListener` and `SetData`. The `TabListener` interface enables this `Fragment` subclass to process user interactions with the tabs in the Action Bar.

❷ The `SetData` interface enables the Fragment subclass contained in the list on the left of the large layout, or the `Activity` that was started to display this `Fragment`, to set the data the `Fragment` displays.

Making Activity, Fragment, Action Bar, and Multiple Layouts Work Together

The example program in this chapter makes activities, fragments, the Action Bar, and multiple layouts using Android's declarative UI system work together to implement the typical app skeleton for a wide range of applications.

Letting the Android system choose layouts is one important part of enabling this design pattern. The other part is a small amount of utility code the `Fragment` and `Activity` classes use to manage tabs in the Action Bar, and the `Fragment` objects selected using those tabs.

Action Bar

Along with the `Fragment` class, the Action Bar enables creation of scalable user interface designs in Android. The Action Bar's part in this is to provide a container for menus, text entry fields, and other "chrome" around the main part of the user interface and a simple way of displaying this part of the user interface on a wide variety of screen sizes. We need to organize our code so that tabs only appear in the Action Bar when there are fragments to be selected using those tabs.

Tabs and Fragments

This is where fragments we use for the list and the tabs, the UI code they contain, and the tabs in the Action Bar we use to navigate between fragments come together. For this framework example, we created a handful of utility methods that can be used by both `Activity` and `Fragment` subclasses to help with fragment and tab interactions. These are static methods, so we organized them into their own class, as shown in the following program listing:

```
package com.finchframework.uiframework;

import android.app.ActionBar;
import android.app.ActionBar.Tab;id
import android.app.ActionBar.TabListener;
import android.app.Activity;
import android.app.Fragment;
import android.content.Intent;
import android.os.Bundle;

public class TabManager { ❶

    /**
     * Common utility code for initializing tabs, shared by activities that have
     * fragments and tabs
     *
     * Assumes the fragments are already instantiated, and that they were
     * specified in resources
     *
     * This can be called without knowing if the tab fragments are present in
     * the layout, fails silently if it can't find the
     *
     * @param activity
     *             The activity that hosts the tabs and corresponding fragments
     * @param defaultIndex
     *             The index of the Fragment shown first
     * @param nameIDs
     *             an array of ID for tab names
     * @param fragmentIDs
     *             an array of IDs of Fragment resources
     */
    public static void initialize(Activity activity, int defaultIndex,
            int[] nameIDs, int[] fragmentIDs) { ❷

        // How many do we have?
        int n = nameIDs.length;
        int i = 0;

        // Find at least one fragment that should implement TabListener
        TabListener f = (TabListener) activity.getFragmentManager()
                .findFragmentById(fragmentIDs[i]);

        // Null check - harmless to call if there are no such fragments
        if (null != f) {

            // Get the action bar and remove existing tabs
            ActionBar b = activity.getActionBar();
            b.removeAllTabs();

            // Make new tabs and assign tags and listeners
            for (; i < n; i++) {
                f = (TabListener) activity.getFragmentManager()
                        .findFragmentById(fragmentIDs[i]);
                Tab t = b.newTab().setText(nameIDs[i]).setTag(f)
```

```
                    .setTabListener(f);
                b.addTab(t);
            }
            b.getTabAt(defaultIndex).select();
        }
    }

    /**
     * If we have tabs and fragments in this activity, pass the bundle data to
     * the fragments. Otherwise start an activity that should contain the
     * fragments.
     *
     * @param activity
     * @param data
     */
    public static void loadTabFragments(Activity activity, Bundle data) {❸
        int n = activity.getActionBar().getTabCount();
        if (0 != n) {
            doLoad(activity, n, data);
        } else {
            activity.startActivity(new Intent(activity,
                    ContentControlActivity.class).putExtras(data));
        }
    }

    /**
     * An interface to pass data to a Fragment
     */
    public interface SetData {
        public void setData(Bundle data);
    }

    /**
     * Iterate over the tabs, get their tags, and use these as Fragment
     * references to pass the bundle data to the fragments
     *
     * @param activity
     * @param n
     * @param data
     */
    private static void doLoad(Activity activity, int n, Bundle data) {
        int i;
        ActionBar actionBar = activity.getActionBar();

        for (i = 0; i < n; i++) {
            SetData f = (SetData) actionBar.getTabAt(i).getTag();
            f.setData(data);
        }
        actionBar.selectTab(actionBar.getTabAt(0));
    }

}
```

❶ In the Fragment class that is selectable with a tab in the Action Bar, we saw that it
also implemented the SetData interface. The definition of that interface is here, along

with a utility method that wraps that interface with code that abstracts the difference between cases where one activity holds all the fragments, and cases where a new activity is started to display the fragments.

❷ The `initialize` method tests if there are fragments to initialize that are associated with tabs. We saw in the preceding program listing that the `Fragment` subclasses that are selectable using tabs in the Action Bar contain the code for handling tab interactions. This `initialize` method is what connects the tabs to the fragments so that the interface actually gets called. But, before doing this initialization, this method tests if there are any fragments to initialize, another example of accommodating layouts with and without the fragments.

❸ The `LoadTabFragments` method is the only place in all of our example app that comes close to "making a decision:" If there are no fragments to load with data, this code will start an activity we know will display those fragments. And, if we need to start that activity, we pass the data to that activity using the `extras` field of the `Intent` argument to `startActivity`.

The Other Activity

Well, what if we are on a small screen? We saw in the previous program listing that the `loadTabFragments` method causes an activity to be started if the fragments selectable with tabs are not on the screen. That activity can be certain that the only thing in it will be the two fragments, and the tabs that do not fit in the activity, that started this activity, another example of knowing about screen geometry without having to ask or decide about it.

Here is the code for that activity:

```
package com.finchframework.uiframework;
import android.app.ActionBar;
import android.app.Activity;
import android.content.res.Configuration;
import android.os.Bundle;
import android.util.Log;


public class ContentControlActivity extends Activity {

    // String for logging the class name
    private final String TAG = getClass().getSimpleName();

    // Turn logging on or off
    private final boolean L = true;

    @Override
    protected void onCreate(Bundle savedState) {
        super.onCreate(savedState);

        // To keep this method simple
```

```
        doCreate(savedState);

        // If we had state to restore, we note that in the log message
        if (L) Log.i(TAG, "onCreate" +
                (null == savedState ? " Restored state" : ""));
    }

    @Override
    protected void onRestart() {
        super.onRestart();
        // Notification that the activity will be started
        if (L) Log.i(TAG, "onRestart");
    }

    @Override
    protected void onStart() {
        super.onStart();
        // Notification that the activity is starting
        if (L) Log.i(TAG, "onStart");
    }

    @Override
    protected void onResume() {
        super.onResume();
        // Notification that the activity will interact with the user
        if (L) Log.i(TAG, "onResume");
    }

    protected void onPause() {
        super.onPause();
        // Notification that the activity will stop interacting with the user
        if (L) Log.i(TAG, "onPause" + (isFinishing() ? " Finishing" : ""));
    }

    @Override
    protected void onStop() {
        super.onStop();
        // Notification that the activity is no longer visible
        if (L) Log.i(TAG, "onStop");
    }

    @Override
    protected void onDestroy() {
        super.onDestroy();
        // Notification the activity will be destroyed
        if (L) Log.i(TAG, "onDestroy"
                // Are we finishing?
                + (isFinishing() ? " Finishing" : ""));
    }

    @Override
    protected void onSaveInstanceState(Bundle outState) {
        super.onSaveInstanceState(outState);
        saveState(outState);
```

```
        // Called when state should be saved
        if (L) Log.i(TAG, "onSaveInstanceState");

    }

    @Override
    protected void onRestoreInstanceState(Bundle savedState) {
        super.onRestoreInstanceState(savedState);
        if (null != savedState) restoreState(savedState);

        // If we had state to restore, we note that in the log message
        if (L) Log.i(TAG, "onRestoreInstanceState" +
                (null == savedState ? " Restored state" : ""));
    }

    /////////////////////////////////////////////////////////////////////////
    // The minor lifecycle methods - you probably won't need these
    /////////////////////////////////////////////////////////////////////////

    @Override
    protected void onPostCreate(Bundle savedState) {
        super.onPostCreate(savedState);
        if (null != savedState) restoreState(savedState);

        // If we had state to restore, we note that in the log message
        if (L) Log.i(TAG, "onCreate" + (null == savedState ? " Restored state" : ""));

    }

    @Override
    protected void onPostResume() {
        super.onPostResume();
        // Notification that resuming the activity is complete
        if (L) Log.i(TAG, "onPostResume");
    }

    @Override
    protected void onUserLeaveHint() {
        super.onUserLeaveHint();
        // Notification that user navigated away from this activity
        if (L) Log.i(TAG, "onUserLeaveHint");
    }

    /////////////////////////////////////////////////////////////////////////
    // Overrides of the implementations ComponentCallbacks methods in Activity
    /////////////////////////////////////////////////////////////////////////

    @Override
    public void onConfigurationChanged(Configuration newConfiguration) {
        super.onConfigurationChanged(newConfiguration);

        // This won't happen unless we declare changes we handle in the manifest
        if (L) Log.i(TAG, "onConfigurationChanged");
    }
```

```
@Override
public void onLowMemory() {
    // No guarantee this is called before or after other callbacks
    if (L) Log.i(TAG, "onLowMemory");
}

//////////////////////////////////////////////////////////////////////
// App-specific code here
//////////////////////////////////////////////////////////////////////


/**
 * This is where we restore state we previously saved.
 * @param savedState the Bundle we got from the callback
 */
private void restoreState(Bundle savedState) {
    // Add your code to restore state here

}

/**
 * Add this activity's state to the bundle and/or commit pending data
 */
private void saveState(Bundle state) {
    // Add your code to add state to the bundle here
}

/**
 * Perform initializations on creation of this Activity instance
 * @param savedState
 */
private void doCreate(Bundle savedState) {
    setContentView(R.layout.content_control_activity);

    if (null != savedState) restoreState(savedState);

    ActionBar bar = getActionBar();
    bar.setDisplayShowTitleEnabled(false);
    bar.setNavigationMode(ActionBar.NAVIGATION_MODE_TABS);

    // Initialize the tabs
    int names[] = {R.string.content, R.string.detail };
    int fragments[] = { R.id.content_frag, R.id.detail_frag };
    TabManager.initialize(this, 0, names, fragments);        ❶


    // Load data if there is some
    Bundle b = getIntent().getExtras();
    TabManager.loadTabFragments(this, b); ❷
}

}
```

The notable lines of code in this activity are:

❶ This activity calls the `Tabmanager.initialize` method, just like the preceding activity. Because the `TabManager` methods work for any layouts the system has chosen for any of the activity classes, there is no conditional logic surrounding this call.

❷ Similarly, the `TabManager.loadTabfragments` method call is identical to the one that caused this activity to be started, except that, in the context of this activity, the tabs and fragments to be loaded with the specified data do exist.

Using Content Providers

When Android applications share data, they rely on the content provider API to expose data within their database. For example, the Android contact content provider allows an unlimited number of applications to reuse contact persistence on the Android platform. By simply invoking this content provider, an application can integrate access to a user's contacts stored locally and synchronized with the Google cloud. Applications can read and write data in content providers without having to provide their own database manipulation code. In this way, content providers provide a powerful feature that allows developers to easily create applications with sophisticated data management—in many cases, applications will end up writing very little data persistence code of their own.

The content provider API enables client applications to query the OS for relevant data using a Uniform Resource Identifier (URI), similar to the way a browser requests information from the Internet. For a given URI query, a client does not know which application will provide the data; it simply presents the OS with a URI and leaves it to the platform to start the appropriate application to provide the result. The platform also provides a permission that allows clients to limit access to content provider data.

The content provider API enables full create, read, update, and delete access to shared content. This means applications can use URI-oriented requests to:

- Create new records
- Retrieve one, all, or a limited set of records
- Update records
- Delete records

This chapter shows you how to write your own content provider by examining the inner workings of an example content provider, `SimpleFinchVideoContentProvider`, included within the Finch source tree. All file references are contained in the source directory for this chapter. Thus, when the *AndroidManifest.xml* file is referenced in this chapter, the *$(FinchVideo)/AndroidManifest.xml* file is assumed. We'll use this code to describe how to create a content provider by implementing each method required by the main content provider API, the class `ContentProvider`. We will also explain how to integrate an SQLite database into that content provider. We'll describe how to implement the basic function of a content provider, which is to provide a mapping between URIs that reference data and database rows. You will see how a content provider encapsulates data persistence functions and enables your application to share data across processes when you declare your provider in *AndroidManifest.xml*. We will show you how to hook content provider data into Android UI components, thus completing the MVC architecture that we have led up to so far in this book. Finally, we will build a data viewing activity that automatically refreshes its display in response to changes in data.

 Throughout this chapter, we make the assumption that local content provider storage uses an SQLite database. Given the content provider `query`, `insert`, `update`, and `delete` API methods, it's actually a bit of a stretch to think about mapping it to anything else, even though, in theory, the API can store and retrieve data using any backend, such as a flat file, that could support the required operations.

We follow this introduction in the next chapter by showing you how to extend and enhance the very concept of a content provider. In the process, you will learn to leverage the content provider API to enable integration of RESTful network services into Android. This simple architecture will prevent many common mobile programming errors, even though it only relies on basic Android components. You will see that this approach leads logically into a mobile application architecture that adds significant robustness and performance improvements to Android applications.

We will walk through a video listing application that provides a simplified illustration of this architecture. This application will follow the suggested approach by loading, parsing, and caching YouTube video content entries from the RESTful web service at *http://gdata.youtube.com*. We'll simply be using gData as an example of a RESTful service that we can integrate into an Android content provider. The application UI will use content providers to dynamically display video entries as they are loaded and parsed from the network. You will be able to apply this approach to integrate the large number of web services available on the Internet into your Android-based application. Incidentally, the gData URI provides a pretty neat demo from Google and is worth checking out in its own right.

Understanding Content Providers

Content providers encapsulate data management so that other parts of an application, such as the view and controller, do not need to participate in persisting application data. Saying this in a different way: content providers persist application data because the view and controller should not handle it. Specialized software layers that do not attempt to perform tasks of other layers are the hallmark of well-crafted code. Bugs and unneeded complexity arise when software layers perform tasks that are beyond their scope. Thus, a UI should consist only of well laid out UI components fine-tuned to collect events from their end user. A well-written application controller will contain only the domain logic of the mobile application. And in connection with this chapter, simplifications arise when both types of code can outsource data persistence to a logical third party: content providers. Recalling the discussion from "SQL and the Database-Centric Data Model for Android Applications" on page 275, content providers are well suited to implementing the nondocument-centric data model.

With the assistance of a content provider, applications do not need to open their own SQLite tables, because that detail will take place behind the content provider interface in tables owned by the content provider. In the past, to share data, mobile applications might have had to store it in files in the local filesystem with an application-defined configuration format. Instead, with Android, applications can often rely solely on content provider storage.

Before digging into the `SimpleFinchVideoContentProvider`, we'll provide an overview of the simple Finch video application and provide background on content provider implementation tasks.

Implementing a Content Provider

To take advantage of this design structure, you will need to write your own content provider, which involves completing the following tasks:

1. Create a content provider public API for client consumption by:
    a. Defining the `CONTENT_URI` for your content provider
    b. Creating the column names for communication with clients
    c. Declaring public static `String` objects that clients use to specify columns
    d. Defining MIME types for any new data types
2. Implement your content provider. This requires the following:
    a. Extending the main content provider API, the `ContentProvider` class, to create a custom content provider implementation
    b. Setting up a provider URI
    c. Creating an SQLite database and associated cursors to store content provider data
    d. Using cursors to make data available to clients while supporting dynamic data updates
    e. Defining the process by which binary data is returned to the client
    f. Implementing the basic `query`, `insert`, `update`, and `delete` data methods of a `Cursor` to return to the client

3. Update the *AndroidManifest.xml* file to declare your `<provider>`.

When we have finished discussing the implementation of a basic content provider, we will describe tasks related to using content providers to develop the more advanced network architecture that we have mentioned.

Browsing Video with Finch

The Finch video viewer enables users to list video-related metadata. We have included two versions of a video listing application and two versions of underlying content providers. The first version, presented in this chapter, is a simple video listing application that uses `SimpleFinchVideoContentProvider`, which is designed to teach you to implement your first content provider. A second version of the app, presented in the next chapter, uses a slightly more complex content provider that adds the ability to pull content from the online YouTube video search service. This second version of the app has the ability to cache results and the ability to show video thumbnails.

Now we will explore the first app in detail. This simple application has one activity: `SimpleFinchVideoActivity`, which allows a user to create and list his own video metadata (e.g., video title, description, URI, and ID), as shown in Figure 12-1.

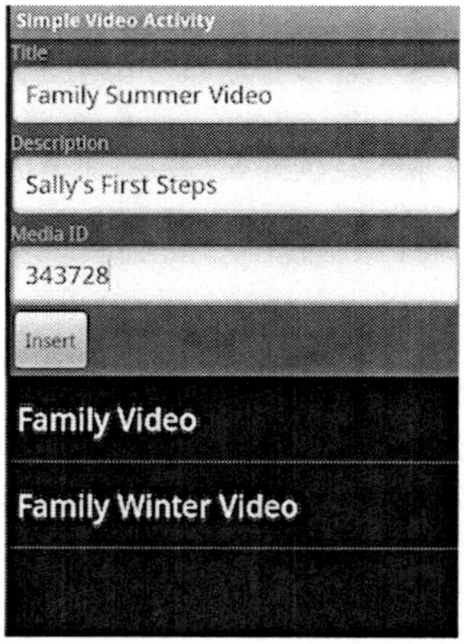

Figure 12-1. An activity for our simple video provider that lets users enter their own video "metadata"

To use this application, simply enter appropriate data for a "video" entry, and then press the Insert button. The list underneath the text fields uses Android MVC to automatically refresh its view of data.

The simple video database

To store the data you enter into this application, the `SimpleFinchVideoContent` `Provider` class creates its database with the following SQL statement:

```
CREATE TABLE video (_id INTEGER PRIMARY KEY, title TEXT, decription TEXT, uri TEXT);
```

The `_id` column is required for use with the Android cursor system. It provides the unique identity of a row in a cursor as well as the identity of an object in the database. As such, you need to define this column with the SQL attributes `INTEGER PRIMARY KEY` `AUTOINCREMENT` to make certain its value is unique.

The `title` and `description` columns store video title and description data, respectively. The `uri` column contains a media URI that could be used to play a video entry in an actual working version of this application.

Structure of the simple version of the code

This section briefly examines relevant files within the simple Finch video application:

AndroidManifest.xml
> We've created a manifest for a simple video content provider application that will contain a reference to our activity `SimpleFinchVideoActivity` as well as our content provider `SimpleFinchVideoContentProvider`.

$(FinchVideo)/src/com/oreilly/demo/pa/finchvideo/FinchVideo.java
> The `FinchVideo` class contains the `AUTHORITY` attribute (discussed later) and the `SimpleVideo` class that defines the names of the content provider columns. Neither the `FinchVideo` class nor the `SimpleVideo` class contains any executable code.

$(FinchVideo)/src/com/oreilly/demo/pa/finchvideo/provider/SimpleFinchVideoContent-Provider.java
> The `SimpleFinchVideoContentProvider` class is the content provider for the simple video database. It handles URI requests as appropriate for the simple video application. This file is the subject of the first half of this chapter.

$(FinchVideo)/src/com/oreilly/demo/pa/finchvideo/SimpleFinchVideoActivity.java
> The `SimpleFinchVideoActivity` class is an activity that allows the user to view a list of videos.

Defining a Provider Public API

Though we saw in Chapter 3 how clients use content providers, we provide more information here for content provider authors to fully implement the provider public API. For clients to use your content provider, you will need to create a public API class that contains a set of constants that clients use to access column fields of `Cursor` objects returned by your provider's query method. This class will also define the content provider authority URI that provides the foundation of the whole provider URI communication scheme. Our class, `FinchVideo.SimpleVideos`, provides the API to our `SimpleFinchVideo`.

First we'll explain the class in pieces, providing background on its fields, and then we'll show a full listing.

Defining the CONTENT_URI

For a client application to query content provider data, it needs to pass a URI that identifies relevant data to one of the Android content resolver's data access methods. These methods, `query`, `insert`, `update`, and `delete`, mirror the methods found on a content resolver that we define in "Writing and Integrating a Content Provider" on page 350. On receiving such an invocation, the content resolver will use an authority string to match the incoming URI with the `CONTENT_URI` of each content provider it knows about to find the right provider for the client. Thus, the `CONTENT_URI` defines the type of URIs your content provider can process.

A `CONTENT_URI` consists of these parts:

`content://`
> This is a prefix that tells the Android Framework that it must find a content provider to resolve the URI.

The authority
> This string uniquely identifies the content provider and consists of up to two sections: the organizational section and the provider identifier section. The organizational section uniquely identifies the organization that created the content provider. The provider identifier section identifies a particular content provider that the organization created. For content providers that are built into Android, the organizational section is omitted. For instance, the built-in "media" authority that returns one or more images does not have the organizational section of the authority. However, any content providers that are created by developers outside of Google's Android team must define both sections of the content provider. Thus, the simple Finch video example application's authority is `com.oreilly.demo.pa.finchvideo.SimpleFinchVideo`. The organizational section is `com.oreilly.demo.pa.finchvideo`, and the provider identifier section is `SimpleFinchVideo`. The Google documentation suggests that the best solution for picking the authority section of your `CONTENT_URI` is to use the fully qualified class name of the class implementing the content provider.

> The authority section uniquely identifies the particular content provider that Android will call to respond to queries that it handles.

The path
> The content provider can interpret the rest of the URI however it wants, but it must adhere to some requirements:

- If the content provider can return multiple data types, the URI must be constructed so that some part of the path specifies the type of data to return.

  For instance, the built-in "contacts" content provider provides many different types of data: people, phones, contact methods, and so on. The contacts content provider uses strings in the URI to differentiate which type of data the user is requesting. Thus, to request a specific person, the URI will be something like this:

  ```
  content://contacts/people/1
  ```

  To request a specific phone number, the URI could be something like this:

  ```
  content://contacts/people/1/phone/3
  ```

  In the first case, the MIME data type returned will be vnd.android. cursor.item/person, whereas in the second case, it will be vnd.android.cur sor.item/phone.

- The content provider must be capable of returning either one item or a set of item identifiers. The content provider will return a single item when an item identifier appears in the final portion of the URI. Looking back at our previous example, the URI *content://contacts/people/1/phone/3* returned a single phone number of type vnd.android.cursor.item/phone. If the URI had instead been *content://contacts/people/1/phone*, the application would instead return a list of all the phone numbers for the person having the person identifier number 1, and the MIME type of the data returned would be vnd.android.cursor.dir/ phone.

As mentioned earlier, content providers can interpret the path portions of the URIs to suit their needs. This means the path portion can use items in the path to filter data to return to the caller. For instance, the built-in "media" content provider can return either internal or external data depending on whether the URI contains the word *internal* or *external* in the path.

The full CONTENT_URI for the simple Finch video is *content://com.oreilly.demo.pa.finch-video.SimpleFinchVideo/video*.

The CONTENT_URI must be of type public static final Uri. It is defined in the Finch Video class of our simple video application. In our public API class we start by extending the class BaseColumns, and then define a string named AUTHORITY:

```
public final class FinchVideo.SimpleVideos extends BaseColumns {
    public static final String SIMPLE_AUTHORITY =
    "com.oreilly.demo.pa.finchvideo.FinchVideo";
```

Then we define the CONTENT_URI itself:

```
public static final class FinchVideo.SimpleVideos implements BaseColumns {
    public static final Uri CONTENT_URI =
    Uri.parse("content://" + AUTHORITY + "/video");
```

Put more simply, defining this URI just involves picking an authority string that should use a Java package used by your application as the organizational identifier—a public API package is likely a better candidate here than an implementation package, as we discussed in "Java Packages" on page 56. The content provider identifier is just the name of your content provider class. The provider URI for our simple Finch video provider looks as follows:

```
"content://" + FinchVideo.FinchVideoContentProvider.SIMPLE_AUTHORITY + "/" +
    FinchVideo.SimpleVideos.VIDEO
```

Creating the Column Names

Content providers exchange data with their clients in much the same way an SQL database exchanges data with database applications: using cursors full of rows and columns of data. A content provider must define the column names it supports just as database applications must define the columns they support. When the content provider uses an SQLite database as its data store, the obvious solution is to give the content provider columns with the same name as the database columns, and that's just what `SimpleFinchVideoContentProvider` does. Because of this, no mapping is necessary between the `SimpleFinchVideoContentProvider` columns and the underlying database columns.

 Not all applications make all of their data available to content provider clients, and some applications that are more complex may want to make derivative views available to content provider clients. The projection map described in "The SimpleFinchVideoContentProvider Class and Instance Variables" on page 355 is available to handle these complexities.

Declaring Column Specification Strings

The `SimpleFinchVideoProvider` columns are defined in the `FinchVideo.SimpleVideos` class discussed in this section. Every content provider must define an `_id` column to hold the record number of each row. The value of each `_id` must be unique within the content provider; it is the number that a client will append to the content provider's *vnd.android.cursor.item* URI when attempting to query for a single record.

When the content provider is backed by an SQLite database, as is the case for `SimpleFinchVideoProvider`, the `_id` should have the type `INTEGER PRIMARY KEY AUTOINCREMENT`. This way, the rows will have a unique `_id` number and `_id` numbers will not be reused, even when rows are deleted. This helps support referential integrity by ensuring that each new row has an `_id` that has never been used before. If row `_ids` are reused, there is a chance that cached URIs could point to the wrong data.

Here is a complete program listing of the simple Finch video provider API, the class `FinchVideo.SimpleVideos`. Note that we have only included constants that serve the purposes we have outlined. We take care not to define content provider implementation constants here, as they will not be useful to a client and might tie clients to using a particular implementation of a content provider. We strive to achieve good software design and ensure that our software layers remain separable where clients should not have direct compilation dependencies on content provider implementation classes. The complete listing of the public API of the Finch video provider API follows.

```
/**
 * Simple Videos columns
 */
public class FinchVideo {
    public static final class SimpleVideos implements BaseColumns {
        // This class cannot be instantiated
        private SimpleVideos() {}

        // uri references all videos
        public static final Uri VIDEOS_URI = Uri.parse("content://" +
                SIMPLE_AUTHORITY + "/" + SimpleVideos.VIDEO);

        /**
         * The content:// style URL for this table
         */
        public static final Uri CONTENT_URI = VIDEOS_URI;❶

        /**
         * The MIME type of {@link #CONTENT_URI} providing a directory of notes.
         */
        public static final String CONTENT_TYPE =
                "vnd.android.cursor.dir/vnd.finch.video";❷

        /**
         * The MIME type of a {@link #CONTENT_URI} sub-directory of a single
         * video.
         */
        public static final String CONTENT_VIDEO_TYPE =
                "vnd.android.cursor.item/vnd.finch.video";

        ❸
        /**
         * The video itself
         * <P>Type: TEXT</P>
         */
        public static final String VIDEO = "video";

        /**
         * Column name for the title of the video
         * <P>Type: TEXT</P>
         */
        public static final String TITLE = "title";

        /**
         * Column name for the description of the video.
         */
        public static final String DESCRIPTION = "description";
```

```
/**
 * Column name for the media uri
 */
public static final String URI = "uri";

/**
 * Unique identifier for an element of media
 */
public static final String MEDIA_ID = "media_id";
}

...
// The API for FinchVideo.Videos is also defined in this class.
}
```

Here are some of the highlights of the code:

❶ We use the VIDEOS_URI to define the value for our CONTENT_URI. The videos URI contains that content URI as described.

❷ This is the MIME type of the video entries that our provider will store. In "Implementing the getType Method" on page 358 we explain how our content provider uses this type.

❸ These are the names of the columns that clients can use to access values in Cursor objects that our provider creates.

Writing and Integrating a Content Provider

Now that we've examined the general structure of the simple video list application and provided a way for clients to access our content provider, it's time to look at how the application both implements and consumes the SimpleFinchVideoContentProvider.

Common Content Provider Tasks

In the following sections, we provide a high-level guide to tasks associated with writing a content provider. We then provide an introduction to Android MVC and finish with an explanation of the SimpleFinchVideoContentProvider code.

Extending ContentProvider

Applications extend the ContentProvider class to handle URIs that refer to a particular type of data, such as MMS messages, pictures, videos, and so forth. For example, for a content provider class that handled videos, the ContentProvider.insert method would insert data that described a video into an SQLite table with columns appropriate for that information, such as a title, description, and similar information.

Start writing your content provider by implementing the following two methods:

onCreate
> This method provides a hook to allow your content provider to initialize itself. Any code you want to run just once, such as making a database connection, should reside in this method.

String getType(Uri uri)
> This method, given a URI, returns the MIME type of the data that this content provider provides at the given URI. The URI comes from the client application interested in accessing the data.

You'll continue to implement by overriding the main content provider data access methods:

insert(Uri uri, ContentValues values)
> This method is called when the client code needs to insert data into the database your content provider is serving. Normally, the implementation for this method will either directly or indirectly result in a database insert operation.

Cursor query(Uri uri, String[] projection, String selection, String[] selectionArgs, String sortOrder)
> This method is called whenever a client wishes to read data from the content provider's database. Normally, here, you retrieve data using an SQL SELECT statement and return a cursor containing the requested data. Developers call this method indirectly using Activity's managedQuery method, or call startManagingQuery on the return values from this method. If your activity fails to "manage" the returned cursor, or fails to close the cursor, your application will contain a serious memory leak that will result in poor performance and, likely, crashes.

update(Uri uri, ContentValues values, String selection, String[] selectionArgs)
> This method is called when a client wishes to update one or more rows in the content provider's database. It translates to an SQL UPDATE statement.

delete(Uri uri, String selection, String[] selectionArgs)
> This method is called when a client wishes to delete one or more rows in the content provider's database. It translates to an SQL DELETE statement.

These four methods each perform an action on data referenced by a given URI parameter. A typical implementation of each of these methods starts with matching the incoming URI argument to a particular type of data. For example, a content provider implementation needs to figure out whether a given URI refers to a specific video or to a group of videos. After a provider matches the URI, appropriate SQL operations follow. Each method then returns a value that either contains referenced data, describes affected data, or refers to the number of elements that were affected by the operation. For example, a query for a specific video would return a cursor that contained a single video element, if the given URI referenced a single element present in a local table.

Matching URIs to table data is an integral part of the job of a content provider. You might not think it would be that hard to parse a content provider URI yourself, but Android provides a nice utility for doing that job for you, which is convenient, but more important, helps developers to standardize on the format of provider URIs that we have discussed. The `URIMatcher` class supports mapping from URIs containing authority, path, and ID strings to application-defined constants usable with `case` statements that handle particular subtypes of URIs. From there, the provider can decide what SQL operations to use to manage actual table rows. A typical content provider will create a static instance of `URIMatcher` and populate it using a static initializer that calls `URIMatcher.addURI` to establish the first-level mapping used later in content provider data methods. Our simple video content provider does this in "The SimpleFinchVideoContentProvider Class and Instance Variables" on page 355.

File Management and Binary Data

Content providers often need to manage large chunks of binary data, such as a bitmap or music clip. Storage of large data files should influence the design of an application and will likely have significant performance implications. A content provider can serve files through content provider URIs in a way that encapsulates the location of actual physical files so that clients can be agnostic about that information. Clients use content provider URIs to access files without knowing where the files actually reside. This layer of indirection enables a content provider to manage these files in a way that makes the most sense for the content provider data without having that information leak into the client—which could end up causing code changes in a client if the content provider needed to make a change in the way the physical files are stored. Generally, it's much easier to change just the provider than all of its potential clients. Clients should not need to know that a set of provider media files might reside in flash memory, on the SD card, or entirely on the network, so long as the provider makes the files accessible from a set of content provider URIs that the client understands. The client will just use the method `ContentResolver.openInputStream` for a given URI and then read data from the resultant stream.

Additionally, when sharing large amounts of data between applications, because an Android application should not read or write files that another application has created, a content provider must be used to access the relevant bytes. Therefore, when the first content provider returns a pointer to a file, that pointer must be in the form of a `content://` URI instead of a Unix filename. The use of a `content://` URI causes the file to be opened and read under the permissions of the content provider that owns the file, not the client application (which should not have access rights to the file).

It's also important to consider that filesystem I/O is much faster and more versatile than dealing with SQLite blobs, and it's better to use the Unix filesystem to directly store binary data. Additionally, there's no advantage to putting binary data in a database, because you can't search on it!

To implement this approach in your app, the Android SDK documentation suggests one strategy where a content provider persists data to a file and stores a `content://` URI in the database that points to the file, as shown in Figure 12-2. Client applications will pass the URI in this field to `ContentProvider.openStream` to retrieve the byte stream from the file it specifies.

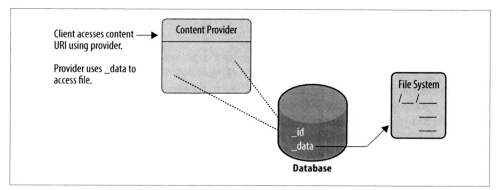

Figure 12-2. Android MVC's typical use of cursors and content providers

In detail, to implement the file approach, instead of creating a hypothetical user table like this:

```
CREATE TABLE user ( _id INTEGER PRIMARY KEY AUTOINCREMENT, name TEXT, password
                         TEXT, picture BLOB );
```

the documentation suggests two tables that look like this:

```
CREATE TABLE user ( _id INTEGER PRIMARY KEY AUTOINCREMENT, name TEXT, password
                         TEXT, picture TEXT );
CREATE TABLE userPicture ( _id INTEGER PRIMARY KEY AUTOINCREMENT,
                         _data TEXT );
```

The `picture` column of the `user` table will store a `content://` URI that points to a row in the `userPicture` table. The `_data` column of the `userPicture` table will point to a real file on the Android filesystem.

If the path to the file were stored directly in the `user` table, clients would get a path but be unable to open the file, because it's owned by the application serving up the content provider and the clients don't have permission to read it. In the solution shown here, however, access is controlled by a `ContentResolver` class we'll examine later.

The `ContentResolver` class looks for a column named `_data` when processing requests. If the file specified in that column is found, the provider's `openOutputStream` method opens the file and returns a `java.io.OutputStream` to the client. This is the same object that would be returned if the client were able to open the file directly. The `ContentResolver` class is part of the same application as the content provider, and therefore is able to open the file when the client cannot.

Later in this chapter, we will demonstrate a content provider that uses the content provider file management facility to store thumbnail images.

Android MVC and Content Observation

It's important to relate a bigger picture of how MVC works with content providers in Android. Additionally, a more detailed discussion of MVC in Android will lead us into "A "Network MVC"" on page 367.

To understand the power of the content provider framework, we need to discuss how cursor update events drive dynamic updates of Android UIs. We think it will help to highlight the often-overlooked communications pathways in the traditional MVC programming pattern, where the following occurs: the View delivers user input events to the Controller; the Controller makes modifications to the Model, and the Model sends update events to the View and to any other observer that registers interest in the Model; the View renders the contents of the Model, usually without directly engaging in application logic, and ideally, just simply iterates over the data in the Model.

In Android, the MVC pattern works as shown in Figure 12-3, where explicitly:

- The Model consists of a content provider and the cursors it returns from its query method, as well as the data it holds in its SQLite tables.

- Content providers should be written to send notification events whenever they change data by calling ContentResolver.notifyChange. Because the provider has sole access to modify the data, it will always know when data changes.

- Notifications are delivered to a UI component, often a ListView, through observation of Cursor objects that are bound to content provider URIs. Cursor update messages fire from the Model to the View in response to the provider's invocation of notifyChange. The View and Controller correspond to Android activities and their views, and to the classes that listen to the events they generate. Specifically, the system delivers ContentObserver.onChange messages to instances of ContentObserver registered using Cursor.registerContentObserver. The Android classes automatically register for cursor changes whenever a developer calls a method such as ListView.setAdapter(ListAdapter). The list view has an internal content observer, and the list adapter will register with the Cursor object.

To think about how this notification works in practice, suppose an activity were to call ContentResolver.delete. As we'll see shortly, the corresponding content provider would first delete a row from its database and then notify the content resolver URI corresponding to that row. Any listening cursors embedded in any view will be notified simply that data has changed; the views will, in turn, get the update event and then repaint themselves to reflect the new state. The views paint whatever state resides in their display area; if that happened to include the deleted element, it will disappear from the UI. The Cursor objects act as a proxy object between cursor consumers and

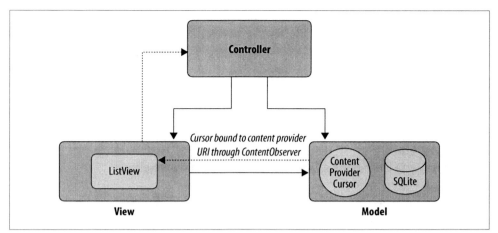

Figure 12-3. Typical use of cursors and content providers in the Android MVC

the content provider system. Events flow from the provider, through the cursor, and into the View system. The degree of automation in this chain of events results in significant convenience for developers who need to perform only the minimum amount of work to put it into action. Additionally, programs don't have to explicitly poll to keep their rendering of the model up-to-date as the model tells the view when state changes.

A Complete Content Provider: The SimpleFinchVideoContentProvider Code

Now that you understand the important tasks associated with writing a content provider and Android MVC—the communication system for Android content providers—let's see how to build your own content provider. The `SimpleFinchVideo ContentProvider` class extends `ContentProvider` as shown here:

```
public class SimpleFinchVideoContentProvider extends ContentProvider {
```

The SimpleFinchVideoContentProvider Class and Instance Variables

As usual, it's best to understand the major class and instance variables used by a method before examining how the method works. The member variables we need to understand for `SimpleFinchVideoContentProvider` are:

```
private static final String DATABASE_NAME = "simple_video.db";
private static final int DATABASE_VERSION = 2;
private static final String VIDEO_TABLE_NAME = "video";
private DatabaseHelper mOpenHelper;
```

DATABASE_NAME

The name of the database file on the device. For the simple Finch video, the full path to the file is */data/data/com.oreilly.demo.pa.finchvideo/databases/simple_video.db*.

DATABASE_VERSION

The version of the database that is compatible with this code. If this number is higher than the database version of the database itself, the application calls the DatabaseHelper.onUpdate method.

VIDEO_TABLE_NAME

The name of the video table within the simple_video database.

mOpenHelper

The database helper instance variable that is initialized during onCreate. It provides access to the database for the insert, query, update, and delete methods.

sUriMatcher

A static initialization block that performs initializations of static variables that can't be performed as simple one-liners. For example, our simple video content provider begins by establishing a content provider URI mapping in a static initialization of a UriMatcher as follows:

```
private static UriMatcher sUriMatcher;

private static final int VIDEOS = 1;
private static final int VIDEO_ID = 2;

static {
    sUriMatcher = new UriMatcher(UriMatcher.NO_MATCH);
    sUriMatcher.addURI(AUTHORITY, FinchVideo.SimpleVideos.VIDEO_NAME, VIDEOS);
    // use of the hash character indicates matching of an id
    sUriMatcher.addURI(AUTHORITY,
        FinchVideo.SimpleVideos.VIDEO_NAME + "/#", VIDEO_ID);
...
// more initialization to follow
```

The UriMatcher class provides the basis of the convenience utilities that Android provides for mapping content provider URIs. To use an instance of it, you populate it with mappings from a URI string such as "videos" to a constant field. Our mappings work as follows: the application first provides an argument, Uri Matcher.NO_MATCH, to the constructor of the provider UriMatcher to define the value that indicates when a URI does not match any URI. The application then adds mappings for multiple videos to VIDEOS, and then a mapping for a specific video to VIDEO_ID. With all provider URIs mapped to an integer value the provider can perform a switch operation to jump to the appropriate handling code for multiple and single videos.

This mapping causes a URI such as content://com.oreilly.demo.pa.finch video.SimpleFinchVideo/video to map to the constant VIDEOS, meaning all videos.

A URI for a single video, such as `content://oreilly.demo.pa.finchvideo.Simple FinchVideo/video/7`, will map to the constant `VIDEO_ID` for a single video. The hash mark at the end of the URI matcher binding is a wildcard for a URI ending with any integer number.

sVideosProjectionMap

The projection map used by the query method. This `HashMap` maps the content provider's column names to database column names. A projection map is not required, but when used it must list all column names that might be returned by the query. In `SimpleFinchVideoContentProvider`, the content provider column names and the database column names are identical, so the `sVideosProjectionMap` is not required. But we provide it as an example for applications that might need it. In the following code, we create our example projection mapping:

```
// example projection map, not actually used in this application
sVideosProjectionMap = new HashMap<String, String>();
sVideosProjectionMap.put(FinchVideo.Videos._ID,
    FinchVideo.Videos._ID);
sVideosProjectionMap.put(FinchVideo.Videos.TITLE,
    FinchVideo.Videos.TITLE);
sVideosProjectionMap.put(FinchVideo.Videos.VIDEO,
    FinchVideo.Videos.VIDEO);
sVideosProjectionMap.put(FinchVideo.Videos.DESCRIPTION,
    FinchVideo.Videos.DESCRIPTION);
```

Implementing the onCreate Method

During initialization of the simple Finch video content provider, we create the video's SQLite data store as follows:

```
private static class DatabaseHelper extends SQLiteOpenHelper {
    public void onCreate(SQLiteDatabase sqLiteDatabase) {
        createTable(sqLiteDatabase);
    }

    // create table method may also be called from onUpgrade
    private void createTable(SQLiteDatabase sqLiteDatabase) {
        String qs = "CREATE TABLE " + VIDEO_TABLE_NAME + " (" +
            FinchVideo.SimpleVideos._ID + " INTEGER PRIMARY KEY, " +
            FinchVideo.SimpleVideos.TITLE_NAME + " TEXT, " +
            FinchVideo.SimpleVideos.DESCRIPTION_NAME + " TEXT, " +
            FinchVideo.SimpleVideos.URI_NAME + " TEXT);";
        sqLiteDatabase.execSQL(qs);
    }
}
```

When creating SQLite tables to support content provider operations, developers are required to provide a field with a primary key called `_id`. While it's not immediately clear that this field is required, unless you read the Android developer docs in detail, the Android content management system actually does enforce the presence of the `_id` field in the cursors that are returned by the query method. `_id` is used in query matching with the # special character in content provider URLs. For example, a URL such as *content://contacts/people/25* would map to a data row in a contacts table with _id 25. The requirement is really just to use a specific name for a table primary key.

Implementing the getType Method

Next, we implement the getType method to determine MIME types of arbitrary URIs passed from the client. As you can see in the following code, we provide URI matching for VIDEOS, and VIDEO_ID to MIME types we defined in our public API:

```
public String getType(Uri uri) {
    switch (sUriMatcher.match(uri)) {
        case VIDEOS:
            return FinchVideo.SimpleVideos.CONTENT_TYPE;

        case VIDEO_ID:
            return FinchVideo.SimpleVideos.CONTENT_VIDEO_TYPE;

        default:
            throw new IllegalArgumentException("Unknown video type: " + uri);
    }
}
```

Implementing the Provider API

A content provider implementation must override the data methods of the ContentProvider base class: insert, query, update, and delete. For the simple video application, these methods are defined by the SimpleFinchVideoContentProvider class.

The query method

After matching the incoming URI, our content provider query method performs a corresponding select on a readable database, by delegating to SQLiteDatabase.query, and then returns the results in the form of a database Cursor object. The cursor will contain all database rows described by the URI argument. After we've made the query, the Android content provider mechanism automatically supports the use of cursor instances across processes, which permits our provider query method to simply return the cursor as a normal return value to make it available to clients that might reside in another process.

The query method also supports the parameters uri, projection, selection, selectionArgs, and sortOrder, which are used in the same manner as the arguments to SQLiteDatabase.query that we saw in Chapter 9. Just as with any SQL SELECT, parameters to the query method enable our provider clients to select only specific videos that match the query parameters. In addition to passing a URI, a client calling the simple video content provider could also pass an additional where clause with where arguments. For example, these arguments would enable a developer to query for videos from a particular author.

As we've seen, MVC in Android relies on cursors and the data they contain, as well as framework-based delivery of content observer update messages. Because clients in different processes share `Cursor` objects, a content provider implementation must take care not to close a cursor that it has served from its `query` method. If a cursor is closed in this manner, clients will not see exceptions thrown; instead, the cursor will always act like it is empty, and it will no longer receive update events—it's up to the activity to properly manage the returned cursors.

When the database query completes, our provider then calls `Cursor.setNotification Uri` to set the URI that the provider infrastructure will use to decide which provider update events get delivered to the newly created cursor. This URI becomes the point of interaction between clients that observe data referenced by that URI and the content provider that notifies that URI. This simple method call drives the content provider update messages that we discussed in "Android MVC and Content Observation" on page 354.

Here, we provide the code for our simple content provider's `query` method, which performs URI matching, queries the database, and then returns the cursor:

```
@Override
public Cursor query(Uri uri, String[] projection, String where,
                    String[] whereArgs, String sortOrder)
{
    // If no sort order is specified use the default
    String orderBy;
    if (TextUtils.isEmpty(sortOrder)) {
        orderBy = FinchVideo.SimpleVideos.DEFAULT_SORT_ORDER;
    } else {
        orderBy = sortOrder;
    }

    int match = sUriMatcher.match(uri);❶

    Cursor c;

    switch (match) {
        case VIDEOS:
            // query the database for all videos
            c = mDb.query(VIDEO_TABLE_NAME, projection,
                    where, whereArgs,
                    null, null, sortOrder);

            c.setNotificationUri(
                    getContext().getContentResolver(),
                    FinchVideo.SimpleVideos.CONTENT_URI);❷
            break;
        case VIDEO_ID:
            // query the database for a specific video
            long videoID = ContentUris.parseId(uri);
            c = mDb.query(VIDEO_TABLE_NAME, projection,
```

```
                    FinchVideo.Videos._ID + " = " + videoID +
                            (!TextUtils.isEmpty(where) ?
                                    " AND (" + where + ')' : ""),
                    whereArgs, null, null, sortOrder);
            c.setNotificationUri(
                    getContext().getContentResolver(),
                    FinchVideo.SimpleVideos.CONTENT_URI);
            break;
        default:
            throw new IllegalArgumentException("unsupported uri: " + uri);
    }

    return c;❸
}
```

Here are some of the highlights of the code:

❶ This matches the URI using our prebuilt URI matcher.

❷ Setting the notification URI to `FinchVideo.SimpleVideos.CONTENT_URI` causes the cursor to receive all content resolver notification events for data referenced by that URI. In this case, the cursor will receive all events related to all videos, as that is what `FinchVideo.SimpleVideos.CONTENT_URI` references.

❸ The cursor is returned directly. As mentioned, the Android content provider system provides support for sharing any data in the cursor across processes. Interprocess data sharing happens "for free" as part of the content provider system; you can just return the cursor and it will become available to activities in different processes.

The insert method

Let's move on to the `insert` method, which receives values from a client, validates them, and then adds a new row to the database containing those values. The values are passed to the `ContentProvider` class in a `ContentValues` object:

```
@Override
public Uri insert(Uri uri, ContentValues initialValues) {

    // Validate the requested uri
    if (sUriMatcher.match(uri) != VIDEOS) {
        throw new IllegalArgumentException("Unknown URI " + uri);
    }

    ContentValues values;
    if (initialValues != null) {
        values = new ContentValues(initialValues);
    } else {
        values = new ContentValues();
    }

    verifyValues(values);

    // insert the initialValues into a new database row
    SQLiteDatabase db = mOpenDbHelper.getWritableDatabase();
```

```
long rowId = db.insert(VIDEO_TABLE_NAME,
        FinchVideo.SimpleVideos.VIDEO_NAME, values);
if (rowId > 0) {
    Uri videoURi =
            ContentUris.withAppendedId(
                    FinchVideo.SimpleVideos.CONTENT_URI, rowId);❶
    getContext().getContentResolver().
        notifyChange(videoURi, null);❷
    return videoURi;
}

    throw new SQLException("Failed to insert row into " + uri);
}
```

The insert method will also match the incoming URI, perform a corresponding database insert operation, and then return a URI that references the new database row. Because the SQLiteDatabase.insert method returns the database row ID of the newly inserted row, which is also its value for the _id field, the content provider can easily put together the right URI by appending the rowID variable to the content provider authority defined in the content provider public API that we discussed in Chapter 3.

Here are some of the highlights of the code:

❶ We use Android's utilities for manipulating content provider URIs—specifically, the method ContentUris.withAppendedId to append the rowId as the ID of the returned insertion URI. Clients can turn around and query the content provider using this same URI to select a cursor containing the data values for the inserted row.

❷ Here the content provider notifies a URI that will cause a content update event to be fired and delivered to observing cursors. Note that the provider's invocation of notify is the only reason an event will be sent to content observers.

The update method

The update method operates in the same manner as insert, but instead calls update on the appropriate database to change database rows that the URI references. The update method returns the number of rows affected by the update operation:

```
@Override
public int update(Uri uri, ContentValues values, String where,
                String[] whereArgs)
{
    // the call to notify the uri after deletion is explicit
    getContext().getContentResolver().notifyChange(uri, null);

    SQLiteDatabase db = mOpenDbHelper.getWritableDatabase();
    int affected;
    switch (sUriMatcher.match(uri)) {
        case VIDEOS:
            affected = db.update(VIDEO_TABLE_NAME, values,
                    where, whereArgs);
            break;
```

```
        case VIDEO_ID:
            String videoId = uri.getPathSegments().get(1);
            affected = db.update(VIDEO_TABLE_NAME, values,
                    FinchVideo.SimpleVideos._ID + "=" + videoId
                        + (!TextUtils.isEmpty(where) ?
                        " AND (" + where + ')' : ""),
                    whereArgs);
            break;

        default:
            throw new IllegalArgumentException("Unknown URI " + uri);
    }

    getContext().getContentResolver().notifyChange(uri, null);
    return affected;
}
```

The delete method

The delete method is similar to update, but will delete rows referenced by the given URI. Like update, delete returns the number of rows affected by the delete operation:

```
@Override
public int delete(Uri uri, String where, String[] whereArgs) {
    int match = sUriMatcher.match(uri);
    int affected;

    switch (match) {
        case VIDEOS:
            affected = mDb.delete(VIDEO_TABLE_NAME,
                    (!TextUtils.isEmpty(where) ?
                        " AND (" + where + ')' : ""),
                    whereArgs);
            break;
        case VIDEO_ID:
            long videoId = ContentUris.parseId(uri);
            affected = mDb.delete(VIDEO_TABLE_NAME,
                    FinchVideo.SimpleVideos._ID + "=" + videoId
                        + (!TextUtils.isEmpty(where) ?
                        " AND (" + where + ')' : ""),
                    whereArgs);

            // the call to notify the uri after deletion is explicit
            getContext().getContentResolver().
                notifyChange(uri, null);

            break;
        default:
            throw new IllegalArgumentException("unknown video element: " +
                    uri);
    }

    return affected;
}
```

Note that the preceding descriptions relate only to our simple implementation of a content provider; more involved scenarios could involve joining across tables for a query or cascaded deletes for deleting a given data item. The content provider is free to pick its own scheme for data management using the Android SQLite API so long as it does not break the content provider client API.

Determining How Often to Notify Observers

As we've seen from our listing of the content provider data management operations, notification does not happen for free in the Android content management system: an insert into an SQLite table does not automatically set up a database trigger that fires notification on behalf of a content provider. It's up to the developer of the provider to implement a scheme that determines the appropriate time to send notifications and decides which URIs to send when content provider data changes. Usually content providers in Android send notifications immediately for all URIs that have changed during a particular data operation.

When designing a notification scheme, a developer should consider the following trade-off: fine-grained notification results in more precise change updates that can reduce load on the user interface system. If a list is told a single element has changed, it can decide to repaint only that element if it happens to be visible. But fine-grained notification also has the drawback that more events get pushed through the system. The UI will likely repaint more times because it will be getting more individual notification events. Coarse-grained notification runs fewer events through the system, but running fewer events often means that the UI will have to repaint more of itself on receiving notifications. For example, a list could receive a single event directing it to update all elements when only three individual elements had actually changed. We suggest keeping this trade-off in mind when picking a notification scheme. For example, you might consider waiting until you finish reading a large number of events and then firing a single "everything changed" event, rather than sending an update for each event.

Often, content providers simply notify clients of whatever URIs were involved when data changes.

Declaring Your Content Provider

In "Using a content provider" on page 81 we saw how clients access and use a content provider. Now that we have our own simple content provider, all that is left is to make it available to clients by adding the following line of XML to your *AndroidManifest.xml*:

```
<provider android:name=".provider.SimpleFinchVideoContentProvider"
    android:authorities="oreilly.demo.pa.finchvideo.SimpleFinchVideo"/>
```

After you have built your application, its *.apk* file contains the provider implementation classes, and its manifest file contains a line similar to the line of XML we just added, all application code on the Android platform will be able to access it, assuming it has requested and been granted permission to do so, as described in Chapter 3.

Having completed the task of creating your own simple content provider in this chapter, it's time to look into some novel content provider patterns, which we'll do in Chapter 13.

A Content Provider as a Facade for a RESTful Web Service

In Chapter 6, we saw that user interfaces that need to interact with remote services face interesting challenges, such as not tying up the UI thread with long-running tasks. We also noted in Chapter 3 that the Android content provider API shares symmetry with REST-style web services. Content provider data operations map straight onto REST data operations, and now we'll show you how to translate content provider URIs to request network data. We suggest taking advantage of this symmetry by writing content providers to operate as an asynchronous buffer between the domain or unique aspects of your application, and the network requests that acquire the data on which your application operates. Writing your application in this way will simplify your application, and will solve common UI and network programming errors encountered in Android and other types of Java programming.

Historically, Java UI programmers, both enterprise and mobile, have written mobile and desktop-based applications in a rather brittle way, and sometimes did run network requests directly on the UI thread, often without caching data obtained from those requests. In most applications, showing anything in a UI would require accessing the network every time a user requested the display of data. Believe it or not, Unix workstations from the 1980s and 1990s would frequently lock up when access to remotely mounted filesystems became unavailable. If applications had used a local dynamic caching scheme, they would have been able to continue running for the duration in which the file server was absent, and then synchronize when it returned. Developers needed to pay conscious attention, but often did not, to make certain that their applications accessed and stored network data correctly.

The trend continued in J2ME, where developers could cache network state in the anemic record management system known as RMS. This library did not support a query language, or an MVC notification system. J2ME developers would need to spawn their own plain Java threads to make network requests, but in many cases did not, which led to brittle applications. If web browsers were to load network data on the UI thread, you would often see them completely freeze to the point where the operating system would have to kill the browser to get rid of it—whenever the network would hang, the UI thread would lock up. Pages and all the images they referenced would always have to be downloaded at every viewing, making for a very slow experience—assuming one of the requests did not hang the whole application. The takeaway from these anecdotes is that traditionally, operating systems have left the loading and caching of network data up to the application, providing little direct library support to help developers implement these tasks correctly.

To resolve these problems, you could use a completely asynchronous interface to handle network interaction and data storage. With such an approach, developers would not have to think about when it was OK to request data from the network—it would always be safe to use such an API, on or off the UI thread. Such considerations become significantly more important in a mobile environment, where intermittent network connectivity increases the likelihood of a hang in incorrectly written code.

We suggest using the content provider API as an asynchronous model of the network, and as a cache of network state so that your application View and Controller do not need their own mechanisms for opening connections or accessing a database. It's easy to map the provider API onto the API of existing REST-based web services—the provider simply sits in between the application, forwarding requests to the network and caching results as needed. In this chapter, we will show you how this approach can simplify your application, and we will explain more general benefits of the technique, including how it introduces some of the more positive characteristics of web and AJAX programming to Android applications. For more information on AJAX programming, go to *http://en.wikipedia.org/wiki/Ajax_(programming)*.

Developing RESTful Android Applications

We are not the only ones who see the benefits of this approach. At the Google I/O conference in May 2010, Virgil Dobjanschi of Google presented a talk that outlined the following three patterns for using content providers to integrate RESTful web services into Android applications:

Activity→Service→ContentProvider
  This pattern involves an activity contacting a service to access application data, which in turn delegates to a content provider to access that data. In this scenario, the activity invokes an asynchronous method on a service that performs asynchronous RESTful invocations.

Activity→ContentProvider→Service
  An activity contacts a content provider, which in turn delegates to a service to asynchronously load data. This approach allows the activity to use the convenience of the content provider API to interact with data. The content provider invokes methods on the asynchronous service implementation to invoke a RESTful request.

This approach capitalizes on the convenient symmetry between the content provider API and RESTful use of HTTP.

`Activity→ContentProvider→SyncAdapter`

Android sync adapters provide a framework for synchronizing user data between a device and the cloud. Google Contacts uses a sync adapter. In this scenario, an activity uses the content provider API to access data synchronized by a sync adapter.

In this chapter, we'll explore the second pattern in detail with our second Finch video example; this strategy will yield a number of important benefits for your applications. Due to the elegance with which this approach integrates network operations into Android MVC, we've given it the moniker "Network MVC."

After you finish reading this chapter, we suggest that you view Google's talk (*http://www.google.com/events/io/2010/sessions/developing-RESTful-android-apps.html*).

A "Network MVC"

We like to think of the second pattern as a networked form of MVC, where the content provider itself pulls data from the network and then pumps it into the regular Android MVC. We'll view the content provider as a model of network state—the provider can fulfill data requests with local state, or can retrieve data from the network. With this approach, the Controller and View code should not directly create network requests to access and manage application data. Instead, your application View and Controller should use the `ContentResolver` API to make data queries through a content provider, which alone should asynchronously load network resources and store the results in a local data cache. Additionally, the provider should always respond quickly to a request by initially avoiding a network invocation that might be needed to fulfill the request by using whatever data is already available in the local database. Executing the request in this manner ensures that the UI thread is blocked for no longer than absolutely necessary, and that the UI has some data to display as soon as possible, thus improving overall snappiness and user satisfaction when using the UI. Here is the provider sequence for querying data, in more detail:

1. The provider matches the incoming URI and queries local database contents for items that previously matched the query.

2. Our provider always attempts to obtain the latest state for the query and subsequently spawns an asynchronous REST request to load content from the network. You could make this behavior configurable based on the request.

3. The provider returns the cursor from the initial local query to the client.

4. The asynchronous loading thread should decide if data in the provider cache needs to be refreshed; if it does, the provider loads and parses data from the network.

5. When content arrives from the network, the provider directly inserts each new data item into the database and then notifies clients of the URIs for the new data. Because the insertion is already happening inside the content provider, there is no need to call `ContentResolver.insert`. Clients holding existing cursors that contain an older version of data can call `Cursor.requery` to refresh their data.

With this sequence, the View and Controller eventually get updated with network data, but only the content provider creates the network request. We view a request for a resource that does not currently exist in the provider's data set as a request to load the resource—the network request that loads data into the cache is a side effect of the activity provider query.

Figure 13-1 illustrates the operations taking place inside the content provider during execution of operations in the sequence.

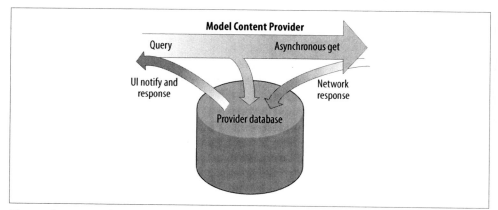

Figure 13-1. Network provider caching content on behalf of the client

For each query, this sequence uses a single `Cursor` object created by a provider and then returned to the View. Only the provider has the requirement to notify the UI when data changes. The View and Controller do not have to collect data, and do not have to update the Model. When data is available, the content provider notifies the cursor for the query. The role of data management is encapsulated inside the content provider, which simplifies the code in the View and Controller. The provider client requests data and receives a cursor quickly; the cursor is notified when network data arrives. It's critical to recall that notification depends on database and `Cursor` objects remaining open as long as content provider clients are using them. Closed cursors and databases will result in client views showing no results, which can make it difficult to know if a component such as a list is empty because its cursor was closed erroneously, or if a given query actually had no results.

Summary of Benefits

It's worth summarizing the benefits of the Network MVC approach:

- Increased perceived performance overall, and increased actual performance from caching, are among the main benefits of this pattern. Mobile programming often performs like the Web would with no caching system.

- Storing data in memory is not a good idea, as you do not know when Android will remove your activity from memory. This pattern emphasizes storing data in the content provider as quickly as possible.

- Most potential UI thread-safety violations cannot happen. Android View components have already been written to dynamically update to reflect current cursor contents. If the size of the data in the model shrinks, `ListView` will make sure to reduce the number of times it iterates over the cursor. Other component systems, for readers familiar with J2SE Swing, would leave this type of task up to the developer, which would leave open the possibility that the list component might iterate beyond the bounds of its model on deletion of data elements.

- This approach leverages the cursor management system and the user interface's built-in capabilities for dynamic updates in response to content observation events. User interface developers don't need to write their own polling and update systems; they just rely on content observation and the content provider interface.

- As with any correct request for network resources, it's not possible for the UI thread to hang on the network.

- Delivery of network events happens without requiring the presence of a user interface. Even if a particular activity is not present when a network event arrives, the content provider will still be around to handle it. When the user loads the activity, a query will reveal the event that arrived in the background. The absence of an active UI activity will not result in events simply getting dropped.

- Elements of the application are encapsulated and have a special purpose, because as we've mentioned, the content provider handles all network and SQLite interactions. The View and Controller just use a provider as a generic system for data management.

- It's easier to write applications because it's difficult to use the API incorrectly—just make content provider calls and the system handles the REST (pun intended).

- Finally, in a book on mobile programming it's easy to focus on device issues, but if clients end up relying on their cache and referring to the network only when absolutely necessary, they will end up significantly reducing the network load on systems that serve data to devices. This pattern provides a significant benefit for servers as well as clients.

Our Approach in Context

To be clear, we are suggesting that applications should write content providers to access and store network data wherever possible. While this might seem like an onerous burden at first, consider that web browsers also use an asynchronous mechanism for loading URI referenced content. For readers familiar with basic web programming, the default Android API may be more flexible and extensive than that found in AJAX, but AJAX has long had a foolproof architecture. Modern browsers load URI data using asynchronous I/O mechanisms (see *http://en.wikipedia.org/wiki/Asynchronous_io*), which prevents most opportunities for a browser user interface to hang. Although it may not seem like the browser is doing much when a given URI fails to load, the UI thread itself is never in danger of blocking due to a network connection becoming unresponsive. If the UI thread were to hang, the whole browser would stop working. It would not even be able to tell you that it was hung—especially because many browsers are entirely single-threaded. Instead, browsers are able to provide you with the opportunity to halt any given page load request, and then load another page that will hopefully be more responsive. Going further, all modern browsers make use of a persistent web cache, and we are simply suggesting that Android applications should also have a similar construct.

Beyond the pattern we are describing, Google provides specific documentation for improving application responsiveness, and reducing the likelihood of "Application Not Responding" notifications, at *http://developer.android.com/guide/practices/design/responsiveness.html.*

Code Example: Dynamically Listing and Caching YouTube Video Content

To demonstrate the prescribed architecture, we present the Finch video listing application that allows a user to perform a mobile video search using the RESTful API, at *http://gdata.youtube.com*. Our example code is written with an eye toward intermittent connectivity in a mobile environment. The application preserves user data so that it will remain usable even when the network cannot be reached—even if that means our application can only display older, locally cached results when that happens.

When a user runs a query, the application attempts to retrieve the latest YouTube results for that query. If the application successfully loads new results, it will flush results that are older than one week. If the application were to blindly drop old results before running an update query, it might end up with no results to view, which would render the app useless until network access returned. The screen in Figure 13-2 shows a query for the keyword "dogs". Pressing Enter in the search box or hitting the refresh button spawns a new query.

Figure 13-2. Finch video SampleApplication

Our application includes a caching content provider that queries the YouTube API to access YouTube video metadata. Query results are cached in an SQLite table called `video`, as part of the content provider `query` method. The provider makes use of the Finch framework for invoking asynchronous REST requests. The UI consists of an activity as shown in Figure 13-2, a list with a search query box, and a refresh button. The list dynamically refreshes on content provider data notification. Whenever the user enters a search query and then presses Enter, the activity invokes the query request on the `FinchVideoContentProvider` with the appropriate URI query. We'll now explore the details of this example.

Structure of the Source Code for the Finch YouTube Video Example

This section briefly examines relevant Java source within the Finch YouTube video application that is unique to the simple version of our video listing application. To start, the files reside in two different directories: that of the Finch video application directory for Chapter 12, and that of the Finch Framework library on which Chapter 12 has a dependency. The source files that make up our YouTube application include:

Chapter 12 files in $(FinchVideo)/src/

> *$(FinchVideo)/src/com/oreilly/demo/pa/finchvideo/FinchVideo.java*
>> The `FinchVideo` class contains the `Videos` class, which serves the same function as `FinchVideo.SimpleVideos` did in the simple video app. The `FinchVideo`

.Videos class defines several more constants in addition to the names of the content provider columns that our simple version defined for the YouTube application. Neither the FinchVideo class nor the Videos class contains any executable code.

$(FinchVideo)/src/com/oreilly/demo/pa/finchvideo/provider/FinchVideoContent-Provider.java

This is the main content provider that serves YouTube metadata and carries out asynchronous RESTful requests on the YouTube GData API.

$(FinchVideo)/lib-src/com/oreilly/demo/pa/finchvideo/provider/YouTubeHandler .java

This parses responses from the YouTube GData API and inserts data entries as they arrive.

Finch framework source code in $(FinchFramework)/lib-src

$(FinchFramework)/lib-src/com/finchframework/finch/rest/RESTfulContent Provider.java

This contains a simple framework for invoking RESTful HTTP requests from within an Android content provider. FinchVideoContentProvider extends this class to reuse behavior for asynchronously managing HTTP requests.

$(FinchFramework)/lib-src/com/finchframework/finch/rest/FileHandler.java
$(FinchFramework)/lib-src/com/finchframework/finch/rest/FileHandlerFactory .java

These are simple frameworks for downloading URI content to a file-based cache. They handle the response when the app requests thumbnail URIs.

$(FinchFramework)/lib-src/com/finchframework/finch/rest/ResponseHandler.java

This provides a simple abstraction layer for handling downloaded HTTP content from the YouTube API. YouTubeHandler extends this class.

$(FinchFramework)/lib-src/com/finchframework/finch/rest/UriRequestTask.java

This is a runnable object specialized to download HTTP content. It uses the Apache HTTP client framework.

Stepping Through the Search Application

In Figure 13-3, we depict the steps involved as our content provider services search requests from the View and Controller using a REST-style network request. The content provider has the opportunity to cache network results in SQLite tables before notifying observers listening to URIs associated with the relevant data. Requests should move asynchronously between components. The View and Controller should not directly or synchronously invoke their own network requests.

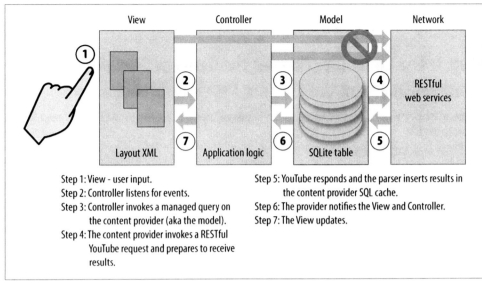

Figure 13-3. *The sequence of events that implement a client request for content provider data*

The rest of this chapter steps through our second Finch video example to implement this pattern in an Android application. We recommend keeping Figure 13-3 and its steps in mind as we move forward. Note that the steps do not always appear in order as we describe the code to you, but we'll note the steps in bold without having to break from the flow of the code.

Step 1: Our UI Collects User Input

Our UI in Figure 13-2 uses a simple EditText to collect search keywords.

Step 2: Our Controller Listens for Events

Our FinchVideoActivity registers a text listener, our "Controller," that receives an event when the user presses the Enter key:

```
class FinchVideoActivity {
...
mSearchText.setOnEditorActionListener(
    new EditText.OnEditorActionListener() {
        public boolean onEditorAction(TextView textView,
            int actionId,
            KeyEvent keyEvent)
    {
...
        query();
...
```

```
        }
    );
```

Step 3: The Controller Queries the Content Provider with a managedQuery on the Content Provider/Model

The controller then invokes the activity's **query** method in response to user text input (for a search):

```
// inside FinchVideoActivity

...

// sends the query to the finch video content provider
private void query() {
    if (!mSearchText.searchEmpty()) {
        String queryString =
            FinchVideo.Videos.QUERY_PARAM_NAME + "=" +
                Uri.encode(mSearchText.getText().toString());
        Uri queryUri =
            Uri.parse(FinchVideo.Videos.CONTENT_URI + "?" +
                queryString);
        Cursor c = managedQuery(queryUri, null, null, null, null);
        mAdapter.changeCursor(c);
    }
}
```

Step 4: Implementing the RESTful Request

Step 4 is quite a bit more involved than the other components of the sequence so far. We'll need to walk through our RESTful `FinchVideoContentProvider` as we did for `SimpleFinchVideoContentProvider`. To start, `FinchVideoContentProvider` extends our utility called `RESTfulContentProvider`, which in turn extends `ContentProvider`:

```
FinchVideoContentProvider extend RESTfulContentProvider {
```

`RESTfulContentProvider` provides asynchronous REST operations in a way that allows the Finch provider to plug in custom request-response handler components. We'll explain this in more detail shortly, when we discuss our enhanced **query** method.

Constants and Initialization

`FinchVideoContentProvider` initialization is pretty close to the simple video content provider. As with the simple version, we set up a URI matcher. Our only extra task is to add support for matching specific thumbnails. We don't add support for matching multiple thumbnails, as our viewer activity does not need that support—it only needs to load individual thumbnails:

```
sUriMatcher.addURI(FinchVideo.AUTHORITY,
    FinchVideo.Videos.THUMB + "/#", THUMB_ID);
```

Creating the Database

We create the Finch video database with Java code that executes the following SQL:

```
CREATE TABLE video (_ID INTEGER PRIMARY KEY AUTOINCREMENT,
    title TEXT, description TEXT, thumb_url TEXT,
    thumb_width TEXT, thumb_height TEXT, timestamp TEXT,
    query_text TEXT, media_id TEXT UNIQUE);
```

Note that we've added the ability to store the following attributes beyond the simple version of our database:

`thumb_url, thumb_width, thumb_height`
This is the URL, width, and height associated with a given video thumbnail.

`timestamp`
When we insert a new video record, we stamp it with the current time.

`query_text`
We store the query text, or query keywords, in the database with each result for that query.

`media_id`
This is a unique value for each video response that we receive from the GData API. We don't allow two video entries to have the same `media_id`.

A Networked Query Method

Here's what we've been leading up to: the implementation of the `FinchYouTube Provider` query method calls out to the network to satisfy a query request for YouTube data. It does this by calling a method of its superclass, `RESTfulContentProvider.asyncQueryRequest(String queryTag, String queryUri)`. Here `queryTag` is a unique string that allows us to reject duplicate requests when appropriate, and `queryUri` is the complete URI that we need to asynchronously download.

Specifically, we invoke requests on the following URI after we have appended `URL Encoder.encoded` query parameters obtained from our application's search text input field:

```
/** URI for querying video, expects appended keywords. */
private static final String QUERY_URI =
        "http://gdata.youtube.com/feeds/api/videos?" +
                "max-results=15&format=1&q=";
```

 You can learn how to create a GData YouTube URI that meets the needs of your application quite easily. Google has created a beta (what else?) utility located at *http://gdata.youtube.com*. If you visit this page in your browser, it will show you a web UI consisting of a plethora of options that you can customize to create a URI like the one shown in the previous code listing. We have used the UI to select up to 15 results, and have selected the use of a mobile video format.

Our networked `query` method does the usual URI match, and then adds the following tasks, which represent step 4, "Implementing the RESTful Request" from our sequence:

```
/**
 * Content provider query method that converts its parameters into a YouTube
 * RESTful search query.
 *
 * @param uri a reference to the query URI. It may contain "q=" terms,
 *   which are sent to the google YouTube
 * API where they are used to search the YouTube video database.
 * @param projection
 * @param where not used in this provider.
 * @param whereArgs not used in this provider.
 * @param sortOrder not used in this provider.
 * @return a cursor containing the results of a YouTube search query.
 */
@Override
public Cursor query(Uri uri, String[] projection, String where,
                    String[] whereArgs, String sortOrder)
{
    Cursor queryCursor;

    int match = sUriMatcher.match(uri);
    switch (match) {
        case VIDEOS:
            // the query is passed out of band of other information passed
            // to this method -- it's not an argument.
            String queryText = uri.
                getQueryParameter(FinchVideo.Videos.QUERY_PARAM_NAME);❶

            if (queryText == null) {
                // A null cursor is an acceptable argument to the method,
                // CursorAdapter.changeCursor(Cursor c), which interprets
                // the value by canceling all adapter state so that the
```

```
            // component for which the cursor is adapting data will
            // display no content.
            return null;
        }

        String select = FinchVideo.Videos.QUERY_TEXT_NAME +
                " = '" +  queryText + "'";

        // quickly return already matching data
        queryCursor =
                mDb.query(VIDEOS_TABLE_NAME, projection,
                        select,
                        whereArgs,
                        null,
                        null, sortOrder);❷

        // make the cursor observe the requested query
        queryCursor.setNotificationUri(
                getContext().getContentResolver(), uri);❸

        /*
         * Always try to update results with the latest data from the
         * network.
         *
         * Spawning an asynchronous load task thread guarantees that
         * the load has no chance to block any content provider method,
         * and therefore no chance to block the UI thread.
         *
         * While the request loads, we return the cursor with existing
         * data to the client.
         *
         * If the existing cursor is empty, the UI will render no
         * content until it receives URI notification.
         *
         * Content updates that arrive when the asynchronous network
         * request completes will appear in the already returned cursor,
         * since that cursor query will match that of
         * newly arrived items.
         */
        if (!"".equals(queryText)) {
            asyncQueryRequest(queryText, QUERY_URI + encode(queryText));❹
        }
        break;
case VIDEO_ID:
case THUMB_VIDEO_ID:
    long videoID = ContentUris.parseId(uri);
    queryCursor =
            mDb.query(VIDEOS_TABLE_NAME, projection,
                    FinchVideo.Videos._ID + " = " + videoID,
                    whereArgs, null, null, null);
    queryCursor.setNotificationUri(
            getContext().getContentResolver(), uri);
    break;
case THUMB_ID:
    String uriString = uri.toString();
```

```
                    int lastSlash = uriString.lastIndexOf("/");
                    String mediaID = uriString.substring(lastSlash + 1);

                    queryCursor =
                            mDb.query(VIDEOS_TABLE_NAME, projection,
                                    FinchVideo.Videos.MEDIA_ID_NAME + " = " +
                                            mediaID,
                                    whereArgs, null, null, null);
                    queryCursor.setNotificationUri(
                            getContext().getContentResolver(), uri);
                    break;

            default:
                throw new IllegalArgumentException("unsupported uri: " +
                        QUERY_URI);
        }

        return queryCursor;
    }
```

Here are some of the highlights of the code:

❶ Extract a query parameter out of the incoming URI. We need to send this parameter in the URI itself and not with the other arguments to the query method, as they have different functions in the query method and could not be used to hold query keywords.

❷ Check first for data already in the local database that matches the query keywords.

❸ Set the notification URI so that cursors returned from the query method will receive update events whenever the provider changes data they are observing. This action sets up step 6 of our sequence, which will enable the view to update when the provider fires notification events when it changes data, as it will when data returns from a given request. Once notification arrives, step 7 occurs when the UI repaints. Note that steps 6 and 7 are out of order in our description, but it's appropriate to talk about those stages here as they relate to the notification URI and the query.

❹ Spawn an asynchronous query to download the given query URI. The method asyncQueryRequest encapsulates the creation of a new thread to service each request. Note that this is step 5 in our diagram; the asynchronous request will spawn a thread to actually initiate network communication and the YouTube service will return a response.

RESTfulContentProvider: A REST helper

Now we'll look into the behaviors that FinchVideoProvider inherits from RESTful ContentProvider to execute RESTful requests. To start we'll consider the behavior of a given YouTube request: as we've seen, query requests run asynchronously from the main thread. A RESTful provider needs to handle a few special cases: if a user searches for "Funny Cats" while another request for the same keywords is in progress, our provider will drop the second request. On the other hand, if a user searches for "dogs" and then "cats" before "dogs" finishes, our provider allows "dogs" to run in parallel to "cats", because the user might search again for "dogs" and then obtain the benefit of cached results in which she had shown some interest.

RESTfulContentProvider enables a subclass to asynchronously spawn requests and, when request data arrives, supports custom handling of the response using a simple plug-in interface called ResponseHandler. Subclasses should override the abstract method, RESTfulContentProvider.newResponseHandler, to return handlers specialized to parse response data requested by their host provider. Each handler will override the method ResponseHandler.handleResponse(HttpResponse) to provide custom handling for HttpEntitys contained in passed HttpResponse objects. For example, our provider uses YouTubeHandler to parse a YouTube RSS feed, inserting database video rows for each entry it reads. More detail on this in a bit...

Additionally, the class RESTfulContentProvider enables a subclass to easily make asynchronous requests and reject duplicate requests. RESTfulContentProvider tracks each request with a unique tag that enables a subclass to drop duplicate queries. Our Finch VideoContentProvider uses the user's query keywords as the request tag because they uniquely identify a given search request.

Our FinchVideoContentProvider overrides newResponseHandler as follows:

```
/**
 * Provides a handler that can parse YouTube GData RSS content.
 *
 * @param requestTag unique tag identifying this request.
 * @return a YouTubeHandler object.
 */
@Override
protected ResponseHandler newResponseHandler(String requestTag) {
    return new YouTubeHandler(this, requestTag);
}
```

Now we'll discuss the implementation of RESTfulContentProvider to explain the operations it provides to subclasses. The class UriRequestTask provides a runnable for asynchronously executing REST requests. RESTfulContentProvider uses a map, mRequestsInProgress, keyed by a string to guarantee uniqueness of requests:

```
/**
 * Encapsulates functions for asynchronous RESTful requests so that subclass
 * content providers can use them for initiating requests while still using
 * custom methods for interpreting REST-based content such as RSS, ATOM,
 * JSON, etc.
 */
public abstract class RESTfulContentProvider extends ContentProvider {
    protected FileHandlerFactory mFileHandlerFactory;
    private Map<String, UriRequestTask> mRequestsInProgress =
            new HashMap<String, UriRequestTask>();

    public RESTfulContentProvider(FileHandlerFactory fileHandlerFactory) {
        mFileHandlerFactory = fileHandlerFactory;
    }
```

```
    public abstract Uri insert(Uri uri, ContentValues cv, SQLiteDatabase db);

    private UriRequestTask getRequestTask(String queryText) {
        return mRequestsInProgress.get(queryText);❶
    }

    /**
     * Allows the subclass to define the database used by a response handler.
     *
     * @return database passed to response handler.
     */
    public abstract SQLiteDatabase getDatabase();

    public void requestComplete(String mQueryText) {
        synchronized (mRequestsInProgress) {
            mRequestsInProgress.remove(mQueryText);❷
        }
    }

    /**
     * Abstract method that allows a subclass to define the type of handler
     * that should be used to parse the response of a given request.
     *
     * @param requestTag unique tag identifying this request.
     * @return the response handler created by a subclass used to parse the
     * request response.
     */
    protected abstract ResponseHandler newResponseHandler(String requestTag);

    UriRequestTask newQueryTask(String requestTag, String url) {
        UriRequestTask requestTask;

        final HttpGet get = new HttpGet(url);
        ResponseHandler handler = newResponseHandler(requestTag);
        requestTask = new UriRequestTask(requestTag, this, get,❸
                handler, getContext());

        mRequestsInProgress.put(requestTag, requestTask);
        return requestTask;
    }

    /**
     * Creates a new worker thread to carry out a RESTful network invocation.
     *
     * @param queryTag unique tag that identifies this request.
     *
     * @param queryUri the complete URI that should be accessed by this request.
     */
    public void asyncQueryRequest(String queryTag, String queryUri) {
        synchronized (mRequestsInProgress) {
            UriRequestTask requestTask = getRequestTask(queryTag);
            if (requestTask == null) {
                requestTask = newQueryTask(queryTag, queryUri);❹
                Thread t = new Thread(requestTask);
```

```
                    // allows other requests to run in parallel.
                    t.start();
                }
            }
        }
    ...
    }
```

Here are some highlights of the code:

❶ The method getRequestTask uses mRequestsInProgress to access any identical requests in progress, which allows the asyncQueryRequest to block duplicate requests with a simple if statement.

❷ When a request completes after the ResponseHandler.handleResponse method returns, RESTfulContentProvider removes the task from mRequestsInProgress.

❸ newQueryTask creates instances of UriRequestTask that are instances of Runnable that will, in turn, open an HTTP connection, and then call handleResponse on the appropriate handler.

❹ Finally, our code has a unique request, creates a task to run it, and then wraps the task in a thread for asynchronous execution.

While RESTfulContentProvider contains the guts of the reusable task system, for completeness we'll show you the other components in our framework.

UriRequestTask. UriRequestTask encapsulates the asynchronous aspects of handling a REST request. It's a simple class that has fields that enable it to execute a RESTful GET inside its run method. Such an action would be part of step 4, "Implementing the RESTful Request," of our sequence. As discussed, once it has the response from the request, it passes it to an invocation of ResponseHandler.handleResponse. We expect the handleResponse method to insert database entries as needed, which we'll see in YouTubeHandler:

```
/**
 * Provides a runnable that uses an HttpClient to asynchronously load a given
 * URI.  After the network content is loaded, the task delegates handling of the
 * request to a ResponseHandler specialized to handle the given content.
 */
public class UriRequestTask implements Runnable {
    private HttpUriRequest mRequest;
    private ResponseHandler mHandler;

    protected Context mAppContext;

    private RESTfulContentProvider mSiteProvider;
    private String mRequestTag;

    private int mRawResponse = -1;

    public UriRequestTask(HttpUriRequest request,
                            ResponseHandler handler, Context appContext)
```

```java
        {
            this(null, null, request, handler, appContext);
        }

        public UriRequestTask(String requestTag,
                              RESTfulContentProvider siteProvider,
                              HttpUriRequest request,
                              ResponseHandler handler, Context appContext)
        {
            mRequestTag = requestTag;
            mSiteProvider = siteProvider;
            mRequest = request;
            mHandler = handler;
            mAppContext = appContext;
        }

        public void setRawResponse(int rawResponse) {
            mRawResponse = rawResponse;
        }

        /**
         * Carries out the request on the complete URI as indicated by the protocol,
         * host, and port contained in the configuration, and the URI supplied to
         * the constructor.
         */
        public void run() {
            HttpResponse response;

            try {
                response = execute(mRequest);
                mHandler.handleResponse(response, getUri());
            } catch (IOException e) {
                Log.w(Finch.LOG_TAG, "exception processing asynch request", e);
            } finally {
                if (mSiteProvider != null) {
                    mSiteProvider.requestComplete(mRequestTag);
                }
            }
        }

        private HttpResponse execute(HttpUriRequest mRequest) throws IOException {
            if (mRawResponse >= 0) {
                return new RawResponse(mAppContext, mRawResponse);
            } else {
                HttpClient client = new DefaultHttpClient();
                return client.execute(mRequest);
            }
        }

        public Uri getUri() {
            return Uri.parse(mRequest.getURI().toString());
        }
    }
```

YouTubeHandler. As required by the abstract method, RESTfulContentProvider.newRes
ponseHandler, we've seen that our FinchVideoContentProvider returns YouTubeHandler
to handle YouTube RSS feeds. YouTubeHandler uses a memory-saving XML Pull parser
to parse incoming data, iterating through requested XML RSS data. YouTubeHandler
contains some complexity, but generally, it's just matching XML tags as needed to
create a ContentValues object that it can insert into the FinchVideoContentProvider's
database. Part of step 5 occurs when the handler inserts the parsed result into the
provider database:

```
/**
 * Parses YouTube Entity data and inserts it into the finch video content
 * provider.
 */
public class YouTubeHandler implements ResponseHandler {
    public static final String MEDIA = "media";
    public static final String GROUP = "group";
    public static final String DESCRIPTION = "description";
    public static final String THUMBNAIL = "thumbnail";
    public static final String TITLE = "title";
    public static final String CONTENT = "content";

    public static final String WIDTH = "width";
    public static final String HEIGHT = "height";

    public static final String YT = "yt";
    public static final String DURATION = "duration";
    public static final String FORMAT = "format";

    public static final String URI = "uri";
    public static final String THUMB_URI = "thumb_uri";

    public static final String MOBILE_FORMAT = "1";

    public static final String ENTRY = "entry";
    public static final String ID = "id";

    private static final String FLUSH_TIME = "5 minutes";

    private RESTfulContentProvider mFinchVideoProvider;

    private String mQueryText;
    private boolean isEntry;

    public YouTubeHandler(RESTfulContentProvider restfulProvider,
                          String queryText)
    {
        mFinchVideoProvider = restfulProvider;
        mQueryText = queryText;
    }

    /*
     * Handles the response from the YouTube GData server, which is in the form
     * of an RSS feed containing references to YouTube videos.
     */
```

```java
public void handleResponse(HttpResponse response, Uri uri)
        throws IOException
{
    try {
        int newCount = parseYoutubeEntity(response.getEntity());❶

        // only flush old state now that new state has arrived
        if (newCount > 0) {
            deleteOld();
        }

    } catch (IOException e) {
        // use the exception to avoid clearing old state, if we cannot
        // get new state.  This way we leave the application with some
        // data to work with in absence of network connectivity.

        // we could retry the request for data in the hope that the network
        // might return.
    }
}

private void deleteOld() {
    // delete any old elements, not just ones that match the current query.

    Cursor old = null;

    try {
        SQLiteDatabase db = mFinchVideoProvider.getDatabase();
        old = db.query(FinchVideo.Videos.VIDEO, null,
                "video." + FinchVideo.Videos.TIMESTAMP +
                        " < strftime('%s', 'now', '-" + FLUSH_TIME + "')",
                null, null, null, null);
        int c = old.getCount();
        if (old.getCount() > 0) {
            StringBuffer sb = new StringBuffer();
            boolean next;
            if (old.moveToNext()) {
                do {
                    String ID = old.getString(FinchVideo.ID_COLUMN);
                    sb.append(FinchVideo.Videos._ID);
                    sb.append(" = ");
                    sb.append(ID);

                    // get rid of associated cached thumb files
                    mFinchVideoProvider.deleteFile(ID);

                    next = old.moveToNext();
                    if (next) {
                        sb.append(" OR ");
                    }
                } while (next);
            }
            String where = sb.toString();

            db.delete(FinchVideo.Videos.VIDEO, where, null);
```

```
                Log.d(Finch.LOG_TAG, "flushed old query results: " + c);
            }
        } finally {
            if (old != null) {
                old.close();
            }
        }
    }

    private int parseYoutubeEntity(HttpEntity entity) throws IOException {
        InputStream youTubeContent = entity.getContent();
        InputStreamReader inputReader = new InputStreamReader(youTubeContent);

        int inserted = 0;

        try {
            XmlPullParserFactory factory = XmlPullParserFactory.newInstance();
            factory.setNamespaceAware(false);
            XmlPullParser xpp = factory.newPullParser();

            xpp.setInput(inputReader);

            int eventType = xpp.getEventType();
            String startName = null;
            ContentValues mediaEntry = null;

            // iterative pull parsing is a useful way to extract data from
            // streams, since we don't have to hold the DOM model in memory
            // during the parsing step.

            while (eventType != XmlPullParser.END_DOCUMENT) {
                if (eventType == XmlPullParser.START_DOCUMENT) {
                } else if (eventType == XmlPullParser.END_DOCUMENT) {
                } else if (eventType == XmlPullParser.START_TAG) {
                    startName = xpp.getName();

                    if ((startName != null)) {

                        if ((ENTRY).equals(startName))
                        {
                            mediaEntry = new ContentValues();
                            mediaEntry.put(FinchVideo.Videos.QUERY_TEXT_NAME,
                                    mQueryText);
                        }

                        if ((MEDIA + ":" + CONTENT).equals(startName)) {
                            int c = xpp.getAttributeCount();
                            String mediaUri = null;
                            boolean isMobileFormat = false;

                            for (int i = 0; i < c; i++) {
                                String attrName = xpp.getAttributeName(i);
                                String attrValue = xpp.getAttributeValue(i);
```

```
                            if ((attrName != null) &&
                                    URI.equals(attrName))
                            {
                                mediaUri = attrValue;
                            }

                            if ((attrName != null) && (YT + ":" + FORMAT).
                                    equals(MOBILE_FORMAT))
                            {
                                isMobileFormat = true;
                            }
                        }

                        if (isMobileFormat && (mediaUri != null)) {
                            mediaEntry.put(URI, mediaUri);
                        }
                    }

                    if ((MEDIA + ":" + THUMBNAIL).equals(startName)) {
                        int c = xpp.getAttributeCount();
                        for (int i = 0; i < c; i++) {
                            String attrName = xpp.getAttributeName(i);
                            String attrValue = xpp.getAttributeValue(i);

                            if (attrName != null) {
                                if ("url".equals(attrName)) {
                                    mediaEntry.put(
                                            FinchVideo.Videos.
                                                    THUMB_URI_NAME,
                                            attrValue);
                                } else if (WIDTH.equals(attrName))
                                {
                                    mediaEntry.put(
                                            FinchVideo.Videos.
                                                    THUMB_WIDTH_NAME,
                                            attrValue);
                                } else if (HEIGHT.equals(attrName))
                                {
                                    mediaEntry.put(
                                            FinchVideo.Videos.
                                                    THUMB_HEIGHT_NAME,
                                            attrValue);
                                }
                            }
                        }
                    }

                    if (ENTRY.equals(startName)) {
                        isEntry = true;
                    }
                }
            } else if(eventType == XmlPullParser.END_TAG) {
                String endName = xpp.getName();

                if (endName != null) {
```

```
            if (ENTRY.equals(endName)) {
                isEntry = false;
            } else if (endName.equals(MEDIA + ":" + GROUP)) {
                // insert the complete media group
                inserted++;

                // Directly invoke insert on the finch video
                // provider, without using content resolver.  We
                // would not want the content provider to sync this
                // data back to itself.
                SQLiteDatabase db =
                        mFinchVideoProvider.getDatabase();

                String mediaID = (String) mediaEntry.get(
                        FinchVideo.Videos.MEDIA_ID_NAME);

                // insert thumb uri
                String thumbContentUri =
                        FinchVideo.Videos.THUMB_URI + "/" + mediaID;
                mediaEntry.put(FinchVideo.Videos.
                        THUMB_CONTENT_URI_NAME,
                        thumbContentUri);

                String cacheFileName =
                        mFinchVideoProvider.getCacheName(mediaID);
                mediaEntry.put(FinchVideo.Videos._DATA,
                        cacheFileName);

                Uri providerUri = mFinchVideoProvider.
                        insert(FinchVideo.Videos.CONTENT_URI,
                                mediaEntry, db);❷
                if (providerUri != null) {
                    String thumbUri = (String) mediaEntry.
                            get(FinchVideo.Videos.THUMB_URI_NAME);

                    // We might consider lazily downloading the
                    // image so that it was only downloaded on
                    // viewing.  Downloading more aggressively
                    // could also improve performance.

                    mFinchVideoProvider.
                            cacheUri2File(String.valueOf(ID),
                            thumbUrl);❸
                }
            }
        }

} else if (eventType == XmlPullParser.TEXT) {
    // newline can turn into an extra text event
    String text = xpp.getText();
    if (text != null) {
        text = text.trim();
        if ((startName != null) && (!"".equals(text))){
            if (ID.equals(startName) && isEntry) {
                int lastSlash = text.lastIndexOf("/");
```

```
                                    String entryId =
                                        text.substring(lastSlash + 1);
                                    mediaEntry.put(FinchVideo.Videos.MEDIA_ID_NAME,
                                        entryId);
                        } else if ((MEDIA + ":" + TITLE).
                                equals(startName))
                        {
                            mediaEntry.put(TITLE, text);
                        } else if ((MEDIA + ":" +
                                DESCRIPTION).equals(startName))
                        {
                            mediaEntry.put(DESCRIPTION, text);
                        }
                    }
                }
            }
            eventType = xpp.next();
        }

        // an alternate notification scheme might be to notify only after
        // all entries have been inserted.

    } catch (XmlPullParserException e) {
        Log.d(Ch11.LOG_TAG,
                "could not parse video feed", e);
    } catch (IOException e) {
        Log.d(Ch11.LOG_TAG,
                "could not process video stream", e);
    }

    return inserted;
    }
}
```

Here are some of the highlights of the code:

❶ Our handler implements handleResponse by parsing a YouTube HTTP entity in its method, parseYoutubeEntity, which inserts new video data. The handler then deletes old video data by querying for elements that are older than a timeout period, and then deleting the rows of data in that query.

❷ The handler has finished parsing a media element, and uses its containing content provider to insert its newly parsed ContentValues object. Note that this is step 5, "Response handler inserts elements into local cache," in our sequence.

❸ The provider initiates its own asynchronous request after it inserts a new media entry to also download thumbnail content. We'll explain more about this feature of our provider shortly.

insert and ResponseHandlers

Going into step 5 in a bit more detail, our Finch video provider implements insert in much the same way as our simple video provider. Also, as we've seen in our application, video insertion happens as a side effect of the query method. It's worth pointing out that our insert method is broken into two pieces. We intend that content provider clients call the first form and that response handlers call the second form, shown in the following code. The first form delegates to the second. We break up insert because the response handler is part of the content provider and does not need to route through the content resolver to itself.

```
@Override
public Uri insert(Uri uri, ContentValues initialValues) {
    // Validate the requested uri
    if (sUriMatcher.match(uri) != VIDEOS) {
        throw new IllegalArgumentException("Unknown URI " + uri);
    }

    ContentValues values;
    if (initialValues != null) {
        values = new ContentValues(initialValues);
    } else {
        values = new ContentValues();
    }

    SQLiteDatabase db = getDatabase();
    return insert(uri, initialValues, db);
}
```

YouTubeHandler uses the following method to directly insert rows into the simple video database. Note that we don't insert the media if the database already contains a video entry with the same mediaID as the one we are inserting. In this way, we avoid duplicate video entries, which could occur when integrating new data with older, but not expired, data.

```
public Uri insert(Uri uri, ContentValues values, SQLiteDatabase db) {
    verifyValues(values);

    // Validate the requested uri
    int m = sUriMatcher.match(uri);
    if (m != VIDEOS) {
        throw new IllegalArgumentException("Unknown URI " + uri);
    }

    // insert the values into a new database row
    String mediaID = (String) values.get(FinchVideo.Videos.MEDIA_ID);

    Long rowID = mediaExists(db, mediaID);
    if (rowID == null) {
        long time = System.currentTimeMillis();
        values.put(FinchVideo.Videos.TIMESTAMP, time);
        long rowId = db.insert(VIDEOS_TABLE_NAME,
                FinchVideo.Videos.VIDEO, values);
        if (rowId >= 0) {
            Uri insertUri =
                    ContentUris.withAppendedId(
                            FinchVideo.Videos.CONTENT_URI, rowId);
            mContentResolver.notifyChange(insertUri, null);
```

```
            return insertUri;
        } else {
            throw new IllegalStateException("could not insert " +
                    "content values: " + values);
        }
    }

    return ContentUris.withAppendedId(FinchVideo.Videos.CONTENT_URI, rowID);
}
```

File Management: Storing Thumbnails

Now that we've explained how our RESTful provider framework operates, we'll end the chapter with an explanation of how the provider handles thumbnails.

Earlier we described the ContentResolver.openInputStream method as a way for content providers to serve files to clients. In our Finch video example, we use this feature to serve thumbnail images. Storing images as files allows us to avoid use of database blobs and their performance overhead, and allows us to only download images when a client requests them. For a content provider to serve files, it *must* override the method ContentProvider.openFile, which opens a file descriptor to the file being served. The content resolver takes care of creating an input stream from the file descriptor. The simplest implementation of this method will call openFileHelper to activate the convenience utility that allows the ContentResolver to read the _data variable to load the file it references. If your provider does not override this method at all, you will see an exception generated that has a message as follows: No files supported by provider at .... Our simple implementation only allows read-only access, as shown in the following code:

```
/**
 * Provides read-only access to files that have been downloaded and stored
 * in the provider cache. Specifically, in this provider, clients can
 * access the files of downloaded thumbnail images.
 */
@Override
public ParcelFileDescriptor openFile(Uri uri, String mode)
        throws FileNotFoundException
{
    // only support read-only files
    if (!"r".equals(mode.toLowerCase())) {
        throw new FileNotFoundException("Unsupported mode, " +
            mode + ", for uri: " + uri);
    }

    return openFileHelper(uri, mode);
}
```

Finally, we use a FileHandler implementation of ResponseHandler to download image data from YouTube thumbnail URLs corresponding to each media entry. Our File HandlerFactory allows us to manage cache files stored in a specified cache directory. We allow the factory to decide where to store the files:

```
/**
 * Creates instances of FileHandler objects that use a common cache directory.
 * The cache directory is set in the constructor to the file handler factory.
 */
public class FileHandlerFactory {
    private String mCacheDir;

    public FileHandlerFactory(String cacheDir) {
        mCacheDir = cacheDir;
        init();
    }

    private void init() {
        File cacheDir = new File(mCacheDir);
        if (!cacheDir.exists()) {
            cacheDir.mkdir();
        }
    }

    public FileHandler newFileHandler(String id) {
        return new FileHandler(mCacheDir, id);
    }

    // not really used since ContentResolver uses _data field.
    public File getFile(String ID) {
        String cachePath = getFileName(ID);

        File cacheFile = new File(cachePath);
        if (cacheFile.exists()) {
            return cacheFile;
        }
        return null;
    }

    public void delete(String ID) {
        String cachePath = mCacheDir + "/" + ID;

        File cacheFile = new File(cachePath);
        if (cacheFile.exists()) {
            cacheFile.delete();
        }
    }

    public String getFileName(String ID) {
        return mCacheDir + "/" + ID;
    }
}

/**
 * Writes data from URLs into a local file cache that can be referenced by a
 * database ID.
 */
public class FileHandler implements ResponseHandler {
    private String mId;
    private String mCacheDir;
```

```
public FileHandler(String cacheDir, String id) {
    mCacheDir = cacheDir;
    mId = id;
}

public
String getFileName(String ID) {
    return mCacheDir + "/" + ID;
}

public void handleResponse(HttpResponse response, Uri uri)
        throws IOException
{
    InputStream urlStream = response.getEntity().getContent();
    FileOutputStream fout =
            new FileOutputStream(getFileName(mId));
    byte[] bytes = new byte[256];
    int r = 0;
    do {
        r = urlStream.read(bytes);
        if (r >= 0) {
            fout.write(bytes, 0, r);
        }
    } while (r >= 0);

    urlStream.close();
    fout.close();
}
}
```

Advanced Topics

In Part IV we cover Android APIs that are important to many applications, but that are not part of the core Android Framework and that not every application is likely to make use of.

Search

When we speak of Android, it's hard to avoid talking also about Google, and Google is almost synonymous with search. Search as a capability has become the entryway for the user to extract specific information based on a query. To this end, Android provides a universal interface, namely the Quick Search Box and Search Bar, to make the idea of search ubiquitous. At the base level, there is a search framework—a UI framework—and its usage is highly encouraged.

Search Interface

The search framework enables your application to be searchable. Be aware that the search framework is just a UI framework and does not provide the underpinnings for the actual search logic. Instead, it provides the UI portions that allow the user to input a search query and execute it. This in turn can call search logic that you specify, and thus return the appropriate results. To show the basics of building out the search logic as well as the search interface, we'll explore an example search application that allows users to search through Shakespeare's sonnets.

Search Basics

Search requires a couple of things from the application. First it requires the actual logic that returns the search results. It also requires the searchable configuration that establishes some of the specifics regarding what occurs when the search UI is initiated and how it is executed. Finally, a searchable activity is launched, receives the query, and after calling upon the search logic, displays the results.

Search logic

There are many ways to create the actual search logic that generates the search results. Here we explore two options: a basic index-based search and a search backed by an SQLite database, `android.database.sqlite` search. In either case, we'll start with the basic building blocks: data objects and a SearchLogic interface.

For data objects, this example essentially has one main object and one lesser subobject. Because we are searching through sonnets, we have a Sonnet class that contains the title, the number of the sonnet, and the sonnet's lines. The lesser subobject is a Sonnet Fragment for when we need to retrieve only a specific line within a sonnet without generating the whole sonnet. The subobject is used primarily for showing the search results.

```
public class Sonnet {
    public int num;
    public String title;
    public String[] lines;
}

public class SonnetFragment {
    public int num;
    public String line;
}
```

From the SearchLogic interface, we need to write two methods that will be called when we actually do the search or sonnet retrieval via the UI: search(), which takes the query string and returns a sorted array of SonnetFragment objects, and getSonnet(), which returns the specific Sonnet object referenced by its number.

```
public interface SearchLogicInterface {
    SonnetFragment[] search(String query);
    Sonnet getSonnet(int i);
}
```

Index-based search logic. In preparation for this, the sonnets are pulled in as a raw file and each line is parsed. Each group of lines making up a sonnet is then processed as a Sonnet object and each word of each line is tallied up into the larger index as a key. Its value is a set in which each member is a SonnetRef object containing the ID of the sonnet that contains the word along with an array of line numbers containing the word. More advanced techniques are certainly available, such as word-location tracking (where the position of the word within the line of the sonnet is included as a value), including metadata to reference the meaning or context of the word within the sonnet, weighting the word within a sonnet so as to create a ranking system per word for each sonnet, and other methods to handle more precise search queries or generate more specific query results. However, here we'll just address the basic index search system.

With the completed index available to the app, when a query specifying a specific word is made, the results are quickly returned because all the logic needs to do is look up that word in the index and the list of referencing sonnets and lines, which are the values in the index. In our example we use a HashMap as the index, with the word as the key and multiple SonnetRef objects, containing the sonnet number and line number, as its values.

```
// the index
private HashMap<String, HashSet<SonnetRef>> termindex;
...
// adding the term to the index
```

```
HashSet<SonnetRef> set = null;
if(index.containsKey(word)) {
    set = index.get(word);
} else set = new HashSet<SonnetRef>();

set.add(new SonnetRef(sons.size() - 1, i));
...
```

To handle multiple terms, the logic gets each set of SonnetRef objects and does an intersection to find the sonnet numbers in common. This intersection is what is ultimately returned.

```
public SonnetFragment[] search(String query) {
    if(query == null || query.trim().length() < 1) return new SonnetFragment[0];
    query = query.trim().toLowerCase();
    ArrayList<SonnetFragment> frags = new ArrayList<SonnetFragment>();
    String[] terms = query.split(" ");

    if(terms == null) terms = new String[]{query};
    ArrayList<HashSet<SonnetRef>> sets = new ArrayList<HashSet<SonnetRef>>();
    for(String term: terms) {
        if(termindex.containsKey(term)) {
            // we get each set of SonnetRefs specific to each term
            sets.add((HashSet<SonnetRef>) (termindex.get(term).clone()));
        }
    }
    if(!sets.isEmpty()) {
        HashSet<SonnetRef> main = null;
        for(HashSet<SonnetRef> set: sets) {
            if(main == null) main = set;
            else {
                // here we do the intersection
                main.retainAll(set);
            }
        }

        if(main != null && !main.isEmpty()) {
            Iterator<SonnetRef> it = main.iterator();
            while(it.hasNext()) {
                SonnetRef s = it.next();
                Sonnet son = sonnets[s.num];
                frags.add(new SonnetFragment(s.num, son.lines[s.line]));
            }
        }
    }

    return frags.isEmpty()
            ? new SonnetFragment[0]
            : frags.toArray(new SonnetFragment[frags.size()]);
}
```

Database-backed search logic. In this implementation, the core of the search is an SQL query against the sonnets stored in the database. When the sonnet data is read in, each sonnet is added to the database. The columns consist of the referencing sonnet number, the sonnet title, the line number, and the line itself.

```
    private SonnetsSQLOpenHelper sql;
    ...
    private static class SonnetsSQLOpenHelper extends SQLiteOpenHelper {
        @Override
        public void onCreate(SQLiteDatabase db) {
                    // create the table
            sonnetdb = db;
            sonnetdb.execSQL("CREATE TABLE "+SONNETTABLE+" ("+
                        BaseColumns._ID +" INTEGER, "+SONNETNUM+
                        " INTEGER, "+SearchManager.SUGGEST_COLUMN_INTENT_DATA_ID+
                        " TEXT, "+SONNETSTR+" TEXT, "+LINENUM+" INTEGER, "+
                        LINETXT+" TEXT);");
        }

            // add the ability to add a sonnet line to the DB
        public long addSonnet(int id, int sonnetnum, String sonnetstr,
                                             int linenum, String line) {
            ContentValues initialValues = new ContentValues();
            initialValues.put(BaseColumns._ID, id);
            initialValues.put(SONNETNUM, sonnetnum);
            initialValues.put(
                        SearchManager.SUGGEST_COLUMN_INTENT_DATA_ID,
                    ""+sonnetnum);
            initialValues.put(LINENUM, linenum);
            initialValues.put(SONNETSTR, sonnetstr);
            initialValues.put(LINETXT, line);

            return sonnetdb.insert(SONNETTABLE, null, initialValues);
        }
    }
    ...
    Sonnet sonnet = new Sonnet(num, ls.toArray(new String[size]));
    if(sql != null) {
        for(int i=0;i<size;i++) {
                // add each line to the db
            sql.addSonnet(id++, sonnet.num, sonnet.title, i, sonnet.lines[i]);
        }
    }
    ...
```

The search query can then be executed using a LIKE clause.

```
    public Cursor searchDB(String query, String[] columns) {
        query = query.toLowerCase();
            // here we specify the specific SQL query.
            //    in this case a LIKE of the query string
        String selection = LINETXT + " LIKE ?";
        String[] selectionArgs = new String[] {"%"+query+"%"};
        return query(selection, selectionArgs, columns, null);
    }

        // here we actually execute the query and return a Cursor
    private Cursor query(String selection, String[] selectionArgs,
                                     String[] columns, String sort) {
        SQLiteQueryBuilder builder = new SQLiteQueryBuilder();
        builder.setTables(SONNETTABLE);
```

```
            Cursor cursor = builder.query(
                            sql.getReadableDatabase(),
                            columns,
                            selection,
                            selectionArgs,
                            null,
                            null,
                            sort);

        if (cursor == null) {
            return null;
        } else if (!cursor.moveToFirst()) {
            cursor.close();
            return null;
        }
        return cursor;
    }
```

Searchable configuration

Once you have the search logic established, you need to get into the search framework. The first step is to create the *searchable configuration*, an XML file placed in the *res/xml* directory and typically named *searchable.xml*. The searchable configuration contains specific attributes that ultimately become the settings for a `SearchableInfo` object that the system instantiates.

The searchable configuration XML file must include the `searchable` element as the root node and must include the `android:label` attribute.

```xml
<?xml version="1.0" encoding="utf-8"?>
<searchable xmlns:android="http://schemas.android.com/apk/res/android"
    android:label="@string/app_label"
    >
</searchable>
```

The full searchable configuration syntax follows:

```xml
<?xml version="1.0" encoding="utf-8"?>
<searchable xmlns:android="http://schemas.android.com/apk/res/android"
    android:label="string resource"
    android:hint="string resource"
    android:searchMode=["queryRewriteFromData" | "queryRewriteFromText"]
    android:searchButtonText="string resource"
    android:inputType="inputType"
    android:imeOptions="imeOptions"
    android:searchSuggestAuthority="string"
    android:searchSuggestPath="string"
    android:searchSuggestSelection="string"
    android:searchSuggestIntentAction="string"
    android:searchSuggestIntentData="string"
    android:searchSuggestThreshold="int"
    android:includeInGlobalSearch=["true" | "false"]
    android:searchSettingsDescription="string resource"
    android:queryAfterZeroResults=["true" | "false"]
```

```
                android:voiceSearchMode=["showVoiceSearchButton" | "launchWebSearch" |
                                                          "launchRecognizer"]
                android:voiceLanguageModel=["free-form" | "web_search"]
                android:voicePromptText="string resource"
                android:voiceLanguage="string"
                android:voiceMaxResults="int"
                >
                <actionkey
                    android:keycode="KEYCODE"
                    android:queryActionMsg="string"
                    android:suggestActionMsg="string"
                    android:suggestActionMsgColumn="string"/>
        </searchable>
```

For more information on the searchable configuration, take a look at the Search Con‐
figuration section of the Android Developers Guide (*http://developer.android.com/*
guide/topics/search/searchable-config.html#searchable-element).

Searchable activity

After defining a searchable configuration, you must create an activity that is searchable.
This activity will ultimately call the search logic and present the results. The system
starts this activity by issuing an intent with the `ACTION_SEARCH` action when a search is
executed in the Search Dialog or Search Widget. The query is contained within the
intent as a `SearchManager.QUERY` string. From there, the activity can call the search logic
with the query string. The logic returns the results, which can then be displayed. In our
example, the query string would be passed to the search logic's `search()` method and
an array of `SonnetFragment` objects would be returned. The activity's logic would then
display the results to the user.

The first step is to declare the searchable activity in the manifest and specify to the
system that this is the activity to which the search query ought to be made. This is done
by adding the `android.intent.action.SEARCH` action to the intent filters and specifying
the searchable configuration.

```
    <application ... >
        <activity android:name=".searchdemo.SearchActivity" >
            <intent-filter>
                <action android:name="android.intent.action.SEARCH" />
            </intent-filter>
            <meta-data android:name="android.app.searchable"
                       android:resource="@xml/searchable"/>
        </activity>
        ...
    </application>
```

The second step is to decide how the search results will be displayed. It is generally
suggested that some form of list be used to display the results. In this example, we chose
to display the results in a `ListView`. To make things simpler, we made our activity extend
`ListActivity`, because it provides a default layout with a `ListView` and with `getList
View()` and `setListAdapter()` convenience methods to access it.

```java
public class SearchActivity extends ListActivity {

    // the Search Logic object
    private SearchLogicInterface SEARCHLOGIC;

    @Override
    public void onCreate(Bundle savedInstanceState) {
        super.onCreate(savedInstanceState);

        setContentView(R.layout.search);

        // initialize the search logic
        initializeSearchLogic();

        // handle intents if any
        handleIntent();
    }

    private void handleIntent() {
        if(getIntent() != null) {
            Intent intent = getIntent();
            if (Intent.ACTION_SEARCH.equals(intent.getAction())) {
                query = intent.getStringExtra(SearchManager.QUERY).toLowerCase();
                search(query);
            }
        }
    }

    private void search(String query) {
        // call search logic
        final SonnetFragment[] sfrags = SEARCHLOGIC.search(query);

        getListView().setVisibility(View.VISIBLE);
        getListView().addHeaderView(
                View.inflate(this, R.layout.searchheader, null), null, false);

        ArrayAdapter<SonnetFragment> arr =
                new ArrayAdapter<SonnetFragment>(this, R.layout.searchrow, sfrags);
        setListAdapter(arr);

        getListView().setOnItemClickListener(new OnItemClickListener() {
            public void onItemClick(AdapterView<?> adpt, View view,
                int pos, long id) {
                // Do something once user clicks the
                //     specific sonnetfragment in the list
            }
        });
    }
}
```

It is important for the code to handle the ACTION_SEARCH intent that the system passes to the activity. Once the SearchManager.QUERY string extra (getStringExtra) is extracted from the intent, it is used as the input to the search logic and the results are returned.

In this case, the array of SonnetFragment objects is put into an ArrayAdapter and this ArrayAdapter is set as the List's adapter, thus displaying the results.

This completes the basic interface work. Next we cover the UI components that the user accesses to execute the search: namely the Search Dialog and the Search Widget. You should use the Search Widget if your target devices run Android 3.0 (Honeycomb/API 11) or later.

Search Dialog

The Search Dialog is a user interface that allows the user to input text and execute a search. It is a component that appears at the top of the screen when initiated. The Android system controls all events in the Search Dialog. When the user enters a query and then submits it, the system sends out the ACTION_SEARCH intent to the activity that was specified in the manifest.

To enable the Search Dialog to send searches to the declared searchable activity from a specific activity, the <meta-data> element must include the android:value attribute that specifies the searchable activity's class name. It must also include, within the specific activity that the manifest designates as the Search Dialog, the android:name attribute with a value of "android.app.default_searchable".

```
<application ... >
    <activity
            android:label="@string/app_name"
            android:name=".searchdemo.MainActivity" >

            <meta-data android:name="android.app.default_searchable"
                        android:value=".searchdemo.SearchActivity" />
    </activity>
    </activity>
    ...
</application>
```

Once this metadata reference is in place, the Search Dialog will activate when the user taps the device's Search button (should the device have one) with this activity in the fore, or when the activity calls the onSearchRequested() method.

```
public class MainActivity extends Activity {

    @Override
    public void onCreate(Bundle savedInstanceState) {
        super.onCreate(savedInstanceState);

        setContentView(R.layout.main);

        findViewById(R.id.search).setOnClickListener(new OnClickListener() {
            @Override
            public void onClick(View v) {
                onSearchRequested();   // activates the Search Dialog
            }
```

```
        });
    }
```

The Search Dialog floats at the top of the screen. It does not cause any change in the activity stack, so when it appears, no life cycle methods—onPause(), and so forth—are called. The activity just loses input focus to the Search Dialog. If the user cancels the search by pressing the Back button, the Search Dialog closes and the activity regains input focus.

Search Widget

The Search Widget (specifically, the SearchView class) is for Android 3.0 (Honeycomb/ API 11) and later only. It is recommended that the SearchView be used in an Action Bar as an action view for a collapsible menu item rather than placing the Search Widget in your activity layout. To put it in an ActionBar, create a custom menu XML file (named *search_menu.xml* in this example) referencing android:actionView Class="android.widget.SearchView" in one of the items, and place the XML file in the *res/menu* directory.

```xml
<?xml version="1.0" encoding="utf-8"?>
<menu xmlns:android="http://schemas.android.com/apk/res/android">
    <item android:id="@+id/menu_search"
        android:icon="@android:drawable/ic_menu_search"
        android:title="@string/search"
        android:showAsAction="ifRoom|withText"
        android:actionViewClass="android.widget.SearchView"
        />
</menu>
```

Once you have the menu XML file, you can inflate it in the activity's onCreateOptions Menu() method. From there, reference SearchView and set setSearchableInfo() with SearchableInfo representing the searchable configuration.

```java
@Override
public boolean onCreateOptionsMenu(Menu menu) {
    // Inflate the options menu from XML
    MenuInflater inflater = getMenuInflater();
    // inflate the search_menu.xml
    inflater.inflate(R.menu.search_menu, menu);

    // Get the SearchView and set the searchable configuration
    SearchManager searchManager =
        (SearchManager) getSystemService(Context.SEARCH_SERVICE);
    SearchView searchView =
        (SearchView) menu.findItem(R.id.menu_search).getActionView();
    searchView.setSearchableInfo(
        searchManager.getSearchableInfo(getComponentName()));

    // Do not iconify the widget; expand it by default
    searchView.setIconifiedByDefault(false);
    // turn on submit button
    searchView.setSubmitButtonEnabled(true);
```

```
        // enable query selection refinement
    searchView.setQueryRefinementEnabled(true);

    return true;
}
```

Query Suggestions

When a user uses the Search Dialog or Search Widget to input the search query, search suggestions may be provided within the interface to make it easier for the user to select possible queries. The basic steps that accomplish this are:

1. The system passes the query text to a defined content provider that contains search suggestions.
2. This content provider returns a Cursor that points to a list of all suggestions based on that query.
3. The system displays the suggestions.

Should the user then select one of the suggestions, an intent is sent to the searchable activity with a custom action and data.

The APIs provide an easy means to show suggestions based on search history (recent queries) as well as a means to create custom (application logic generated) suggestions.

Recent Query Suggestions

The SearchRecentSuggestionsProvider class is the basis for a provider that holds past searches as search suggestions and does most of the logic necessary for returning the proper results. This cuts down on the amount of code and configuration necessary to implement a search history suggestion system.

To do all this, create a class that extends SearchRecentSuggestionsProvider and define the authority and mode within it by calling the setupSuggestions() method.

```
package com.oreilly.demo.android.pa.searchdemo;

import android.content.SearchRecentSuggestionsProvider;

public class CustomSearchSuggestionProvider extends
                    SearchRecentSuggestionsProvider {
    public final static String AUTHORITY =
        "com.oreilly.demo.android.pa.searchdemo.CustomSearchSuggestionProvider";

    public final static int MODE = DATABASE_MODE_QUERIES;

    public CustomSearchSuggestionProvider() {
        super();
        setupSuggestions(AUTHORITY, MODE);
    }
}
```

After the provider is established, it must be declared in the manifest. The key here is to reference the same authority string that is defined in the custom SearchRecent SuggestionsProvider.

```
<application>
    ...
    <provider android:name=".searchdemo.CustomSearchSuggestionProvider"
        android:authorities=
            "com.oreilly.demo.android.pa.searchdemo.CustomSearchSuggestionProvider"
    />
    ...
</application>
```

This authority must also be referenced in the searchable configuration XML file as an android:searchSuggestAuthority attribute. You must also define an android:search SuggestSelection with the value " ?" (note the initial space), thus passing the query through as an SQLite selection argument.

```
<?xml version="1.0" encoding="utf-8"?>
<searchable xmlns:android="http://schemas.android.com/apk/res/android"
    android:label="@string/app_name"
    android:hint="@string/search_hint"
    android:voiceSearchMode="showVoiceSearchButton|launchRecognizer"
    android:searchSuggestAuthority=
        "com.oreilly.demo.android.pa.searchdemo.CustomSearchSuggestionProvider"
    android:searchSuggestSelection=" ?"
    >
</searchable>
```

Finally, now that the SearchRecentSuggestionsProvider has been coded, declared, and configured, the queries must be added to the search history. This is done by calling saveRecentQuery() on SearchRecentSuggestions and passing the query to it.

To clear the history call, issue clearHistory().

```
SearchRecentSuggestions suggestions =
                new SearchRecentSuggestions(this,
                        CustomSearchSuggestionProvider.AUTHORITY,
                        CustomSearchSuggestionProvider.MODE);

suggestions.saveRecentQuery(query, null);  // save query

suggestions.clearHistory();  // clear history
```

Custom Query Suggestions

To create custom query suggestions supplied by some application logic, the primary thing to consider is the content provider that receives the query and returns a Cursor. This Cursor references what are, essentially, rows of suggestion data that the system displays to the user. In this particular case, the system expects the data to have some specific columns defined, as shown in Table 14-1. Some are required and the rest are optional.

Table 14-1. Cursor data for custom query suggestions

Column	Base class	Meaning	Required?
_ID	android.pro vider.BaseColumns	Unique integer ID for that row	Yes
SUGGEST_COLUMN_TEXT_1	android.app.Search Manager	The suggestion string	Yes
SUGGEST_COLUMN_TEXT_2	android.app.Search Manager	Secondary line of text to be displayed	No
SUGGEST_COLUMN_ICON_1	android.app.Search Manager	Drawable resource or file URI for the icon to be displayed on the left	No
SUGGEST_COLUMN_ICON_2	android.app.Search Manager	Drawable resource or file URI for the icon to be displayed on the right	No
SUGGEST_COL UMN_INTENT_ACTION	android.app.Search Manager	Specifies the intent action for this suggestion, and should be taken from the value of the android:search SuggestIntentAction element in the searchable configuration	No
SUGGEST_COL UMN_INTENT_DATA	android.app.Search Manager	Specifies the intent data for this sug-gestion, and should be taken from the value of the android:searchSug gestIntentData element in the searchable configuration	No
SUGGEST_COL UMN_INTENT_DATA_ID	android.app.Search Manager	A URI path string that is appended to the data field in the intent	No
SUGGEST_COL UMN_INTENT_EXTRA_DATA	android.app.Search Manager	Extra data to be put into the EXTRA_DATA_KEY key of the intent	No
SUGGEST_COLUMN_QUERY	android.app.Search Manager	Included data in the QUERY key of the intent	No
SUGGEST_COLUMN_SHORT CUT_ID	android.app.Search Manager	Used only for the Quick Search Box. This is the ID referred to when the search suggestion is to be stored as a shortcut.	No
SUGGEST_COLUMN_SPIN NER_WHILE_REFRESHING	android.app.Search Manager	Used only for the Quick Search Box. This is a drawable resource or file URI used for the icon to be displayed on the right, while the shortcut of this suggestion is being refreshed in the Quick Search Box instead of the icon defined by SUGGEST_COL UMN_ICON_2.	No

It is important to note that if your search suggestions are not stored in a table format (such as an SQLite table) and thus can be easily made to conform to the columns necessary for the system, you should create a `MatrixCursor` with the required columns and add data using the `addRow(Object[])` method.

Regardless of the `Cursor` specifics, the content provider's `query()` method must return this `Cursor` as defined earlier. The `query()` method is defined as follows:

```
public Cursor query(Uri uri, String[] projection, String selection,
                    String[] selectionArgs, String sortOrder)
```

It receives the following parameters from the system:

uri
: Explained following this list.

projection
: Always null.

selection
: The value of `android:searchSuggestSelection` in the searchable configuration.

selectionArgs
: Contains the search query as the single element of the array, if you have declared the `android:searchSuggestSelection` attribute in the searchable configuration, else null. This is essentially the term or terms that the user is searching for.

sortOrder
: Always null.

The `uri` format is:

```
content://your.authority/optional.suggest.path/some_uri_path_that_you_defined/query
```

your.authority is the previously defined `android:searchSuggestAuthority` attribute in the searchable configuration XML file. The *optional.suggest.path* is the optionally defined `android:searchSuggestPath` attribute in the searchable configuration XML file. This ensures that you can distinguish among the activities that are potential sources for the query when you have multiple searchable activities for the same content provider. The *some_uri_path_that_you_defined* element is a constant string you define, and *query* is the actual query string passed by the user. This query string may be URI-encoded, so decoding may be needed.

An example `query()` method follows.

```
public class SearchDBProvider extends ContentProvider {
    ...
    public final static String AUTHORITY =
            "com.oreilly.demo.android.pa.searchdemo.SearchDBProvider";
    ...
    // build a uri matcher based on the AUTHORITY
    private static final UriMatcher matcher = buildUriMatcher();
    ...
    @Override
```

```
public Cursor query(Uri uri, String[] projection, String selection,
                        String[] selectionArgs, String sortOrder) {
    switch (matcher.match(uri)) {
        // we figure out it is a suggestion call
        case SEARCH_SUGGEST:
            return getSuggestions(selectionArgs[0]);
        ...
    }
}

private Cursor getSuggestions(String query) {
    query = query.toLowerCase();
    String[] columns = new String[] {
                            BaseColumns._ID,
                            SearchDBLogic.SONNETNUM,
                            SearchDBLogic.LINETXT,
                            SearchManager.SUGGEST_COLUMN_INTENT_DATA_ID
                        };

    // do a search against the search
    //    logic to come up with suggestions
    return ((SearchDBLogic) SearchActivity.SEARCHLOGIC).
                                        searchDB(query, columns);
}
...
}
```

You must also specify the content provider in your manifest.

```
<application>
    ...
    <provider android:name=".searchdemo.SearchDBProvider"
        android:authorities=
            "com.oreilly.demo.android.pa.searchdemo.SearchDBProvider"
    />
    ...
</application>
```

Then configure your searchable configuration with at least an android:searchSuggest
Authority set to the authority string previously defined.

```
<?xml version="1.0" encoding="utf-8"?>
<searchable xmlns:android="http://schemas.android.com/apk/res/android"
    android:label="@string/app_name"
    android:searchSuggestAuthority=
            "com.oreilly.demo.android.pa.searchdemo.SearchDBProvider"
    >
</searchable>
```

Other things such as the custom intent can be specified within the searchable configuration as well, using the android:searchSuggestIntentAction. By providing a custom
intent, the searchable activity can be made to distinguish between a regular search query
(provisioned with the android.Intent.action.SEARCH intent) and a suggested search
query. An example follows that uses the android.Intent.action.VIEW for the custom
intent.

```
<?xml version="1.0" encoding="utf-8"?>
    <searchable xmlns:android=
                "http://schemas.android.com/apk/res/android"
     android:label="@string/app_name"
     android:searchSuggestAuthority=
       "com.oreilly.demo.android.pa.searchdemo.SearchDBProvider"
     android:searchSuggestIntentAction="android.Intent.action.VIEW"
     >
</searchable>
```

In this case, the searchable activity needs to handle the `Intent.ACTION_VIEW` as well as the `Intent.ACTION_SEARCH`.

```
Intent intent = getIntent();

if (Intent.ACTION_SEARCH.equals(intent.getAction())) {
    String query = intent.getStringExtra(SearchManager.QUERY).toLowerCase();
    search(query);  // go do the search against the searchlogic
} else if (Intent.ACTION_VIEW.equals(intent.getAction())) {
    Uri data = intent.getData();
    loadData(data);  // do something with this data
}
```

Finally, if you wish to expose the search suggestions to the Quick Search Box, the searchable configuration must set the `android:includeInGlobalSearch` element to true. Suggestions that the user selects from the Quick Search Box can be automatically exposed as shortcuts by the system. These are suggestions that the system has cached from your content provider so that it can quickly access the suggestion. Once you make your application's search suggestions available to the Quick Search Box, its ranking determines how the suggestions are exposed to the user for a particular query. This might depend on how many other apps have results for that query, and how often the user has selected your results compared to those from other apps. There is no guarantee concerning how your suggestions are ranked, or whether your app's suggestions show at all for a given query. In general, you can expect that providing quality results increases the likelihood that your app's suggestions are provided in a prominent position, and that apps that provide low-quality suggestions are more likely to be ranked lower or not be displayed.

Location and Mapping

Ever since mobile phones started to incorporate standalone GPS receivers, developers have foreseen a new era of location-based applications. Location awareness enables a new generation of mobile applications. If your application is looking up restaurants, it's clearly advantageous if you can restrict your search to the area around you. It's even better if you can see a map of the restaurants' locations, and perhaps be able to look up driving or walking directions. If you're looking for a temporary job, as in the MJAndroid application highlighted in "Using the Database API: MJAndroid" on page 280, it's definitely a benefit to be able to graphically view job opportunities on a map.

Navigation is really just the first generation of location-based services (LBS). Applications that enable users either to opt in to allow sharing of their location with friends, such as Google Latitude, or to attach importance to geographic sites, such as Foursquare, have arrived in a big way. The world of LBS has really taken off, and as we'll see, Google's Android provides powerful features that greatly simplify development of this type of application.

In economic terms, location-based applications are a major factor in mobile telephony, making up a significant portion of the revenue from mobile applications, and growing fast. Because they are based on the ability of the mobile network to locate devices and the relationship of mobility and location, location-based applications are as fundamental to mobile telephony as communication.

Applications often combine location awareness with search: Where are my contacts? Where are services or products I'm looking for? Where are people with common interests?

In this chapter, we'll explore how the MJAndroid application uses Android to address some of these questions.

Location-Based Services

Mobile phones use several related methods, alone and in combination, to determine where they are:

Cell ID

> Whether you're actually talking on the phone or not, as long as it's powered up, your mobile phone carries on a constant conversation with nearby cell towers. It has to do this to be able to respond when someone calls you, so every few seconds it "pings" the cell tower it was using last to tell it that it's still in range and to note network parameters such as the current time, the current signal strength (uplink and downlink), and so on.
>
> If you happen to be moving, your phone may initiate a handover to another cell tower, all in the background and without you having to intervene. Each cell tower worldwide has a unique identifier called, appropriately enough, its Cell ID, and each tower knows its latitude and longitude, so it's easy enough for a mobile phone to know *approximately* where you are located by noting the current Cell ID's geographic location. Cell network sizes vary depending on the expected traffic in an area, but in the United States their radius ranges from a half mile (cities) to five miles or more (wide-open spaces).

Triangulation

> Most of the time your mobile phone is in range of more than one cell tower. In 2G and later mobile technologies, the cell tower has the ability to tell what direction your signal is coming from. If there are two or three towers that can see your phone, together they can triangulate on your phone's location. With some operators, your phone then has the ability to query the network to find out its location. This sounds a little backward, but it can be very accurate, and it doesn't depend on any extra hardware on the mobile phone.

GPS

> The satellite-based Global Positioning System is ubiquitous these days, found in car navigation units, handheld navigators, and mobile phones. The good news is that, using GPS, your mobile phone can determine its location very accurately, including its altitude if that's important for some particular application. There are several downsides to GPS, but it is gaining popularity nonetheless. The downsides are:

Increased cost

> GPS radios and processors are fairly inexpensive, but still, an increase of even $10 in the bill-of-materials cost of a mobile phone is considerable.

Reduced battery life

> There have been great strides in reducing the power required by GPS radios and processors, but they still suck battery power. Most phones that include GPS also have a feature that lets the user turn it on and off. If your application depends on GPS accuracy, it's good to remember that your application might

have to check to see whether the GPS device is turned on, and notify the user if it isn't.

Unreliable availability

Nothing "always works," but GPS in particular depends on your mobile device being able to see the satellites currently overhead. If you're in the basement of a high-rise building, surrounded by steel-reinforced concrete, you probably aren't going to be able to use GPS.

It's reasonable to expect that all Android phones will include one or all of these location finding methods. Most recent Android phones, in particular, can use them all. So now we'll proceed to techniques for using the location capabilities.

Mapping

Google is most famous for its search engine, but not far behind that comes the acclaim of Google Maps. When creating Android, the folks at Google could easily see the potential in LBS and how well it fit with their mapping expertise. Most LBS applications end up displaying a map. Meanwhile, Google already had the technology to display and update interactive maps, and the business processes in place to allow others to use those maps and add features for their own websites. It still required a significant leap to make that mapping technology available to application developers for mobile phones, but Google has certainly answered the challenge in Android.

The Google Maps Activity

One of the applications that comes with Android is the Google Maps application itself. If it's appropriate, you can start Google Maps from your application the same way you start any other `Activity`:

1. Create an `Intent` (`new Intent(String action, Uri uri)`) that says you need to display a map. The parameters are:

   - An `action`, for which you must specify `ACTION_VIEW`
   - A `Uri`, for which you should specify one of the following URI schemes, substituting your data:
     - —geo: *latitude, longitude*
     - —geo: *latitude , longitude* ?z= *zoom*
     - —geo:0,0?q *my_street_address*
     - —geo:0,0?q *business_near_city*

2. Call `startActivity(Intent intent)`, using the intent you just created.

An example that creates a map is:

```
Intent intent = new Intent(ACTION_VIEW, "geo:37.422006,-122.084095");
startActivity(intent);
```

This is certainly easy, and it gets you all the power of Google Maps, but you can't really integrate the map into your application this way. Google Maps is an application unto itself, and there's no way for you to change anything about the user interface or add overlay graphics to the map to point out whatever is of interest to your users. Android provides more flexible packages to add that power.

The MapView and MapActivity

Chapter 9's MJAndroid sample application needs to add overlays that show the locations for jobs in the area. So, instead of using the Google Maps application, we will use a `MapView`, which we can overlay with graphics as needed. You can have only one `MapView` per `Activity`, and that `Activity` has to extend `MapActivity`. As you'll see, that's a small price to pay for the powerful geographic functions that `MapView` adds to your application.

There are a couple of unique prerequisites for using `MapView`s, and we touched on both of them when we looked at the initialization of MJAndroid in Chapter 9:

Include the `MapView`'s library

The `MapView` is not included in the default Android libraries. Instead, you need to specify in *AndroidManifest.xml* that you are using this additional library:

```
<application android:icon="@drawable/icon2">
        <uses-library android:name="com.google.android.maps" />
```

You can't put the `uses-library` line just anywhere in *AndroidManifest.xml*; it needs to be within the `<application>` tag and outside the `<activity>` tag definitions.

Sign your application and obtain a Maps API key from Google

When you use a `MapView` in your application, you are using actual Google Maps data to draw the map. For legal reasons, Google needs to track who is using its map data. Google doesn't care what your application does with the data, but you need to register with Google for an API key and agree to appropriate Terms of Service. This tells Google your application is using mapping data, and whether you are also using the routing data that is available from Google Maps. "Google Maps API Keys" on page 143 covered the processes of signing your application and getting an API key.

 Remember that programs using a `MapView` must be signed. To build the MicroJobs application, you'll need to get your own key, as described in "Google Maps API Keys" on page 143.

Working with MapViews

The `MapView` encapsulates a lot of very complex mapping software and is available for you to use in your Android applications—for free. Here are some of the things you can do with a `MapView`, with only a little programming on your part:

- Show a street map of any area in the world, with up-to-date mapping information courtesy of Google.
- Change the map view to show:

  Street view
  > Photographs taken at street level for many areas in North America

  Satellite view
  > An aerial, photographic view of the area

  Traffic view
  > Real-time traffic information superimposed on the map or satellite views

- Move the map under program control.
- Plot your own graphics in overlays on top of the map.
- Respond to user touch events on the map.

MapView and MyLocationOverlay Initialization

The map in MicroJobs has two modes:

- At startup, and when we select Current Location from the Spinner, we want to display a map of our current location, and we want that map to track us as we move around. For this map, we will use the `MyLocationOverlay` class.
- When we select a specific location from the Spinner, we want to display a map of that location, turn off location updates, and not track movement.

Let's look at the code in *MicroJobs.java* that initializes the `MapView` and the `My LocationOverlay` that tracks our current location:

```
@Override
public void onCreate(Bundle savedInstanceState) {

    // code elided ...
    mvMap = (MapView) findViewById(R.id.mapmain); ❶

    // get the map controller
    final MapController mc = mvMap.getController(); ❷

    mMyLocationOverlay = new MyLocationOverlay(this, mvMap); ❸
    mMyLocationOverlay.enableMyLocation();
    mMyLocationOverlay.runOnFirstFix(❹
        new Runnable() {
            @Override
```

```
            public void run() {
                mc.animateTo(mMyLocationOverlay.getMyLocation());❺
                mc.setZoom(16);
                updateCurLocation(mMyLocationOverlay.getMyLocation());
            }
        });

        Drawable marker = getResources().getDrawable(R.drawable.android_tiny_image);❻
        marker.setBounds(0, 0, marker.getIntrinsicWidth(), marker.getIntrinsicHeight());
        mvMap.getOverlays().add(new MJJobsOverlay(marker));

        mvMap.setClickable(true);❼
        mvMap.setEnabled(true);
        mvMap.setSatellite(false);
        mvMap.setTraffic(false);

        // start out with a general zoom
        mc.setZoom(16);❽

        // code elided ...
    }

    /** Required method to indicate whether we display routes */
    @Override
    protected boolean isRouteDisplayed() { return false; }❾
```

Here are some of the highlights of the code:

❶ We first find the MapView in the *main.xml* layout file the same way we find any other view, and assign it to the variable mvMap, of type MapView, so that we can refer to it when we need to.

❷ We also get a handle on the MapController associated with MapView. We'll use that to pan (animate) the map, zoom in, zoom out, change views, and so on.

❸ To use MyLocationOverlay, we create a new instance, giving it the highly creative name MyLocationOverlay.

❹ The first thing we do with mMyLocationOverlay is define a method that Android will call when we receive our first location fix from the location provider.

❺ This runOnFirstFix method moves the map to the current location (given by MyLocationOverlay.getMyLocation()), and zooms to a reasonable level for us to see nearby job prospects.

❻ Next we identify a marker that we've decided to use on mMyLocationOverlay to mark available jobs. We use an image that's stored in our *res/drawable* directory, called *android_tiny_image*. It's a picture of a little Android robot. We define the bounds of the Drawable, and add the marker overlay to the list of overlays for the MapView mvMap.

❼ Now we'd like to set some initial attributes for mvMap, described later in this section. We'll allow the user to change most of these through menu buttons.

❽ Then, following a belt-and-suspenders philosophy, just in case there isn't a location provider to trigger `runOnFirstFix`, we'll set the zoom level again here.

❾ Finally, `MapView` requires us to override the `isRouteDisplayed()` method to indicate whether we are displaying route information on our map. We are not, so we return `false`.

`MyLocationOverlay` encapsulates a wealth of location and mapping code. In our single call to the constructor we:

- Ask Android to figure out what location providers are available in our environment (GPS, Cell ID, triangulation).
- Connect to the "best" of those location providers.
- Ask the location provider to provide us with periodic location updates as our handset moves.
- Link to routines that will automatically move our map as needed to track any changes in location.

`MyLocationOverlay` also allows us to place a compass rose on the `MapView` and have that updated as well, but we won't be using that in MJAndroid.

The map attributes set by the code are:

setClickable
> We want users to be able to tap on a job to cause MJAndroid to display more detail about that job, so we set this to `true`.

setEnabled
> This method is actually inherited from `android.view.View`. Google doesn't tell us exactly what this means in the case of a `MapView`, but presumably it enables the standard map functions—zooming, panning, and so on.

setSatellite
> Setting this flag adds a satellite view from the composite map, whereas clearing the flag removes the view. We don't want to start with satellite information on the map.

setTraffic
> Similarly, setting or clearing this flag adds or removes current traffic information from the map, respectively. Again, we don't want to start with traffic information on the map.

Zooming in Android Maps

Android maps come equipped with support for zooming in and out. The "i" key zooms in on the map, whereas the "o" key zooms out. Maps can also zoom in and out under program control, through the `MapController`.

Several methods are defined for zooming, all using the `MapController`. Android defines 21 zoom levels for maps. At zoom level 1, the equator of the Earth is 256 pixels long. Every step up in zoom level multiplies that by 2. Google warns that the higher-resolution maps are not available worldwide. All the zoom methods clamp the zoom level to the range 1 through 21 if you ask it to go beyond those limits.

The methods that control zoom, along with their parameters, are:

`zoomIn`
> Zooms in one level.

`zoomOut`
> Zooms out one level.

`setZoom(int zoomlevel)`
> Zooms to the given level, restricting it to the range 1 to 21.

`zoomInFixing(int xpixel, int ypixel)`, `zoomOutFixing(int xpixel, int ypixel)`
> Zoom in or zoom out one level, but keep the given point fixed on the screen. Normally when you zoom in and out, the center of the screen is the only point that stays fixed. These routines let you pick any point on the map to be the fixed point.

`zoomToSpan(int latSpanE6, int longSpanE6)`
> Attempts to zoom so that the given span is displayed on the map. What it actually does is select the zoom level that is the closest match for the span requested. The latitude and longitude span parameters are expressed as integers with a value 10^6 times the actual value in degrees. For instance, a latitude/longitude span of 2.5 degrees by 1.0 degrees would be expressed as `zoomToSpan(2500000, 1000000)`.

Pausing and Resuming a MapActivity

For a minute, let's focus on map activities and note a way we can help save battery power. The good news is that Android makes this pretty easy.

In a mobile environment, battery life is everything, and if we're not the application that is currently being displayed, we want to do everything we can to minimize the power we consume. Recall from the discussion of the Android life cycle ("Visualizing Life Cycles" on page 296) that when an `Activity` (such as MicroJobs) starts another `Activity` (such as MicroJobsList), the new `Activity` takes over the screen, and the calling `Activity` gets pushed onto a stack of activities that are waiting to run. At that time, Android calls the `onPause` routine in the calling `Activity` so that it can prepare itself to go into hibernation. At this point, in *MicroJobs.java* (or just about any `MapActivity` that uses location updates), we want to turn off location updates. Doing so will at least save the cycles devoted to doing the update, and may allow the handset to save even more power by putting the location provider in a quiescent state that uses less power.

When the called `Activity` (in our case, MicroJobsList) exits and the calling `Activity` is popped off the stack and takes control of the screen, the framework calls the onResume method in the calling `Activity`. In a `MapActivity`, we want to turn on location updates again when this method is invoked.

In MicroJobs, the onPause and onResume methods are straightforward:

```
/**
 * @see com.google.android.maps.MapActivity#onPause()
 */
@Override
public void onPause() {
    super.onPause();
    mMyLocationOverlay.disableMyLocation();
}

/**
 * @see com.google.android.maps.MapActivity#onResume()
 */
@Override
public void onResume() {
    super.onResume();
    mMyLocationOverlay.enableMyLocation();
}
```

Note that if we'd had a compass rose as part of our `MyLocationOverlay`, we would have to disable and enable it as well. Otherwise, the system would be wasting cycles and battery updating the direction of the compass rose, even though it wasn't visible on-screen.

Controlling the Map with Menu Buttons

We want to give the user the ability to turn on satellite, traffic, and street views of the map. In addition, we'll throw in a few menu buttons to enable zooming and another way to get to the Jobs list.

Android has a sophisticated set of menu capabilities that includes three types of menus (options, context, and submenus), each with its own capabilities, icon menu buttons, and other advanced features. We just use text-based menu buttons (we did this before, in "The Menu and the Action Bar" on page 199). We need to do two things:

1. Create the menu of buttons that will be displayed.
2. Catch the menu events and invoke appropriate actions.

The following code creates the menu in *MicroJobs.java*:

```
/**
 * Set up menus for this page
 *
```

```
 * @see android.app.Activity#onCreateOptionsMenu(android.view.Menu)
 */
@Override
public boolean onCreateOptionsMenu(Menu menu) {
    boolean supRetVal = super.onCreateOptionsMenu(menu);
    menu.add(Menu.NONE, 0, Menu.NONE, getString(R.string.map_menu_zoom_in));
    menu.add(Menu.NONE, 1, Menu.NONE, getString(R.string.map_menu_zoom_out));
    menu.add(Menu.NONE, 2, Menu.NONE, getString(R.string.map_menu_set_satellite));
    menu.add(Menu.NONE, 3, Menu.NONE, getString(R.string.map_menu_set_map));
    menu.add(Menu.NONE, 4, Menu.NONE, getString(R.string.map_menu_set_traffic));
    menu.add(Menu.NONE, 5, Menu.NONE, getString(R.string.map_menu_show_list));
    return supRetVal;
}
```

We create menu buttons by overriding the onCreateOptionsMenu method, where we are passed a menu parameter for the Activity's menu. After dutifully allowing the superclass a chance to do what it needs to do, we simply add items (buttons) to the menu using menu.add. The version of menu.add that we've chosen takes four parameters:

int groupid

> Android allows you to group menu items so that you can quickly change the whole menu at once. We don't have a need for that in MicroJobs, so Menu.NONE says we don't need it.

int itemid

> We need a unique identifier for this menu item so that we can tell later whether it was picked.

int order

> The itemid we defined in the second parameter does not imply order. If we cared about the order in which the items were presented, we'd do that with this parameter. Because we don't care, we use Menu.NONE again.

int titleRes

> This is the ID of the string resource we want to use for the button title. Note that this is an Integer, not a String, so the menu strings need to be predefined in *string.xml*, under the *res* directory. Recall that Android takes care of compiling the strings in *res/strings.xml* into a *.java* file (*R.java*) that assigns an integer to each string. The getString method retrieves that integer for you (despite the name, the method returns an integer and not a string).

To catch the menu events, we override the onOptionsItemSelected method:

```
/**
 * @see android.app.Activity#onOptionsItemSelected(android.view.MenuItem)
 */
@Override
public boolean onOptionsItemSelected(MenuItem item) {
    switch (item.getItemId()) {
        case 0:
            // Zoom in
            zoomIn();
            return true;
```

```
            case 1:
                // Zoom out
                zoomOut();
                return true;
            case 2:
                // Toggle satellite views
                mvMap.setSatellite(!mvMap.isSatellite());
                return true;
            case 3:
                // Launch StreetView with lat/lon of center of current map
                String uri = "google.streetview:cbll="+curlocation[0]+","+curlocation[1]+
                                "&cbp=1,0,,0,1.0&mz="+mvMap.getZoomLevel();
                Intent streetView = new Intent(
                                    android.content.Intent.ACTION_VIEW,
                                    Uri.parse(uri)
                                );
                startActivity(streetView);
                return true;
            case 4:
                // Toggle traffic views
                mvMap.setTraffic(!mvMap.isTraffic());
                return true;
            case 5:
                // Show the job list activity
                startActivity(new Intent(MicroJobs.this, MicroJobsList.class));
                return true;
        }
        return false;
    }
```

We use the MenuItem parameter, and the switch has a case for each button that we
defined for the menu. We've already seen code similar to that contained in each case.

Controlling the Map with the Keypad

Some users might prefer to control the map through the keypad (generally one "click,"
versus two "clicks" to cause a menu event). Enabling this behavior again demonstrates
how to respond to KeyPad events in general. We've added some code to zoom in, zoom
out, and back out of the current activity:

```
/**
 * @see android.app.Activity#onKeyDown(int, android.view.KeyEvent)
 */
@Override
public boolean onKeyDown(int keyCode, KeyEvent event) {
    switch (keyCode) {
        case KeyEvent.KEYCODE_DPAD_UP: // zoom in
            zoomIn();
            return true;
        case KeyEvent.KEYCODE_DPAD_DOWN: // zoom out
            zoomOut();
            return true;
        case KeyEvent.KEYCODE_BACK: // go back (meaning exit the app)
```

```
            finish();
            return true;
        default:
            return false;
    }
}
```

To catch key-down events, we simply override onKeyDown (as described in "Listening for Key Events" on page 192) and provide a switch for the different keys that are of interest. In addition to the keycodes you would expect (KEYCODE_A, ...KEYCODE_Z; and things like KEYCODE_SPACE, KEYCODE_SHIFT_LEFT, and KEYCODE_SHIFT_RIGHT), Android includes keycodes that may or may not appear on any particular device (KEYCODE_CAMERA and KEYCODE_VOLUME_UP). A complete set of keycodes can be found at *http://code .google.com/android/reference/android/view/KeyEvent.html.*

Location Without Maps

What if your activity needs to access location information, but it doesn't include a MapView? When you use a MapView, Android makes everything very easy with My LocationOverlay, but if you don't need a map it still isn't that hard to get location information. The code in this section is not part of MJAndroid, but it shows how you obtain location information independent of MapView.

Let's look at a very simple, one-activity application that displays the current location in a TextView.

The Manifest and Layout Files

An appropriate *AndroidManifest.xml* file follows. The only change we need to make here is to add the uses-permission tag for android .permission.ACCESS_FINE_LOCATION (in the next-to-last line of the file). We always need this permission to get location information from a GPS location provider.

```
<?xml version="1.0" encoding="utf-8"?>
    <manifest xmlns:android="http://schemas.android.com/apk/res/android"
        package="com.microjobsinc.dloc"
        android:versionCode="1"
        android:versionName="1.0.0">
        <application android:icon="@drawable/icon" android:label="@string/app_name">
            <activity android:name=".Main"
                    android:label="@string/app_name">
                <intent-filter>
                    <action android:name="android.intent.action.MAIN" />
                    <category android:name="android.intent.category.LAUNCHER" />
                </intent-filter>
            </activity>
        </application>

    <uses-permission android:name="android.permission.ACCESS_FINE_LOCATION">
```

```
        </uses-permission>
        </manifest>
```

We'll use a very simple layout file with four TextViews: one label and one text box each for latitude and longitude.

```xml
<?xml version="1.0" encoding="utf-8"?>
<LinearLayout xmlns:android="http://schemas.android.com/apk/res/android"
    android:orientation="vertical"
    android:layout_width="fill_parent"
    android:layout_height="fill_parent"
    >
<TextView
    android:id="@+id/lblLatitude"
    android:layout_width="fill_parent"
    android:layout_height="wrap_content"
    android:text="Latitude:"
    />
<TextView
    android:id="@+id/tvLatitude"
    android:layout_width="fill_parent"
    android:layout_height="wrap_content"
    />
<TextView
    android:id="@+id/lblLongitude"
    android:layout_width="fill_parent"
    android:layout_height="wrap_content"
    android:text="Longitude:"
    />
<TextView
    android:id="@+id/tvLongitude"
    android:layout_width="fill_parent"
    android:layout_height="wrap_content"
    />
</LinearLayout>
```

Connecting to a Location Provider and Getting Location Updates

Let's start with an activity that just connects with the GPS LocationProvider and gets and displays our current location (no updates):

```java
package com.oreilly.demo.pa.microJobs;

import android.app.Activity;
import android.content.Context;
import android.location.Location;
import android.location.LocationManager;
import android.os.Bundle;
import android.widget.TextView;

public class Main extends Activity {
    /** Called when the activity is first created. */
    @Override
    public void onCreate(Bundle savedInstanceState) {
        super.onCreate(savedInstanceState);
```

```
            setContentView(R.layout.main);

            // find the TextViews
            TextView tvLatitude = (TextView)findViewById(R.id.tvLatitude);
            TextView tvLongitude = (TextView)findViewById(R.id.tvLongitude);

            // get handle for LocationManager
            LocationManager lm = (LocationManager)
                getSystemService(Context.LOCATION_SERVICE);❶

            // connect to the GPS location service
            Location loc = lm.getLastKnownLocation("gps");❷

            // fill in the TextViews
            tvLatitude.setText(Double.toString(loc.getLatitude()));❸
            tvLongitude.setText(Double.toString(loc.getLongitude()));
        }
    }
```

The procedure is pretty straightforward. Here are some of the highlights of the code:

❶ This code connects to the LocationManager using getSystemService(Context.LOCA TION_SERVICE).

❷ This code asks the LocationManager where we are using getLastKnownLocation("pro vider").

❸ This code gets the latitude and longitude from the Location returned and uses it as needed.

But we also want to get periodic location updates from the LocationManager so that we can track our location as we move about. For that we need to add a listener routine and ask the LocationManager to call it when it has an update.

Location updates from the LocationManager are accessible to an application through a DispLocListener class, so we will create an instance of this class in the onCreate method of our main activity. We are required to override a number of methods in DispLoc Listener to meet the LocationListener interface definition, but we don't need them for this application, so we'll leave the definitions empty. The full implementation follows.

```
    package com.oreilly.demo.pa.MicroJobs;

    import android.app.Activity;
    import android.content.Context;
    import android.location.Location;
    import android.location.LocationListener;
    import android.location.LocationManager;
    import android.os.Bundle;
    import android.widget.TextView;

    public class Main extends Activity {
        private LocationManager lm;
        private LocationListener locListenD;
        public TextView tvLatitude;
```

```java
public TextView tvLongitude;

/** Called when the activity is first created. */
@Override
public void onCreate(Bundle savedInstanceState) {
    super.onCreate(savedInstanceState);
    setContentView(R.layout.main);

    // find the TextViews
    tvLatitude = (TextView)findViewById(R.id.tvLatitude);
    tvLongitude = (TextView)findViewById(R.id.tvLongitude);

    // get handle for LocationManager
    LocationManager lm =
      (LocationManager) getSystemService(Context.LOCATION_SERVICE);

    // connect to the GPS location service
    Location loc = lm.getLastKnownLocation("gps");

    // fill in the TextViews
    tvLatitude.setText(Double.toString(loc.getLatitude()));
    tvLongitude.setText(Double.toString(loc.getLongitude()));

    // ask the Location Manager to send us location updates
    locListenD = new DispLocListener();
    lm.requestLocationUpdates("gps", 30000L, 10.0f, locListenD);
}

private class DispLocListener implements LocationListener {

    @Override
    public void onLocationChanged(Location location) {
        // update TextViews
        tvLatitude.setText(Double.toString(location.getLatitude()));
        tvLongitude.setText(Double.toString(location.getLongitude()));
    }

    @Override
    public void onProviderDisabled(String provider) {
    }

    @Override
    public void onProviderEnabled(String provider) {
    }

    @Override
    public void onStatusChanged(String provider, int status, Bundle extras) {
    }
}
}
```

Our onCreate method creates an instance of DispLocListener and requests that the LocationManager update it as needed using requestLocationUpdates. This method takes four parameters:

String provider
> Which location provider to use. We assume GPS is available in this case.

long minTime
> Minimum update time, in milliseconds. The LocationManager will wait at least this long between updates. Here's an opportunity to tune your application for battery life: more frequent updates mean more battery usage.

float minDistance
> Minimum distance, in meters, required to trigger an update. The Location Manager will update us only if we've moved at least this far since the last update.

LocationListener listener
> The name of the listener method to call when there is an update. This is the DispLocListener instance we just created.

Finally, we want to add the onPause and onResume code to turn location updates off when we're not actually displaying on the user's screen, and turn them back on when we are:

```
/**
 *  Turn off location updates if we're paused
 */
@Override
public void onPause() {
    super.onPause();
    lm.removeUpdates(locListenD);
}

/**
 * Resume location updates when we're resumed
 */
@Override
public void onResume() {
    super.onResume();
    lm.requestLocationUpdates("gps", 30000L, 10.0f, locListenD);
}
```

Updating the Emulated Location

While developing and debugging an application like the one shown in the preceding section, you're normally running on the emulator. It would be nice (maybe even essential) to be able to update the current location that the emulator uses as it's running your code. Such a mock location provider can get very fancy, but Android provides some built-in ways of updating the emulated location:

- The geo program built into the Android shell

- One-time updates via DDMS
- Tracks that are sequentially updated via DDMS

We'll look at each of these.

Using geo to update location

The geo utility is built into the Android image that runs on the emulator. It has a number of capabilities and can be used, for instance, to inject a mock location. Do this by telnetting to the emulator console and using the geo fix command like this:

`geo fix`

> You can use the `geo fix` command to send a location to Android by telnetting to the console of the emulated Android. The `LocationProvider` will then use this as the current location.

```
telnet localhost 5554
Android Console: type 'help' for a list of commands
OK
geo fix -122.842232 38.411908 0
OK
```

The three parameters passed to the `geo fix` command are:

longitude
> Specified in decimal

latitude
> Also specified in decimal

altitude
> Specified in meters

Using DDMS to update location

In Chapter 1, we discussed the Dalvik Debug Monitor Server (DDMS). Here we will discuss two features of this tool related to location updates. The Emulator Control pane of the DDMS screen provides several ways to control the running emulator. After switching to the DDMS perspective (click on DDMS in the upper right of the Eclipse window) you should see the Emulator Control pane in the middle left of the DDMS window (Figure 15-1). You will probably have to scroll down in that pane to see the controls related to Location Controls.

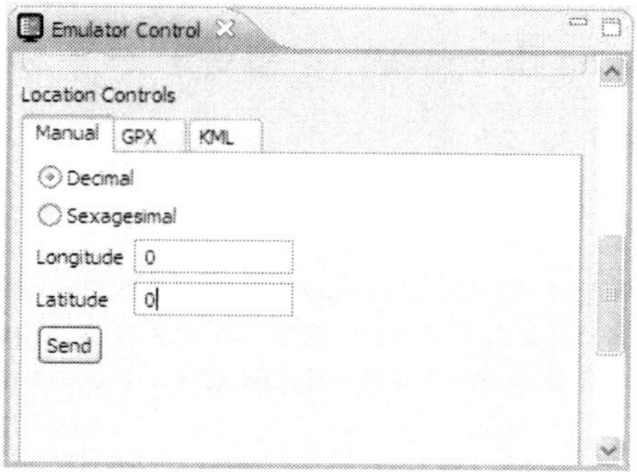

Figure 15-1. DDMS Emulator Control pane

To send a one-time update of a location to the emulator, just enter the longitude and latitude in the appropriate boxes and click Send.

If you click on either the GPX or KML tab, you will be able to load a GPX or KML file that describes a path, as shown in Figure 15-2. Here we've already loaded the file *OR.kml*, which is included on the website for this book. It traces a path near O'Reilly headquarters in Sebastopol, California.

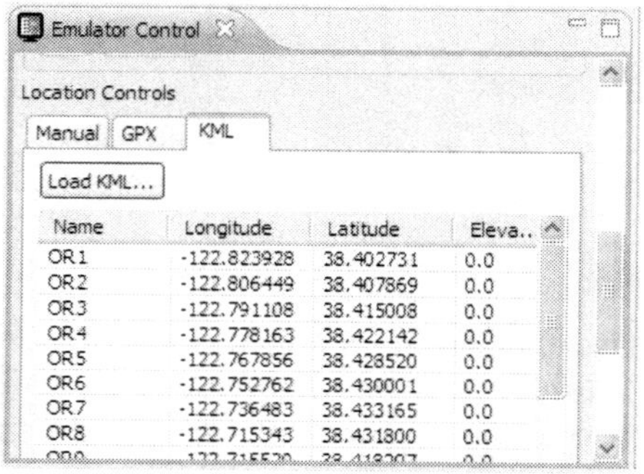

Figure 15-2. DDMS emulator with KML location updates

You can create GPX tracks with many GPS navigation software tools, and KML tracks with Google Earth or many other navigation programs. The *OR.kml* file was generated by plotting a series of Google Earth placemarks and concatenating them together into a single file. Here's an excerpt of *OR.kml*:

```xml
<?xml version="1.0" encoding="UTF-8"?>
<kml xmlns="http://earth.google.com/kml/2.2">
<Document>
    <name>OR1.kml</name>
    <StyleMap id="msn_ylw-pushpin">
```

```
        <Pair>
            <key>normal</key>
            <styleUrl>#sn_ylw-pushpin</styleUrl>
        </Pair>
        <Pair>
            <key>highlight</key>
            <styleUrl>#sh_ylw-pushpin</styleUrl>
        </Pair>
    </StyleMap>
    <Style id="sh_ylw-pushpin">
        <IconStyle>
            <scale>1.3</scale>
            <Icon>
             <href>http://maps.google.com/mapfiles/kml/pushpin/ylw-pushpin.png</href>
            </Icon>
            <hotSpot x="20" y="2" xunits="pixels" yunits="pixels"/>
        </IconStyle>
        <ListStyle>
        </ListStyle>
    </Style>
    <Style id="sn_ylw-pushpin">
        <IconStyle>
            <scale>1.1</scale>
            <Icon>
             <href>http://maps.google.com/mapfiles/kml/pushpin/ylw-pushpin.png</href>
            </Icon>
            <hotSpot x="20" y="2" xunits="pixels" yunits="pixels"/>
        </IconStyle>
        <ListStyle>
        </ListStyle>
    </Style>
    <Placemark>
        <name>OR1</name>
        <LookAt>
            <longitude>-122.7583711698369</longitude>
            <latitude>38.38922415809942</latitude>
            <altitude>0</altitude>
            <range>14591.7166300043</range>
            <tilt>0</tilt>
            <heading>0.04087372005871314</heading>
            <altitudeMode>relativeToGround</altitudeMode>
        </LookAt>
        <styleUrl>#msn_ylw-pushpin</styleUrl>
        <Point>
            <coordinates>-122.8239277647483,38.40273084940345,0</coordinates>
        </Point>
    </Placemark>
    <Placemark>
        <name>OR2</name>
        <LookAt>
            <longitude>-122.7677364592949</longitude>
            <latitude>38.3819544049429</latitude>
            <altitude>0</altitude>
            <range>11881.3330990845</range>
            <tilt>0</tilt>
```

```
          <heading>-8.006283077460853e-010</heading>
          <altitudeMode>relativeToGround</altitudeMode>
      </LookAt>
      <styleUrl>#msn_ylw-pushpin</styleUrl>
      <Point>
          <coordinates>-122.8064486052584,38.40786910573772,0</coordinates>
      </Point>
  </Placemark>
  <Placemark>
      <name>OR3</name>
      <LookAt>
          <longitude>-122.7677364592949</longitude>
          <latitude>38.3819544049429</latitude>
          <altitude>0</altitude>
          <range>11881.3330990845</range>
          <tilt>0</tilt>
          <heading>-8.006283077460853e-010</heading>
          <altitudeMode>relativeToGround</altitudeMode>
      </LookAt>
      <styleUrl>#msn_ylw-pushpin</styleUrl>
      <Point>
          <coordinates>-122.7911077944045,38.41500788727795,0</coordinates>
      </Point>
  </Placemark>
  ...
```

StreetView

Prior to Android 2.3 the Google Maps API library had a `setStreetView(boolean)` method with the `MapView`. However, this is now deprecated (the method is a no-op method) and today Google encourages the use of its StreetView app. The Google StreetView application is provided in most Android phones. If it is not preinstalled it is available for download from the Android Market.

To use the StreetView app, as with other applications, generate an intent with an appropriate `URI` and then use it to launch the `Activity`. Here is the `URI` to launch the StreetView application (note that the `cbll` parameter is required but `cbp` and `mz` are optional):

```
google.streetview:cbll=lat,lng&cbp=1,yaw,,pitch,zoom&mz=mapZoom
```

The specific variables within the `Uri` are defined as follows:

- `lat`: Latitude
- `lng`: Longitude
- `yaw`: Panorama center-of-view horizontally in degrees clockwise from North (the two commas that follow must be kept for backward compatibility)
- `pitch`: Panorama center-of-view vertically in degrees from −90 to 90 (up to down)
- `zoom`: Panorama zoom; 1.0 = normal, 2.0 = 2x, 3.0 = 4x
- `mapZoom`: The zoom amount for the map itself

An example of setting up and launching the `streetView` intent follows.

```
String uri = "google.streetview:cbll=42.352299,-71.063979&cbp=1,0,,0,1.0&mz=12";
Intent streetView = new Intent(android.content.Intent.ACTION_VIEW, Uri.parse(uri));
startActivity(streetView);
```

Multimedia

In today's world of converging technologies, the mobile phone is used for a variety of tasks beyond simple voice calls. Multimedia capabilities, or the playing and recording of audio and video, is one such significant task that many users find to be of great value. Take a quick look around and you will find people using the phone as a means to enjoy a variety of programs as well as share self-recorded media among friends. Android provides the APIs to easily access this capability as well as embed multimedia and its manipulation directly within an application.

Audio and Video

Android supports playback of most popular audio and video formats. It also lets you record some formats. Recordings are stored in files, and can optionally be put in a persistent media store. The MediaStore is the content provider within Android that enables the storing and sharing of media data such as images, video, and audio. Once placed within this content provider, metadata associated with the media files becomes available for other applications to use.

As of this writing, most Android devices currently on the market support the following audio and video formats. Note that device makers can add support for other formats not listed here.

Audio

        AAC LC/LTP *
        HE-AACv1 (AAC+)
        HE-AACv2 (enhanced AAC+)
        AMR-NB *
        AMR-WB *
        MP3
        FLAC (Android 3.1+)
        MIDI
        Ogg Vorbis

PCM/WAVE

Video

H.263 *
H.264 AVC * (encode Android 3.0+)
MPEG-4 SP
VP8 (Android 2.3.3+)

The asterisk (*) indicates the formats for which encoding is available. For all others, only decoding is possible.

Check the Developers site at *http://developer.android.com/guide/appendix/media-formats.html* for further details and changes.

Playing Audio and Video

Android provides a standard means to play audio and video: the `MediaPlayer` class. For audio content, you can also play back raw data, which is useful in sophisticated applications where you generate the audio dynamically.

A `MediaPlayer` goes through several states during its life cycle:

Idle
> The `MediaPlayer` is instantiated.

Initialized
> The media source is set.

Preparing
> The `MediaPlayer` is preparing the media source for playback.

Prepared
> The `MediaPlayer` is prepared for playback.

Started
> Playback is in progress.

Paused
> Playback has been paused.

Playback Completed
> Playback of source is done (the playback can be started again).

Stopped
> The `MediaPlayer` is no longer prepared to play the source.

End
> The `MediaPlayer` is no more, and all associated resources are released.

For details on these states, view the state diagram provided on the Developers site at *http://developer.android.com/reference/android/media/MediaPlayer.html#StateDiagram*. To get started with `MediaPlayer`, it's useful at this point to view it as a series of steps in your application:

1. Create a `MediaPlayer` instance through the `create()` method (idle state).
2. Initialize the `MediaPlayer` with the media source to play (initialized state).
3. Prepare the `MediaPlayer` for playback through the `prepare()` method (preparing and prepared states).
4. Play the `MediaPlayer` through the `start()` method (started state).
5. During playback, if desired, you can pause, stop, or replay the `MediaPlayer` (started, paused, playback completed, and stopped states).
6. Once playback is finished, make sure to release the `MediaPlayer`'s associated resources by calling `release()` (end state).

The following sections provide more detail.

Audio Playback

Audio can be played through two methods, `MediaPlayer` and `AudioTrack`. `MediaPlayer` is the standard, simple way to do playback. Its data must be in a file or be stream-based. `AudioTrack`, in contrast, provides direct access to raw audio in memory.

MediaPlayer audio playback

When you first start using `MediaPlayer`, you should determine whether a file placed within the application's resources is to be used. If so, `MediaPlayer` has a convenient static method that will set up the data source and prepare the player:

```
MediaPlayer mediaplayer = MediaPlayer.create(this, R.raw.example);
```

If you are not using an application resource, such as referencing an audio file residing on the filesystem (SD card and the like) or on a website (e.g., *http://<SomeServer>/<SomeAudioFile>.mp3*), you'll have to manually set up and call your data source. You can take the data from a URI through a call to:

```
setDataSource(context, uri)
```

The context in the first argument is a means for the `MediaPlayer` to access the resources of the application itself, and thus be able to resolve the URI. Either the application or the activities context will do.

The alternative is to specify an absolute file path through:

```
setDataSource(path)
```

API version 9 lets you attach some auxiliary effects (such as reverb) to the player. Set any effects you want while setting the data source, before calling `prepare()`:

```
MediaPlayer mediaplayer = new MediaPlayer();

// Uri mediaReference = "http://someUriToaMediaFile.mp3";
// mediaplayer.setDataSource(this, mediaReference);

// use absolute path
mediaplayer.setDataSource("/sdcard/somefile.mp3");

// prepare mediaplayer
mediaplayer.prepare();
```

Once the MediaPlayer is prepared, you can play it:

```
mediaplayer.start();
```

During play, the player can be paused or stopped. When in the paused state, it may be unpaused simply by calling start() again. Once the MediaPlayer is stopped, you can't start it again without resetting it through the reset() method, reinitializing it with the data source as shown earlier, and issuing prepare(). However, look at the following:

```
mediaplayer.pause();    // pausing
mediaplayer.start();    // going from pause to play

mediaplayer.stop();     // stopping

...

// to be able to play again reset must be called
mediaplayer.reset();
// now the media player must be reinitialized to play again
```

While the MediaPlayer is playing, you can track its current position in the file through getCurrentPosition(). This returns the amount of time played through in the file, in millisecond units:

```
mediaplayer.getCurrentPosition();
```

Once the MediaPlayer is no longer needed, make sure to release it so that the resources are cleaned up and made available for the system:

```
mediaplayer.release();
```

AudioTrack audio playback

AudioTrack provides a much more direct method of playing audio. The following example shows the parameters required to set up an AudioTrack:

```
File mediafile = new File(mediaFilePath);
short[] audio = new short[(int) (mediafile.length()/2)];

// read in file and fill up audio[]

AudioTrack audiotrack = new AudioTrack(
                        // stream type
                AudioManager.STREAM_MUSIC,
                        // frequency
```

```
11025,
                // channel config–mono, stereo, etc.
AudioFormat.CHANNEL_CONFIGURATION_MONO,
                // audio encoding
AudioFormat.ENCODING_PCM_16BIT,
                // length
audio.length,
                // mode
AudioTrack.MODE_STREAM
);
```

The `AudioTrack` method provides the type of audio stream (music, ringtone, alarm, voice call, etc.), the sample rate in Hertz (44100, 22050, 11025), the audio configuration (mono or stereo), the audio format/encoding, the length of the audio in number of bytes, and the mode (static or stream). Android's `AudioTrack`, once configured, will automatically know how to interface with the hardware on the device, thus providing a painless experience.

To play the audio, issue the `play()` method and write the data out to the hardware:

```
// start playing state
audiotrack.play();

// write audio to hardware
audiotrack.write(audio, 0, audio.length);
```

To pause the track, utilize the `pause()` method:

```
// pause
audiotrack.pause();
```

To stop playing the track, set it to the stopped state. If you don't need the track anymore, release it. Otherwise, to replay the audio, you must reinitialize it:

```
// stop
audiotrack.stop();

// release all resources
audiotrack.release();
```

Video Playback

Video playback, unlike audio playback, can use only the `MediaPlayer`. There is no video equivalent of `AudioTrack`. Video uses the `MediaPlayer` similarly to audio files, but you must additionally specify a view (called a *surface*) on which the video can be displayed. Android offers a convenient control that includes its own surface: the `VideoView` view. An example of its use follows. It includes the addition of an optional controller that lets the user control the playback through a simple interface that includes buttons to start, stop, and pause the playback, as well as a seek bar to skip forward or back within the video's playback progress.

```
// create the view (in this case it is already included in the layout resource)
VideoView videoview = (VideoView) findViewById(R.id.videoview);
videoview.setKeepScreenOn(true);

// used if streaming
if (videouri != null) videoview.setVideoURI(videouri);
// absolute path if it is a file
else videoview.setVideoPath(videopath);

// let's add a media control so we can control the playback
mediacontroller = new MediaController(this);
mediacontroller.setAnchorView(videoview);
videoview.setMediaController(mediacontroller);
if (videoview.canSeekForward())
  videoview.seekTo(videoview.getDuration()/2);

// start the playback
videoview.start();
```

Recording Audio and Video

The standard class that supports recording is the `MediaRecorder`. Much like the `Media Player`, it passes through various states during its life cycle. The states are as follows (for more details, view the state diagram provided by the Developers site, at *http:// developer.android.com/reference/android/media/MediaRecorder.html*):

Initial
> The `MediaRecorder` class is instantiated.

Initialized
> The `MediaRecorder` is ready to be used.

DataSource Configured
> The media source (where the output will be placed) is configured.

Prepared
> The `MediaRecorder` is prepared to record.

Recording
> Recording is underway.

Released
> All resources are released.

To utilize the `MediaRecorder`, some permissions may need to be set in the manifest:

- To enable video recording, enable `RECORD_VIDEO` and the `CAMERA`:

    ```
    <uses-permission android:name="android.permission.RECORD_VIDEO"/>
    <uses-permission android:name="android.permission.CAMERA"/>
    ```

- To record audio, enable `RECORD_AUDIO`:

    ```
    <uses-permission android:name="android.permission.RECORD_AUDIO"/>
    ```

Audio Recording

There are three methods to record audio. The `MediaRecorder` is the standard method; using an `Intent` is the simplest method; and the `AudioRecorder` can be used to record directly from hardware buffers.

MediaRecorder audio recording

First, initialize the `MediaRecorder`. Then set the data source information (the audio input source, the output format, the encoding type, where the file is to be recorded to, etc.). Starting with version 8, you can set the bit rate and sampling rate. Once all this is done, call the `prepare()` method:

```
// initialize the MediaRecorder
MediaRecorder mediarecorder = new MediaRecorder();

// configure the data source
    // the source of the audio input
    mediarecorder.setAudioSource(MediaRecorder.AudioSource.MIC);
    // output format
    mediarecorder.setOutputFormat(MediaRecorder.OutputFormat.THREE_GPP);
    // encoding
    mediarecorder.setAudioEncoder(MediaRecorder.AudioEncoder.AMR_NB);
    // use absolute path to file where output is stored
    mediarecorder.setOutputFile("/sdcard/audiorecordexample.3gpp");

    // prepare to record
    mediarecorder.prepare();
```

Then when the recoding needs to start, call the `start()` method:

```
mediarecorder.start();
```

When the recording needs to be stopped, call the `stop()` method. If you want to continue recording after this, call `reset()` to force the `MediaRecorder` back to the idle state. Then reconfigure the data source to prepare the `MediaRecorder` again:

```
mediarecorder.stop();
...
mediarecorder.reset();
```

Once the `MediaRecorder` is no longer needed, make sure to release it:

```
mediarecorder.release();
```

The following example is a convenient little app that uses the code we developed to provide a "record" button for the user. When the button is clicked, the `record` method executes with the file path already referenced. A "stop" button is then made visible and the "record" button becomes invisible. When the "stop" button is clicked, the `stop Record` method is called and the "record" button comes back.

```java
public class AudioRecorder extends Activity {
  private MediaRecorder mediarecorder;

  public void onCreate(Bundle savedInstanceState) {
      super.onCreate(savedInstanceState);

      setContentView(R.layout.audiorecorderlayout);

      ImageButton recordbutton = (ImageButton) findViewById(R.id.record);
      recordbutton.setOnClickListener(new OnClickListener() {
          public void onClick(View v) {
              record("/sdcard/audiorecordexample.3gpp");
          }
      });

      ImageButton stopbutton = (ImageButton) findViewById(R.id.stop);
      stopbutton.setOnClickListener(new OnClickListener() {
          public void onClick(View v) {
              stopRecord();
          }
      });
  }

  private void record(String filePath) {
          try {
              File mediafile = new File(filePath);
              if(mediafile.exists()) {
                  mediafile.delete();
              }
              mediafile = null;

              // record button goes away
              ImageButton button = (ImageButton) findViewById(R.id.record);
              button.setVisibility(View.GONE);
              // stop button shows up
              ImageButton stopbutton = (ImageButton) findViewById(R.id.stop);
              stopbutton.setVisibility(View.VISIBLE);

              // set up media recorder
              if(mediarecorder == null) mediarecorder = new MediaRecorder();
              mediarecorder.setAudioSource(MediaRecorder.AudioSource.MIC);
              mediarecorder.setOutputFormat(MediaRecorder.OutputFormat.THREE_GPP);
              mediarecorder.setAudioEncoder(MediaRecorder.AudioEncoder.AMR_NB);
              mediarecorder.setOutputFile(filePath);

              // prepare media recorder
              mediarecorder.prepare();
              // start media recorder
              mediarecorder.start();
          } catch (Exception e) {
              e.printStackTrace();
          }
      }
  }
}
```

```
        private void stopRecord() {
                // stop media recorder
            mediarecorder.stop();
                // reset media recorder
            mediarecorder.reset();

            // record button shows up
            ImageButton button = (ImageButton) findViewById(R.id.record);
            button.setVisibility(View.VISIBLE);
            // stop button goes away
            ImageButton stopbutton = (ImageButton) findViewById(R.id.stop);
            stopbutton.setVisibility(View.GONE);
        }
    }
```

Intent audio recording

Recording via Intent is the easiest of the methods. Just construct the Media Store.Audio.Media.RECORD_SOUND_ACTION intent, and start it using the startActivity ForResult() from within the Activity. This will launch the default audio recorder that is provided in most Android devices and proceeds to record some audio:

```
Intent intent = new Intent(MediaStore.Audio.Media.RECORD_SOUND_ACTION);
startActivityForResult(intent, 1); // intent and requestCode of 1
```

Once the recording is complete and the audio recorder finishes, your Activity that originated the call to startActivityForResult() will be brought back to the fore. When that occurs, your Activity's onActivityResult() method will be triggered with the requestCode you provided (in this case, 1), a result code (OK or error), and an intent carrying the URI referencing the recorded audio file:

```
protected void onActivityResult(int requestCode, int resultCode, Intent intent) {
    // is it our requestCode?
  if (requestCode == 1) {
      // is the resultCode OK?
    if (resultCode == RESULT_OK) {
          // lets get the uri
        Uri audioUri = intent.getData();
          // lets play the uri or do something with it.
        playAudio(audioUri);
      }
    }
  }
```

AudioRecorder audio recording

In parallel with AudioTrack, AudioRecorder provides a much more direct recording experience:

```
short[] buffer = new short[10000];

recorder = new AudioRecord(    // source to record from
                MediaRecorder.AudioSource.MIC,
                        // frequency
```

```
                11025,
                                // channel config-mono, stereo, etc.
                AudioFormat.CHANNEL_CONFIGURATION_MONO,
                                // audio encoding
                AudioFormat.ENCODING_PCM_16BIT,
                                // buffer size
                buffer.length
        );
```

The AudioRecord method provides the type of source to record audio from (Mic, Camcorder [mic facing the same direction as the camera], or VoiceCall), the sample rate in Hertz (44100, 22050, or 11025), the audio configuration (mono or stereo), the audio format/encoding, and the length of the buffer in number of bytes. Note that the size of this buffer determines how long an AudioRecord can record before "over-running" data that has not been read yet. Data should be read from the audio hardware in chunks of sizes less than the total recording buffer size. Android's AudioRecord, once configured, will automatically know how to interface with the hardware on the device, thus providing a painless experience.

To start recording, set the AudioRecord's state to the Record state and read data repeatedly from the hardware buffer:

```
recorder.startRecording();
while(recordablestate) {
    try {
        // read in up to buffer size
        int readBytes = recorder.read(buffer, 0, buffer.length);

        // do something with the bytes that are read
    } catch (Exception t) {
        recordablestate = false;
    }
}
```

To stop recording, set the AudioRecord's state to Stop. If you no longer wish to record, do not forget to release all resources associated with the recording. Otherwise, you may call startRecording() to start recording again:

```
    // stop recording
recorder.stop();

    // release recording resources
recorder.release();
```

Video Recording

You can record video in two ways: by using the MediaRecorder or by using an Intent. Raw recording is not supported, as it is for audio.

MediaRecorder video recording

The process for recording video with the `MediaRecorder` is much the same as that for recording audio: initialize the `MediaRecorder`, prepare the data source, and start the `MediaRecorder`. You can offer the user a preview window so that he can preview the video being captured, by providing a surface as shown earlier for playing back video. Generally, a `VideoView` is used:

```
// initialize
MediaRecorder mediarecorder = new MediaRecorder();

// set data source
mediarecorder.setAudioSource(MediaRecorder.AudioSource.MIC);
mediarecorder.setVideoSource(MediaRecorder.VideoSource.CAMERA);
mediarecorder.setOutputFormat(MediaRecorder.OutputFormat.DEFAULT);
mediarecorder.setAudioEncoder(MediaRecorder.AudioEncoder.DEFAULT);
mediarecorder.setVideoEncoder(MediaRecorder.VideoEncoder.DEFAULT);
mediarecorder.setOutputFile("/sdcard/someexamplevideo.mp4");

// provide a surface to show the preview in.  in this case a VideoView is used
videoview = (VideoView) findViewById(R.id.videosurface);
SurfaceHolder holder = videoview.getHolder();
mediarecorder.setPreviewDisplay(holder.getSurface());

// prepare
mediarecorder.prepare();

// start recording
mediarecorder.start();
```

Intent video recording

Intent-based video recording is like using an intent to record audio. The intent to use is `MediaStore.ACTION_VIDEO_CAPTURE`, and the resultant data is the URI of the video file.

Stored Media Content

Even when media is saved to a file (as in the case of recording), the media file is not immediately available to other applications. To make the file available, you must insert it into the MediaStore. The MediaStore is a content provider dedicated to the storage and retrieval of media data (images, video, audio) with the device. To store a reference to the file, create a `ContentValues` object and insert it into the appropriate MediaStore content provider. The following example inserts an audio file with appropriate metadata, such as title and artist:

```
// generate ContentValues and add appropriate metadata values

ContentValues content = new ContentValues();

// VERY IMPORTANT!  Must reference the absolute path of the data.
content.put(MediaStore.MediaColumns.DATA, "/sdcard/AudioExample.3gpp");
```

```java
content.put(MediaStore.MediaColumns.TITLE, "AudioRecordExample");
content.put(MediaStore.MediaColumns.MIME_TYPE, "audio/amr");
content.put(MediaStore.Audio.Media.ARTIST, "Me");
content.put(MediaStore.Audio.Media.IS_MUSIC, true);

// get the Content Resolver
ContentResolver resolve = getContentResolver();

// insert into the content resolver
Uri uri = resolve.insert(MediaStore.Audio.Media.EXTERNAL_CONTENT_URI, content);

// announce to everyone that cares that it was inserted
sendBroadcast(new Intent(Intent.ACTION_MEDIA_SCANNER_SCAN_FILE, uri));
```

Sensors, NFC, Speech, Gestures, and Accessibility

Thanks to advances in technology, both the environment and the user can interact with devices in a variety of ways, from external sensors that can detect when a device has changed orientation within an environment, to touch-screen adaptations that enable complex gestures to trigger an event within the device. Android provides APIs that enable the developer to access these sensors and the user to interact with these devices in a variety of ways. In this chapter, we will explore some of these APIs—sensors, NFC (Near Field Communication), the Gesture libraries, and accessibility.

Sensors

The modern smartphone provides more than just the ability to send and receive communication in various forms. The addition of external sensors that can report information about the environment the phone is in has made the phone more powerful and useful for the user as well as the developer. Starting with Android 1.5 (API level 3), a standard set of sensors are available. The physical sensors include, but are not limited to, accelerometers that measure acceleration along various axes, gyroscopes that measure rotational change around some axes, magnetic field sensors that sense the strength of magnetic fields along a set of axes, a light sensor that measures the amount of ambient light, a proximity sensor that measures external objects' proximity to the device, temperature sensors that measure ambient temperature, and pressure sensors that act as a barometer. The direct measured value of each sensor is considered a raw measurement, and thus the associative sensor is a "raw sensor." With some of the sensors, the measurements can be combined or collected and calculations can be made over the collected measurements to show a more complex measurement. For example, by integrating the gyroscope's measurements of rotational change over time you can measure the rotational vector. This sort of complex measurement is often derived from a composite sensor.

To access a sensor or set of sensors, Android provides a convenient system service called the SensorManager. This can be accessed via the `getSystemService()` method of the Context with the argument of `Context.SENSOR_SERVICE`. With the SensorManager you then can get a specific sensor via the `getDefaultSensor()` method.

However, a composite sensor may sometimes be returned, so if you wish to get access to the raw sensor and its associated data, you should use `getSensorList()`:

```
SensorManager mngr =
    (SensorManager) context.getSystemService(Context.SENSOR_SERVICE);
// getting the default accelerometer
Sensor accel = mngr.getDefaultSensor (Sensor.TYPE_ACCELEROMETER);
// getting the raw accelerometer
List<Sensor> list = mngr.getSensorList(Sensor.TYPE_ACCELEROMETER);
```

Once you get a sensor or set of sensors, you can actually enable them and start getting their data by registering a listener against the sensors. Data should begin to come in at the rate you give as an argument. This rate can be `SENSOR_DELAY_NORMAL`, `SENSOR_DELAY_UI` (a rate appropriate for basic UI interaction), `SENSOR_DELAY_GAME` (a high rate that many games would find sufficient), `SENSOR_DELAY_FASTEST` ("give it to me as fast as you can"), or a specified delay between events in units of milliseconds:

```
SensorEventListener listener = new SensorEventListener() {
    @Override
    public void onAccuracyChanged(Sensor sensor, int accuracy) { }

    @Override
    public void onSensorChanged(SensorEvent event) { }
};

// registering a listener
mngr.registerListener(listener, sensor, SensorManager.SENSOR_DELAY_UI);
```

The two methods in a `SensorEventListener`—`onAccuracyChanged()` and `onSensorChanged()`—are called when data from the sensor in question is available. `onAccuracyChanged()` is called whenever a change to the degree of error or accuracy with the sensor occurs. The `onSensorChanged()` method is perhaps the more interesting method, in that the data the sensor is measuring is passed to it wrapped in a `SensorEvent` object.

It is incredibly important to unregister the listener and thus disable the sensor when you no longer need it (e.g., when an activity is paused); otherwise, the device will continue to use resources and drain power. The system will not take care of this for you even when the screen is turned off:

```
mngr.unregisterListener(listener);
```

While the sensor is on, `SensorEvent` is passed to the listener via the `onSensorChanged()` method. It is in this `SensorEvent`'s values that each sensor type differs.

Position

The phone's coordinate system is based on the screen and default orientation of the phone. The x-, y-, and z-axes are as shown in Figure 17-1 and work as follows:

x-axis
>   Horizontal, with positive values to the right and negative values to the left

y-axis
>   Vertical, with positive values upward and negative values downward

z-axis
>   Positive values coming out of the screen toward the front and negative values behind the screen (the z zero point rests on the screen)

When the user moves the phone, the axes follow the phone's movement and do not swap places.

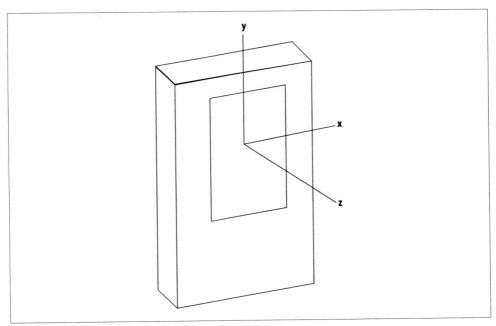

Figure 17-1. Phone coordinate system

The accuracy and variance of the various sensors depend on the quality of hardware. In many cases, significant levels of jitter/noise will need to be eliminated (through the use of low-pass filters, for example). The type of filter and its construction is up to the developer to design and create.

Accelerometer

The accelerometer measures the acceleration applied to the device and returns values along the three axes (value[0] for the x-axis, value[1] for the y-axis, and value[2] for the z-axis). The values are in SI units (m/s^2). It is important to note that the force of gravity is not eliminated from the values returned. Thus, when the device is sitting on a table (say, face up) value[2] will read 9.81 m/s^2.

Because it became a fairly common need to eliminate or determine the force of gravity along the various axes, Android 2.3 (API level 9) also supports a linear acceleration sensor and a gravity sensor, discussed later in this chapter.

Gyroscope

The gyroscope measures the angular speed or rate of rotation around the three axes. All values are in radians/second. Rotation is positive in the counterclockwise direction. That is, an observer looking at the device screen normally—located at 0, 0, 100 in device coordinates—would report positive rotation if the device appeared to be rotating counterclockwise. Because this is angular speed, to calculate an angle you must integrate the values over a period of time:

```
private static final float NS2S = 1.0f / 1000000000.0f;
private float timestamp;
private float[] angle;

@Override
public void onSensorChanged(SensorEvent event) {
    float gyrox = event.values[0];
    float gyroy = event.values[1];
    float gyroz = event.values[2];

    // here we integrate over time to figure out the rotational angle around
    each axis if (timestamp != 0) {
        final float dT = (event.timestamp - timestamp) * NS2S;
        angle[0] += gyrox * dT;
        angle[1] += gyroy * dT;
        angle[2] += gyroz * dT;
    }

    timestamp = event.timestamp;
}
```

Because this is a common problem set, Android 2.3 (API level 9) supports a rotation vector sensor, which we discuss in the following section.

Rotation vector

The rotation vector, in Android 2.3 and later versions, represents the orientation of the device as a combination of an angle and an axis, in which the device has rotated through an angle Θ around an axis <x, y, z>. Even though this can be calculated via the gyroscope, many developers ended up doing this often enough that Google provided the rotation vector to help simplify the use case.

The three elements of the rotation vector are <x*sin(Θ/2), y*sin(Θ/2), and z*sin(Θ/2)>, such that the magnitude of the rotation vector is equal to sin(Θ/2) and the direction of the rotation vector is equal to the direction of the axis of rotation. The three elements of the rotation vector are equal to the last three components of a unit quaternion <cos(Θ/2), x*sin(Θ/2), y*sin(Θ/2), and z*sin(Θ/2)>. Elements of the rotation vector are unitless.

Linear acceleration

Another sensor type is supported by Android 2.3 (API level 9) to simplify a common calculation with the use of the accelerometer. The value sent is a three-dimensional vector indicating acceleration along each device axis, not including gravity. This means the values are the result of linear acceleration on each axis minus the effects of gravity along that axis. This makes it easier to filter out gravity's constant effects for those of us using the phone while on Earth. All values have units of m/s^2.

Gravity

The values resulting from this sensor make up a three-dimensional vector indicating the direction and magnitude of gravity. This too is an Android 2.3 (API level 9) sensor that provides a common calculation. Units are m/s^2.

Other Sensors

Android also supports the following sensors:

Light
> This sensor provides a single-valued array (value[0]) that represents the ambient light level in SI lux units (lx).

Magnetic
> This sensor measures the ambient magnetic fields in microteslas (μT) along the x-, y-, and z-axes.

Pressure
> Not many devices provide this sensor. Those that do will provide the values in kilopascals (kPa) or mbar.

Proximity
> This sensor measures a single-valued array (value[0]) representing distance measured in centimeters (cm) to the sensor. In some cases, the proximity sensor may provide only a "near" (0) versus "far" (1) binary measurement. In that case, a distance equal to or greater than the sensor's `getMaximumRange()` value will return "far" and anything less than that will return "near."

Temperature

> This is another sensor that not many devices provide. This is the device's temperature. The values will be in centigrade (°C). Deprecated in Android 4.0 (API Level 14).

Ambient Temperature

> This is another sensor that not many devices provide. This is the ambient air temperature. The values will be in centigrade (°C). Supported Android 4.0 (API Level 14) and later.

Relative Humidity

> This is another sensor that not many devices provide. This is the ambient relative humidity. The values will be in percentages (%). Supported Android 4.0 (API Level 14) and later.

Near Field Communication (NFC)

Near Field Communication is a short-range (up to 20 cm), high-frequency, wireless communication technology. It is a standard that extends the Radio Frequency Identification (RFID) standard by combining the interface of a smartcard and a reader into a single device. This standard is primarily built for mobile phone use, and thus is attracting a lot of attention among vendors that are interested in contactless data transmission (such as credit card sales). The standard enables NFC to be used in three specific ways:

Card emulation

> The device is a contactless card (and thus can be read by other readers).

Reader mode

> The device can read RFID tags.

P2P mode

> Two devices can communicate back and forth and exchange data.

In Android 2.3 (API level 9), Google introduced the Reader Mode NFC functionality. Starting in Android 2.3.3 (API level 10), the ability to write data to an NFC tag and exchange data via P2P mode is also available.

NFC tags consist of data encoded in NFC Data Exchange Format (NDEF), a message format specified by the NFC Forum Type 2 Specification. Each NDEF message consists of one or more NDEF records. The official technical specification for NFC can be found at *http://www.nfc-forum.org/*. To develop and test an NFC reading application it is highly suggested that you get an NFC-compliant device (such as the Nexus S, at *http://www.google.com/phone/detail/nexus-s*) and an NFC-compliant tag.

To use NFC functionality in your application, you need to declare the following permission in your manifest:

```
<uses-permission android:name="android.permission.NFC" />
```

To restrict the installation of the application to devices that can use NFC, add the following to your manifest as well:

```
<uses-feature android:name="android.hardware.nfc" />
```

Reading a Tag

Reader mode is for receiving notices when an RFID/NFC tag is scanned. In Android 2.3 (API level 9), the only means to do this is to create an `Activity` that listens for the `android.nfc.action.TAG_DISCOVERED` intent, which is broadcast when a tag is read. Android 2.3.3 (API level 10) offers a more comprehensive means to receive this notice, following the process shown in Figure 17-2.

In Android 2.3.3 (API level 10) and later, when an NFC tag is discovered the tag object (a `Parcelable`) is placed into an `Intent` as an `EXTRA_TAG`. The system then begins to follow a logic flow to determine the best `Activity` to which to send the intent. This is designed to give a high probability of dispatching a tag to the correct activity without showing the user an activity chooser dialog (i.e., in a transparent manner), and thus prevent the connection between the tag and the device from being broken by unneeded user interaction. The first thing that is checked is whether there is an `Activity` in the foreground that has called the `enableForegroundDispatch()` method. If so, the intent is passed to the `Activity` and things stop there. If not, the system inspects the first `NdefRecord` in the first `NdefMessage` of the tag's data. If the `NdefRecord` is URI, Smart Poster, or MIME data, the system then checks for an `Activity` registered for the `ACTION_NDEF_DISCOVERED` intent (`android.nfc.action.NDEF_DISCOVERED`) with that type of data. If this exists, the `Activity` that matches (the narrower the match, the better) receives the intent and things stop there. If this is not the case, the system seeks an `Activity` that is registered for `ACTION_TECH_DISCOVERED` and that matches the specific set of technologies of the tag (again, the narrower the match, the better). If there is a match, the intent is passed to that `Activity` and everything is settled. However, should no `Activity` exist that passes the prior checks, the intent is finally passed as an `ACTION_TAG_DISCOVERED` action, much as Android 2.3 (API level 9) handles the tag.

To set up a foreground `Activity` to be the first to receive the tag, you must retrieve the NFC device adapter and call `enableForegroundDispatch` with the `Activity`'s context reference. The actual NFC device adapter is represented by the `NfcAdapter` class. To retrieve the actual adapter of the device, issue `getDefaultAdapter()` in Android 2.3 (API level 9) or `getDefaultAdapter(context)` in Android 2.3.3 (API level 10):

```
NfcAdapter adapter = NfcAdapter.getDefaultAdapter();

// --- for API 10 only
// NfcAdapter adapter = NfcAdapter.getDefaultAdapter(context);

if(adapter != null) {
        // true if enabled, false if not
    boolean enabled = adapter.isEnabled();
}
```

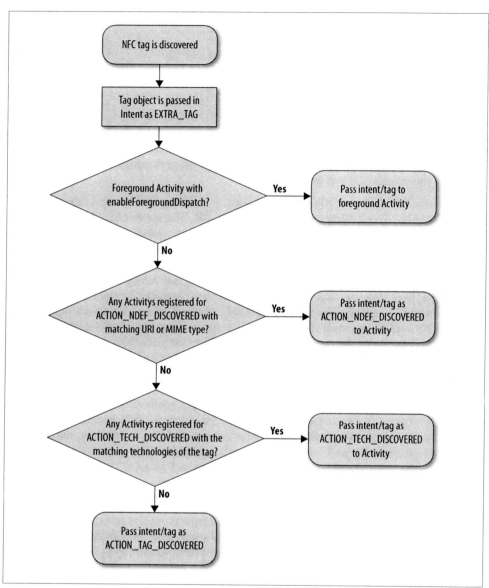

Figure 17-2. NFC tag flow in Android 2.3.3 (API level 10)

Once the NFC device adapter is retrieved, construct a PendingIntent and pass it to the enableForegroundDispatch() method. This method must be called from the main thread and only when the Activity is in the foreground (after onResume() has been called):

```
PendingIntent intent =
        PendingIntent.getActivity(this, 0,
```

```
        new Intent(this, getClass()).addFlags(Intent.FLAG_ACTIVITY_SINGLE_TOP),
        0);

NfcAdapter.getDefaultAdapter(this).enableForegroundDispatch(this, intent,
    null, null);
```

It is extremely important that when the Activity leaves the foreground (when onPause() is called) you call the disableForegroundDispatch() method:

```
@Override
protected void onPause() {
    super.onPause();
    if(NfcAdapter.getDefaultAdapter(this) != null)
        NfcAdapter.getDefaultAdapter(this).disableForegroundDispatch(this);
    }
}
```

In the case of registering an Activity for ACTION_NDEF_DISCOVERED, the Activity must have android.nfc.action.NDEF_DISCOVERED as an intent-filter and any specific data filters in the manifest file:

```
<activity android:name=".NFC233">
        <!-- listen for android.nfc.action.NDEF_DISCOVERED -->
        <intent-filter>
            <action android:name="android.nfc.action.NDEF_DISCOVERED"/>
            <data android:mimeType="text/*" />
        </intent-filter>
    </activity>
```

This goes for the TECH_DISCOVERED case as well (the following example also includes a metadata resource describing the specific technology that resides in the NFC tag that we are narrowing in on, such as NDEF content):

```
<activity android:name=".NFC233">
        <intent-filter>
            <action android:name="android.nfc.action.TECH_DISCOVERED" />
        </intent-filter>

        <meta-data android:name="android.nfc.action.TECH_DISCOVERED"
            android:resource="@xml/nfcfilter"
        />
</activity>
<?xml version="1.0" encoding="utf-8"?>
    <!-- capture anything using NfcF or with NDEF payloads-->
<resources xmlns:xliff="urn:oasis:names:tc:xliff:document:1.2">
    <tech-list>
        <tech>android.nfc.tech.NfcF</tech>
    </tech-list>

    <tech-list>
        <tech>android.nfc.tech.NfcA</tech>
        <tech>android.nfc.tech.MifareClassic</tech>
        <tech>android.nfc.tech.Ndef</tech>
    </tech-list>
</resources>
```

An example of registering for the `ACTION_TAG_DISCOVERED` intent would be written in the manifest file like this:

```
<!-- this will show up as a dialog when the nfc tag is scanned -->
<activity android:name=".NFC" android:theme="@android:style/Theme.Dialog">
    <intent-filter>
        <action android:name="android.nfc.action.TAG_DISCOVERED"/>
        <category android:name="android.intent.category.DEFAULT"/>
    </intent-filter>
</activity>
```

When a tag is read, the system broadcasts an intent with the payload as the associated data. In Android 2.3.3 (API level 10), a `Tag` object is also included as an `EXTRA_TAG`. This `Tag` object provides a means to retrieve the specific `TagTechnology` and to perform advanced operations (such as I/O). Be aware that `Arrays` passed to and returned by this class are not cloned, so be careful not to modify them:

```
Tag tag = (Tag) intent.getParcelableExtra(NfcAdapter.EXTRA_TAG);
```

In Android 2.3 (API level 9) and later, the ID of the tag is wrapped within the intent and keyed with the term "android.nfc.extra.ID" (`NfcAdapter.EXTRA_ID`) as a byte array:

```
byte[] byte_id = intent.getByteArrayExtra(NfcAdapter.EXTRA_ID);
```

This data is packaged up as an array of `Parcelable` objects (`NdefMessage`) keyed with the term "android.nfc.extra.NDEF_MESSAGES" (`NfcAdapter.EXTRA_NDEF_MESSAGES`):

```
Parcelable[] msgs =
    intent.getParcelableArrayExtra(NfcAdapter.EXTRA_NDEF_MESSAGES);
NdefMessage[] nmsgs = new NdefMessage[msgs.length];
for(int i=0;i<msgs.length;i++) {
    nmsgs[i] = (NdefMessage) msgs[i];
}
```

Within each `NdefMessage` is an array of `NdefRecord`. This record will always include a 3-bit TNF (type name format), the type of record, a unique ID, and the payload. For specifics look at the *NdefRecord* doc (*http://developer.android.com/reference/android/nfc/NdefRecord.html*). Currently there are several known types, of which we cover the four most common: TEXT, URI, SMART_POSTER, and ABSOLUTE_URI:

```
// enum of types we are interested in
private static enum NFCType {
    UNKNOWN, TEXT, URI, SMART_POSTER, ABSOLUTE_URI
}

private NFCType getTagType(final NdefMessage msg) {
    if(msg == null) return null;
    // we are only grabbing the first recognizable item

    for (NdefRecord record : msg.getRecords()) {
        if(record.getTnf() == NdefRecord.TNF_WELL_KNOWN) {
            if(Arrays.equals(record.getType(), NdefRecord.RTD_TEXT)) {
                return NFCType.TEXT;
            }
            if(Arrays.equals(record.getType(), NdefRecord.RTD_URI)) {
```

```
                return NFCType.URI;
            }
            if(Arrays.equals(record.getType(), NdefRecord.RTD_SMART_POSTER)) {
                return NFCType.SMART_POSTER;
            }
        } else if(record.getTnf() == NdefRecord.TNF_ABSOLUTE_URI) {
            return NFCType.ABSOLUTE_URI;
        }
    }
    return null;
}
```

To read the payload of an NdefRecord.RTD_TEXT type, the first byte of the payload will define the status, and thus the encoding type of the text payload:

```
/*
 * the First Byte of the payload contains the "Status Byte Encodings" field,
 * per the NFC Forum "Text Record Type Definition" section 3.2.1.
 *
 * Bit_7 is the Text Encoding Field.
 * * if Bit_7 == 0 the the text is encoded in UTF-8
 * * else if Bit_7 == 1 then the text is encoded in UTF16
 * Bit_6 is currently always 0 (reserved for future use)
 * Bits 5 to 0 are the length of the IANA language code.
 */
private String getText(final byte[] payload) {
    if(payload == null) return null;
    try {
        String textEncoding = ((payload[0] & 0200) == 0) ? "UTF-8" : "UTF-16";
        int languageCodeLength = payload[0] & 0077;
        return new String(payload, languageCodeLength + 1,
                          payload.length - languageCodeLength - 1, textEncoding);
    } catch (Exception e) {
        e.printStackTrace();
    }
    return null;
}
```

When reading in the payload of a standard URI (NdefRecord.RTD_URI) type, the first byte of the payload defines the URI's prefix:

```
/**
 * NFC Forum "URI Record Type Definition"
 *
 * Conversion of prefix based on section 3.2.2 of the NFC Forum URI Record
 * Type Definition document.
 */
private String convertUriPrefix(final byte prefix) {
    if(prefix == (byte) 0x00) return "";
    else if(prefix == (byte) 0x01) return "http://www.";
    else if(prefix == (byte) 0x02) return "https://www.";
    else if(prefix == (byte) 0x03) return "http://";
    else if(prefix == (byte) 0x04) return "https://";
    else if(prefix == (byte) 0x05) return "tel:";
    else if(prefix == (byte) 0x06) return "mailto:";
    else if(prefix == (byte) 0x07) return "ftp://anonymous:anonymous@";
```

```
            else if(prefix == (byte) 0x08) return "ftp://ftp.";
            else if(prefix == (byte) 0x09) return "ftps://";
            else if(prefix == (byte) 0x0A) return "sftp://";
            else if(prefix == (byte) 0x0B) return "smb://";
            else if(prefix == (byte) 0x0C) return "nfs://";
            else if(prefix == (byte) 0x0D) return "ftp://";
            else if(prefix == (byte) 0x0E) return "dav://";
            else if(prefix == (byte) 0x0F) return "news:";
            else if(prefix == (byte) 0x10) return "telnet://";
            else if(prefix == (byte) 0x11) return "imap:";
            else if(prefix == (byte) 0x12) return "rtsp://";
            else if(prefix == (byte) 0x13) return "urn:";
            else if(prefix == (byte) 0x14) return "pop:";
            else if(prefix == (byte) 0x15) return "sip:";
            else if(prefix == (byte) 0x16) return "sips:";
            else if(prefix == (byte) 0x17) return "tftp:";
            else if(prefix == (byte) 0x18) return "btspp://";
            else if(prefix == (byte) 0x19) return "btl2cap://";
            else if(prefix == (byte) 0x1A) return "btgoep://";
            else if(prefix == (byte) 0x1B) return "tcpobex://";
            else if(prefix == (byte) 0x1C) return "irdaobex://";
            else if(prefix == (byte) 0x1D) return "file://";
            else if(prefix == (byte) 0x1E) return "urn:epc:id:";
            else if(prefix == (byte) 0x1F) return "urn:epc:tag:";
            else if(prefix == (byte) 0x20) return "urn:epc:pat:";
            else if(prefix == (byte) 0x21) return "urn:epc:raw:";
            else if(prefix == (byte) 0x22) return "urn:epc:";
            else if(prefix == (byte) 0x23) return "urn:nfc:";
            return null;
    }
```

In the case of an absolute URI (NdefRecord.TNF_ABSOLUTE_URI) type, the whole payload is encoded in UTF-8 and makes up the URI:

```
if(record.getTnf() == NdefRecord.TNF_ABSOLUTE_URI) {
    String uri = new String(record.getPayload(), Charset.forName("UTF-8");
}
```

The special Smart Poster (NdefRecord.RTD_SMART_POSTER) type consists of multiple subrecords of text or URI (or absolute URI) data:

```
private void getTagData(final NdefMessage msg) {
    if(Arrays.equals(record.getType(), NdefRecord.RTD_SMART_POSTER)) {
        try {
                // break out the subrecords
            NdefMessage subrecords = new NdefMessage(record.getPayload());
                // get the subrecords
            String fulldata = getSubRecordData(subrecords);
            System.out.println("SmartPoster: "+fulldata);
        } catch (Exception e) {
            e.printStackTrace();
        }
    }
}

// method to get subrecord data
```

```
    private String getSubRecordData(final NdefRecord[] records) {
        if(records == null || records.length < 1) return null;
        String data = "";
        for(NdefRecord record : records) {
            if(record.getTnf() == NdefRecord.TNF_WELL_KNOWN) {
                if(Arrays.equals(record.getType(), NdefRecord.RTD_TEXT)) {
                    data += getText(record.getPayload()) + "\n";
                }
                if(Arrays.equals(record.getType(), NdefRecord.RTD_URI)) {
                    data += getURI(record.getPayload()) + "\n";
                } else {
                    data += "OTHER KNOWN DATA\n";
                }
            } else if(record.getTnf() == NdefRecord.TNF_ABSOLUTE_URI) {
                data += getAbsoluteURI(record.getPayload()) + "\n";
            } else data += "OTHER UNKNOWN DATA\n";
        }
        return data;
    }
```

Writing to a Tag

As of Android 2.3.3 (API level 10), the ability to write data to a tag is available. To do this, the Tag object must be used to get the appropriate TagTechnology within the tag. NFC tags are based on a number of independently developed technologies and offer a wide range of capabilities. The TagTechnology implementations provide access to these different technologies and capabilities. In this case, the NDEF technology is needed to retrieve and modify the NdefRecords and NdefMessages in the tag:

```
// get the tag from the Intent
Tag mytag = (Tag) intent.getParcelableExtra(NfcAdapter.EXTRA_TAG);

// get the Ndef (TagTechnology) from the tag
Ndef ndefref = Ndef.get(mytag);
```

Note the following requirements when performing I/O operations with a Tag Technology:

- connect() must be called before using any other I/O operation.
- I/O operations may block, and should never be called on the main application thread.
- Only one TagTechnology can be connected at a time. Other calls to connect() will return an IOException.
- close() must be called after completing I/O operations with a TagTechnology, and it will cancel all other blocked I/O operations on other threads (including connect()) with an IOException.

Therefore, to write data to a tag, a connect() is called from within a thread that is separate from that of the main thread. Once this is done, isConnected() should be checked to verify that the connection has been established. If the connection is established, `writeNdefMessage()` with a constructed `NdefMessage` (containing at least one `NdefRecord`) may be called. Once the data is written, `close()` is called to cleanly terminate the process.

The full code to write a text record to a tag using its NDEF `TagTechnology` reference is as follows:

```
// pass in the Ndef TagTechnology reference and the text we wish to encode

private void writeTag(final Ndef ndefref, final String text) {
    if(ndefref == null || text == null || !ndefref.isWritable()) {
        return;
    }

    (new Thread() {
        public void run() {
            try {
                Message.obtain(mgsToaster, 0,
                    "Tag writing attempt started").sendToTarget();
                int count = 0;
                if(!ndefref.isConnected()) {
                    ndefref.connect();
                }
                while(!ndefref.isConnected()) {
                    if(count > 6000) {
                        throw new Exception("Unable to connect to tag");
                    }
                    count++;
                    sleep(10);
                }
                ndefref.writeNdefMessage(msg);
                Message.obtain(mgsToaster, 0,
                    "Tag write successful!").sendToTarget();
            } catch (Exception t) {
                t.printStackTrace();
                Message.obtain(mgsToaster, 0,
                    "Tag writing failed! - "+t.getMessage()).sendToTarget();
            } finally {
                // ignore close failure...
                try { ndefref.close(); }
                catch (IOException e) { }
            }
        }
    }).start();
}

// create a new NdefRecord
private NdefRecord newTextRecord(String text) {
    byte[] langBytes = Locale.ENGLISH.
                            getLanguage().
                            getBytes(Charset.forName("US-ASCII"));

    byte[] textBytes = text.getBytes(Charset.forName("UTF-8"));

    char status = (char) (langBytes.length);
```

```
        byte[] data = new byte[1 + langBytes.length + textBytes.length];
        data[0] = (byte) status;
        System.arraycopy(langBytes, 0, data, 1, langBytes.length);
        System.arraycopy(textBytes, 0, data, 1 + langBytes.length, textBytes.length);

        return new NdefRecord(NdefRecord.TNF_WELL_KNOWN,
                              NdefRecord.RTD_TEXT,
                              new byte[0],
                              data);
    }
```

P2P Mode and Beam

P2P mode is enabled in Android 2.3.3+ (API level 10) when one device is set up to transmit data over NFC to another device that can receive NFC data. The sending device may also receive data from the receiving device, leading to peer-to-peer (P2P) communication. In API level 10 this is done through a foreground push. But that method is deprecated in later API releases (API level 14+, Android 4.0+), which include a newer push API called Beam in its place. We describe both methods in this section.

API levels 10–13

In API 10, the enableForegroundNdefPush() method in the NfcAdapter class does a P2P NFC message exchange. This enables the Activity to transmit an NdefMessage, when it is in the foreground, to another NFC device that supports the com.android.npp NDEF push protocol. The enableForegroundNdefPush() method must be called from the main thread before communication starts (such as in its onResume() method) and should be disabled when the Activity goes into the background (in its onPause() method):

```
    @Override
    public void onResume() {
        super.onResume();

        NdefRecord[] rec = new NdefRecord[1];
        rec[0] = newTextRecord("NFC Foreground Push Message");
        NdefMessage msg = new NdefMessage(rec);

        NfcAdapter.getDefaultAdapter(this).enableForegroundNdefPush(this, msg);
    }

    // create a new NdefRecord
    private NdefRecord newTextRecord(String text) {
        byte[] langBytes = Locale.ENGLISH.
                                  getLanguage().
                                  getBytes(Charset.forName("US-ASCII"));

        byte[] textBytes = text.getBytes(Charset.forName("UTF-8"));

        char status = (char) (langBytes.length);
```

```
byte[] data = new byte[1 + langBytes.length + textBytes.length];
data[0] = (byte) status;
System.arraycopy(langBytes, 0, data, 1, langBytes.length);
System.arraycopy(textBytes, 0, data, 1 + langBytes.length, textBytes.length);

return new NdefRecord(NdefRecord.TNF_WELL_KNOWN,
                      NdefRecord.RTD_TEXT,
                      new byte[0],
                      data);
}
```

While `enableForegroundNdefPush()` is active, standard tag dispatch is disabled. Only the foreground activity may receive tag-discovered dispatches via `enableForegroundDispatch()`. This ensures that other activities and services do not intercept an NFC tag that is being scanned at that moment and thus that the foreground activity receives the data.

It is important that when the `Activity` is no longer in the foreground (`onPause()`) `disableForegroundNdefPush()` is called:

```
@Override
protected void onPause() {
    super.onPause();
    if(NfcAdapter.getDefaultAdapter(this) != null) {
        NfcAdapter.getDefaultAdapter(this).disableForegroundNdefPush(this);
    }
}
```

Beam: API level 14+

To use Android Beam, the respective devices must have their screens unlocked and the device initiating the beam must have the `Activity` in question in the foreground.

In API level 14 and later, Android Beam is accomplished through the use of two methods of `NfcAdapter`: `setNdefPushMessage()` and `setNdefPushMessageCallback()`. `setNdefPushMessage()` accepts an `NdefMessage` as an argument and sends out the message immediately, whereas `setNdefPushMessageCallback()` works asynchronously and is provided with an `NfcAdapter.CreateNdefMessageCallback` interface. This interface's `createNdefMessage()` method is called when the device is within NFC transmission range of another device. If both `pushMessage` methods are in use, `setNdefPushMessageCallback()` takes precedence.

```
// here we use the callback to push a message via the NfcAdapter
NfcAdapter nfcadapter = NfcAdapter.getDefaultAdapter(this);

// here a callback is generated
CreateNdefMessageCallback nfccallback = new CreateNdefMessageCallback() {

    @Override
    public NdefMessage createNdefMessage(NfcEvent event) {
        String text = "Beaming via callback";
        byte[] mimeBytes =  "application/com.oreilly.demo.android.pa.sensordemo".
```

```
        getBytes(Charset.forName("US-ASCII"));NdefRecord mimeRecord = new Ndef
        Record(NdefRecord.TNF_MIME_MEDIA, mimeBytes, new byte[0], text.getBytes());

        NdefMessage msg = new NdefMessage(new NdefRecord[] {mimeRecord});

        return msg;
    }

};

nfcadapter.setNdefPushMessageCallback(nfccallback, this);


// here we just push a message directly

String directtext = "Beaming Directly";
byte[] directMimeBytes = "application/com.oreilly.demo.android.pa.sensordemo".
getBytes(Charset.forName("US-ASCII"));NdefRecord directMimeRecord = new NdefRecord
(NdefRecord.TNF_MIME_MEDIA, directMimeBytes, new byte[0], directtext.getBytes());
NdefMessage directmsg = new NdefMessage(new NdefRecord[] {directMimeRecord});

nfcadapter.setNdefPushMessage(directmsg, this);
```

In the preceding example, an Android Application Record (AAR) is not being used, so the portion of the manifest for the activity's definition would include the following intent filter:

```
<activity android:name=".NFC40">
    <intent-filter>
        <action android:name="android.nfc.action.NDEF_DISCOVERED"/>
        <category android:name="android.intent.category.DEFAULT"/>
        <data android:mimeType="application/com.oreilly.demo.android.pa.sensordemo"/>
    </intent-filter>
</activity>
```

It is highly recommended that you use an AAR instead of the intent filter when you wish to handle the NFC action at an application level (AAR does not work at the activity level due to the package name constraint) so that other applications can't interfere with the handling of this specific NFC action.

```
// generate the NdefMessage with an AAR

NdefMessage msg = new NdefMessage(new NdefRecord[] {mimeRecord,
        NdefRecord.createApplicationRecord("com.oreilly.demo.android.pa.sensordemo")});

nfcadapter.setNdefPushMessage(msg, this);
```

Gesture Input

In the world of touch-screen devices, the use of complex gestures (such as multiple swipes of the finger in different directions on the screen) is a great way to make interactions both fun and easy to do. Starting with Android 1.6 (API level 4), a gestures API is available for use. Within this API, the easiest way to add gesture input capability to an app is to use `android.gesture.GestureOverlayView`:

```
<!-- an example usage of GestureOverlayView in a layout xml -->

<android.gesture.GestureOverlayView
        xmlns:android="http://schemas.android.com/apk/res/android"
    android:id="@+id/gestures"
    android:layout_width="fill_parent"
    android:layout_height="fill_parent"
    android:gestureStrokeType="multiple"
    android:eventsInterceptionEnabled="true">
</android.gesture.GestureOverlayView>
```

`GestureOverlayView` is a specialized `FrameLayout` that you can place over other widgets or that can contain other widgets. It can capture strokes on the touch screen as well as display a colored line (the default is yellow) representing the stroke path. A `GestureOverlayView.OnGesturePerformedListener` interface is provided to enable the ability to react to a gesture that has been performed:

```
GestureOverlayView gestures = (GestureOverlayView) findViewById(R.id.gestures);
gestures.addOnGesturePerformedListener(
                            new GestureOverlayView.OnGesturePerformedListener() {
    @Override
    public void onGesturePerformed(GestureOverlayView overlay, Gesture gesture) {
        // do nothing for now
    }
});
```

Once the gesture is performed, you can see if it is recognized within the Gesture library. The Gesture library can be read in via various means using the `GestureLibraries` class's static methods. Once the library is loaded (loading a `GestureStore`), the performed gesture can be passed to it and then analyzed using the `recognize` method. This method returns a list of `Predictions`, each holding a score and name, with the score indicating the closeness to the named gesture within the library:

```
final GestureLibrary library = GestureLibraries.fromFile("/Some/File/Path");
library.load();            // load library

GestureOverlayView gestures = (GestureOverlayView) findViewById(R.id.gestures);
gestures.addOnGesturePerformedListener(
                            new GestureOverlayView.OnGesturePerformedListener() {

    @Override
    public void onGesturePerformed(GestureOverlayView overlay, Gesture gesture) {
            // do the recognize
        ArrayList<Prediction> predictions = library.recognize(gesture);
        if (predictions.size() > 0) {
            for(Prediction prediction: predictions) {
                // the score is high enough that we know it's a hit
                if (prediction.score > 1.0) {
                    // let's show a toast telling us what the gesture is named
                    Toast.makeText(this,
                        prediction.name, Toast.LENGTH_SHORT).show();
```

```
                }
            }
        }
    }
});
```

The basic anatomy of a `Gesture` consists of multiple `GestureStroke` objects, and each `GestureStroke` object is made up of `GesturePoint` objects. The `GesturePoint` is made up of *x* and *y* spatial coordinates and a single timestamp indicating when the point was generated. When a `Gesture` is stored in a `GestureStore` (within a `GestureLibrary`) it is keyed with a name (`String`).

Adding a `Gesture` to a `GestureLibrary` is pretty straightforward. You provide a name to associate the gesture, as well as the `Gesture` object, and then save it to the library. Note that a library must be read from an external file source (such as the SD card or private file) for the library to be modifiable and, thus, a gesture store. A library read from a raw resource is read-only (use of `GestureLibraries.fromRawResource(context, resId)`):

```
public void saveGesture(String name, Gesture gesture) {
    library.addGesture(name, gesture);
    library.save();
}
```

Accessibility

Starting with Android 1.6 (API level 4), an accessibility API designed to make Android apps more widely usable by blind and low-vision users is available. The core of the accessibility API is the `AccessibilityService`, an abstract class that is run in the background.

This use of the `AccessibilityService` ultimately means you are extending it, and thus it is a service and must be declared within the manifest. Not only must the declaration be made, but this type of service also has a specific intent it must handle (`android.accessibilityservice.AccessibilityService`):

```
<service android:name=".Accessibility">
    <intent-filter>
        <action android:name="android.accessibilityservice.AccessibilityService" />
    </intent-filter>
</service>
```

When creating an `AccessibilityService` class you must declare the feedback and event types. You do this by generating an `AccessibilityServiceInfo` object, setting the various variables, and then passing it to the `setServiceInfo()` method. Please note that the system will pick up this information only after it has bound to the class/object:

```
AccessibilityServiceInfo info = new AccessibilityServiceInfo();
info.eventTypes = AccessibilityEvent.TYPES_ALL_MASK;
// timeout (ms) after the most recent event of a given type before notification
info.notificationTimeout = 50;
info.feedbackType = AccessibilityServiceInfo.FEEDBACK_GENERIC |
```

```
                        AccessibilityServiceInfo.FEEDBACK_AUDIBLE |
                        AccessibilityServiceInfo.FEEDBACK_HAPTIC |
                        AccessibilityServiceInfo.FEEDBACK_SPOKEN |
                        AccessibilityServiceInfo.FEEDBACK_VISUAL;
    info.packageNames = new String[1];
    // only handle this package
    info.packageNames[0] = getPackageName();
    setServiceInfo(info);
```

Once the service has started and the system has bound to it, events will be received and
passed to the onAccessibilityEvent() method:

```
@Override
public void onAccessibilityEvent(AccessibilityEvent event) {
    // here we check to see if it was a 'click' event
    if(event.getEventType() == AccessibilityEvent.TYPE_VIEW_CLICKED) {
        // do something with the click event
    }
}
```

At this point, you have various options to react to the event. Usually the Vibrator Service
is used to provide a haptic response along with sound or speech. The Vibrator is a
system-level service that is retrieved via the context getSystemService() method. Once
the Vibrator object is retrieved, a pattern of vibrations can be applied when reacting to
an event:

```
// get Vibrator
Vibrator vibrate = (Vibrator) getSystemService(Service.VIBRATOR_SERVICE);
// pattern to vibrate with
long[] pattern = new long[] { 0L, 100L };
// vibrate
vibrate.vibrate(pattern, -1);
```

Android provides a TextToSpeech engine that you can use to provide speech. To use
this you instantiate an android.speech.tts.TextToSpeech class, which initializes the
TextToSpeech engine. Once initialized, speech can be produced by calling the speak
method on the class. A variety of methods and options can be called, such as setting
locale, pitch, or speech speed. Be sure to call the shutdown method when the TextTo
Speech instance is no longer needed so that its resources can be recovered:

```
TextToSpeech tts = new TextToSpeech(thisContext,
    new TextToSpeech.OnInitListener() {
    @Override
    public void onInit(int status) {
        // notification when the TextToSpeech Engine has been initialized
    }
);

// say 'click'
tts.speak("Click", 2, null);
// no longer needed and thus we shut down and release the resources
tts.shutdown();
```

For more accessibility-related resources check out the Eyes-Free open source project (*http://code.google.com/p/eyes-free*).

Communication, Identity, Sync, and Social Media

One of the primary data types that is stored and used (and reused) in Android is contact data. This consists of the various pieces of information associated with a contact—name, phone number, email, and so on. In Android 2.0 (API level 5), contact data was significantly expanded (allowing access to multiple accounts and support for aggregation of similar contacts). In earlier chapters we covered the use of content providers and Android database classes, so we will not cover that preliminary material in this chapter. Instead, we will focus on the use of the ContactsContract content provider.

Account Contacts

To access the account contacts the following permissions must be provided in the manifest:

```
<uses-permission android:name="android.permission.GET_ACCOUNTS" />
<uses-permission android:name="android.permission.READ_CONTACTS" />
<uses-permission android:name="android.permission.WRITE_CONTACTS" />
```

Within an Activity, we can use the managedQuery method to query the Contacts Contract.Contacts data and return a Cursor for our use:

```
private Cursor getContacts() {
    Uri uri = ContactsContract.Contacts.CONTENT_URI;

    String[] projection = new String[] {
            ContactsContract.Contacts._ID,
            ContactsContract.Contacts.LOOKUP_KEY,
            ContactsContract.Contacts.DISPLAY_NAME
    };

    String selection = null;
    String[] selectionArgs = null;
    String sortOrder = ContactsContract.Contacts.DISPLAY_NAME +
                                            " COLLATE LOCALIZED ASC";
```

```
        return managedQuery(uri, projection, selection, selectionArgs, sortOrder);
    }
```

For complete information on the columns and constants available in the `Contacts Contract.Contacts` class, refer to the developer documentation at *http://developer.an droid.com/reference/android/provider/ContactsContract.Contacts.html*.

Once we have the `Cursor`, we can load it within a `SimpleCursorAdapter` and have it display the specific data fields we want, in this case the "display name" of the contact:

```
String[] fields = new String[] {
        ContactsContract.Data.DISPLAY_NAME
};
SimpleCursorAdapter adapter = new SimpleCursorAdapter(this,
                                            R.layout.contact,
                                            cursor,
                                            fields,
                                            new int[] {R.id.name});
    // get the listview
ListView contactlist = (ListView) findViewById(R.id.contactlist);
    // set the adapter and let it render
contactlist.setAdapter(adapter);
```

Here is the layout that contains the `ListView` (referenced as `R.id.contactlist`):

```
<?xml version="1.0" encoding="utf-8"?>
<LinearLayout xmlns:android="http://schemas.android.com/apk/res/android"
    android:orientation="vertical"
    android:layout_width="fill_parent"
    android:layout_height="fill_parent"
    android:background="#fff"
    >
    <ListView android:id="@+id/contactlist"
        android:layout_width="fill_parent"
        android:layout_height="wrap_content"
        />
</LinearLayout>
```

Here is the contact layout (referenced as `R.layout.contact`) used for the `SimpleCursor Adapter`:

```
<?xml version="1.0" encoding="utf-8"?>

<LinearLayout xmlns:android="http://schemas.android.com/apk/res/android"
        android:layout_width="wrap_content"
        android:layout_height="wrap_content"
        android:background="#fff"
        >
<TextView android:id="@+id/name"
        android:layout_width="fill_parent"
        android:layout_height="wrap_content"
        android:textColor="#000"
        android:textSize="25sp"
        android:padding="5dp"
```

```
        />
    </LinearLayout>
```

Here we delete a contact by providing the `Cursor` and the position within the `Cursor` to delete:

```
private void deleteContact(Cursor cursor, int position) {
    cursor.moveToPosition(position);
    long id = cursor.getLong(0);
    String lookupkey = cursor.getString(1);
    Uri uri = ContactsContract.Contacts.getLookupUri(id, lookupkey);

    String[] selectionArgs = null;
    String where = null;
    ContentResolver cr = getContentResolver();
    cr.delete(uri, where, selectionArgs);
}
```

To add a contact in this example we construct a collection of `ContentProvider` `Operations` and batch-apply them. Note that we first insert the new contact and then add the phone information should it be available (as it is in this case). To do the inserts, we generate an insert-specific `ContentProviderOperation` by creating a `ContentProviderOperation.Builder` with the `SimpleCursorContentProviderOperation` `.newInsert()` method and then building with the `build()` method:

```
String accountNameWeWant = "SpecialAccount";

String phone = "8885551234";
String name = "Bob";

String accountname = null;
String accounttype = null;

Account[] accounts = AccountManager.get(this).getAccounts();

// find the account we want.  if we don't find it we use 'null' - the default
for(Account account : accounts) {
    if(account.equals(accountNameWeWant)) {
        accountname = account.name;
        accounttype = account.type;
        break;
    }
}

ArrayList<ContentProviderOperation> ops =
  new ArrayList<ContentProviderOperation>();

ops.add(ContentProviderOperation.newInsert
    (ContactsContract.RawContacts.CONTENT_URI)
        .withValue(ContactsContract.RawContacts.ACCOUNT_TYPE, accountname)
        .withValue(ContactsContract.RawContacts.ACCOUNT_NAME, accounttype)
        .build());

// create the new contact
ops.add(
```

```
ContentProviderOperation.newInsert(ContactsContract.Data.CONTENT_URI)
    .withValueBackReference(ContactsContract.Data.RAW_CONTACT_ID, 0)
    .withValue(ContactsContract.Data.MIMETYPE,
        ContactsContract.CommonDataKinds.StructuredName.CONTENT_ITEM_TYPE)
    .withValue(ContactsContract.CommonDataKinds.StructuredName.DISPLAY_NAME,
        name)
    .build());

// if there is a phone num we add it
if(phone.getText() != null
    && phone.getText().toString().trim().length() > 0) {
    ops.add(ContentProviderOperation.newInsert
            (ContactsContract.Data.CONTENT_URI)
        .withValueBackReference(ContactsContract.Data.RAW_CONTACT_ID, 0)
        .withValue(ContactsContract.Data.MIMETYPE,
            ContactsContract.CommonDataKinds.Phone.CONTENT_ITEM_TYPE)
        .withValue(ContactsContract.CommonDataKinds.Phone.NUMBER,
            phone)
        .withValue(ContactsContract.CommonDataKinds.Phone.TYPE,
            ContactsContract.CommonDataKinds.Phone.TYPE_HOME)
        .build());
}

try {
    getContentResolver().applyBatch(ContactsContract.AUTHORITY, ops);
} catch (Exception e) {
    e.printStackTrace();
    }
```

Authentication and Synchronization

Starting with Android 2.0 (API level 5), it is possible to write custom sync providers to integrate with system contacts, calendars, and so forth. Synchronizing with a remote service at this time is unfortunately a precarious endeavor, as any misstep at particular points can literally cause the Android system to crash and reboot (with very little indication as to what was done incorrectly). Hopefully, as Android evolves, synchronizing will become easier and less tricky. For now, the process consists of two parts—authentication (Account Authenticator) and synchronization (Sync Provider).

Before diving into the details of the two parts, we would like to note that the examples we provide here have two components—a server side and the Android client side. The server side that we use is a basic web service that accepts specific GET requests and responds back with a JSON-formatted response. The relevant GET URI as well as the example response are provided within each section. The source that comes with this book includes the full server-side source for completeness.

The other thing to note is that in the example we provide, we choose to sync up with the account contacts. This is not the only thing with which you can sync up. You can sync up with any content provider you have access to, or even to application-specific stored data.

Authentication

To get the client to authenticate with a remote server using the Android Account Authenticator system, three pieces must be put into place:

- A service that is triggered by the `android.accounts.AccountAuthenticator` intent and that, in its `onBind` method, returns a subclass of `AbstractAccountAuthenticator`
- An activity that prompts the user to enter her credentials
- An XML file describing how your account should look when displayed to the user

Let's address the service first. In the manifest we need `android.permission.AUTHENTICATE_ACCOUNTS` to be enabled:

```
<uses-permission android:name="android.permission.AUTHENTICATE_ACCOUNTS" />
```

Then the service needs to be described in the manifest. Note that the `android.accounts.AccountAuthenticator` intent is included within the `intent-filter` descriptor. The manifest also describes a resource for the `AccountAuthenticator`:

```
<service android:name=".sync.authsync.AuthenticationService">
    <intent-filter>
        <action android:name="android.accounts.AccountAuthenticator" />
    </intent-filter>
    <meta-data android:name="android.accounts.AccountAuthenticator"
                android:resource="@xml/authenticator" />
</service>
```

The resource we indicated in the manifest follows. In particular, it describes the `accountType` that will distinguish this authenticator from other authenticators using the account's definition. Be very careful with this XML document (e.g., do not directly assign a string to the `android:label` or have a missing drawable indicated), as Android will crash and burn the moment you attempt to add a new account (from within the Account & Sync settings).

```
<?xml version="1.0" encoding="utf-8"?>

<account-authenticator xmlns:android="http://schemas.android.com/apk/res/android"
    android:accountType="com.oreilly.demo.android.pa.clientserver.sync"
    android:icon="@drawable/icon"
    android:smallIcon="@drawable/icon"
    android:label="@string/authlabel"
/>
```

Now that the service is described within the manifest, we can turn to the service itself. Note that the `onBind()` method returns an `Authenticator` class. This class extends the `AbstractAccountAuthenticator` class:

```
package com.oreilly.demo.android.pa.clientserver.client.sync.authsync;

import android.app.Service;
import android.content.Intent;
import android.os.IBinder;
```

```
public class AuthenticationService extends Service {
    private static final Object lock = new Object();
    private Authenticator auth;

    @Override
    public void onCreate() {
        synchronized (lock) {
            if (auth == null) {
                auth = new Authenticator(this);
            }
        }
    }

    @Override
    public IBinder onBind(Intent intent) {
        return auth.getIBinder();
    }
}
```

Before we get to the full source of the `Authenticator` class, there is a method within the `AbstractAccountAuthenticator` that is important—addAccount(). This method ultimately is called when the button indicating our custom account is selected from the Add Account screen. A `LoginActivity` (our custom `Activity`, which will ask the user to sign in) is described within the `Intent` that is placed within the `Bundle` that is returned. The `AccountManager.KEY_ACCOUNT_AUTHENTICATOR_RESPONSE` key included in the intent is vital, as it includes the `AccountAuthenticatorResponse` object that is needed to ship back the account keys once the user has successfully certified against the remote service.

```
public class Authenticator extends AbstractAccountAuthenticator {

    public Bundle addAccount(AccountAuthenticatorResponse response,
            String accountType, String authTokenType,
            String[] requiredFeatures, Bundle options) {

        Intent intent = new Intent(context, LoginActivity.class);
        intent.putExtra(AccountManager.KEY_ACCOUNT_AUTHENTICATOR_RESPONSE, response);
        Bundle bundle = new Bundle();
        bundle.putParcelable(AccountManager.KEY_INTENT, intent);
        return bundle;
    }

}
```

Now for the full `Authenticator` activity that extends the `AbstractAccountAuthenticator`:

```
package com.oreilly.demo.android.pa.clientserver.client.sync.authsync;

import com.oreilly.demo.android.pa.clientserver.client.sync.LoginActivity;
import android.accounts.AbstractAccountAuthenticator;
import android.accounts.Account;
import android.accounts.AccountAuthenticatorResponse;
import android.accounts.AccountManager;
import android.content.Context;
import android.content.Intent;
import android.os.Bundle;
```

```java
public class Authenticator extends AbstractAccountAuthenticator {
    public static final String AUTHTOKEN_TYPE
                    = "com.oreilly.demo.android.pa.clientserver.client.sync";
    public static final String ACCOUNT_TYPE
                    = "com.oreilly.demo.android.pa.clientserver.client.sync";

    private final Context context;

    public Authenticator(Context context) {
        super(context);
        this.context = context;
    }

    @Override
    public Bundle addAccount(AccountAuthenticatorResponse response,
            String accountType, String authTokenType,
            String[] requiredFeatures, Bundle options) {

        Intent intent = new Intent(context, LoginActivity.class);
        intent.putExtra(AccountManager.KEY_ACCOUNT_AUTHENTICATOR_RESPONSE, response);
        Bundle bundle = new Bundle();
        bundle.putParcelable(AccountManager.KEY_INTENT, intent);
        return bundle;
    }

    @Override
    public Bundle confirmCredentials(AccountAuthenticatorResponse response,
        Account account, Bundle options) {
        return null;
    }

    @Override
    public Bundle editProperties(AccountAuthenticatorResponse response,
            String accountType) {

        return null;
    }

    @Override
    public Bundle getAuthToken(AccountAuthenticatorResponse response,
            Account account, String authTokenType, Bundle loginOptions) {

        return null;
    }

    @Override
    public String getAuthTokenLabel(String authTokenType) {
        return null;
    }

    @Override
    public Bundle hasFeatures(AccountAuthenticatorResponse response,
            Account account, String[] features) {
        return null;
```

```
    }

    @Override
    public Bundle updateCredentials(AccountAuthenticatorResponse response,
            Account account, String authTokenType, Bundle loginOptions) {
        return null;
    }

}
```

For this exercise, the remote server has a login API call (accessed via an HTTP URI) that takes the username and password as variables. Should the login succeed, the response comes back with a JSON string containing a token:

```
uri: http://<serverBaseUrl>:<port>/login?username=<name>&password=<pass>

response: { "token" : "someAuthenticationToken" }
```

The LoginActivity that requests the user to input the username and password for the account then proceeds to contact the remote server. Once the expected JSON string is returned, the handleLoginResponse() method is called and passes the relevant information about the account back to the AccountManager:

```
package com.oreilly.demo.android.pa.clientserver.client.sync;

import org.json.JSONObject;

import com.oreilly.demo.android.pa.clientserver.client.R;
import com.oreilly.demo.android.pa.clientserver.client.sync.authsync.Authenticator;
import android.accounts.Account;
import android.accounts.AccountAuthenticatorActivity;
import android.accounts.AccountManager;
import android.app.Dialog;
import android.app.ProgressDialog;
import android.content.ContentResolver;
import android.content.Intent;
import android.os.Bundle;
import android.os.Handler;
import android.os.Message;
import android.provider.ContactsContract;
import android.view.View;
import android.view.View.OnClickListener;
import android.widget.EditText;
import android.widget.Toast;

public class LoginActivity extends AccountAuthenticatorActivity {
    public static final String PARAM_AUTHTOKEN_TYPE    = "authtokenType";
    public static final String PARAM_USERNAME          = "username";
    public static final String PARAM_PASSWORD          = "password";

    private String username;
    private String password;

    @Override
    public void onCreate(Bundle savedInstanceState) {
```

```java
        super.onCreate(savedInstanceState);
        getVars();
        setupView();
    }

    @Override
    protected Dialog onCreateDialog(int id) {
        final ProgressDialog dialog = new ProgressDialog(this);
        dialog.setMessage("Attemping to login");
        dialog.setIndeterminate(true);
        dialog.setCancelable(false);
        return dialog;
    }

    private void getVars() {
        username = getIntent().getStringExtra(PARAM_USERNAME);
    }

    private void setupView() {
        setContentView(R.layout.login);

        findViewById(R.id.login).setOnClickListener(new OnClickListener() {
            @Override
            public void onClick(View v) {
                login();
            }
        });

        if(username != null) {
            ((EditText) findViewById(R.id.username)).setText(username);
        }
    }

    private void login() {
        if(((EditText) findViewById(R.id.username)).getText() == null ||
            ((EditText) findViewById(R.id.username)).getText().toString().
                trim().length()
                < 1) {
            Toast.makeText(this, "Please enter a Username",
                Toast.LENGTH_SHORT).show();
            return;
        }
        if(((EditText) findViewById(R.id.password)).getText() == null ||
            ((EditText) findViewById(R.id.password)).getText().toString().
                trim().length()
                < 1) {
            Toast.makeText(this, "Please enter a Password",
                Toast.LENGTH_SHORT).show();
            return;
        }

        username = ((EditText) findViewById(R.id.username)).getText().toString();
        password = ((EditText) findViewById(R.id.password)).getText().toString();

        showDialog(0);
```

```java
        Handler loginHandler = new Handler() {
            @Override
            public void handleMessage(Message msg) {
                if(msg.what == NetworkUtil.ERR) {
                    dismissDialog(0);
                    Toast.makeText(LoginActivity.this, "Login Failed: "+
                                    msg.obj, Toast.LENGTH_SHORT).show();
                } else if(msg.what == NetworkUtil.OK) {
                    handleLoginResponse((JSONObject) msg.obj);
                }
            }
        };

        NetworkUtil.login(getString(R.string.baseurl),
                        username, password, loginHandler);
    }

    private void handleLoginResponse(JSONObject resp) {
        dismissDialog(0);

        final Account account = new Account(username, Authenticator.ACCOUNT_TYPE);

        if (getIntent().getStringExtra(PARAM_USERNAME) == null) {
            AccountManager.get(this).addAccountExplicitly(account, password, null);
            ContentResolver.setSyncAutomatically(account,
                ContactsContract.AUTHORITY, true);
        } else {
            AccountManager.get(this).setPassword(account, password);
        }

        Intent intent = new Intent();
        intent.putExtra(AccountManager.KEY_ACCOUNT_NAME, username);
        intent.putExtra(AccountManager.KEY_ACCOUNT_TYPE,
                        Authenticator.ACCOUNT_TYPE);
        if (resp.has("token")) {
            intent.putExtra(AccountManager.KEY_AUTHTOKEN, resp.optString("token"));
        }
        setAccountAuthenticatorResult(intent.getExtras());
        setResult(RESULT_OK, intent);
        finish();
    }
}
```

The LoginActivity's layout XML is:

```xml
<?xml version="1.0" encoding="utf-8" ?>
<LinearLayout
    xmlns:android="http://schemas.android.com/apk/res/android"
    android:orientation="vertical"
    android:layout_width="fill_parent"
    android:layout_height="wrap_content"
    android:background="#fff">
    <ScrollView
        android:layout_width="fill_parent"
        android:layout_height="0dip"
```

```
        android:layout_weight="1">
        <LinearLayout
            android:layout_width="fill_parent"
            android:layout_height="wrap_content"
            android:layout_weight="1"
            android:orientation="vertical"
            android:paddingTop="5dip"
            android:paddingBottom="13dip"
            android:paddingLeft="20dip"
            android:paddingRight="20dip">
            <EditText
                android:id="@+id/username"
                android:singleLine="true"
                android:layout_width="fill_parent"
                android:layout_height="wrap_content"
                android:minWidth="250dip"
                android:scrollHorizontally="true"
                android:capitalize="none"
                android:hint="Username"
                android:autoText="false" />
            <EditText
                android:id="@+id/password"
                android:singleLine="true"
                android:layout_width="fill_parent"
                android:layout_height="wrap_content"
                android:minWidth="250dip"
                android:scrollHorizontally="true"
                android:capitalize="none"
                android:autoText="false"
                android:password="true"
                android:hint="Password"
                android:inputType="textPassword" />
        </LinearLayout>
    </ScrollView>
    <FrameLayout
        android:layout_width="fill_parent"
        android:layout_height="wrap_content"
        android:background="#fff"
        android:minHeight="54dip"
        android:paddingTop="4dip"
        android:paddingLeft="2dip"
        android:paddingRight="2dip">
        <Button
            android:id="@+id/login"
            android:layout_width="wrap_content"
            android:layout_height="wrap_content"
            android:layout_gravity="center_horizontal"
            android:minWidth="100dip"
            android:text="Login" />
    </FrameLayout>
</LinearLayout>
```

At this point, the account is established and is ready to be used to synchronize data.

Synchronization

To synchronize an account's data we once again are dealing with three pieces—a service that is registered to listen for an `android.content.SyncAdapter` intent and that returns an `AbstractThreadedSyncAdapter` extended class on the `onBind()` method, an XML descriptor describing the structure of the data that is to be viewed and synced, and a class extending the `AbstractThreadedSyncAdapter` that handles the actual sync.

For our example, we wish to sync up with contact information for the account that we described in the preceding section. Do note that contact information is not the only information with which you can sync up. You can sync up with any content provider you have access to, or even to application-specific stored data.

The following permissions are indicated in the manifest:

```
<uses-permission android:name="android.permission.GET_ACCOUNTS" />
<uses-permission android:name="android.permission.READ_CONTACTS" />
<uses-permission android:name="android.permission.WRITE_CONTACTS" />
<uses-permission android:name="android.permission.AUTHENTICATE_ACCOUNTS" />
<uses-permission android:name="android.permission.USE_CREDENTIALS" />
<uses-permission android:name="android.permission.MANAGE_ACCOUNTS" />
<uses-permission android:name="android.permission.INTERNET" />
<uses-permission android:name="android.permission.WRITE_SETTINGS" />
<uses-permission android:name="android.permission.WRITE_SECURE_SETTINGS" />
<uses-permission android:name="android.permission.READ_SYNC_STATS" />
<uses-permission android:name="android.permission.READ_SYNC_SETTINGS" />
<uses-permission android:name="android.permission.WRITE_SYNC_SETTINGS" />
```

Now we describe the service we intend to use. Note that the manifest specifies both the intent `android.content.SyncAdapter` and two data structures; one for the contact data and one for the SyncAdapter:

```
<service android:name=".sync.authsync.SyncService">
    <intent-filter>
        <action android:name="android.content.SyncAdapter" />
    </intent-filter>
    <meta-data android:name="android.content.SyncAdapter"
                               android:resource="@xml/syncadapter" />
    <meta-data android:name="android.provider.CONTACTS_STRUCTURE"
                               android:resource="@xml/contacts" />
</service>
```

In the `sync-adapter` XML resource, note the `accountType` descriptor. The content we intend to work with is the Android contacts data:

```
<?xml version="1.0" encoding="utf-8"?>

<sync-adapter xmlns:android="http://schemas.android.com/apk/res/android"
    android:contentAuthority="com.android.contacts"
    android:accountType="com.oreilly.demo.android.pa.clientserver.client.sync"
/>
```

Here is the contacts descriptor XML. Note the names of the various columns we described.

```xml
<?xml version="1.0" encoding="utf-8"?>
<ContactsSource xmlns:android="http://schemas.android.com/apk/res/android">

    <ContactsDataKind
        android:mimeType=
"vnd.android.cursor.item/vnd.com.oreilly.demo.android.pa.clientserver.sync.profile"
        android:icon="@drawable/icon"
        android:summaryColumn="data2"
        android:detailColumn="data3"
        android:detailSocialSummary="true" />

</ContactsSource>
```

The SyncService we created returns the SyncAdapter class. This is our custom class that extends AbstractThreadedSyncAdapter:

```java
package com.oreilly.demo.android.pa.clientserver.client.sync.authsync;

import android.app.Service;
import android.content.Intent;
import android.os.IBinder;

public class SyncService extends Service {
    private static final Object lock = new Object();
    private static SyncAdapter adapter = null;

    @Override
    public void onCreate() {
        synchronized (lock) {
            if (adapter == null) {
                adapter = new SyncAdapter(getApplicationContext(), true);
            }
        }
    }

    @Override
    public void onDestroy() {
        adapter = null;
    }

    @Override
    public IBinder onBind(Intent intent) {
        return adapter.getSyncAdapterBinder();
    }
}
```

Continuing with this exercise, we create a getfriends method on the remote server side. This takes the token that was passed back and stored by the successful login coded up in the previous section, and a time indicating the last time the call was made (if it is the first time, 0 is passed). The response is another JSON string describing the friends (with ID, name, and phone), the time the call was made (in Unix time on the server), and a history describing additions and deletions of friends for this account. In the history, the type field is 0 to add and 1 to delete. The who field is the ID of the friend, and the time shows when the operation occurred.

```
uri: http://<serverBaseUrl>:<port>/getfriends?token=<token>&time=<lasttime>
```

response:

```
{
    "time" : 1295817666232,
    "history" : [
        {
            "time" : 1295817655342,
            "type" : 0,
            "who" : 1
        }
    ],
    "friend" : [
        {
            "id" : 1,
            "name" : "Mary",
            "phone" : "8285552334"
        }
    ]
}
```

The AbstractThreadedSyncAdapter class, extending SyncAdapter, follows:

```java
public class SyncAdapter extends AbstractThreadedSyncAdapter {
    private final Context context;

    private static long lastsynctime = 0;

    public SyncAdapter(Context context, boolean autoInitialize) {
        super(context, autoInitialize);
        this.context = context;
    }

    @Override
    public void onPerformSync(Account account, Bundle extras, String authority,
                ContentProviderClient provider, SyncResult syncResult) {
        String authtoken = null;
        try {
            authtoken = AccountManager.get(context).blockingGetAuthToken(account,
                            Authenticator.AUTHTOKEN_TYPE, true);

            ListFriends friendsdata =
                ListFriends.fromJSON(
                    NetworkUtil.getFriends(context.getString(R.string.baseurl),
                    authtoken, lastsynctime, null));

            lastsynctime = friendsdata.time;

            sync(account, friendsdata);
        } catch (Exception e) {
            e.printStackTrace();
        }
    }

    private void sync(Account account, ListFriends data) {
```

```
                // MAGIC HAPPENS
        }
    }
```

The full SyncAdapter class follows, demonstrating the actions that occur when the sync method receives data. The various additions and deletions of the contact information are included. (Contact and ContentProvider operations are covered in previous chapters and sections.)

```
    package com.oreilly.demo.android.pa.clientserver.client.sync.authsync;

    import java.util.ArrayList;

    import android.accounts.Account;
    import android.accounts.AccountManager;
    import android.content.AbstractThreadedSyncAdapter;
    import android.content.ContentProviderClient;
    import android.content.ContentProviderOperation;
    import android.content.ContentUris;
    import android.content.Context;
    import android.content.SyncResult;
    import android.database.Cursor;
    import android.os.Bundle;
    import android.provider.ContactsContract;
    import android.provider.ContactsContract.RawContacts;

    import com.oreilly.demo.android.pa.clientserver.client.R;
    import com.oreilly.demo.android.pa.clientserver.client.sync.NetworkUtil;
    import com.oreilly.demo.android.pa.clientserver.client.sync.dataobjects.Change;
    import com.oreilly.demo.android.pa.clientserver.client.sync.dataobjects.ListFriends;
    import com.oreilly.demo.android.pa.clientserver.client.sync.dataobjects.User;

    public class SyncAdapter extends AbstractThreadedSyncAdapter {
        private final Context context;

        private static long lastsynctime = 0;

        public SyncAdapter(Context context, boolean autoInitialize) {
            super(context, autoInitialize);
            this.context = context;
        }

        @Override
        public void onPerformSync(Account account, Bundle extras, String authority,
                    ContentProviderClient provider, SyncResult syncResult) {
            String authtoken = null;
            try {
                    // get accounttoken.  this eventually calls our Authenticator
                    // getAuthToken()
                authtoken = AccountManager.get(context).blockingGetAuthToken(account,
                        Authenticator.AUTHTOKEN_TYPE, true);

                ListFriends friendsdata =
                    ListFriends.fromJSON(
                        NetworkUtil.getFriends(context.getString(R.string.baseurl),
```

```
                        authtoken, lastsynctime, null));

                lastsynctime = friendsdata.time;

                sync(account, friendsdata);
        } catch (Exception e) {
            e.printStackTrace();
        }
    }

    // where the magic happens
    private void sync(Account account, ListFriends data) {
        User self = new User();
        self.username = account.name;

        ArrayList<ContentProviderOperation> ops =
                                new ArrayList<ContentProviderOperation>();

        // cycle through the history to find the deletes
        if(data.history != null && !data.history.isEmpty()) {
            for(Change change : data.history) {
                if(change.type == Change.ChangeType.DELETE) {
                    ContentProviderOperation op = delete(account, change.who);
                    if(op != null) ops.add(op);
                }
            }
        }

        // cycle through the friends to find ones we do not already have and add them
        if(data.friends != null && !data.friends.isEmpty()) {
            for(User f : data.friends) {
                ArrayList<ContentProviderOperation> op = add(account, f);
                if(op != null) ops.addAll(op);
            }
        }

        if(!ops.isEmpty()) {
            try {
                context.getContentResolver().applyBatch(ContactsContract.AUTHORITY,
                                                ops);
            } catch (Exception e) {
                e.printStackTrace();
            }
        }
    }

    // adding a contact.  note we are storing the id referenced in the response
    // from the server in the SYNC1 field - this way we can find it with this
    // server based id
    private ArrayList<ContentProviderOperation> add(Account account, User f) {
        long rawid = lookupRawContact(f.id);

        if(rawid != 0) return null;
        ArrayList<ContentProviderOperation> ops =
          new ArrayList<ContentProviderOperation>();
```

```java
        ops.add(ContentProviderOperation.newInsert(
                ContactsContract.RawContacts.CONTENT_URI)
            .withValue(RawContacts.SOURCE_ID, 0)
            .withValue(RawContacts.SYNC1, f.id)
            .withValue(ContactsContract.RawContacts.ACCOUNT_TYPE,
                    Authenticator.ACCOUNT_TYPE)
            .withValue(ContactsContract.RawContacts.ACCOUNT_NAME,
                    account.name)
            .build());

        if(f.name != null && f.name.trim().length() > 0) {
            ops.add(ContentProviderOperation.newInsert(
                    ContactsContract.Data.CONTENT_URI)
                .withValueBackReference(ContactsContract.Data.RAW_CONTACT_ID,
                                0)
                .withValue(ContactsContract.Data.MIMETYPE,
                    ContactsContract.CommonDataKinds.StructuredName.CONTENT_ITEM_TYPE)
                .withValue(ContactsContract.CommonDataKinds.
                    StructuredName.DISPLAY_NAME, f.name)
                .build());
        }

        if(f.phone != null && f.phone.trim().length() > 0) {
            ops.add(ContentProviderOperation.newInsert
                (ContactsContract.Data.CONTENT_URI)
                    .withValueBackReference(ContactsContract.Data.RAW_CONTACT_ID, 0)
                    .withValue(ContactsContract.Data.MIMETYPE,
                            ContactsContract.CommonDataKinds.Phone.CONTENT_ITEM_TYPE)
                    .withValue(ContactsContract.CommonDataKinds.Phone.NUMBER, f.phone)
                    .withValue(ContactsContract.CommonDataKinds.Phone.TYPE,
                            ContactsContract.CommonDataKinds.Phone.TYPE_HOME)
                    .build());
        }

        ops.add(ContentProviderOperation.newInsert(ContactsContract.Data.CONTENT_URI)
                .withValueBackReference(ContactsContract.Data.RAW_CONTACT_ID, 0)
                .withValue(ContactsContract.Data.MIMETYPE,
"vnd.android.cursor.item/vnd.com.oreilly.demo.android.pa.clientserver.client.sync.profile")
                .withValue(ContactsContract.Data.DATA2, "Ch15 Profile")
                .withValue(ContactsContract.Data.DATA3, "View profile")
                .build()
                );
        return ops;
    }

    // delete contact via the server based id
    private ContentProviderOperation delete(Account account, long id) {
        long rawid = lookupRawContact(id);
        if(rawid == 0) return null;
        return ContentProviderOperation.newDelete(
                ContentUris.withAppendedId(
                        ContactsContract.RawContacts.CONTENT_URI,
                rawid))
                .build();
    }
```

```
// look up the actual raw id via the id we have stored in the SYNC1 field
private long lookupRawContact(long id) {
    long rawid = 0;
    Cursor c = context.getContentResolver().query(
                    RawContacts.CONTENT_URI, new String[] {RawContacts._ID},
                    RawContacts.ACCOUNT_TYPE + "='" +
                    Authenticator.ACCOUNT_TYPE + "' AND "+
                    RawContacts.SYNC1 + "=?",
                    new String[] {String.valueOf(id)},
                    null);
    try {
        if(c.moveToFirst()) {
            rawid = c.getLong(0);
        }
    } finally {
        if (c != null) {
            c.close();
            c = null;
        }
    }
    return rawid;
}
}
```

An important detail might be missed in the previous SyncAdapter class: during the onPerformSync() call, we attempt to get the authtoken from the AccountManager by using the blockingGetAuthToken() method. This eventually calls the AbstractAccount Authenticator that is associated with this account. In this case, it calls the Authentica tor class we provided in the previous section. Within the Authenticator class, the method getAuthToken() is called. An example follows:

```
@Override
public Bundle getAuthToken(AccountAuthenticatorResponse response, Account account,
                    String authTokenType, Bundle loginOptions) {
    // check and make sure it is the right token type we want
    if (!authTokenType.equals(AUTHTOKEN_TYPE)) {
        final Bundle result = new Bundle();
        result.putString(AccountManager.KEY_ERROR_MESSAGE,
            "invalid authTokenType");
        return result;
    }
    // if we have the password, let's try and get the current
    // authtoken from the server
    String password = AccountManager.get(context).getPassword(account);
    if (password != null) {
        JSONObject json = NetworkUtil.login(context.getString(R.string.baseurl),
                                    account.name, password, true, null);
        if(json != null) {
            Bundle result = new Bundle();
            result.putString(AccountManager.KEY_ACCOUNT_NAME, account.name);
            result.putString(AccountManager.KEY_ACCOUNT_TYPE, ACCOUNT_TYPE);
            result.putString(AccountManager.KEY_AUTHTOKEN,
                            json.optString("token"));
            return result;
```

```
            }
        }
        // if all else fails let's see about getting the user to log in
        Intent intent = new Intent(context, LoginActivity.class);
        intent.putExtra(LoginActivity.PARAM_USERNAME, account.name);
        intent.putExtra(AccountManager.KEY_ACCOUNT_AUTHENTICATOR_RESPONSE, response);
        Bundle bundle = new Bundle();
        bundle.putParcelable(AccountManager.KEY_INTENT, intent);
        return bundle;
    }
```

Bluetooth

Bluetooth was the nickname for King Harald of Denmark. The following article on Sun's developer site (*http://developers.sun.com/mobility/midp/articles/bluetooth1/*) contains a variety of information about Bluetooth, including the possibly apocryphal assertion that a runic stone erected in honor of Harald states:

Harald Christianized the Danes

Harald controlled Denmark and Norway

Harald thinks notebooks and cellular phones should communicate seamlessly

To show you how to use Android's Bluetooth classes in your applications, we will create a utility for connecting to and transferring data to and from Bluetooth devices. This code is based on the BluetoothChat example in the Android SDK. It has been generalized to cover more applications of Bluetooth, and it has been modified to make it easier to adapt to your purposes.

As we explore Android's Bluetooth APIs, we will see how this code makes use of these APIs, and how you can use the code for application-specific purposes, including as a diagnostic tool for Bluetooth development.

First we will learn more about how Bluetooth works, and how it is implemented in Android.

The Bluetooth Protocol Stack

This section takes a look at the standards and protocols that make up the Bluetooth protocol stack (see Figure 18-1). These protocols and standards are what characterize Bluetooth: the kinds of data Bluetooth is designed to move, how many devices can be connected at the same time, latency, and so on.

Bluetooth has emerged as a separate form of networking because it is a "personal area network," or PAN, also referred to as a piconet. Bluetooth is designed to connect up to eight devices and to carry data at a maximum of approximately three megabits per second. The connected devices must be close to one another: within about 10 meters. Bluetooth operates at very low power levels, in milliwatts. That means very small batteries can last a long time: a Bluetooth headset with a tiny, lightweight battery can

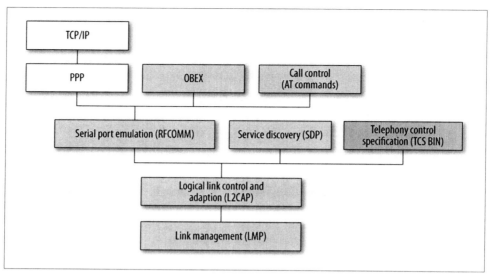

Figure 18-1. The Android Bluetooth protocol stack

last for hours of talking—about as long as the much larger battery in your mobile handset can last, because the mobile radio signal must be able to reach a relatively distant antenna.

The kinds of devices for which Bluetooth is useful include low and medium data-rate devices such as keyboards, mice, tablets, printers, speakers, headphones, and headsets, and the mobile and personal computing devices those peripheral devices may want to talk to. Bluetooth also supports connections among PCs and mobile handsets.

Bluetooth-specific protocols and adopted protocols

One useful way of thinking about the Bluetooth protocol stack is to separate it into Bluetooth-specific protocols and "adopted" protocols that run on top of Bluetooth. Taken together, Bluetooth and the adopted protocols can be dauntingly complex, but if you temporarily set aside the fact that large, complex protocols such as OBEX and TCP/IP run on top of Bluetooth, it's more understandable. Therefore, we will start with the lower layers of Bluetooth and emphasize how these layers shape how you can make use of Bluetooth.

Another useful mental model of Bluetooth is that it replaces serial ports. This means the lower layers of Bluetooth emulate, and enable you to manage, a virtual set of serial cables between peripherals. This is the type of Bluetooth protocol we will be using. This, in turn, enables us to use the simple `java.io` classes `InputStream` and `Output Stream` to read and write data.

BlueZ: The Linux Bluetooth Implementation

A mobile handset may want to connect to all kinds of Bluetooth devices, unlike peripheral devices that need to be connectable only to a computer or handset. That means a mobile handset wants to have a fairly complete implementation of Bluetooth and the adopted protocols, as well as a user interface that enables the necessary interactions for making and managing connections and for using applications that communicate over Bluetooth.

Android uses the BlueZ Bluetooth stack, which is the most commonly used Bluetooth stack for Linux. BlueZ supercedes a project called Open BT. Information on BlueZ can be found at the BlueZ project site, *http://www.bluez.org*.

BlueZ was developed at Qualcomm, and has been adopted into the Linux kernel. The project was begun in 2001 and has been an active and well-supported project ever since. BlueZ is, therefore, a stable and compatible implementation—another reason Linux is a good choice for handset operating systems.

Using Bluetooth in Android Applications

Using Bluetooth in Android means using classes that were designed to encapsulate the way Bluetooth works in the Android operating system: the BlueZ stack provides ways to enumerate devices, listen for connections, and use connections; the `java.io` package provides classes for reading and writing data; and the `Handler` and `Message` classes provide a way to bridge between the threads that manage Bluetooth input and output and the user interface. Let's take a look at the code and how these classes are used.

Compiling and running this code will give you an idea of what Android's Bluetooth classes can do for applications that need to build simple connections to nearby devices.

The first step in trying out this Bluetooth application is to pair your handset with a PC. Then you need a program that monitors what the PC has received via Bluetooth to see that what you send from this application got to your PC. In this case we'll use the Linux utility `hcidump`.

Start the program under the debugger if you want to set some breakpoints and step through it, especially the parts of the application that open and accept connections. You can create the connection from your PC, using the Blueman applet in Linux, or from the app. Once the connection is created, start `hcidump` in a terminal to see that what you typed into the app is received by the PC. Use the following flags to show only the content of the Bluetooth connection:

```
sudo hcidump -a -R
```

Now what you send from your device should show up as the output of `hcidump` on your PC.

Bluetooth and related I/O classes

This program relies on the `BluetoothAdapter` class to control the device's Bluetooth adapter, the `BluetoothDevice` class to represent the state of the connected device, and the `BluetoothSocket` class to represent sockets for listening for and making connections:

```
package com.finchframework.bluetooth;

import android.os.Handler;
import android.os.Message;

public class BtHelperHandler extends Handler {

    public enum MessageType {
        STATE,
        READ,
        WRITE,
        DEVICE,
        NOTIFY;
    }

    public Message obtainMessage(MessageType message, int count, Object obj) {
        return obtainMessage(message.ordinal(), count, -1, obj);

    }

    public MessageType getMessageType(int ordinal) {
        return MessageType.values()[ordinal];
    }

}
```

The `BtHelperHandler` class defines some constants and provides a little bit of wrapper code that makes message-related methods cleaner.

`BtSPPHelper.java` is what encapsulates our use of the Bluetooth Serial Port Protocol (SPP):

```
package com.finchframework.bluetooth;

import java.io.IOException;
import java.io.InputStream;
import java.io.OutputStream;
import java.util.UUID;

import com.finchframework.finch.R;

import android.bluetooth.BluetoothAdapter;
import android.bluetooth.BluetoothDevice;
import android.bluetooth.BluetoothServerSocket;
import android.bluetooth.BluetoothSocket;
import android.content.Context;
import android.os.Bundle;
import android.os.Message;
import android.util.Log;
```

```java
/**
 * Helper class that runs AsyncTask objects for communicating with a Bluetooth
 * device. This code is derived from the BluetoothChat example, but modified in
 * several ways to increase modularity and generality: The Handler is in a
 * separate class to make it easier to drop into other components.
 *
 * Currently this only does Bluetooth SPP. This can be generalized to other
 * services.
 */
public class BtSPPHelper {
    // Debugging
    private final String TAG = getClass().getSimpleName();
    private static final boolean D = true;

    public enum State {
        NONE,
        LISTEN,
        CONNECTING,
        CONNECTED;
    }

    // Name for the SDP record when creating server socket
    private static final String NAME = "BluetoothTest";

    // Unique UUID for this application
    private static final UUID SPP_UUID =
      UUID.fromString("00001101-0000-1000-8000-00805F9B34FB");

    // Member fields
    private final BluetoothAdapter mAdapter;
    private final BtHelperHandler mHandler;
    private AcceptThread mAcceptThread;
    private ConnectThread mConnectThread;
    private ConnectedThread mConnectedThread;
    private State mState;
    private Context mContext;

    /**
     * Constructor. Prepares a new Bluetooth SPP session.
     * @param context  The UI Activity Context
     * @param handler  A Handler to send messages back to the UI Activity
     */
    public BtSPPHelper(Context context, BtHelperHandler handler) {
        mContext = context;
        mAdapter = BluetoothAdapter.getDefaultAdapter();
        mState = State.NONE;
        mHandler = handler;
    }

    /**
     * Set the current state of the chat connection
     * @param state  The current connection state
     */
    private synchronized void setState(State state) {
```

```
            if (D) Log.d(TAG, "setState() " + mState + " -> " + state);
            mState = state;

            // Give the new state to the Handler so the UI Activity can update
            mHandler.obtainMessage(BtHelperHandler.MessageType.STATE,
                                   -1, state).sendToTarget();
        }

        /**
         * Return the current connection state.
         */
        public synchronized State getState() {
            return mState;
        }

        /**
         * Start the session. Start AcceptThread to begin a
         * session in listening (server) mode.
         *
         * Typically, call this in onResume()
         */
        public synchronized void start() {
            if (D) Log.d(TAG, "start");

            // Cancel any thread attempting to make a connection
            if (mConnectThread != null) {mConnectThread.cancel(); mConnectThread = null;}

            // Cancel any thread currently running a connection
            if (mConnectedThread != null) {
                mConnectedThread.cancel();
                mConnectedThread = null;
            }

            // Start the thread to listen on a BluetoothServerSocket
            if (mAcceptThread == null) {
                mAcceptThread = new AcceptThread();
                mAcceptThread.start();
            }
            setState(State.LISTEN);
        }

        /**
         * Start the ConnectThread to initiate a connection to a remote device.
         * @param device  The BluetoothDevice to connect
         */
        public synchronized void connect(BluetoothDevice device) {
            if (D) Log.d(TAG, "connect to: " + device);

            // Cancel any thread attempting to make a connection
            if (mState == State.CONNECTING) {
                if (mConnectThread != null) {
                    mConnectThread.cancel();
                    mConnectThread = null;
                }
            }
```

```java
        // Cancel any thread currently running a connection
        if (mConnectedThread != null) {
            mConnectedThread.cancel();
            mConnectedThread = null;
        }

        // Start the thread to connect with the given device
        mConnectThread = new ConnectThread(device);
        mConnectThread.start();
        setState(State.CONNECTING);
    }

    /**
     * Start the ConnectedThread to begin managing a Bluetooth connection
     *
     * @param socket
     *            The BluetoothSocket on which the connection was made
     * @param device
     *            The BluetoothDevice that has been connected
     */
    private synchronized void connected(BluetoothSocket socket,
            BluetoothDevice device) {
        if (D)
            Log.d(TAG, "connected");

        // Cancel the thread that completed the connection
        if (mConnectThread != null) {
            mConnectThread.cancel();
            mConnectThread = null;
        }

        // Cancel any thread currently running a connection
        if (mConnectedThread != null) {
            mConnectedThread.cancel();
            mConnectedThread = null;
        }

        // Cancel the accept thread because we only want to connect to one
        // device
        if (mAcceptThread != null) {
            mAcceptThread.cancel();
            mAcceptThread = null;
        }

        // Start the thread to manage the connection and perform transmissions
        mConnectedThread = new ConnectedThread(socket);
        mConnectedThread.start();

        // Send the name of the connected device back to the UI Activity
        mHandler.obtainMessage(BtHelperHandler.MessageType.DEVICE, -1,
                device.getName()).sendToTarget();
        setState(State.CONNECTED);
    }
```

```java
/**
 * Stop all threads
 */
public synchronized void stop() {
    if (D) Log.d(TAG, "stop");
    if (mConnectThread != null) {
        mConnectThread.cancel();
        mConnectThread = null;
    }
    if (mConnectedThread != null) {
        mConnectedThread.cancel();
        mConnectedThread = null;
    }
    if (mAcceptThread != null) {
        mAcceptThread.cancel();
        mAcceptThread = null;
    }
    setState(State.NONE);
}

/**
 * Write to the ConnectedThread in an unsynchronized manner
 * @param out The bytes to write
 * @see ConnectedThread#write(byte[])
 */
public void write(byte[] out) {
    ConnectedThread r;

    // Synchronize a copy of the ConnectedThread
    synchronized (this) {
        if (mState != State.CONNECTED) return;
        r = mConnectedThread;
    }
    // Perform the write unsynchronized
    r.write(out);
}

private void sendErrorMessage(int messageId) {
    setState(State.LISTEN);
    mHandler.obtainMessage(BtHelperHandler.MessageType.NOTIFY, -1,
    mContext.getResources().getString(messageId)).sendToTarget();
}

/**
 * This thread listens for incoming connections.
 */
private class AcceptThread extends Thread {
    // The local server socket
    private final BluetoothServerSocket mmServerSocket;

    public AcceptThread() {
        BluetoothServerSocket tmp = null;

        // Create a new listening server socket
        try {
```

```java
            tmp = mAdapter.listenUsingRfcommWithServiceRecord(NAME, SPP_UUID);
        } catch (IOException e) {
            Log.e(TAG, "listen() failed", e);
        }
        mmServerSocket = tmp;
    }

    public void run() {
        if (D) Log.d(TAG, "BEGIN mAcceptThread" + this);
        setName("AcceptThread");
        BluetoothSocket socket = null;

        // Listen to the server socket if we're not connected
        while (mState != BtSPPHelper.State.CONNECTED) {
            try {
                // This is a blocking call and will only return on a
                // successful connection or an exception
                socket = mmServerSocket.accept();
            } catch (IOException e) {
                Log.e(TAG, "accept() failed", e);
                break;
            }

            // If a connection was accepted
            if (socket != null) {
                synchronized (BtSPPHelper.this) {
                    switch (mState) {
                    case LISTEN:
                    case CONNECTING:
                        // Situation normal. Start the connected thread.
                        connected(socket, socket.getRemoteDevice());
                        break;
                    case NONE:
                    case CONNECTED:
                        // Either not ready or already connected.
                        // Terminate new socket.
                        try {
                            socket.close();
                        } catch (IOException e) {
                            Log.e(TAG, "Could not close unwanted socket", e);
                        }
                        break;
                    }
                }
            }
        }
        if (D) Log.i(TAG, "END mAcceptThread");
    }

    public void cancel() {
        if (D) Log.d(TAG, "cancel " + this);
        try {
            mmServerSocket.close();
        } catch (IOException e) {
            Log.e(TAG, "close() of server failed", e);
```

```
            }
        }
    }

    /**
     * This thread runs while attempting to make an outgoing connection
     * with a device. It runs straight through; the connection either
     * succeeds or fails.
     */
    private class ConnectThread extends Thread {
        private final BluetoothSocket mmSocket;
        private final BluetoothDevice mmDevice;

        public ConnectThread(BluetoothDevice device) {
            mmDevice = device;
            BluetoothSocket tmp = null;

            // Get a BluetoothSocket for a connection with the
            // given BluetoothDevice
            try {
                tmp = device.createRfcommSocketToServiceRecord(SPP_UUID);
            } catch (IOException e) {
                Log.e(TAG, "create() failed", e);
            }
            mmSocket = tmp;
        }

        public void run() {
            Log.i(TAG, "BEGIN mConnectThread");
            setName("ConnectThread");

            // Always cancel discovery because it will slow down a connection
            mAdapter.cancelDiscovery();

            // Make a connection to the BluetoothSocket
            try {
                // This is a blocking call and will only return on a
                // successful connection or an exception
                mmSocket.connect();
            } catch (IOException e) {
                sendErrorMessage(R.string.bt_unable);
                // Close the socket
                try {
                    mmSocket.close();
                } catch (IOException e2) {
                    Log.e(TAG, "unable to close() socket during connection failure",
                        e2);
                }
                // Start the service over to restart listening mode
                BtSPPHelper.this.start();
                return;
            }

            // Reset the ConnectThread because we're done
            synchronized (BtSPPHelper.this) {
```

```
                mConnectThread = null;
            }

            // Start the connected thread
            connected(mmSocket, mmDevice);
        }

        public void cancel() {
            try {
                mmSocket.close();
            } catch (IOException e) {
                Log.e(TAG, "close() of connect socket failed", e);
            }
        }
    }

    /**
     * This thread runs during a connection with a remote device.
     * It handles all incoming and outgoing transmissions.
     */
    private class ConnectedThread extends Thread {
        private final BluetoothSocket mmSocket;
        private final InputStream mmInStream;
        private final OutputStream mmOutStream;

        public ConnectedThread(BluetoothSocket socket) {
            Log.d(TAG, "create ConnectedThread");
            mmSocket = socket;
            InputStream tmpIn = null;
            OutputStream tmpOut = null;

            // Get the BluetoothSocket input and output streams
            try {
                tmpIn = socket.getInputStream();
                tmpOut = socket.getOutputStream();
            } catch (IOException e) {
                Log.e(TAG, "temp sockets not created", e);
            }

            mmInStream = tmpIn;
            mmOutStream = tmpOut;
        }

        public void run() {
            Log.i(TAG, "BEGIN mConnectedThread");
            byte[] buffer = new byte[1024];
            int bytes;

            // Keep listening to the InputStream while connected
            while (true) {
                try {
                    // Read from the InputStream
                    bytes = mmInStream.read(buffer);

                    // Send the obtained bytes to the UI Activity
```

```
                    mHandler.obtainMessage(BtHelperHandler.MessageType.READ,
                            bytes, buffer).sendToTarget();
            } catch (IOException e) {
                Log.e(TAG, "disconnected", e);
                sendErrorMessage(R.string.bt_connection_lost);
                break;
            }
        }
    }

    /**
     * Write to the connected OutStream.
     * @param buffer  The bytes to write
     */
    public void write(byte[] buffer) {
        try {
            mmOutStream.write(buffer);

            // Share the sent message back to the UI Activity
            mHandler.obtainMessage(BtHelperHandler.MessageType.WRITE, -1, buffer)
                    .sendToTarget();
        } catch (IOException e) {
            Log.e(TAG, "Exception during write", e);
        }
    }

    public void cancel() {
        try {
            mmSocket.close();
        } catch (IOException e) {
            Log.e(TAG, "close() of connect socket failed", e);
        }
    }
}
}
```

The BtSPPHelper class brings the use of these classes together, and also contains the definition of private Thread subclasses that listen for, establish, and run connections.

This is also where the java.io package meets Android Bluetooth: the Bluetooth Socket objects contain methods that return references to InputStream and Output Stream objects to be used to read and write data on the socket connection:

```
package com.finchframework.bluetooth;

import java.util.Set;

import com.finchframework.finch.R;

import android.app.Activity;
import android.bluetooth.BluetoothAdapter;
import android.bluetooth.BluetoothDevice;
import android.content.BroadcastReceiver;
import android.content.Context;
import android.content.Intent;
```

```java
import android.content.IntentFilter;
import android.os.Bundle;
import android.util.Log;
import android.view.View;
import android.view.Window;
import android.view.View.OnClickListener;
import android.widget.AdapterView;
import android.widget.ArrayAdapter;
import android.widget.Button;
import android.widget.ListView;
import android.widget.TextView;
import android.widget.AdapterView.OnItemClickListener;

/**
 * Derived from the BluetoothChat example, an activity that enables
 * picking a paired or discovered Bluetooth device
 */
public class DeviceListActivity extends Activity {
    // Debugging
    private static final String TAG = "DeviceListActivity";
    private static final boolean D = true;

    // Return Intent extra
    public static String EXTRA_DEVICE_ADDRESS = "device_address";

    // Member fields
    private BluetoothAdapter mBtAdapter;
    private ArrayAdapter<String> mPairedDevicesArrayAdapter;
    private ArrayAdapter<String> mNewDevicesArrayAdapter;

    @Override
    protected void onCreate(Bundle savedInstanceState) {
        super.onCreate(savedInstanceState);

        // Set up the window
        setContentView(R.layout.device_list);

        // Set result CANCELED in case the user backs out
        setResult(Activity.RESULT_CANCELED);

        // Initialize the button to perform device discovery
        Button scanButton = (Button) findViewById(R.id.button_scan);
        scanButton.setOnClickListener(new OnClickListener() {
            public void onClick(View v) {
                doDiscovery();
                v.setVisibility(View.GONE);
            }
        });

        // Initialize array adapters. One for already paired devices and
        // one for newly discovered devices
        mPairedDevicesArrayAdapter = new ArrayAdapter<String>(this,
            R.layout.device_name);
        mNewDevicesArrayAdapter = new ArrayAdapter<String>(this,
            R.layout.device_name);
```

```
        // Find and set up the ListView for paired devices
        ListView pairedListView = (ListView) findViewById(R.id.paired_devices);
        pairedListView.setAdapter(mPairedDevicesArrayAdapter);
        pairedListView.setOnItemClickListener(mDeviceClickListener);

        // Find and set up the ListView for newly discovered devices
        ListView newDevicesListView = (ListView) findViewById(R.id.new_devices);
        newDevicesListView.setAdapter(mNewDevicesArrayAdapter);
        newDevicesListView.setOnItemClickListener(mDeviceClickListener);

        // Register for broadcasts when a device is discovered
        IntentFilter filter = new IntentFilter(BluetoothDevice.ACTION_FOUND);
        this.registerReceiver(mReceiver, filter);

        // Register for broadcasts when discovery has finished
        filter = new IntentFilter(BluetoothAdapter.ACTION_DISCOVERY_FINISHED);
        this.registerReceiver(mReceiver, filter);

        // Get the local Bluetooth adapter
        mBtAdapter = BluetoothAdapter.getDefaultAdapter();

        // Get a set of currently paired devices
        Set<BluetoothDevice> pairedDevices = mBtAdapter.getBondedDevices();

        // If there are paired devices, add each one to the ArrayAdapter
        if (pairedDevices.size() > 0) {
            findViewById(R.id.title_paired_devices).setVisibility(View.VISIBLE);
            for (BluetoothDevice device : pairedDevices) {
                mPairedDevicesArrayAdapter.add(device.getName() +
                    "\n" + device.getAddress());
            }
        } else {
            String noDevices =
              getResources().getText(R.string.none_paired).toString();
            mPairedDevicesArrayAdapter.add(noDevices);
        }
    }

    @Override
    protected void onDestroy() {
        super.onDestroy();

        // Make sure we're not doing discovery anymore
        if (mBtAdapter != null) {
            mBtAdapter.cancelDiscovery();
        }

        // Unregister broadcast listeners
        this.unregisterReceiver(mReceiver);
    }

    /**
     * Start device discovery with the BluetoothAdapter
     */
```

```java
private void doDiscovery() {
    if (D) Log.d(TAG, "doDiscovery()");

    // Indicate scanning in the title
    setProgressBarIndeterminateVisibility(true);
    setTitle(R.string.scanning);

    // Turn on sub-title for new devices
    findViewById(R.id.title_new_devices).setVisibility(View.VISIBLE);

    // If we're already discovering, stop it
    if (mBtAdapter.isDiscovering()) {
        mBtAdapter.cancelDiscovery();
    }

    // Request discovery from BluetoothAdapter
    mBtAdapter.startDiscovery();
}

// The on-click listener for all devices in the ListViews
private OnItemClickListener mDeviceClickListener = new OnItemClickListener() {
    public void onItemClick(AdapterView<?> av, View v, int arg2, long arg3) {
        // Cancel discovery because it's costly and we're about to connect
        mBtAdapter.cancelDiscovery();

        // Get the device MAC address, which is the last 17 chars in the View
        String info = ((TextView) v).getText().toString();
        String address = info.substring(info.length() - 17);

        // Create the result Intent and include the MAC address
        Intent intent = new Intent();
        intent.putExtra(EXTRA_DEVICE_ADDRESS, address);

        // Set result and finish this Activity
        setResult(Activity.RESULT_OK, intent);
        finish();
    }
};

// The BroadcastReceiver that listens for discovered devices and
// changes the title when discovery is finished
private final BroadcastReceiver mReceiver = new BroadcastReceiver() {
    @Override
    public void onReceive(Context context, Intent intent) {
        String action = intent.getAction();

        // When discovery finds a device
        if (BluetoothDevice.ACTION_FOUND.equals(action)) {
            // Get the BluetoothDevice object from the Intent
            BluetoothDevice device =
                intent.getParcelableExtra(BluetoothDevice.EXTRA_DEVICE);
            // If it's already paired, skip it, because it's been listed already
            if (device.getBondState() != BluetoothDevice.BOND_BONDED) {
                mNewDevicesArrayAdapter.add(
                    device.getName() + "\n" + device.getAddress());
```

```
            }
        // When discovery is finished, change the Activity title
        } else if (BluetoothAdapter.ACTION_DISCOVERY_FINISHED.equals(action)) {
            setProgressBarIndeterminateVisibility(false);
            setTitle(R.string.select_device);
            if (mNewDevicesArrayAdapter.getCount() == 0) {
                String noDevices =
                    getResources().getText(R.string.none_found).toString();
                mNewDevicesArrayAdapter.add(noDevices);
            }
        }
    }
};

}
```

The DeviceListActivity class

This activity displays a dialog that lists known devices and enables the user to request a scan for devices. Unlike those parts of the app where Thread subclasses are used to implement asynchronous I/O and Handler subclasses pass the results to the UI thread, the startDiscovery method of the BluetoothAdapter class kicks off a separate thread and communicates results using broadcast intents. A BroadcastReceiver is used here to process those results.

The BtConsoleActivity class

The BtConsoleActivity class creates a chat-like activity for interacting with a Bluetooth device. The menus in this activity enable connecting to a device, and the main view in this activity is a scrolling list of data sent and received. At the bottom of the screen, there is an EditText view for entering text to be sent to the other end of the SPP connection.

Handler classes are used to glue the single-threaded UI to the threads that listen for, establish, and perform I/O on socket connections.

The Android Native Development Kit (NDK)

Java Native Interface (JNI) is a part of the Java standard that enables developers to write methods in languages that are compiled to native code, such as C and C++, and call those methods from Java code. JNI is also what connects the Java runtime environment to the underlying operating system. For details on JNI and how it can be used with Java code, see the Java Native Interface Specification (*http://download.oracle.com/javase/1 .5.0/docs/guide/jni*).

To make things as easy as possible for the Java developer, JNI lets a native method use Java objects in the same way that Java code uses these objects. Within the native method, Java objects can be created and used. This ability to access and use Java objects enables the native method to use other Java objects through references passed to it from a Java application.

JNI is especially useful when you want to use platform-specific features or take advantage of hardware in the platform that can't be accessed through Android APIs, such as accessing faster numerical computation by taking advantage of FPU instructions. Graphics-intensive code that makes extensive use of the OpenGL API is another place to use JNI.

This chapter covers JNI basics for programmers using the Android Native Development Kit (NDK). The NDK makes it more convenient to compile native code that can be used with Android programs.

When deciding whether you should develop in native code, think about your requirements and consider whether the Android SDK already provides the functionality you need. Using JNI makes your program harder to debug, and it ties it to the CPU types supported by the NDK, currently two variants of ARM, and x86.

Native Methods and JNI Calls

JNI specifies conventions allowing calls to methods implemented in other languages. Native methods require more changes, to comply with the conventions, than Java methods.

Conventions in Native Method Calls

When a virtual machine (VM)—in Android's case, Dalvik—invokes a function implemented in C or C++, it passes two special parameters:

- A `JNIEnv` pointer, which identifies the thread in the VM that called the native method
- A `jobject` type, which is a reference to the calling class

These parameters are passed transparently to Java code. That is, they do not appear in the method signature declared in the calling Java code. The Java call just explicitly passes any other parameters needed by the called function.

A JNI function may look like this:

```
/* sample method where the Java call passed no parameters */
void Java_ClassName_MethodName (JNIEnv *env, jobject obj) {
    /* do something */
}

/* another sample method with two parameters passed, returning a double */
jdouble Java_ClassName_MethodName ( JNIEnv* env, jobject obj,
                                    jdouble x,  jdouble y) {
    return x + y;
}
```

These examples show the two parameters passed automatically to every native method, and explicit parameters with types that map to Java types.

When a native method is called, it runs in the same process and the same thread as the Java code that calls it. As we will see later in this chapter, it can allocate memory from the Java heap to take advantage of garbage collection, or outside the Java heap to circumvent Java memory management. Variables allocated on the stack in C or C++ code have the same semantics as in native executables in those languages. They are allocated from the stack space for the process they run in.

JNI provides types that correspond to Java types, as shown in Table 19-1.

Table 19-1. Data mapping

Native type	Java type	Description
boolean	jboolean	Unsigned 8 bits
byte	jbyte	Signed 8 bits
char	jchar	Unsigned 16 bits
short	jshort	Signed 16 bits
int	jint	Signed 32 bits
long	jlong	Signed 64 bits
float	jfloat	32 bits
double	jdouble	64 bits
void	void	N/A

In compound types such as objects, arrays, and strings, the native code must explicitly convert the data by calling conversion methods, which are accessible through the JNIEnv pointer.

Conventions on the Java Side

Before native methods can be used within a Java class, the library containing native methods must be loaded by calling System.loadLibrary. Typically, the class that needs the native method would statically load this. Native methods accessed by a class are declared in the class using the **native** keyword:

```java
public class ClassWithNativeMethod {

    public native double nativeMethod();    // native method

    static {
        System.loadLibrary("sample");  // load lib called 'sample'
    }

    public static void main(String[] args) {
        ClassWithNativeMethod cwnm = new ClassWithNativeMethod();

        double answer = cwnm.nativeMethod();  // call native method

        System.out.println("Answer is : "+answer);
    }
}
```

The Android NDK

The Android Native Development Kit (NDK) is a companion tool to the Android SDK. If you use the NDK to create native code, your applications are still packaged into an *.apk* file and run inside a Dalvik VM on the device. The fundamental Android application model does not change.

Setting Up the NDK Environment

To use the NDK, you must first install and set up the SDK. The system requirements for installing and using the NDK are as follows:

- Windows XP (32-bit) or Vista (32- or 64-bit) with Cygwin 1.7 or later, or Mac OS X 10.4.8 or later, or Linux (32- or 64-bit)
- GNU Make 3.81 or later
- GNU AWK or nawk

First, download and install the latest version of the NDK (*http://developer.android.com/sdk/ndk/index.html*). Installation is simple: unzip the archive. The name of the top-level directory will include the version number of the NDK. Here we will refer to that directory as *ndk*. If the version currently available is newer than the one we use in this chapter, you may find there are more native APIs supported.

Once the NDK is downloaded and installed, you will find extensive documentation in the *ndk/docs* directory. We highly recommend that you read the documentation, starting with *OVERVIEW.html*. Also included in the NDK are samples (located in *ndk/samples*). The samples cover quite a bit more than this chapter will, so after you have used the NDK a bit, we recommend that you go through the samples.

Editing C/C++ Code in Eclipse

To make the best use of Eclipse to edit C code, you should install the Eclipse C/C++ Development Tooling, or Eclipse CDT. This will equip your Eclipse environment with an editor that can edit C code with syntax coloring, formatting, and other features that are comparable to Eclipse's Java editing capabilities.

The name of the repository for the correct version of CDT depends on your version of Eclipse. For Eclipse Indigo, use the repository at *http://download.eclipse.org/tools/cdt/releases/indigo* in the Install New Software dialog. See Chapter 5 for more information about using Eclipse, adding packages to your Eclipse environment, and using static analysis.

Compiling with the NDK

To develop native code with the NDK, you will need to do the following:

1. Create a *jni* directory within your project.
2. Place your native source in the *jni* directory.
3. Create a makefile called *Android.mk* (and, optionally, an *Application.mk* file) in the *jni* directory.
4. Run the *ndk*/ndk-build command from within the *jni* directory.

The optional *Application.mk* file describes what native modules are needed for your application as well as specific ABI types to build against. In this case, we use all to indicate we want all the available API types. As of this writing, this includes ARM5, which is called armeabi in the NDK; ARM7, which is called armeabi-v7a; and the Intel x86 architecture, which is called x86. For more details, check *APPLICATION-MK.html* in the documentation. A sample *Application.mk* file follows:

```
# Build all available ABIs
APP_ABI := all
# What platform (API level) to build against
APP_PLATFORM := android-14
```

The *Android.mk* file describes your source to the build system. It is really a tiny GNU Makefile fragment that is parsed by the build system when building your app. For more details, read the *ANDROID-MK.html* file in the NDK documentation. A sample *Android.mk* follows:

```
# Must define the LOCAL_PATH and return the current dir
LOCAL_PATH := $(call my-dir)

# Cleans various variables... making a clean build
include $(CLEAR_VARS)

# Identify the module/library's name
LOCAL_MODULE    := sample
# Specify the source files
LOCAL_SRC_FILES := sample.c
# Load local libraries (here we load the log library)
LOCAL_LDLIBS    := -llog

# Build the shared library defined above
include $(BUILD_SHARED_LIBRARY)
```

Once you have written your *Android.mk* makefile and, optionally, an *Application.mk* makefile, as well as the native source files themselves, run *ndk*/ndk-build within the project directory to build your libraries. If the build is successful, the shared libraries will be copied into your application's root project directory and added to its build.

If you download and peruse the Android source code, makefiles that closely resemble this one are used throughout the Android build system. Writing a simple application that uses the Android NDK is a good way to familiarize yourself with the use of JNIs, native code, and how native code is built in Android itself.

JNI, NDK, and SDK: A Sample App

To help you understand how the SDK and native source can be put together, we provide the following sample app. It describes an activity called `SampleActivityWith NativeMethods`. The Android manifest fragment declaring this activity is shown here:

```
<activity android:name=".SampleActivityWithNativeMethods"
          android:label="Sample Activity With Native Methods"
          android:debuggable="true" />
```

The `SampleActivityWithNativeMethods` activity uses the following layout:

```
<?xml version="1.0" encoding="utf-8"?>
<LinearLayout xmlns:android="http://schemas.android.com/apk/res/android"
    android:orientation="vertical"
    android:layout_width="fill_parent"
    android:layout_height="fill_parent"
    >
<Button
    android:id="@+id/whatami"
    android:layout_width="fill_parent"
    android:layout_height="wrap_content"
    android:paddingTop="5dp"
    android:paddingBottom="5dp"
    android:text="What CPU am I?"
    />
</LinearLayout>
```

The sample C library source has a method called `whatAmI`, which our Java activity will hook to the button with the `whatami` ID. We also define a function named `LOGINFO`, resolving to an `__android_log_print` call. This is how the Android log is written:

```
// the jni library MUST be included
#include <jni.h>
// the log lib is included
#include <android/log.h>

// usage of log
#define  LOGINFO(x...)  __android_log_print(ANDROID_LOG_INFO,"SampleJNI",x)

jstring
Java_com_oreilly_demo_android_pa_ndkdemo_SampleActivityWithNativeMethods_whatAmI(
                                        JNIEnv* env,jobject thisobject) {
    LOGINFO("SampleJNI","Sample Info Log Output");

    return (*env)->NewStringUTF(env, "Unknown");
}
```

Our *Android.mk* file follows. Note that it causes the log library to be loaded:

```
LOCAL_PATH := $(call my-dir)
```

```
include $(CLEAR_VARS)

LOCAL_MODULE    := sample
LOCAL_SRC_FILES := sample.c
LOCAL_LDLIBS    := -llog

include $(BUILD_SHARED_LIBRARY)
```

Finally, here is the SampleActivityWithNativeMethods Java activity's source code. The class loads the sample library and declares the whatAmI() native method. When the button is clicked, the whatAmI() method is called and returns "Unknown". This then shows a Toast with the string "CPU: Unknown". If you find the output uninformative, rest assured that we will include the CPU information in a later section.

```
package com.oreilly.demo.android.pa.ndkdemo;

import com.oreilly.demo.android.pa.ndkdemo.R;
import android.widget.Toast;

public class SampleActivityWithNativeMethods extends Activity {

    static {
        System.loadLibrary("sample");  // load our sample lib
    }

    @Override
    public void onCreate(Bundle savedInstanceState) {
        super.onCreate(savedInstanceState);
        setContentView(R.layout.sample);

        setupview();
    }

    public native String whatAmI();  // sample lib native method

    private void setupview() {
        findViewById(R.id.whatami).setOnClickListener(
                                   new View.OnClickListener() {

            public void onClick(View v) {
                String whatami = whatAmI();
                Toast.makeText(getBaseContext(), "CPU: "+whatami,
                                    Toast.LENGTH_SHORT).show();
            }
        });
    }
```

Native Libraries and Headers Provided by the NDK

The NDK comes with the following set of headers for stable native APIs:

- libc (C library) headers
- libm (math library) headers

- JNI interface headers
- libz (Zlib compression) headers
- liblog (Android logging) header
- OpenGL ES 1.1 and OpenGL ES 2.0 (3D graphics libraries) headers
- libjnigraphics (pixel buffer access) header (for Android 2.2 and later)
- A minimal set of headers for C++ support
- OpenSL ES native audio libraries
- Android native application APIs

 Except for the libraries just listed, native system libraries in the Android platform are not stable and may change in future platform versions. Your applications should use only the stable native system libraries provided in the NDK.

Some libraries, such as libc and libm, are automatically referenced in the build and thus need to be referenced only in the source code as includes. However, some libraries are not automatically referenced, and thus require specific statements within the *Android.mk* build file.

Here is a sample *Android.mk* file that imports the cpufeatures module, which will give us the information missing from our earlier whatAmI example:

```
LOCAL_PATH := $(call my-dir)

include $(CLEAR_VARS)

LOCAL_MODULE    := sample
LOCAL_SRC_FILES := sample.c
LOCAL_LDLIBS    := -llog
  # Here we reference the cpufeatures module
LOCAL_STATIC_LIBRARIES := cpufeatures

include $(BUILD_SHARED_LIBRARY)

  # Here we import the cpufeatures modules
$(call import-module,cpufeatures)
```

The following source (extending the whatAmI function we showed in the previous section) utilizes the cpufeatures module we have included:

```
// Include the cpu-features module
#include <cpu-features.h>
#include <jni.h>
#include <android/log.h>

#define  LOGINFO(x...)   __android_log_print(ANDROID_LOG_INFO,"SampleJNI",x)

jstring
Java_com_oreilly_demo_android_pa_ndkdemo_SampleActivityWithNativeMethods_whatAmI(
```

```
                                         JNIEnv* env, jobject thisobject) {
    LOGINFO("SampleJNI","Sample Info Log Output");

        // -- Here we use the cpufeatures -- //
    uint64_t cpu_features;

    if (android_getCpuFamily() != ANDROID_CPU_FAMILY_ARM) {
        return (*env)->NewStringUTF(env, "Not ARM");
    }

    cpu_features = android_getCpuFeatures();

    if ((cpu_features & ANDROID_CPU_ARM_FEATURE_ARMv7) != 0) {
        return (*env)->NewStringUTF(env, "ARMv7");
    } else if ((cpu_features & ANDROID_CPU_ARM_FEATURE_VFPv3) != 0) {
        return (*env)->NewStringUTF(env, "ARM w VFPv3 support");
    } else if ((cpu_features & ANDROID_CPU_ARM_FEATURE_NEON) != 0) {
        return (*env)->NewStringUTF(env, "ARM w NEON support");
    }
        // -- End cpufeatures usage -- //

    return (*env)->NewStringUTF(env, "Unknown");
}
```

Building Your Own Custom Library Modules

This section combines several techniques shown throughout the chapter to create and use a simple C module that uses the math library to calculate a power. We'll start with the *Android.mk* file. Notice that we need to build the library (sample_lib) and export the includes. This library is then referenced in the sample.

```
LOCAL_PATH := $(call my-dir)

  # this is our sample library
include $(CLEAR_VARS)

LOCAL_MODULE    := sample_lib
LOCAL_SRC_FILES := samplelib/sample_lib.c
  # we need to make sure everything knows where everything is
LOCAL_EXPORT_C_INCLUDES := $(LOCAL_PATH)/samplelib

include $(BUILD_STATIC_LIBRARY)

  # sample uses the sample lib we created
include $(CLEAR_VARS)

LOCAL_MODULE    := sample
LOCAL_SRC_FILES := sample.c
LOCAL_LDLIBS    := -llog
  # We load our sample lib
LOCAL_STATIC_LIBRARIES := sample_lib

include $(BUILD_SHARED_LIBRARY)
```

We have a short header file, *sample_lib.h*:

```
#ifndef SAMPLE_LIB_H
#define SAMPLE_LIB_H

extern double calculatePower(double  x, double  y);

#endif
```

The source code for our function, *sample_lib.c*, is:

```
#include "sample_lib.h"
  // we include the math lib
#include "math.h"

  // we use the math lib
double calculatePower(double  x, double  y) {
    return pow(x, y);
}
```

Following is the *sample.c* file that glues our `sample_lib` library to the Java code:

```
  // we include the sample_lib
#include "sample_lib.h"
#include <jni.h>
#include <android/log.h>

#define  LOGINFO(x...)  __android_log_print(ANDROID_LOG_INFO,"SampleJNI",x)


jdouble
Java_com_oreilly_demo_android_pa_ndkdemo_SampleActivityWithNativeMethods_calculatePower(
                      JNIEnv* env, jobject thisobject, jdouble x, jdouble y) {

    LOGINFO("Sample Info Log Output");

    // we call sample-lib's calculate method
    return calculatePower(x, y);
}
```

The layout the `Activity` will use is:

```
<?xml version="1.0" encoding="utf-8"?>
<LinearLayout xmlns:android="http://schemas.android.com/apk/res/android"
    android:orientation="vertical"
    android:layout_width="fill_parent"
    android:layout_height="fill_parent"
    >
<EditText
    android:id="@+id/x"
    android:layout_width="fill_parent"
    android:layout_height="wrap_content"
    android:paddingTop="5dp"
    android:paddingBottom="5dp"
    android:textColor="#000"
    android:hint="X Value"
    />
```

```
<EditText
    android:id="@+id/y"
    android:layout_width="fill_parent"
    android:layout_height="wrap_content"
    android:paddingTop="5dp"
    android:paddingBottom="5dp"
    android:textColor="#000"
    android:hint="Y Value"
    />
  <Button
    android:id="@+id/calculate"
    android:layout_width="fill_parent"
    android:layout_height="wrap_content"
    android:paddingTop="5dp"
    android:paddingBottom="5dp"
    android:text="Calculate X^Y"
    />
</LinearLayout>
```

Following is the SampleActivityWithNativeMethods activity that we have modified to use with this new library. The sample library is loaded and the calculatePower() method is declared. When the "calculate" button is clicked, we then take the numbers provided from the two edit text boxes (using a default of 2 if the text is missing or is not a number) and pass them to the calculatePower() method. The returned double is then popped up as part of a Toast.

```
package com.oreilly.demo.android.pa.ndkdemo;

import com.oreilly.demo.android.pa.ndkdemo.R;
import android.app.Activity;
import android.os.Bundle;
import android.view.View;
import android.widget.EditText;
import android.widget.Toast;

public class SampleActivityWithNativeMethods extends Activity {

    static {
        System.loadLibrary("sample");  // load our sample lib
    }

    @Override
    public void onCreate(Bundle savedInstanceState) {
        super.onCreate(savedInstanceState);
        setContentView(R.layout.sample);

        setupview();
    }

    // sample lib native method
    public native double calculatePower(double x, double y);

    private void setupview() {

        findViewById(R.id.calculate).setOnClickListener(
```

```
                                            new View.OnClickListener() {

    public void onClick(View v) {
        String answer = "";
        double x = 2;
        double y = 2;

        String sx = ((EditText) findViewById(R.id.x)).getText().toString();
        String sy = ((EditText) findViewById(R.id.y)).getText().toString();

        if(sx == null) {
            answer = "X defaults to 2\n";
        } else {
            try {
                x = Double.parseDouble(sx);
            } catch (Exception e) {
                answer = "X is not a number, defaulting to 2\n";
                x = 2;
            }
        }

        if(sy == null) {
            answer += "Y defaults to 2\n";
        } else {
            try {
                y = Double.parseDouble(sy);
            } catch (Exception e) {
                answer = "Y is not a number, defaulting to 2\n";
                y = 2;
            }
        }

        double z = calculatePower(x, y);

        answer += x+"^"+y+" = "+z;

        Toast.makeText(SampleActivityWithNativeMethods.this, answer,
                                        Toast.LENGTH_SHORT).show();
    }
});
    }
}
```

Native Activities

Android 2.3 (API level 9) and Android NDK revision 5 let you write entire activities and applications as native source by using the NativeActivity class to access the Android application life cycle.

To utilize this method, the android.app.NativeActivity needs to be referenced in the Android manifest file. Note that the application reference has a hasCode attribute. This attribute should be set to false if there is no Java in the application (only the

NativeActivity). In this case, however, because we do have Java code, we set the value
to true:

```
<!-- This .apk has Java code, so set hasCode to true which is the default. -->
<!-- if this only had a native app (only the activity
     called 'android.app.NativeActivity') -->
<!-- then set to false -->

<application android:icon="@drawable/icon" android:label="@string/app_name"
    android:hasCode="true" >

    <activity android:name=".NDKApp" android:label="@string/app_name">
        <intent-filter>
            <action android:name="android.intent.action.MAIN" />
            <category android:name="android.intent.category.LAUNCHER" />
        </intent-filter>
    </activity>

    <activity android:name="android.app.NativeActivity"
                        android:label="SampleNativeActivity"
                        android:debuggable="true" >

        <!-- here we declare what lib to reference -->
        <meta-data android:name="android.app.lib_name"
                            android:value="sample_native_activity" />
    </activity>

</application>
```

In this example, we use the *android_native_app_glue.h* header file instead of *native_
activity.h*. The *native_activity.h* interface is based on a set of application-provided callbacks that will be called by the Activity's main thread when certain events occur. This
means callbacks should not block, and therefore it is constraining. The *android_
native_app_glue.h* file exposes a helper library with a different execution model that
provides a means for the application to implement its own main function in a different
thread. The function must be named android_main(), and is called when the application
is created and an android_app object is passed to it. This provides a means to reference
the application or activity and listen in on various life cycle events.

The following simple nativeactivity example constructs an Activity and listens in on
Motion events. The Motion events' *x* and *y* screen coordinates are then sent to LogCat.

```
#include <jni.h>
#include <android/log.h>
#include <android_native_app_glue.h>

// usage of log
#define LOGINFO(x...) __android_log_print(ANDROID_LOG_INFO,"SampleNativeActivity",x)

// handle commands
static void custom_handle_cmd(struct android_app* app, int32_t cmd) {
    switch(cmd) {
        case APP_CMD_INIT_WINDOW:
        LOGINFO("App Init Window");
```

```
            break;
        }
    }

    // handle input
    static int32_t custom_handle_input(struct android_app* app, AInputEvent* event) {
            // we see a motion event and we log it
        if (AInputEvent_getType(event) == AINPUT_EVENT_TYPE_MOTION) {
        LOGINFO("Motion Event: x %f / y %f", AMotionEvent_getX(event, 0),
                AMotionEvent_getY(event, 0));
        return 1;
        }
        return 0;
    }

    // This is the function that application code must implement,
    // representing the main entry to the app.
    void android_main(struct android_app* state) {
        // Make sure glue isn't stripped.
        app_dummy();

        int events;
        // set up so when commands happen we call our custom handler
        state->onAppCmd = custom_handle_cmd;
        // set up so when input happens we call our custom handler
        state->onInputEvent = custom_handle_input;

        while (1) {
            struct android_poll_source* source;

            // we block for events
            while (ALooper_pollAll(-1, NULL, &events, (void**)&source) >= 0) {

                // Process this event.
                if (source != NULL) {
                    source->process(state, source);
                }

                // Check if we are exiting.
                if (state->destroyRequested != 0) {
                    LOGINFO("We are exiting");
                    return;
                }
            }
        }
    }
```

This is the *Android.mk* file for the sample nativeactivity. Note that it loads and refers to the android_native_app_glue module.

```
LOCAL_PATH := $(call my-dir)

# this is our sample native activity
include $(CLEAR_VARS)

LOCAL_MODULE    := sample_native_activity
```

```
LOCAL_SRC_FILES := sample_nativeactivity.c
LOCAL_LDLIBS    := -llog -landroid
LOCAL_STATIC_LIBRARIES := android_native_app_glue

include $(BUILD_SHARED_LIBRARY)

$(call import-module,android/native_app_glue)
```

Following is the main Java Android activity that is called when the user launches the application. Clicking on the button launches the `NativeActivity` that we have provided.

```
package com.oreilly.demo.android.pa.ndkdemo;

import com.oreilly.demo.android.pa.ndkdemo.R;
import android.app.Activity;
import android.content.Intent;
import android.os.Bundle;
import android.view.View;

public class NDKApp extends Activity {
    @Override
    public void onCreate(Bundle savedInstanceState) {
        super.onCreate(savedInstanceState);
        setContentView(R.layout.main);

        findViewById(R.id.nativeactivity).setOnClickListener(
          new View.OnClickListener() {

            public void onClick(View v) {
                startActivity(new Intent(getBaseContext(),
                    android.app.NativeActivity.class));  // call nativeactivity
            }

        });
    }
}
```

If you compile and run this example, you will note that when the native activity is launched, the screen is blank, and if you are viewing LogCat you will see various log messages appear (especially when moving your finger across the screen). This, however, is not much fun. So to spruce things up, we wish to do something with the screen. The following example adds the use of OpenGL ES to change the screen's color.

Here is the native source with the additional OpenGL ES material. It simply turns the screen bright red when the activity is displayed.

```
#include <jni.h>
#include <android/log.h>
#include <android_native_app_glue.h>

#include <EGL/egl.h>
#include <GLES/gl.h>

// usage of log
#define LOGINFO(x...)
```

```
    __android_log_print(ANDROID_LOG_INFO,"NativeWOpenGL",x)

struct eglengine {
    EGLDisplay display;
    EGLSurface surface;
    EGLContext context;
};

// initialize the egl engine
static int engine_init_display(struct android_app* app, struct eglengine* engine) {
    const EGLint attribs[] = {
            EGL_SURFACE_TYPE, EGL_WINDOW_BIT,
            EGL_BLUE_SIZE, 8,
            EGL_GREEN_SIZE, 8,
            EGL_RED_SIZE, 8,
            EGL_NONE
    };
    EGLint w, h, dummy, format;
    EGLint numConfigs;
    EGLConfig config;
    EGLSurface surface;
    EGLContext context;

    EGLDisplay display = eglGetDisplay(EGL_DEFAULT_DISPLAY);
    eglInitialize(display, 0, 0);
    eglChooseConfig(display, attribs, &config, 1, &numConfigs);
    eglGetConfigAttrib(display, config, EGL_NATIVE_VISUAL_ID, &format);

    ANativeWindow_setBuffersGeometry(app->window, 0, 0, format);

    surface = eglCreateWindowSurface(display, config, app->window, NULL);
    context = eglCreateContext(display, config, NULL, NULL);

    if (eglMakeCurrent(display, surface, surface, context) == EGL_FALSE) {
        LOGINFO("eglMakeCurrent FAIL");
        return -1;
    }

    eglQuerySurface(display, surface, EGL_WIDTH, &w);
    eglQuerySurface(display, surface, EGL_HEIGHT, &h);

    engine->display = display;
    engine->context = context;
    engine->surface = surface;

    glHint(GL_PERSPECTIVE_CORRECTION_HINT, GL_FASTEST);
    glEnable(GL_CULL_FACE);
    glShadeModel(GL_SMOOTH);
    glDisable(GL_DEPTH_TEST);

    return 0;
}

// draw to the screen
static void engine_color_screen(struct eglengine* engine) {
```

```
    if (engine->display == NULL) {
        return;
    }

    glClearColor(255, 0, 0, 1);  // let's make the screen all red
    glClear(GL_COLOR_BUFFER_BIT);

    eglSwapBuffers(engine->display, engine->surface);
}

// when things need to be terminated
static void engine_terminate(struct eglengine* engine) {
    if (engine->display != EGL_NO_DISPLAY) {
        eglMakeCurrent(engine->display, EGL_NO_SURFACE, EGL_NO_SURFACE,
            EGL_NO_CONTEXT);
        if (engine->context != EGL_NO_CONTEXT) {
            eglDestroyContext(engine->display, engine->context);
        }
        if (engine->surface != EGL_NO_SURFACE) {
            eglDestroySurface(engine->display, engine->surface);
        }
        eglTerminate(engine->display);
    }
    engine->display = EGL_NO_DISPLAY;
    engine->context = EGL_NO_CONTEXT;
    engine->surface = EGL_NO_SURFACE;
}

// handle commands
static void custom_handle_cmd(struct android_app* app, int32_t cmd) {
    struct eglengine* engine = (struct eglengine*)app->userData;
    switch(cmd) {
        // things are starting up... let's initialize the engine and color the screen
        case APP_CMD_INIT_WINDOW:
            if (app->window != NULL) {
                engine_init_display(app, engine);
                engine_color_screen(engine);
            }
            break;
        case APP_CMD_TERM_WINDOW:  // things are ending...let's clean up the engine
                engine_terminate(engine);
            break;
    }
}

// handle input
static int32_t custom_handle_input(struct android_app* app, AInputEvent* event) {
    // we see a motion event and we log it
    if (AInputEvent_getType(event) == AINPUT_EVENT_TYPE_MOTION) {
    LOGINFO("Motion Event: x %f / y %f", AMotionEvent_getX(event, 0),
                AMotionEvent_getY(event, 0));
    return 1;
    }
    return 0;
}
```

```
// This is the function that application code must implement,
// representing the main entry to the app.
void android_main(struct android_app* state) {
    // Make sure glue isn't stripped.
    app_dummy();

    // here we add the eglengine to the app
    struct eglengine engine;
    memset(&engine, 0, sizeof(engine));
    // set engine as userdata so we can reference
    state->userData = &engine;

    int events;
    // set up so when commands happen we call our custom handler
    state->onAppCmd = custom_handle_cmd;
    // set up so when input happens we call our custom handler
    state->onInputEvent = custom_handle_input;

    while (1) {
        struct android_poll_source* source;

        // we block for events
        while (ALooper_pollAll(-1, NULL, &events, (void**)&source) >= 0) {

            // Process this event.
            if (source != NULL) {
                source->process(state, source);
            }

            // Check if we are exiting.
            if (state->destroyRequested != 0) {
                LOGINFO("We are exiting");
                return;
            }
        }
    }
}
```

The *Android.mk* file for the sample_native_activity_opengl activity loads the EGL and
GLESv1_CM libraries:

```
LOCAL_PATH := $(call my-dir)

# this is our sample native activity with opengl
include $(CLEAR_VARS)

LOCAL_MODULE    := sample_native_activity_opengl
LOCAL_SRC_FILES := sample_nativeactivity_opengl.c
  # loading the log , android, egl, gles libraries
LOCAL_LDLIBS    := -llog -landroid -lEGL -lGLESv1_CM
LOCAL_STATIC_LIBRARIES := android_native_app_glue

include $(BUILD_SHARED_LIBRARY)

$(call import-module,android/native_app_glue)
```

Index

Symbols

% (percent sign), wildcard character in SQL, 274
. (period), sqlite3 commands beginning with, 272
.exit command, 273
9-patch, 27
; (semicolon), ending SQL commands, 273
= (equals sign)
    assignment operator, 35
| (pipe character), use by sqlite3, 274

A

aapt tool, 203
aapt utility, 94
AAR (Android Application Record), 461
ABSOLUTE_URI NFCType, 454
abstract classes, 45
AbstractAccountAuthenticator class, 471, 484
    addAccount method, 472
AbstractThreadedSyncAdapter class, 480
AccelerateInterpolator objects, 255
accelerometer, 447
access modifiers, 57–59
accessibility, 463
AccessibilityEvent objects, 464
AccessibilityService class, 463
AccessibilityServiceInfo objects, 463
account contacts, 467–470
AccountAuthenticator objects, 471
AccountAuthenticatorResponse objects, 472
AccountManager objects, 474
Action Bar, 200, 333
    SearchView in, 403

ACTION_NDEF_DISCOVERED intent, 451
activities, 15
    connecting to GPS LocationProvider, 423
    ContentControlActivity in UI, 336–340
    defined, 77
    Fragment, Activity, and scalable design, 317
    fragments and, 205
    Google Maps, 413
    keeping references to Activity objects, discouraged, 78
    life cycle, 83
    life cycle of activity that spawns a task, 114
    native, 512–518
    searchable, 400–402
    SimpleFinchVideoActivity class (example), 344
    tasks comprised of, 78
    visualizing Activity component life cycle, 296–308
        configuration changes and life cycle, 305
        life cycle methods of Activity class, 304
        memory recovery and life cycles, 302
        minor life cycle methods of Activity class, 307
        saving and restoring instance state, 304
      working together with other UI elements, 333
Activity class, 77, 78
    (see also activities)
    findViewById method, 180
    life cycle methods, 304
    minor life cycle methods, 307
    onCreate method, 83

We'd like to hear your suggestions for improving our indexes. Send email to *index@oreilly.com*.

Verizon Developer Community websites, 141

DeviceListActivity class, 500

.dex files, transformation of .class files into, 151

directories

Android application projects, 86

disableForegroundDispatch method, 453

disableForegroundNdefPush method, NfcAdapter class, 460

dispatchDraw method, ViewGroup objects, 231

dispatchKeyEvent method, View object, 173

dispatchTouchEvent method, 190

dispatchTrackballEvent method, 190

DispLocListener class, 424

distribution of applications

alternative, 139–142

in Android Market, 135–138

document-centric applications, 275

doInBackground method, AsyncTask object, 109

dot commands, sqlite3, 272

double type, 34

Draw 9-patch, 27

draw method, View objects, 231

Drawable class, 232

drawable directory, 88

Drawable objects, 242–246

AnimationDrawable, 256

BitmapDrawable, 248

FaderDrawable (example), 245

transformations of, 244

wrappers supporting special effects, 245

Drawable.Callback interface, 256

DrawableContainer class, 246, 256

drawCachedBitmap method, 248

drawCircle method, 234

drawFrame method, 259, 261

drawing

drawing text with Canvas, 235

main classes used in Android UI framework, 232

drawPosText method, 236

drawText method, 236

drawTextOnPath method, 236

DROP TABLE statement, 265

dynamic declarations, 43

E

Eclair, 232

Eclipse IDE, 3, 147–167

and Android, 158

Android projects, basic organization of, 86

associations, 153

builders and artifacts, 151

creating Android project, 12

documentation, 148

editing C/C++ code in, 504

idiosyncrasies of, 166

installing, 5

Java coding in, 156

editing Java code and code completion, 156

refactoring, 157

Java environments, 150

application runtime, 150

Java compiler, 150

Java Runtime Environment, 150

keeping up-to-date, 29

observing Activity life cycle using LogCat view, 296

plug-ins, 148

preventing bugs and keeping code clean, 158

applying static analysis to Android code, 163

limitations of static analysis, 166

using static analyzers, 159

projects, 151

refactoring tools, 88

views and perspectives, 153–156

workspaces, 149

Eclipse iDE

extensions, 151

editors

new layout editor introduced by Google Android Tools team, 180

UI editor, 319

editors for Eclipse, 152

EditText object, 99

invalidate method, 181

Emulator Control pane, DDMS window, 427

enableForegroundDispatch method, 451

enableForegroundNdefPush method, NfcAdapter class, 459

encapsulation, 60

getters and setters, 60

life cycle methods of Application class, 312–313

visualizing Activity life cycle, 296

visualizing Fragment life cycle, 308–310

friends and events, finding, 281

fromRawResource method, GestureLibrary objects, 463

G

garbage collection (Java), 55

gen directory, 87
    R class, 89

generics, 54

geo utility, using to update location, 427

gesture handling
    provided by MotionEvent, 188

gesture input, 462–463

Gesture objects, 463

GestureDetector objects, 192

GestureLibraries class, 462

GestureLibraries objects
    fromRawResource method, 463

GestureOverlayView objects, 462
    OnGesturePerformedListener interface, 462

GesturePoint objects, 463

gestures
    multiple, tracking by a device, 190

GestureStore objects, 463

GestureStroke objects, 463

getArguments method
    Fragment object, 211

getConfigSpec method, 259

getCurrentPosition method
    MediaPlayer, 436

getDefaultAdapter method, NfcAdapter class, 451

getFragmentManager method, 210

getHistoricalX method, 188, 191

getHistoricalY method, 188, 191

getLastKnownLocation method, 424

getLastNonConfigurationInstance method, 307

getMatrix method, Canvas transformations, 241

getMeasuredHeight method, 229

getMeasuredWidth method, 229

getMode and getSize methods, MeasureSpec objects, 228

getPointerCount method, 191

getPointerId method, 191

getRepeatCount method, KeyEvent object, 193

getResources method, Context class, 89

getSensorList method, 446

getSuggestedMinimumHeight method, 229

getSuggestedMinimumWidth method, 229

getSystemService method, Context objects, 446

getter and setter methods, 60

getting paid for apps distributed via Android Market, 138

getType method
    implementing for content provider, 351
    implementing for simple Finch video content provider (example), 358

getX method, 191

getY method, 191

Global Positioning System (see GPS)

GLSurfaceView class, 259

GLSurfaceView.Renderer interface, 259

Google Checkout, 138

Google Maps, 413

Google Maps API keys, 143

GPS (Global Positioning System), 412

GPU (Graphics Processing Unit), 259

GPX location updates, DDMS emulator, 428

gradients, 251

graphics and animation, 225–261
    animation, 253–258
        background, 256–258
        surface view, 258
        transitions, 253–255
    creating your own widgets, 225–248
        Canvas drawing, 231–242
        layout, 226–231
    graphics effects, 248–252
        Effects application (example), 249
        Effects widget (example), 249
        shadows, gradients, filters, and hardware acceleration, 251
    OpenGL graphics, 258–261

gravity, 229, 449

GUIs (graphical user interfaces)
    Android GUI architecture, 171–175
        complete UI system, 173
        Controller, 173
        Model, 171

N

*_NAME constant, database column names, 279
namespaces, 56
    content provider, 81
    package attribute in the manifest, 89
native methods and JNI calls, 502–504
    conventions in native method calls, 502
NativeActivity class, 512
NAVBuilder Inside (NBI), 141
NDEF TagTechnology reference, 458
NdefMessage objects, 454, 459
    writeNdefMessage method, 458
NdefRecord objects, 454, 458
    createApplicationRecord method, 461
    RTD_SMART_POSTER type, 456
    RTD_TEXT type, 455
    RTD_URI type, 455
    TNF_ABSOLUTE_URI type, 456
NDK (Native Development Kit) (see Android Dative Development Kit)
Near Field Communication (see NFC)
network API, Verizon carrier network, 141
network communication
    using serialization for, 119
network MVC, 367
    summary of benefits, 369
network, content provider API as asynchronous model of, 366
NetworkException object, 49
new keyword
    creating an object or instance of a class, 35
nextFocusDown, nextFocusLeft, nextFocusRight, and nextFocusUp properties, 196
NFC (Near Field Communication), 450–462
    P2P mode and beam, 459
        API levels 10-13, 459
        Beam, API level 14+, 460
    reading a tag, 451–457
    writing to a tag, 457–459
NfcAdapter class, 451
    disableForegroundNdefPush method, 460
    enableForegroundNdefPush method, 459
    EXTRA_ID, 454
    EXTRA_TAG, 454
    setNdefPushMessageCallback method, 460
    setNdePushMessage method, 460

NfcAdapter.CreateNdefMessageCallback interface, 460
no-arg constructors, 36
NOT NULL constraint, 268
notification of content observers, 363
notify( ) and wait( ) methods, thread control with, 71–72
notifyChange method, ContentResolver class, 354

O

Object class, 37
object relational-mapping (ORM), 119
ObjectInputStream objects, 119
ObjectOutputStream objects, 119
objects, 35
    created using anonymous classes, 63
    creating, 35
    inheritance and polymorphism, 39
oeg.w3c.dom package, 98
onAccessibilityEvent method, 464
onAccuracyChanged method, 446
onActivityCreated method, 310
onActivityResult method, 441
onAnimationEnd method, AnimationListener objects, 255
onAttach method
    Fragment objects, 310
onChange method
    ContentObserver class, 354
onClick method
    OnClickListener interface, 181
OnClickListener interface, 181
onContextItemSelected method, 202
onCreate method
    Activity class, 77, 304
    Fragment objects, 207, 209, 310
    implementing for simple Finch video content provider, 357
    SQLiteOpenHelper class, 277
    YouTubeDbHelper class (example), 279
onCreateContextMenu method, 202
onCreateOptionsMenu method, 420
onCreateView method, 320
    Fragment objects, 208, 310
onDestroy method
    Activity class, 304
onDraw method
    text rendering methods, 235

refactoring, 157
references
    holding reference to a parameter, causing
        concurrency problems, 112
registerContentObserver method, 82, 354
relational database management systems
    (RDBMSs), 264
relative humidity sensor, 450
RelativeLayout objects, 208
release method
    AudioRecorder, 442
    AudioTrack, 437
    MediaPlayer class, 436
    MediaRecorder, 439
remote procedure calls
    AIDL and, 124
rendezvous process for concurrent threads,
    105
requestChildFocus method, 197
requestFocus method, 196, 197
requestLayout method, 227
requestLocationUpdates method, 426
res directory, 87
    content of, 88
    conversion of contents of packaged resource
        file and R class, 94
reset method
    MediaPlayer, 436
    MediaRecorder, 439
resource qualifiers
    and screen sizes, 145
resources
    frame-by-frame animation, 256
    loading anew for configuration changes in
        activity, 306
    multiple versions of, using configuration
        qualifiers, 217
Resources class
    getDrawable method, 248
resources for Android applications, 88
REST (Representational State Transfer), 80
RESTful web service
    YouTube video content entries, 342
RESTful Web service
    content provider as facade for, 365–392
        code example, Finch video application,
            370
        developing RESTful Android
            applications, 366

implementing RESTful request, 374–
    392
network MVC, 367
source code structure, Finch video
    application, 371
stepping through search application,
    372
RESTful web services, contentProvider
    operations and, 80
RESTfulContentProvider (example)
    a REST helper, 379
ResultSet object, 111
RFID/NFC tags, 451
rotate method, 237
RotateAnimation objects, 255
RotateDrawable objects, 245
rotation vector, 449
RTD_TEXT type, NdefRecord, 455
runAnimation method, 255
Runnable interface, 67
runtime environment, Android applications,
    95–98
    Android libraries, 96
    Dalvik VM, 95
    sandboxing processes and users, 96
    Zygote, forking a new process, 95
RuntimeException
    caused by multiple threads accessing a View,
        198
RuntimeException class, 51

S

SampleActivityWithNativeMethods
    (example), 506, 507
sandboxing processes and users, 96
satellite view, 415
scalable UI, folding and unfolding, 326–333
    decisions on screen size and resolution, 326–
        330
    delegating to Fragment classes, 330–333
scale method, 237
ScaleAnimation objects, 255
ScaleDrawable objects, 245
ScaleGestureDetector objects, 192
scope, 55–59
    access modifiers and encapsulation, 57–59
    Java packages, 56
screens
    compatibility with many kinds of, 145

control over, with Paint class, 233
TreeMap object, 53
triangulation, 412
triggers, database, 271
try-catch blocks, 49
tweened animations, 253
type casting, 40
type safety
    AsyncTask maintaining, 110
    parcelable types and, 124
type safety in Java, 59–62
    encapsulation, 60
        getters and setters, 60
type system (Java) (see data types)

U

UIs (user interfaces), 315
    activities, fragments, action bar, and
            multiple layouts working
            together, 333–336
        action bar, 333
        tabs and fragments, 334–336
    adapting to multiple devices, using
            configuration qualifiers, 217
    Android applications versus servlets, 77
    Android's single-threaded UI, 118
    AsyncTask and UI thread in Android apps,
            105–116
    attaching the UI to its behaviors, 100
    ContentControlActivity, 336–340
    folding and unfolding scalable UI, 326–333
        decisions on screen size and resolution,
                326–330
        delegating to Fragment classes, 330–
                333
    laying out the fragments, 323
        multiple layouts, 325
        using visual editor, 324
    saving state of the UI, 85
    selecting among styles, 219
    small screens versus tablet screens, 205
    starting with blank slate, 319–323
        Fragment subclasses, 320
        QueryResultsListFragment class source
                code, 320
    top-level design, 316
        Fragment, Activity,a nd scalable design,
                317
    visual editing of user interfaces, 319

UNIQUE constraint, 268
unlockCanvasAndPost method, SurfaceView
        objects, 258
unmarshaling, 118
UNSPECIFIED measurement specification
        mode, 230
update method, 290
    ContentProvider objects, 351
    implementing for simple Finch video
            content provider (example), 361
UPDATE queries (SQL), 274
UPDATE statement, 270
updating existing database data, 290
updating tools, 28
    Android SDK, keeping up-to-date, 28
    Eclipse and ADT plug-in, 29
    JDK, 29
uploading application to Android Market, 137
URI NFCType, 454
URIMatcher class, 352
UriMatcher class, 375
UriReqestTask class (example), 379
UriRequestTask class (example), 381–383
URIs
    content provider, using to call data
            operations, 81
    defining CONTENT_URI, 346–348
    GData YouTube URIs, 376
    launching StreetView app, 430
    reading payload for NdefRecord.RTD_URI,
            455
    setting notification URI used by content
            provider for cursors, 359
    standardizing format of content provider
            URIs, 352
    use in content provider queries, 341
URLs
    content provider, 81
USB debugging, 20
uses-permission tag for
        android.permission.ACCESS_FINE_
        LOCATION, 422

V

VALUES clause, INSERT INTO statements,
        274
values directory, 89
variables
    anonymous classes and, 64

About the Authors

Zigurd Mednieks is a consultant to leading OEMs, enterprises, and entrepreneurial ventures creating Android-based systems and software. Previously he was chief architect at D2 Technologies, a Voice-over-IP (VoIP) technology provider. There he led engineering and product definition work for products that blended communication and social media in purpose-built embedded systems and on the Android platform.

Laird Dornin is a mobile development architect with extensive experience in Java, Android, J2ME, SavaJe, and the WebKit browser library. He was a member of the J2SE development team at Sun Microsystems specializing in Java RMI and Jini technology. He is currently a senior engineer at a major wireless carrier, where he provides Android architectural guidance and Network API support to members of the carrier's developer community.

G. Blake Meike is a software engineer with more than 20 years of experience, much of it with Java. He has built systems as large as Amazon's massively scalable AutoScaling service and as small as a pre-Android OSS/Linux-based Java-like platform for cellphones. Blake is currently an Android Evangelist, working at Marakana. He is co-author of two O'Reilly books on Android, including the bestselling *Programming Android*.

Masumi Nakamura, with more than a decade of software engineering experience, has worked in various positions within the mobile technology arena, from building out mobile infrastructure to founding his own mobile company. He was one of the primary Android developers of the Where (Where, Inc.) Android app and is now a senior manager/architect for Paypal's Data Science group. Outside of coding, he spends his time practicing Ba Gua Zhang, playing with UAVs, and caring for his cats.

Colophon

The animal on the cover of *Programming Android, Second Edition* is a pine grosbeak (*Pinicola enucleator*). A member of the finch family, these largest of the so-called "winter finches" can be found throughout the coniferous forests of the northern hemisphere: in Alaska, Canada, Scandinavia, and Siberia. More rarely, during the winter some individuals stray as far south as the upper Midwest and New England portions of the United States, and on occasion even into temperate Europe.

Adult pine grosbeaks are rather distinctive looking. Both males and females have long forked black tails and black wings with white wing bars. The remainder of a male's plumage is predominantly red, while females display an olive color on the head and rump and gray on the back and underside. Conversely, colors on young pine grosbeaks are noticeably more subdued.

Pine grosbeaks feed mostly on vegetable matter, including the buds, seeds, and fruit of various varieties of tree, though they will also eat insects, and in fact prefer to feed such to their young. Interestingly, breeding adults will develop pouches in the floor of its mouth specifically designed to carry this food back to the nest.

The cover image is from *Johnson's Natural History*. The cover font is Adobe ITC Garamond. The text font is Linotype Birka; the heading font is Adobe Myriad Condensed; and the code font is LucasFont's TheSansMonoCondensed.

Have it your way.

Get even more for your money.

Join the O'Reilly Community, and register the O'Reilly books you own. It's free, and you'll get:

- $4.99 ebook upgrade offer
- 40% upgrade offer on O'Reilly print books
- Membership discounts on books and events
- Free lifetime updates to ebooks and videos
- Multiple ebook formats, DRM FREE
- Participation in the O'Reilly community
- Newsletters
- Account management
- 100% Satisfaction Guarantee

Signing up is easy:

1. **Go to: oreilly.com/go/register**
2. **Create an O'Reilly login.**
3. **Provide your address.**
4. **Register your books.**

Note: English-language books only

To order books online:
oreilly.com/store

For questions about products or an order:
orders@oreilly.com

To sign up to get topic-specific email announcements and/or news about upcoming books, conferences, special offers, and new technologies:
elists@oreilly.com

For technical questions about book content:
booktech@oreilly.com

To submit new book proposals to our editors:
proposals@oreilly.com

O'Reilly books are available in multiple DRM-free ebook formats. For more information:
oreilly.com/ebooks

O'REILLY®

Spreading the knowledge of innovators   oreilly.com

CPSIA information can be obtained at www.ICGtesting.com
Printed in the USA
BVOW02s0021170714

359407BV00024B/493/P